Afro-American Anthropology:
Contemporary Perspectives

Edited by Norman E. Whitten, Jr. and John F. Szwed

Afro-American Anthropology

CONTEMPORARY PERSPECTIVES

Foreword by Sidney W. Mintz

The Free Press, New York · Collier-Macmillan Limited, London

Extract from *Shadow and Act* by Ralph Ellison, © Copyright 1964 by Ralph Ellison, reprinted by permission of Random House, Inc., and Martin Secker & Warburg Limited.

Copyright © 1970 by The Free Press
A DIVISION OF THE MACMILLAN COMPANY
Printed in the United States of America

All rights reserved. No part of this book may be reproduced or transmitted in any form or by any means, electronic or mechanical, including photocopying, recording, or by any information storage and retrieval system, without permission in writing from the Publisher.

Collier-Macmillan Canada, Ltd., Toronto, Ontario

Library of Congress Catalog Card Number: 79-93109

Printing Number
1 2 3 4 5 6 7 8 9 10

CONTENTS

CONTRIBUTORS vii
FOREWORD, *by Sidney W. Mintz* 1
PREFACE 17
PICTORIAL ESSAY, *by George A. Talbot following page* 22
INTRODUCTION, *by Norman E. Whitten, Jr. and John F. Szwed* 23

PART I: CULTURAL PATTERNING

1. ETHNOHISTORY AND SELF-IMAGE IN THREE NEW WORLD NEGRO SOCIETIES, *by Thomas J. Price* 63
2. REFERENTIAL AMBIGUITY IN THE CALCULUS OF BRAZILIAN RACIAL IDENTITY, *by Marvin Harris* 75
3. RITUAL DISSOCIATION AND POSSESSION BELIEF IN CARIBBEAN NEGRO RELIGION, *by Erika Bourguignon* 87
4. CRISIS, CONTRACULTURE, AND RELIGION AMONG WEST INDIANS IN THE PANAMA CANAL ZONE, *by R. S. Bryce-Laporte* 103
5. NON-STANDARD NEGRO DIALECTS: CONVERGENCE OR DIVERGENCE? *by J. L. Dillard* 119
6. CULTURAL AND LINGUISTIC AMBIGUITY IN A WEST INDIAN VILLAGE, *by Karl Reisman* 129
7. TOWARD AN ETHNOGRAPHY OF BLACK AMERICAN SPEECH BEHAVIOR, *by Thomas Kochman* 145
8. PATTERNS OF PERFORMANCE IN THE BRITISH WEST INDIES, *by Roger Abrahams* 163
9. THE HOMOGENEITY OF AFRICAN–AFRO-AMERICAN MUSICAL STYLE, *by Alan Lomax* 181
10. PERSONAL NETWORKS AND MUSICAL CONTEXTS IN THE PACIFIC LOWLANDS OF COLOMBIA AND ECUADOR, *by Norman E. Whitten, Jr.* 203
11. AFRO-AMERICAN MUSICAL ADAPTATION, *by John F. Szwed* 219

PART II: SOCIO-ECONOMIC ADAPTATIONS

12. TOWARD A DEFINITION OF MATRIFOCALITY, *by Nancie L. González* 231
13. BLACK TRADERS OF NORTH HIGHLAND ECUADOR, *by Kathleen Klumpp* 245
14. DIFFERENTIAL ADAPTATIONS AND MICROCULTURAL EVOLUTION IN GUYANA, *by Leo Despres* 263
15. A RESPONSE TO MARGINALITY: THE CASE OF BLACK MIGRANT FARM WORKERS, *by Dorothy Nelkin* 289
16. THE KINDRED OF VIOLA JACKSON: RESIDENCE AND FAMILY ORGANIZATION OF AN URBAN BLACK AMERICAN FAMILY, *by Carol B. Stack* 303
17. WHAT GHETTO MALES ARE LIKE: ANOTHER LOOK, *by Ulf Hannerz* 313
18. STRATEGIES OF ADAPTIVE MOBILITY IN THE COLOMBIAN-ECUADORIAN LITTORAL, *by Norman E. Whitten, Jr.* 329

PART III: "BLACK CULTURE" AND GHETTO ETHNOGRAPHY

19. BLACK CULTURE: MYTH OR REALITY? *by Robert Blauner* 347
20. SOUL MUSIC AND BLUES: THEIR MEANING AND RELEVANCE IN NORTHERN UNITED STATES BLACK GHETTOS, *by Michael Haralambos* 367
21. THE SOCIAL ORGANIZATION OF A MOVEMENT OF REVOLUTIONARY CHANGE: CASE STUDY, BLACK POWER, *by Luther P. Gerlach and Virginia H. Hine* 385
22. MAKING THE SCENE, DIGGING THE ACTION, AND TELLING IT LIKE IT IS: ANTHROPOLOGISTS AT WORK IN A DARK GHETTO, *by Charles A. Valentine and Betty Lou Valentine* 403

REFERENCES CITED 419

PICTURE CREDITS 451

INDEX 453

CONTRIBUTORS

ROGER D. ABRAHAMS is Professor of Anthropology and English, and Associate Director of the Center for Intercultural Studies in Folklore and Oral History at the University of Texas, Austin. His major publications include *Deep Down in the Jungle: Negro Narrative Folklore from the Streets of Philadelphia* (Hatboro, 1964) and *Positively Black* (Englewood Cliffs, 1969). He is the author of other books, articles, and reviews and has undertaken extensive field research in the urban United States, and in the Caribbean.

ROBERT BLAUNER, Associate Professor of Sociology at the University of California, Berkeley, has published a book, *Alienation and Freedom* (Chicago, 1964) and articles focusing on ghetto revolts and contemporary race relations in the United States.

ERIKA BOURGUIGNON is director of the Cross-Cultural Study of Dissociational States at The Ohio State University, where she is also Professor of Anthropology. The author of many articles, Dr. Bourguignon has worked for years on cross-cultural studies, with particular reference to Afro-American research within the Caribbean area.

ROY SIMON BRYCE-LAPORTE, a West Indian born in the Republic of Panama, is Assistant Professor of Anthropology at Yale University, and Director of the Afro-American Studies Program at that university. The research reported in this volume is the result of a personal experience in which he was both mediator and scientific observer. He has done research with rural and urban ethnic minorities in Panama, Honduras, Costa Rica, Puerto Rico, Los Angeles, and Syracuse.

LEO A. DESPRES is Chairman of the Department of Anthropology at Case–Western Reserve University. The author of a recent book, *Cultural Pluralism and Nationalist Politics in British Guiana*, Professor Despres has contributed to knowledge of social structure, political anthropology, and cultural ecology through various articles and reviews.

J. L. DILLARD, Visiting Lecturer in Linguistics at the Ferkauf Graduate School of Humanities and Social Sciences at Yeshiva University, is well known in the area of Afro-American Studies for his research in the Caribbean. The paper in this book is an advance sample of work forthcoming in a book, tentatively entitled, *Black English and White Professors*. He is past director of Urban Language Study at the Center for Applied Linguistics.

LUTHER GERLACH is Associate Professor of Anthropology at the University of Minnesota. VIRGINIA H. HINE, with whom Gerlach has worked on a joint forthcoming book, *Prometheus Unbound: A Study of Movements of Personal Transformation and Revolutionary Change* (New York, 1970), resides in Miami, Florida. Professor Gerlach has produced a sound-color film, *People, Power, Change: A Study of Movements of Revolutionary Change*.

NANCIE L. GONZÁLEZ, Professor of Anthropology at the University of Iowa, has done extensive work with Spanish-Americans in New Mexico and with the Black Carib of Honduras. She has recently returned from a field trip to the Dominican Republic. She has published two books, *The Spanish-Americans of New Mexico: A Distinctive Heritage* (Los Angeles, 1967) and *Migration and Modernization: Adaptive Reorganization in the Black Carib Household* (Seattle, 1969), and a number of articles on Black Carib life and social adaptations to the larger industrial societies.

ULF HANNERZ, Lecturer in Social Anthropology at the University of Stockholm, Sweden, has been staff anthropologist at the Center for Applied Linguistics in Washington, D.C. He has published a book on Nigeria (in Swedish) and several papers, which he has just published as a collection of his own essays in a book entitled *Soulside*.

MICHAEL HARALAMBOS presents the first results of his field work with black Americans in this book. He is a graduate student and teaching assistant at the University of Minnesota. He has also done field work among the Teton Sioux.

MARVIN HARRIS is the author of the distinguished book, *The Rise of Anthropological Theory* (New York, 1968), *Patterns of Race in the Americas* (New York, 1964), and *The Nature of Cultural Things* (New York, 1966). He is past chairman of the Department of Anthropology at Columbia University, where he is Professor of Anthropology. His many articles, reviews, and lectures are drawn from his ethnographic work in Brazil, Ecuador, and Mozambique.

KATHLEEN M. KLUMPP publishes her first article in this volume. She is a graduate student in anthropology at the University of Illinois and has carried out field work in the highlands of Ecuador, where she will shortly be returning to complete work for her Ph.D. in anthropology.

THOMAS KOCHMAN is Assistant Professor in the Department of Linguistics at Northeastern Illinois State College,

CONTRIBUTORS

and Instructor at the Center for Inner City Studies. His major research interests include the vocabulary analysis of the black idiom and a compilation of a black American lexicon.

ALAN LOMAX, Director of the Cantometrics Project at Columbia University, is the author of *Folk Song Style and Culture* (Washington, 1968). He has produced many records from both field recordings and his own talented singing, as well as scholarly articles and popular pieces for various magazines.

SIDNEY W. MINTZ is the author of *Cañemelar: The Subculture of a Rural Sugar Plantation Proletariat* (in Steward et al., *The People of Puerto Rico*) and *Worker in the Cane: A Puerto Rican Life History*, as well as a number of articles on the Caribbean. He is one of the few scholars to have carried out extensive field research in the British, Hispanic, and Gallic subareas of the Caribbean. He is now chairman of the Social Science Research Council Committee on Afro-American Societies and Cultures and President of the American Ethnological Society. He is Professor of Anthropology at Yale where he is also the chairman of the faculty committee on Afro-American studies.

DOROTHY NELKIN, Research Associate at the New York School of Industrial and Labor Relations at Cornell University, has done research on the development of labor unions in sub-Saharan Africa as well as more recent work with migrant farm labor in the eastern United States.

THOMAS J. PRICE has worked in Colombia, Nicaragua, Surinam, French Guiana, and various parts of the Carribean on a variety of problems pertaining to Afro-American studies. He is currently Associate Professor of Anthropology at Williams College. The author of many articles and a handbook, *Problems of American Minorities*, Professor Price is now in Surinam completing work on the changing social and cultural orientations of the Boni Bush Negroes.

KARL REISMAN is Assistant Professor of Anthropology at Brandeis University. He has been conducting field work on the Island of Antigua for a number of years.

CAROL B. STACK is a graduate student in anthropology at the University of Illinois. Her principal research interests lie in the areas of urbanization and family structure in the urban United States and the Caribbean, and in the analysis of cognatic kinship systems. She is particularly interested in black American family organization and urban education.

JOHN F. SZWED is Director of the Center for Urban Ethnography at the University of Pennsylvania. He has carried out field work among Afro-Americans in Philadelphia and Trinidad as well as with Newfoundland peasants. His monograph, *Private Cultures and Public Imagery: Interpersonal Relations in a Newfoundland Peasant Society*, complements several articles on Afro-American cultures.

GEORGE A. TALBOT is Assistant Professor of Anthropology, Livingston College, Rutgers University, and Associate Editor and Art and Production Director of *Trans-action* magazine. His principal interests are social organization and urban anthropology with special concerns for the role of buildings and housing in social behavior. He is also concerned with the use of photography as a documentary tool in the social sciences.

CHARLES A. and BETTY LOU VALENTINE are, in their own words, "a black and white, husband-wife (and son) participant ethnographic team, working among poor urban Afro- and Spanish-Americans in the northern United States." They are interested in discovering whether there is any such thing as either "poverty culture" or "black culture," and if so what their natures may be and what the implications of change are for Afro-Americans, for poor people in the United States, and for the future of the larger society as a complex plural system. The Valentines are also particularly interested in the role of anthropologists in relation to movements for ethnic and self-assertion and broad sociopolitical change. Charles A. Valentine is Associate Professor of Anthropology at Washington University and the author of *Culture and Poverty: Critique and Counter Proposals* (Chicago, 1968).

NORMAN E. WHITTEN, JR., Associate Professor of Anthropology at Washington University and Visiting Professor of Anthropology at the University of California, Los Angeles (1969–70), has worked with black sub-cultures in North Carolina, Ecuador, Colombia, and Nova Scotia. He is the author of *Class, Kinship, and Power in an Ecuadorian Town: The Negroes of San Lorenzo* (Stanford, 1965), a record of black Ecuadorian-Colombian music, and a number of articles on South American lifeways. He is also a member of the black studies program at Washington University and is currently working on a book entitled *Black Subculture in Northern South America*.

FOREWORD*

Sidney W. Mintz

* The author wishes to thank Jacqueline W. Mintz and Richard Price for valuable criticisms of earlier drafts of this paper. Professors Richard M. Morse and Norman E. Whitten, Jr., also provided useful comments. The arguments set forth here, however, are the responsibility of the author alone.

In the course of nearly five hundred years since the "Discovery" of the New World, millions of migrants from every corner of the earth became "Americans." While doing so they transformed aboriginal American Indian life, such that even the most isolated and self-sufficient Indian communities of the Hemisphere were profoundly modified. "Becoming American," that is to say, has been a process of change defining the history of the Americas and affecting every inhabitant of the Hemisphere. Though the people of the United States persist in regarding themselves as *the* Americans, all who live in the Americas have a proper claim on that title, and those to our south commonly refer to us as "*Norteamericanos*" to make the point.

If we ask what, in some essential sense, makes one an American, the first answer is likely to be geography; only the Amerindians, of all Americans, can really lay prior claim to a world that was to become "new"—in total ethnocentric innocence—in 1492. But if this answer fails to satisfy, we may seek to specify further. We who are Americans live in societies and bear cultures whose origins are elsewhere, transformed by the migrations of our ancestors and by the novel challenges this New World imposed upon them. Today, the consequences of transplantation and of adjustment during a period nearly five centuries long define us, even those of us who are American Indians.

Such a definition may seem irrelevant when one considers the profound gaps—cultural, economic, linguistic, political, physical—that divide New World peoples, both within the component American polities and among them. But from the point of view of those of the Old World we are, in some fundamental way, of the New. That even slight additional refinement may appear to dissolve the contrast—we are rich and poor, Spanish-speaking and Quechua-speaking, Haitian and Canadian, black and white —does not really alter so central a historical feature of the New World reality.

From one vantage-point, then, we of the Hemisphere are a people whose ways of being share the common quality of a foreign past. From another, this reality seems unimportant, in our daily lives and in our social relationships. We "Americans"—in this widest sense—share too little. That we are all in part from somewhere else fails of itself to provide us with any sense of common identity or destiny. (In fact, some would even argue that the lack of an understanding based on the acknowledgment of the shallowness of our own roots typifies the American experience, dividing us rather than bringing us together.) From the vantagepoint of an Egypt, a China, an India—or even a Europe—we of the Americas are raw and callow, the bearers of diluted civilizations. Our awareness of such disdain is often blurred, but the Limeño in Madrid, the Bostonian in London and the Martiniquan in Paris—not to mention the Trinidad-born Indian in New Delhi—share some knowledge of what it means to be an American, in this most ample of senses. That we more commonly experience our "American-ness" as something else—Blackness, Indian-ness, Third-World-ness, anti-yanquismo, or North American xenophobia-at-large—is a reflection both of the highly differentiated character of the peoples of these continents, and of the relative rarity of social situations in which some generalized Hemispheric identity might take precedence over other allegiances. In other words, what is implicitly shared by all Americans is usually ignored in the midst of more pressing priorities of consciousness.

And yet it should be within this widest context—the Hemisphere and its five short centuries of newness—that North Americans begin to explore Afro-America. The very word is a hybrid, expressing symbolically the linkage of two worlds—but it is innocent, as is Euro-America, or Mestizo-America (Service 1955), and no more hybridized. We who think of ourselves as athwart the American tradition may claim to feel no need for hybrid words and hyphens, and resent their implications—except, of course, on St. Patrick's Day, Columbus Day, and certain other Days, and in memories, dreams, and subtly persistent insecurities. Hyphens are supposedly laid aside, together with old languages, old costumes, and old habits of thought. Shiny new unhyphenated North Americans—*gringos*, the Mexicans might say—usually prefer the image of a past uncluttered by any realities, and marked by such cozy symbols as Washington's hatchet, Franklin's kite, Boone's bear, Crockett's coonskin cap, and Teddy's Rough Riders. We claim to honor a past; yet we have difficulty in admitting that it ever had a beginning, for particular ones of us.

This unease, this nervous joy, is part of a very North American style; Henry Ford's dictum that history is bunk is a North American dictum. We do not question the American past, most of us, in part because we covertly recognize that we are not altogether part of it. It is a seamless past, summed up in Jamestown, Sturbridge, and Freedomland; we make the Pilgrims' Pride our pride and our reality; it is Ellis Island and the village slums of Europe that become our fantasies. Nor should it surprise that a new and insistent demand that the Afro-American past be identified and explicated excites a certain amount of resistance. After all, if ancience of pedigree were enough to win membership in the D.A.R., those worthy ladies might be

FOREWORD

aghast at the company they would have to keep. How much more anxiety-provoking, then, to the Johnny-come-latelies, is a pedigree search by the anciently disinherited!

But a genuine search for that hidden past has begun, and it requires of the interested that they think through seriously what "Afro-American" can mean. The term implies two backgrounds, or some kind of interpenetration of one background by another. This book is largely concerned with just such implications; their meanings are various and complex. Terms like "Afro-American" and "African"—or any comparable geographical term used adjectivally—are not self-explanatory. When one speaks of an "African" food, an "African" dance, or an "African" custom, for instance, one may mean any of several quite different things. An African food may be a crop domesticated in Africa, or native to Africa—such as okra (*Hibiscus esculentus* L.) and ackee (*Blighia sapida* Koen.). Or an African food may be a food processed in a distinctively African fashion, such that certain sorts of cassava cakes—the Haitian *bambouri* or Jamaican "bammy"—might justifiably be considered African, even though the cassava itself is a New World cultigen, and only diffused to Africa after 1492. Conceivably, an African food could be a food eaten regularly by a group of Africans working at the United Nations—in which case one assumes that it would be a food they typically ate in Africa, and now continue to eat in a new setting, rather than assuming that anything eaten by people from Africa thereby becomes African. One might be impelled to wonder, though, whether anyone feels that pigs' ears, turnip greens and grits—items from the cuisine now popularly called "soul food" in the United States—could qualify as African, even if these foods are not (or were not) eaten in Africa. Most reflective persons would, one supposes, think not; but the confusion here is real, even if its implications are not wholly intellectual in character.

If we turn from such things as foods to human beings, the confusion is compounded. When a person is described as an African, one is prepared to assume that this means someone born in Africa, or a citizen of an African country or colony—that, at least, is parallel to the way we North Americans define an "American." The term "African," that is, refers to someone from a definable geographical area, the African continent. But if that is the meaning, are not the children of Kenyan Indians, Nigerian Lebanese, and Dutch *voortrekkers* Africans all? And of course this is part of the confusion, because, for at least some people, the term "African" carries clear overtones of physical type. Such confusion inevitably returns us to puzzles of culture such as cuisine, to ask again whether a food might be classified as "African" according to the physical type of those who eat it.

For most of those interested in defining Afro-American studies, the term "Afro-Americana" has to do with culture—that is, with patterns of socially learned behaviors expressed in artifacts, languages, traditions, values, and the like. In the case of Afro-American cultures, these patterns of socially acquired behaviors and their consequences are principally carried in time and space by those descended from African slaves whose histories involved enslavement, forced transatlantic migration, protracted and complex servitude, and persisting social isolation and exclusion, over centuries. But the physical type of the individuals who carry out and maintain those behavioral patterns, hold those values, and use those languages is a relevant datum only to the extent that it affects behavior socially—that is, through the perceptions of the persons involved in the social relationships. There is, in other words, no genetic relationship between a particular mode of learned behavior—eating turnip greens, dancing the frug, standing or gesturing or intoning in some patterned way—and the physical type of those who behave in these ways.

Yet there is a noticeable readiness on the part of contemporary observers to attribute such behavioral patterns to heredity rather than to learning. In the case of white North Americans observing Afro-Americans (and it must be repeatedly stressed that some Afro-Americans are phenotypically white, while some white North Americans are not), such attributions are not explainable purely on grounds of a lack of observational keenness. While we may expect to see English children dance Morris dances, we are neither startled nor amused to see them dance a waltz or even a mambo. Polish children do dance polkas; but the news that they knew how to dance the watusi and preferred it probably would be received calmly by most of us. And yet too many of us, when we see Black North American children dancing, too often expect them to dance in ways that are *somehow* connected to the way they *look*—even though we are not always prepared to admit freely to such expectations.

The implications of an underlying assumption that learned behavior is genetically transmitted behavior are of immense importance, and not only because of the intellectual errors that flow from such an assumption. Here, however, it concerns us only with reference to the study of Afro-Americana. In recent years in the United States, this assumed or imputed connection between physique and behavior appears to have become more widespread, rather than less, among Afro-Americans; its presence among North American whites is ancient. Malcolm X tells us in his autobiography (1966:57) that learning to dance appropriately was difficult for him at first; but soon his African ancestry—his "long-suppressed African instincts," as he puts it—"broke through." There may be a full circle here: from the imputation of "inborn rhythm" to Afro-Americans by whites who cannot (or will not) distinguish between physique and culture, to the pseudo-scientific question of the difficulties of finding "a gene for rhythm," to the assertion of "African instincts" for dancing by a black militant. To some extent, this conceptual merging of physique and behavior is expressed in common parlance by the use of such terms as "black" and "soul" without any clear attempt to specify that African or Afro-American cultures are socially learned and socially perpetuated phenomena. Discussions of Afro-Americana and Afro-American studies today thus must take into account the fact that terms like "Afro-American" may be used in ordinary discourse with either physical or cultural associations, or both, in mind.

The distinction between physique and culture was once drawn carefully by Afro-Americanists, as in the work of Melville Herskovits (1930:145–55). The apparent linkage between physique and culture is difficult to dispute, however, in regard to such items as intonation, facial expression, gesture, and posture—of the sort Herskovits himself once labeled (1945:22) "cultural imponderables." It is easy to see why these aspects of behavior might be thought to be innate or genetically transmitted, since their manifestation seems "automatic" or "natural." But the socially acquired character of these traits is demonstrable;

the learned and patterned motor habits that we usually pick up unconsciously and at very early ages from our parents and other kinsmen and carry into adolescence and adulthood are both difficult to become aware of, and difficult to change; the covert and unnoticed character of social transmission of such habits is of course the principal reason why they are commonly perceived as "innate," rather than learned. Motor habits of speech are similarly learned, in good part unconsciously, and carried unnoticed; these, too, though to a lesser extent, may be perceived as "part of" a person because they seem to be linked phenomenologically to the very way in which he is defined.

It is of interest that these seemingly minor behavioral patterns are also closely tied to the expressive media, such as music, dance, drama, voice, and the like, and that it is in these aesthetic spheres, once again, that linkages between physique and culture are often imputed to Afro-Americans. In fact, rather than "explaining" such behavioral patterns by vague reference to racial or instinctual responses, it is reasonable to view these expressions as continuities with the African past, and as some evidence of the success of Afro-Americans in conserving cultural materials that could not be conserved in other aspects of life. Patterns of socially learned motor behavior are probably not readily destroyed, even by extremely repressive conditions; and the aesthetic and creative possibilities implicit in these traditional patterns and their cognitive accompaniments may have been among those cultural traditions most readily maintained under slavery.

Nonetheless, there is a strong predisposition to view the connections between physical type, learned motor behavior, and aesthetic expression as genetic rather than cultural, and it is not difficult to see why. What is more, the perceptions of persons who assume a genetic connection between perceived physical characteristics and socially learned behavior become cultural data themselves by virtue of the effects such perceptions may have upon behavior. That is, physical type and culture are not biologically linked, but certain kinds of social behavior, based on the assumption that they are, can produce clear correlations between them. This assertion in no way qualifies a historical reality—that those African peoples torn from their ancestral homelands whose descendants are today's Afro-Americans both carried with them elements of different cultures, and were of different physical appearances, from those who frequently became their masters. But the assumption that the linkage is biological rather than social lies buried beneath the whole of Afro-American social history and is—in some deformed and refracted way—the mirror image of the Afro-American tradition itself. In what sense this may be so will become clearer at a later point.

The first African slaves to be transported to the New World arrived during the first decade following the Discovery, and slavery did not end in the New World until Brazilian abolition was decreed by the Imperial Government at Rio de Janeiro in 1888. Hence the involuntary servitude of Africans and their descendants in this Hemisphere lasted nearly four centuries; its initiation predated the North American Declaration of Independence by nearly three. The precise number of enslaved Africans who reached the New World alive will never be known—nor will the numbers who died in slaving wars and in the hideous "coffles" to the coast, during the Middle Passage, or before being debarked in the Americas. It would not be rash to suppose, however, that upwards of fifteen million African slaves reached this Hemisphere—in what may have been the most massive acculturational event in human history (Mintz 1961:580).

Aside from special circumstances—as when hispanicized slaves of African origin served as subalterns and assistants to the *conquistadores*—nearly all the slaves were allocated in terms of the needs of large-scale agriculture. This was especially the case for the production of subtropical commodities, such as tobacco, sugar, and spices, which were finding large and sometimes new markets in Europe. Hence the African slave trade and slavery itself were intimately bound up with the spread of European military and colonial power, and with commercial developments, especially in overseas capitalistic agriculture.

New World plantation organization during the sixteenth century and the subsequent two centuries, though of course agricultural, had a very modern—even industrial—cast for its time. This was particularly true for sugar production, where mill operations were tied closely to those of the field, and capital investment in equipment was necessarily heavy. Slaves were used extensively for sugar-cane cultivation and sugar production in Brazil and the Hispanic Caribbean in the sixteenth century; in later centuries, similar patterns developed along the Guiana coasts, through the Caribbean islands, on the Pacific coasts of Peru, on portions of the Caribbean Littoral, in Mexico, and in Louisiana. The relatively highly-developed industrial character of the plantation system meant a curious sort of "modernization" or "westernization" for the slaves—an aspect of their acculturation in the New World that has too often been missed because of the deceptively rural, agrarian, and pseudo-manorial quality of slave-based plantation production.

Moreover, the development of plantations to produce commodities for European markets was a vital first step in the history of overseas capitalism. Even more than the exploitation of mines, the plundering of native treasures, or the development of trade patterns with viable indigenous societies, as in much of Asia and parts of Africa, the establishment of the plantation system meant a rooted overseas capitalism based on conquest, slavery and coercion, investment and entrepreneurship. The stimulus to overseas commodity production originated in European developments accompanying the accelerated breakdown of European feudalism, the growth and unification of international trade, and the disfranchisement of vast rural European populations as part of the creation of factory cities. Thus, the growth of slave-based economies in the New World was an integral part of the rise of European commerce and industry, while European factory workers were in a position structurally parallel to that occupied by the enslaved and forced-labor strata of New World colonial societies.

Finally, it should be pointed out that the slave-produced commodities of the subtropical areas outside Europe, particularly in the West Indies, were sold to Europe's working masses and, at a later time—especially with the growth of factory-based cotton textile production and that of other industrial fibers—to local populations in the "underdeveloped" world as well. Here, again, we discern direct relationships between New World slave-based societies and the growth of European power and influence.

Hence the development of slave systems outside Europe was important to European development; the slave economies were in fact dependent parts of European economies; and slavery itself, as it grew in the New World, was an essential ingredient of that westernization of the world outside Europe that has typified the last four centuries of world history.

While the demographic spread of peoples of African or part-African ancestry has not been confined solely by labor demands, those demands have dominated such spread through the centuries. Though granting the provisional nature of his data, Zelinsky (1949) demonstrates that the peoples of African origin are still concentrated heavily in the Antilles, coastal Latin America (particularly the Caribbean and Atlantic coasts, but also along the Pacific Littoral), and in the South of the United States. Morse (1964:3) points out that, in spite of the obvious inexactness of such calculations, 95% of the Negroes and mulattoes in Middle America in 1950 were in the Antillean islands, while 76% of the Negroes and mulattoes in South America in that year were to be found in Brazil. "In short, of the 33 million Negroes and mulattoes in Latin America in 1950, 27 million were in the Antilles and Brazil," Morse (*ibid.*) has written.

In any case, however, the distribution of *peoples* must be carefully distinguished from the distribution of *cultures*, even though cultural elements of demonstrable African provenience probably tend to be concentrated in those same areas where peoples whose ancestry is in some degree originally African are found. When we turn to the distribution of cultures, of course, we are dealing with phenomena that can diffuse freely between individuals, and from group to group, without genetic change of any kind. Folklore, dance forms, cuisine, music, aesthetic traditions, even language and all else that is cultural require no genetic transmission—only a readiness to learn new forms. These forms, moreover, may be taken on with their old meanings, or with new meanings added; in fragments (a word, an exclamation, a gesture) or in "complexes"; to replace older forms or to supplement them—or, perhaps most commonly, to mix together in some way with older forms. The word "goober" (from Kongo *nguba*) need not displace "peanut" in everyday speech, but its use may lend a sentence regional flavor; "Creole" cookery can combine African and European and other elements in a new and distinctive cuisine that differs from all the traditions that sired it; Br'er Rabbit may learn new tricks, some of them European; and the blues may even incorporate a few European elements—instrumental, melodic, rhythmic—that seem to serve the musician's purposes.

A thorough discussion of Afro-American cultures is impossible here, and it would be pretentious to attempt it; only several general points may be suggested. The ancestors of Afro-Americans could not transfer their cultures to the New World intact; they differed in this regard in degree, though significantly so, from other migrants. To begin with, enslaved Africans were quite systematically prevented—with few exceptions (see, for instance, Pierson 1942: 73; and Pierson 1953)—from bringing with them the personnel who maintained their homeland institutions; the complex social structures of the ancestral societies, with their kings and courts, guilds and cult-groups, markets and armies were not, and could not be, transferred. Cultures are linked as continuing patterns of and for behavior to such social groupings; since the groupings themselves could not be maintained or readily reconstituted, the capacities of random representatives of these societies to perpetuate or to re-create the cultural contents of the past were seriously impaired. Again, the slaves were not usually able to regroup themselves in the New World settings in terms of their origins; the cultural heterogeneity of any slave group normally meant that what was shared culturally was likely to be minimal. It was not, after all, some single "African culture" that was available for transfer, nor even some generalized African cultural substratum, as has sometimes been suggested. There is, moreover, some tendency to think of those ancestral African cultures as changeless and pure, and such a presupposition interferes with our discernment of the changeable quality of all cultures, including those of Africa itself. Just as cultures were transmuted in the New World, so too, they changed (and continued to change, after 1492) in the societies of the Old.

Inevitably, Afro-American cultures would take on their characteristic forms under the social and physical conditions with which the slaves themselves had to deal. To probe the consciousness of those millions of Africans as they sought to survive as functioning human beings in the settings into which slavery thrust them is a task which will concern (and, hopefully, intimidate) generations to come of serious students of Afro-Americana. Surely these human beings like all others sought to make comprehensible the destinies imposed upon them by brute force. The daily job of living did not end with enslavement, and the slaves could and did create viable patterns of life, for which their pasts were pools of available symbolic and material resources.

These creative processes had a two-way character, however; not only did the cultures of the slaves come to implicate features of other, non-African origins, but the cultures of non-slaves also assimilated important materials from the African heritage. Such assimilation was especially strong in the expressive aspects of culture, as in Brazilian, Cuban, and North American music, dance, and folklore. So interpenetrated became the heritages of Afro-Americans and other Americans, in fact, that it is very difficult (if not impossible) in many cases to speak of an "Afro-American culture" that is rigorously distinguishable from the wider national culture. This assertion has been put eloquently by Ralph Ellison (*Shadow and Act*, New York: Random House, Inc., 1964, pp. 254–256):

> Slavery was a vicious system, and those who endured it a tough people, but it was *not* (and this is important for Negroes to remember for the sake of their own sense of who and what their grandparents were) a state of absolute repression.
> A slave was, to the extent that he was a *musician*, one who expressed himself in music, a man who realized himself in the world of sound. Thus, while he might stand in awe before the superior technical ability of a white musician, and while he was forced to recognize a superior social status, he would never feel awed before the music which the technique of the white musician made available. His attitude as "musician" would lead him to possess the music expressed through the technique, but until he could do so he would hum, whistle, sing or play the tunes to the best of his ability on any available instrument. And it was, indeed, out of the tension between desire and ability that the techniques of jazz emerged. This was likewise true of American Negro choral singing. For this, no literary explanation, no cultural analyses, no political slogans—indeed, not even a high degree of social or political freedom—was required. For the art—the blues, the spiritual, the jazz, the dance—was what we had in place of freedom.
> Technique was then, as today, the key to creative freedom, but before this came a will toward expression. . . . Negro musicians have never, as a group, felt alienated from any music sounded within their hearing, and it is

my theory that it would be impossible to pinpoint the time when they were not shaping ... the mainstream of American music. Indeed, what group of musicians has made more of the sound of the American experience? Nor am I confining my statement to the sound of the slave experience, but am saying that the most authoritative rendering of America in music is that of American Negroes.

For as I see it, from the days of their introduction into the colonies, Negroes have taken, with the ruthlessness of those without articulate investments in cultural styles, whatever they could of European music, making of it that which would, when blended with the cultural tendencies inherited from Africa, express their own sense of life—while rejecting the rest. Perhaps this is only another way of saying that whatever the degree of injustice and inequality sustained by the slaves, American culture was, even before the official founding of the nation, pluralistic; and it was the African's origin in cultures in which art was highly functional which gave him an edge in shaping the music and dance of this nation.

The question of social and cultural snobbery is important here. The effectiveness of Negro music and dance is first recorded in the journals and letters of travelers but it is important to remember that they saw and understood only that which they were prepared to accept. Thus a Negro dancing a courtly dance appeared comic from the outside simply because the dancer was a slave. But to the Negro dancing it—and there is ample evidence that he danced it well—burlesque or satire might have been the point, which might have been difficult for a white observer to even imagine. During the 1870's Lafcadio Hearn reports that the best singers of Irish songs, in Irish dialect, were Negro dock workers in Cincinnati, and advertisements from slavery days described escaped slaves who spoke in Scottish dialect. The master artisans of the South were slaves, and White Americans have been walking Negro walks, talking Negro flavored talk (and prizing it when spoken by Southern belles), dancing Negro dances and singing Negro melodies far too long to talk of a "mainstream" to which they're alien.

Ellison is making an exceedingly important point, not only about the innovative resiliency and creative integrity of the slaves, but also about the nature of culture. When we speak of Afro-American cultures, we are speaking of mangled pasts; but those pasts were carried by successive generations of men, dealing with the daily challenges of oppression. The glory of Afro-Americana inheres in the durable fiber of humanity, in the face of what surely must have been the most repressive epoch in modern world history. It has depended upon creativity and innovation, far more than upon the indelibility of particular culture contents.

The terms "culture" and "society" have been employed with considerable freedom in this essay, and it may be useful to attempt to specify their meaning with more precision—even though there is no generally accepted agreement on such meanings among social scientists. A particularly relevant contrast is drawn by Wolf (1959: 142):

> By culture I mean the historically developed forms through which the members of a given society relate to each other. By society I mean the element of action, of human manoeuver [sic] within the field provided by cultural forms, human manoeuver which aims either at preserving a given balance of life-chances and life risks or at changing it. Most "cultural" anthropologists have seen cultural forms as so limiting that they have tended to neglect entirely the element of human manoeuver which flows through these forms or around them, presses against their limits or plays several sets of forms against the middle. . . . Dynamic analysis should not omit note of the different uses to which the form is put by different individuals, of the ways in which people explore the possibilities of a form, or of the ways in which they circumvent it. Most social anthropologists, on the other hand, have seen action or manoeuver as

primary, and thus neglect to explore the limiting influences of cultural forms. Cultural form not only dictates the limits of the field for social play, it also limits the direction in which the play can go in order to change the rules of the game, when this becomes necessary. . . . Past culture certainly structures the process of perception, nor is human manoeuver always conscious and rational: by taking both views—a view of cultural forms as defining fields for human manoeuver, and a view of human manoeuver always pressing against the inherent limitations of cultural forms—we shall have a more dynamic manner of apprehending the real tensions of life.

Here we see culture depicted as a kind of resource, and society as a kind of arena—the distinction is between sets of historically available alternatives or forms on the one hand, and the societal circumstances or settings within which these forms may be employed, on the other. This is a critical distinction, consistent with Ellison's view of the individual artist, which enables us to conceptualize Afro-American cultures—not simply as historically derived bodies of materials, of patterns of and for behavior, but of such materials actively employed by organized human groupings in particular social contexts. Without the dimension of human action, of choices made and pursued—of maneuver—culture could be thought to be a lifeless collection of habits, superstitions, and artifacts. Instead, we see that culture is *used*; and that any analysis of its use immediately brings into view the arrangements of persons in social groups, for whom cultural forms confirm, reinforce, maintain, change, or deny particular arrangements of status, power, and identity.

But such validations or denials through the employment of cultural forms depend upon the symbolic associations—the meaning or significance—of each usage to those who hold positions within a given social system or sub-system. Whether it be drinking tea, wearing an "Afro" haircut, or employing some particular idiomatic expressions rather than some others, usages are endowed with meanings apparent to those who habitually practice them, acquire them, or invent them; and appropriate practice confirms a network of understandings, of symbolic accord, corresponding to the networks of social relations within which persons define themselves, act, and interact.

In attempts to trace or to recapture the history of a particular culture, both the significance of the employment of cultural materials for social maneuver and the symbolic meanings of the forms themselves may be ignored. Yet the social and symbolic significance of such forms in maintaining or changing society, or in changing the relative positions of the individuals and groups within it, is of first importance. In fact, the very search for the "origins" of cultural forms may itself be part of social maneuver; if we seek to "prove" that the North Americans invented political democracy, there is implicit in the search the premise that political democracy is a good thing to have invented. Much the same for monotheism, the phonetic alphabet, and the fuel combustion engine; few polemicists set out to prove that their own ancestors invented blood sacrifice, the sexual double standard, or the ambush, unless these practices have been either ennobled or repudiated in the interim.

This is by no means to say that the study of historical origins and diffusion is intellectually empty of meaning. Demonstrating that the aboriginal peoples of the New World, Asia, and Africa have contributed massively to the world's total repertory of skills and resources, as in terms of domesticated plants and animals, engineering and the sciences, philosophy and aesthetics, has had tremendous influence, both intellectually and politically. The findings have done much to restore a sense of balance and modesty to the Western view of the world outside.

But the history of a particular skill, artifact, belief, plant, or food is not the same as its employment and the symbolic meanings it has for the members of a continuing society. Culture has "life" because its content serves as resources for those who employ it, change it, incarnate it. Human beings cope with the demands of everyday life through their interpretive and innovative skills, and their capacity for employing symbolism—not by ossifying their behavioral forms, but by using them creatively. Thus, quite aside from the question of historical origins, the cultural resources of Afro-Americans and of Afro-American cultures are by no means limited to those elements or complexes that are provably African historically; such origins are far less significant than the continuing creative employment of forms, whatever their origins, and the symbolic usages imparted to them.

The argument here is that the culture concept can be best applied in the analysis of the Afro-American world if distinctions between form and meaning on the one hand, and between culture and society on the other, are kept clearly in view. Such a position raises questions about "levels" or "spheres" of culture, when one attempts to deal with complex societies of the Western sort, as many of the contributors to this volume are doing. The quite puzzling problems of the relationships among class and culture, race and culture, and poverty and culture are not new to the social sciences, but Afro-American studies have brought their reconsideration once more sharply into focus.

Valentine (1968) has pointed out that many theses concerning "lower-class culture," "Black culture" and the "culture of poverty" have been set forth without any solid rooting in ethnography—in long-term, face-to-face anthropological fieldwork, that is to say—and the point is well taken. Yet it must also be stressed that even good ethnography will not solve some of the theoretical questions with "yes" and "no" answers, since the relationships between culture, class, society, and "race" are extremely intricate. This assertion will not be news to some, but it badly needs to be reiterated because the usages of such terms as "sub-culture" and "class culture" have grown looser and more careless in recent years.

Assertions of relationship between membership in a certain class and "carrying" a certain sub-culture are not, in fact, new. For instance, just such a relationship was suggested in studies of Puerto Rican rural proletarian communities made some time ago, wherein the community constituted what was almost a mono-class isolate, and proletarianization appeared to have brought clear sub-cultural accompaniments in its wake (Mintz 1951; 1953a; 1953b; 1956). Moreover, it should be mentioned that while the social dimension of "race" entered into the perceived composition of such communities, it was neither an important criterion of social position nor a significant marker of distinction within the community. People of highly variable physical appearance could not be said to have participated in clearly different sub-cultures in these settings.

Studies of class groupings in which "race" is a critical factor of social assortment, or which function in large urban centers as in the United States, pose more serious methodological and conceptual problems. Urban North American neighborhoods lack homogeneity of the sort typical of rural proletarian communities; they lack the physical isolation and boundedness often characteristic of rural communities; and the marked sociological significance of "race," though by no means fully understood in such cases, is nonetheless real, creating additional complexity for both fieldworker and social analyst.

The deepest and most subtle aspects of this last difference cannot be treated here, though it is often touched upon by the contributors to this volume. Suffice it to say that the United States probably stands alone in the Hemisphere in the way that the sociological aspects of perceived physical differences express themselves in behavior. Some scholars are convinced that, in the United States, race differences are really reducible to matters of class; others hold that perceived physical differences constitute a qualitatively different barrier to mobility and cohesion in North American society. A resolution of this controversy will emerge from fieldwork—not from either programmatic claims or an academic sophistication of the relevant theories. But it is possible to predict that, in the elaboration of concepts to deal with the North American case, a new conception of Afro-Americana, or of Afro-American "cultures," will develop.

At an earlier point in this essay, it was suggested that an assumption of direct linkage between physique and behavior underlay the whole of Afro-American social history, constituting, in some twisted fashion, a reflection of the Afro-American tradition itself. In practice, and throughout the Hemisphere, it has been the perceived physical differences between Afro-Americans and other Americans that served as a basis for social exclusion and isolation. In turn, this enforced separation, probably clearer and more inviolable in the United States than in most of the Americas, has simplified the oppression of Afro-Americans and has limited strictly their access to mobility within the wider society. Exclusion has been by no means complete, even in the United States, nor are the people who call themselves Afro-Americans in this country genetically homogeneous, or even necessarily identifiable in individual cases as having any African ancestry. Hence, if there is a community of Afro-Americans in the United States (in the widest sense of the term "community"), then it is bound by social ties and by cultural affinities. It is not "race," that is, *but the perception of race differences by the majority*, which has provided an apparent genetic underpinning to the Afro-American community in this country. Since the cultural development of Afro-Americans has—over time and in most cases in the United States—been accompanied both by the majority imputation of an inherent linkage between physique and behavior, and by profound social and economic exclusion of Afro-Americans from large sectors of the national society and its institutions, Afro-American culture in this country has of course been significantly affected by these accompaniments. It is, then, the sociology of prejudice, economic exploitation, and discrimination based on perceived differences which illuminates the arena within which Afro-American culture in this country has taken on its characteristic shape.

At the same time, surely one of the most remarkable aspects of Afro-American culture in the United States is its relative lack of provable African content. This fact has been used to argue both that North American slavery was the most vicious and dehumanizing of all, on the one hand; and that North American society gave the slaves the maximum opportunity to acculturate to the majority society, on the other. Whatever the final answer to this controversy—we have long to wait—it needs to be said again that the content of Afro-American cultures in this Hemisphere takes on its significance in what those who are Afro-Americans have done with it, not in whether its origins are demonstrably African.

A presentation of this kind cannot conclude without mentioning the relevance—if any—of anthropology to the continuing study of Afro-Americana. The history of North American anthropology was for very long closely bound up with the study of the American Indian, and particularly the North American Indian. The Bureau of American Ethnology, for instance, was specifically established to provide the Congress with information on North American Indians. The first graduate Department of Anthropology, initiated at Columbia University in 1899 by Franz Boas, trained scores of anthropologists in the first half-century of its existence, and fathered many new departments—almost all the students of all of them became specialists in North American Indian studies. What is more, before the onset of the Second World War, almost all of the anthropological studies carried out by North Americans among the Indians were concerned with the "retrieval" of Indian cultures at an earlier time—ideally, "before the white man."

This striking emphasis on "our own primitives"—and upon their pasts, since few North American Indians could have been called "primitive" in any legitimate sense, by the time Boas was training his students—stands in noticeable contrast to the emphases typifying European schools of anthropology, where students were prepared for the most part to carry out fieldwork among the colonies of the metropolitan power. Put another way, one might say that the Europeans were engaged in documenting their colonial present, while the North Americans studied their colonial past.

Among the rather rare exceptions to the North American rule was Melville J. Herskovits, a Boas student who early undertook to specialize in the study of Afro-Americans. Although Herskovits carried out most of his research in Latin America and in Africa rather than in the United States, his most influential work, *The Myth of the Negro Past* (1941), was a studied attempt to establish the culture-history of Afro-American peoples (including those of the United States), confirming the presence of substantial African materials in their cultures. Herskovits' work deviated from the mainstream of Boasian ethnography in its emphasis on Afro-Americana; yet it probably conformed all the same to the Boasian emphasis, insofar as it was heavily historical in direction. Like other Boas students, Herskovits was engaged in good part in documenting the past. Viewed from the vantage-point of the sociology of knowledge, one might suppose that Herskovits felt he had first to prove that there *was* such a past, in order to validate Afro-Americans as a fit subject of anthropological study. Surely, to judge by the ordinary canons of North American anthropological prestige, fieldwork among Afro-Americans was not the way to get ahead.

The reasons for the general lack of interest in Afro-Americana on the part of North American anthropologists are doubtless diverse. There was first the question whether North American Negroes could be said to have a different culture from that of the majority—the very asking of which was unpopular. Moreover, as Dr. Ann Fischer has pointed out in a recent (1969) paper, white anthropologists found themselves compelled to conform to local *mores* in doing fieldwork among Afro-Americans in this country, such that their ethnographies usually became studies of the etiquette of race relations, rather than studies of Afro-American communities and subcultures. Other, possibly more subtle reasons may be linked to the relativistic posture of many ethnographers; it can be embarrassing to defend the values of one's informants, when those same informants are members of an oppressed minority, while the ethnographer—like it or not—is a member of the oppressing majority. Moreover, such embarrassment is likely to be more acute when one seeks to study one's fellow-citizens; Dr. Fischer notes that most of us—the writer included—have been far readier to study Afro-American cultures elsewhere than to study Afro-American culture in our own country.

There is, however, yet another dimension to the laggardness of North American anthropologists toward the study of Afro-American cultures which requires mention. Anthropology has its own preoccupation with purity, and this is the purity of primitivity—what one cynical colleague has dubbed "the search for the uncontaminated McCoy." This preoccupation has persisted until the present among North American anthropologists, even though the insistence on North American Indian studies has not. Whereas anthropologists from this country now move throughout the whole world in search of peoples to study, the unarticulated preference for "naked savages" still hovers around us. Peoples who have been influenced by "civilization," especially "Western civilization," are somehow less interesting, not more, because of it; and peoples who are superficially "just like us" are the least interesting of all. This bias—for that is what it is—has tended to preclude the study not only of Afro-Americans, but of many other categories of human beings as well. And while a very good case can be made for insisting that students deal early in their careers with cultures that are significantly different from their own, it is more difficult to maintain the view that one is disqualified automatically and perpetually from studying peoples who share something culturally with the observer.

Thus, while even the Afro-Americanists among us were more disposed to study Afro-Americans in Brazil or in Haiti than in the United States, it is also true that Afro-Americanist studies generally have won little attention or prestige in North American anthropology. One reason, related neither to racism nor to the failure of cultural relativity, is that Afro-Americans, nearly everywhere in the Hemisphere, are very Western, culturally. Houses constructed of old Coca-Cola signs, a cuisine littered with canned corned beef and imported Spanish olives, ritual shot through with the cross and the palm leaf, languages seemingly pasted together with "ungrammatical" Indo-European usages, all observed within the reach of radio and television—these are not the things anthropologists' dreams are made of.

Yet we have begun to learn that it is the carriers of *these* cultures, both as victims and aggressors, who are asking today's questions, and providing irresistible answers. It becomes no longer a matter of what we shall do for them, but of what they must know, and have, in order to do for themselves. The search for an anthropology concerned with the widest issues of modern life has hence paralleled the search of the westernized for a voice in the modern world. That this picture is changing is suggested by the papers in the present collection, many of which give evidence of the new willingness of young North American anthropologists to advance a pressing intellectual task—one that should have been undertaken decades ago, and in which our pioneer predecessors were few.

Here we have, it seems to me, the major thrust of this book. It is a book about peoples who cannot escape and who indeed, are choosing in many cases not to escape but to belong, though, reasonably enough, on their own terms. Their ordinariness is distinguished precisely by its lack of the exotic, a word that has too long laid a curse on anthropology as a science of man. The mystery of the human condition is not what man has, but what he does with what he has; this is as true of the people who walk these pages as it once was of those naked savages who inspired anthropology.

No one has said it better than Joseph Mitchell (1938), whose ethnographies of the North American city properly belong on the same shelf as Malinowski's on the Trobrianders:

> The people in a number of the stories are of the kind that many writers have recently got in the habit of referring to as "the little people." I regard this phrase as patronizing and repulsive. There are no little people in this book. They are as big as you are, whoever you are.

REFERENCES CITED

ELLISON, R.
    1964 Shadow and act. New York: Random House, Inc.

FISCHER, A.
    1969 The effect upon anthropological studies of U.S. Negroes of the professional personality and subculture of anthropologists. (mimeo.)

HERSKOVITS, M. J.
    1930 The Negro in the New World: the statement of a problem. American Anthropologist 32(1):145–55.
    1941 The myth of the Negro past. New York, Harper and Brothers.
    1945 Problem, method and theory in Afroamerican studies. Afroamérica I(1–2):5–24.

MINTZ, S.
    1951 Cañamelar: the contemporary culture of a rural Puerto Rican proletariat. Unpublished Ph.D. thesis, Columbia University.
    1953a The folk-urban continuum and the rural proletarian community. The American Journal of Sociology LIX(2):136–43.
    1953b The culture history of a Puerto Rican sugar cane plantation, 1876–1949. Hispanic American Historical Review 33(2):224–51.
    1956 Cañamelar: the subculture of a rural sugar plantation proletariat. *In* J. Steward *et al.*, The people of Puerto Rico. Urbana: University of Illinois Press.
    1961 Review of Elkins' Slavery. American Anthropologist 63(3):579–87.

MITCHELL, J.
    1938 McSorley's wonderful saloon. New York, Grosset and Dunlap.

MORSE, R.
    1964 Negro-white relations in Latin America. *In* Reports and speeches of the ninth Yale conference on the teaching of the social studies, April 3–4, New Haven, 13pp.

PIERSON, D.
    1942 Negroes in Brazil. Chicago: University of Chicago Press.

1953 Africans and their descendants at Bahia, Brasil. *In* Les Afro-Américains, Mémoires de l'Institut Français d'Afrique Noire No. 27:153–56.

SERVICE, E. R.
1955 Indian-European relations in colonial Latin America. American Anthropologist 57(1):411–25.

VALENTINE, C.
1968 Culture and poverty: critique and counter-proposals. Chicago: University of Chicago Press.

WOLF, E.
1959 Specific aspects of plantation systems in the New World: community subcultures and social class. *In* Plantation systems of the New World. Washington, D.C.: Pan American Union, Social Science Monographs, II.

X, MALCOLM
1964 The autobiography of Malcolm X. New York: Grove Press.

ZELINSKY, W.
1949 The historical geography of the Negro population of Latin America. Journal of Negro History 34(2):153–221.

PREFACE

Anthropologists are people who specialize in the study of the culturally exotic. They traditionally gather their own data through intensive participation in the lifeways of a people chosen for investigation, and analyze these data in the broadest possible perspective of space and time. When cultural anthropologists think about a new problem they frequently focus on areas and people about which little or nothing is known. Research often comes to mean the gathering of new information with which established theoretical propositions may be confronted, tested and refined.

For nearly 400 years Africans were brought to the New World to work in what were to become the least developed areas of developing societies. They were to serve primarily agrarian aspects of industrializing economies, and were relegated to socio-economic sectors in which direct competition with Euro-colonists was minimal. More often than not their attention was turned to the need for a cash income, while their actual labor was turned to subsistence pursuits. In most of the Caribbean-United States regions they remained enslaved well into the nineteenth century to serve plantation interests, while the peripheral regions, including maritime Canada and the west coast of northern South America and the Andes, saw an earlier freedom, and plantations exerted little or no force.

In various ways, and by various mechanisms, populations of Afro-Americans have been excluded from full participation in the nations, states, and territories to which they were brought. Subject to English, French, Dutch, Spanish, Portuguese, and a bevy of "Creole" colonial policies, by a number of methods and through various ideologies, Negroes in the New World have diversified and endured until the picture today is one of multiple cultures and subcultures existing in various environments and participating in multiple ways in the socio-economic lives of their respective societies. High in the Andes of Colombia and Ecuador, in the "yungas" of Bolivia, the tropical rainforests of the north Pacific and Atlantic coasts and in most of the tropical lowlands of South America, through Central America and Mexico, in the Caribbean Islands, on the desert slopes of Ecuador, and the arid coast of Peru, in southern South America in varied rural enclaves, in cities and towns throughout the Americas, in the northern temperate zones of Canadian Maritimes and Canadian Great Plains, Afro-Americans have adapted to their enormously varied ecological niches, and have expanded their specific populations. They represent tribal, state, peasant, rural and urban proletariat, middle class, and elite levels of sociocultural integration. For many laymen and scholars, however, Afro-Americans are not as well known in their variety as are American Indians, or other New World ethnic aggregates.

For anthropology, contemporary studies of New World Negroes have emphasized historical depth and contemporary geographic spread. The tendency has been to examine the African background, slavery and its effects, the dispersal of Afro-Americans throughout the New World, and the multiple cultures of Afro-Americans. The assumption has usually been that research in American cities is better left to other professionals: sociologists, economists, historians, political scientists—to professionals especially equipped to work in the great "melting pots" of America. We have assumed that other professionals would use our data on temporal and spatial distribution, that they would come to see Afro-American adaptations in terms of a multiplicity of responses to innumerable hardships and pressures. We have assumed that those seeking to understand the problems of contemporary urban ghetto life, whether the ghetto be black or white or defined by religious preference, would approach their problems not only with reference to immediate socio-economic pressures, but with the sophistication derived from anthropological studies of New World Negro cultures.

We have been wrong. It is necessary to state positively and illustrate judiciously the contribution which anthropology is making to the understanding of New World Negro societies. Current interest in Afro-American anthropology must be brought under the aegis of contemporary trends in theory and method, and where possible, the theory and method must be set in terms of contemporary relevance. This book purports to take some steps in these directions.

Afro-American Anthropology will be considered by some as a pretentious title for this book. "There is no special sub-field of anthropology devoted to Afro-America," many will say, and many others will say, "There is no Afro-America." Such criticisms are fully justified and we hereby acknowledge them.

But there is a counter argument to which we have succumbed. This argument is predicated on the assumption that the literary function of title semantics is primarily connotative. Anthropologists tend to be comparative in perspective, and inductive in their generalizations from field data. The combination of field work, inductive generalization, and subsequent construction of relevant categories for purposes of inter- and intra-cultural comparison does lend a distinctiveness of approach to definable black aggregates throughout the New World. Although Afro-American anthropology is not a distinctive sub-discipline (and, we hope, it never will be), "anthropology" in the title does connote a range of approaches, which, although overlapping with other disciplines, nevertheless characterizes the congeries of studies reported in this book.

"Afro-American" refers to two presently interrelated, but fundamentally independent constructs. First, it refers to carriers of culture—a cultural stream of elements, complexes, and themes characteristic of Africa south of the Sahara that seem to persist in the New World, regardless of the carriers. Let us be clear. Afro-America, in its real anthropological perspective, must include information about the Afro-rhythms of the Cayapa Indians of western Ecuador, about West African Ashanti concepts about blood probably manifest among the Guajiro Indians of northeastern Colombia and Venezuela, about African animal tales found today among the Indians of Amazonia and, about culinary habits of white Mississippians.

This book is deficient in that it fails to include an analysis of a current of an Afro-American stream among non-"blacks."

Second, "Afro-American" presently refers to an important identity referent of black aggregates within societies where "non-whiteness" is an important criterion for categorical social relationships which differentiate (i.e., segregate) people on the basis of observable, or imputed, ethnicity. Afro-American, in this social structural sense, refers to people classed as "black" or "Negro" or 'Preto" or "Noire" or "colored" as a distinctive portion of a "non-white" population within a social system which stresses color or descent from color as one means of sorting people into political, prestige, or economic classes for particular purposes.

The authors of the papers in this volume have ranged freely through such terms as "Afro-America," "black," and "Negro," usually without explaining fully their usage. The one author, Marvin Harris, who devotes full attention to the calculus of Brazilian racial identity, shows us how terribly complicated clarity about ethnicity can be, particularly in contexts where the calculus of identity itself is subject to strategic ambiguity. We have encouraged authors to seek their own terms, eschewing imposed categories drawn from professional or ethical biases in an area in which there is enormous variety in the folk and professional classes, and which, sadly, continues to confuse racial and cultural criteria. For example, in contemporary America. "Afro-America" is once again being used to refer to a cultural stream, sometimes to an idealized, non-existent, or newly created stream; it also refers to communities of American Negroes involved in cultural revitalization. "Black" refers to a color category in the United States which connotes non-mainstream aggregates with positive identity referents to "Afro-American communities." Obviously, "mainstream" and "Afro-American communities" are both concepts for which one should do a calculus of cultural identity to portray the full range of connotations attached to the concepts. "Negro" seems to refer to a category of "non-white" with or without posiitve identity referents to an Afro-American community. For the most part, we have let context determine the denotations and connotations of such terms.

We do not see this book as representative of a sub-field of Afro-American anthropology. We do see it as bringing theoretical and methodological perspectives associated with anthropology to bear on some of the persistent problems in Afro-American research—problems of family, kinship, ethnicity, and economics; of bilingualism and code-switching; of unconventional politics; of adaptations to marginality; and in the problems of "building black identities" as such problems exist in the context of New World ethnic exclusion.

As much as possible, we have also sought to broaden the perspective of the Afro-American geographical range by including recent studies by anthropologists from regions in which descriptions of black people have been previously unknown to the discipline. The book introduces new studies from the Ecuadorian Andes and the rain-forest coast, from Colombia, Panama, and Honduras. It also includes materials on the better studied regions in the West Indies (Trinidad, Nevis, Antigua), and from San Andrés, Haiti, Guyana, and Brazil. In the United States we have included material from the urban north, the rural north, and the rural south.

The editors met for the first time during the American Anthropological Association meetings held in Pittsburgh in November, 1966. Whitten had just returned from his first summer among Nova Scotian Negroes with whom he had begun to work after two years of field work with Ecuadorian and Colombian blacks. He was primarily interested in socio-economic adaptation and the political consequences of exclusion and marginality. Szwed for years had been working on pieces written on American Negro sub-cultures, had spent a summer in Trinidad, and had begun a long range study of symbolic adaptation of urban black aggregates in Philadelphia. Together, the editors first discussed areas of mutual interest (Szwed had worked for two years in the Canadian Maritimes, but with non-Negroes; Whitten had been working on Negro folklore in South America and North America, but lacked a broad, comparative base-line), and decided to organize a symposium to bring together scholars who wished to discuss matters pertaining to the contemporary "Black Americas."

During this meeting the editors talked with several people who had worked in two or more areas of the New World with Afro-American aggregates about the possibility of reassessing the direction and understanding of contemporary Afro-American research. There was general agreement that reassessment was needed, and heightened communication between scholars interested in New World Negro studies might be affected expeditiously through an open conference. Toward this end the editors organized a day-long symposium of twelve anthropologists to consider studies of New World Negroes made since 1941, the date of publication of Melville J. Herskovits' important book, *The Myth of the Negro Past*. The symposium was held at the 1967 A. A. A. meetings in Washington, D.C., the following papers being presented in this order:

Norman E. Whitten, Jr. (Washington University, St. Louis)
Adaptation and adaptability as processes of microevolutionary change in New World Negro communities
Thomas J. Price (Williams College)
Ethnohistory and self-image in three New World Negro societies
Bette E. Landman (Temple University)
Homebodies vs. wage-earners: a case of male role conflict in the British West Indies
Ann Fischer (Tulane University)
Fertility and the matrifocal tradition in Negro families
Erika Bourguignon (Ohio State University)
Religious syncretisms among New World Negroes
Daniel J. Crowley (University of California, Davis)
The creolization of Africanisms
John F. Szwed (Temple University)
Expressing the changes: musical adaptation among New World Negroes
Alan Lomax (Columbia University)
The homogeneity of African-New World Negro musical style
Roger D. Abrahams (University of Texas)
Patterns of performance in the British West Indies
Karl Reisman (Brandeis University)
Code variability in a West Indian village
Guy B. Johnson (University of North Carolina)
The Gullah dialect revisited: a note on linguistic acculturation
Charles A. Valentine (Washington University, St. Louis)
The Negro problem: a critique

The symposium members agreed to raise the question of whether there were similarities among Negroes living in distinctly different sociocultural systems in the New World which were in contrast with non-Negroes in similar socio-economic situations. Each anthropologist prepared a paper indicating the nature of his theoretical or methodological contribution; the plan was to first focus on data from an area in which he had done field work, and then to discuss his position by reference to data from other areas. We planned an overall discussion in which more solid generalizations could be made and checked against findings on a wide variety of New World Negro cultures, including urban ghettos in the northern United States. One anthropologist with considerable experience in civil-rights activities then designing (and now carrying out) field work in an urban ghetto, Charles A. Valentine, was invited to make a critique of the papers at the end of the symposium. Authors of other volunteered papers at the same meeting also attended and contributed to the general discussion. This book is an eventual outgrowth of the symposium and ensuing discussion.

For Whitten, this volume represents the first synthesis of work begun at the University of North Carolina in 1959. Research during the past ten years has largely been supported by the National Institute of Mental Health. Aspects of the field work leading to the 1967 symposium were made possible by Public Health Service Fellowship MH 14333 and by supplements M-54447 SSS and MH 06978-01SSS RO4 from the National Institute of Mental Health, by National Institutes of Health Grant 1-SO1-FR5444, and by National Institute of Mental Health Small Grants MH 12809-01 and MH 13750-01. The manuscript was completed under NIMH Grant No. 1 PO 1 MH15567-01, which also allowed the senior editor released time to develop a model of adaptation to economic marginality. Tulane University and the Universidad del Valle in Cali, Colombia, provided an opportunity for Whitten to explore some aspects of Afro-America in a broad perspective during 1964 and 1965. Washington University has been generous in support of his work, providing faculty grants for the summers of 1966 and 1968, and by helping to defray expenses of the symposium and the assemblage of materials during 1967 and 1968. Latin American Studies at Washington University has also helped defray expenses pertaining to the Ecuadorian work.

A Lehigh University Summer grant allowed John F. Szwed time to develop some of this material during 1965.

We are indebted to the following persons who offered valuable suggestions and provided constructive criticism at various stages of preparation of the manuscript: John W. Bennett, Erika Bourguignon, Mary Farvar, Thrace Harris, James R. Jaquith, Ann Harris, Pertti Pelto, Nadia Ramzy, Ted Polhemus, William Stewart, George Talbot, Charles A. Valentine, and Alvin W. Wolfe. Sue Szwed and Sibby Whitten, our wives, have contributed considerably to this effort. The Free Press provided a grant to cover some expenses involved in typing the manuscript and in developing the photographic essay.

Finally, we wish to express our sincere gratitude to Mrs. Rose Marie Jaquith who served as editorial assistant and typist during the final compilation of papers at Washington University between November, 1968, and April, 1969, and to Miss Cynthia Gillette who worked under heavy pressures to collate and synthesize bibliography and references. Both Mrs. Jaquith and Miss Gillette have shown an indefatigable drive to complete this book on schedule. Without this assistance we would have been unable to devote our own time to the necessary job of editing and writing.

Norman E. Whitten, Jr.
John F. Szwed

Preface to the Pictorial Essay

My interest in preparing this essay stems from my professional concerns as an anthropologist, my activities as Associate Editor, and more especially, Art Director of *Trans-Action* magazine. The essay concentrates on largely visual information to amplify and comment on major elements and themes raised in the body of the book. Such a portrayal demands a high degree of cooperation among contributors, photographers, editors, and publisher. It was first necessary to consider all articles (in preliminary drafts, as well as final form) and to discuss them with Norman E. Whitten, Jr. Then, the contributors to this volume, other specialists who had worked in the areas under consideration, freelance photographers, and photo agencies were contacted with a request for pictures of high quality and "human interest" which could also be used to represent complex concepts used in the various articles. Although much of what we asked for rarely appears in the index to the filing systems of photographers and agencies the response was tremendous. As might be expected, however, the coverage was extremely uneven, and the limitations imposed by space and cost ultimately structured our final selection.

From the outset there was a general agreement that we should avoid the "typical" and the "common" portrayals of Afro-American societies and cultures, and that we should seek photographs that were not readily accessible in other photographic sections dealing with black lifeways. Such decisions, when translated into production of a scholarly photographic essay, pose very special problems.

Norman E. Whitten, Jr., who originally suggested the essay to me, and to The Free Press, has contributed many suggestions and collaborated on the written text. Ann Novotny of Research Reports assisted in the picture research. Charles Reynolds and Sam Holmes and the staffs of several photographic agencies were also helpful, particularly Betty Dornhiem, Jimmy Fox, Dave Wilson, Natalie Smith, Liz Tamiso and Ted Leighton. The sections on *Ecstasy on Maxwell Street* and *Migratory wage labor*, were dependent upon the photographic documentation of James Newberry and Richard Bellak, respectively.

Many anthropologists and photographers contributed material of very high quality which unfortunately could not be used because of space limitations, cost, or balance. We are indebted to all those who sent material and sincerely regret that more could not be printed. Some of the original picture research was done for the article, "Negroes in the New World: Anthropologists Look at Afro-Americans," which appeared in the July/August issue of *Trans*-Action (1968). *Trans*-Action's staff contributed both to that effort and to the current one.

Funds for this essay were made possible by a grant from African Studies at Washington University, a grant from The Free Press, and by Norman E. Whitten, Jr. Finally, I am indebted to Miss Sara Miller, who coordinated and contributed to the exchange of information among contributors, photographers, and my own staff.

George A. Talbot

Afro-Americans

> *". . . You Got to Walk that Lonesome Valley*
> *You Got to Go There by Yourself . . ." (American Spiritual)*

This essay represents a convergence of skills—the ability of photographers to visually portray diverse lifeways and the anthropological stress on comparison of specific items of culture.

"*. . . and I feel like traveling on . . .*" (Negro spiritual). Above, a Gullah-speaking man from the "Sea Island" coast of Georgia returns to his small home. In the 1930's many Gullah-speaking folk migrated to Harlem.

Gullah speech is unintelligible to a speaker of "standard American English"; it represents the most exotic black language spoken in North America.

Going up river in Boni Country.

The origins of the carving traditions shown below lie in 17th and 18th century Africa. But the products are Afro-American creations—productions of art growing out of the New World contexts and experiences, built upon patterns from past African civilization.

A grave yard at Sunbury, Georgia, circa 1930.   Carvings from the Georgia coastal area.

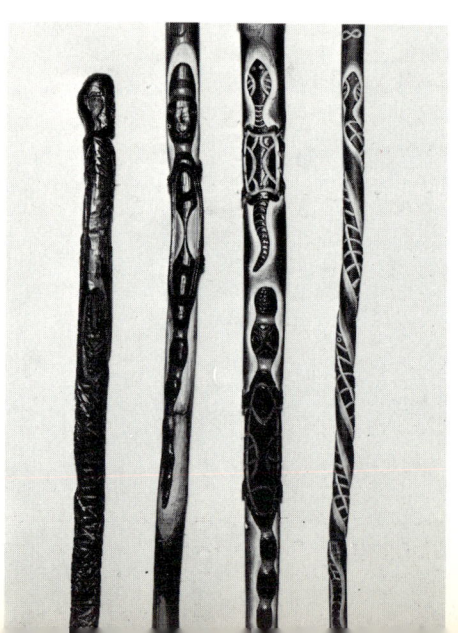

The Search for Origins

In their search for "Africanisms" and in their desire to contribute to the knowledge of exotic lifeways, anthropologists have frequently "gone into the bush." The mere identification of Afro-American cultural traits, unfortunately, may tell us little about how black people have adapted to varied environments in northern and southern hemispheres. Afro-American cultures may be seen as streams of elements that take on meaning and relevance in specific social and environmental settings.

Oracle divination among the Boni.

Carving a Djuka stool.

A Boni girl—scarification is a trait with clear African origin.

A Boni village.

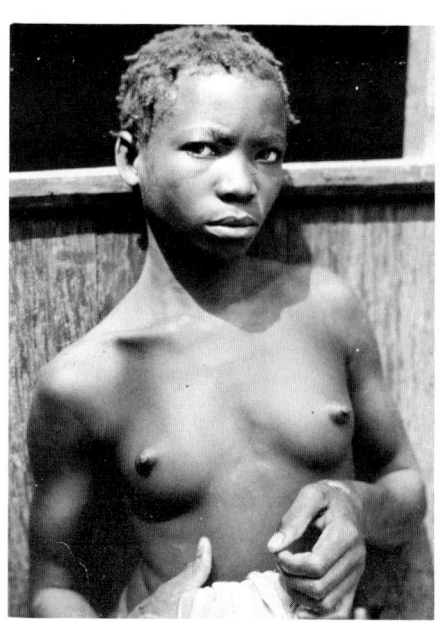

Slash and burn agriculture.

Bush People

The so-called Bush Negroes make up several tribal groups of Afro-Americans inhabiting the inland waterways of Surinam and French Guiana. Such groups include the Boni (Aluku), Djuka (Aucaner), Saramacca, Mataway, and Paramaka. These groups have been adapting to their natural environment since the end of the 17th century, when they first escaped from slavery and began to form into tribal groups patterned on life and organizations characteristic of their West African homeland.

At a Boni wake, a coffin rests unsteadily on the heads of the pallbearers. The movement of the box as it is carried is supposed to reveal the cause of the deceased's death by tilting itself toward the person guilty of witchcraft.

In the context of the money economy a new element enters the environment of the bush Negroes. On the Maroni River, a Boni family must enter the cash economy through white traders who represent the "white environment."

Race and Ethnicity

"... to the white mind, prefixing anything with "Negro" automatically consigned it to an inferior category" (Cleaver, Soul on Ice, 80). Ethnicity is not really a matter of "race" nor are categorical social relationships necessarily determined by specific degrees of "color consciousness."

Individuals, if not groups, may show considerable warmth across categorical barriers.

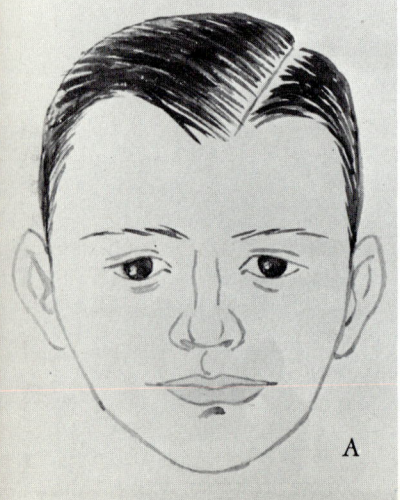
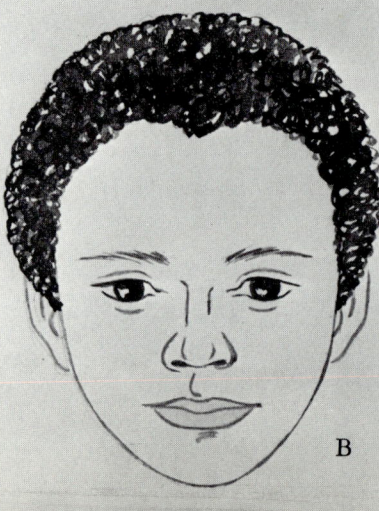

A B C

Rio de Janeiro, Brazil.

What is a Negro? Who are to be placed in the "inferior category" by the "whites"? What criteria exist in a particular culture for racist thought? Although North Americans think in *Negro–non-Negro* binary categories, such is not the case in Brazil. Marvin Harris, using male and female drawings such as these, elicited varied responses. For example, Brazilians agree that A is "white" (*branco*) and E is "black" (*preta*). But C and D elicited responses ranging from black to white, with a number of other categories also suggested. B has no adequate English gloss, or translation, but the Brazilians agree on the category *sarará*. A, C, D, are male. B and E are female.

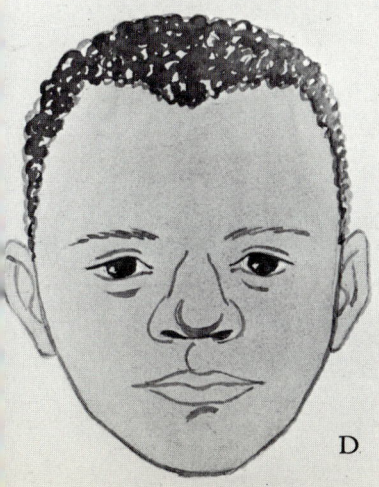 

Barbados.

Favela, Rio de Janeiro, Brazil.

Right, Chocó, Colombia.

Rural Paraguay.

The Black Americas

Throughout the Americas Negroes have often been relegated to the agricultural aspects of industrializing economies. The results lead to social and economic marginality which may make similarities in patterns of social organization understandable. Frequently, black people in such circumstances must adapt to both cash and subsistence economies.

Haiti—crippled beggars in the market place, at Fonds des Nègres.

Below, slum, Atlanta, U.S.A.

A Diversity of Contexts

Specific cultural and political contexts are very different in the Americas, and within them many Afro-Americans have adapted to their specific niches. It is clear that any similarities between Afro-American social systems must also be seen with reference to ethnic diversity within the "Afro-American community" and by specific reference to varied cultural, economic, and political settings.

Eastern Canada, where black power is in its infancy.

New political ideology, Cuba.

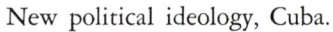

"*La Violencia,*" Colombia—two parties strive for control within a "coalition government."

Above, mending the *Atarraya* in western Colombia; right, a Gullah fisherman throws the same kind of net on the south coast of the U.S.A.

Traders and Markets

Black traders from the Chota Valley and Otavalo Indians compete over sales of potatoes, corn, and *fresca* at a rail stop in the Ecuadorian Andes.

Favela market, Brazil.   *Marchanta,* Dominican Republic.

Maxwell Street market, Chicago, U.S.A.

Trading is the core of an internal marketing system which is necessary for survival in a cash economy to which direct access is restricted to those classed as "non-Negro." The internal marketing system must be seen in terms of degrees of articulation to a national and international money economy, not in terms of ethnicity or cultural traits, except where ethnicity itself becomes a significant variable in bargaining and marketing procedures.

Shopkeeper, San Lorenzo, western Ecuador.

Black Representatives of an Indian Culture

West Indian slaves escaped, just as the Bush Negroes of the Guianas did. Some took refuge with the Carib Indians on the Island of St. Vincent, adopting their language and customs. By the end of the 18th century most Carib had become black. Their deportation to the Island of Roatán off the coast of Honduras began their penetration into Honduras and Nicaragua, where they now represent the last living remnant of Carib culture. They also exhibit characteristic forms of "Afro-American" family and household composition, which suggests that their social system is a result of adaptation to socio-economic conditions, not a carry-over from an "Afro-Indian" past.

Street dancer.

Fish market, Stann Creek.

Below, local pub in Belize City, British Honduras.

Family and Household

A middle class family shopping, deep South, U.S.A.

Headman of a cooperative farm and his family, Jamaica.

A Carib man and child, British Honduras.

Mother and child, Haiti.

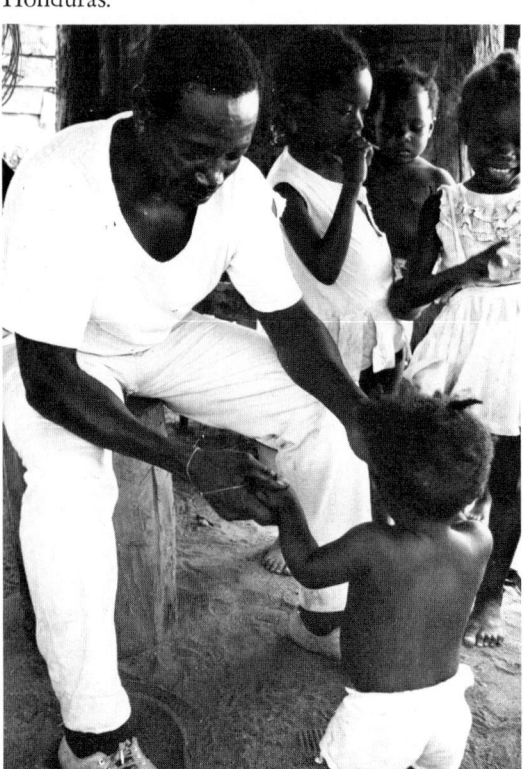

A farm family in the deep South, U.S.A.

The role of family and household organization in economic activities and transmitting culture has long plagued Afro-American research. Consistencies are not always what they seem. Perhaps we have too readily employed the "middle class" perspective of a "stable parent-child nucleus" as an explanatory factor in human behavior. Perhaps a larger grouping of kinsmen constitutes the "minimal social grouping" in systems of marginality.

Below, corner boys in the Hough district, Cleveland, U.S.A.

Paul Evans is typical of many migrants who join work crews in an attempt to support themselves and their families. Each year he leaves his family home in Tennessee to join a crew going east.

A common way to organize a crew is to select a leader who can mobilize his kinsmen. Such organization in response to migratory wage labor suggests that family life in such circumstances should be seen in terms of ramifying networks of kinsmen oriented toward opportunism in gaining cash.

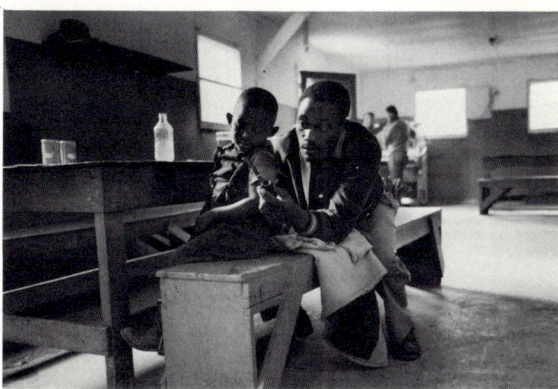

Migratory Wage Labor

The migrant is exposed to exploitation by his employers and others who come to camp to hustle the workers. Right, local whites sell used appliances at high prices to camp workers.

Many migrants come from the deep South—some come from as far as the West Indies.

Religion

Laying on of hands at a street revival in Chicago, U.S.A.

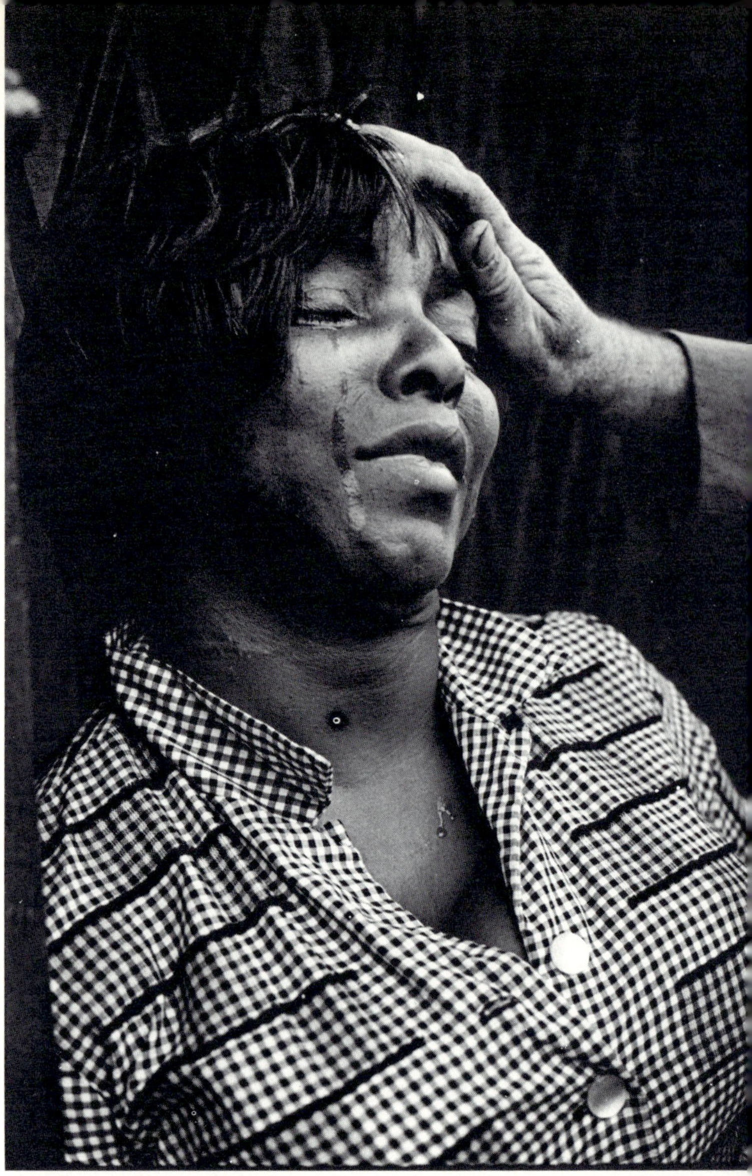

Below, Seventh Day Adventists, Trinidad.

River funeral, northwest Ecuador.

Gospel preacher, Chicago, U.S.A.

Haiti—rural folk prepare for a ceremony of *Vodû*.

Syncretisms—amalgamations of different traditions to form unique configurations in the New World—are common among Afro-Americans in their respective cultures. Protestant, Catholic, Jewish and Muslim traditions have taken on a variety of traits, both African and European.

A Macumba ceremony, Brazil.

Music is more often than not the domain in which the most strikingly African forms are to be found. Music may often be thought of as a cultural "focus," defined by Melville J. Herskovits as "that area of activity or belief where the greatest awareness of form exists, the most discussion of values is heard, the widest difference in structure is to be discerned" (Cultural Dynamics, 183).

Drum tuning, Trinidad.

Negro beggar joins an Indian pan-pipe player, Quito, Ecuador.

Carib drummers, British Honduras.

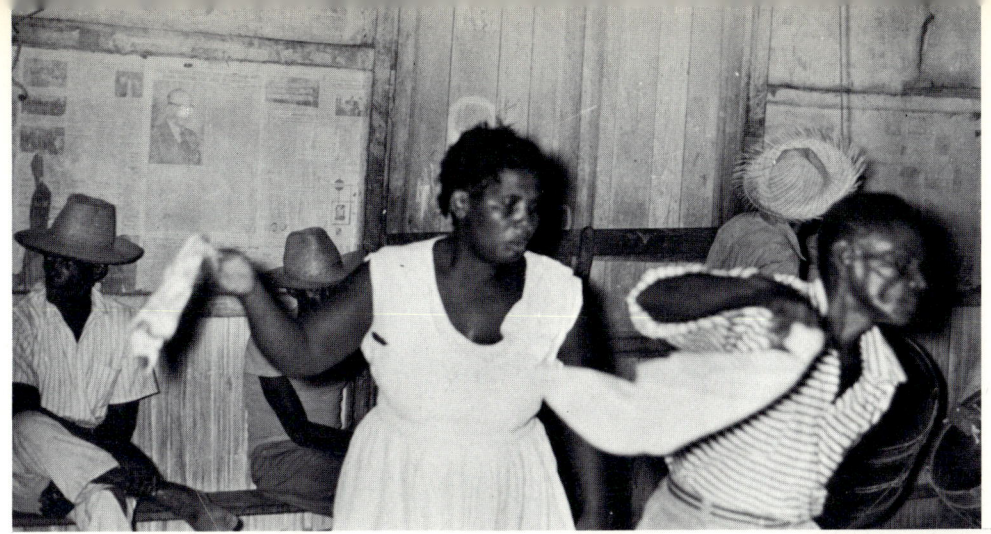

Music as a Focus

The currulao, or marimba dance. Above and right, some of the most African music in the New World is played in western Ecuador and Colombia.

String band, Carnival, Martinique.

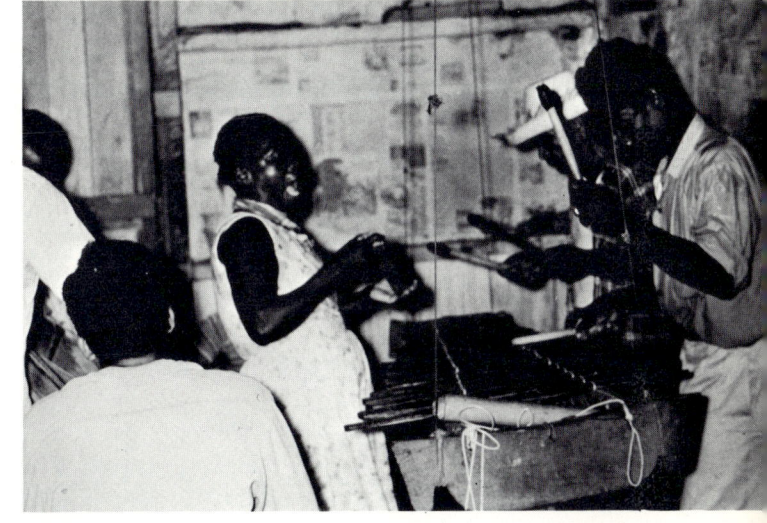

Ecstasy on Maxwell Street

Perhaps due to their emphasis on going into the bush in a search for the exotic, anthropologists have tended to avoid direct contact with subcultures within their own nation. Such avoidance includes a failure, until recently, to come to grips with contemporary Afro-American culture in its richness and diversity.

Maxwell Street was the market of the old Jewish Ghetto on Chicago's near south side. Serving eastern European immigrants who clung to old world ways, it was the subject of Louis Wirth's famous book, The Ghetto. *The market has seen changes in the ethnic composition and the physical destruction of its milieu through urban renewal. But its functions of providing a center for trade and ritual activity remain.*

Top row, bottom row—secular contexts provide outlets for cultural expression.

Revivalist.

Revivalist.

Black Jews.

Patterns of Performance

Above, The Giant of Despair, Nevis.   Below, Carnival, New Orleans, U.S.A.

One of the concomitants of creole culture has been a rich harvest of performance styles and patterns throughout the Americas.

Carnival—above, Haiti; below, Trinidad.

Philadelphia, U.S.A.

Like It Is

"Soul" represents the expressive core of contemporary Afro-American life. Soul is black. To have soul is to be black. To be black is to live without fear in a hostile and often deadly white-dominated environment. To be black is to stand up to the hitherto unquestioned power of white America and say "I'm black and I'm proud."

New York, U.S.A.

Wilson Pickett, soul singer.

A conversation about what to do if attacked by a man with a gun.

In the Colombian Andes conservative and liberal parties cut across ethnic lines.

Right, Milwaukee, U.S.A.

Below, in the plural society, such as Guyana, two sectors (Afro-American and East Indian) may divide into opposing parties, but power and control often remain with the white European minority.

Power and Politics

In the United States polarity created by the system of separating "Negroes" from "non-Negroes" is reflected in the contemporary concepts of ethnicity and power. The black power movement now seems to hang together in a segmentary way—through series of ritual linkages between groups with differing ideologies but playing complementary strategies. Segmentary systems confuse white politicians who are accustomed to a pyramid model, in which Afro-Americans are relegated to the bottom, or base.

Washington, D.C., Spring 1968.

New York, U.S.A.

"... Ain't Nobody Else Can Go There for You
You Got to Go There by Yourself."

"... we survived our forced march and travail through the Valley of Slavery, Suffering, and Death.... And we had thought that our hard climb out of that cruel valley led to some cool, green and peaceful, sunlit place—but it's all jungle here, a wild and savage wilderness that's overrun with ruins" (Cleaver, Soul on Ice, 210).

Above, Bobby Seale, Chairman and co-founder of the Black Panther Party, Aug. 25, 1968, Los Angeles, U.S.A.

INTRODUCTION

Norman E. Whitten, Jr. and John F. Szwed

Melville J. Herskovits' *The Myth of the Negro Past* (1941) was the first major publication about Afro-America by an American anthropologist.[1] This book presents some of the methodological, theoretical, and substantive developments since 1941, in an attempt to update Afro-American studies in anthropology since publication of *The Myth*.

The Myth of the Negro Past was the initial publication of the 1938 Carnegie project, headed by Gunnar Myrdal, which also produced such classics as *An American Dilemma*.[2] Herskovits had made earlier statements about Afro-American culture patterns. He reviewed the importance of Afro-American research for a professional audience in 1930, and in 1935 he summarized the available anthropological literature for social scientists generally.[3]

In preparing his book, Herskovits made use of Sir Harry H. Johnston's important traveler's account (1910). Although classifiable as racist and imperialist in our present sense, Johnston's work is nevertheless impressive in its extent. Due recognition is given to it by Herskovits' comments (1958:10):

> That the Negro peoples in the New World offer unusual opportunities for research has been remarked by several students. Sir Harry H. Johnston, in the volume wherein he reports a visit to the West Indies and the United States in 1910, shows with clarity how rich a yield can be provided by knowledge of the ancestral continent when directed toward the New World scene. Despite the shortness of his stay, and the undisciplined observation and analysis of data that here, as in other works, characterize the writings of this soldier, writer and artist, his book is illuminating. For it demonstrates how much in the way of aboriginal tradition exists in West Indian and South American regions where, in disregard of even its surface manifestations, it has been overlooked by those students from

Portions of this section are reprinted with permission from *Trans-Action*, Vol. 5, No. 8 (July–August 1968), pp. 49–56.

the United States, who, without grounding in African culture and equipped only with the hypothesis of the disappearance of African customs as a frame of reference, have tended to minimize African retentions.

The reader interested in renewing his acquaintance with Afro-America is well advised to peruse the photos and chapters of Sir Harry Johnston. This book will certainly give a sense of the extent of Afro-American penetration into the New World. This penetration, in spite of current interest, is frequently forgotten, or ignored, by contemporary scholars seeking cultural patterns and adaptive strategies of Negroes in New World nations and territories.[4]

Herskovits' early work in the United States was strongly influenced by that of his mentor, Franz Boas, with whom he studied from 1920–23. Boas' strong stand against racism in anthropology (and other disciplines) is most clearly set forth by George W. Stocking, Jr., in his recent book, *Race, Culture and Evolution* (1968).[5] In keeping with the thrust of early American anthropology, Herskovits first turned to the social problem of American racism. His earliest publications and activities showed the same blending of science and political ideology that his teacher had displayed. From his readings on Africa and his research in physical anthropology, Herskovits assaulted current notions of race with a series of articles in popular magazines (Herskovits 1924a, 1924b), with reviews, and public lectures. In order to shed light on genetic "intermixing" of African with non-African, his early technique was to measure American Negroes with calipers and a tape measure to ascertain such features as the breadth of their noses and the length of their limbs, and to compare these measurements with those from whites. He combined his anthropometric techniques with genealogical method by asking the people measured about their ancestry, and then compared their reported genealogies with their phenotypic, or visible, characteristics. Between 1924 and 1928, while conducting this research among American Negroes, he published some 29 articles on Negro growth, development, pigmentation, and other phenotypic characteristics. In 1928, culminating four years of work, he wrote (Midland paperback 1964:17):

> We speak of Negroes in this country, but plainly this is nonsense if we are employing the word "Negro" in its biological sense. The American Negro is an amalgam, and the application of the term "Negro" to him is purely sociological.

Herskovits went on to demonstrate that Negroes, as an aggregate of identifiable people, make up an ethnic category within the United States. He thereby implied that the cultural adaptations of the ethnic category must be considered if we are to comprehend the varieties of sub-cultural traits reputed to contrast between American categories. He followed this popular book with a technical monograph (1930c), by which time he had turned increasing attention to the cultures of New World Negroes. Writing about her late husband's early work and formative ideas, Mrs. Frances B. Herskovits (1966:vii) tells us:

> His field experience in Surinam in 1928 and 1929 had a profound influence on his thinking, and though he was scarcely conscious of this at the time, the findings in both the Bush and the city of Paramaribo began shaping his concepts of acculturation. In the Guiana Bush, among the Saramacca peoples, he saw nearly all of western sub-Saharan Africa represented, from what is now Mali to Loango and into the Congo.

After more field work in Surinam (cf. Herskovits and Herskovits 1934, 1936) and

Haiti (Herskovits 1937b)—during which time he maximized opportunities for comparative work within the Caribbean (Herskovits 1966:viii–ix)—West Africa (Herskovits 1938), and later Trinidad (Herskovits and Herskovits 1947a), and Brazil (Herskovits and Herskovits 1943; Herskovits 1946), Herskovits published his major statement on New World Negroes to which we have alluded above. In the preface Herskovits (1958 edition:xiii) immediately raised the issue of the relevance of his work to the United States:

> The approach ... though oriented toward the study of the Negro in the United States, takes into full account the West African, South American, and West Indian data, lacking which, I am convinced, true perspective on the values of Negro life in the country cannot be had, either by the student treating the larger problems of cultural change or by the practical man seeking to lessen racial tension.[6]

HERSKOVITS AND HIS RESEARCH

Obviously, if we are to update Afro-American anthropology since 1941, we must consider the field as it stood nearly 30 years ago. This involves a systematic review of Herskovits' work and writing and some attention to why Herskovits relied so heavily on data from the Caribbean and Africa to understand black American lifeways. In his early years his insistence on detaching race concepts from culture concepts—particularly where confusion of the two affected government policies of immigration, education, and psychological testing (Herskovits 1926, 1927)—often led him to deny cultural differences between white and black American ethnic groups. Thus, in the midst of the Harlem Renaissance (one of the American Negro's first cultural revitalization movements), Herskovits (1925b) in *The Negro's Americanism* (Locke 1925, 1968 edition:359–60) argued that total cultural assimilation had already occurred:

> That they have absorbed the culture of America is too obvious, almost, to be mentioned. They have absorbed it as all great racial and social groups in this country have absorbed it. And they face much the same problem as these groups face. The social ostracism to which they are subjected is only different in extent from that to which the Jew is subjected. The fierce reaction of race-pride is quite the same in both groups. But, whether in Negro or Jew, the protest avails nothing, apparently. All racial and social elements in our population who live here long enough become acculturated, Americanized in the truest sense of the word.... As we turn to Harlem we see its social, economic and political make-up as a part of the larger whole of the city—separate from it, it is true, but still essentially not different from any other American community in which the modes of life and action are determined by the great dicta of "what is done." In other words, it represents, as do all American communities which it resembles, a case of complete acculturation. And so I return to my reaction on first meeting this center of Negro activity, as the complete description of it: "Why, it's the same pattern, only a different shade!"

When Herskovits was forced to consider arguments for cultural differences between American Negro and white aggregates (as when he reviewed Newbell Niles Puckett's *Folk Beliefs of the Southern Negro* [1926] in 1927), he argued that the only possible survivals of African culture were those which were practiced in secrecy, such as Haitian voodoo.[7] Perhaps Herskovits sensed that if a case could be made for the survival of Africanisms among United States Negroes, racists might be able to justify policies of exclusion and segregation by arguing that black Americans had not yet reached the point at which they could qualify as "100 per cent American."[8] At any rate, he was strongly committed (as were sociologists of the time) to the notion of "melting pot" assimilation in America, and his early work shows no sign of his eventual interest in demonstrating otherwise.

But after his Surinam fieldwork in 1928 and 1929 (undertaken with his wife and Morton Kahn [Herskovits and Herskovits 1934, 1936; Kahn 1931]) he showed a new willingness to recognize the possibility of contrasting cultural aspects of blacks and whites in the United States:

> What do the Africans do that the inhabitants of the Negro quarter of New York City also do? May we find perhaps, on closer examination that there are some subtle elements left of what was ancestrally possessed? May not the remnant, if present, consist of some slight intonation, some quirk of pronunciation, some temperamental disposition? (Herskovits 1930b in Herskovits 1966:6).

By the mid-1930's, after a field trip to West Africa, he seriously argued that differences in cultural behavior between whites and Negroes in the United States were a concern for historical and ethnohistorical research, and he began to list some of these differences in his writing. Apparently thinking of the impact that his ideas and data might have on a society that already asserted such differences from a folk perspective, he chose to present his work in such a way as to put the white public on the defensive: first, by showing that cultural differences had an "honorable" basis in legitimate African cultures, and second, by boldly asserting that Afro-American customs and beliefs had affected mainstream culture to the degree that they had already been accepted as American. In a popular article (1935b) he claimed that spirituals, jazz, and certain aspects of southern dialect, etiquette, cuisine, and religion were all African in origin.

Herskovits' great concern for the relativity of cultural behavior often turned up in critical asides aimed at then current liberal concerns with the "pathology" of the Negro family and with solving the "Negro Problem" through education. There is a contemporary ring to passages such as the following (Herskovits 1938–39, in Herskovits 1966:121):

> When for instance, one sees vast programs of Negro education undertaken without the slightest consideration given even to the possibility of some retention of African habits of thought and speech that might influence the Negroes' reception of the instruction thus offered, one cannot but ask how we hope to reach the desired objectives. When we are confronted with ... sociological analyses of Negro family life which make not the slightest attempt to take into account even the chance that the phenomenon being studied might in some way have been influenced by the carryover of certain African traditions ... we can but wonder about the value of such work.

The Herskovitses went to Haiti in 1934, drawn to the island by the publication of J. C. Dorsainvil (1931) and J. Price-Mars (1928) on folk religion. From this work came *Life in a Haitian Valley* (Herskovits 1937b), a book illustrating Herskovits' new consciousness of African contributions to family organization, economics, and religion. But perhaps the most interesting notion presented in this work was his concept of "socialized ambivalence." Sidney Mintz comments (1964:46):

> In this book Herskovits advances the ... idea that Haitian culture is not really an amalgam of two traditions, but two sets of counterposed values or behavioral alternatives, one "African" and the other "European." ... the items he contrasts are of interest: monogamic morality vs. the African tradition of polygyny; obligations toward the

ancestral gods of Africa vs. the threats of eternal damnation; the substitution of games of chance for games of skill; and so on. "In its broader implications, as a matter of fact," Herskovits writes, "it is entirely possible that this socialized ambivalence underlies much of the political and economic instability of Haiti, so that, arising from a fundamental clash of custom within the culture, it is responsible for the many shifts in allegiance that continually take place as it is for the change in attitudes in everyday association."

In commenting upon Herskovits' theoretical foci in *Life in a Haitian Valley* Mintz clearly regrets that the author never followed up on his hypothesis of "socialized ambivalence" in later works (1964:46). Mintz (1964:46–47) properly places Herskovits' emphasis and goals in terms of his interests on finding "Africanisms":

> ... one sees the author adding new information for plotting on his scale of intensities of Africanisms, though there is no indication of how different items can be weighted relatively in each case. *Nor is it entirely clear why formal similarity, especially rather strained similarity, necessarily argues for historical connection or common origin* ... (emphasis added).

We will return to this point later.

The Herskovitses' interest in folk religion (this time the Shango cult) later led them to Trinidad in 1939. Although *Trinidad Village* was not published intil 1947, Herskovits' ideas of African continuity and the processes of cultural change in Afro-America began to be spelled out in numerous publications in the early 1940's.[9]

THE SEARCH FOR AFRICANISMS: SOME CONSEQUENCES

Herskovits' strategy in *The Myth* was to focus on *trait similarities* among the cultures of black people in various social and economic circumstances. He saw similarities as reflecting various degrees of "Africanisms," and in other publications even devised a "scale of intensity of Africanisms" (Herskovits 1945b:14; 1948b:615; M. G. Smith 1965:24–29) to portray to a general public processes of culture change among Negroes in the New World. Herskovits referred to the continuity of African cultural forms in terms of processes of "retention," by which he meant that, somehow, components of African lifeways were retained through several hundred years of slavery and oppression. Where Herskovits could not find clear-cut Africanisms, but still felt that differences between black cultural patterns and white middle class norms needed historical explanation, he referred to a process of "reinterpretation." For example, he argued that features regarded by most as typically European—such as self-sufficient women, common-law marriages, the respect shown to grandmothers, and even the custom of a man's asking a woman's family for her hand in marriage—would justify classifying the social organization of Negroes in both urban and rural United States as "quite African" (Herskovits 1958:167–86).

The term "syncretism" refers to the processes whereby an amalgamation of cultural elements results from joining one cultural tradition with another (Herskovits 1958: xxii). For example, Herskovits found that in areas such as Brazil, Haiti, Cuba, and the American Deep South, Catholic saints and African deities had merged to produce a new set of spirits. Herskovits considered the idea of the devil in the United States as an illustration of syncretism. Presumably, for whites the devil represents the "... fallen Angel of European dogma, the avenger who presides over the terrors of hell and holds the souls of the damned to their penalities ..."

(Herskovits 1958:252). In Negro churches, on the other hand, Herskovits felt that the devil represented more a capricious and powerful trickster who might successfully compete with God. He found the prototype of *this* devil in the mythology of the Dahomean peoples of West Africa, who have a divine trickster known as "Legba" (cf. Herskovits 1958:252–53).

Herskovits (1945b:5–24; 1948a:1–10; 1948b:542–44) also developed a notion of "cultural focus,"[10] which he outlined as follows in the 1958 version of *The Myth* (xxvi: see also 136ff.):

> Every people tend at a given time in their history to lay stress on that aspect, or those aspects, of their culture which are of greatest interest to them.... In a situation of cultural contact where free choice is not allowed, they retain elements of [these] focal aspects, either in unchanged or reinterpreted form, more tenaciously than those of other aspects.

The Myth of the Negro Past sought to *destroy* the idea of American Negroes as a disorganized people with attenuated cultural resources by demonstrating the historical depth and continuing force of their African heritage. In large part, the book was aimed at Herskovits' major critic, the Negro sociologist E. Franklin Frazier.[11] Where Herskovits saw the female-centered households and serial marriages as reinterpretations of African polygyny serving new needs in the New World, Frazier was committed to the idea that slavery had so destroyed African social patterns that Afro-American kinship arrangements could only be seen as unsuccessful attempts to emulate American kinship patterns which were perpetuated through socio-economic deprivation (Frazier 1939). Considerable attention has been given to this controversy (cf. Herskovits 1940; Frazier 1957a; Keil 1966:4–5), probably less for the merit of the arguments than for the political implications of the issues (cf. Bastide 1967:9–10). But whatever the importance of this dispute, Herskovits' field work in Bahia, Brazil, in 1941–42—an area in which Frazier had also worked—added fuel to the fire (Frazier 1942; Herskovits 1943b).

It is difficult to convey in a brief summary the breadth and expanse of Herskovits' work. He frequently turned to scholars' unanalyzed data from the fields of folklore, ethnomusicology, religion, dance, art, literature, ethnohistory, psychology, and linguistics. And at some points he drew on material—today referred to as "microcultural" behavior (kinesics, proxemics)—that anthropologists had not yet developed concepts to deal with.[12] He did not, however, attempt generalizations pertinent to social organization.

Except for a brief interlude in 1949 at the International Congress of Americanists (Tax 1952:143–217), and in spite of increasing work by contemporary scholars,[13] the impact of "Afro-America" (as an assemblage of cultural traits) on anthropology declined. This does not mean, however, that contributions to Afro-American systems of adaptation were not being made. The work of Wagley and his co-investigators (1952), R. T. Smith (1956), M. G. Smith (1955; 1960; 1962a; 1962b), Nancie L. Solien (1958), Marvin Harris (1956), Harry W. Hutchinson (1957), and Edith Clarke (1957), to name only a few, made clear breakthroughs in conceptualizing problems pertinent to (but not exclusively oriented toward) Afro-Americans.[14] On the whole, Herskovits' analysis of "retentions," "reinterpretations," and "syncretism"; his reliance on psychological principles for an understanding of cultural processes; his use of vague concepts such as "focus"; and his negation of social structural approaches turned many anthropologists away from the comparative, generalizing study of Afro-American systems of adaptation. *The Myth* had a negative effect outside anthropology as well. It seemed to exaggerate differences between Negroes and non-Negroes in the Americas. And it implied that "Negro culture" in the United States was not whole, but made up of fragments of retentions, reinterpretations, and syncretized aspects of other cultures, most of which were unknown to present carriers.

The greatest sustained critical challenge to Herskovits and to Afro-American studies was launched by British social anthropologists. The emphases of the British social anthropologists were sufficiently different from those of most American anthropologists to produce conflicts in and of themselves. And the fact that the British developed many of their theories in African societies meant that Afro-American studies were more likely to be challenged than cultural anthropological studies, say, among American Indians. New sophistication in data collection combined with expanding knowledge of West African societies made many of Herskovits' claims appear unreliable.

The work of Raymond T. Smith (1956) is illustrative. In the process of analyzing the household structure of Negro families in British Guiana, in the context of national economic patterns, he found himself facing the Herskovits-Frazier controversy. Like other British scholars, he was drawn toward Frazier's methodological emphasis on statistical data and the analysis of interactional processes of culture contact under slavery. Rereading the treatment of kinship and household organization in *Trinidad Village*, Smith was disturbed by Herskovits' field techniques, particularly as they related to household composition and status differentiation. Noting that Herskovits' best analyses emerged from cultural patterns such as life cycle and child training practices, behaviors most susceptible to his theory of culture change and reinterpretation, R. T. Smith (1956:231–32) pointed out:

> It is in the discussion of ritual and symbolism that the Herskovitses' thesis is most convincing, and here their analyses are remarkably penetrating and well documented. This brings us up against the core of the problem, which concerns the validity of a theoretical system based upon an all-embracing concept of culture. Once the assertion is made that social structure is an aspect of culture, capable of transmission in exactly the same way as symbolism, the way is open for confusion. . . . However, *the study of social structure does not respond to the models used by Prof. and Mrs. Herskovits, and the prior task of sociology in this field is the elucidation of the social structure of a functioning system within a general theoretical framework which permits of comparative study at a higher level of abstraction than the purely descriptive* (emphasis added).

Since Herskovits put primary emphasis on symbolic elements and treated social structure as part of culture, while British scholars of the period were doing just the opposite, theoretical opposition over the significance of Afro-American data was inevitable.

There are further objections to Herskovits' work. In a major critique of his Caribbean studies, M. G. Smith (1965:24–37)—an anthropologist who, unlike Herskovits, had first studied Africa and *then* Afro-America—raises questions about his theory of cultural change, as well as his methods. Concepts such as "focus" and "Africanism" disturbed Smith, and he argued that their generality and imprecision enabled Herskovits to find in the Caribbean what he was after all looking for—a continuity of African culture. Because it is difficult to recognize African cultural elements in modified form and in alien contexts, he asked for better evidence of provenience in both Africa and Europe (M. G. Smith 1965:28–36). Since Herskovits sometimes took unusual liberties in treating Africa and Europe as a common Old World cultural area (Herskovits 1958:18), the problem of discovering sources of cultural traits was, to say the least, compounded.

M. G. Smith objected with equal vigor to Herskovits' lack of attention to the culture contact situation itself, both during and after slavery, where different degrees of freedom and independence existed. Herskovits' sweeping treatment of culture change situations—usually without reference to different institutions of slavery, plantation life, patron-client relationships, and the like —left his work open to serious question as to just *how* African cultural traits came to be "reinterpreted."

The total effect of social anthropological criticisms of Herskovits' approach to Afro-American studies was such as to lead scholars to deemphasize historical studies in favor of synchronic, problem-oriented investigation, with careful attention to techniques of data-gathering and analysis.[15] A few studies directly attempted to reconcile historical and structural concerns (Henriques 1953; M. G. Smith 1955; Greenfield 1966), but most investigators limited themselves to the kind of conceptual approaches that had been used successfully in Africa by such scholars as Meyer Fortes (1949, 1958).[16]

Students of New World cultures continued to write about American Indians, *mestizo* (people of Indian and European descent) America, or Latin and Anglo-America. But after 1941 Negroes as a New World ethnic category received less and less attention in anthropological publications, while the Caribbean as a plural society received more and more.[17] Anthropologists continued to study Negroes living in ethnically identifiable communities,[18] but their findings were subsumed under other rubrics and questions of commonalty of cultural traits among Afro-Americans were "explained" by other factors. Anthropologists focused on "plantation America," on race relations in the Americas, on the Caribbean as a plural society, and on the family and household composition of migratory wage laborers vis-à-vis the larger society.[19] In the United States, a few anthropologists worked in the Deep South (cf. Powdermaker 1939; Rohrer and Edmonson 1960), but most avoided working with Negroes in the urban North, leaving the field to sociologists, political scientists, and "urbanologists" who continued to specialize in urban problems and race relations.[20] While anthropologists thought that their findings were being ignored or distorted, it seemed to sociologists and others that anthropology—the discipline based on a tradition of field work and comparison—consistently ignored the great subculture at our door, that of the urban black American.

THE ROMANCE OF AFRO-AMERICAN FOLKLORE[21]

Before moving to contemporary issues and perspectives it is instructive to briefly review contributions from the field of folklore, for anthropology and folklore have often been closely related in the study of Afro-Americans.

The treatment of the folklore of American Indians and Afro-Americans in writings on the folklore of the United States offers an interesting contrast. The symbol systems of Indian Americans presented severe problems to those attempting to understand them: they required translation, which often led to incoherence in English, and they rested on cultural bases too alien for most white American tastes. Even Boas, in his time the outstanding scholar of American Indian studies, had difficulty understanding and appreciating the structure of the Indian's tales and myths (Boas 1916:878). Finally, Indians were located in the least accessible regions of America, and were frequently hostile to American whites.

Negroes, on the other hand, were located in the most populous portions of the United States, were more or less under the control of the white man, and spoke English. The early nineteenth-century writings on Negro folklore were, for the most part, condescending portraits of inferior beings in a complex society (cf. Jackson 1967:xv–xxiii). During the same period minstrelsy developed a similar view of the Negro on the stage, and most whites came to think that such shows were accurate pictures of Negro life and lore.

The first serious work on Negro folklore and culture appeared in the middle 1800's, with a scattering of articles on music in such journals as *Century*, *Atlantic*, and *New England Magazine* (Jackson 1967); but the signal event was the publication of W. F. Allen's, Charles P. Ware's and Lucy McKim Garrison's *Slave Songs of the United States* (1867). This first collection of Negro folk songs was an exceptional achievement for the time. Plagued with the difficulties of notating folk music, the authors came to realize that they were dealing with a musical sensibility startlingly different from that encountered in Western music. But they were also aware of the existence of a different social reality underlying the songs, and their notes describe the relationship of leader to singing group, and even make a gesture at describing the social function of the music.

Yet these commentators of the middle to the late nineteenth century were far from being ethnographers. They were ministers, abolitionists, educators, military officers, and members of the Freedman's Bureau, all intent on making the Negro appear a pitiable creature in the hands of white slave owners. In their attempts to show the Negro's primitive humanity and spirituality they carefully selected their material for social approval, presenting only sacred songs and songs of remorse. In effect, they created a new stereotype: that of humble, God-fearing, simple folk. Even so, their efforts opened up the study of Negro folklore as a serious enterprise, and countered the casual treatment of Negro life with a pseudo-scholarly approach.

The importance of Afro-American folklore was broadly emphasized by the publication of Joel Chandler Harris' *Uncle Remus: His Songs and His Sayings* in 1881, which opened the way for a string of literary treatments of Negro folklore and folk themes. Lafcadio Hearn, for example, used Negro material regularly in his reporting, and later, after moving to New Orleans, began to study Creole language and folklore (1885, 1890).

Serious collecting of Afro-American folklore was generally recognized by the end of the nineteenth century. The second issue of the *Journal of American Folklore* (1888) called for the study of the "lore of Negroes in the Southern States of the Union," along with that of Indians, Mexicans, and others; and the second and third *Memoirs* of the American Folklore Society were devoted to folk tales and folk songs of Louisiana Negroes and those of Andros Island, Bahamas (Fortier 1895; Edwards 1895).

Within a few years numerous publications containing Afro-American folklore began to appear outside of the United States—in Jamaica (Jekyll 1907), Cuba (Ortiz 1917), Dutch Guiana (Ortiz 1912; F. P. and A. P. Penard 1912), and Haiti (Price-Mars 1928).

In the same period European journals such as *Folk-lore* in England and *Bijdragen tot de Taal-, Land-, en Volkenjunde van Nederlandsch-Indie* and *De West-Indische Gids* in the Netherlands began to publish articles on folk tales, music, and religion in the West Indies.

In the United States, H. E. Krehbiel (1914) introduced an argument for the African sources of Negro music that set off a controversy lasting thirty years (Wilgus 1959: 345–64). The 1920's became an important decade for Afro-American folklore collections: Dorothy Scarborough (1925), Newman I. White (1928), James Weldon Johnson (1925, 1926), and N. G. J. Ballanta-Taylor (1925) published folk songs from various parts of the U.S. South, while the Gullah regions of Georgia and South Carolina became the subject of other folklore studies (A. González 1922, 1924; Johnson 1930).

Activities in Afro-American folkloristics between 1850 and 1930 produced an impressive bulk of publications, but in retrospect most of it suggests increasing numbers of problems without solutions. By the time folk song collecting had begun, for example, minstrelsy had already made an impression on the folk themselves, and the collectors were often confused by this interweaving of oral and literate traditions, and some were unable to tell one from the other. The collections of folklore in general were preselected and set to conform to either the positive or negative stereotype of the collector. Beyond this, folklore scholarship of this period was generally noncomparative, eclectic, and unsystematic. Still, even though little attention was paid to the cultural setting of the singers and taletellers, folklore studies may be regarded as paving the way for later ethnographic descriptions of Negro life.

Sociologists Howard W. Odum and Guy B. Johnson (1925, 1926) took the next step by shifting attention from the songs to the singers. These investigators' attempts to reach the "inner life" of the singers led them to examine the context of folk songs with great care. They were among the first to publicly observe the manner in which particular southern Negroes were able to "use" the white man by choosing to present a certain face in order to gain favors. Odum and Johnson gave accounts of the organization of Negro singing groups and the manner in which leader and group coordinated their efforts, and they advanced folklore scholarship by their discovery that text (lexical meaning) was often secondary to the overall emotional tone of the song.

Another sociologist, Newbell Niles Puckett (1926), published an oddly constructed and biased work that nevertheless used interviews and questionnaires as a basis for gathering information. Inadequate as the book is, it remains the first serious attempt at collating occult and mundane beliefs and practices.

Anthropology and folklore come together with the first of Boas' students to show serious interest in Afro-Americans, Elsie Clews Parsons. Her independent means permitted her to travel widely in the Americas, as well as to support the American Folklore Society and a number of Boas' students. As early as 1917 Parsons began publishing her collections of folk tales from the United States South and the Bahamas. By the end of her life she had assembled an enormous body of data on Afro-American folklore, covering the French and English Antilles, Santo Domingo, Barbados, Bermuda, and the Cape Verde Islanders in the New World (Parsons 1918; 1923a; 1923b; 1933–35; 1943).

In some ways Parsons' folk tale collections resemble those of Joel Chandler Harris. She usually chose to let her collections stand on their own, making little reference to other aspects of her informants' lives and drawing few inferences from her work. Yet her anthropological training under Boas shows through. The size and breadth of her collections, her scrupulous notes on informants, on time and place of collection, and her careful comparisons with other African and Afro-American collections were all new to Afro-American studies. Only American Indian cultures had received such serious attention from anthropological folklorists. Parsons' collections were the first to avoid the preselection of material that had resulted in an overabundance of animal tales in earlier collections. In addition, she developed considerable sensitivity to linguistic style in her as yet unpublished notes to her Antilles collection.

Herskovits (1943a:1) notes that Parsons conceived of her Afro-American folklore collections as the study of processes of diffusion. Herskovits (1958:272–83) found these and other collections useful for diffusional and acculturative studies, and they remain an important source for students interested in historical and linguistic processes.

Perhaps the least known of Boas' students was the Negro novelist Zora Neale Hurston, who studied at Columbia in the late 1920's, where she also came under the influence of the folkloristic approaches of Gladys Reichard and Ruth Benedict. Boas provided her with a fellowship that enabled her to do fieldwork in Georgia, New Orleans, and her native home of Polk City, Florida, resulting in her book, *Mules and Men* (1935). In the foreword to this anecdotal collection of tales, songs, and folk religion, Boas (1935) pointed to the complex relationship between African and European elements underlying Afro-American culture. This point is all too often ignored in later distributional studies seeking to separate "Africanisms" from "Europeanisms."

After her trip to the South, Hurston traveled to the Bahamas and then returned to New York City to sponsor a concert tour of Bahamian singers and dancers (Hurston 1942). She later worked in Mobile, Alabama, with Cudjo Lewis, an aged slave who had come from Nigeria in 1859, and prepared one of the first personal documents in anthropology. She traveled to Haiti in the 1930's, furthering her interests in Afro-American folk religion and magic with *Tell My Horse* (1938). Subsequently she devoted herself more and more to writing a series of novels that drew on folk themes.

Beyond being the most successful Negro collector of Afro-American folklore, Zora Neale Hurston provided the most richly documented portrait of black folk religion and magic in North America. Scattered through her writings are full accounts of folk cures, "hoodoo" rituals, descriptions of the paraphernalia of conjure, and portraits of occultists in various parts of the black Americas.

One other folklorist of the period, Martha W. Beckwith, deserves mention. Throughout the 1920's Beckwith published intensively on her fieldwork in Jamaica, an effort that reached its peak with the publication of the first book on Afro-America that deserves the tag ethnography: *Black Roadways: A Study of Jamaican Folklife* (1929). Although far from being a holistic study of Jamaican life, Beckwith's treatment of economics and marketing practices, rites of passage, festivals, technology, ethnobotany, religious sects, and magical practices was a great advance over the impressionistic and fragmentary studies that preceded her work. Beckwith was torn between an appreciation for the indigenous strength of the folk cultures, and what struck her as the pitiful condition of lower class Negro life. In her final pages she speaks of "degrading" practices, "shiftlessness," and "inertia," and calls for the intervention of "trained social workers" who might help solidify the people "upon a higher plane of genuine folk culture" (Beckwith 1929:225–26). Here she and the early Afro-American folklorists rested, between an earlier condescension and later liberal social science.

By the end of the 1930's the study of Afro-American folklore declined in popularity, partly due to a poverty of theory in the study of folklore itself, but more directly as a result of the migration of Negroes to northern cities during the period. The Federal Writer's Project stimulated work in the 30's, the most important contribution being B. A. Botkin's editing of salvage folklore, which is published in part in *Lay My Burden Down* (1945). It is hoped that someday an anthropologist will undertake a serious analysis of the 10,000 pages from which Botkin culled his illustrations. Herein lie many of the data necessary to begin a synthesis of work as widely diverse as, for example, that of Stanley Elkins (1959) and Herbert Aptheker (1943). Other important books in the Federal Writer's Project which are today scarcely known to anthropologists are *Gumbo Ya-Ya* (1945) and *Drums and Shadows* (1940). The latter of the two is packed with evidence in support of Herskovits' principal contentions. Guy B. Johnson (1940:vii), however, sets a note in the Foreword which has been sounding down into the 1960's:

> ... I believe that there are a few important African survivals in the United States, but that the degree of significance of these African heritages is questionable in view of the overwhelming tendency of the culture of the white man to displace the Negro's African culture, and that their influence on the everyday problem of race relations is relatively inconsequential.

With the exception of an occasional origins controversy (Jackson 1943; Fisher 1953; Whitten 1962), most folklorists in the United States increasingly came to share the view of Richard Dorson (1959:166–98) that Afro-American folklore was, in the main, part of Euro-tradition, together with bits of other traditions. Such a view stimulated some collecting (e.g., Dorson 1956), but contributed no advances in theoretical or methodological perspectives.[22]

The reason for this failure of Afro-American folklore studies to advance theory and method lies not in the controversies themselves, nor even in the relative weighting of Africanisms and Europeanisms in New World cultures. Rather, it seems to lie in the complete failure of the folklorists to consider *social organization*. Commenting on a research project, an Africanist, Alvin W. Wolfe (personal communication), makes a telling point:

> When I did library research on a paper on voodoo in Haiti and Louisiana I was appalled at the complete lack of information anywhere about the people who were engaged in all these exotic rites that were described in such precise detail. It always seemed to me that it was nice to know just how much cornmeal was at what point on the ground in front of the altar, but it would also have helped enormously to know whether the person who put it there (and who cleaned it up afterward) was an X or a Y, and whether he ever saw Z except during the ritual.

AN ATTEMPT AT REASSESSMENT: THE 1967 A.A.A. SYMPOSIUM

The Preface of this book sets forth the structure of the 1967 Symposium on

INTRODUCTION

Negroes in the New World held at the American Anthropological Association Meeting in Washington, D.C. Some symposium members chose to update New World Negro studies by referring to the continuing advantages of cultural approaches stemming from the work of Melville J. Herskovits, while others swung to social structural analyses based on adaptational theory to direct attention to new possibilities. We did not oppose the Herskovits "cultural mechanism school" with the social anthropological "model building school." Rather we sought generalizations at various levels of analysis, admitting the differential value of several explanatory models for different sociocultural sub-systems. What emerged from the symposium seemed to be a series of problems in cultural analysis, together with new directions for research in the area of social adaptation. Concepts of how to update Afro-American studies since 1941 diverged radically according to whether the participant was primarily concerned with social or cultural organization and change.

In this Introduction we have chosen to present significant aspects of the papers of Erika Bourguignon (which was read by Esther Pressel) and Daniel Crowley, as illustrative of directions growing directly out of Herskovits' traditional approach to cultural change, and Whitten's approach to social processes which stems from social anthropological and neoevolutionary theory. Although the social organizational section preceded the cultural at the A.A.A. symposium, the order is here reversed for continuity with previous sections.

Syncretism: Religions and Creole Cultures

In thinking about Afro-American, or black, religion, the casual scholar, and even the professional anthropologist of religion, is still frequently drawn to notions of retention, reinterpretation, and syncretism (for recent developments cf. Leacock 1964a; 1964b). In a search for such cultural processes the mundane symbolic realms of Afro-American religions are sometimes obscured by descriptions of the obviously exotic syncretisms such as are manifest in voodoo in Haiti and Louisiana, *Shango* in Trinidad, *Candoblé* and *Macumba* in Brazil, and *Obeah* in other parts of the Caribbean. Store front churches in the United States, Black Muslim ideology, and various revitalization movements with or without obvious political impact are also fascinating for the student of Afro-American religions. Our attention is usually turned to the Caribbean, in the broad sense of an arc drawn from Brazil through the southern United States. There is good reason for such a focus, for, as M. G. Smith (1965:19) tells us, "The historical conditions that define the area from Brazil to the United States as the broad comparative context of Caribbean studies . . . consist in the expansion of Europe to the New World, to the common historical patterns of conquest, colonization, peonage, or slavery, and the development of multiracial and multicultural societies throughout this area."

The notion of syncretism has not been significantly developed since Herskovits' publications.[23] Researchers in various parts of the New World have reported the rise and fall of cults, religious movements, and belief systems, some of which show mixtures of African and non-African traits. It is clear, however, that there is no common "Afro-American" religion nor systematic body of African belief that is reinterpreted in various ways throughout the New World. After surveying recent historical work in the Caribbean, Erika Bourguignon turned to the varieties of religious syncretisms apparent in New World Negro communities to suggest directions for continuing research. Her paper, in part, follows.[24]

In discussing Afro-American religious variation we may begin by noting that, in Haiti, *vodû* is widespread throughout the society, and may be said to represent the classical example of a syncretic Afro-Catholic religion (Herskovits 1934; Métraux 1959; Bourguignon 1965). In Martinique and Guadeloupe, on the other hand, such a syncretic religion appears to be absent (Leiris 1955; Horowitz 1967). An explanation is offered by Wagley and Harris (1958a:99):

> The relative lack of African survivals in the culture of Martinique can be accounted for to some extent by several rather obvious factors. Chief among them is that Martinique is a small island. Escaped slaves were not able to form communities— as in Jamaica, Surinam, Brazil and Haiti— which could perpetuate African conditions. Supervision of slaves was strict and close contact with the whites has been the rule ever since the time when the first slaves found themselves working side by side with the French *engagés*. Furthermore, unlike the population of Haiti, for whom independence severed contact with France, the people of African origin in Martinique have had continuous relations with metropolitan French.

True enough, independence severed the Haitian's relations with France as early as 1804, but the cults were clearly in existence before them. Haitian school books are fond of giving the cult leaders great credit for the development of the Haitian revolution. Why were such cults absent in Martinique at the same time? Because there were no maroons? But the groups Moreau de St. Méry (1797–98) described in prerevolution Haiti were present on plantations, not hidden in the hills. The maroons of Jamaica, on the other hand, have not maintained the purest African tradition on that island. And in Haiti as well as in Martinique Africans worked side by side with French *engagés* and were subject to the same French policies. How then can we account for the differences between these two French colonies prior to 1804, if the size of the islands appears to be the principle difference between them?

In the subsequent period, the histories of the two islands diverge and the differences are accentuated. While slavery was terminated in Haiti with the French revolution in 1789 it endured in Martinique until 1848. And if independence severed Haiti's contact with France, it also severed contact both with Africa and with the Catholic Church. For with the end of slavery and colonial status, the slave trade ceased. With independence came severe conflict with the Church which led to an open break lasting for more than half a century. The special character of *vodû* after 1804 can be ascribed to the peculiar history of Haiti.

The continuation of slavery and French influence in Martinique after 1804 may well have led to a suppression of cults or incipient cults that had existed there before. More intensive efforts at conversion and education there are also to be considered. Furthermore, French centralization in contrast to Haitian local diversity and lack of effective national control should be investigated as possibly significant elements in this situation. Also, as shown by the recent work of Price (1964), there seems to have been a much greater traceable influence of American Indians in Martinique than in Haiti. Finally, since the end of slavery an East Indian population has been introduced, as in Trinidad and Guyana. These, however, are only some suggestions as to the possible reasons for the presence and absence of cult formation. The problem is still open.

We may take the case of Trinidad as a further example. Trinidad became a British possession in 1797 and since then has been exposed to strong British (including Protestant) influences. But, prior to that time, Trinidad had been a Spanish possession and large numbers of French planters had settled there in the last quarter of the 18th century. Slavery was abolished in 1833, but this did not terminate contact with Africa. Indeed, some free African immigrants arrived in Trinidad as late as about 1855 (e.g., Carr 1953). Moreover, large numbers of East Indians and Chinese were also brought to the island in the 1840's. The resulting religious scene is one of great variety. Thus the Rada (Dahomean)

INTRODUCTION

community which Carr (1953) describes is traced directly to its founder in 1855. He was a free African immigrant who came to Trinidad as a mature man and who had been a *bokono* (diviner) in his native country. Although Catholic elements have been syncretized with African traditions in this group, particularly with respect to the names of the saints, the African tradition has remained remarkably pure. Of a more mixed nature is the better known *shango* cult (Herskovits and Herskovits 1947a; F. Mischel 1958; Mischel and Mischel 1958; Henry 1965; Simpson 1962b, 1965). Here the mixture includes predominantly Yoruba elements on the African side and both Catholic and Baptist elements on the Christian side. Shango is identified with St. John the Baptist. Among elements of the shango cult which are reminiscent of Pentecostal Protestantism is speaking in "unknown tongues" (*glossolalia*) and the intensive use of the Bible. In addition to being affiliated with the Catholic Church, shango participants may also be members of Spiritual Baptist ("Shouter") groups or have contacts with them (Mischel 1958; Simpson 1966). Spiritual Baptists represent the most attenuated form of Africanisms in this continuum of Afro-American religions in Trinidad (Herskovits & Herskovits 1947a). In spite of the overlap in membership that exists between them, however, these groups maintain their separate institutional character.

That cult groups need *not* keep separate identities is illustrated by the innovations of M. G. Smith's *Dark Puritan* (1957a) which is an account of a Grenadian who had at various times lived in Trinidad, and who founded a cult which derived from a very personal synthesis of Seventh Day Adventism, Shouterism and shango, which itself contains both African and Catholic elements. While this case is perhaps unique, it does indicate the possibility of a type of multiple syncretism which appears to overcome, in an act of personal innovation, the differences between the beliefs of these various groups.

Spiritual Baptists, called "Shakers," whose activities resemble those of Trinidad are also found on St. Vincent. However, there is no cult of syncretized African spirits such as the shango cult of Trinidad there (Henney 1967; 1968a; 1968b).

Perhaps the most highly eclectic and complex form of syncretism is the Umbanda religion of Brazil. Umbanda integrates features of African religions, Catholicism, Brazilian Indian contributions and aspects of the belief system developed by the French 19th century spiritualist theoretician, Alan Kardec.[25] African elements are clearly recognized as such by the participants who represent practically the whole broad ethnic spectrum of Brazilian society. In spite of its strongly marked African roots, Umbanda can no longer be identified as an Afro-American, Afro-Catholic or Negro religion. Furthermore, unlike the other Afro-American religions discussed in this paper, it does not have its principal appeal and support among the disinherited members of the lower class. In São Paulo its appeal appears to be to the upwardly mobile members of the lower and lower middle class (Pressel 1968a, 1968b; see also Bastide 1961b; Camargo 1961; McGregor 1967). Umbanda, then, perhaps alone among the various syncretic religions with African components, has made the transition to a religion of the social whole. Indeed, one is tempted to see it as a new religion facilitating as well as symbolizing the development of a new society. Yet Umbanda seems to lack some of the key characteristics of a revitalization movement (Wallace 1956; Pressel 1968b).

The study of Umbanda, which is only in its beginnings, introduces a new perspective into our theoretical analysis of syncretic religions. By looking at what New World Negroes have retained from their African past we tend to focus on the conserving and conservative function of the religions. Some authors (e.g., Courlander and Bastien 1966: 39–68) tend to see Haitian *vodû* and other Afro-American religions as obstacles to culture change and as instruments of political conservatism and control. The example of Umbanda would tend to suggest that this is not necessarily so. A detailed comparison between *vodû* and Umbanda, for example, might help us delineate the social, economic and political features of a society which might influence the character of a syncretic movement in this respect. It may well be that *vodû* is a conservative force, while shango in Trinidad provides compensatory outlets for its members in their strivings for prestige and power (Mischel and Mischel 1958).

Umbanda appears to be able to provide its members with help in the processes of decision making and in dealing with the inventory of new statuses and roles provided by the rapid social and economic changes inherent in the development of new social forms in contemporary urban Brazil.

Umbanda, then, furnishes us with an important contrast to the Afro-American religions of the Caribbean and to the orthodox Afro-Brazilian religions as well. . . .

Dr. Bourguignon has contributed another paper on cults and possession beliefs for this volume. Also, Professor R. S. Bryce-Laporte takes us a step further toward updating Afro-American studies by presenting a paper dealing with an occult event in the context of black-white relationships in the Panama Canal Zone.

The term "Creole" is often used by Afro-American scholars to refer to new syncretisms arising in the lifeways of New World peoples, including New World Negroes. At the symposium Daniel Crowley suggested that Creole culture is an enormously varied complex of notions and definitions that cannot be used with analytical precision. Placing his paper in historical perspective, he began by asserting:

If this symposium does nothing more than to direct attention to what Herskovits actually wrote, rather than to the sometimes naive, sometimes malicious misinterpretations of his position in secondary or tertiary sources, it will have served its purpose admirably. . . .

The burden of this paper is that the term "creolization" today describes more generally the processes of adaptation Herskovits synthesized as retention, reinterpretation and syncretism, and that the concept it represents is applicable not only in the Latin America of Gillin's "creole culture," the Caribbean, southern Louisiana and the west coast of Africa, but also in any area where a culture neither aboriginal nor alien but a mixture of the two, with retentions on both sides and ample borrowing from other outside sources is in the process of becoming dominant—which is to say, most of the world. The Afro-American cases studied by Herskovits represent some of the most spectacular examples because even the extreme social distance between slave and master was ultimately destroyed by this inexorable process, so that the remaining biologically unmixed local descendants of the planter dance in the streets during Carnival in Trinidad beside their mixed-blood, African and East Indian compatriots, the latter carefully eschewing "creolization" while they dance.

Crowley went on to demonstrate the tremendous range of syncretisms arising in the lifeways of New World peoples, making it quite clear that "the term creole is no longer necessarily related to race. An unmixed European (Louisiana, Argentina), African (Trinidad, Haiti, Sierra Leone), or aboriginal Indian (Peru, Bolivia), or any or all mixtures thereof may be creole, and the term is even used in Alaska for the native-born descendants of Russians and Eskimos!"

The fact that two anthropologists, Bourguignon and Crowley, who have spent years of field work in the Caribbean area, stress that we must *not* speak of "New World Negro religion," or "New World Negro culture," is indeed significant. In other words, the symposium participants regarded the self-image, religion, and cultural characteristics of the peoples studied as being in a process of *continuing adaptation* to the vicissitudes of everyday life in the New World. Possible economic bases for such continuing adaptation will be discussed presently.

INTRODUCTION

The Sounds and Voices of Afro-Americans

In the area of communication, unlike those of religious syncretism and creolization, the 1967 symposium took another turn. Some participants agreed that certain common stylistic features did characterize New World Negroes in their respective cultures and social systems. But at the same time that style in a general sense was regarded as containing some similarities, the specific functions and uses of communication were seen as quite variable in different settings. Alan Lomax, whose expanded paper is reproduced in this volume, argues from the standpoint of Cantometrics, a system for rating song performance, that "although European folk singing has strongly influenced the content of the music of the United States, Afro-American style is virtually identical with that of the African heartland." The methods used to reach this conclusion, and indeed the conclusion itself, deserve careful attention. The article by Whitten and the one by Szwed approach, in different ways, the curious persistence of African musical forms in totally different sociocultural contexts. Whitten considers music in western Ecuador to be a cultural focus, a tenacity of form allowing for flexibility in socio-economic adaptation by providing a continuing symbol stream which can be manipulated according to context. In such an argument, however, the reader must be advised of another approach, that of M. G. Smith (1965:26–27), who writes in criticism of Herskovits' "scale of intensity":

> ... Africanisms in music have a higher level of intensity than those in any other field, in terms of this scale. Now it is possible to exclude music from the comparison effectively by treating it as a pattern of motor behavior of the type which is liable to persist in a very marked degree, even though marginal to the culture focus.

Clearly the area of contemporary ethnomusicology has much to offer, and studies are now being published which contribute to our knowledge of stylistic continuity and social diversity (cf. Keil 1966; Haralambos in this volume). But much synthesis remains to be done; that such synthesis is possible is illustrated by the papers of Szwed and Lomax.

The idea of stylistic continuity in the area of folklore is considered by Abrahams. These ideas together with those presented by Dillard and Reisman again give the scholar of Afro-Americans some baselines for new research, as well as introducing a number of legitimate warnings about reifying ideas and overgeneralizing across levels of sociocultural processes. Particularly needed, in terms of contemporary research, are analyses of style that consider the nature of the similarities and differences that lie within a culture area—Daniel Crowley's (1966) study of Bahamian folk tales remains almost the only work of its kind. The applications of linguistic theory to folk tale collecting—as it is being attempted by William Stewart (1968) and J. L. Dillard (1962, 1963)—also shows promise, both for the study of folklore and for the light it sheds on linguistic processes in general. Historical factors also remain to be integrated into analyses of Afro-American folklore, with Trinidad so far being almost the only area to be studied in this fashion (Pearse 1955; Elder 1966b).

In order to explain the dialects of diverse groups of Negroes in the New World, early observers assumed that the Negro had neither the physical nor the mental ability to learn and speak "correct" English. Antiracist literary scholars accepted the "myth of the Negro past"—the notion that no African influence could have survived the slavery experience. Just as early cultural anthropologists had confronted racists by arguing that Negroes were really not culturally different from white Europeans, scholars such as G. P. Krapp and Cleanth Brooks claimed the following:

> The first conclusion to be drawn ... is that the speech of the Negro and the white is essentially the same, the characteristically Negro forms turning out to be survivals of earlier native English forms (Brooks 1935:63).

Negroes were seen to be living archives of forms of English that had been spoken in England a century or so previously. In order to sustain this argument in the face of dialects as distinct as Gullah, spoken on the Sea Islands off the coast of Georgia and South Carolina, some even postulated a French Canadian source (Norton 1921: 149)!

Herskovits (1966:117–35; 1958:275–91) and Lorenzo Turner (1949) came to understand Negro speech in the United States as falling on a continuum of dialects that included various "Creoles" in the West Indies, South America, and West Africa. Although they were interested primarily in another version of the Africanisms vs. Europeanisms debate, by shifting emphasis from the study of lexical items in isolation to analysis of patterns of syntax, Herskovits and Turner pointed the way to seeing Negro speech in the United States as a generalized "Creole" speech system once broadly distributed in the southern states. Dillard, in this volume, summarizes the available publications (see also Stewart 1962, 1966).

Once Afro-American dialects are understood as distinct levels of *social* communication coexisting with other levels in a single society, contemporary interests of sociolinguistics become very important. Reisman, for example, confronts data very similar to those assembled by Herskovits (1937b) in Haiti, but instead of finding it necessary to "resolve" ambiguities by postulating vague cultural processes, he argues in this book that ambiguity itself is *part* of the communication system of the Negroes of the British West Indian island of Antigua. Along similar lines, at least by implication, is the paper by Kochman which demonstrates how style categories in the black ghetto serve different offensive and defensive functions.

SOCIAL ORGANIZATION: CONTEMPORARY PERSPECTIVES

Novelist Norman Mailer (1969:60) tells us, "The American Black has survived—of all the peoples of the Western World, he was the only one in the near seven decades of the twentieth century to have undergone the cruel weeding of real survival."

"Real survival" for American Indians and for black Africans in America could not follow the course of survival strategies of white Europeans. Survival has meant adapting not only to exigencies in the natural environments, but to the continuing vicissitudes of life imposed by dominating white social, political, and economic systems. That black aggregates have survived under enormous pressures, and have expanded into most New World environmental niches, would suggest some powerful adaptive mechanisms. In such a discussion ideas of "family" and "household" seem to loom large, for it is within such minimal clusters that basic human properties are preserved, and through which the lifeways of a people are transferred and transformed.

INTRODUCTION

With such a focus it would seem that the positive benefits in Negro family organization within a white-dominated system should be explored. Such exploration is legion (cf. Otterbein 1965), but the resulting confusion about "mother-centeredness" is more often than not unenlightening.

In this book Nancie L. González attempts to bypass sterile arguments over "organization vs. disorganization" by giving us a definition of "matrifocality" from the standpoint of processes of adaptation within "neoteric societies" (societies defined as "newly created" or "recent in origin"). By so defining the problem, Afro-American family studies are placed in a context of cross cultural comparison, where regularities are sought according to environing features, not in terms of imposed racial categories.

From the beginning of New World Negro studies in the Americas, scholars and laymen have commented on the social organization of Negro families and households by comparing them with white middle class norms. Writings on Negro life abound in discussions of disorganization, disorientation, retention, deviance, and other terms that show the failure of scholars to come to grips with the organization of family and household life under certain circumstances. In the early 1960's pioneering steps toward a synthesis of Carribbean materials were taken by Mintz and Davenport (1961). Let us reconsider the problems posed by similarities in New World Negro household and family composition among lower class black people living in *ethnically identifiable rural communities*. At the 1967 A.A.A. symposium Whitten presented data indicating general similarities ranging from the back roads of Nova Scotia to the forests of western Ecuador. Herskovits would have taken such findings as evidence of African retention and reinterpretation. A number of sociologists, following the tradition established by E. Franklin Frazier (Valentine 1968:20–24), would argue that they are evidence of disorganization resulting from the effects of slavery and subsequent disorientation toward the standards of "mainstream" society (cf. Rainwater 1966a; Blake 1961; Bernard 1966; Moynihan 1965; Billingsley 1968). Whitten argued, however, that there was no possible way to preserve African residence and family forms through the complex history of slavery and freedom of Negroes in the Canadian Maritimes and western Ecuador and Colombia. He also rejected the idea that all such similarities could be attributed to urbanization or to plantation life or to the peripheral effects of either. In effect he attempted an analysis of "characteristic" social organizational features which would complement M. G. Smith's (1962a) analysis of the "unique" organization of Carriacou.

Following suggestions by anthropologists Mintz and Davenport (1961) and sociologist St. Clair Drake (1966) he suggested three concepts to clarify recent findings on the social organization of New World Negroes: *exclusion from direct access to capital resources; subsequent economic marginality; and an adaptation to marginality*.

The use of these concepts necessitates clarification of assumptions in regard to the relations between structural analysis and the role of history. We do not wish to be caught in the "historicism-ahistoricism" dilemma (Herskovits 1960). There are two processes of reasoning by which Afro-American scholars can assemble an argument— *reasoning by analogy* and *reasoning by homology* Both combine historical and ahistorical approaches. In the case of Afro-America the latter process assumes formal similarities of African background and raises the question, "What differences have resulted and why?" Concepts of evolutionary *divergence* are immediately raised and ideas of causal relationships stress contemporary difference while similarities are assumed to perpetuate through processes of retention and reinterpretation. Herskovits argued by homology.

Reasoning by analogy does not negate historical derivation from a common source, but it does stress that structure cannot be *explained* by common tradition. Similarities are sought without regard for common roots, the crucial evolutionary question being why similarities should exist, and the cause of such similarities. Causality is sought in terms of similar environing pressures. The questions raised about Afro-America then become centered on the idea of evolutionary *convergence* and it is to this idea that this section will be addressed.[26] Obviously, our ultimate interest is the combining of analogous and homologous reasoning in a full understanding of the relationship of historical and structural variables. But for now, we regard the structural problem as the most pressing.

An analysis of structural analogues assumes a cultural materialist strategy which Marvin Harris (1968:241) has most recently articulated as follows:

> This strategy states that the explanation for cultural differences and similarities is to be found in the techno-economic processes responsible for the production of the material requirements of biosocial survival. It states that the techno-economic parameters of sociocultural systems exert selective pressures in favor of certain types of organizational structures and upon the survival and spread of definite types of ideological complexes. It states that, in principle, all of the major problems of sociocultural differences and similarities can be solved by identifying the precise nature of these selective parameters; yet as a general principle, it does not commit itself to the explanation of any specific sociocultural type or any specific set of institutions.

Harris demonstrates the value of this strategy in a book (1964b) which clearly establishes that a viable approach to race relations demands clear concepts of manpower allocations within specific economic systems. He sums up the results of his work (1968:243) by noting the critical difference between race relations in Brazil and the United States:

> The United States whites invoked a rule of descent whereby mixed types were jammed into the Negro category, while Brazil had already evolved a system for establishing racial identity which did not depend on a descent rule. Hence, the United States acquired the conflict-ridden two-caste system in contrast to the continuous color spectrum of Brazilian multiracialism.

At this level of analysis the cultural materialist strategy is particularly effective, but we diverge from its application in our search for regularities among black aggregates in the New World—first, because of a slightly different emphasis on concepts of ethnicity, and second, due to a different emphasis on what is crucial in the techno-economic system affecting specific aggregates defined by the larger society in "racial" terms. These points will be made more specifically on pages 45 to 48 in this Introduction.

To provide a framework for reexamining some characteristic features of Afro-American social organization let us direct our attention to two areas beyond the Caribbean sphere—western Ecuador and Colombia, and eastern Canada—for these areas lie beyond Herskovits' Afro-America. Yey they lead scholars back to the well known problems set forth by Herskovits and recently reexamined by M. G. Smith (1965: 24-37). Although the techno-economic systems are very different in Nova Scotia and the Pacific Littoral of Colombia and Ecuador, we will argue that the *effect* of the economy on aggregates of people usually called "Negro" or "moreno" in the Pacific Littoral and "colored" or "Negro" in Nova Scotia, is similar in some crucial respects. Both serve to create a condition of economic marginality to which the response is a similar network-based social system in each area. Due to environing differences, however, the functions of the network bases diverge radically in the two regions.

ADAPTATION, ADAPTABILITY, AND MICROEVOLUTIONARY CHANGE[27]

On the periphery of the New World, in western Ecuador and western Colombia, and in the Maritime provinces of Canada, freedom came by the end of the eighteenth century, and plantations exerted little or no influence. In the former area Negroes mined alluvial gravels for placer gold, gaining their freedom by escaping, by buying it, and by default as gravel deposits were depleted (cf. West 1952). In the Canadian Maritimes economic pressures during the 1700's were unfavorable to perpetuating slavery, while overt beneficence by British and United Empire Loyalists during the early 1800's freed American slaves through the British-Canadian port of Halifax and the Bay of Fundy and Nova Scotian Eastern Shore *entrepôts* (cf. Smith 1899; Fergusson 1948; Dallas 1803).

Freedom itself in western Colombia and Ecuador and in the Canadian Maritimes did not provide economic security due to the difficulties imposed on subsistence by the natural environment and to the general exclusion of Negroes from direct competition over strategic resources within the money economy. What seems remarkable today is that in these fringe areas household and kinship organization of lower class Negroes in ethnically identifiable communities seems very similar to the structure reported from the urban and rural United States, from the Caribbean, and from Central America, Brazil, and the Guianas.[28] It is difficult to attribute similarities in these fringe areas to slavery itself, to urbanization, the plantation, or to such processes as retention or diffusion. One thing we can do is to raise the question: *What consistent economic regularity faces lower class Negroes in ethnically identifiable communities throughout the New World?* We can then ask how this economic modality could influence processes of adaptation and adaptability. This section will direct attention to the *lower sectors of rural communities* and suggest that economic marginality is a critical constant effecting adaptive processes in many rural New World Negro communities. According to Kalervo Oberg (1955:478), "Marginality in the economic sense implies a margin of subsistence to sporadic and uncertain surpluses . . . [he goes on to suggest that] economic insurance is secured through dependence upon near relatives." Although this concept has been developed for "tribal" marginals of South America, it also may be valuable as a basis for considering lower class marginals in complex sociopolitical settings.[29] Economic marginality may be a concomitant of poverty, or it may be characteristic of populations where "boom and bust" periods of fluctuation are common. When people are caught up in a cash economy, and are dependent on cash for *part* of their livelihood, while being excluded from power over economic resources, then a situation of economic marginality probably necessitates a heavy reliance on kinsmen, friends, and exploitable companions. With sporadic and uncertain surpluses potentially available, people may be thought of as building ties to a variety of neighbors, relatives, and friends, trying to tap some of the surplus of their associates when it is available.

Frequently, in underdeveloped countries, land and subsistence economies balance the lack of cash income, the result being a tenuous peasant or rural proletariat adaptation to the prevailing money economy (cf. Adams 1964:49–78; Erasmus 1956, 1961a; Frucht 1967). Anthropologists have frequently sought to classify people characterized by an adaptation to economic marginality according to cultural criteria, thereby missing the point of adaptation to economic circumstance. In urban settings, and in rural areas where land is becoming increasingly scarce, reliance on sociopolitical techniques in times of scarce money can define the coping mechanisms of specific aggregates. In the urban and rural United States racism directed toward black aggregates creates the economic analog of underdeveloped countries.

Let us explore certain consistencies in ethnically identifiable communities of New World Negroes a bit further before considering microevolutionary processes proceeding from a primary adaptation to economic marginality. Raymond T. Smith (1963), in a review article on "Caribbean social structure," singles out the most consistent aspect of lower class Negro social relationships, using Nancie L. González' data on the Black Carib as a basis. González noted:

> ... the nuclear family unit among the [Black] Carib may be scattered in several different households. For example, the husband-father may be living with his own mother, one or more children may be with their maternal relatives or with non-Caribs, while the mother may be working and "living-in" as a maid in one of the port towns (Smith 1963:33, from Solien 1958:104).

Commenting on this statement, R. T. Smith (1963:33) asserts:

> Her observations could be duplicated from every report that has ever been written on lower-class Negro family life, and it is quite true that the concentration of attention upon the household as a functioning unit of child-care and economic organization *has tended to divert attention from the networks of relationship linking households to each other* (emphasis added).[30]

Pinpointing and programing a focus on networks instead of family and household in what Nancie L. González calls neoteric societies is a clear advance. Consider the problem of studying social structure in rural Negro communities in the New World. Anthropologists with an ethnohistorical bent, such as Herskovits, have traditionally analyzed African lineages, clans, compounds, secret societies, and even voluntary groupings within cities to gain an understanding of boundaries imposed by custom on social interaction. The boundaries are inevitably those of the tribal and tribal adjusting-to-urban groups. A concept of *group* which proceeds from African to Afro-American material is likely to flounder in search of remnants, retentions, survivals, or hints of *prior* group organization in neoteric societies. With adaptation rather than tradition as our dominant concept in a search for regularities, African groupings can be dismissed as irrelevant for a discussion of New World neoteric societies. For example, Marshall Sahlins (1961:330) notes that "lineages do not form in the absence of long-term exploitation of restricted dom-

INTRODUCTION

ains." Social structure in many Negro communities in the New World has probably developed, and would seem to continue to develop, through indirect, short-term exploitation of relatively open domains.[31] The relatively open domains are characterized by changing economic and political structures to which direct access is restricted to people classed as non-Negro.[32]

Proceeding from an analysis of New World bureaucratized sectors central to economic growth (or "primary development," Adams 1967), another confusion arises. The study of voluntary and institutional *groups* which cope directly with economic growth reinforces a theory of society as made up *exclusively* of bounded social entities. Looking from the industrial-bureaucratized part of New World society, Negro communities often do not seem to fit the social model; they seem not to work properly through channels connecting one institution to another—the picture has been presented as one of disorganization, disorientation, disintegration. And when we look at the group-based model of society in terms of an emphasis on the family group as *the* primary socializing agency, our image of disorganization and cyclical disorientation is a theoretical *fait accompli*.

We suggest that in many New World Negro rural communities, where by one means or another individuals are kept effectively outside of the sources of economic change, *definable, bounded groups are maladaptive, and survival value for them is thereby limited*. Constant subjection to varying inputs from externally generated cash nexi seems to favor the development of *networks* of individuals, making up strings of *quasi-groups*. According to Adrian Mayer (1966: 97–98) these are "first . . . ego-centered, in the sense of depending for their very existence on a specific person as a central organizing focus; . . . [and] second, the actions of any member are relevant only in so far as they are interactions between him and ego or ego's intermediary."

It is important to note here that ramifying ties, inherent in the nature of ego-centered networks, can coalesce for purposes of short-run gain into "action sets" which contain (Mayer 1966:109) "paths of linkages, and are thus a combination of relationships linking people directly to ego, and of those linking people to intermediaries who are themselves in direct contact with ego." An illustration of an action set with sociopolitical impact is given in Whitten's article in Part II of this volume.

New World Negro community adaptive potential is conceived of as frequently being dominated by two types of social relationships, neither forming classical groups (in Mitchell's sense [1966:51–52], of "structural relationships") but both contributing to quasi-group formation. One is the categorical relationship, the other the personal network. Both mechanisms contribute to the formation of action sets in times of crisis for the exploitation of perceived resources. According to J. Clyde Mitchell (1966:52–53) categorical relationships are those in which people "tend to categorize people in terms of some visible characteristic and to organize their behavior accordingly . . . *It is essential to categorical relationships that the . . . internal divisions within a category should be ignored*" (emphasis added, see also Southall 1961:1–46). Throughout the New World *cultural definitions of visible characteristics vary from place to place, but generally impose a negative value on aggregates of individuals with African Negro features* (cf. Wagley and Harris 1958: 117; Hoetink 1967; Mörner 1967; Bastide 1967; Pitt-Rivers 1967; Lowenthal 1967). Some elaboration of this statement is necessary because it will illustrate, among other things, our departure from Harris' cultural materialist strategy, and should serve to explain why we are focusing on the internal adaptive capacity of New World Negro aggregates, rather than on the external environing system. Although the latter can enlighten us to differences such as those existing in Brazilian and United States race relations, it can also obscure significant convergences between the two nations.

In his seminal work *Race Relations* Michael G. Banton (1967:138) offers a generalization which can help us understand microevolutionary change:

> The pattern of countervailing checks and balances characteristic of community relations is distorted where there are cleavages and one category of people cannot adequately press its claims. When this happens, those who gain most immediately from their rivals' weakness ... acquire a strategically advantageous position. They press their short-term sectional interests at the expense of the long-run interests of their social category, and, indeed, of the whole regional society.

Harris (1964b:54) typifies the lowland Latin American pattern of racial definitions in terms of fluid categorical relationships. Writing about the Brazilian pattern he states, "... neither the Negroes nor the mixed or mulatto types nor the whites may be said to constitute by themselves separately identifiable, significant social segments." But Banton (1967:259) tells us:

> Historically, one of the more striking features is that Brazilian society moved away from a threatened two-category system towards an integrated order, in which *dark-skinned people were concentrated at the bottom of the social scale*, but the sign value of racial appearance could be outweighed by wealth or other claims to status. In more recent times it has seemed that *industrialization is strengthening racial distinctions*, but the trend in race relations cannot be considered independently of changes in the politico-economic structure.

Pierson (1942) makes similar observations as does Harris himself (Wagley 1952:47–81; Harris 1956). It would seem, in terms of social structure, that ethnic exclusion is occurring in Brazil just as it is in the United States and Canada and throughout the Caribbean. It is true that there are more channels for upward mobility and there are subtleties of classification that allow money to "lighten" people. But unlike Harris' interpretation, it seems crucial to note that there is a general sense in which a lower stratum can be considered in ethnic terms for particular purposes and placed in a disadvantageous position vis-à-vis the larger system. In many parts of the New World concepts of "Negroness" are used pejoratively by those standing in various degrees of "whiteness." Where this occurs "Negroness" is usually *associated with lower economic strata*, whether or not avenues of mobility are open to those classed as "Negroes" to change their ethnic identity. Under such circumstances the concept(s) of "Negroness" has (have) deterring effects on those in the category who may wish to rise within the broad confines of their techno-economic system. Furthermore, to the degree that a pejorative sense of "Negroness" is internalized within Negro ethnic categories, "white" interests become part of the larger environment. One does not become that which he perceives as environing; rather one copes with environing forces as external, potential resource factors (necessitating means of exploitation). The crucial factor in Negroes' environments in much of the New World has been people standing in a contrasting categorical relationship, the general criterion for which we call "whiteness." It is through this categorical relationship that cash economic inputs are usually made. Let us continue to develop a sense of analysis by using contemporary social anthropological

INTRODUCTION

theory with a modified cultural materialist strategy.

Personal networks, according to Mitchell, refer to "the network of personal links which individuals have built up around themselves..." (1966:54). Everyone builds networks around himself: within households, between households, within communities, and between communities. Networks, inasmuch as they can be tapped in times of need, provide an ego with a measure of social capital resources. Some networks in any community radiate, at any time, from successful individuals, from people who have effectively manipulated strategic resources to advance socially, economically, and politically. A personal network seen from the perspective of successful individuals may be regarded as a strategic adaptive mechanism since success defines progress, from an individual standpoint, within the larger society.

If we consider that uprooted people adapt first to the dominant modalities in their environment by using their most accessible social capital—kinship—in such a way as to maximize flexible networks, then the idea of ego-centered kinship networks oriented toward exploitation of the "white world" becomes reasonable. It is sufficiently reasonable, in fact, to make one wonder why there has been so much controversy over the concepts of family and household. Both of these are definable groups probably often submerged in arrangements of individuals, within relatively successful ego-centered, adaptable, interpersonal networks of relationship.[33]

The papers by Whitten and Stack for this volume illustrate the value of this approach. Each focuses on the kindred as the minimal economic unit. At the 1967 A.A.A. meeting Whitten went on to argue that in the Pacific Littoral of Ecuador and Colombia people can rise in their natal community by strategically employing their social capital through a corporate action set which he called a stem kindred. Nova Scotian Negroes could not mobilize the *same sort* of network base for mobility purposes. Some of the reasons for the differences in mobility patterns could be seen in the larger system of ethnic exclusion, but another section of Whitten's paper dealt with the "game of mobility" itself as played in two different areas. His work is spelled out in methodological perspective (1969) in an article entitled *Network Analysis and Processes of Adaptation among Negroes in Ecuador and Nova Scotia*. He concludes this article by asserting that such a contrast between Negro *costeños* of Ecuador and Colombia and Negro maritimers of eastern Canada demonstrates theoretically important cultural variability arising from similar network bases. Here again it should be noted that cultural materialist strategy is being employed, not in the sense of searching out techno-economic differences, but by asking what regularities exist at the community level which seem crucial in defining parameters of adaptation. The next question relates to the extent to which parallel patterns of adaptation appear in the social system. This raises the issue of the symbolic content attached to action sets which function to exploit marginal resources of larger societies. And it suggests that the symbol system attached to one social structural set of rules may further mobility under conditions of economic gain, while another set may actually retard the adaptive potential of definable aggregates with a similar social system. Unlike Harris, Whitten focuses on the internal system of adaptation (following the lead of Murphy and Steward 1956). He assumes that cultural rules "feed back" to social system adjustments, sometimes facilitating adaptation, but sometime retarding adaptation.

Network analysis is fundamental to an understanding of the adaptive capacity of aggregates within neoteric societies, *particularly, though not exclusively* those of New World Negroes in ethnically identifiable rural communities. Here they are forced to adapt to a changing bureaucratized universe on the basis of expendable social capital through the categorical relationship "whiteness."

Adaptation in cultural anthropology is sometimes productively conceived of in terms of game theory. Alexander Alland (1967:312) tells us that a valuable concept, central to adaptive processes, is that of "minimax":

> The term refers to strategies in which the attainment of net gain is maximized through attention to potential loss as well as potential gain. A good strategy in game theory is one in which a player protects himself against excessive loss as he attempts to win at the expense of his adversary.... If human behavior involves adaptive mechanisms, then one would expect successful strategies to develop through time which minimax behavior in relation to specific environments.

Davenport (1960) has initiated this approach in anthropology. The article by Kochman in this book is directly concerned with the game of survival in ghetto life. Marshall Sahlins (Tax 1964:136) relates the notion of minimax to the symbol content of a particular adaptive organization:

> Adaptation implies maximizing the social life chances. But the maximization is almost always a compromise, a vector of the internal structure of culture and the external pressure of environment. Every culture carries the penalty of a past within the frame of which ... it must work out its future.

Whitten's argument herein developed implies that generalization from the Pacific Lowlands of Colombia and Ecuador and the Canadian Maritimes, can, the necessary changes having been made, be applied throughout the New World to identifiable ethnic aggregates, many of which are composed of classes of black people in various nations and territories.[34] The crucial environmental element in such Negroes' environments from tropics to temperate zones does seem to be "the white man" (or whiteness as the criterion for a categorical relationship), for it is usually through white-dominated economic resources that Negroes' adaptive potential is channeled. Where organizational similarities among Negro communities exist, then we can expect the reasons to lie in their developing similar strategies to survive in a position of economic marginality. In the following papers Nelkin uses a cognatic concept of social marginality, while Whitten attempts to demonstrate the value of a concept of strategy for understanding social organization in western Colombia and Ecuador. Despres further contributes by relating the concept of ecological niche to those of adaptation and strategy. By focusing on a nation, Guyana, as an ecosystem, Despres demonstrates the explanatory power of an analysis of complementary adaptive strategies in a plural society.

If, as we now think, Negroes' exclusion from economic control appears to favor networks and action sets rather than bounded groups which support short-run exploitation of human resources (including "whiteness") our corollary is that ego-centered networks can be analyzed as the minimal economic unit in a system of economic marginality. Viewed from this perspective, a "family" or "household" should be thought of at any time as providing two or more possible linkages in a chain of economic exchange. If it is demonstrated

INTRODUCTION

that neither family nor household is the minimal productive or exploitive unit in a system of economic marginality, we should seek out the crucial factors, understand the intersecting of competitive strategies and analyze resulting patterns. And we should do so without regard for contemporary middle class norms that assume a minimal family group as a *primary* social and economic unit. Such a perspective does not deny the function of family and household organization in the analysis of social systems. It does challenge the *primacy* of family and household composition as explanations of economic and socialization processes in systems adapting to economic marginality. Documentation necessary to constructive work in this direction has recently been done in Washington, D.C., by Elliot Liebow (1967). In the area of ideology Roger Bastide (1967:217–18, 227) uses a similar approach to analyze and explain the growth and tendencies of Negritude. In this volume Hannerz illustrates adaptation and network analysis, as do Stack, Whitten, Nelkin, and Despres.

Neglect of Contemporary Problems

At the 1967 A.A.A. symposium Charles A. Valentine voiced concern about the policy issues included in Afro-American research. He stressed not only the failure of anthropologists to adequately understand the role of white domination of Negroes throughout the New World, but also anthropologists' reticence to speak out on crucial policy issues. He moved from the analytical to the applied role of anthropology: "Despite shibboleths to the contrary, our roles as scholars cannot be separated from our influence as citizens. Whatever we say or fail to say about New World Negro life will be used or misused in the wider world. We cannot escape our relevance to the increasingly critical areas of policy decisions and action initiatives." As for the symposium papers, Valentine pointed out that:

> ... nearly all of these papers deal exclusively with Negro communities that are exotic and/or marginal in one sense or another. Conspicuously omitted from systematic attention here are the masses of urban and largely northern Negroes who are presently facing the most powerful nation in the world with an extreme sociopolitical crisis that has world-wide international implications. It is almost as if we had unintentionally defined the New World Negro so as to exclude the principal mass of black people in our hemisphere who are really in movement and making history.... Can it be that some of us find this aspect of the New World Negro too overwhelming and too close to home for us to deal with as we would our favorite marginals and exotics?... If this is the case, then New World Negro studies are in danger of becoming merely one more anachronistic ornament of a privileged subculture in our own complex and conflicted society.

Until very recently, neglect of contemporary American urban problems has been characteristic of anthropology as a discipline —just as anthropologists have neglected the urban milieux of other countries.[35] Many American anthropologists assume that, with American culture all around us, it is important to make careful reports on *other* peoples in order to avoid possible bias when we do make comparisons.

We have endeavored to round out this book by including reports of several ongoing studies in northern United States urban areas. It is worth noting, however, that some 70% of New World Negroes live outside the U.S. (cf. Harris 1964b:127–31). The articles by Kochman, Hannerz, and Stack in Part II and Gerlach and Hines, Haralambos, and the Valentines in Part III range from language to roles, from soul stations to black power. Other papers draw comparisons with the work being done in the urban North.

Valentine made three additional criticisms that are well worth noting as anthropologists begin to reemphasize studies of Afro-American communities:

1. Ethnography has its own built-in bias toward internal characteristics of the particular part-society under study. Unless one carefully guards against and compensates for this bias, it can lead him to underestimating the effects of external forces originating elsewhere in the larger system.
2. The built-in bias of ethnography may lead anthropologists and others to attribute certain features to Negro part-societies without adequately exploring *the possible occurrence of the same culture pattern in non-Negro communities.*
Perhaps the most striking movement in this direction is the notion of the mother-centered family as an exclusively Negro phenomenon. Such prejudicial biases have recently reached major policy levels, as evidenced by the *Moynihan Report.*[36]
3. Tendencies such as the two just mentioned may lead to the use of models constructed from lower class data only, thereby *confounding Negroes with poor people in general.*[37]

Valentine referred specifically to the failure of anthropologists to compare New World Negroes and non-Negroes living under the same circumstances and subject to the same pressures. This criticism is particularly relevant to the "exclusion" hypothesis formulated above by Whitten, to the discussion of matrifocality developed in this book by Dr. González, and to the discussion of the kindred by Mrs. Stack. For if there are whites and Negroes equally excluded by the larger society and living under the same conditions of economic marginality, then similarities should fit some of the generalizations drawn above. And differences between them could be linked either to specific aspects of their respective histories or to specific divergent adaptive responses to environing qualities of the larger societies. As long as New World racism attaches a negative valence to black aggregates, then we should expect not to find black and white aggregates under the *same* circumstances within a racist society.

Some mention should be made here of the relationship between Indians and Negroes, especially in Latin America, where Indianness may carry a negative social valence, particularly when combined with marginal economic means. An important step in Afro-American studies will be taken when scholars make careful intranational comparisons of the adaptive strategies of Indians and Negroes, under conditions where they share complementary ecological niches vis-à-vis a national system and under conditions where they share competitive niches. Such a study might help us to approach parallelisms and divergences in "Indigenismo" and "Négritude" (cf. Coulthard 1968). Miss Klumpp's article moves toward an analysis of people in the highlands of Ecuador who share the Indians' undesirable ethnic identity. Another glaring need in Latin America is a full-scale ethnography of urban black aggregates, ghettoized to some extent because of overt ethnicity. Cities such as Guayaquil, Panama City, Cayenne, Paramaribo, and Barranquilla would all be desirable locations.

In considering concepts which should be explored in updating Afro-American studies by anthropologists, we might well examine M. G. Smith's comment (Despres 1967:ix) on the relationship of different organizational emphases in plural societies. He states: "Eufunctional for its adherents, a distinctive ethnic structure may be positively dysfunctional for the society. Alternatively, once conditions have changed, such a structure may lose its functional values with minimal changes of form, or it may preserve these values despite formal changes." It would seem that the *only* avenue to economic

INTRODUCTION

betterment in a system where people are excluded on the basis of ethnic appearance would be through unconventional strategies with marked dysfunctional results in the larger societies. However, the nature of national social structure itself would seem crucial in the *creation* of its subsectional groupings. Despres' article in this book demonstrates the inner workings of a national system with distinctive ethnic sectors without the "eufunctional-dysfunction" dichotomy. Valentine, in his conclusion, suggests roles for the ethnographer which are directly relevant to his participation in different sectors of a complex nation.

We must recognize sociopolitical and cultural movements which emphasize the internationality of contemporary Afro-American cultures. For example, Stokely Carmichael is quoted in *Muhammad Speaks* (1967, Dec. 15:2) as stating:

> For me the African world stretches from South America through the African continent, to the northern part of South America (that is, through Brazil, Venezuela, and Colombia): through the Caribbean Islands, the Antilles, through Central America and Mexico to the United States and Nova Scotia.

With the exception of Mexico and Venezuela this book touches on every area mentioned by Carmichael, including even the large population of Ecuadorian Negroes (both highland and lowland), people apparently still unrecognized by contemporary black power advocates.[38]

AFRO-AMERICAN ANTHROPOLOGY: CULTURAL PATTERNING AND SOCIO-ECONOMIC ADAPTATIONS

The structure of this book follows the ideas and issues raised in this Introduction. *Part I, Cultural Patterning*, includes papers which demonstrate theoretical and methodological consequences of cultural diversity and similarity as they relate to recurrent issues in the study of Afro-Americans. Thomas J. Price, with experience in Colombia, Surinam, Honduras, and various parts of the Caribbean begins by demonstrating how Afro-Americans' images of Africa are influenced by the attitudes of non-Negroes. Marvin Harris, who works primarily in Brazil and has done research in Ecuador and Mozambique, continues to refine techniques through theoretical and methodological sophistication applied to ethnic categories. Erika Bourguignon, who has carried out field investigations in Haiti, gives us new material on possession and dissociation in ritual contexts, while Bryce–Laporte reports on a specific occult event in the context of Panamanian ethnic and cultural plurality. Professor J. L. Dillard, a scholar of both Africa and the Caribbean, updates our understanding of contemporary theories and issues in Creole speech patterns. Reisman and Kochman, who work in Antigua and the urban United States, respectively, contribute to a sense of patterning by the analysis of codes and strategies. Roger Abrahams, with considerable experience in the urban United States and in Trinidad and Nevis, attempts to present patterning of performances in diverse areas, a theme which also pervades the work of Lomax. Whitten's paper demonstrates the need for social anthropological perspectives, even in the area of music, while Szwed's article attempts to tie together stylistic and social structural variables offered by Lomax and Whitten in an historical and programmatic manner.

Part II, Socio-economic Adaptations, is designed to provide a basis for the analysis of Afro-American aggregates that is essentially cross cultural. Adaptational theory is the core around which the papers are oriented, though each of the authors presents his own special viewpoint according to the specific problem confronting him. We begin with Nancie L. González' definition of matrifocality. This sort of family structure has pervaded most writing about Afro-Americans. Also, her general frame of reference serves to direct our attention away from Afro-America *per se* and toward cross cultural categories of adaptive response in neoteric societies. Kathleen Klumpp, who has worked with Indians and Negroes in highland Ecuador, contributes to our knowledge of Afro-America by examining data from the Andes, and also to our knowledge about internal marketing systems. Leo Despres' article on Guyana demonstrates the explanatory and organizational value of contemporary ecological theory by discussing different adaptive strategies according to a number of niches occupied by different ethnic groups. Adaptation to marginality itself is the subject of the paper by Mrs. Dorothy Nelkin, while Mrs. Carol Stack focuses directly on the kindred as a means of understanding resource allocation by urban black Americans. By making a network analysis of ghetto male relationships and by adopting an ecological frame of reference, Ulf Hannerz (who has also done field work in Nigeria) gives us fresh insights into social structural and cultural consequences of urban marginality all too frequently ignored by anthropologists. Finally, Whitten attempts to present the adaptive strategies of west Ecuadorian and Colombian black people by a developmental model of mobility processes. Concepts developed in this section may well be relevant to contemporary black America, especially where adaptation to "ghetto life" has been important.

Psychologist Kenneth Clark (1965:11) tells us that:

"Ghetto" was the name for the Jewish quarter in sixteenth century Venice. Later it came to mean any section of a city to which Jews were confined. America has contributed to the concept of the ghetto the restriction of persons to a special area and the limiting of their freedom of choice on the basis of skin color. The dark ghetto's invisible walls have been erected by the white society, by those who have power, both to confine those who have *no* power and to perpetuate their powerlessness. The dark ghettos are social, political, educational, and — above all — economic colonies. Their inhabitants are subject peoples, victims of the greed, cruelty, insensitivity, guilt and fear of their masters.

Part III, "Black Culture" and Ghetto Ethnography, begins with an article on "Black Culture" by a sociologist, Robert Blauner. It is followed by three papers reporting on recent, on-going research by anthropologists in urban ghetto settings. Luther Gerlach and Virginia H. Hine report on the value of a "segmentary model" for understanding the contemporary black power movement, while Michael Haralambos contributes to our understanding of the "anthropology of complex societies" with his analysis of the cultural content of "soul stations."

To close this volume, Charles and Betty Lou Valentine report on their first months of field work in a contemporary urban black ghetto, finding that the stereotypes and models thus far applied to such situations are indeed to be questioned and reexamined. Generalizations are judiciously few, but the provocative challenge to established explicit and implicit models of what "the ghetto" ought to be like are manifest and must be considered by future investigators and writers. The paper represents an anomaly for anthropology because the anthropologists in this setting seem compelled to *write from the field*; in some recent work these investigators have altered their names and disguised the location of their field site. That they feel that writing for varied reading publics is part of a field experience presents us with an intriguing new perspective of continuing field work in complex societies.

It is the hope of the authors of this Introduction that the articles which follow will lead the readers to seek new theories and new data with which to challenge established notions, and newly developing notions. In other words, it is our hope that the traditional anthropological fiat of confrontation of established theories with fresh data, inductively derived, can be expanded to the benefit not only of anthropology, but also to those self-identifying as Afro-Americans.

NOTES

1. *The Myth of the Negro Past* is a milestone in Afro-American studies, and the reader of this book should consider it to be a substantial complement to our edited volume. Among other things, a 1958 paperback edition contains a supplemental bibliography considerably updating the earlier work, together with a new Preface by the author.

This book, however, is designed neither as *Festschrift* to, nor criticism of, Herskovits and his work. Such *Festschriften* and criticism, together with comment and reply, are already extensive. The obituaries by Merriam (1963; 1964a) and Bascom (1964) point out many of Herskovits' strengths, while tributes are paid to him by Dillard (1964) and Mintz (1964). R. T. Smith (1956) and M. G. Smith (1955) raise a number of critical issues, and Herskovits' reaction to a number of his critics is presented in his 1960 paper, *The Ahistorical Approach to Afroamerican Studies*, which is reprinted, together with others of Herskovits' publications, in *The New World Negro* (1966) edited by his wife, Mrs. Frances Herskovits. At the 1967 A. A. A. symposium Guy B. Johnson raised fresh issues. His paper is reprinted in Johnson (1968: xiii–xvii).

2. *An American Dilemma* was first published in 1944. In 1964 it was republished in a convenient 2 volume paperback edition, with materials in a Foreword and a new Preface which set the book in a contemporary perspective by noting changes in the past 20 years. The Carnegie charge to the project headed by Gunnar Myrdal was to prepare "a comprehensive study of the Negro in the United States, to be undertaken in a wholly objective and dispassionate way as a social phenomenon" (Myrdal 1964:ii). Memoranda on Negro life in the United States were prepared by dozens of scholars, many of whom published their findings in individual books due to uncertainty about Myrdal's return to the United States to complete his work. The full list of publications by 1944 is given by Myrdal (1964:liv–lv). All the research manuscripts are deposited in the Schomburg Collection of the New York Public Library. A condensation of *An American Dilemma* was published by Arnold Rose in a book entitled *The Negro in America* (1944), a Beacon Paperback edition being published in 1956.

Prior to the 1938 Carnegie project a general summary of knowledge in the 1920's was published in *The American Negro* (1928) as Volume CXXX, No. 229, of *The Annals of the American Academy of Political and Social Science*. Between 1928 and 1938 and into the time of Myrdal's work a number of good studies were published, such as *Black Manhattan* by James Weldon Johnson (1930), *Preface to Peasantry* by Arthur F. Raper (1936), *The Negro's God* by Benjamin E. Mays (1938), and *After Freedom* by Hortense Powdermaker (1939), to mention only four books now available in paperback republished by Atheneum Press under the general editorship of August

Meier. A comprehensive bibliography of American Negro studies is given by Elizabeth W. Miller (1966), and Erwin K. Welsch has recently provided a select annotated bibliography on American Negroes as a research guide (1965).

3. In "The Negro in the New World: The Statement of a Problem", published in the *American Anthropologist*, Herskovits (1930b) established the basis for his chart of cultural intensity and the basis for his subsequent analyses of cultural change. It is interesting to note that he also published an article on "The Culture Areas of Africa" (1930a) and several articles on his work in Surinam during the same year. The 1935a article was entitled "Social History of the Negro" and spelled out many of Herskovits' ideas of the value of combining historical and ethnohistorical analysis with distributional studies, using theories of psychological process to account for similarities and differences in what was regarded as a continuing process of acculturation. During the same year he published a popular article entitled "What Has Africa Given America?" (1935b). Ideas first expressed in the 1935 articles were not fully elaborated and formalized until after publication of *The Myth* in the *American Anthropologist* article, "The Contribution of Afroamerican Studies to Africanist Research" (1948a).

A complete bibliography of Herskovits' writings is given as an appendix to Merriam (1964): "Bibliography of Melville J. Herskovits," by Anne Moneypenny and Barrie Thorne.

4. References pertinent to the spread and distribution of Afro-American culture and to identifiable black aggregates may be gleaned from Johnston (1910), J. King (1945), Hudson (1964), Bernard and Bernard (1928:306–18), Mörner (1966:17–44; 1967), Franco (1961), Bastien (1964), Aguirre Beltrán (1946), Ramos (1937, 1939), Zelinski (1949), and Bastide (1967). See also the United Nations Demographic Yearbook (1956:259–61; 1963:311–13).

Ideas pertaining to "race relations" will help the reader evaluate information on distribution. The recent works by Banton (1967, with *Current Anthropology* reviews 1969), van den Berghe (1967), Hunter et al. (1965), and Hoetink (1967) provide important concepts.

For a sample of some national, regional and community studies of Negroes in the New World nations exclusive of the northern United States see Aguirre Beltrán (1958), Taylor (1951), González (1969), West (1952, 1957), Escalante (1964), Whitten (1965), Liscano (1950), Carvalho-Neto (1965), Pierson (1942), Ramos (1939), Da Costa Eduardo (1948), Hutchinson (1957), Harris (1956), Freyre (1964), Herskovits (1937b), Herskovits and Herskovits (1934; 1936; 1947a), Hurault (1961, 1965), Neumann (1961; 1965a; 1965b; 1967), Davis (1952), Kahn (1931), Dark (1954), Price-Mars (1928), Ortiz (1916, 1924, 1947), Beckwith (1929), M. G. Smith (1962a; 1962b; 1965), Clarke (1957), Greenfield (1966), Otterbein (1966), R. T. Smith (1956), Despres (1967), Henriques (1953), Woofter (1930), Johnson (1930), Rohrer and Edmonson (1960), and Powdermaker (1939).

5. For a broader view of Boas' position see his books (1911, 1940). Boas' contributions are brilliantly articulated by Stocking (1968:133–60, 161–95). That racism was integrally a part of British and American anthropology prior to the untiring academic and administrative work of Franz Boas is adequately documented in Banton (1967:12–35, 36–54) and Stocking (1968:42–68, 110–32). To fully appreciate the sociopolitical as well as the academic setting surrounding Boas during the time when Melville J. Herskovits was just beginning his academic career it is essential that one read Stocking (1968:270–307, particularly 298–301). See also Harris (1968:250–300) and Goldschmidt (1959). For a very critical review of Boas' work which bluntly asserts that "Boas' influence was reactionary and antiscientific at some points, such as for example, in his attitude toward cultural evolutionism" (White 1966:55), see White's short monograph (1966).

6. Herskovits' political concerns led him into involvement with civil rights activities of his day. Many of his first publications were in the Urban League Journal *Opportunity* and in the magazine of the National Association for the Advancement of Colored People (NAACP),

Crisis; and at W. E. B. Du Bois' invitation, he addressed the Fourth Pan-African Congress in 1927. For a number of years he commented on the state of American race relations for the *American Journal of Sociology* (Herskovits 1929, 1932, 1933) and warned intellectuals of new racist literature by writing in liberal journals such as *The New Republic* and *The Nation*. Throughout, his concern was to promote the Boasian position separating concepts of race and culture. That such a position, now accepted in contemporary "liberalism", demanded continuous defense is well demonstrated by the references given in Footnote 5 above.

7. Whitten feels that the idea of the survival of "secret" or "private" African elements, perhaps even in masked form, lends an aura of mysticism to the unraveling of cultural history. Obviously, it also provides a polemic for those unable to find evidence of Africanisms in published sources. Perhaps this explains why Herskovits never fully considered it in his later works. Szwed disagrees with this interpretation, arguing that covert linguistic categories and features are examples of cultural elements that are perpetuated "in secret."

8. A similar argument can be made, of course, for *any* complex of traits, and can be particularly well made for large-scale societies such as the United States. See, for a dramatic example, "One Hundred Percent American," by Ralph Linton (1937:427–29). Roger Bastide (1967:14–16) suggests that Nina Rodriguez (1900) in Brazil and Fernando Ortiz (1917) in Cuba were concerned with similar problems.

9. See Herskovits (1940; 1941; 1943a; 1945a; 1945b). In Trinidad Herskovits began to grapple with the complexities evident where "folk religion" competed with established religions for acceptance among folk and non-folk. For other examples see Métraux (1959), Tallant (1962), and Bastide (1961a; 1961b). Bourguignon and Bryce-Laporte both help clarify such issues in this volume.

10. In terms of intellectual history it is important to note that it was in 1945b, in the article "Problem, Method and Theory in Afroamerican Studies" (in Herskovits 1966:43–61), that Herskovits first explicitly states that he "will discuss three elements in the scientific study of the New World Negro and his African background, that hitherto in large measure has been *implicit* in [his] ... writings on the subject ... (1966:43), emphasis added). In this article Herskovits, for the first time, identifies and labels his notions of scale of intensity and cultural focus, both having been introduced implicitly in previous publications (e.g., 1930b; 1941).

11. For a critical review of traditions of sociological thought established and perpetuated by Frazier see Valentine (1968:20–25). Lest the reader judge Frazier too harshly, however, on the basis of *The Negro Family in the United States* (1939, revised paperback edition 1966), he is also urged to read *The Negro in the United States* (1957a) in order to grasp Frazier's full perspective. Among other things, Frazier was able to understand the significance of different processes operating at different levels of sociocultural systems, and to raise the question of impact of such different processes (e.g., cultural persistence, social structural adaptation) on actual groupings of people in particular economic settings. For a perspective on the Frazier-Herskovits controversy see Frazier (1939), Herskovits' (1940) review of this book, Frazier's (1942) and Herskovits' (1943b) concepts of Bahia family structure, Frazier's (1957a) extended reply to Herskovits, and Keil's (1966:4–5) and Mintz' (1961) more recent discussions.

12. For definitions and contemporary references on such approaches see Birdwhistell (1952; 1968a; 1968b), Goffman (1963), and E. Hall (1963, 1966).

13. Exceptions, of course, are Herskovits himself, some of his students, and a few others. (For a bibliography of Herskovits' work see Moneypenny and Thorne [1964)].) Scholars who continued Herskovits-style work include Crowley (1958–59, 1962), Simpson (1945; 1955a; 1962b; 1965; 1966), Bastide (1961b; 1967), Bastien (1951a; 1951b), Price (1954), Aguirre Beltrán (1946, 1958), Ortiz (1940, 1947, 1952–55), Taylor (1951), Carvalho-Neto (1962, 1965), Bascom

(1941, 1952), Waterman and Bascom (1949), Pollak-Eltz (1966, 1967, 1968), and Hogg (1960).

14. Most of these publications were community studies which attempted to describe and analyze social organization in terms of relationships to environing characteristics of larger systems. The foci of each investigator varied, but all sought to place data first in the context of the continuing social life of the people examined, and secondly, to establish the relationships between the elements themselves and a larger system of economic, social, and political relationships.

15. Studies such as those conducted by R. T. Smith (1956), Edith Clarke (1957), and M. G. Smith (1962a) clearly departed from Herskovits' interests. R. T. Smith (1963:29) remarks, however, that the concentration on domestic organization by British social anthropologists was prompted by the need to demonstrate the organization lying behind flexible kinship systems. In this sense it would seem that R. T. Smith and Herskovits, different though their work was in other respects, can be regarded as seeking similar ends, in contrast with those of E. Franklin Frazier, at least on the level of "family analysis."

16. Again, Herskovits and his students are an exception to this generalization. A crucial article defining the approach, and the assumptions behind the approach, of the more influential of British investigators (with the exception of M. G. Smith) is Meyer Fortes' (1953:17-41) article "The Structure of Unilineal Descent Groups." In this article Fortes sought to understand the perpetuity of unilineal groupings of kinsmen through an analysis of household dynamics which promoted segmentation in larger units through fission in the domestic unit. By analyzing the processes of replication Fortes was able to handle concepts of perpetuity of whole units, seen as abstractions, while at the same time accounting for internal conflict, fission, and segmentation, seen as aspects of continuing daily life. R. T. Smith's (1956) work is a direct outgrowth of this approach. The idea of the replication of processes in the domestic domain which can be used to construct a model of a social system without reference to "disorganization-organization" dichotomies is later formalized by Fortes in his Introduction to Goody (1958) and is spelled out in terms of Caribbean social organization by R. T. Smith (in Rubin 1957:67-75).

17. An important confusion resulted from this rise and fall of emphases in Charles Wagley's (1957:3) article on "Plantation America" (in Rubin 1957), where he wrote:

The purpose of this paper is to delimit three cultural spheres of the New World which can serve as a frame of reference for our own studies of the contemporary societies and cultures of the Americas. These three American culture-spheres, here to be called Euro-America, Indo-America, *and* Plantation-America, *are set off one from the other by a series of interdependent and interrelated differences deriving mainly from the New World context itself* (emphasis added).

In replying to Wagley, Frazier (1957c:v) wrote "Since the other culture spheres are described in ethnic terms ... the reader may ask why 'Plantation-America' was not designated 'Negro-America.'" Herskovits (1960) reviews this conceptual confusion, yet oddly does not make a strong case for a concept of "Afro-America" instead of "Negro-America" or "Plantation-America." This controversy is most recently discussed by Gwendolyn Mildo Hall in a popular article in the *Negro Digest* (Feb. 1969:35-44). Strategic review of many such concepts are given in Rubin (1957, 1960) and in the Pan American Union publication, *Plantation America* (1959). The reader is also referred to M. G. Smith's (1965) illuminating discussion of the value of concepts of "the plural society." Smith (in Despres 1967:xi) has recently summed up the state of "Caribbean studies" as follows:

Ever since the decline of Afro-American orientations to Caribbean studies, the sociology of this region has been canvassed by three competing theoretical approaches; the "plantation" framework of Wagley (1957), Rubin (1957, 1959) and Mintz (1959b); Parsonian structural-functionalism in various modes (Braithwaite 1953, 1960; R. T. Smith 1956); and analysis based on the model of plural societies advanced by J. S. Furnivall (1948).

INTRODUCTION

18. See note no. 4 for a list of some important community studies.

19. See notes 4 and 16.

20. The results of some of such work is given by Thomas F. Pettigrew (1964), and most recently, and most completely, in *The Negro American*, edited by Talcott Parsons and Kenneth Clark (1965). Earlier summaries include Myrdal's *American Dilemma*, and Rose, *The Negro in America* (see note no. 2).

21. For other reviews of the history of Negro folklore studies see Dorson (1959:166–81), Bruce Jackson (1967:xv–xxiii), and Crowley (1962).

22. For other references see Herskovits (1941; 1944; 1945a), Herskovits & Herskovits (1936; 1947b), Ortiz (1950, 1952–55), Ramos (1935), Merriam (1951), Waterman (1943, 1952), Courlander (1960, 1963), Bourguignon (1959; 1968c), Bastide (1959) and Crowley (1956a; 1956b; 1958–59).

23. A recent exception is Bastide (1965). For discussions of syncretisms among non-Afro-Americans see Edmonson *et al.* (1960).

24. This section of the Introduction is a reproduction of part of a paper entitled "Religious Syncretism among New World Negroes," which Erika Bourguignon prepared for presentation at the 1967 A. A. A. meetings as part of the symposium entitled "Negroes in the New World: Problems in Theory and Method." It is used here by permission of the author.

25. It is interesting that the writings of Allan Kardec also influenced the development of another complex syncretic religion—the Cao-Dai movement in Viet Nam.

26. These ideas are not new to scholarship. Lowie (1912), for example, wrote ". . . the apparent mysticism in the doctrine of convergence disappears at once if the supposed identities are recognized not as ethnological realities, but as logical abstractions; not as homologies, but as analogies." Charles J. Erasmus (1950) has presented anthropology with a brilliant reassessment of the importance of these principles in his analysis of parallel systems of organization.

27. This section was first prepared as a paper delivered at the 1967 A. A. A. meeting in Washington, D. C., for the symposium entitled "Negroes in the New World: Problems in Theory and Method." The theoretical section is herein expanded, but the actual comparisons between Ecuador and Nova Scotia have been minimized. The comparative material has been developed as a long paper on methodology and is published in the book *Marginal Natives: Anthropologists in Cross-Cultural Research* (1969), edited by Morris Freilich. For other illustrations of anthropologists' use of concepts of adaptation see the readings in Cohen (1968, Vol. 2) and Alland (1967). For an earlier set of warnings about such models see Harris (1960).

28. A notable exception, which will be handled below, is the organization of Carriacou as presented by M. G. Smith (1962a).

29. We use this simple definition by Oberg rather than the more elaborated concepts of Oscar Lewis (1966a; 1966b) or Alexander Leighton (1959, 1965) for one very important reason. The thrust of this paper is to explore consistencies in organizational responses to fluctuation in a money economy where *surplus is sporadic* for definable aggregates. Lewis chooses "poverty" as a constant aspect of the economic order to explain the total culture of people living in urban part-societies. This paper assumes cultural variability as part of social organizational similarity, and furthermore assumes that important feedback mechanisms are at work in determining the specific reaction of a given social system to change within an economic order. If we were to follow Lewis' lead we would be unable to analytically separate cultural feedback mechanisms from social organizational adjustment to economic regularities, and would therefore lose, we feel, our evolutionary perspective. Without this perspective labeling and classification could supplant a search for processes of change in contemporary organizations of people classified as

"black" within complex societies. For another perspective on the same sort of problem see Myrdal (1964:1065–70).

30. As stated above, Carriacou, a small island in the British West Indies, offers an exception to this generalization. M. G. Smith (1962a:57) states that here:

> The local combination of production for exchange and subsistence assumes a complementary division of economic roles between the sexes and their cohabitation. Domestic units consisting of spouses and their children, or of old women and their sons, are better adapted to the local economy than are units containing adults of one sex only.... The important point is that men should contribute towards the upkeep of a household, whether living there or not.

Unlike the rest of the New World, Carriacou is characterized by patrilineal lineages ramifying from household organizations. Again, unlike much of the rest of the New World, categorical relationships (those which frequently separate "black" from "white" for economic purposes) do not segregate color aggregates on Carriacou (M. G. Smith 1962a:61). When confronted with the need for men to emigrate, Carriacou residents have not made the more typical adaptation to serial polygyny, but rather have turned to heightened lesbian behavior as a balancing adaptation to household stability and male migration (Smith 1962a:198ff.).

This study by Smith in many ways supports our own position. Note, for example, how he explains the organization of Carriacou:

> Carriacou economic conditions place special value on the cohabitation of man and woman. In these circumstances the woman is perhaps less dependent on her mate than he is on her, although the complementary economic roles of man and woman provide a firm basis for their continuing cohabitation. To pursue exchange activities effectively, the man needs a woman to care for his house, garden, and his children. A woman, on the other hand, can fend for herself provided she receives enough cash gifts from men related to her in various ways. Although "the man is the head of the house" and owns and controls it, his wife has charge of the internal economy (Smith 1962a:203).

Smith (1962a:304–5) himself notes that Carriacou "... is probably unique in the British West Indies in having 92 per cent of its male population married, in its high rate of marital stability, in its exclusion of keeping unions, in its demographic structure, and in its systematic combination of marriage and extra-residential mating."

Most important in this book by Smith is that he does not dichotomize household and family from the ramifying network of kinship relationships. He chooses, rather, to see both as aspects of the same system of social organization in adaptation to economic factors.

31. A domain is a "field or sphere of activity or influence: as, the domain of science" (Webster's Third International Dictionary). For a discussion of "power domain" relevant to ideas presented in this paper see Adams (1964:49–78; 1967:36–49).

32. Again, the social structure of Carriacou which contains patrilineages is an exception to this generalization (M. G. Smith 1962a).

33. M. G. Smith (1962a:311–12) makes a similar point from a slightly different perspective in his analysis of Carriacou.

34. Again, this does not imply that *all* black aggregates will be characterized by this sort of adaptation. The example of Carriacou has already been noted. What this argument does suggest is that where the sort of system previously labeled "disorganized" or "loose" is found, the type of analysis herein presented should prove of value, and should also contribute to theory construction in anthropology by seeking out patterns of evolutionary convergence under similar conditions. In fact, it seems to us that the strength of M. G. Smith's analysis of the patrilineal descent system and family and household composition on Carriacou rests on his maximal kinship segments in relationship to economic conditions.

35. Urban anthropology such as that being done by Leeds (1965) in Brazil; Mangin (1967a;

1967b) in Peru; Gulick (1967) in Lebanon; Plotnicov (1967), Mitchell (1966), Bascom (1955), Little (1966), Banton (1957), Marris (1961), H. Kuper (1965), Meillassoux (1968), and others in Africa; Belshaw (1957) in New Guinea; Lewis (1966a; 1959; 1961) in the United States, Puerto Rico, and Mexico; and the work of Firth (1956), Frankenburg (1966), Bott (1957), and others in England, and the Andersons (1965) in France, illustrate anthropology's rapid involvement with urban settings (see also Eddy 1969). Dozens of studies are now underway which have not yet been published.

Banton's edited book, *The Social Anthropology of Complex Societies* (1966); Steward et al., in *The People of Puerto Rico* (1956), and Valentine's *Culture and Poverty* (1968, see also *Current Anthropology* reviews 1969) all offer important guidelines.

36. The Moynihan Report was first presented anonymously to the President and his staff as *The Negro Family: The Case for National Action*, Office of Policy Planning and Research of the Department of Labor (1965). The full sociopolitical context is detailed in Rainwater and Yancey (1967) *The Moynihan Report and the Politics of Controversy* and given critical treatment by Charles A. Valentine in *Culture and Poverty* (1968). Moynihan comments on Valentine's and our perspectives in a letter to *Trans-action* (1968:Nov.:63) and comments on Valentine's treatment in *Current Anthropology*, which also contains a reply by Valentine. Whitten wishes to note that we are concerned with what Moynihan *wrote* specifically for the President of the United States to read. Moynihan accuses us of ignoring what he publicly says. We leave it to the reader to decide the issues, which are now set forth in print in the sources given above.

37. Valentine's position is fully articulated in *Culture and Poverty* (1968) which is given *Current Anthropology* review treatment (1969).

38. For a recent overview of Afro-American studies see Roger Bastide (1967), *Les Amériques Noires: Les Civilisations Africaines dans le Nouveau Monde*.

Part one

CULTURAL PATTERNING

One

ETHNOHISTORY AND SELF-IMAGE IN THREE NEW WORLD NEGRO SOCIETIES

Thomas J. Price

A shorter version of this essay appeared in *Trans-Action*, Vol. 5, No. 8 (July–August, 1968), pp. 71–75.

Until recently, the cultural self-image of Negroes living in "part-societies" has been given slight attention. Ethnologists and social anthropologists alike, concentrating on the problems of African retentions, various features of social and economic organization, and other matters often have left unexplored the general question of the particular people's view of the origins of their cultural forms, the role played by larger social and political organizations in the formation of that view, and the extent to which cultural self-image both affects communication with members of larger organizations and gives direction to acculturative processes. To a large extent this omission is undoubtedly a reflection of the covert element, grounded in African tradition and the responses to slavery (M. G. Smith 1953), which runs through Afro-American cultural forms. The use of indirection and "half answers," noted in *The Myth of the Negro Past*, has certainly been a major source of frustration to all field workers in the area; indeed, Herskovits generally cautioned his students against readily accepting the initial responses to questions. In this book, Karl Reisman has given the best analysis to date concerning the problem of obtaining statements of underlying norms and values.

The present paper attempts to explore one aspect of cultural self-image in three New World societies which have strikingly different ethnohistories: the Boni Bush Negroes (or *Aluku*, the term they themselves use) of French Guiana and Surinam, Colombian coastal villages, and the island of San Andrés (Colombia).[1] All three societies share the belief that the African cultural heritage played some role in forming their present ways of life, although wide differences in attitude exist with regard to the relationship between what is felt to be

African (whether or not this evaluation is ethnohistorically valid) and their respective ideal cultural self-images.

THE BONI

Although the various tribal groupings of Bush Negroes—the Djuka (also termed "Aucaners" and "Tapanahoni"), the Saramaca, the Matawey, the Paramaka, and the Boni—have undergone differing degrees of acculturation, they are generally agreed to be the most culturally African groups in the New World. The Boni have a strong sense of ethnohistory; with the exception of various items of technology, most maintain that their beliefs and practices were originally brought to Surinam by their African ancestors, including traits which are readily identified by the outsider as European.

According to their world view there are four categories of human beings: themselves, the *Bushinenge* or Bush Negroes; the *Bakka* (white people); the *Bakkanenge* (town Negroes, literally "white Negroes"); and the *Ingi* (aboriginal Indians). For reasons not yet entirely clear to this author, their ancestors were believed to have brought supernatural disfavor on themselves, for which they were punished through enslavement to the white man. There is little to suggest that the Boni interpretation of slavery carries the implication of cultural or racial inferiority, for the gods and *obias* of the ancestors enabled them to launch a successful revolt, guided them to their present locale, and aided their descendants in the continuing struggle to remain independent despite sporadic skirmishes with whites, Indians, and the Djuka.

History has provided and maintained barriers to communication and cultural exchange between the Bushinenge and the white man, save in selected technological sectors; and although the "old people" of the Boni escaped from slavery in Surinam and found a haven in French territory, the traditional antipathy toward whites has been extended to include French officialdom, missionaries, and medical personnel. The Boni and Bakkanenge view each other with a mixture of awe and contempt. On the one hand, the Boni take considerable pride in the "fact" that the ancestors of town Negroes lacked the courage to run away and cope with the severe conditions and dangerous supernatural forces encountered in jungle life. On the other, the Bakkanenge see themselves, and are seen in turn by the Boni, as having considerable economic and political power and, at least in town, as enjoying relatively superior social status. Yet the two groups realize that their destinies are inextricably interwoven due to their common racial and cultural histories.

Similarly, the Boni view their present location as a flawed blessing. In discussing their territory and life there, all agree that they are not where they ought to be, that they are paying for ancestral sins by living a life of punishment (*pina*) in a hostile and alien environment. For older people release comes only with death, when one of the multiple souls returns to Africa, and for the young who are able to make the transition to town life. Nevertheless, for the bulk who remain, it is their way of life which enables them to exist there, to cope with the dangerous bush and river beings, to obtain food; and they are quick to point out that without their help, whites and Bakkanenge from the outside world could not survive.

On the other side of the coin, it is only through their present situation that freedom and dignity have remained possible. They are easily identified in the coastal cities of Cayenne and Paramaribo and are automatically relegated to the lowest social rank and most menial jobs. On my first trip into Boni territory, I was struck by the transformation in my boatman when the journey began. From hat in hand subservience in St. Laurent he became a dashing, ten-feet-tall extrovert on the river. Until recently, bush and town cultures were both accorded their proper places; and save for new technological items, the bush people have been singularly uninterested in non-bush ways. Voluntary migration to the city was rare, and when it did occur it was generally confined to marginal personalities, individuals cast as scapegoats, and those with exceptional entrepreneurial skills. Through the years the *Granman*, the tribal leader, himself constituted an important agent in maintaining social and cultural isolation. He severely regulated the length of time a man could work outside the territory before returning, and prohibited women from leaving the territory unless in the company of their husbands. Battery-powered radios were not permitted, and a ban was placed on various dance forms which originated in the city. These restrictions vanished with the death of the Granman in 1965. The interim period before the installation of the new Granman was marked by the sudden appearance of radios, instantly bringing the outside world into the smallest village. In addition, as a result of the political ramifications of multi-ethnicity in Paramaribo, Bush Negroes are now being accorded more important roles in the economic and political life of Surinam, a policy which has abetted a quickening flow of the young to the city.

Boni resistance to ethnographic probing is the natural result of the belief that if their ways are revealed to the outside world they will no longer work for them and the people will either die or be forced to resume the ancestral roles vis-à-vis the white man. Further sanctions are provided by both the gods and the ancestors, and by the Granman, who is viewed as the principal buffer between themselves and external political authority.

The first line of defense against curious outsiders is provided by language. *Takitaki*, the *lingua franca*, or hybrid dialect, of Surinam, serves as the vehicle of communication between the Boni and townspeople from Surinam. However, ordinary discourse within the group is carried out in their own dialect, variously termed *Bushinenge tongo* and *Aluku tongo*. Pronunciation and vocabulary are sufficiently different from those of ordinary Takitaki to prevent eavesdropping by outsiders. In addition, many Boni words are further translatable into what is termed *Dipitaki*, which involves both a layer of vocabulary they formerly believed to be totally African, and the shortening of non-Dipi words. In the case of some words, the African provenience can probably be demonstrated. Thus, "rattle," *sekseki* (shake-shake) in Aluku, becomes *adjawala* in Dipi. Others, however, are of undoubted European derivation, as in the case of "promise"—*pamishi* in Aluku, *prometi* in Dipi. Creoles who have spent years in Boni territory and speak Aluku tongo generally find Boni conversation incomprehensible when the Dipi mode is employed.[2]

The term "Dipi" may be applied to anything which should not be revealed. In order to retain their cultural privacy in their communication with outsiders, the Boni have made a high art of institutionalized prevarication. The mastery of the art of indirection and of giving misleading but logical answers is shared by all members of the society and characterizes communication both among themselves and when dealing with non-Boni. Thus, the crude wooden cross draped with cloths which is found in all villages is readily identified for the foreigner as the *faaka tiki*. When pressed for an explanation, faaka is indicated to mean "dress" (from "frock"), tiki as stick. Eventually one learns that in this case faaka is derived from the contraction of *fu aka*, "for the souls." In fact, it marks the spot where the spirits of the ancestors congregate and where libations are made.[3] In dealing with outsiders, one set of terms for villages, rivers, ritual objects, and the like, are employed, another set when speaking to one another. In a sense, a layer of spurious culture has, through the years, been created to shield Boni custom from the outside world.

Participation in village life by a visiting investigator is also highly structured. Assuming the Granman's consent has been obtained, the village headman then decides where the visitor may live, his choice generally being a location which affords a limited view of activities. Furthermore, the kind of quasi-membership which many anthropologists are able to establish in the societies they study is simply not possible with the Boni, and one is rarely invited to participate in the more fundamental aspects of life. Initiative must come completely from the outsider, but his presence at the most neutral of activities is often viewed as an imposition. As to wakes or religious ceremonies in villages other than the one in which he is residing, protocol demands that one go through the proper channels for permission to attend; but even when the response is positive, it is likely to come after the more important phases of the observance have been completed. There are some ceremonials and shrines which are yet to be observed by outsiders (Hurault 1965).

Verbal information obtained from two or more Boni is quite unreliable, such is the strength of social pressure. Conversation is limited to the exchange of pleasantries and to the sectors of life which are both readily observable and can be discussed in terms of form; but further probing into meanings, complex social arrangements, and supernatural usages are greeted with protestations of ignorance. Sessions with informants must be carried out in privacy, if not secrecy. However, with a conception of their ethnohistory in mind, a general knowledge of African cultures is invaluable to a researcher. The Boni are exceedingly interested in Africa and the contemporary life of the people with whom they share ancestral ties. On the one hand, such knowledge generates the suspicion that the foreigner knows more about local custom than is actually the case. On the other hand, although they are highly conservative, they generally realize that many of the old traditions have probably been lost; and the anthropologist's acquaintance with African backgrounds raises his status above that of ordinary bakra.

COASTAL COLOMBIA[4]

During an initial survey of possible communities for a study of African retention, numerous leads given by white nationals who had traveled extensively in the relevant parts of the country were followed, and a considerable period of time was devoted to investigating remote villages in the Chocó, along the Pacific coast, and in the Department of Córdoba. In each case, the promise of a primitive village whose inhabitants "live like Africans" and speak an "unintelligible dialect" went unfulfilled. With the possible exception of one or two quite isolated communities, the Colombian Negro has undergone a rather advanced form of acculturation. Music, the dance, and folklore in many areas remain dominated by African forms, but, contrary to the role played by Catholicism in the retention of African traits in other countries, there is no evidence of the survival of the more formal religious aspects.[5] Nor is there any evidence that these existed in the recent past. Economic life is nearly indistinguishable from that of the mestizo peasant, and family life and organization differ but slightly from the lower class Caribbean model. Coastal Spanish, though undoubtedly shaped by the slave's linguistic heritage, can hardly be categorized with either Gullah or Takitaki. It would seem quite logical, then, that the coastal Negro would consider himself from a cultural point of view to be of the Colombian peasantry, and that given the attitudes of the dominant group toward African culture, he would be ashamed of the African heritage. However, only the latter part of this characterization holds true. There is no conception of what the African past really was, and any discussion of it is likely to make the coastal Negro peasant uncomfortable; but there is much to be found in the interaction between him and both coastal city dwellers and highland whites to support the deep-seated suspicion that a good deal of his culture may, in fact, be African.

It was realized at an early point that the best ploy to be used in establishing rapport was to explain the work in terms of a personal desire to learn "Colombian customs." Originally, the mistake was made of expressing an interest in Afro-American cultures, a bit of intelligence which virtually destroyed communication. In addition, even when the later rationale was adopted and seemingly accepted and the people began to show some curiosity about the investigator's own cultural background, they continued to be uncommunicative when they believed that the questions which were asked involved African words or practices. In most communities, folklore about slavery is virtually impossible to obtain, and the conclusion is inescapable that this sort of lore has been lost through shame and disuse.

The opinion that the lowland Negro is both racially pure and quite African in culture is held rather widely in Colombia, an attitude of which coastal Negroes are aware. Highland whites, especially, claim that "Negro Spanish" is unintelligible to them, an opinion which they make no attempt to hide from the Negro. Visitors to the coastal villages discuss within earshot of the inhabitants the primitiveness of the house types and technology, the purity of the physical type, and the negative psychological and behavioral stereotypes which are generally held concerning Negroes. On one occasion during a wake in Arrollo de Piedra, a village near El Manzanillo, the white owner of a nearby farm arrived on horseback, spotted the American anthropologist, and immediately launched into a loud discussion of the Negro's "lack of respect for the dead," an opinion undoubtedly based on ignorance concerning the reasons behind story-telling, joke-telling, and gaming during such rites. On the few occasions when priests and nuns visit these small villages, the people are harangued for their immoral characters, lack of religious fervor, and for their "superstitious ways."

The extent to which the cultural traits which separate black and white in Colombia may be attributed to the African heritage, to survivals of colonial Spanish folk beliefs and practices, or to syncretisms between the two, constitutes an issue which lies outside the scope of the present paper. Suffice to say that the Negro shares the average white Colombian's ignorance concerning Spanish and Indian culture at the time of the conquest, and so finds the notion of African provenience unavoidable. Verbally, the Negro blames cultural differences on ignorance, poverty, and the lack of education. If he views his way of life as a matter of racial determinism (an opinion which many Colombian whites hold), the belief is not articulated. However, it is apparent that, unlike the Boni, white standards of beauty have been completely internalized by most.

These negative aspects of the coastal Negro's self-view are somewhat ameliorated by the possibility of socio-economic mobility. Although the positive psychological ramifications of the Bush Negro's sense of tribe and political autonomy are absent, he is aware that individuals with his physical type have accumulated considerable wealth in the city, and that *de facto* segregation in housing, quality of schooling, and the like, are economic, not racial matters. In supernatural terms, unlike either of the opposing folk beliefs encountered in North America, that either the tables are turned in the afterlife, or that Heaven is segregated, there is nothing in the doctrine which the coastal Negro has internalized which suggests that God is black, nor that some of the *Almas de Purgatorio* (souls of Purgatory) must continue to employ hair-straighteners.

Nevertheless, the Colombian Negro is aware of his lowly social position; and although he does not share the Boni's anxiety about the possible reinstitution of slavery, the somewhat cloudy picture of land tenure has fostered a generalized concern about the possible reassertion of white economic power. He is aware that the land he now works and to which he has title was once owned by whites, and many hold that the descendants of the original owners may one day return and claim their "rights." It is also widely believed, with some justification, that in any court case involving white and black, the decision invariably favors the former.

Rapport in these villages is obviously facilitated if the ethnographer is an *extranjero* (foreigner) rather than *forastero* (stranger), particularly if he is white. Any white who is believed to be a Colombian national might be a political informer, a police agent investigating either the contraband trade or the outlawed practice of dynamiting fish, or a descendant of the original land owner. A foreigner is unlikely to be any of these, and, where ethnography is concerned, finds it easier to avoid the Afro-American interpretation of his work. Nevertheless, once the serious business of ethnography begins, suspicions are rekindled. Resistance is particularly marked when inquiry is directed toward those cultural areas which are the most suspect from the standpoint of African origins: saint worship, rites for the dead, witchcraft, and marital institutions. As implied earlier, the most effective strategy is one which stresses a comparison between the foreign investigator's cultural background and what he finds in the villages. Eventually, little attempt is made to shut him out of any activity, and he is invited to all social and religious events.

SAN ANDRÉS[6]

The cultural self-image of the people of San Andrés is composed of four elements: Anglo-American, Islander, Afro-American, and Colombian. Traditionally, the preferred self-image involved the first two of these. Originally settled by English-speaking Protestants and their slaves, St. Andrews, together with Providencia ("Old Providence"), eventually became Colombian property. Although, as expressed by the people, "The English gave us their customs and then left us to the Spaniard," the people of San Andrés continued to identify themselves as "Islander," or simply as being "from San Andrés."

Until the last twenty years or so, their ideal self-image was buttressed by several conditions. Bogotá had little interest in the island beyond supplying it with governors. And aside from these and itinerant peddlers, few mainlanders were willing to undertake the arduous trip in the small, antiquated vessels which maintained communication and trade with Cartagena and Barranquilla. Continuous economic and social contacts were maintained with the neighboring English-speaking communities of Corn Island (Nicaragua), and Bluefields, a mainland Nicaraguan port. In addition, strong ties began to develop with the United States through the arrival of American vessels engaged in the copra trade, the advent of American missionaries, and the job market made available through the opening of the Panama Canal. As American enterprise developed on the Colombian mainland, San Andresanos were generally preferred as workers by monolingual managers; and equally monolingual and ethnocentric wives began to compete for the limited number of island women seeking work as domestics. Finally, Americans working on the Spanish-speaking mainland began to visit San Andrés while on vacation, and their latent anti-Hispanic ethnocentrism created a high acceptant attitude toward Islanders and island ways.

The people themselves have long shared a deep antipathy toward mainland culture and people, expressed in the sayings, "Spanish is the language of the dogs," and "Me no like Spaniard nohow," and in the derogatory labels for mainlanders, "Continental" and "Panya." When in a particularly contemptuous mood the even stronger term "Panyabawstid" is used. Mainland Colombians are said to be deceitful, devious, and unscrupulous in business transactions, or, as Islanders put it, "The Panya machét cut on both side."

The people point with pride to their relatively high standard of living, especially when compared to coastal Colombian Negroes. This assessment is shared by white Colombians. And although San Andresanos are referred to as "the Negroes of San Andrés," from a cultural point of view the label carries English rather than Afro-American connotations. As further proof of their believed superiority, they cite the fact that individual Islanders have had successful careers in both business and the armed forces, and have made substantial fortunes in the contraband trade.

However, the basis of the preferred self-view was rendered increasingly shaky as the result of several factors; and some of the elements which earlier had supported the identity turned out, like the Panya's machete, to be a two-edged sword. Of critical importance was a sharp change in the pattern of political and economic relations between island and mainland. Island economy was gradually integrated into the national one and, in the people's view, the community was subjected to a program of political, religious, and cultural harassment designed to obliterate the non-Hispanic identity. These pressures generated widespread hostility, but they also served to heighten long-standing divisive elements in the society. The organized rebellion which many predicted never materialized. As late as 1954 it was firmly believed that the United States would eventually step in and "liberate" the island. Whenever an unidentified plane flew over the island, people would nod their heads wisely saying,

"Uncle Sam know what happen here." An American Seventh Day Adventist missionary was jailed for protesting too loudly the temporary closing of the Protestant schools. Rumors of annexation were rampant, culminating in the appearance of an American naval plane; but the bubble burst when it became evident that the crew's orders did not extend beyond removing the missionary. Finally, San Andrés was designated a free port, and was soon deluged with continentals and foreigners. Today, the people have virtually become a minority on their own island.

Catholic parochial education had already become highly successful through a system of scholarships to mainland high schools, obtainable after the completion of the required number of years in the schools, whose courses are all taught in Spanish, run by the Church on the Island. This program found ready acceptance in the lower socioeconomic sectors, among those who saw fluency in Spanish as a tool for upward mobility.

As in the case of coastal Colombia, San Andresanos have been well aware of the behavioral distance which separates them from the carriers of the desired cultural model. Once more, the most striking barrier is language. The forms of communication which are employed vary, according to socio-economic group, from a type of English which would put most American college students to shame, to a dialect variously termed "broken English," *Patois*, and *Bende*. The latter form is the object of considerable ambivalence. It is the more expressive medium of communication where island values and humor are concerned, and a story or joke told in it is invariably characterized as "sweet." The same story rendered in "good English" elicits only a mild response. Also, as in the case of the Dipitaki of the Boni, it serves to foster group solidarity and functions as a defensive language when used in the presence of outsiders. Nevertheless, fluency in the Bende is associated with the lower class and with the inability to speak "good English" which, many maintain, is more difficult to learn than Spanish. Most are aware of its African roots although, once more, there may be an overestimation of the role played in its genesis by African forms. Similarly, Islanders are conscious of the possibility that some aspects of family life, some of the beliefs concerning the dead, and the obia [obeah] complex are not of English origin, due in part to their condemnation by Protestant missionaries from the States.[7] In the past, many have verbalized the belief that most missionaries, both Protestant and Catholic, picture them as "African savages" during their home leaves in order to obtain more funds for their work.

Like most Caribbean peoples, the Islanders have had a long tradition of travel and work abroad. Whatever their reasons for going—unemployment, shame, and paranoia engendered by envy and gossip in a little community,[8] or simply the desire to travel—those who have come to the States have inevitably encountered discrimination. The belief is also expressed that white outsiders, the bakra, hide their feelings about color while visiting San Andrés, but that "back home" they are probably indistinguishable from other whites in their treatment of Negroes.

The result of these conditions has been the growing conviction that the adherence to "old Island ways" has been a sign of backwardness and is not a source of kinship with white North Americans. Consequently, the self-image has begun to shift in the direction of the Colombian model. Bilingualism began to increase appreciably by

1960 among all but the elderly. It is no longer unusual for Islanders to carry on conversations in Spanish among themselves. In their relations with mainland Colombians, with whom they can now converse easily, they stress their national loyalty and considerable knowledge of Colombian history and geography. But at the same time, their Anglo-American cultural roots serve to separate them in the minds of white Colombians from the poor Afro-American peasants of the mainland coast.

Incipient Colombianization is also apparent in a new identity projected by Islanders in their relationships with Americans in the United States. Whereas "old Island" immigrants in New York City continue to identify themselves as being from San Andrés and are totally monolingual, younger immigrants refer to themselves as Colombians, communicate with one another in Spanish, and use Spanish kinship terms and terms of address when white Americans are present.

Any analysis of the view which Afro-American societies and part-societies in the Caribbean and Latin America have of their sociopolitical situations must take into consideration sub-cultural differences, as well as the interpretations of those differences both by the people in question and the members of larger social and political entities into which they have, to one degree or another, been integrated. The extent to which the European cultural models have come to be accepted as a cultural ideal has, of course, been intertwined with the psychological ramifications of slavery and the emergence of new national identities and social structures in the New World. The continuing association of low social rank, racial and sub-cultural differences, together with differing degrees of integration into a larger social system, has led to divergent responses in the three societies examined here. These are the maintenance of an autonomous cultural identity which places high value on the African heritage (Surinam), acculturation in the direction of the desired or ideal model (Colombia), and the adoption of an entirely new, but previously denigrated model (San Andrés).

NOTES

1. Research in Colombian Negro communities was sponsored by a grant from the Grace and Henry Doherty Foundation, 1952–53, and was continued under the auspices of the Instituto Nacional de Antropología (Bogotá) the following year. Further study was made possible by the Medical School, Universidad del Valle (Cali), 1958–60. Field work on San Andrés was originally subsidized by the Instituto Nacional, and during the summer of 1956 by a grant from the Research Institute for the Study of Man. The Universidad del Valle sponsored my return in 1960. Research on the Boni was carried out through a grant from the National Science Foundation, 1964–65. During the academic year 1968–69, return visits were paid to coastal Colombia, the Boni, and San Andrés, and comparative research carried out both on Corn Island (Nicaragua), and Roatán, one of the Bay Islands off the coast of Honduras.

2. The belief in the African provenience of *Aluku tongo* may now be undergoing some modification. There is a growing realization that many words are, indeed, derived from English. One informant in 1969 used the term "broken English" to describe his language, a notion which had obviously been picked up on the outside.

3. As pointed out by Richard Price in the discussion following the 1967 A. A. A. symposium, *faka* is also defined by the Bush Negroes as "flag," which, in the case of *faaka tiki*, serves as an additional linguistic layer.

4. The material presented in this part of the paper is based on work in El Manzanillo, La Boquilla, and Punta Canoa, small coastal villages near Cartagena.

5. Price, Thomas J., "Estado y Necesidades de las Investigaciones Afro-Colombianas," *Revista Colombiana de Antropología,* II (1955), 11–36. For a recent discussion of the Colombian Negro's tribal backgrounds, see Pavy, David, "The Provenience of Colombian Negroes," *The Journal of Negro History,* Vol. III, No. 1, 1967. For an analysis of social structure in a largely Negro community in Ecuador and one which has relevance for the Colombian coastal Negro, attention is called to Norman E. Whitten, Jr., *Class, Kinship, and Power in an Ecuadorian Town* (Stanford 1965).

6. Price, T. J., "Algunos Aspectos de Estabilidad y Desorganizacion Cultural en una Comunidad Islena del Caribe Colombiana," *Revista Colombiana de Antropología,* III (1955), 13–54. See also Lowenthal, David, "Race and Color in the West Indies," *Daedalus,* Spring 1967.

7. The fact that American Protestant missionaries (generally from the Southern Baptist Convention) have seen a need for their work on San Andrés, has, in itself, contributed to the Islanders' confusion concerning their identity.

8. The belief that their socio-economic problems at least in part stem from envy among their peers finds expression in the frequently heard sentiment, "The people of San Andrés are like crabs in a bucket; when one gets to the top, the others reach up and pull him down." It should also be pointed out that for many the additional jobs and somewhat higher pay which resulted from the economic boom have been counterbalanced by higher food prices engendered by the strains on locally grown produce and the consequent need to import food of all types. Also, real estate values have increased more than tenfold, putting new land acquisition beyond the reach of the relatively poor.

Two

REFERENTIAL AMBIGUITY IN THE CALCULUS OF BRAZILIAN RACIAL IDENTITY[1]

Marvin Harris

This article is reprinted by permission of the *Southwestern Journal of Anthropology*.

The comparative study of race relations in Brazil and the United States has brought to light important differences in culturally controlled systems of "racial" identity. Many observers have pointed out the partial subordination of "racial" to class identity in Brazil exemplified in the tendency for individuals of approximately equal socioeconomic rank to be categorized by similar "racial" terms regardless of phenotypic contrasts, and by the adage "money whitens" (Pierson 1942, 1955; Wagley *et al.*, 1952; Harris 1956; Azevedo 1956). Other aspects of the Brazilian calculus of "racial" identity lead to categorizations which are inconceivable in the cognitive frame of descent rule which underlies the division of the United States population into "whites" and "Negroes" (now more politely, "blacks"). Experimental evidence indicates that phenotypically heterogeneous full siblings are identified by heterogeneous "racial" terms. Children of racially heterogeneous Brazilian marriages are not subject to the effects of hypodescent[2]: if the phenotypes are sharply different, full siblings may be assigned to contrasting categories (Harris and Kottak 1963). It has also long been observed that the inventory of terms which define the Brazilian domain of "racial" types exceeds the number of terms in the analogous domain used by whites in the United States (and probably by blacks as well).

The suggestion has been made that the most distinctive attribute of the Brazilian "racial" calculus is its uncertain, indeterminate, and ambiguous output. Subordination of race to class, absence of descent rule, and terminological profusion all contribute to this result (Harris 1964a; 1964b). Several different indications of the absence of a common shared calculus should be pointed out: ego lacks a single sociocentric racial identity; the repertory of racial terms varies widely from one person to another (holding region and community constant); the referential meaning of a given term varies widely (i.e., the occasions in which one term rather than another will be used); and the abstract meaning of a given term (i.e., its elicited contrasts with respect to other terms) also varies over a broad range even within a single community.

Clarification of the nature of the ambiguity in the Brazilian "racial" calculus awaits the development of cross culturally valid methods of cognitive analysis. In this essay, I report on a preliminary attempt to employ a test instrument to elicit the Brazilian lexicon of "racial" categories and to provide a measure of referential ambiguity and consensus with respect to the elicited terms.

The instrument employed consisted of a deck of seventy-two full face drawings constructed out of the combination of three skin tone, three hair form, two lip, two nose, and two sex types. All other features were held constant. The drawings were presented in a standardized random order. Each respondent was permitted to glance at the whole deck before being asked to identify the first drawing. Responses were initiated without using terms presumed to be part of the domain. In general it was found that a question involving a request for the "qualidade" or "typo" or "raça" of the person depicted in the drawing was adequate to prime the response process. The word "cor" was used as a last resort.

The deck was shown to 100 native born adult Brazilians, 39 women and 61 men at sites in five different states: Bahia 28; Alagoas 30; Pernambuco 12; Ceará 7; Brasília 8; São Paulo 15. From occupational data and place of birth, the respondents could be classified into the following socio-economic strata: Urban Upper Class 18; Urban Middle Class 31; Urban Lower Class 13; Rural Upper Class 12; Rural Lower Class 26. On the basis of objective criteria (photo portraits were taken of most respondents) their phenotypes can be classified as: predominantly caucasoid 42; marked caucasoid-negroid mix 32; predominantly negroid 16; predominantly caucasoid-negroid-indian mix 6; other types 4. The size of the sample and its non-random nature obviously render all conclusions highly tentative.

The lexical productivity of the graphic stimuli exceeded expectations. In a strictly lexical count, the sample responded with 492 different categorizations. Twenty-five per cent of the sample responded with fifteen or more categorizations, with the range extending from two to seventy categorizations per respondent, and the median at nine per respondent.

The diversity of response is the salient characteristic of the domain under study. Although under other circumstances (as, for example, scientific, chemical, or botanical terminologies) large numbers of terms correlate with precise usage, this is not the case with Brazilian racial categories. Disagreement appears to be a fundamental characteristic of the area defined by these terms. The most frequently employed terms were, in fact, applied to almost all the drawings, and each of the drawings was identified by at least twenty different lexical combinations.

It would be incorrect to conclude that this is a totally orderless domain. On the contrary, cognitive models can be constructed which maximize the order inherent in the raw data. The problem, however, is to provide a model which maximizes the order without ignoring the pronounced tendency toward ambiguity, which is also a real aspect of the raw data.

With this objective in mind, the drawings were analyzed in relation to response patterns, utilizing only the twelve most commonly employed terms, each of which occurred more than one hundred times. These terms are: *moreno, branco, mulato, preto, negro, alvo, moreno-claro, cabo verde, claro, sarará, escurinho, escuro*.

In Figures 2-1 to 2-5 the drawings which were most frequently identified by some of the most popular terms are shown

It is apparent that associated with each of the more popular terms is a particular combination of skin color, hair form, and nose and lip width. Were this the only information available, these components could be used to define cognitive categories which would appear to be in complementary distribution in the manner of componential schemes now enjoying wide interest among anthropologists (see below). Thus a *branco* could be defined as an individual of either sex, with light skin, thin lips, straight to wavy hair, and a thin nose; a *preto*, as an individual of either sex, with kinky hair, dark skin tone, narrow or wide nose, and thick lips; and so on.

Such definitions, however, would neglect over 50% of the occasions which in fact furnished the stimuli for eliciting the terms *branco, preto*, and the like. Moreover, such a scheme would leave no room for the fact that for many Brazilians these terms are not in complementary distribution. Indeed, almost every "key" term was found to be modifiable by another "key" term by someone or other in the sample.

Among the more significant lexical combinations turned up by the presentation of the drawings, special attention should be accorded to the items listed in the next column.

Now we turn to the problem of translating these responses. Since the cognitive domain

branco africano
(*white African*)
branco amarelo
(*yellow white*)
branco indio
(*Indian white*)
branco mestiço
(*mestizo white*)
branco nagó
(*)
branco sarará
(*)
caboclo preto
(*)
claro branco
(*)
indio preto (*black Indian*)
indio moreno
(*)
moreno caboclo
(*)
moreno cabo verde
(*)
moreno escuro claro
(*)
moreno mestiço
(*)
moreno preto
(*)
moreno sarará
(*)

mulato branco
(*white mulatto*)
mulato caboclo
(*)
mulato indio (*Indian mulatto*)
mulato mestiço
(*mestizo mulatto*)
mulato sarará
(*)
negro branco
(*white Negro*)
negro mulato escuro
(*dark mulatto Negro*)
negro preto
(*black Negro*)
preto amarelo
(*yellow black*)
preto claro (*light black*)
preto louro (*blond black*)
preto mestiço
(*mestizo black*)
preto moreno
(*)
preto negro (*Negro black*)
preto sarará
(*)

---

under discussion is radically unconformable with the experience of non-Brazilians, any gloss into English is misleading. To achieve operationally valid definitions of these terms, each should be paired with the drawings which elicited them. Nonetheless, since this would involve extravagant typographical displays in the interest of being precise about what is *ex hypothesi* ambiguous, I have yielded to the expedient of glossing some of the conventionally more acceptable examples. The phrases marked with an asterisk contain terms for which any tendency to think of conventional glosses would be counter-productive in relation to the basic task of setting forth the cognitive specialities of the Brazilian system.

The complexities involved in attempting any conventional gloss can be grasped by comparing curves of the frequencies with which particular pictures were paired with the most popular terms.

In Figure 2-1 the vertical axis was constructed by arranging the thirty-six male drawings in the descending (from top to bottom) order of frequency with which the term *branco* was applied to each. The horizontal axis indicates with what frequency each of the drawings was called either *branco*, *preto*, or both. The resulting curves show how certain drawings are called either *branco* or *preto* and seldom or never both *branco* and *preto*; while other drawings are called both *branco* and *preto* with moderate to low frequency. The latter condition is characteristic of almost half of the drawings. It should also be pointed out that the drawing which was most frequently called *branco* was also the drawing which was most frequently identified by any single term among all the drawings. Yet the number of respondents calling that drawing by some term other than *branco* exceeded the number who called it *branco*.

In Figure 2-2 a similar procedure is employed to show the relationship between the frequency with which each of the female drawings was called either *branca* or *preta* or both *branca* and *preta*. Although essentially similar to the *branco-preto* pattern, there appears here to be somewhat more overlapping and scattering.

Figure 2-3 plots female drawings against male drawings for frequency of *branco* and *branca* identification. In this graph, each female drawing is equated with the male drawing which it resembles in all diagnostics except sex. The parallel nature of the two curves indicates that an essentially similar calculus is at work in the case of both the male and female drawings, at least with respect to the *branco-preto* distinction.

In Figure 2-4 the frequency of *alvo* and *claro* identifications are plotted along the *branco-preto* axes. These terms exhibit maximum contrast with *preto* and considerable similarity to *branco*. Nonetheless, we must guard against the conclusion that *branco-alvo-claro* are "synonyms" in some absolute sense. There are many operations which might be utilized to arrive at different measures of and hence different definitions of synonymy. One might insist, for example, that two terms were referentially equivalent only when they were applied to both similar and different stimuli with precisely the same frequencies. If *branco* and *alvo* mean precisely the same thing, why are they not elicited with precisely the same frequency? "Noise" introduced by the observational operations accounts for some, but not all, of the difference.

Figure 2-5 compares the terms *cabo verde*, *alvo*, and *sarará*. *Cabo verde* and *sarará* tend to occur in complementary distribution with respect to each other, yet the relatively low overall frequency with which they occur limits our ability to confirm the trend. *Alvo*, however, overlaps markedly and systematically with both *cabo verde* and *sarará*. Since *branco*, *preto*, *alvo*, and *claro* are systematically related along the same set of dimensions, we now can confirm the existence of a calculus by which the probability that a given drawing will be identified as either *alvo*, *branco*, *claro*, *preto*, *cabo verde*, or *sarará* can be stated.

With the generous assistance of Douglas White, I have attempted to discover the

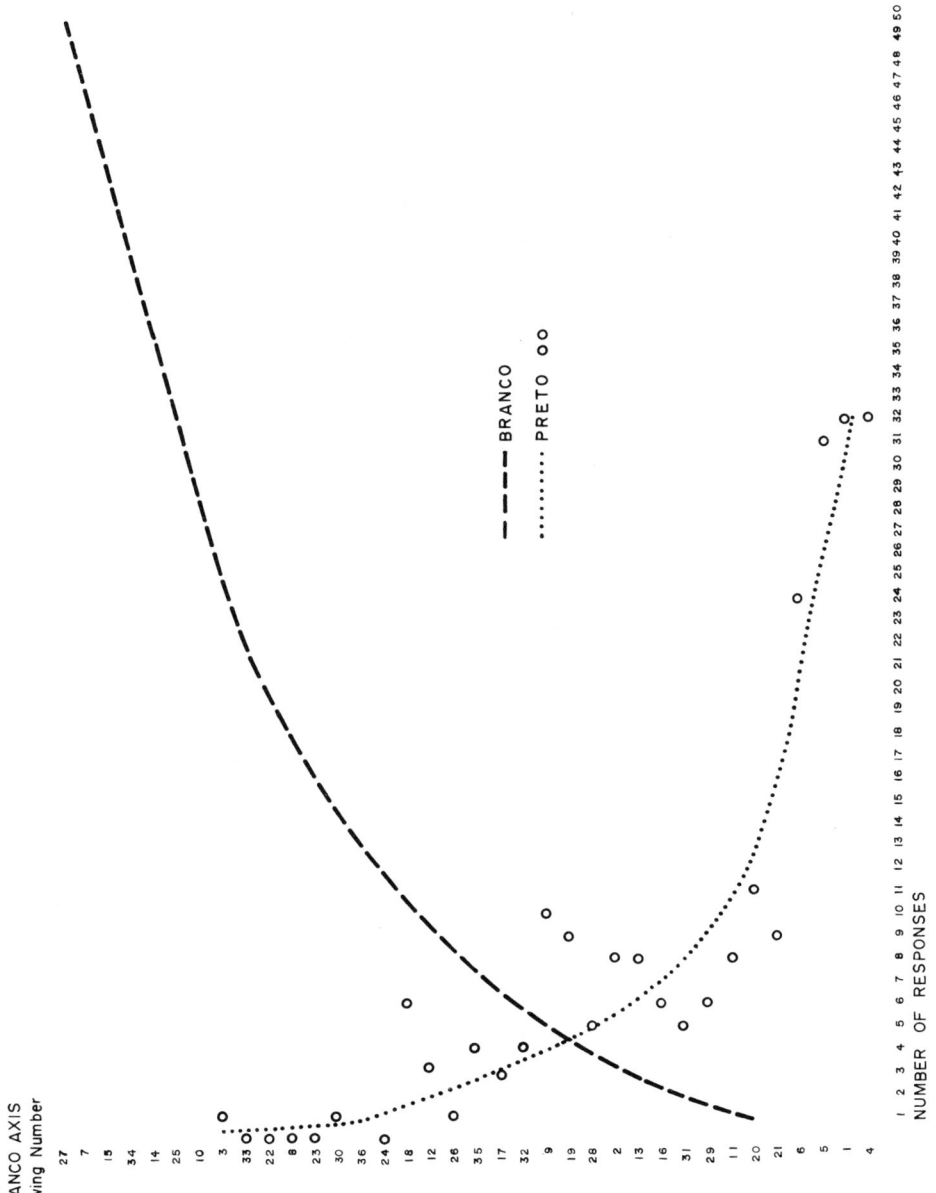

FIGURE 2-1. *Branco-Preto* Comparison: Male Drawings.

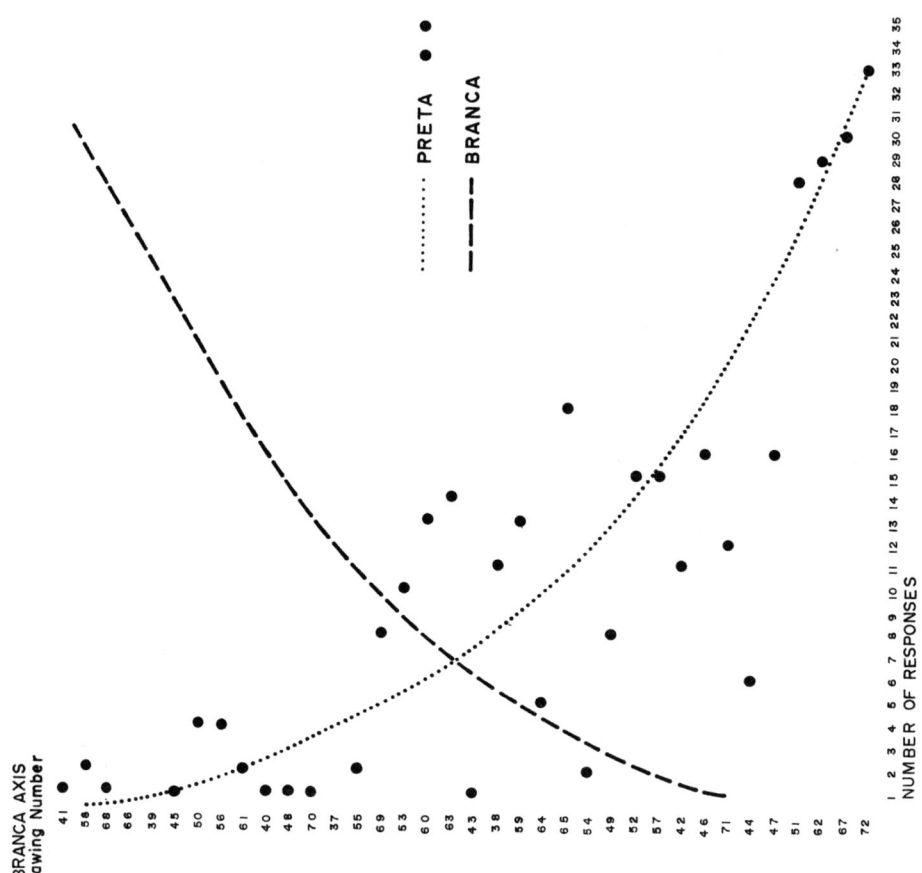

FIGURE 2-2. *Branca-Preta* Comparison: Female Drawings.

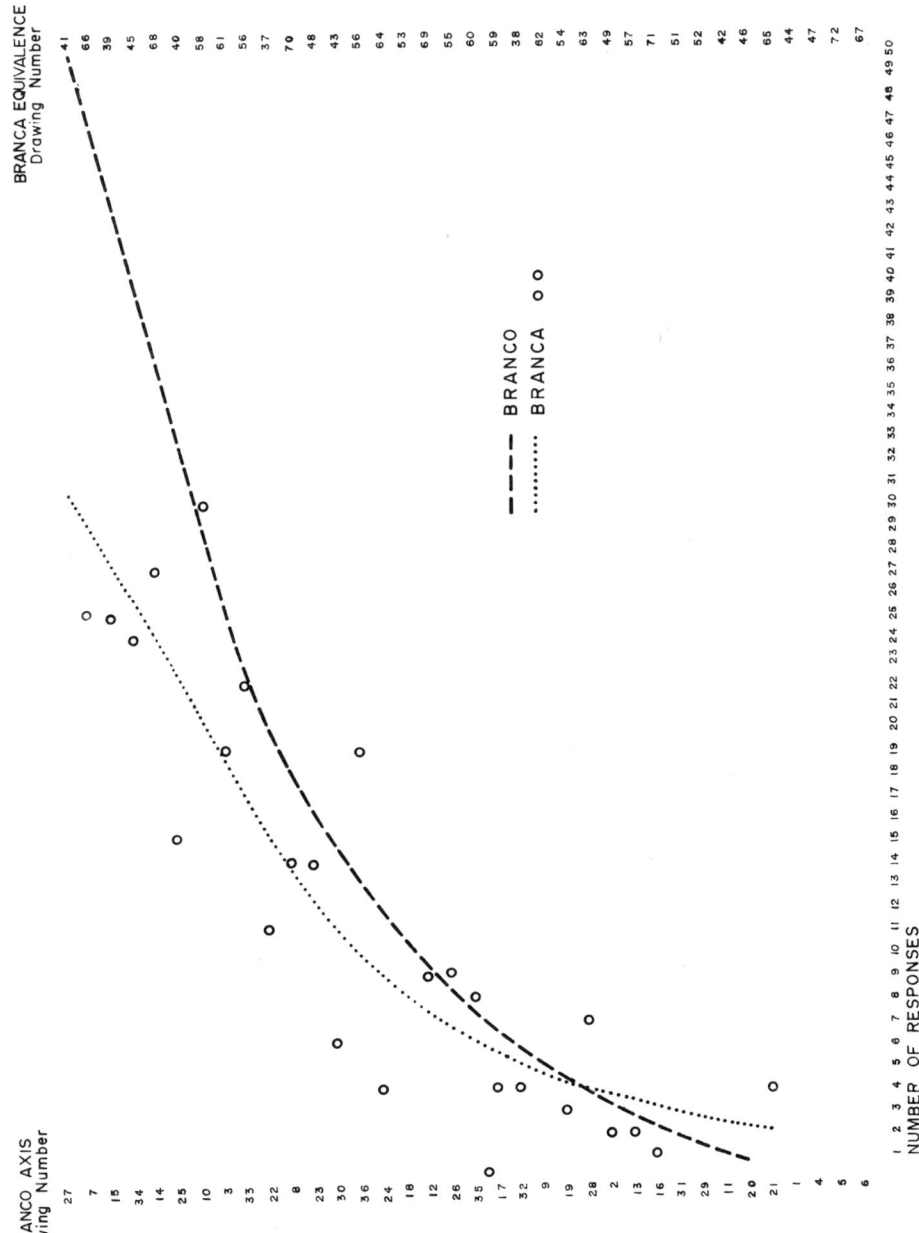

FIGURE 2-3. *Branco-Branca* Equivalence: Male-Female Comparison.

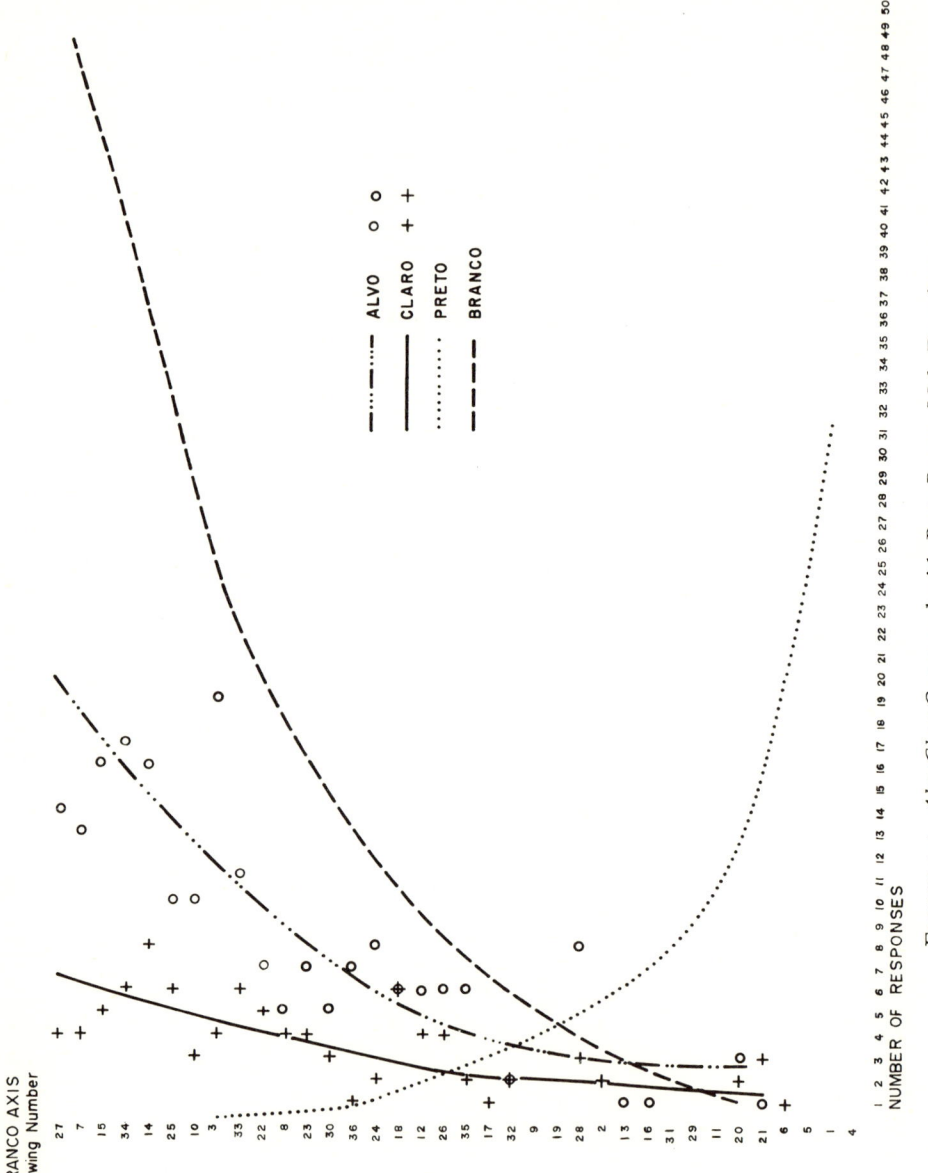

FIGURE 2-4. *Alvo-Claro* Compared with *Preto-Branco*: Male Drawings.

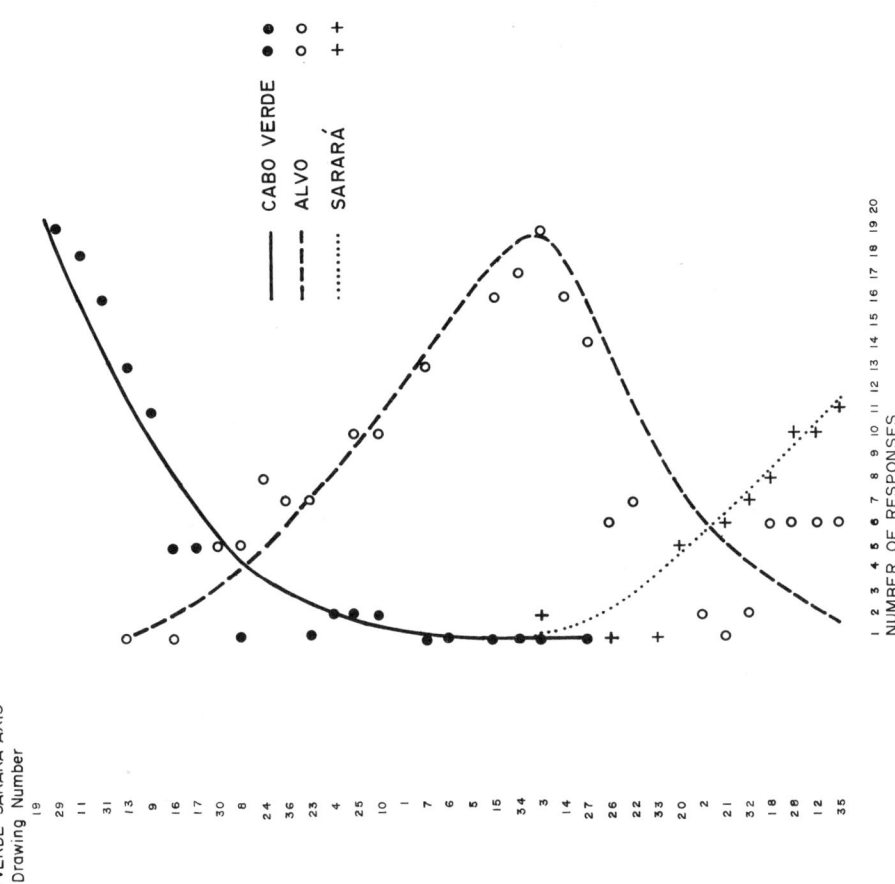

FIGURE 2-5. *Cabo Verde–Alvo–Sarará* Comparison: Male Drawings.

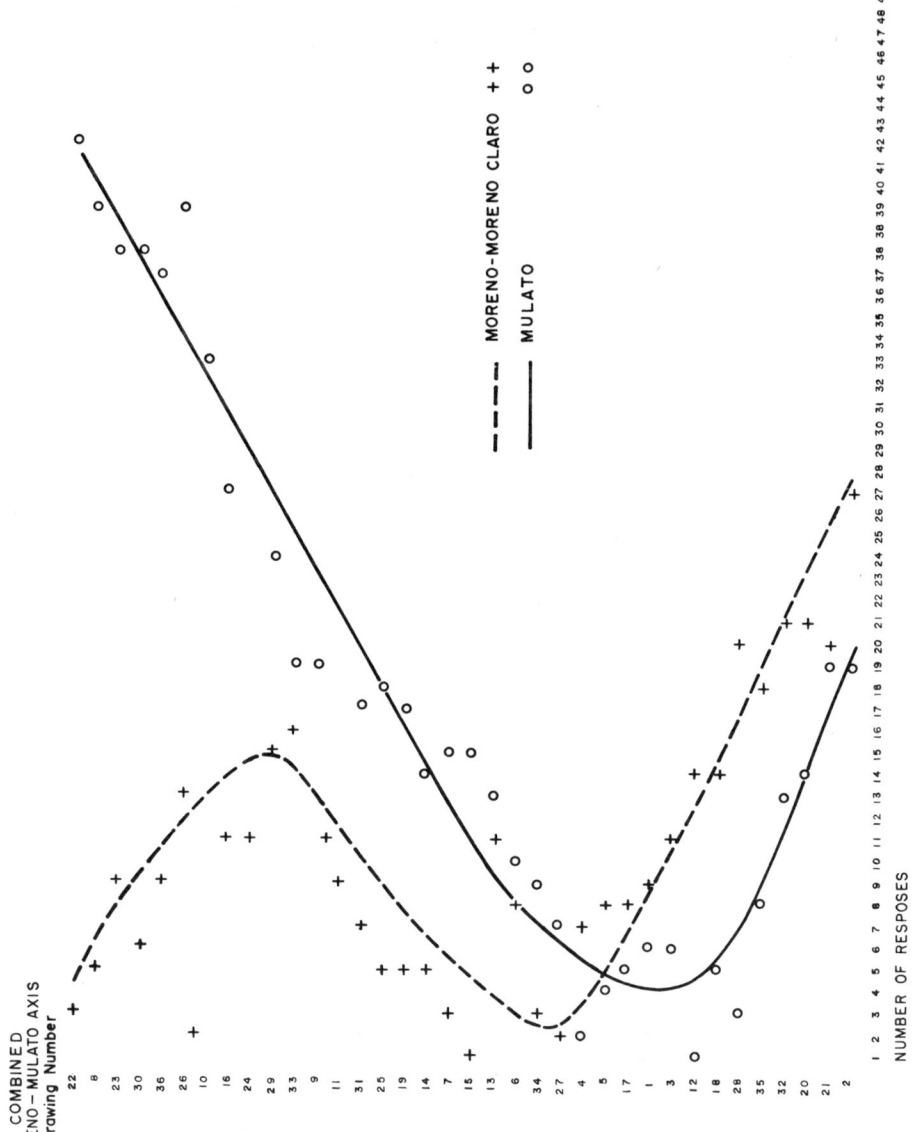

FIGURE 2-6. *Moreno-Mulato* Comparison: Male Drawings.

patterned relationship between these seven terms and *moreno, moreno claro, moreno escuro,* and *mulato*. The relationship between *mulato* frequencies and the sum of *moreno* and *moreno claro* frequencies is depicted in Figure 2-6. All of our attempts to relate these curves to the *branco-preto* axes have been unsuccessful. If there is an orderly principle by which *morenos* or *mulatos* are distinguished from *brancos, pretos, sararás, alvos, claros,* and *cabo verdes*, it is an extremely complex one. At the moment it seems as if Brazilians will call almost any combination of facial features by the terms *moreno* or *mulato* with a high but unpatterned frequency.

It should be pointed out, in conclusion, that this analysis of the calculus of "racial" identity in Brazil has been carried out in conformity with an epistemological and methodological model which challenges certain assumptions about domains now popular among anthropologists. According to the strategists of the "New Ethnography" (Sturtevant 1964; Frake 1964; Hammel 1965; Colby 1966) culture is the manifestation of a finite shared code, the code being a set of rules for the socially appropriate construction and interpretation of messages. This school has published numerous descriptions of what are alleged to be the shared finite sets of rules which account for the terminological distinctions in several different areas. The principal domains studied have been: kinship terminologies (e.g., Hammel 1965; Lounsbury 1965; Goodenough 1965a; Romeny and D'Andrade 1964; and Wallace and Atkins 1960); deference patterns (Goodenough 1965b); disease categories (Frake 1961); color categories (Conklin 1955); firewood categories (Metzger and Williams 1966); and the spacing of house sites (Frake 1962). The ambiguous output of the Brazilian "racial" calculus casts doubt on the assumption that the codes or rules associated with the abstract distinctions and actual identification of many classes of phenomena constitute intersubjectively uniform sets. Equally plausible is the assumption that actual classificatory performance is the expression of indeterminate and variable "competence" (cf. Chomsky 1965:4). This assumption is especially attractive if the prime social function of the rules is not the maintenance of orderly distinctions but the maintenance or even maximization of noise and ambiguity. Brazilian racial categories appear to constitute such a domain. Lacking caste distinctions based on racial identity, Brazilian social structure contains no evident practical requirements for achieving high levels of intersubjective "competence" with respect to racial classifications. On the other hand, given the highly stratified nature of Brazilian society, there may be a positive, conservative, structural reason for maintaining and maximizing the noise and ambiguity in the calculus under discussion. Objectively, there is a correspondence between class and race in Brazil (cf. Fernandes 1964); the more negroid the phenotype, the lower the class. Prevention of the development of racial ideology may very well be a reflex of the conditions which control the development of class confrontations. In the United States, racism and racial caste divisions have split and fragmented the lower class. "Black Power" in the United States lacks the revolutionary potential of the preponderant mass; "Black Power" in Brazil contains this potential. The ambiguity built into the Brazilian calculus of racial identity is thus, speculatively at least, as intelligible as the relative precision with which blacks and whites identify each other in the United States.

NOTES

1. I wish to acknowledge the indispensable assistance rendered by Ruth Martinez, Douglas White, Rojer Sanjek, David Epstein, Sam Gorenstein, William McGuire, Sanders Kirsch, Paul Byers and George Morren's mother.

2. Hypodescent involves the assignment of the children of a marriage between spouses of unequal status to the descent group of the lower-ranking parent.

Three

RITUAL DISSOCIATION AND POSSESSION BELIEF IN CARIBBEAN NEGRO RELIGION[1]

Erika Bourguignon

The Caribbean is a region of particular cultural complexity, distinctive in its history and geography, which may serve us as a laboratory for testing a variety of hypotheses concerning cultural change and cultural integration. This distinctiveness has been pointed out by anthropologists approaching the area from rather different theoretical vantage points. Thus, Herskovits (1941) stressed the common African heritage which Caribbean Negroes share and which also relates them to Negroes in the rest of the Afro-American area, including in particular the United States and Brazil. M. G. Smith, forsaking this view of cultural homogeneity, instead has focused on the region as one exemplifying cultural pluralism (Smith 1960, 1965). Mintz (1966), on the other hand, characterizes the region as having a series of common societal features (such as being multi-ethnic immigrant societies, having colonial status, one-crop economies, and so on) accompanying great cultural variety, as well as some widely shared cultural elements.

Perhaps nowhere are both variety and similarity demonstrated better than in the area of religion, the area which Herskovits (1958) considered to be the cultural focus of Negro societies. If we concern ourselves, as we shall in the following pages, with the religion of the Negro masses of the Caribbean region, we are, in fact, limiting ourselves to only one aspect, albeit a major one, of the total religious situation in the area. Catholicism, Anglicanism, and the various major Protestant denominations officially hold sway everywhere. Spiritualism has made significant inroads, particularly in Puerto Rico (Rogler and Hollingshead, 1961, 1965). Where Indians, Chinese, and Indonesians have appeared in large numbers, as in Trinidad and in the Guianas, Islam, Hinduism, and Buddhism play major roles (Despres 1967; Klass 1961).

Our concern, however, is with a more circumscribed field: we wish to examine the role of dissociational states and possession beliefs in two types of religious groupings among the Negro lower class populations throughout the region. The two types are the Afro-American, Afro-Catholic spirit cults on the one hand and the independent fundamentalist Pentecostal churches on the other. We may consider them to be polar types with regard to their cultural affiliations. The former are widespread in Cuba, Jamaica, Haiti, Trinidad, and the Guianas. Haitian *vodû* may serve as the prototype to be examined most closely in the following pages.[2] The churches, on the other hand, are found in the Virgin Islands and throughout the (British) West Indies. The Spiritual Baptists ("Shakers") of St. Vincent may serve us as a prototype for this group.[3]

The phenomenon referred to as "spirit possession" is the central experiential fact in lower class Negro religious life in the Caribbean, whether we deal with the Afro-American syncretic spirit cults or with the independent fundamentalist churches. (It also plays a major role, of course, in the growing spiritualist movement.) Because this phenomenon is, in fact, surrounded by a great deal of conceptual and terminological confusion, it may be well worth our effort to examine it in some detail before dealing with our specific examples.

What is generally spoken of as "spirit possession" actually involves two distinct aspects, two distinct levels of ethnographic "fact": an observable behavior pattern and a system of cultural beliefs and interpretations. These, however, in turn structure expectations and therefore behavior. In the following paragraphs, we shall restrict the term "possession" to native beliefs concerning certain potential relations between human beings and postulated spiritual entities. The behavior itself, and the psychophysiological state exhibited through it, will be called, where appropriate, "dissociation" or "trance" (Bourguignon 1965; 1968a). Other terms which have been suggested are "altered states of consciousness" (Ludwig 1968) and "exceptional states" (*Ausnahmezustände*, Pfeiffer, ms.).

We know from a world-wide survey of data that not all beliefs concerning possession refer to dissociation; indeed, as we shall see, this is also true in the Caribbean, where other possession beliefs exist as well. Furthermore, not all states of dissociation find their native explanation in possession belief, and this too is true in the region under discussion. It thus behooves us to consider the native theory and the observable behavior each in its own right, without committing the anthropologist to native beliefs. Because, as was indicated above, beliefs do structure behavior, this is at times difficult. In what follows, we shall refer to dissociational states, expressing a belief in possession, as "possession trance," in order to distinguish such states from other types of trance and other types of possession beliefs as well. This usage corresponds rather closely to that of Haitian and French authors who speak of "crise de possession" and "crise de *loa*" (e.g., Mars 1946).

It must be pointed out that these terminological distinctions merely state the obvious, yet any search of the publications in this area will rapidly reveal the verbal and conceptual chaos which exists even in recent writings. Some of the sources of this difficulty have been analyzed elsewhere (Bourguignon and Pettay 1964), but the fact that possession belief is deeply rooted in the cultural tradition of the Western observer, going back to both Hebrew and Greek sources, makes it particularly difficult to establish order and objectivity in this area.

We begin our discussion by comparing the possession trance as it appears in Haitian *vodû* and in Vincentian Shaker ritual. In *vodû*, possession trance is the central ritual action, the focus of attention of both participants and foreign observers alike, and a great deal has consequently been written on the subject. *Vodû* is based on a belief in a large number of anthropomorphic spirits who are summoned, on ritual occasions, to participate in the dancing and feasting, at times to offer advice or to perform a cure. Many of these spirits have names and attributes which are recognizably and obviously West African, most specifically derived from the Fon of Dahomey or the neighboring Nago and other Yoruba groups. The spirits are grouped into "nations" called Rada, Nago, Ibo, Congo, and so on. At the same time, they may be represented by chromolithographs, depicting Catholic saints and referred to by the names of those saints. These correspondences, which are also found in Cuba, in Trinidad, and in Brazil, have been the subject of a number of studies (Herskovits 1937a; 1937b; Métraux 1959; Courlander 1960; Simpson 1962, 1965 among others). While some spirits are clearly African, others appear to have arisen or been invented locally, a process which is still going on under the eyes of observers (e.g., Menneson-Rigaud 1946). The African and Catholic elements sharply reveal the syncretism that has been the subject of so much discussion (Herskovits 1937a; 1937b; 1941; 1958). Other aspects of the identity of the spirits directly reveal the present Haitian social structure and the self-perception of cult members: spirits are identified with respect to power and class position and skin color and other racial attributes. Their tastes in food and clothing, their speech patterns, and their specific powers reveal them to be reflections of the society in which the *voduists* live. Spirits are believed to be interested in human beings and to be responsive to their appeal, specifically to drum rhythms, songs, and food offerings. In response to these they may "mount" individuals, displacing their personalities temporarily and using their bodies as vehicles. The person is then referred to as the spirit's "horse," a term which, incidentally, is also found in similar contexts in various parts of Africa and Asia (Bourguignon 1964). Facial expressions, bearing, patterns of behavior and of speech, and the like, are transformed and the individual's own presence is obliterated by that of the possessing spirit. Indeed, male spirits may possess women and, less frequently, female spirits may possess men. "Mounting" by the spirits is preceded by a brief period of intense concentration or of distraction, and is frequently followed by a moment of collapse or unconsciousness. Métraux writes (1959:121–122):

> The symptoms of the opening phase of trance are clearly psychopathological. They conform exactly, in their main features, to the stock clinical conception of hysteria. People possessed start by giving the impression of having lost control of their motor system. Shaken by spasmodic convulsions, they pitch forward, as though projected by a spring, turn frantically round and round, stiffen and stay still with body bent forward, sway, stagger, save themselves [*sic*! Mistranslation; should read: run away EB], again lose balance, only to fall finally in [i.e., into EB] a state of semi-consciousness.

It should be noted, however, that there is a very great individual variation both in respect to which of these symptoms is exhibited and in their violence. These factors are related, or are supposed to be related, to the nature of the possessing spirit and in particular to the "horse's" relationship to the spirit. Extreme violence reveals the spirit's anger. The symptoms also appear to be related to the degree of habituation—i.e., the more frequently the subject has experienced possession trance, the greater the ease with which he attains the state. Haitians also say that persons who resist possession will experience a more violent seizure, and this does indeed make good psychological sense. It is expected that there will be no memory of the events that take place during the minutes or hours that possession trance lasts. In some people it is possible to observe a brief period of disorientation as they regain consciousness.

A number of important points must be stressed here. During the state of dissociation, the individual plays a complex role or roles, indeed often veritable short plays are enacted. He (or more often, she) has a large inventory of roles available from which to "choose." Not only are many spirits known, but new ones may be introduced; furthermore, there is expected to be individual variety in the aspects and behavior manifested by a given spirit "in the head" of two or more persons. Some people may be possessed by several spirits, often in immediate succession. This is quite at variance with the possession trance pattern as it is found in the cognate Fon-Yoruba group of societies. There, each cult house concerns itself with a limited number of spirits of a single group, and each devotee is dedicated to only one single spirit. Innovation seems to be far more limited and individual choice much more severely restricted. Indeed, the very susceptibility of *vodû* to innovation appears to be one of its most distinctive characteristics. As has been indicated, there also is great leeway for individual variation. Some people, for example, have spirits whose character resembles their own, while in other cases the spirits behave in ways totally opposite to those of their mounts. Consequently, there are great personal differences not only in the manifestations of possession trance but also in the personal significance of the experience. There are also considerable differences in any given individual's level of dissociation and the violence of his seizures from occasion to occasion. To play complex roles satisfactorily the individually expressive and the socially patterned must be well harmonized; awareness of social cues must be maintained during dissociation, while at the same time experiencing an alteration of self-perception, self-control, memory functions, and a variety of sensory modalities. The character of a given spirit personality is expected to remain fairly constant from one occasion to another. The result is frequently a structure of multiple personalities as striking as any recorded by psychiatrists. I have elsewhere suggested how such opportunity for dissociated role-playing enlarges the individual's field of action (Bourguignon 1965).

Possession trance may also occur outside the ritual context in two situations: in situations of crisis and fear in which, as it were, the personality of the protective spirit comes to the rescue. Dissociation may then help to master pain and fear. Spontaneous possession trances of a more disorganized type also may occur, particularly as first possessions or possessions of non-initiates and may indicate the need for a ritual of initiation. The absence of detailed patterning along traditional lines in such first seizures is underscored by the fact that divination is called for in order to identify the spirit that must be responsible for these states.

Haitians do not, however, limit their definition of possession by spirits to those manifested in trance states. For example, it is believed that speaking in one's sleep is an expression of possession and that the words are those of the spirit. The head washing (*lavé tête*) initiation ritual fixes a person's principal spirit in his head, so that, theoretically, possession is a permanent attribute of the initiate, although the presence of the spirit is manifested only during trance states or, as just indicated, during certain moments of sleep. In fact, a spirit established in a person's head in this manner must be removed after the "horse's" death by a special ritual called *dessunin*. (This view of the permanent presence of the spirit in the person's head is concurred in by certain Protestants who drive it out by striking the head with a Bible!)

The background of the Haitian possession trance practice and possession belief in this context is clearly West African. As we have indicated, similarities can be and have been traced in vocabulary, in the specific attributes of certain of the spirits, in details of rituals, musical rhythms, dance steps, and the like. M. G. Smith has argued (1957c: 36), although not specifically with respect to Haiti, that not all African societies exhibit possession. It is therefore interesting to note that in a sample of 114 societies representing all parts of sub-Saharan Africa, 82% exhibited institutionalized forms of dissociational states, 81% some type of possession belief, and 66% possession trance (Bourguignon 1968b).

Vodû and other Afro-Catholic syncretic cults share a particularly significant feature with the spirit cults of the Fon and the Yoruba: initiation into these cults is not prompted by *illness interpreted as arising from possession*. This is quite different, for example, to the *Ndoep* cult of Senegal (Wolof, Lebu, Serer) (Zempléni 1966), or the *Zar* cult of Ethiopia and neighboring areas, to which vodû has been specifically compared (Leiris 1958a). In Haiti, illness may precede initiation and the spirits may be blamed for it, but it is *not* called possession, but rather being "troubled" (*kembé*) by them. The distinction is of some importance, for the Fon-Yoruba group of cults were not marginal, therapeutic societies ("cults of deprivation," as Lewis [1966] has phrased it) but cults of worship, linked to the power structure and the establishment, whether of kingship and the state or of the kin group and the ancestors (Herskovits 1938; Mercier 1954; Verger 1957; Bascom 1944; Frobenius 1913; Simpson 1962b; Parrinder 1953).

On the other hand, no patterns of possession trance comparable to those of Haiti and its cognate societies are found in the European Judeo-Christian tradition. Demonic possession trance, unlike the Afro-Haitian pattern, is a feared pathological phenomenon which is treated ritually by exorcism (Oesterreich 1922; Lhermitte 1946–7, 1963).

Before proceeding with an examination of other applications of the terms "possession" and "trance" to the Haitian situation, we should compare what has been said so far with the "spirit possession" of the enthusiastic Pentecostal churches, with special reference to the Spiritual Baptists ("Shakers") of St. Vincent. This group appears to be the source for the Spiritual Baptists ("Shouters") of Trinidad (Herskovits and Herskovits 1947a). However, while the Trinidadian groups have had contact with *shango* cults and there has been some borrowing between these groups (Simpson 1965), no spirit cults exist on St. Vincent and no such influences have been exerted on the Shakers.

Shakers experience dissociational states in the course of their lengthy prayer meetings. These states are induced through prolonged preaching, testifying, and singing. There is no dancing and there are no musical instruments, but a strong beat is marked by hand-clapping, foot-tapping, and beating a leather strap on a table serving as an altar. Behavior during dissociation is individualized, although a choral phase of joint rhythmic movement and breathing patterns has been identified. The trancers tremble and perspire, they may move vigorously, hyperventilate (overbreathe), shout and speak in tongues. Such states are believed to be manifestations of the Holy Spirit who shakes the trancers and causes these various forms of behavior. Awareness is constricted and although individuals say they are conscious of their surroundings, they are attentive only to the actions of the Spirit, and later have only a blurred memory of what happened during their trance states.

It may be justifiable to call both the Haitian and the Vincentian phenomenon "possession trance," but the differences must be stressed as well as the similarities. While the Haitian impersonates specific, well-delineated anthropomorphic entities, with complex personalities and a great range of possible activities, the Vincentian does not. The Haitian trancer sings and dances, smokes, drinks and eats; he may climb trees or dive into water and otherwise carry out a variety of actions. The Vincentian jerks, rocks, trembles, but there is no patterned choreography and he does not move far from the spot on which he was standing or sitting when the trance began. He sings hymns and he shouts and speaks in tongues but his range of actions is restricted. Most importantly, while the Haitian interacts with others during his possession trance, with spirits possessing people and with human beings, the Vincentian does not. Even his speaking in tongues is his communication, his "telephone" to God, and no specific message is transmitted to himself or to others. The attention of the Vincentian trancer is drawn inward to his interaction with the Spirit, which shakes both him and all the other trancers in his group. They participate in a common experience as members of a group and each as a separate individual. The Haitian trancer, on the other hand, interacts with others from the standpoint of a personal transformation. The Vincentian may feel happy, purged of sin, a child of God, as a result of his experience; but he has not modified his position in relation to his fellows through the intervention of a possessing spirit, as the Haitian may be able to do. The Haitian, in fact, affirms his individuality by his temporary transformation; the Vincentian shows himself a worthy member of his group, of his church. Both experiences are, undoubtedly, cathartic as well as ego-enhancing, but the manner of operation is distinct in its formal and in its ideological features.

The differences between the Haitian and the Vincentian manifestations of possession are so great that the use of the same term for the two phenomena can be questioned, particulatly, in its application to the Vincentian case. The German word *Ergriffenheit* has been suggested as more appropriate (Pfeiffer 1968; Benz 1968). However, this term, for which there is no good English counterpart, other than the very approximate word "seizure," has been given a rather special meaning by Frobenius (Jensen 1963:54,56). Our justification in speaking of possession trance with reference to the Shakers is this: their beliefs and practices very clearly derive from traditional Christian, particularly early Methodist, beliefs and practices. In Protestantism, the term *possession* represents standard English usage. Thus, we read in Hasting's *Dictionary of the*

Bible (rev. ed., 1963:782) that possession is "the coercive seizure of the spirit of man by another spirit" and that "the Holy Spirit may also seize and possess a man." The authors of the article furthermore cite both Old and New Testament sources for their statements. Similarly, the report on glossolalia of the Episcopal Diocese of California (1963) uses the term in this sense of seizure by the Holy Ghost, and raises the theological question of whether people speaking in tongues may be considered to be possessed.

In any comparative study, a variety of native formulations of the notion of possession must be recognized, which share, however, a core of significant features. Among these is the idea of substituting an agency (one or more spirits or powers) for at least part of that control which the self normally exerts over itself—over the body, the personality, the will. That is, what underlies any idea of possession is a conceptual separation of such elements of the self as the body, the personality, and the executive functions into elements that can be isolated from one another; this is then often phrased as a temporary removal of one or more souls to be replaced by some other force. This basic animism accounts apparently in part for the very wide distribution of the concept of possession in its many diverse forms. That is to say, once it is admitted that there is a body and one or more separable principles which activate and animate it, it is possible as well to admit of a substitution or addition of some other principle or agency for one or more of those "normally" associated with the body in the native view. The conception of the nature of the principle which is removed, or in temporary abeyance, varies widely, as we know, and so does the conception of the substituted principle and the actions for which it is held responsible. A more detailed examination of these considerations, however, would take us too far afield and is not quite germane to our present concerns.

As already indicated, formal similarities to the Haitian pattern of possession trance as well as evidence of its origins can be found in other Afro-American and West African spirit cults; the origins of the Vincentian pattern, on the other hand, are to be found easily in the history of Methodism. The Shakers claim their religion was founded by John and Charles Wesley and, indeed, Methodist missionary activities began during the lifetime of John Wesley. While Methodism later gave up its appeal to emotionalism in its search for converts, the early history of Methodism is marked by violent conversions and dramatic seizures, both in Europe and America. Descriptions of seizures among English, Welsh, Scottish, and Irish converts are very similar to those reported for converts among the Negro slaves in the British West Indies islands. Thus Wesley's biographer, Southey, writes with obvious disapproval (1925:II:170; orig. 1825):

> ... like Mesmer and his disciples, he had produced a new disease, and he accounted for it by a theological theory instead of a physical one. As men are intoxicated by strong drink affecting the mind through the body, so are they by strong passions influencing the body through the mind. Here there was nothing but what would naturally follow when persons, in a state of spiritual drunkenness, abandon themselves to their sensations, and such sensations spread rapidly, both by voluntary and involuntary imitation.

The seizures experienced by those who listened to the preaching of Wesley and his followers appear, on the whole, to have been unpatterned but relatively violent. Wesley's own descriptions are found in his journal, as for example in the following entry for Sunday, July 1, 1739:

> Some sunk down, and there remained no strength in them; others exceedingly trembled and quaked; some were torn with a kind of convulsive motion in every part of their bodies, and so violently that often four or five persons could not hold one of them. I have seen many hysterical and many epileptic fits; but none of them were like these in many respects (quoted in Sargant 1959:87).

Sargant discusses these reports in the context of conversion and brain-washing, and speaks of the neuro-physiological significance of these violent experiences. It seems clear from the materials provided by him and by Southey that these were single dramatic events in the life of an individual, the experience of conversion, rather than recurrent ritual events.[4]

The patterned, repetitive trances appear to have evolved only somewhat later, where the ecstatic experiences became institutionalized. Methodism abandoned these practices, however, even in the lifetime of Wesley. The opportunity thus existed for a variety of distinct patterns to arise in different communities, as for example the type known as "Jumpers" which developed in Wales during the eighteenth century (Southey 1925:II:100-101). In the Caribbean area we consequently find some differences in the details of patterning of the trances among the Methodist-derived churches as we move from island to island. Moore, for example, writing of Jamaican revivalists, speaks of "trumping" and "laboring," a pattern of hyperventilation linked to a dance step. The dancers expel the breath on a deep forward bend and suck it in with a grunting sound as they straighten up (Moore 1965:64–5; see also Simpson 1956). This serves to induce possession trance; however, it is also continued during the trance itself. Such a pattern of induction is absent in St. Vincent, although hyperventilation occurs during the trance.[5]

It is also likely that prior familiarity with African patterns of possession trance set the stage, as it were, for the slaves, to whom the Methodists appealed in particular. We know very little of the religious beliefs and practices of the slaves in the British possessions, such as St. Vincent, prior to the arrival of the Moravian and Methodist missionaries in the middle of the eighteenth century. The Anglican Church, generally, did not address itself to them. However, there is some evidence to suggest that African-derived religions did exist during the eighteenth century in areas where they are no longer to be found today.[6] Thus, Goveia writes (1965:247–48, references are to Caines 1804:I:130–35):

> The persistence of the African traditions was also reflected in the religious and magical beliefs and rituals of the Negro slaves in the Leeward Islands. Caines notes the use of dancing in their religious ceremonial, and the high place accorded to spirit possession—"the most envied condition at which a Confuist can arrive"—as a form of religious experience. Confu was said to be a sect of the cult of Obeah, which was still very widespread among the Negroes, though Caines thought that its influence was declining somewhat due to the spread of scepticism or of the Christian religion.

With reference to St. Vincent and with respect to the pre-Methodist period, we know that the slaves were not welcome in the Anglican Church. We also know that slavery was originally introduced by French planters and that Catholic missionaries did work among the slaves. To this day, many Shakers receive their first religious training in the Catholic Church, and certain minor Catholic influences are to be seen in their practices: the references to saints, the use of chromolithographs representing various saints, and the use of a bell during the ritual being perhaps the most noteworthy.

In addition to the possession trance to be seen in public ceremonies, St. Vincent Shakers experience another type of dissociation. This occurs during a retreat, called "mourning," which is undergone by individual members to further their spiritual growth and to advance in the hierarchy of the church. The experience is likened to a spiritual journey undertaken by the candidate, a journey of visionary revelations. The mourning ritual has been analyzed by Henney (1967), who compares it in detail with experiments in sensory deprivation, which have often been reported to produce hallucinations and other pseudo-perceptions. The mourning ritual, which lasts an indeterminate number of days, is undergone individually under conditions of restricted movement, reduced diet (which may cause hypoglaecemia), and other elements of deprivation. It is linked not only to specific expectations of rewards, but also to considerable fear about the outcome. An individual may be found to be unworthy or revelations may not be forthcoming or may not be accepted by the cult leader. Some individuals — sinners — have been known to go insane during the period of seclusion.

Similar rituals are reported for the Spiritual Baptists of Trinidad (Herskovits and Herskovits 1947a: 204-209; Simpson 1965, 1966) and for the revivalists of Jamaica (Simpson 1966). I am not aware of any Christian or specifically Methodist precedent for this practice. No visions or spiritual journey are found in Haitian *vodû*, related Afro-Catholic cults elsewhere, or in the detailed relevant writings on the Fon and Yoruba cults (Herskovits 1938; Verger 1957; Bascom 1944). On the other hand, in Haitian *vodû* and in the cognate cults in the New World as well as in West Africa, we do find a pattern of retreats and isolation linked to a theory of spiritual death and rebirth. In Haiti, specifically, this is found in abbreviated form prior to the headwashing ritual of initiation (*lavé tête*) and in greater complexity in the longer retreats preceding the *kanzo* ritual and the ritual of "taking the *asson*" (i.e., becoming a priest or priestess). As indicated, it is said that a person dies when he goes into the retreat and I recall seeing a woman and her relatives weep bitterly at the moment of the preparatory ritual when she was being led away into the sanctuary. However, there is none of the dramatic falling to the drums, which Verger has so brilliantly photographed in Dahomey and in Bahia (1957 photos 13-15, 16-21). There is no prolonged state of catalepsy and no pattern of extreme regression during which the initiate must be socialized again with a new personality (*ibid.*, photos 38-40). Quite to the contrary, in Haiti the retreat is also sometimes conceptualized as a marriage between the candidate (most often a woman) and the spirit for whom the initiation is undergone. She must buy a trousseau—a white dress and shirt—new sheets to lie on the ground on a mat, and acquire a *vodû* necklace which is likened to a wedding ring. The spirits call women initiates "my wife." As among Vincentian Shakers, the candidate is alone much of the time, lies on the ground, may not freely move or speak, communicates with an attendant by using a bell, and receives a reduced diet of *acassan* without sugar and *calalu* (okra) without salt. Yet during this retreat a series of rituals are carried out: special herb baths are given to the candidate, cuts are made in the scalp. Relatively little is, in fact, known about this period which is shrouded in a certain esoteric secrecy.[7] However, visions and trance states are not expected, nor are they reported in writings on Haiti or of the cognate cults elsewhere (see also Bastide 1958, 1961b for Brazil). It may be questioned, however, whether dissociations of the hallucinatory kind do not actually occur during the period of seclusion, or whether it is that they have either not been discovered or reported by anthropologists. It may well be, in fact, that they do occur at times as a result of the relative deprivations and the heightened emotional state and attendant tensions, but do not represent an expected and patterned phenomenon, and have therefore tended to escape detection. As I have indicated elsewhere, at least one informant reported a confused state developing as a result of the experiences of a short retreat. She stated that the spirits were talking the esoteric cult language in her head (Bourguignon 1965:50).

Ludwig (1968) has classified altered states of consciousness (i.e., what we are here calling "dissociation" or "trance") according to how they are induced. Like the "experimental sensory deprivation states" which he lists, and to which we have referred earlier, Vincentian "mourning" trance belongs to the category of states resulting from a "reduction of exteroceptive stimulation and/or motor activity" (Ludwig 1968:71). Possession trance, on the other hand, whether among Vincentian Shakers, Haitian *voduists*, or the Yoruba and Fon spirit worshipers, rather results from an "increase of exteroceptive stimulation and/or motor activity and/or emotion" (Ludwig 1968:72). It is interesting that the cataleptic trance state, which is an integral part of the beginning of the retreat prior to the initiation among the Yoruba and Fon and their Brazilian counterparts, is interpreted not as arising from possession but from death of the former self and is induced in the course of a public ritual. It is not associated with a "reduction of exteroceptive stimulation and/or motor activity" but is induced by the very factors which induce possession trance in others: dance, music, expectations, and crowds—i.e., an increase in exteroceptive stimulation together with both motor activity and emotion. It would appear, then, that the categories into which trance-inducing factors may be grouped cut across the manifestations of trance; forms as distinct as the passive cataleptic trance and hyperactive possession trance may be induced by the same set of stimuli, in fact in the very same situational context. Ludwig (1968:77–85) also points out that the types of altered states of consciousness which he distinguishes share a series of characteristics, in spite of their great apparent diversity. Among these characteristics are changes in thought patterns, a disturbed time sense, loss of control, changes in emotional expression, and a number of others. Furthermore, he has found it possible under experimental conditions to transform one type of trance into another through altered hypnotic suggestion—e.g., a hyper alert, hyper kinetic state induced by appropriately active methods into a relaxed hypokinetic one (Lyle and Ludwig 1964). These observations justify our contention that it is desirable not to discuss possession trance, as has often been the case, without taking into consideration other types of trance that may also exist in the same society or group. Furthermore, as we shall see in a moment, it is also necessary to consider what other applications of the concept of possession may exist. And third, we may wish to know whether, particularly in relatively complex differentiated societies, there may be other (or competitive) institutional settings for dissociation than the one on which we happen to focus.

Concerning this last point, we might mention that there are some pentecostal groups in Haiti, although they have not been the subject of systematic study. *Voduists* who have seen rituals of the Pentecostalists, interestingly enough, attribute their possession trance to "mounting" by *vodû* spirits and find the contrasting explanation of Pentecostals (when they are on speaking terms, to get such an explanation) meaningless. In Trinidad, possession by the *shango* "powers" sometimes appear in the context of Spiritual Baptist ritual, "a slightly embarrassing situation" (Simpson 1965:115). This is possible because of the close contacts between the two groups, even to the point of overlapping membership. Thus, whatever the observable and historical differences between possession trance in the Afro-Catholic cults and in the Pentecostal churches, there is an underlying kinship in these forms of behavior and experience which is felt and perceived by the participants.

As indicated above, in addition to possession trance and other forms of trance we must also concern ourselves with possession beliefs in other contexts. In Haiti we find a belief in possession by the dead, which unlike *vodû* worship, exists in a context of sorcery and is probably shared more widely among the population than *vodû* practices. The same thing may be said for possession belief in St. Vincent. In *vodû* ritual, worshipers are possessed, as we have seen, by individualized spirits and this possession is acted out in dramatic trance performances. The spirits are welcomed and their appearance in a ritual context is generally encouraged. Furthermore, they come, it is believed, on their own volition. In the form of possession under consideration here, neither trance nor dramatic performance is involved. Rather the concept of possession by the dead serves as an explanation for certain apparently intractable types of illness, particularly when an enemy can be identified. In fact, the motive behind dispatching one or more spirits of dead persons against a victim is to cause his death, not merely illness. The diagnosis is made by divination and the cure involves exorcism, compelling the possessing spirit or spirits to depart. However, contrary to the Judeo-Christian or Moslem practice of exorcism, the spirit is not questioned or identified. The aim of the divination is to identify the enemy, not the spirits, who appear to be credited with little volition. The spirits of the dead are not individualized and no roles are played. Also, this type of possession is distinguished terminologically and conceptually from possession by spirits associated with the possession trance of *vodû* ritual.

A similar category of possession illness resulting from sorcery exists in St. Vincent. The belief is not linked to Shakerism, however, but exists generally in the population; formerly, it appears to have been more widespread. Again, as in Haiti, a sorcerer can send a spirit (possibly a ghost) called "jumby" against a person; such a jumby then invades the person and must be exorcized. Little detail is available on this pattern, but it appears similar to the one found in Trinidad (Simpson 1965:76–8).

In recent years, another fundamentalist group has appeared in St. Vincent. This is a Dutch healing cult, known as Streams of Power, which stresses faith healing, glossolalia, and other manifestations of the spirit. Periods of glossolalia are very brief but involve light trance states and constitute an important part of their public prayer meetings. While they thus engage in possession trance, they disapprove of the behavior of the Shakers. They do not experience visionary trances but do believe in demoniac possession, which causes illness. Streams of Power represents an alternative pattern to possession trance and possession illness beliefs of the Shakers.

Thus in Haiti and St. Vincent we find possession trance occurring in public ceremonials, and induced through an increase in exteroceptive stimulation. The difference lies in some of the specific behaviors exhibited and in the underlying belief system. In both places we find two stages of initiation preceded by periods of seclusion. However, while there are patterned expectations of visionary experiences in St. Vincent, there are no such expectations in Haiti. Shakers in seclusion experience visionary trances on which their future status in the group depends. In Haiti such occurrences, if they exist, are not patterned and not reported. They play no significant role in the life of the cult. In both places we find possession by harmful spirits linked to sorcery practices and beliefs rather than to the spirits and practices grouped with activities that center on worship. In fact, Haitians distinguish between these two sets of activities as those of the right hand and those of the left, and a *vodû* priest who also engages in sorcery is said to serve "with both hands."

IMPLICATIONS

We may now pause briefly to examine the implications of these descriptive materials. Haitian *vodû* and St. Vincent Shakerism represent, as already indicated, polar types on historic grounds. *Vodû* has close African affinities, known both to participants and observers. Shakers reject all possible African ties, and those that may in fact exist—beyond those to be found in the rhythms of the hymns—are somewhat tenuous. Several comparative references have been made to Trinidad. Trinidad has preserved strong French and Catholic patterns, but it has also come under British and Protestant, particularly Methodist, influences. Here there exists both an Afro-American spirit religion in the form of *shango* and a Methodist-derived Pentecostal church in the form of the Spiritual Baptists. The *shangoists*, while preserving strong Yoruba patterns (Simpson 1962b; 1965) have also undergone Protestant influences as evidenced by the fact that Shango is syncretized with St. John the Baptist. On the other hand, unlike Haitian *vodû*, there appear to be fewer fusions of African elements from different sources, so that the picture of a Yoruba-Catholic-Protestant mixture emerges rather clearly. There is also a strong trace of African elements in the belief system and the practices of the Spiritual Baptists—e.g., in the form of animal sacrifices (Herskovits and Herskovits 1947a; Simpson 1965, 1966). Whether this is due to the "original" retention of African elements or the borrowing of such elements from *shangoists* is probably beyond discovery and also somewhat immaterial. The influences work both ways, with *shangoists* participating in Spiritual Baptist mourning ritual, a ritual which they at times feel they need but which their cult group does not supply.

As indicated above, Trinidadians share with Vincentians and Haitians a belief in malevolent possession caused by sorcery, which is unrelated to the possession trance pattern. It may well be that this malevolent possession-sorcery complex links, in reinterpreted form, African concerns with sorcery and divinatory practices, as well as with the dead on the one hand, to European beliefs in demoniac possession and practices of exorcism on the other. The evidence on this point is, however, inconclusive. With regard to African-derived features and resulting syncretisms we find a continuum ranging from *vodû* at one pole with the most evident number of African features and Vincentian Shakerism at the other, with the fewest such features. *Shango* and Trinidadian Spiritualist Baptists occupy the middle range between these extremes. However, on the basis of our categories of possession, possession trance, and trance, the beliefs and practices of Vincentian Shakers and Trinidadian Spiritual Baptists on the one hand and of Haitian *vodû* and Trinidadian *shango* on the other all appear to fall into the same basic pattern. This pattern involves the primacy of public possession trance ritual, seclusion, and sensory deprivation as a part of initiation and a folk belief in malevolent possession associated with sorcery. This pattern, furthermore, is similar to that of the Yoruba-Fon group of cults in that possession illness is not associated with cult initiation, but rather exists as a distinct and unrelated group of beliefs and practices. I have elsewhere attempted to delineate two types of African possession cults (Bourguignon 1969) in which cults of this sort ("West African" type) are distinguished from those of the possession illness variety ("East African" type). Regardless of the degree of African influence that we can discover among the Shakers of St. Vincent, then, all of the groups under discussion here *on typological grounds* belong to this first, or "West African," type.

While the implications of our categories remain to be explored more fully, I should like to argue that for certain research problems a typological analysis of this sort may prove to be more fruitful than an historical one. For example, it may provide us with insights into the relations between social control, religion, and concepts of folk illness as that term has been used by Rubel (1964). Thus, in Haiti possession illness constitutes one type of folk illness. Ideas and practices concerning it are tied in with beliefs and practices of *vodû* and sorcery and with a complex centering around the concept of the *zombi* (Bourguignon 1959).

To pursue this point a little further, in Haiti (and elsewhere in the Caribbean) spirits are dichotomized into two categories: on the one hand, those who are potentially helpful and whose presence is experienced in public rituals of possession trance, and on the other hand, those who cause possession illness. These are spirits of dead persons over whom sorcerers have gained control—because they have been neglected by their relatives—and who can be used to cause harm to human beings through malevolent possession.[8] These two types are behaviorally and conceptually distinct and complementary. Spirits who are worshipped are powerful; some are ancestors, who, as the Haitians say, have been "canonized." The dead who may be dispatched to cause illness, on the other hand, resemble *zombis* in that they have not been revered but have been neglected. They are not intrinsically evil, but powerless and at the mercy of a sorcerer. That is, they cause evil to human beings while they are (or because they are) victims themselves. The danger inherent in the neglect of one's duty to the dead resides not only in their potential anger but also in their potential victimization.

Such a view of the world of spirits contrasts sharply with the situation in the "East African" cults in which a single type of spirit can cause both malevolent possession, bringing on illness, and also ritual possession trance as part of cure and of worship, and where, furthermore, a spirit can be transformed from being harmful into being protective by means of ritual manipulation. As we have seen, in Haiti and in the other cases which we have examined, there exists a system of worship centering about possession trance which finds its mirror image in a parallel system of sorcery in which possession illness is a key concept. Together, they provide not only a structured world view but also a system of defense and attack in an essentially hostile society and a hostile world.

What is required now is a fuller analysis of concepts of folk illness in the Caribbean area, as well as studies of sorcery and of other mechanisms of social control. Africanists have pointed the way in this respect (e.g., Marwick 1965; Middleton and Henker 1963). Possession beliefs and dissociational states in their many forms and complex interrelations will then be found to be significantly related to aspects of social control and, consequently, to aspects of social change.

NOTES

1. This paper is part of a larger investigation which was supported in whole by Public Health Service Research Grant MH 07463 from the National Institute of Mental Health.
2. Much of the data on Haiti are drawn from my own field work, carried on during 1947–48. I am indebted to the Carnegie Corporation of New York and the Graduate School of Northwestern University, which made this research possible. The writings on *vodû* are extensive, but include, in addition to scholarly work and excellent observational materials, much that is superficial and flamboyant. Principal sources are cited.
3. This discussion is based on the only anthropological field work conducted on that island, the recent work of J. H. Henney (1967; 1968a; 1968b). This research was part of the Cross-Cultural Study of Dissociational States, of which the present paper is also a product.
4. This point is of some significance to Sargant's argument. It is therefore surprising to find that he groups with conversion experiences in early Methodism and elsewhere the trance states of ecstatic "primitive" religions, such as, specifically, Haitian "voodoo." In the latter instance trance experiences are repeated and not limited to conversion experiences, whose very existence, in this context, may be questioned.
5. It is noteworthy that some of the physiological features of trance may at times be used to induce the state, by imitative anticipation.
6. This point also applies to Martinique and Guadeloupe. Various arguments have been suggested to account for the absence of Afro-Catholic cults in these islands (Leiris 1958a; Bourguignon 1967). It should be noted, however, that Father Labat, writing of his stay in Martinique in 1701, comments in regard to cases of dissociation which he witnessed that the slaves are so obsessed by the Devil that when he appears to them they fall into convulsions like epileptics (Labat 1724:I:458).
7. Métraux (1959:199–202) has described this period in some detail, attempting to piece together the sometimes conflicting reports of several informants. His picture varies on several points from mine. Remember, however, that there is extreme local variation and not all the rituals described are practiced everywhere. In fact, in some regions the pattern of the *kanzo* initiation under discussion here is altogether absent (cf. Herskovits 1937b).
8. Whiting and Child (1953) categorized "possession" as one of two types of "dependence explanation of illness." There is no distinct category for sorcery in their scheme and most magic would be classified by them as "oral" or "anal" explanations of illness.

Four

CRISIS, CONTRACULTURE, AND RELIGION AMONG WEST INDIANS IN THE PANAMA CANAL ZONE

R. S. Bryce-Laporte

This paper centers on an incident which occurred in the early 1950's in a now nonexistent border town of the Panama Canal Zone.[1]

One night two young men, both Panamanian Negroes of West Indian origin, were involved in a fiery discussion during the first showing of a picture at the local movie theater. The boys exchanged insults and challenges. As soon as the picture ended both boys left with their respective entourage. The argument was resumed in the hallway of the local clubhouse. One boy struck the other on his head with a cue stick from a nearby billiard table. The victim, who later died, supposedly attempted to conceal his injury from his mother and at first gave the doctor an alibi rather than disclose the real cause.

The other boy was arrested by the Zone police (American white) but was quickly released on bail. His mother, in anxiety, sought all the assistance she could possibly obtain to influence the outcome of the pending court trial in favor of her son. In so doing she consulted, among others, the principal of the local high school (which her son attended and where she was employed as a custodian), the official public defender, her son's employers and a student leader and acquaintance of her son. All of these individuals expressed their firm opinion that in view of the circumstances of the crime and the comparative "better" reputation of her son to his victim, the sentence would be minimal. It is said that the principal (an American white) had relayed to the student leader (Panamanian-West Indian black) the firm opinion of the public defender and other judicial and police authorities (all American whites) that her son would not only receive the minimum sentence for the crime but that the sentence would be suspended for a period of probation if her son's employers (Panamanian whites) would assure them that he would continue to be in their service. It is believed that the woman obtained this assurance from the employers, who also informed her that they had already notified the zone authorities of their disposition.

Despite these assurances, the woman solicited the aid of at least two occult agencies.

During the period preceding the trial she held a series of spiritual-like meetings or ceremonies at her home. They were conducted by a quasi-revivalist sect known locally as the "Jump-up" or "Benjinite" Church [which had apparent elements of Africanism, Catholicism, and Evangelical Protestantism in its ritual and belief systems]. In addition, she allegedly solicited the aid of an Obeah-Man (shaman) in hope of influencing the outcome of the trial in her son's favor.

It is believed by the townspeople that when the family of the deceased boy learned of her activities they solicited a similar medium, to make sure that their son's killer would pay for his crime. Neither of the two families denied these rumors nor was there any attempt made by them or the townspeople to observe complete secrecy regarding these doings.

The trial found the boy guilty. He was given the minimum period of confinement and then sentence was immediately suspended in favor of a period of probation. In the near future, however, he and his family began to experience many misfortunes and difficulties which culminated with their being ejected from the Zone. As far as the majority of the townspeople were concerned the "Thing" [as Obeah and Benjinite were sometimes called] had worked for both parties!

The major portion of this paper will be directed to answering three questions: First, why did the families of both boys resort to occult means? Second, why did they overlook their own Episcopal churches and seek the services of folk media? Third, why did their solicitations and subsequent rituals take place in relative, but not absolute, secrecy?

My effort to answer these questions requires reconstruction and *post factum* explanation. Merton (1957:93–101) criticizes such explanations on the grounds of their limited rigor and validity but concedes that they have high plausibility and are therefore revealing. I hope to draw attention to a people and to an area about which social scientists know little and to demonstrate the need for further reconsideration and modification of present concepts and methods to meet the challenges presented by these and other people in similar situations. The paper also constitutes an effort to share information from the position of a native and principal participant in a series of events rather than from the perspective of an alien investigator.

THE CANAL ZONE: ITS POWER STRUCTURE, RACE RELATIONS, PLURAL ARRANGEMENTS, AND STRATIFICATION

The Canal Zone is a strip of land which runs across the narrowest part of the Isthmus of Panama and borders the Panama Canal on both sides. Technically and geographically the Zone continues to be a contiguous territorial part of the Republic of Panama. However, for all practical and legal purposes it is under the complete and perpetual jurisdiction of the United States of America. The Canal Treaty provides for the United States to utilize the Zone for the construction, operation, maintenance, and defense of the Canal. Hence, all activities, enterprises, and organizations within the Zone are devised to comply with one or more of those functions. The following paragraphs of this section will attempt to present a picture of certain aspects of the Zone as it was even up to the mid-1950's. After that time certain marked superficial changes have become noticeable—i.e., the integration of the police force on the lower levels and the conversion of colored English language schools to "Latin American" Spanish language schools. However, many of the major structural characteristics have remained fundamentally intact.

The Canal Zone was governed by a

quasi-military bureaucratic government. Its populace had no electoral vote (though Americans were eligible for jury posts and could exercise absentee voting rights). Popular voice in Zone affairs was restricted to United States labor unions and a few professional, fraternal, or patriotic pressure groups (mostly American). The Canal Zone government held totalitarian authority, jurisdiction, and control over all phases of life or organization, e.g., law, labor, capital, defense, communication and transportation, business, and services (save the churches and a few private enterprises). For all purposes, despite its non-agricultural emphasis and its principal economic functions (maritime services), the Canal Zone was a closed system reminiscent of the plantation estate which once dominated socio-economic life in most of the Circum-Caribbean (Angelli 1962:119–29; Bryce-Laporte 1962:9–91; Greaves 1959:13–22; McBride 1937:148; Mintz 1959b:42–53; Rubio 1957; Wagley 1957:3–13; Wilson 1947). Only employees of the Zone could live in the Zone, in quarters built, rented, and maintained by the Zone. Only they could purchase in its commissary stores and utilize its recreational facilities. Only they could be taught in its schools, be treated in its hospitals and clinics, and be buried in its cemeteries. Not all the employees of the Zone lived there, of course. Many lived in the terminal cities of Panama and Colón just outside its usually unmarked borders. Even these people were not fully outside the embrace of the Zone—they all treasured and utilized their "privileges" as employees to shop at its cheaper stores, to attend its more efficient and modern hospitals, to use its cleaner toilets. The Zone then was not only closed but it was also exclusive and prized.

The government pursued a rigid policy of discrimination and segregation based on race and nationality, which affected every facet of life and organization within the borders of the Zone. There were remarkably few American Negroes and few non-American whites in the civilian structure of the Zone's labor force. Hence, for all purposes the population and the labor force of the Zone fitted neatly into the two official categories: United States employee-resident (paid one rate of compensation) and local employee-resident (paid a lower rate of compensation).[2] U.S.-rate employee-residents were in general the occupants of the official, administrative, technical, professional, and skilled occupations and offices. As such they were much better paid, unquestionably privileged, and definitely allowed superior facilities. In addition, they lived in U.S.-rate towns, attended U.S.-rate schools, and utilized U.S.-rate services. Local-rate employee-residents, on the other hand, were the usual occupants of semi-skilled and menial positions, a few becoming junior clerical and supervisory personnel or semi-professionals—i.e., teachers. They were underpaid, underprivileged, and offered substandard facilities. They lived segregated from the U.S.-raters, to whom they were subordinate. The few marginal cases in either segment sought refuge in the Republic, where the economic and other material standards of living were distinctly inferior but the social climate distinctly more liberal.

The Zone situation was a quasi-caste system; its strata were rigid and the relationships between them were stable and asymmetrical. Every white American was ascribed at birth or upon entering the Zone as superordinate over every colored person, regardless of nationality, age, years of service, sex, and the like. This *de facto* relationship was an apparent extension of the *de jure* subjugation intertwined in the official structure of the Canal Zone and was undoubtedly reinforced by it in every institutional way of life in the Zone.

A glance at the judicial-police system (the official legal institution) would serve as an adequate illustration: the law and court systems were American and their implementations were reminiscent of Deep South standards. All the judicial authorities—judges, prosecutors and defenders, and jurors—were white Americans. There were only two prominent West Indian members of the Zone's bar; the remaining non-whites were minor court clerks and custodians. The police organization was all white, with the exception of prison guards. Previously, there were West Indian foot police but they could not arrest a white American even for a traffic violation in a colored neighborhood. They were assigned only to local-rate neighborhoods, never could become officers or members of motorized units, and were paid less than their white counterparts.

To a people who were migrants, or descendants of migrants, from the rural West Indies many of the laws seemed illogical, unfair, limited, strange, and contradictory to the norms of the sub-culture of the local-rate communities or the old culture of the islands. Furthermore, many of the Zone laws were contradictory to those of nearby Panama and so too the system and sentences. Furthermore, conviction, and more so, confinement, could result in the loss of one's job and the privilege of obtaining another job or other supplementary benefits of Canal Zone employment. Yet these people constituted the major part of the prison population, because their low earnings prohibited them from paying fines meted out by the court. White prisoners were rare. It was the general belief of the West Indian-Panamanian black people that the Zone law was one-sidedly severe and that on the other side it was lenient and unjust. Americans who got in trouble were often pardoned, released on bail or, after stern admonition, treated as insane or sent away quietly to the United States. When whites and blacks were indicted, the whites were used as capital witnesses against their colored cohorts and given lighter sentences and less rigorous prison duties whenever confined. Incidents to support these stereotypic beliefs formed part of the anthology of legend and folklore of West Indian-Panamanian blacks. Many local-rate teachers scolded their unruly students saying, "Why can't you be like those children over there?" (i.e., the whites).

The discrepancies between official laws and local customs had their effects even in the intimate institution of the family. The Panamanian-West Indian kinship system is bilateral and women seem central in the domestic domain. Family life was made up of a wide range of structural variations and a great deal of permissive relations. This was much more true in the Republic than in the Canal Zone, where the housing authorities and regulations imposed some far-reaching restrictions. Only legal spouse and primary relatives—parents, children, and sometimes sibling peers—were considered eligible for residence as dependents of the applicant. Only on rare occasions would the government consider a woman, even though she might be employed in its service, as an eligible holder of family quarters (that is, as the head of the household). These restrictions led to various sorts of accommodations, legal and illegal, by the local-rate residents to resolve the dilemma of maintaining Canal Zone quarters without completely disrupting the traditions of extended or compound families or matrifocal households. These housing regulations made the father's status that of recognizable head of the household or the sole "legal holder of family quarters." This status implied the role of economic locus and thereby gave him greater *de jure* authority than his West Indian counterpart.³

In spite of the strengthening of the husband-father role, the mother was the central figure of the local-rate family. She exercised discipline and represented the household in the absence of the father. She was responsible for the care of the children as well as for other domestic matters. In such matters she was assisted by the older children. She was considered with such reverence that any insult of her name or person was considered a dishonor to her offspring.

Children sought playmates from their peer groups at an early age, but were expected to respect all adults. Nevertheless, joking relations were most prevalent among children and non-related adults and intergenerational conflicts stemmed from differences in the standards and traditions between the old and new culture. The traditional adult-dominated relations, which never release the child, regardless of his age and status, from the dominance of parents and elders, could not persist under Canal Zone laws. People were limited in regard to how much of the law could be taken into their own hands, whether in family or non-family affairs.

EL RABO: A LOCAL-RATE COMMUNITY AS A SOCIOCULTURAL SYSTEM

El Rabo was a local-rate colored community within a ten-minute ride or about an hour's walk from the border of Panama City. It was located at the terminal of the Canal and the site of a ferry which connected it with the west bank of the waterway. Hemmed in on most sides by the largest and most important (white) American community in the Zone, it was typical of the segregated, sub-standard ghettos which provided residence for the local-rate employees of the Canal Zone. Its houses consisted of over-crowded, wooden, gray-colored, barrack-type buildings. Some housed bachelors and a few spinsters, but the large majority served multi-family units. All of these structures were raised from the earth by pillars varying in length from five to ten feet, which created unpaved open basements which the local people called "cellars." These cellars were utilized for every conceivable purpose, from religion to romance. All public facilities were minimal replicas of the services extended to U.S.-rate communities. Only the church buildings, the lodge-hall, and the labor union office were not subjected to the curfew regulations and surveillance of the Zone government.

The town consisted of a rather broad lower class with a peripheral lower-middle class minority. There was limited upward movement outside the class although there was almost free movement across or within the class. The limited degree of prestige differential that was attainable in the local community was made possible within the rather restrictive borders of the socio-economic structure imposed by the Canal Zone government and the equally restrictive control system of the community itself. The few who were successful in achieving some increase in prestige often did so through a combination of education, occupation, civic-church position, and individual ambition and perseverance. A few attained some prestige through inheritance. Hence, teachers, ministers, and a few clerical or skilled supervisors, and those in close association with them, could enjoy relatively high local prestige. Such people were often called "butches" by the rest of the community.

The term "butch" connotes prestige, not popularity. The phrases "playing butch" or "acting stuck-up" imply snobbishness, social-climbing, or status-steeking — all distasteful and deviant categories vis-à-vis the larger community. It is important that one capture the subtle difference between prestige and popularity as established by the people of this community. Prestige was a classificatory attribute acquired by those who excelled in their efforts to conform to the standards of the superordinate culture—an outward orientation. Popularity was acquired by those who were considered successful or outstanding in demonstrating the "good" aspects or ideals of the subordinate culture—an inward orientation. Each carried with it a somewhat fixed range of role expectations and a corresponding set of reactive behavior patterns.

Among the qualities associated with the superordinate culture were some of definite American origin and others traceable to the "old aristocratic" culture of the middle and upper classes of the British West Indies. Those considered West Indian-Panamanian were not only those indigenous qualities of the subordinate subculture, but also those American and British traits which had been internalized or assimilated so completely by this element that they were not conceived by the community as false, foreign, nor formal — e.g., speaking with an American or British accent was considered false, foreign, and formal; playing baseball or cricket was considered normal, natural, and native!

Distinct from prestige, then, popularity was usually derived from athletic feats, public relations occupations, wealth, conspicuous friendliness, apparent freedom from bias or snobbery, and ostentatious dressing. Thus, athletes, musicians, singers, delinquents, bus drivers, salesclerks, clandestine lottery vendors, drug addicts, petty criminals, and "funny" characters might be "popular." Perhaps the only ones who lacked either attribute in distinguishing measure were the "average citizens" or "nobodys." The few with a distinguishing measure of both were those individuals who had learned to balance or to appropriately demonstrate different traits at their respectively "proper" times. Then there were those who had both "no" prestige and "no" popularity, such as effeminate men, suspected male homosexuals, girls believed to be promiscuous with white men, alleged stoolpigeons or "squealers," prisoners, and openly practicing lay members of "spirit" churches. In some cases these people with negative amounts of both attributes were often subjected to ridicule, ostracization, and persecution because they represented that which the community could not be proud of and which made the community susceptible to the ridicule of white people.

Inasmuch as these two attributes were largely aquisitive, they could be lost or threatened by the individual's overly deviating from his idiosyncratic credit (the permissible range of deviation from norms and role expectations earned or assigned to each individual in accordance with his status). Inasmuch as the community was neither simple, isolated, nor static, many conflicts arose due to inconsistencies between status and roles perceived by those acting and those judging. Nevertheless, the apparently independent attributes of prestige and popularity seemed to constitute a sort of unwritten frame of reference within the larger norm, value, and control systems of the community. As such the attributes provided guidelines for establishing status differentiation and regulating social behavior among community members.

ANALYSIS

I shall now analyze the event by reinterpreting the three questions previously presented and answer them against the background of the proposed prestige-popularity situation.

1. *What social conditions seemed to be related to the effort of both families to seek the assistance of extra-legal agencies (in this case magical-religious media) to resolve what appears to be a purely criminal concern?*

To answer this question, and the others to come, one must first try to locate the two families involved along the scales of prestige and popularity. Both families were of equally low prestige. The boy who killed and his family were somewhat more popular than the victim and his family. In the town's jargon they were "popular guys" not "butches"; in the study's jargon they were much more "inwardly oriented" than "outwardly oriented" and almost equal in status. Hence, what applies to one family also applies to the other for the purposes of this study.

These people were members of an immigrant minority which voluntarily came to the Isthmus under the auspices of an alien but superordinate American majority. The Americans created an exclusive and closed system in which their imported culture became the official norm system. This norm system was reinforced by the rigid asymmetrical power structure, race relations, and stratification system. From the very beginning the West Indian minority had no opportunity to establish their own legal institution side by side or within the official judicial-police system of the Zone. The American majority, while imposing its laws, minimized and eventually eliminated all opportunities for active political and legal participation of the West Indian minority. In a sense it was more selective giving than selective borrowing.

West Indians have been known to boast of how they were constables, soldiers, court officers, and barristers in their home government. They often decried the Zone's and Panama's legal and police system as inferior to that of the British. They even boasted that in the past when local-raters were employed as foot police there were fewer cases of crime, disrespect, and delinquency, so much so that after every major disturbance or crime these people would engage in rumor-spreading and what seemed then to be wishful thinking that colored policemen would soon be brought back into service. As the people contended, those colored policemen were men of the community, they knew the boys and their parents, would take things into their hands to chase children home, see that they went to school, whip wayward boys and complain to their parents who in turn would chastize the children again. They knew the hoodlums and their ways so well that they could anticipate their acts and capture them before they could escape. These apparently nativistic rumors expressed the yearning for more participation in law-enforcement and for an avenue within the official structure to practice the kind of law and enforcement (which include close parent-police cooperation and stern corporal discipline) more in line with their own sub-culture.

They were not very trustful of the law, as can be seen from the legends and folklore of incidents which were mentioned earlier. Neither did they really understand how it worked. The very schools which were the principal agencies of acculturation, where American methods, textbooks, curricula, and administrative policies were official, were affected by the ambivalence toward acculturation. Its faculty, (made up of West Indian and Panamanian blacks) while teaching American democracy and preparing their students to enter the Zone's labor force, knew only from textbooks the complicated processes and ideals behind American laws. As members of the subordinate minority they were equally subjugated to the one-sided Canal Zone system. Most of them, while ranking very high in prestige (index of high outward orientation), had doubts about the American Democratic system and resented the local situation due to the inconsistencies between what they taught and what they met as persons. They were the leaders and most militant faction of the local labor union (which at one time was allegedly Communist affiliated). But even among them there were cases of solicitations to folk magical-religious media and other extra-legal agencies in times of crisis. The school administration was never successful in getting these teachers to refrain from the use of severe corporal punishment as a means of discipline. Parents requested and supported the teachers' right to use this kind of discipline. Principals were high in the local communal power structure and like clergymen often exercised their powers as law enforcers, judges, and executors in communal conflicts.

In effect, while it is not easy to say why people would choose to solicit folk magic (or religion), it can be seen why they would find it difficult to rely solely on the Zone's judicial system. They feared, resented, mistrusted, did not understand, and were not a part of it. This was clearly demonstrated in some of the common sayings of the people. "Man can change. He is only human. He can plan and promise but you can never tell what will make him change his mind ... Man proposes but God disposes ... So you better do something to make sure nothing upset de plans."

The Canal Zone judiciary system simply did not have the same functions nor meaning for local-raters as it had for U.S.-raters. It reflected a different world view and rationale. It did not recognize Obeah as a social reality nor the manipulation of spirits as cause nor cure for ill-will or illness. It made no provision to prevent, protect from, nor punish the use of sorcery. In the West Indies where there was less inequality in the twentieth century, more participation in the official legal machinery, and the persecution of Obeah practitioners, these people nevertheless clung to their folk religion as an extra-judicial mechanism. It seems natural then to expect similar manifestations in the Canal Zone, where there was greater inequality, fewer opportunities for participation in legal machinery, and no direct persecution of Obeah. If the more acculturated and well-to-do "butches" often sought this medium as well as lawyers and influential friends in times of crisis, if to lose a case could mean the loss of popularity and, perhaps, a source of livelihood, then these are enough reasons for poor families (like the two involved) to seek the assistance of Obeahmen and "Jump-up" churches. From their perspective these agencies were less expensive, more readily available, more effective, and more understandable.

2. *Why did neither family, both members of the Episcopal church, consult their clergy rather than turn to other occult media?*

The community enjoyed full religious freedom, variety, and fluid choice. While the population was predominantly Protestant, the Catholic Church was strong. The formal churches were more permanent, better organized and attended, but the nativistic churches were more numerous, often duplicated, and were constantly undergoing change. It is impossible to generalize regarding the type of person or family which would belong, much less attend, one of these churches. While there are some families who subscribed to but one traditional church, in other families individual members belonged to or attended different churches. There were even cases of single individuals belonging to or attending more than one church.

The church buildings were the only public services found in multiple numbers, and, of course, they were privately owned. Consequently, they served multiple purposes or functions aside from being the sites of religious activities. The churches seemed to be involved in a similar classificatory scheme along the lines of prestige and popularity congruent with the ranking of individuals. The churches seem to range along a continuum from formal to folk. A formal church includes clergy, ritual, organization, theology, and activities governed or patterned after a larger and universal conventional religious denomination; a folk-church is governed or developed by the local minority caste and with minimal international or foreign connections. While most formal churches were considered prestige churches, it does not hold that most folk churches were considered popular, for just as there were individuals who were able to attain prestige by not being "stuck-up," some of the formal churches, being richer, better attended, and better organized, were able to sponsor or participate in activities of a "popular" nature. On the other hand, some folk churches not only had "no" prestige but were normally associated with actions considered bad, shameful, or ridiculous by even the majority of the community—hence were not popular either.

The Anglican church was the state church of the British West Indies where it was largely associated with the upper and middle classes. It was one of the few avenues from which the lower classes could derive minimal status. On the Isthmus both West Indian Anglicans and North American Episcopalians were under the jurisdiction of the American Episcopal church. In this community almost the entire population was of British West Indian nationality or ancestry, and the Episcopal Church was the largest and most populous. While it was closely related and governed by British traditions and American authorities, the local clergy was black, native, and educated. The activities of this church were of the widest variety, touching every class. It enjoyed the highest prestige and the greatest popularity among local churches. But the issue facing the two families was not solely social in nature; prestige was not involved; popularity was to some extent; but more immediately important was the need for a religious ritual to bolster their security for their respective problems. This called for either a church whose rituals and theology corresponded to that of the world view of these people or one whose atmosphere and rituals were conducive to secret participation of the nature required by the two cases. In these respects the Episcopalian Church was of little or no use.

Opposing the Episcopal and Roman Catholic churches in style, and in popularity, are the Benjinite or Jump-up sects. They do not have an elaborate or extensive formal structure. They do not embrace a large scope of the lives of their members, nor are they usually related to other national or international denominations. Some isolated churches are affiliated with or patterned after North American evangelical sects and among other isolated churches there may be visiting and irregular joint activities. In general each sect represents a small network of brethren. It is usually led by a woman called a Mother, at whose home or on whose property most of the ceremonies are celebrated. The remaining officers usually consist of a Deacon or Deaconess, a Shepherd Boy, and an Armor-Bearer. Brothers and Sisters and a group of non-members, who range from the believing well-wishers to curious or critical observers, make up the church.

The word "Benjinite" derives from Bedwardite, an Afro-Christian revival group which was founded in Jamaica around the beginning of the twentieth century. The practices and paraphernalia of the Isthmian cult seem to approximate African-oriented West Indian cults such as myalism, kumina, convince, and pocomania (Beckwith 1923:32–45; Hogg 1960, 1964; Simpson 1956). There has been no drumming in the Isthmian cults in recent times, but there has been increasing evidence of Roman Catholic or Anglican High Church influence among the cults. West Indian pidgin English is the principal form spoken in services. While participants may dress in ordinary clothing, special habits are usually worn by women. The most common habit is generally a long white, brown, blue, or mauve dress, with a cord and a single or multi-colored turban or headwrap and regular shoes or sandals. Men usually wear black or white trousers and white shirts, but on some occasions may dress like either Christian pastors or like monks.

The Benjinite meeting begins with low-keyed prayers and singing and gradually increases in intensity and tempo as people begin to testify, shout, shake, clap, and finally prance forward and sideways in a counter-clockwise promenade. Then some individual (usually a member or officer) gets a "calling." He (or she) falls out of the group or spins into the center of the circle, starts to shake, to grunt or moan ecstatically and, as he gyrates, his body and face contort, his limbs are flung about wildly, and he is said to be "in (or catching) the spirits." The Mother, with the help of other officers, "works with him" while the brethren sing and stomp in a very deliberate and heavy tempo. As he is being "worked out of the spirits," he quiets down and slips into a trance-like state. The singing gets softer and slower as he "travels off to distant places," "hears voices," "sees visions," and "gets messages." He begins to sing or speak in "unknown tongues" or makes scribblings on the ground, and one of the participants or leaders suddenly screams out the "message" for which the entire audience and membership have been anxiously waiting. The message usually takes the form of a symbol which is interpreted as a "warning," such as "sudden death," or an indictment or caution to some *specific* person in the group. The warning usually represents "disaster" and triggers off anxieties associated with crisis situations. Sometimes the message is a "rake" which indicates a number which may be a "winner" in the various lotteries bought by Isthmian people. Sermons, singing, and feasting usually bring the official service to an end. As people leave they discuss or transmit the message or sermon to other interested parties.

In El Rabo such services were usually held at night in the open basement and were open to the public. Only day services were held indoors and they were usually to protect the ceremony from the ridicule and distractions of the larger number of passers-by who would ordinarily not be present at night. In the case of the accused (discussed in the beginning of this paper) the services were held in his home even though they were carried out at night. The curtains were drawn, the ceremony itself was performed in a large inner room, and the main door to the house was closed although not locked. One of my notes describes the sessions as follows:

> As one opened the main door he encountered a crowd of curious observers, many of them friends of the accused. To get into the inner room where the ceremony took place one had to "spin his role" (turn around counter-clockwise three times under the supervision of one of the cult members) before a "seal" (a Bible with a candle and other chalk markings on the floor). Candles, flowers, Bibles, religious pictures and statuettes, crucifixes, chalk-drawings, herbs, twigs, incense, smoke, and medicated water were in abundance. The brethren performed in a circle and the accused was placed in the center. He had on a white head wrap with a candle and Bible in his hands and was promenaded and gyrated about by a presiding cult member. He perspired, gazed, and permitted himself to be led. He seemed afraid but not embarrassed. And as for the onlookers there was not time for ridicule.

The basic idea behind the ceremony was to appeal to and marshall spirits who would intercede in his behalf.

The Obeah-Man that both families allegedly visited is believed to have secret powers to deal with spirits and ghosts of "duppies" (spirits of dead people) and to be able to communicate with God, Satan, and specific dead people. He is able to get such deities to do "good" or "bad." Among the secrets he knows are the proper formulae, prayers, vows, sacrifices, and other "things" that people must do to get "things" done or to "fix" other people. He also administers baths, potions, and prescriptions, fixes penances, and makes "guards" for his clients. The Obeah-Man is regarded with awe by many Isthmians (including Americans and Latins too). The saliency of his presence is disclosed by the words of this local calypso which the accused himself had sung many times before in his heyday of popularity:

> Obeah-mancy—West and South,
> Dats how the Obeah-Man "wash dem out"
> Dey give him dey money to kill everybody;
> The people believe in too much Negro-mancy [necromancy].

The families resorted to these available folk media. Were such media unavailable they might have gone to the Roman Catholic Church or to a folk agency outside of town. More active, high prestige Episcopalians would have done this anyway rather than risk their prestige in a local folk-like church. In the case of low prestige families there was no need for substitution. Folk churches were available as were media where they could experiment and ritualize the latent but still surviving beliefs of their quasi-African world view without violating the local normative system. It was commonplace in the community to hear discussions, rumors, or tales of people of varying degrees of prestige who resorted to or have employed "God" and/or other supernatural beings to carry out evil as well as good.

3. *What is the function of semi-secrecy in the folk rituals?*

The community was homogeneous. There was very little preoccupation with prestige and vertical mobility, for there were few opportunities for upward movement. The community members were nearly unanimously anti-white, anti-government, and opposed to Anglo-American attitudes, for they correctly perceived themselves as being repressed by and without power vis-à-vis the white majority. The "butches" were seen as symbols of submission to or stooges for the repressive white caste. The "popular guys" were perceived as heroes, symbolically representing resistance, disrespect, or defeat of the cultural invasion and socio-economic and political imposition of the ruling white majority caste. Pressure toward conformity was strong and popularity rather than prestige was the big issue among the majority of the townspeople.

The two families involved, while not concerned with losing prestige, saw their popularity at stake. They could well afford to go openly to a folk medium, whereas a high-prestige family could not. But privacy, if not secrecy, was necessary.

The defendant's mother held the meetings in her home (rather than "under the cellar" where they were usually held) to avoid endangering the family's popularity by being mistaken for completely converted Benjinite people. Yet when rumors started to circulate neither family attempted to deny their acts. They were not violating any community norms so long as their occultism was "privately" practised. It was common to hear rumors about people of all classes and denominations employing ghosts, saints, spirits, demons, potions, and/or charms for various reason—i.e., for escape, revenge, cursing, healing, luck, power, and protection. While privacy was regarded as necessary to protect popularity, secrecy was not necessary, inasmuch as the system of norms and world view of the community renforced sympathy toward such action. Occultism under such circumstances was expected behavior. To quote a popular saying: "Everybody does their little business when they are in a tough spot but the whole world don't have to know about it. After all, when a man is in trouble, you can't blame him for trying 'anything' to get out. . . ."

The need for continuing popularity permeates the incident. The boy who was killed accepted the challenge in the first place for fear of losing his popularity. The challenger struck his younger adversary with a cue stick rather than risk loss of popularity in a fist fight. The first boy did not want to disclose the incident even after being mortally wounded lest he be considered a "squealer" (to a white doctor) and thus lose popularity. The defendant's people struggled to win the case to avoid their son's losing popularity (and prestige) by becoming a prisoner. The town considered that Obeah and Benjinite were successful when the defendant and his family were reduced to a non-popular, non-prestige level, even though he escaped going to jail. And neither family could stand to be criticized by the community for being so "stuck up" and "stupid" as not even to try Obeah and Benjinite to "make things work out" in its respective favor.

SUMMARY AND CONCLUSION

The Panama Canal Zone, up until the early 1950's, was a closed, exclusive system. Its government and organization resembled the plantation estate in that it was rigidly hierarchical, bureaucratic, pluralistic, paternalistic, authoritarian, and totalitarian.[4] The West Indian immigrants, who constituted its main civilian labor force, were in every sense subordinate to the white American majority, dependent on the Canal Zone government, and as such were exposed to the cultural standards and pressures of the latter.

The incident discussed and analyzed in this paper points to one basic area of cultural contradiction and complementarity: the United States legal code and West Indian folk magic. To complete the analysis it is necessary to discuss participation in its total setting.

The Canal Zone today may best be regarded as a colonial, conflict-based, plural system.[5] Even though West Indians have shown signs of assuming American behavior, it must be remembered that they came to the Zone as strangers to provide labor that was not forthcoming from the natives for various reasons. It was expected that each wave would be repatriated upon completion of the specific missions for which it came (Panama Railroad, French and American Canals, United Fruit Company Railroad, Third Locks Project). Inasmuch as they came in the first instance with no intentions of staying; inasmuch as one of the reasons they were imported involved their skills, attitudes, language, and cultural traditions; and inasmuch as they were led to share in the ethnocentric claim of superiority over the Panamanian natives, West Indians had no basic reason for striving to acquire Panamanian rather than American ways of life. In each instance, however, as their mission approached its end, the West Indians were discouraged from returning to their homeland by various means. They were encouraged instead either to stay in the employ of the Zone or to proceed to seek employment in various parts of the Republic, especially its two terminal cities and on the plantation and properties of the United Fruit Company. In the Canal Zone (and also in the territories of United Fruit Company) the American elite confined itself to exclusive enclaves and built adjacent "company towns." These towns were systems in which the West Indian stranger group constituted the principal employee-residents. The resulting structural asymmetry, or "two-caste" system, persisted despite shared language and tradition and despite the operation of an official school system in the Zone for training West Indians in occupations reserved for them in the Zone's bureaucratic structure. While school programs were designed to acculturate West Indians to American culture, they were not designed to prepare them for assimilation, upward socio-economic mobility, or increased participation in the power structure of the Zone.

It is generally conceded that in most societies the use of religion and magic is intimately tied up with *crisis situations*—perplexing situations in which participants experience unusually heightened anxiety because of their perceived inability to cope with or resolve a given problem. Homans (1950:321–30) in his synthesis of the Malinowski–Radcliffe-Brown controversy demonstrated that the consequence of *primary anxiety* (due to the feeling of personal inadequacy) and *secondary anxiety* (which persists until the socially prescribed religious means are utilized) are really not contradictory but complementary claims. Both forms of anxiety combine to bolster traditional religious beliefs and practices of the society in question. The incident described in this paper does not deny this relationship but rather alludes to its complication as a consequence of the Zone's social structure.

In the Canal Zone the *primary anxiety* of the West Indian stranger was not due solely to a feeling of ignorance or powerlessness but also to distrust of the superordinate and alien Americans and their judiciary system. The *secondary anxiety* did not serve to perpetuate the established (American/Anglo) religions, not even the one to which the accused overtly belonged, but rather to denigrate them in favor of older African-Antillean cultural traditions. The two families did not worry about their status (nor their "sinning") as they openly and purposefully solicited the aid of the folk media. Seemingly, their affiliation with the Episcopal (or other established) Church was not for religious but social reasons. It was necessary and expected by the community that they would have solicited such aid, and the community was willing to tolerate and even prescribe that they do so. Folklore, gossip, and rumor served to maintain the aura of awe and anxiety. They were also the media by which the community was informed of adherence to prescribed occult traditions. Thus for all reasons *some degree of obvious or advertised secrecy* rather than total secrecy or total openness was necessary.

In the Islands as well as on the Isthmus (and this includes Central America) West Indians tend to retain some of the African-West Indian traditions. Occult practices of the kind described here have been reported in fact about Afro-American peoples in various parts of the continent. Ethnohistorians have argued that the widespread practice of such occultism among Afro-Americans testifies to the focal position occupied by religion in West African culture (Herskovits 1958). Notwithstanding the criticism directed toward this kind of reasoning (M. G. Smith 1965), the position of religion among West Indians, especially this particular kind of occultism, is not to be denied but further analyzed. Even if they brought this tradition from Africa via the West Indies to Panama the question arises concerning the nature of the situations which make them conducive to retention, particularly when the West Indians had an opportunity to learn and practice openly the religions of the dominant section. In other words, our question becomes: Why does *cultural* (religion) pluralism *continue* (or even take new forms) even when the subordinate carrier population is being exposed intensely to the new culture (religion) of the dominant section?

The case of the West Indians in the Canal Zone shows that they did not view themseves as *permanent* immigrants until late in their stay on the Isthmus. Even if they were educated in American culture and institutions they were denied commensurate economic access, social status, and political power to control the social determinants of their fate. They—as total dependents in a closed single-authority system—were *always* living on the *brink of crisis*. People in such situations are likely to make greater demands on their gods, spirits, and their clergy than would be expected of ordinary Protestant Christians. Consequently, most Christian (Protestant) forms could not *fully* substitute for their religions and rituals, thus perpetuating cultural-religious distinction between them as strangers and both their Panamanian hosts and their American superordinates.

In conclusion, this paper has sought to describe an occult crisis-sponsored event in such a way as to present pertinent implications which may be helpful in understanding the position of a totally dependent stranger group in a closed and stabilized plural system. The conclusions are:

1. In stabilized, asymmetrical relations within a plural society there will be a tendency for the subordinate minority to observe at least two norms of social behavior—one representing the official superordinate culture and the other representing the subordinate stratum's own subculture. In other words, such a minority is likely to become *bicultural* rather than simply *"creolized"* or *"marginal"* (cf. Polgar 1960:232–33; Shibutani 1965:282–312).

2. The subordinate stratum will tend to classify social behavior as such behavior seems to correspond to the two (or at least

three in case of *stranger* groups) cultures. Where distance, differences, discrimination, or dislike seem to characterize the relations between the two strata, the subordinate one will tend to consider some cultural aspects of the superordinate as false, foreign, or formal and its own (or any of the superordinate or other cultures which it has assimilated) as native and normal.

   a. All persons and institutions of the subordinate community will be seen, categorized, and be reacted to in accordance with their status, which would be related to the degree and direction of their orientation and to their conformity to either set of norms.

   b. The choice of behavior of the members of the subordinate stratum would be closely related to their status when the alternatives are seen in terms of the superordinate cultural standards versus subordinate cultural standards.

   c. The choice of alternatives will also be related to the question of whether the institution or standard has been sufficiently assimilated by the subordinate stratum or is believed to be sufficiently appropriate to meet the demands of the situation.

3. In cases (a) where the plural society is contained within a closed, exclusive context so that the subordinate minority is localized into segregated communities, and (b) where by contact or acculturating agencies the subordinate stranger group is exposed to the culture of the dominant section but cannot at the same time experience structural advancement commensurate to their cultural acquisition there is likely to emerge among the strangers a *contra-cultural* system of values and institutions (an *underlife*).[6]

   a. This contra-cultural system or underlife will serve as the basis of consensus, cohesion, and guide to relationships among members of the stranger or subordinate section as well as vis-à-vis the superordinate section.

   b. Even if the system is characterized by parallel or common institutions these institutions will have different meanings for the subordinate strangers as compared to the dominant donor elite.

   c. In times of *crisis*, which in their opinions cannot be resolved adequately by the institutions or roles of the dominant or official section, the subordinate strangers will refer (openly if necessary) to their traditional institutions (which may remain active or latent) or to any new institution that they have come to assimilate into their cultural system.

NOTES

1. I wish to acknowledge the aid extended to me by Donald Hogg, Hilda Kuper and Norman Whitten in preparing drafts of this paper.

2. While the Canal was being built, white Americans were paid in gold coins and colored non-Americans in silver. Thus, each set of employees was known as white or "gold" employees and colored or "silver" employees, respectively. The terms "U.S.-raters" and "local-raters" or "American citizens" and "Latin Americans" are modern and more euphemistic mechanisms distinguishing basically the same divisions and eliciting similar forms of discrimination (Biesanz 1955:6). For additional social scientific treatment of the race relations in the Canal Zone see Biesanz (1950, 1951, 1953) and Westerman (1948, 1954).

3. A perennial theme of interest in West Indian family organization has been the role of the woman as the central figure of authority and the only stable adult in the household. More details on the subject are covered in this collection in the article by Nancie L. González. Details of the family life of Panamanian-West Indians are comparable to some extent to that of the Islanders (Biesanz 1955:314–23).

4. These various contextual-structural features of the plantation and the concomitant behavior of its personnel have led to consideration of the adequacy of including it among the category of formal-communal organization called *broad organization settlement institution* or *total institution* (Bryce-Laporte 1968; Etzioni 1961; Goffman 1961a; Hillery 1963:779–90; R. T. Smith 1967; Thompson 1959:26–37).

5. The conflict orientation of West Indian plural society is discussed by Professor M. G. Smith (1965) and other students of the area. Among the specific conceptual-methodological questions raised about Smith's work which are relevant to this paper are (1) the appropriate approach for studying social cohesiveness within individual plural segments, (2) the nature of social cohesiveness within such segments, and (3) the reasons for the perpetuation of cultural pluralism among them (Bryce-Laporte 1968:114–20).

6. The concept of *contraculture* was suggested by Yinger (1960) to refer to the culture of a subordinate or minority people which does not represent a mere sub-cultural variant but stems from frustration and conflict, in their interactions with the superordinate segment of the population. Goffman (1961a) refers to such usually elusive or illegitimate adjustive cultures among inmate populations as *underlife*. Unlike the more widely used descriptive term of *creole* or *immigrant* sub-culture (Adams 1959:73–78; Crowley 1960:850–54) which tend to emphasize acculturation and adaptation as principal sociocultural processes, the concepts of Yinger and Goffman embrace and emphasize power differentiation, control, and conflict as the influential factors in shaping the culture of stranger groups.

Five

NON-STANDARD NEGRO DIALECTS: CONVERGENCE OR DIVERGENCE?

J. L. Dillard

Reprinted with permission from *The Florida FL Reporter* (Fall 1968), Vol. 6, No. 2, pp. 9-12.

The English of the Negro in the United States has recently become the subject of many research projects—some of them under euphemistic names which try either to avoid mentioning ethnicity[1] or to mitigate it by incorporating Negro dialect features into some other variable in the research description such as geographic dialect.[2] Although the issue may be considered to be formally opened, the degree of aperture permitted varies from scholar to scholar. The degree to which historical considerations are to be taken into account is particularly variable.

For those to whom the issue is a closed one, that closing might be taken to have been effected by Krapp (1924, 1928). Yet, carefully reconsidered, all Krapp did was to minimize the number of *Africanisms* in American Negro speech. Krapp (1928) treated Negro dialect as a literary dialect, with more than a hint that it had been *invented* by the authors of the fictional works which he cited. (He apparently did not consider the inconsistency involved in also citing works of Cotton Mather, Benjamin Franklin, and other writers of non-fiction.) His thesis, insofar as the inconsistency of his presentation will allow it to be determined, was that authors improvised Negro speech patterns roughly on the model of Gullah but without checking Negro speech patterns existing in their own time and area. Since Krapp and others of his persuasion considered Gullah to be limited to the Sea Islands, the picture of Negro dialect elsewhere as identical to regional white dialects—despite the evidence from presumably irresponsible writers of fiction—accorded with the developing thesis, actually articulated by Kurath (1928), that the English of the southeastern United States reflected specifically the East Anglian dialect of British English. Kurath allowed for the influence of Irish and Scottish speakers, but by implication restricted the Negro's function in American English to an imitative one.

Krapp's collection of literary attestations documents with some precision the thesis, first advanced by William A. Stewart, that a Pidgin English used as *lingua franca* by the slaves was creolized to form the language of the vast majority of slaves on the large plantations, then was de-creolized (i.e., changed in the direction of Standard English as a norm when slave speakers tried to approximate the English of their masters) to form Negro Non-Standard or Black English. (There is not general agreement on the term to be used; however, Negro Non-Standard—NNS—will be used throughout this paper.) Krapp specifically set about to minimize the number of Africanisms in American Negro speech. Being, apparently, entirely unaware of the nature of Pidgin and Creole languages, he assumed that an absence of African vocabulary precluded any influence from any other source except British English.

Herskovits (1941) shows a recognition of the cultural implications of the conclusion that the slaves were purely imitative in terms of language, and Herskovits and Herskovits (1936) offer some material to rebut the position of the dialect geographers. Turner (1949), squarely in the Herskovits tradition, offered abundant evidence that African language vocabulary and naming traditions survived in Gullah; unfortunately, Turner's really outstanding fieldwork has been misinterpreted as meaning that the investigator turned up a dialect which was virtually unknown and which could be heard only by a Negro who won the confidence of the Sea Island people. Turner himself (1949: 5–14) really made it quite clear that there had been a rather long tradition of study of the Gullah dialect, and that it was the *Africanisms* which provide the "Difficulties which have confronted investigators of Gullah" (Turner's sub-heading, p. 11). Since neither Herskovits nor Turner had considered the implications of Pidgin languages and of the creolization process, their expositions had to be incomplete. For those who were unwilling to concede the influence of any other variety but British English on American English, it was easy to assume that Gullah was isolated, spoken only in the Sea Islands and that the Africanisms simply did not exist in the other parts of the United States. Actually, there is a great deal of evidence that day names (Cuffy, Quaco, Cudjo) were used in all parts of the United States, that a few other names of African etymology (notably Sambo; see Turner 1949:155) were extremely widespread, and that African words like *goober* and *buckra* (Mason 1960) long ago spread far beyond the Sea Islands. Yet the apparent promise of Turner's work was not fulfilled; such articles as R. A. Hall (1950) and McDavid (1951) proved to be dead ends in the works of the authors and of their students.

As long as etymology is allowed to be the deciding factor, it is all too easy to return to the other half of a prefabricated dilemma, to assert that since only a few etyma, or original forms of words, could be shown to go back to African languages the only real influence on American dialects must have been from British dialects, transmitted almost in a direct line from England. It would then follow that any differences in American Negro English would be the result of some "selective cultural differentiation,"[3] although that rather impressive term has so far not been well defined.

Whether the dilemma—African influence or pure British influence—constitutes a real one is a question which has hardly been raised until recently, and largely through the efforts of William A. Stewart, some of whose most telling examples significantly enough were taken from the chapter in Krapp mentioned above. As Stewart (1967) points out, the enclitic vowels that are added to, and treated as a part of, the preceding word, in *makee*, *wantuh*, etc.; the use of *me* as a subject pronoun and as a possessive, along with other examples of "possession by juxtaposition;" and many other details of syntactic construction which are inadvertently pointed up by the "literary dialect" examples in Krapp (1928:246–73) are too much like the Pidgin and Creole varieties of the West Indies, Surinam, and West Africa to be believably the product of some writer's invention. That Krapp stigmatized these forms as "puerile" (p. 126) reflects seriously upon his professional preparation; the concept of linguistic relativity was not new in the 1920's. One wonders what kind of linguistic theory Krapp, Brooks (1935), and the others who were dismissing the subject of Negro influence upon American English were familiar with. Even the modestly technical concept of the phoneme does not appear in their works.

The dilemma may be refuted in the usual way; the possibility which Stewart suggests of influence from a Pidgin is an effective third possibility. The Pidgin may or may have not been of African origin, but it apparently was widely distributed in West Africa in the comparatively early days of the slave trade. The historical problem itself is complex and intriguing but its resolution is not essential to a discussion of Pidgin influence on the English of the slaves. The theory of Pidgin influence itself is not especially new; it is apparently implicit in Bloomfield (1933), accounting for American Negro dialects in terms of de-creolization, since de-creolization presupposes prior creolization, and creolization is usually taken to presuppose the prior existence of a Pidgin. Bloomfield himself and R. A. Hall (1966) would apparently have anticipated the Stewart position on present-day American Negro dialects if they had been aware of the implications of age-grading. Lack of that awareness, which has been promoted almost exclusively by Stewart and then almost entirely in public lectures, has led most of the big research projects to use adult informants, who have been most able to reflect changes in their speech in the direction of regional and national norms. The followers of Herskovits and of Turner have been led somewhat astray into a kind of quibbling about details of African influence.[4] Analyzing Negro dialects as de-creolized creole languages, with a great deal of their apparent variability between Creole-like forms and Standard English forms resulting from code-switching (Bailey 1965), constitutes a still virtually unexplored possibility.

Like any new trend in thinking, this one comes up against an Establishment position, which seems to group itself into two tenets: (1) everything in American dialects must somehow either come from Great Britain or constitute a New World innovation, and (2) investigation of social differences need go no further than the inclusion of elderly, rural, not-too-well-educated informants (the Class I of the familiar Dialect Atlas approach).

These assumptions have not gone unchallenged in the past, although the challenges have been largely ignored. Pickford (1956) is sharply critical of Atlas sociological and sampling techniques, and points out clearly that the whole Linguistic Atlas tradition, European as well as American, has overlooked such plausible factors in language variation as age, social class, urban vs. rural residence, and membership in ethnic groups. Pickford, working apparently without a hint of the great differences which some linguists are now finding between Non-Standard Negro English and Standard American English, was almost prophetic in her theoretical statement of what Stewart and others have demonstrated concretely in the case of American Negro dialects. Her influence may be partly responsible for the sudden rash of urban dialect studies in recent years; in other areas, her warnings have been largely ignored.

But the Creole twist to dialect studies, except for an occasional fore-shadowing by such a linguist as Bloomfield, has not been widely appreciated. The issue comes almost to a direct confrontation: are the admitted differences between the speech of American whites (pointed up inadvertently in even such a traditional, Atlas-oriented work as Atwood 1953) traceable to (1) selective cultural differentiation, or (2) some other factor?[5] Although the mechanisms of the historical transmission of American dialect traits have been studied extensively, the possibilities have not been exhausted at all. For example, even the most traditionally problematic aspects of American Negro lexicophonology can be explained with surprising ease in terms of the "relexification" concept which Stewart (1962) and Taylor (1960) developed in Caribbean historical linguistics.

Perhaps the easier explanation of relexification comes in the example of the use of *done* as an immediate perfective in Negro Non-Standard English, like Gullah /dʌn/. Examples of *done* + *V*(*erb*), in earlier British dialects, are known from such works as Curme (1935); but these are examples of causative *done*, the past participle of causative *do*. (*The king has done close the door* means "The king has caused the door to be closed.") The Negro Non-Standard and Gullah forms (and probably the southern dialect usage in general) looks much more like a replacement for Portuguese Trade Pidgin *kaba*, with about the same time reference as Spanish *acabar de*. Sranan Tongo, in Surinam, retains the Portuguese form even though it is called an English-based Creole. Weskos, of the Cameroun and Nigeria, has relexified the Portuguese form with /dɔn/ and is thus rather close to Gullah and NNS in this respect. Melanesian Pidgin English uses *finish* in about the same function, although with some different word-ordering rules; Hawaiian Creole— usually called "Pidgin"—makes Hawaiian *pau* function the same way, through the same kind of word substitution process. Haitian /fɛk/, ultimately from French *faire*, represents relexification with French material. Outside the verb system, slightly de-creolized Gullah uses *white folks* (singular) for former *bakra* and *y'all* (plural) for former *unu*. The Stewart paper on relexification remains unpublished; it is one of the major gaps in availability of materials on Creole studies. Still, the process of relexification is a known one; it is a proven necessity in Caribbean studies.

On the other hand, *selective cultural differentiation*, its traits, and its mechanisms, remain apparently unstudied, except insofar as certain linguistically naïve investigations of the "limitations" of the speech of uneducated Negroes are concerned. The literature of speech correction as applied to Negro dialect is surveyed in Baratz (forthcoming).

It is difficult and, therefore, probably unfair to speculate about the exact mechanisms of selective cultural differentiation. The nature of the process itself is even in some doubt. Perhaps it is within the range of fairness to examine the example given by McDavid (1967:35ff.), *he do*—well known as a Negroism in the United States. Does selective cultural differentiation mean that something in the culture of the Negro causes him to "drop" a final *-s* which earlier generations (presumably of Negroes) articulated—or, more likely, to select from alternate possibilities among British-based dialects, *he do* rather than *he does*? This would mean, according to McDavid (1967) a Negro proclivity for East Anglian forms rather than for those of other parts of England. This is a conceivable—if somewhat mystifying—possibility if Negro *he do* continues to function like British dialectical *he does~he do*, where the presence or absence of an inflectional suffix signals nothing in the grammar.

The Creolist remembers such rebukes as that administered by Taylor (1957) to Élodie Jourdain, who made a parallel assumption about the relationship between verbal suffixes and grammatical function in Haitian Creole and Standard French, and such demonstrations as those of Taylor (1959, 1963), wherein the Creolist position of investigating syntactic distribution independently of affix considerations (itself not radically different from the position of the Transformational-Generative syntacticians, although arrived at independently) is well illustrated.

The mystifying consideration of how socio-economic deprivation correlates with the "deprivation" of an inflectional suffix must be replaced by the really important consideration of whether Negro *he do* is simply a grammatical equivalent of *he does*, differing only in a "dropped" inflectional ending. Consider the forms *go* and *goes* in the following sentences:

1. They caught the old man because he go round telling these stories all the time.

The informant, asked by Loflin (1967) whether it would be acceptable to say

2.* ... he went around telling these stories,

rejected it because *he do it all the time*. While sentences like

3.* They caught the old man because he goes around telling these stories

may be considered acceptable (NOT grammatical) by some informants who speak Standard American English, in that they involve the suspension of a sequence of tense rule which does not operate in Negro Non-Standard English. Tense is not an obligatory category in the verbal auxiliary system of Negro Non-Standard English.[6] The mere addition of an inflectional ending to NNS (Non-Standard Negro English) does not produce SE (Standard English). Under the impression that it does, NNS speakers attempting to switch codes—perhaps under the urging of teachers who also misunderstand the grammatical relationships—produce sentences like

> Dr. Jackson wrapted the wheels with rope.
> They stopted to watch a dog fight.

Selective cultural differentiation, if taken to be fairly represented by the *he does* (or *goes*)~*he do* (or *go*) example, would seem to fail on two counts: (1) it does not really describe the grammatical facts, and (2) it is unnecessary, since another mechanism is already available for explaining the same phenomena. Here, the concept of relexification is necessary, for it shows that such Negro dialect uses of *go* (or *goes*) and *went* may represent the grafting of these lexical products of traditional English verbal morphophonemics onto what are essentially creole grammatical categories.

This is not to say that cultural differentiation in language is a topic unamenable to study, but it is apparently not the subject of grammatical study—insofar as the examples considered so far tend to indicate. It would seem that cultural differentiation, selective or not, would be applicable more easily to less central areas of language. Hannerz (forthcoming) gives an excellent demonstration of how the widened currency of the term *soul* "typically Negro"—NOT, it should be noted, the etymology of the term—is linked to a changing social situation in which certain Negroes (especially young men) develop an attachment, expressed in the "soul" vocabulary, for some of the Negro life style as a reaction to their possible failure in moving up. It would seem to be in these areas, not in the deeper areas of grammatical categories, that cultural differentiation and language could profitably be studied.

In particular, one must be on guard against the persuasive powers of the impressive and scientific-looking occurrence lists, frequency tables, and maps which are so often used by dialect geographers to make or prove a particular point. For it is often the case that the sheer order and beauty of these devices may mask an otherwise obvious faultiness or incompleteness of the data presented. The three maps in McDavid (1967) which purport to show something about the relationship of the speech of Negroes to that of whites illustrate this problem rather well. The first map indicates that the occurrences of *he do* (as opposed to *he does*) have been heard from speakers in various parts of Great Britain, particularly in the East Anglian region. The other maps show that *he do* is also used widely by whites in the American South Atlantic states, and by Negroes there and elsewhere. The use of *do* (as opposed to *does*) in *he do* is presented as evidence of the distribution and use of the Standard English third person singular agreement marker, used with present tense verbs, so that the fact that British dialect speakers and southern American whites are found to say *he do* is taken as an indication that the Negro dialect "lack" of the *-s* verbal marker (*he do, she teach, it hurt*) is fully within the British (and American white) dialect tradition.

In fact, as William A. Stewart has pointed out to me, the works of many of the better southern dialect writers furnish a great deal of counter evidence to McDavid's conclusions about the distribution of verbal *-s*. For example, the poor whites of eastern North Carolina in Paul Green's *Wide fields* (1928) regularly use it in the Standard English way with main verbs (e.g., "Bring your hankerchief and an'int it, fer she smells like the Queen of Sheby," p. 70), while the local Negroes usually do not (e.g., "When he lift up his arm, de muscle swell out same as a stump," p. 108). That literary sources are often more useful than Dialect Atlas materials in determining the grammar of a given dialect is one of the stronger pieces of evidence in the indictment of the Linguistic Atlas for failure to give adequate grammatical information.

The very neatness of Linguistic maps hides the inconclusive character of the data they present. There is no indication at all whether the *do* in question is a main verb (as in *he does his work* or *he do his work*), or the auxiliary or pro-verbal *do* (as in *does he work?* or *do he work?* and *I know he does* or *I know he do*). Yet, the rules for the use of *-s* may be very different for these two kinds of *do*. Some dialect speakers may use *-s* with the main verb, but not with the auxiliary or pro-verb, saying *he does it*, but *I know he do* (or even *he does it, he do*). Others—this is, in fact, quite common—may use the *-s* with the auxiliary or pro-verb in the affirmative, but not in the negative, saying *he does* and *he don't*. Thus, although the facts may well be presented in the maps, they do not necessarily indicate that the Negro dialect "lack" of *-s* with main verbs (e.g., *he like it*) is of a kind with the British *he do* of East Anglia—particularly in view of the English-based Pidgin and Creole use of verbs without *-s*.

At any rate, the problem of Non-Standard Negro dialect has raised the interesting issue of a case in which the typical atlas, with dots for occurrences of *he do*, from Negro and white informants, is useless, and may tend to obscure the grammatical (and therefore the basic linguistic) facts rather than to reveal them. If, as I obviously believe, there is really the kind of historical difference between NNS and white dialects which Stewart suggests, it may be necessary only to specify that Atlas productions mark essentially white dialect areas, to the exclusion of the NNS group (and, of course, of Cajuns, Mexican Americans, and others). There is already considerable precedent for such a step in the omission of Gullah from Atlas material. Atwood (1953:41) says that "The speech of the Gullah Negroes, which was hardly touched in the Atlas survey, has been shown to contain a good many unique morphological features."

The shotgun divorce of Gullah from other Negro dialects in the United States never produced consistently happy results, even for the dialect geographers who engineered it. From presumably reassuring reminders that the English of the Negro is exactly like that of the whites, except perhaps slightly archaic, they have vacillated to the most extreme limits of exoticism. In Atwood (1953:44) there is even speculation about the forms of "primitive Negro speech"—a phrase which is enough to make any Creolist and probably any West Africanist shudder. Inadvertently, Atwood put his finger on typically Negro forms (*ibid.*, 11, 27, 28, 41, *et passim*). One is never sure at what level of disputation, pedagogical demonstration, or polemic the representatives of the geographic approach are operating. At times, they seem to be trying to convince straw man opponents that Non-Standard dialects have structure (Shuy 1968).

In spite of the received opinion, there is abundant evidence that Gullah is not and never has been limited to the Sea Islands. Gullah or an inland dialect based upon it was spoken at the time of A. B. Lindley's *Love and Friendship* (1807; see Stewart 1967); such a dialect is widely spoken even in metropolitan South Carolina today, as the recent field trips of Stewart have revealed. Except for his observations, there is little to go on; but residents of the area do not consider statements that Gullah is spoken in downtown Charleston, S.C., to be extreme or far-fetched. Popular literature and recordings like Dick Reeves' *Gullah*[7] illustrate quite clearly the existence in metropolitan Charleston not only of Gullah but of mixed dialects intermediate between Gullah and NNS. A personal friend of mine, a 19-year-old (white) girl, learned something which she calls Gullah during a stay in Charleston between the ages of eight and fourteen. The "Gullah" which she speaks reflects such apparent relexifications as *be -in'* for /dɛ/ (e.g., "I be layin' linoleum" in a mildly risque joke). And Stewart tells me that one can encounter today any number of Negro children born and raised in downtown Charleston who, in spite of school attendance, are virtually monolingual in this kind of urban Gullah. These facts would seem to indicate that Charleston is linguistically much more like a Caribbean city than like other American cities—having a full-fledged Creole language (Gullah) and a variety of Standard English in diglossic relationship to each other.

If this is true, the role of Gullah in that

city ought to bring it more recognition than mere whitewashing statements of the type "Negro speech, in general, seems to have the same speech forms as white speech" or trivial acknowledgments like "Grammatically, the most old-fashioned Negro speech shows a lack of inflection of both noun and verb" (McDavid 1955:35–49). If, as seems even more highly likely, diglossic areas of the same type existed at many places in the United States in the past (not only with Black English varieties, but with American Indian Pidgin English or Chinese Pidgin English and Standard English), there should be some recognition of that relationship in the standard works on American English.

The most extreme form of NNS (what Stewart [1962] calls basilect) seems to be essentially a relexified form of Gullah—or, more precisely, of a generalized Plantation Creole of which Gullah may be the only surviving regional form. Other U.S. Negro dialects constitute a rough continuum from Sea Island Gullah through urban Gullah to basilect and other mixed varieties and to the virtually unmixed StE of certain groups. Future dialect studies will be leaving out a great deal if they continue to suppress reference to that relationship. Age and other sociological factors will be important correlates of the degree of convergence with StE, but it appears unlikely that geography will prove to be of any significance. There seems to be nothing to be gained by continuing the reconstructive tradition[8] as represented by e.g., Pederson (1968). It may be an accidental result of the format of the journal, but it may also be an unwitting indication of just what this emphasis has been that the title of this article on middle-class Negro speech in Minneapolis appears just below the section heading *Domaine germanique*.

NOTES

1. For example, the Detroit Dialect Study, the Chicago Dialect Study (Communication Barriers to the Culturally Deprived), and the Urban Language Study (later Sociolinguistics Program) of the District of Columbia.

2. In extreme cases, Negro dialect may even be lumped together with foreign language behavior (e.g., Labov, Cohen, and Robins 1965).

3. The term and the statement appear in McDavid 1967.

4. For example, Turner 1949; R. A. Hall 1950; Taylor 1963.

5. It is, of course, assumed that physiological and mental considerations—or others capable of racist interpretations—are not live issues in this context.

6. This example is taken from a paper by Marvin D. Loflin (1967). I am indebted to Loflin for many parts of the discussion about final -*s* in the verb system; however, Loflin and I arrived at our conclusions independently and our methods of investigation were entirely different. It is probably obvious throughout that this paper owes a great deal to William A. Stewart in all parts and at all stages.

A preliminary version of this paper appeared in *The Florida FL Reporter* (1968).

7. Lenwal Enterprises, Charleston, S. C., 1965.

8. Bloomfield (1933) makes it perfectly clear that this was the original focus of dialect geography.

Six

CULTURAL AND LINGUISTIC AMBIGUITY IN A WEST INDIAN VILLAGE[1]

Karl Reisman

English-based Creole on the island of Antigua, West Indies, serves as part of a more general way of handling cultural symbols, a way which uses and increases their ambiguity. Ambiguities of cultural reference and of associated expressive and moral meaning pervade symbolic expression and are a focus for constant play and manipulation. There is a duality of cultural patterning, both of Creole vs. English speech and of "African" vs. English culture. But this duality is denied and covered by what is both a historical process and by an ongoing symbolic technique of "taking on" dominant cultural forms and "remodeling" them so that the two cultural strands are woven into a complex of cultural and linguistic expression.

Antiguan speech is midway along a range of liguistic assimilation of African populations in the New World.[2] Creole exists but is denied. The ambiguities between Creole and standard English are maximized and the shading of linguistic features back and forth from one to the other is subtly manipulated. External linguistic models of bilingualism, dialect variation, linguistic continua, or simplification are inadequate pictures of such a situation (Hymes 1967; Gumperz 1967; DeCamp 1968). They usually reinforce a bias toward English intrinsic to the image of itself that West Indian society wishes to project. In so doing these models overlook much of what is going on linguistically and the complex nature of the processes they are meant to describe. Only by looking at the overall way in which speech is handled in the cultural conceptions and practices of people can we begin to know how varieties of speech are demarcated and used in a particular community.

The way symbols are handled, the techniques of "masking," "reinterpretation," and "remodeling" (see below) relate to fundamental value patterns first extensively noted by Herskovits (1958:150–58). He argued that certain norms of behavior, of reticence and discretion, of respect and acceptance rather than confrontation, were closely related to an indirect and ambiguous mode of expression and reaction.

Both reticence and discretion are valued qualities of character. Both indicate a strong sense of the bounds of other people's personality and privacy, and both show a concern with avoiding "shaming" another person by revealing something hidden ("calling his name," "spreading news," "tearing off clothes") or arousing envy by showing something of one's own (strong norms of sexual discretion are justified in this way). Reticence extends to cultural matters. The African game of Wari is "hidden" (at least from Herskovits); one should not, in the Bush Negro proverb, "tell more than half of what one knows (1941:156). (The West African Yoruba says, "Half a word is enough for the wise.") These qualities are thus both valued in themselves and, in part, motivated by a fear of reprisal.

"Acceptance" and "respect" are also ambivalent notions in Antigua. There is acceptance and respect for the nature of life itself, of what life brings to one. To challenge what life brings may in some circumstances be taken as a sign of weakness rather than strength. For example, the words "resignation" and "predestination" are reinterpreted to demonstrate the force and nature of one's character. Respect extends to this force of character and also to genuine authority that has its source in personal worth and personal power. There are also strong norms about age respect. In these senses there is genuine respect connected with the acceptance of, and the search to master, situations in the forms *in which they present themselves*. But acceptance in these forms may lead to forms of respect that are much more artificial. People tend to "accept," with varying degrees of sincerity, the surface forms of their culture. In the Antiguan situation one accepts with "respect" both the status system, with its concomitant self-definition as "low," and the total superiority of the standards and value of English culture.[3] In seeking these values one is said to possess "ambition" and "respect."

That this respect is ambivalent can be seen in a number of ways. There is a calypso by The Mighty Sparrow which goes:

> *According to the education you get when you small,*
> *You'll grow up with true ambition and respect from one and all.*
> *But in my days in school they teach me like a fool,*
> *The things they teach me I should be a block headed mule.*
>
> (Slinger Francisco)

"I don't respect anybody" is a remark commonly heard in the village. This may be a piece of wisdom spoken to intimates, or a claim to equality, calling down somebody else's pretensions, or it may be a threatening or boastful assertion of one's self. A common complaint is "People don't have any respect."

Herskovits summed up the whole complex of values and behaviors in the term "indirection." Norms of respect and discretion imply an avoidance of direct confrontation. One quickly learns not to confront directly anyone who has wronged you, for this merely provides fodder for the community's "gossip" and "teasing." Even when no complaint is involved the most casual remarks about another person, about his appearance, for example, may set off a storm of "scandal" and retribution which comes back on their author. One also learns from experience not to trust people with one's thoughts. Only certain people are truly loyal, and only the long testing and observation of their behavior can lead to a sufficiently secure judgment.

Indirect modes of reprisal and expression are the natural consequence of seeking to avoid direct confrontation and of accepting the cultural forms of whatever situation one finds oneself in. The principle of indirect reprisal is involved in recourse to Obeah and in the suspicion of the motives of others, which is rampant in the West Indies. But its normative status is better illustrated by the following incident. A man returned to his village after two years away on contract. During that time he had sent money regularly to a woman with whom he had a child. He returned to find her living with another man. From about 4 p.m. until midnight he was able to maintain his control. As the villagers say, in a seventeenth-century phrase, you have to "know yourself (control yourself) in anything you do." But after drinking with the boys he had to pass the woman's house on his way to sleep, and could control himself no longer. He ran down, beat on the door, and started to fight with the other man. This behavior was not at all approved. He would have been better advised, it was said, to have taken his time, gone to the woman, been sweet, and slowly eased out the other man by his generosity and the claim he had on the woman because of the child. When she had finally dismissed the other man, and had no other resources, then and only then he should abandon her.

In the area of symbolic expression "indirection" takes more complex forms. Because they do not express themselves directly nor wish to reveal differences from others, people "take on" forms from the immediate environment as a mask behind which, or through which, alternate meanings are conveyed. Or they may transform the meanings of forms which are forced on them. Let us call such transformations "masking" or "transvaluation," depending on context. What we are seeking in using such concepts is the formation of syncretisms. I tend to agree with Métraux (1959) rather than Herskovits that most syncretisms are maskings or transvaluations of Euro-American forms, rather than reinterpretations of African forms. Syncretisms increase the area of conscious or unconscious double statement and the possibility of symbolic play. They are not merely the passive results of history.

There is another process at work which increases the ambiguity of the symbols we are discussing. This involves reshaping the forms of symbols to resemble as closely as possible both the historical source and the forms current in the environment. Following Douglas Taylor, who once again has helped us to understand better the question of the origin of cultural forms and its close relation to synchronic technique or style, we call this "remodeling." Discussing the origin of certain words in Saramaccan (Surinam), Taylor (1964:436) points out:

> The words for *sit* and *stand* provide good examples of a process that appears to be fairly common in Saramaccan, and which might be called "remodelling." Thus early Saramaccan sindá *sit*, like Papiamentu sínta and Haitian Creole šita with the same meaning, most probably has its source in Ibero-Romance (cf. Ptg. assentar, sp. assentar, sp. sentado). But modern Saramaccan sindó is one step nearer to its Sranan equivalent, sidón, whose model is usually assumed to have been Eng. sit down. And similarly, Saramaccan tán a pê (tá na pê?, also táanpê, cf. Ptg., estar em pê) *stand* has a variant, táanpu, that no longer contains pê, and is closer to Sranan tanápu *stand* (supplied by the reviewer from another record), whose model is usually assumed to have been Eng. stand up. (Cf. also Saramaccan giín ~ gúun *green*, where we observe a word of

presumably English ancestry in process of replacement, through what appears to be free variation, by one of presumably Dutch ancestry, Sranan grun.) It therefore seems not improbable that a further period of contact between speakers of these two Surinamean creoles should bring the Saramaccan words for *sit* and *stand* still closer to their Sranan equivalents. And if this were to happen, at what point in such an evolutionary series as sindá>sindó>*sindón>sidón *sit* could we say (if we could) that the word changes its genetic relationship?!"

Some forms as recorded by Schumann indicate a source other than that which might have been assumed from the word in its modern shape alone. Thus, Saramaccan and Sranan lóntu *round* might well be assigned to Dut. rond (cf. sónu *sun* sándu *sand*) rather than to Ptg. Sp. redondo were it not for Schumann's *luntu, luluntu*; and Saramaccan mi ii *child* could be identified with its Yoruba equivalent, mi, were it not for Schumann's minini, which suggests, rather, Ptg. menina, menino. And it would still be hazardous to affirm that Ibero-Romance alone determined the adoption and shaping of these creole words.

Both the reshaping of symbols and their reinterpretation so that they can mediate at least two sets of cultural identities and meanings are ongoing creative processes. They are not limited to language, but spread into the nooks and crannies of Caribbean life.

In British Honduras one of the villages on the coast prides itself on the number of white sailors and passersby who have entered into its ancestry. These men are called, appropriately enough, "ships that pass in the night." A second example concerns a man who was church organist in the village where I did my fieldwork. His first name at that time was Wisemore. He has since come to Boston, where he worked for a time at the Beth Israel hospital. I ran into him there by accident, and he immediately took pains to see that I called him by his new name, Seymour, pronounced, obviously enough, *see-more*.

There are other clear cases of maintained double meanings. Some of these are very homely, with no immediate outside audience. Thus there is in Antigua a variety of sweet potato known as [kɔ̃go hoᵒm] which is translated alternately as "come go home" and as "Congo home." The form of the name is capable of either gloss, and is thus a remodeling (a function, we shall see, for which Creole has special mechanisms). The full meaning depends on the association of both glosses. Less close phonetically, but with the same double nature, are two names for a particular hair style: [kiᵉn ro] and [kɔ̃go], respectively, "cane row" and "Congo."

People may "take on" forms from the immediate environment as a mask behind which, or through which, alternate meanings are conveyed. Or they may reinterpret the meanings of forms they have always used. But the meaning of Taylor's notion of remodeling is that they are most likely to do both at once. A form that is retained is likely to be one that can be interpreted in several ways, as related to a number of traditions.

There is a series of "gestures" which are maintained in Antigua as greetings to people passing by. One of these, a side-up turn of the head (jaw to the right), clearly has an African origin—on stylistic grounds.[4] Its meaning there as in Antigua is a sign of recognition to people passing (to be distinguished from a greeting gesture found in Antigua and apparently among Scotch-Irish peasants in Newfoundland, involving a quick "cocking" of the head to one side, jaw to the left).[5] One could regard the persistence of the head-turn simply as a case of continuity. But the gesture is very close to, and easily mistaken for, a Euro-American head gesture meaning, "Come over here!" (either as a command or as a familiar come-hither sign). Clearly, in a plantation slavery environment it was useful to be able to interpret commands to approach as greetings. Parallel to this gesture is a rising intonation when calling people's names, again used to recognize them as they pass by but equally carrying the intonation of the Anglo-American call to "come here." Origin in this case is obscure. The recent report by Jan Daeleman S.I. of the preservation of tone on 67 items in Saramaccan borrowed from Kongo, the retention of distinctive tone in Saramaccan, as well as in occasional one word sentences in Antigua ("How" with falling tone "question,"; "How" with rising tone "of course"), suggests that what happens to intonation should not be thought of as outside the focus of West Indian attention. Remodelings were not only useful but were a way to redress the harshness of the slavery situation, by turning commands into forms of politeness. The intonation used in "please" in shops in Antigua today is the same as that used in American caricatures of haughty British ladies giving commands to servants.

While admittedly speculative from an historical point of view, these suggestions gain probability from the elaboration of devices in Antigua permitting people to communicate in front of outside third parties, such as "passing remarks" without giving the usual face and lip signals which indicate that a person is about to speak, directional speech focused in one direction so that people standing elsewhere cannot understand it, and others. It is one characteristic of remodeled symbols that they do not force their multiplicity. It is up to the listener to "take" or to "get" the multiple meanings. It is a characteristic of Antiguan conversation, for example, for a word to become popular as a token which is tossed into conversations to see how many meanings the group can give to it by placing it in different contexts. Interesting new contexts are quickly spread about, and the word steadily gains meanings until it is worn out and a new one comes on the scene. One such word was "knuckle," which was something one "got" when one's girl was unfaithful. There arose questions over whether one should "take" it or "give" it. Girls, in a mild wave of feminism, decided they were not going to "keep" it, but would "give it back," and so on. The characteristic feature is that the person introducing the word into the conversation does not have to have a clear idea of the meanings he wants it to take on. This is a collective process. It is thus distinguished from the predominant forms of English "wit," in which the person playing with a word controls the contexts in which he presents it, seeking subtlety in the way the meanings are related.

The pattern of values and expression we have been describing is intimately connected with the maintenance of cultural duality. That Caribbean Negro culture is often characterized by a hidden, underlying set of values and cultural patterns is becoming ever more clear. Herskovits' chasing after Africanisms was in part motivated by his awareness of duality, of something hidden beneath the surface. M. G. Smith (1953:70) also acknowledges its presence: "But apart from this there was a definite reluctance among the slaves to let white people know more about their behavior and institutions than was strictly necessary." As we shall see, Raymond T. Smith (1956) has recognized a dual value system in the villages and its relation to the status system. Peter Wilson (1969)[6] has seen its relation to age and sex patterns. And in this volume Thomas Price has set his revealing gaze on the underlying culture, asserting again that it is not merely dual, but deep and hidden.

There has, in fact, been some disagreement about the extent to which one can elicit statements of underlying norms and values. Thus R. T. Smith (1956:149) has recognized the role of low status definition in making possible and defending an alternate set of values. But he seems to have felt that these alternate values were next to impossible to find expressed.

> However, it must be recognized that the permissible deviations from the ideal pattern within the sub-system must themselves be governed by a different ideal pattern and in fact we find that this is the case. There is a moral system within a moral system so to speak, and although the over-all moral system is accepted as being "right" for the subgroup, at the same time people will say that because they are black people they do things in a different way. . . . In our Guianese villages one gets the impression that it would be quite immoral for any person to show open disrespect to his mother, but this is merely an inference. There is no overt expression of this moral norm, nor are there any easily recognizable symbols of its generality. The most one can say is that one never observed anyone showing disrespect to their own mother.

I can only say that I have heard this moral norm overtly expressed countless times, as well as the more general norms of age respect. Appropriate context, appropriate intimacy, and appropriate questions can elicit their clear and strong expression. West Indians in strange cultural contexts, as would be expected, are also highly articulate of their values. Once one knows a value one can almost always re-elicit it at will, usually accompanied by comments indicating how strongly it is held, and often with amplifications. One's very familiarity with it breaks down discretion.[7]

One process that makes it hard to elicit clear statements of alternate values is what we can call negative definition. This is one variation on the process of accepting forms and changing their meaning. Values are often named by the negative terms applied to slave behavior (such terms sometimes being given a "positive" feeling), or approved behavior may be described as an absence of a trait considered desirable in the official system. We shall see below how this may be used to build ambiguous patterns into village life. Here we can begin by noting that passivity, pliability, resignation, "predestination," acceptance, and "mastery of the situation as it is " are all terms that have been used to refer to the same thing.

The term "resignation," as we have seen, is used by some Antiguans to refer to a desirable trait by which one makes the best of a situation and shows one's "virtue" by mastering it, rather than by complaining or trying to change it. To complain about conditions, or indeed to worry too much about them, are deeply felt to be signs of weakness and a character defect. We should point out that this emphasis on "resignation" is not intended to encourage "passivity" but on the contrary, stresses such qualities as "hardness," strength, or "force."

The principle was eloquently stated by one of the villagers this way: "I have some pear trees (avocado) and when those pears are bearing there is nothing I like more than pear. My mouth water for pear. But when my trees finish bearing, my mind not pan pear—done with that!" The value is expressed not only by the shift in meaning of "resignation," but also by a change in the term "predestination," defined by a villager as "What a man have is what he born with." One recalls the title of Billie Holiday's song, "God bless the child that's got his own." The ambiguities in these two phrasings express the value. Not only are you born into a certain condition of life, but you are also born with a certain force of character or person which is the measure of what you will be.

There is, of course, negative definition of the same value, and not only from outside. This centers on such terms as "care less" [nɔ kɛ], "don't care," and [mi naa nak ɔp], "I don't worry," and so on. These terms are ambiguous. They may describe the same value we have just been examining, or they may be used to characterize or express genuine irresponsibility. The line is hard to draw, for people who subscribe to a value of "resignation" may often be irresponsible by Euro-American standards. So it is ambiguous from which point of view the judgement is being made. Similarly, there is ambiguity about whether the term should be taken positively or negatively. It may, for instance, show up in dramatic low status assertions, as in

[mi nɔ kɛ wa mi du	I don't care what I do
kaz mi bIg, mi bad, an mi buɔ	cause I'm big, I'm bad and I'm boast-(ful) ('proud')
an mi jain di polis fuɔs]	and I've joined the police force.

In America it becomes the stereotype of "shiftlessness" and Faulkner's mystical "They endure."

The remodeling of symbols and the maintenance of a dual value system are thus intertwined. But we have seen that the maintenance of this system itself depends on values and patterns of expression that can be stated coherently only in terms of the *underlying* system. The values Herskovits noted are not English. We can see this by looking at one of the gestures indicating respect: turning the face, not looking directly into the eyes. Ask people why they don't look at you when they speak and they say things such as, "Wasn't I? an honest man looks you straight in the eye." This not only avoids the gesture but the whole idea of deference. Only if one starts with knowledge of the gestures and their meanings can one perhaps tease a person about his disrespectful behavior or otherwise elicit the principles involved. One's eyes should be turned aside in respect, one should not be "barefaced" or [fiɛsi] 'face-y.' (Yoruba informants have an explicit set of rules for these eye behaviors.)

Thomas J. Price in this volume has shown us that these underlying, hidden, "African" components of Caribbean societies have different cultural content in different sociohistorical contexts. But in the case of highly personal moral values and personal styles of verbal play of the kind we have been looking at, it would be gratuitous to overlook persuasive and reasonable African parallels. Often West African informants have been able to provide more explicit formulations than could be elicited in Antigua. When these were later tried out they proved to be applicable. The principle we have called "resignation" was recorded fully and explicitly from a Yoruba student while discussing the alternatives open to another student in a difficult situation.

In the last analysis, however, the ambiguities of symbol and value we have been looking at become effective by being built into village life and village social structure. Not surprisingly, a good part of the social relations of Antigua can be accounted for in terms of a color-class system and the norms and attitudes of status that accompany it. Yet lower class status, for rural villagers, is not just a position which one happens to occupy. It is also an *assertion*. There are both positive and negative aspects to low status membership. So there are a number of contexts in which, rather than simply conforming to the deference patterns accompanying such status, one asserts the status—and its lowness—by unruly, disorderly, and non-English behaviors associated with it. Low status and its attributes itself are thus themselves remodeled.

There are two techniques for this: overacceptance and the association of lowness with a brutish unruliness or natural disobedience. The latter process can be seen in the shifts of meaning of the terms "ignorant" and "stupid." These no longer describe a condition, but contain an assertion; for they have come to mean precisely "unruly" and "disobedient" and "stubborn." A low status person has the privilege of dramatizing his feelings by "going on ignorant." Overacceptance involves defining oneself as so low that no judgments are possible. One is characterized by an "absence." This can be seen in what happens to the terms "behavior" and "conduct" which form part of a formula which begins many village formal gatherings: A is for Attention, B is for Behavior, C is for Conduct, D is for Dignity.[8] The two middle terms are shifted so that they parallel the first and the last. That is, the adjectives "good" and "bad" no longer apply to them. "Conduct" and "Behavior" are transformed into high status qualities which one tends to *lack*. So people will say, "Have some behavior," or "You haven't any conduct." As we shall see, by polarizing action and speech between Conduct and the lack of it, such gatherings act out, in a ritualized, symbolic way, the claims and counter claims of high status model behavior and the reassertion of low status privileges and values. This may help explain the extraordinary amount of time devoted to such activity.

The ambiguity thus surrounding status is worked out in the religious scheme of things. Those who raise themselves up from low status are clearly using bad means, the devil's means, for only in the Lord will one be washed "Whiter than snow." In a sense then only the low are virtuous. On the other hand, being low they are unable to live up to any of the formal moral standards of the church. An interesting set of mechanisms in the structural relations of village to church ensure that the church should never come down from its high standards and actually discriminate villagers one from another on the basis of some adaptation of moral criteria.

It is in relation to these backgrounds that we must now look at the relations of Creole to English and their meaning in Antigua.

THE MEANING AND STATUS OF CREOLE

If there is a set of forms that are recognized as norms of Creole speech, to explain which we must assume a "competence" in Creole, then in some sense Creole must be said to exist. It is clear that for Antiguans, officially, no such competence exists. To understand the peculiar role of Creole in Antigua we must begin by understanding the dominance of English and of the idea of English in Antigua. A form of negative definition operates. All varieties of speech are considered to partake in varying degrees of the nature of *language*—that is, of English. Speech may be defined by villagers as lacking in language—that is, it may be "broken" or [brɔkɔp], as indeed the English have long defined it. A little more positively it may be "back way," a term also used for a man's children by women apart from his main household. Or it may be "bad language," a term which is purposely blurred into the meaning of "obscenity." Informally, however, one may hear such phrases as "our bad language" or remarks such as "It's ours and we love it." As we shall see, "to speak" may be called "to make noise." No term as positive, as the term "jagwa taak" that Beryl Bailey found in Jamaica (1966:6) exists in Antigua (if positive it is), although the term "rawback" [raabak] was sometimes used.

But English domination affects more than the names of speech. In speaking with non-Creole speakers, or in any formal context that uses English as a main code, villagers are almost universally both unwilling and unable to cite Creole forms, to translate from English to Creole, or to repeat Creole utterances in even vaguely the same form. Translation from Creole to English is possible if the speaker is willing to be aware of the Creole form he has used. The situation in Jamaica is probably not too much different, though Beryl Bailey found Jamaicans who could, as she says, "translate." From the point of view of linguistic institutions we should point out that the term "dialect" has found some acceptance in Jamaica as identifying alternative ways of speaking. This is essentially not so for Antigua.

Having understood all this, however, we must not make the error of assuming that as a result there are no norms for Creole forms. English penetrates, mixture is plentiful, if not predominant. But if we avoid starting with English, if we begin with Creole, or creolized forms, it can be relatively easy to find that there are standard forms and a normative pattern for Creole.[9]

One way is to begin with reduced forms. There are a number of ways in which forms, particularly Creole forms, may be changed or reduced by optional assimilations, ellipsis, or haplology (dropping of syllables), such changes usually being marked by features of vowel length, nasalization, and intonation. These changes are relevant in two ways. First, they are usually applied only to Creole forms (at least in the village). Second, and this is the immediate point here, these forms are explained in Creole. That is, if one of these reduced forms is spoken and someone asks what it was that was said, one is given not the English form but the Creole. Thus if one questions [bɔ́tnɔ táal ɔ́pnɔɔ bíɛs], one is not told, "But nothing at all is up at the base" or a variant of this. Rather, one is told [bɔ́t nɔ́tn taal ɔ́p ínɔ i bíɛs].

A second example, slightly more complex, reveals more about the workings of the reduction system. There is a contrast between the forms [mí nɔ waak], "I don't walk," as in [mi nɔ waak fo pöpɔs], "I don't walk unless I have to," and [míinɔ wáak], "I was walking." The only difference between these two is the length of the first vowel (also indicated by a shift in pitch). But the second form with the long or geminate vowel is actually one of a series of possible reductions of a full Creole form [mí mÍn dɛ́ wáak], "I was walking." The series of possible forms is:

[mí mÍn dɛ́ wáak
mí Ín dɛ́ wáak
mí Ínɔ wáak
míinɔ wáak]

Questioning any of the reduced forms will prompt people to cite the full Creole form, not a variant of the equivalent English form such as [a wɔz waakIn].

Another way to get at Creole normative patterns, and in one case directly at Creole competence, is through cases of misunderstanding resulting from the interference of linguistic systems. For there is system interference between Creole and local English norms at all levels: phonological, grammatical, and semantic. Again our point is not to establish this, although it has some interesting consequences, but rather to show how cases of interference bring out articulate awareness of Creole principles in village speakers. One fundamental phonological conflict is the distinctive use of vowel length in Creole.

[han] "hand" vs. [haan] "horn"
[wan] "one, a" vs. [waan] "want, warn"
[ba^i] "buy, by" vs. [baa^i] "boy"

(Nasalization is also distinctive and used for various functions: [ɔgli] "ugly" vs. [ɔ̃gli] "only.")

We pointed out above a contrast between [mi nɔ], "I don't," and [miinɔ], "I was ___ing" which depends on the distinction between long and short vowels. On one occasion I was speaking with several men. One of them used the form with the long vowel. He "was doing" something or other. I argued with him about it and a friend rushed to his defense. But the friend took his remark as a negative, the short vowel, and was defending the wrong position. I was trying to tell him he hadn't understood, when the original speaker broke in, "He's right. I said it *the long way*." So the fundamental distinctions are not only there, but may be brought to consciousness.

The other case I want to mention where interference brought out a Creole pattern is less dramatic. The English interogatives "where" and "why" have Creole alternants [wa paat] and [wa mɛk]. Occasionally the English form will not be understood by some speakers in some contexts. Thus trying to get into a building through a mass of construction work I asked, "Where is the best way to go in?" After this and variants of it had drawn several blanks a friend who was with me suggested that I ask instead [wa paat a di bɛs we fo go In].

To sum up, the point I am making here is not a formal point about the relations between varieties, although there are formal points to be made. It is precisely a sociocultural point—namely, that there is in speakers' minds a frame of reference, which if we like we may call a "Creole" model of linguistic competence. This model is maintained by—and must be discovered by—the same indirect means that maintain other low status values.

How the patterns of relationship between Creole and English are felt and conceived can best be seen by examining the parallels with relationships of other low status value patterns. All the cases of indirect maintenance of values we have looked at involve (1) remodeling of symbols, as well as extensive symbolic play and control, (2) both positive and negative definition and valuation, with negative terms likely to be ambiguous, and (3) the formal acceptance of "English" forms and discretion in revealing "non-English" forms and meanings. Creole is both characterized by and serves these processes.

1. One aspect of this is the way Creole lends itself to the creation of remodeled utterances. The assimilations, ellipses, and haplologies that we have already examined were, as we noted, optional and are subject to much more conscious control than are the reductions that normally occur in our casual speech. Along with a certain freedom in stress and juncture phonomena, they may, apart from disguise functions, be used in remodeling to increase the number of multi-meaning utterances available to a speaker. Although in Antigua these phenomena are primarily characteristic of, and mark, Creole speech; they play a significant role, in much Afro-American speech. Thus an example relevant to Americans comes from

the chairman of the delegation of the Mississippi Freedom Democratic Party, the alternate, primarily Negro, delegation from Mississippi to the 1964 Democratic National Convention, when he was being interviewed on network television. He referred to his group consistently as the Mississippi Free Dumocratic Party ([mIsIsIpríi]). There are at least three levels of meaning here: the actual name of the party; the free, not just the Freedom, Democratic party—long vowel; the Mississippi Democratic Party—no fourth word; and, if you like, an implication that the Democratic Party was being just a little dumb. Among other resources, this game used vowel length to mark the haplology, and a shift from labio-dental to bilabial fricative blurred with bilabial stop, all extremely common in the West Indies. See for example the alternation [bɛks] ~ [vɛks] "angry" and the words for the song "Archie Fuck Me Up." published as "Archie Buck Me Up" and sung with a bilabial fricative.

2. The acceptance of English and the negative definition of Creole as an absence (along with the positive standards for it we have tried to indicate) have their consequence in variation, a surprising amount of it controlled, and some of it not. Although one result is undoubtedly a large amount of mixed or loosely shifting speech, it is nevertheless surprising how much of this can be accounted for as "correction." The slightest modulation of situation or imagined role can cause a shift, as can any repetition. One lovely case involved an old country woman calling her donkey to "come here," a good fifty yards at least down the road from the gate to the British Administrator's residence. She was calling vigorously [kɔ̃ ya, kɔ̃ ya] when the Administrator appeared briefly at the gate from inside. The old lady immediately switched to a vociferous [keⁱm hⁱa, keⁱm hⁱa]. The extent to which the "high" variety and the notion of "correction" to it are part of the structure is testified to by the early age at which both learned. Thus I was bouncing a five-year-old child on my knee and talking to her, using Creole forms, when she turned to me and said, "You talk bad," and proceeded to turn my remarks into English. This girl came from a very ordinary village household both in terms of education and ambition.

The degree of creolization observed, for example, at a school fete depended, among other things, on the age of speaker and addressee, sex, general status and particular role, topic, genre, time of day, state of excitement, loudness of voice (i.e., distance between speakers), and so on.

3. The exceptional amount of attention Antiguans pay to speech variation would help to account for certain phenomena associated with discretion—both the fading effect and methods of speech disguise. By the fading effect I mean the tendency of Creole speech to fade or disappear without any marked or noticeable shift in the manner of speaking when outsiders, particularly whites, and even white investigators of language, approach. As far as disguise is concerned we have barely hinted at the repertoire of sound shifts available for this purpose. But there is also available an obverse of the fading effect—namely, that one can shade one's grammar and idiom away from parallels with standard English to forms which may have been rarely heard by an outsider.

While talking about disguise one should mention again a number of other devices which permit one to "pass remarks" in front of somebody's face. Allusion, of course, plays a large role, not only in disguised speech. Thus at a christening party instead of complaining directly about the absence of the baby, one may include as a passing reference, "And behold wise men came from the East saying, Where is He that is king of the Jews?" More linguistic, and suggestive of a range of techniques that should be investigated, is the avoidance of the mouth and face signals normally given in advance of speaking which usually prepare the listener for what is to be said. When these are omitted, unless one is accustomed to the practice, the message is finished before one is set to listen.

CREOLE AS SYMBOL

To complete our understanding of how Creole is felt and conceived, we should notice the degree and the ways in which Creole comes to symbolize just what is kept inside, just what is covered up, just what is "natural," and how at the same time there is an association between Creole and low status character, between Creole and noise, speaking Creole and "making noise."

Creole occurs in contexts of relaxation, expressiveness, involvement, and letting go. A phrase often associated with Creole is to "break away" into Creole, meaning also to let go of constraints, to be "natural." (But notice the pun with the negative term "broken language.") The constraints may, typically enough, be of two kinds. On the one hand there are the norms against direct confrontation. On the other are "English" standards of order, decorum, quietness, and authority.

Breaking the norms of non-confrontation is regularly associated with the use of Creole. When one can hold it no longer, one "gets vex" and one's feelings pour out in a stream of Creole. If the situation is severe and one feels that a public airing would help, this turns into a ritualized, dramatized behavior called a "cursing." The depth of the association of Creole with these kinds of release is illustrated by the fact that "getting vex" is the one context in which creolized speech still persists among adult members of the "middle class."

The power of Creole to symbolize what is inside a person, an unveiling of his nature, may be seen in another way in what happens to personal names with age or after death. Among the many names a person has is a nickname. The content of these nicknames may show traces of the old use of kin terms as respect greetings, as in [brɔdɔ], [ɔŋkl brɔdɔ], [graandi], and so on, or a birth order name such as [fɔs] "first." Most of them characterize the person in some way, as [lafi], [buuz], [waap]: "smile," "warp," and the like. They all represent a simplification in phonological shape, and a closer approximation to Creole norms of shape, than regular names do. Thus where connections can be established, "Norriston" becomes [naani], and others similarly. What is interesting in this for us is that as a person grows older these nicknames, with their old shape and old-style meanings, will be used more and more. After he dies, a person's formal name is soon lost completely, remembered perhaps by one or two people, so that there is a whole group of people, dead perhaps only ten years, remembered in the village only by their nicknames.

Creole is intrinsically felt to be the code of the genuine. School teachers, even head teachers, may, or may be forced to, move into Creole to convince the children that they really mean what they are saying. Thus other forms of speech carry some aura of falseness.

Since confrontation and Creole are associated, it is natural to expect that arguments would tend to creolize. This fact is used to provide a bridge between the two kinds of constraints Creole is felt to break, non-confrontation and "English" standards of decorum. Argument, as it breaks one norm and involves Creole, also comes to symbolize the breaking of the second set of constraints. An association is set up between argument, Creole, noise, and disorder. Both Creole and argument are referred to as "making noise." This, of course, is negative definition. People take great joy in making noise, as a matter of fact. As the Barbadian writer George Lamming put it, "So I made a heaven of noise, which is characteristic of my voice and an ingredient of West Indian behavior" (1960:62).

This is the basis of the symbolism of most village rituals. Meetings begin with a call for Conduct, and descend into "noise" and Creole via argument. In one case, christening parties, there is a ritual argument simply to make sure the inevitable happens. Two plates are provided at each end of the table. Money is placed on one to indicate that the cake on the table should be cut. "I say the cake must cut." On the other plate money is placed to support the contention that the cake should not be cut. "I am determined on my determination that this cake mustn't cut." Such a structure is an invitation to a general argument, with everybody talking at once and with increasing creolization of speech down from the chairman's formal English. When the noise becomes too great there will be a call to Conduct and a temporary reestablishment of order.

The oscillation between noise and order may thus be seen as tied in part to the alternations between Creole and standard language. The alternations are related to the dual pattern of values and of cultural and linguistic expression, which this paper has tried to explore.

But the maintenance of this dual pattern itself depends on the *underlying* values associated with "indirection," as we have tried to show above. In other words, there may well be an underlying continuity in certain fundamental orientations and forms of expression. In this light the pattern of argument and order may be seen as a form of expression that has persisted independently of its involvement in (and remodeling to fit) the cultural situation we have been describing. Suggestive from this point of view is a description by Bowen (Laura Bohannan) in *Return to Laughter* (1954:51–52):

> In this case, however, it was quite clear that the two men had brought a dispute for arbitration. At Kako's sign, one began his story, interrupted by questions from all the notables and punctuated by sarcastic comment and injured denial from the other. Soon everyone was saying so much, and so loudly, that no one could hear. Then someone screamed, "Shut up! Shut up!" until all had taken up the cry. Then a silence, and the case slowly warmed up to a shouting point again.

George Herzog and C. G. Blooah (1936) report a Jabo drum signal, used for controlling meetings, that goes, "Stop ye the noise: speak ye one by one."

CONCLUSION

If we are to look at linguistic codes as part of human communication in a social and cultural setting, then we have to ask how the codes themselves are identified and maintained. How are their patterns of relationship felt and conceived. As Dell Hymes has said, "If the community's own theory of code repertoire and code switching is considered, as it should be in any serious descriptive approach, matters become even more complex and interesting" (1967:20). We have seen that Antiguans maintain a covert duality of both cultural and linguistic values. Their "theory of code repertoire" is communicated by ambiguities of naming, expressions, and form. It is ambiguity of variety and meaning which is at the heart of the code system. This imposes important qualifications on just what is being explained by grammatical theories that rely on speakers' intuitions and yet describe "an idealized speaker-hearer in a homogenous speech situation" (Chomsky 1965:3). Understanding these ambiguities is a prerequisite to understanding the role of language in much of Afro-Caribbean culture.

NOTES

1. Field research was conducted in Antigua in 1960–61 under a grant from the Institute of Caribbean Studies, University of Puerto Rico. I should like to express my appreciation to its then director Dr. Richard Morse, and to the late Hans Wolff, who gave me much useful advice in preparing my research. J. Oliver Davis and his family have given to this work at every turn. There is no adequate repayment for their concern.

2. Duality is shared along almost the whole linguistic range. The exception is Haiti, where national independence has been accompanied by a relatively monolingual population. Over a good part of the range the duality involves as one code a set of grammatical, phonological, and semantic features to which the term "Creole" has been applied. The functions this Creole performs and the degree to which it is institutionalized are patterned differently over the range. So we may move from the monolingual Creole speakers of rural Haiti, through the coexistence of English-based Creole and Dutch in Surinam, to the coexistence of named Creoles with similar European languages in Martinique and British Honduras (Belize), to what we may call the "hidden" Creoles of Jamaica and the Leeward Islands, to a number of (relatively unstudied) American Negro dialects, to the in-group style shifts of middle class American Negroes. All of these, including varieties to which no one would dream of extending the term "Creole," share certain phonological processes and a number of other features.

3. Some Americans who have read this in draft have assumed that the relationships involved are white-black. As anyone involved with the Caribbean knows, this is not the case. The society may be described as organized in a "color-class" system (R. T. Smith 1956:191–96), most of whose status and cultural relations exist within a category that would be called black in the United States (from certain points of view). While the white presence is crucial to the system, the actual number of whites on Antigua has varied considerably. At the time of the fieldwork, they could almost be counted on both hands.

4. My thanks to William Stewart for forcefully pointing this out in discussion, thus leading me to clarify my whole thinking on the subject of transvaluation and persistence.

5. John Szwed, personal communication.

6. Since this was first written, Peter Wilson has tried to show how this duality pervades village structure throughout the various metropolitan spheres of the Caribbean (ms.). He has characterized it by an opposition of respect vs. reputation, the first external and status oriented, the latter internal and focusing on personal values. He has tied this division to age and sex roles (ms. and 1969), older people and women being more closely associated with respect, younger

men being more closely organized around reputation. As my discussion of respect shows, I feel that the notion is itself quite divided and ambivalent and tied to fundamental philosophical values deeply held, as well as to notions of status. That older people re-enact the value and status hierarchy within the village is very true, however. Their relation to the church and other external institutions is in fact a mechanism that insures that these will maintain a sufficiently lofty tone and outlook so as not to interfere with the actual conduct of village life. I am less clear about the ease with which one places women's roles and values in this scheme.

7. This discussion raises methological problems of some concern and interest. For if proper relationship to people, enough time, and sensitivity are necessary to elicit the values, then there is a real sense in which such material is *not* replicable by different field researchers in any automatic way, and in which there are no "procedures" which will automatically lead to significant categories or ways of relating them. And yet this is not to say that the material is not replicable by the same field worker or by more than one field worker if they have sufficient mastery of the cues. The material may then be subject to test, yet there is no guarantee that two researchers will be led to the same formulation or awareness.

In this case there has been notable convergence with the perceptions of Peter Wilson, operating with a different theoretical framework, different interests, and working on a very different West Indian island.

8. Roger Abrahams in this volume has noted similar formulas on Nevis.

9. We might point out that this pursuit of Creole is not uninteresting on formal grounds, for it would make some sense out of the fact that in purely formal terms Antiguan creolized English or English-based Creole speech closely parallels the named, conscious Creole of British Honduras (Belize), and more distantly parallels, and has some reconstructable historical relationships with, the form of Sranan. Mervyn Alleyne has rejected such a common classification of Creoles on the grounds that in some of the cases the codes function in intelligibility chains ("language simplexes") (i.e., Jamaica, Haiti, Antigua) while in other cases they do not (i.e., (Surinam). "The reality is that Jamaican Creole is a dialect of English. . . . Sranan and Papiementu are languages, not 'creoles'" (1967:93). But Gumperz (1967) has shown how languages which on formal grounds must be classified as belonging to distinct genetic families can nevertheless function in an intelligiblity chain and formal divergence is not simple or clear. Thus I see no ground for separating the Caribbean Creoles—certainly not the Creoles of the same vocabulary base—one from another. Alleyne(1968) has somewhat modified his position on this, at least enough to have carried out very exciting comparisons of the codes involved and significantly reconsidering their historical development.

Seven

TOWARD AN ETHNOGRAPHY OF BLACK AMERICAN SPEECH BEHAVIOR

Thomas Kochman

A shorter version of this essay appeared in *Trans-Action*, Vol. 6, No. 4, (February 1969), pp. 26–34.

In the black idiom of Chicago and elsewhere, there are several words that refer to talking; *rapping*, *shucking*, *jiving*, *running it down*, *gripping*, *copping a plea*, *signifying*, and *sounding*. Led by the assumption that these terms, as used by the speakers, referred to different kinds of verbal behavior, this writer has attempted to discover which features of form, style, and function distinguish one type of talk from the other. In this pursuit, we would hope to be able to identify the variable threads of the communication situation: speaker, setting and audience, and how they influence the use of language within the social context of the black community. We also expect that some light would be shed on the black perspective behind a speech event, on those orientating values and attitudes of the speaker that cause him to behave or perform in one way as opposed to another.

The guidelines and descriptive framework for the type of approach used here have been articulated most ably by Hymes in his introduction to the publication, *The Ethnography of Communication* (Gumperz and Hymes 1964: 2ff.), from which I quote:

> In short, "ethnography of communication" implies two characteristics that an adequate approach to the problems of language which engage anthropologists must have. Firstly, such an approach cannot simply take results from linguistics, psychology, sociology, ethnology, as given, and seek to correlate them, however partially useful such work is. It must call attention to the need for fresh kinds of data, to the need to investigate directly the use of language in contexts of situation so as to discern patterns proper to speech activity, patterns which escape separate studies of grammar, of personality, of religion, of kinship and the like, each abstracting from the patterning of speech activity as such into some other frame of reference. Secondly, such an approach cannot take linguistic form, a given code, or speech

itself, as frame of reference. It must take as context a community, investigating its communicative habits as a whole, so that any given use of channel and code takes its place as but part of the resources upon which the members of the community draw.

It is not that linguistics does not have a vital role. Well analyzed linguistic materials are indispensable, and the logic of linguistic methodology is a principal influence in the ethnographic perspective of the approach. It is rather that it is not linguistics, but ethnography—not language, but communication—which must provide the frame of reference within which the place of language in culture and society is to be described.

The following description and analysis is developed from information supplied mainly by blacks living within the inner city of Chicago. Their knowledge of the above terms, their ability to recognize and categorize the language behavior of others (e.g., "Man, stop shucking!"), and on occasion, to give examples themselves, established them as reliable informants. Although a general attempt has been made here to illustrate the different types of language behavior from field sources, I have had, on occasion, to rely on published material to provide better examples, such as the writings of Malcolm X, Robert Conot, Iceberg Slim, and others. Each example cited from these authors, however, is regarded as authentic by my informants. In my own attempts at classification and analysis I have sought confirmation from the same group.

Rapping, while used synonymously to mean ordinary conversation, is distinctively a fluent and lively way of talking which is always characterized by a high degree of personal narration, a colorful rundown of some past event. A recorded example of this type of rap follows, an answer from a Chicago gang member to a youth worker who asked how his group became organized.

Now I'm goin tell you how the jive really started. I'm goin tell you how the club got this big. 'Bout 1956 there used to be a time when the Jackson Park show was open and the Stony show was open. Sixty-six street, Jeff, Gene, all of 'em, little bitty dudes, little bitty. . . . . Gene wasn't with 'em then. Gene was cribbin (living) over here. Jeff, all of 'em, real little bitty dudes, you dig? All of us were little.

Sixty-six (the gang on sixty sixth street), they wouldn't allow us in the Jackson Park show. That was when the parky (?) was headin it. Everybody say, If we want to go to the show, we go! One day, who was it? Carl Robinson. He went up to the show . . . and Jeff fired on him. He came back and all this was swelled up 'bout yay big, you know. He come back over to the hood (neighbourhood). He told (name unclear) and them dudes went up there. That was when mostly all the main sixty-six boys was over here like Bett Riley. All of 'em was over here. People that quit gang-bangin [fighting, especially as a group], Marvell Gates, people like that.

They went on up there, John, Roy and Skeeter went in there. And they start humbuggin (fighting) in there. That's how it all started. Sixty-six found out they couldn't beat us, at *that* time. They couldn't *whup* seven-o (70). Am I right Leroy? You was cribbin over here then. Am I right? We were dynamite! Used to be a time, you ain't have a passport, Man, you couldn't walk through here. And if didn't nobody know you it was worse than that. . . .

Rapping to a woman is a colorful way of "asking for some pussy." "One needs to throw a lively rap when he is 'putting the make' on a broad" (Horton 1967:6).

According to one informant the woman is usually someone he had seen or just met, looks good, and might be willing to have sexual intercourse with him. My informant remarked that the term would not be descriptive of talk between a couple "who have had a relationship over any length of time." Rapping then, is used by the speaker at the beginning of a relationship to create a favorable impression and be persuasive at the same time. The man who has the reputation for excelling at this is the pimp, or mack man. Both terms describe a person of considerable status in the street hierarchy, who, by his lively and persuasive rapping (*macking* is also used in this context), has acquired a stable of girls to hustle for him and give him money. For most street men and many teenagers he is the model whom they try to emulate. Thus, within the community you have a pimp walk, pimp style boots and clothes, and perhaps most of all "pimp talk." A colorful literary example of a telephone rap, which one of my informants regards as extreme, but agrees that it illustrates the language, style, and technique of rapping, is set forth in Iceberg Slim's book *Pimp: The Story of My Life* (© 1967 Holloway House, Los Angeles; used by permission), p. 179. "Blood" is rapping to an ex-whore named Christine in an effort to trap her into his stable.

> Now try to control yourself baby. I'm the tall stud with the dreamy bedroom eyes across the hall in four-twenty. I'm the guy with the pretty towel wrapped around his sexy hips. I got the same hips on now that you x-rayed. Remember that hump of sugar your peepers feasted on?
> She said, "Maybe, but you shouldn't call me. I don't want an incident. What do you want? A lady doesn't accept phone calls from strangers.
> I said, "A million dollars and a trip to the moon with a bored, trapped, beautiful bitch, you dig? I'm no stranger. I've been popping the elastic in your panties ever since you saw me in the hall...."

Field examples of this kind of rapping were difficult to obtain primarily because talk of this nature generally occurs in private, and when occurring in public places such as parties and taverns, it is carried on in an undertone. However, the first line of a rap, which might be regarded as introductory, is often overheard. What follows are several such lines collected by two of my students in and around the south and west side of Chicago:

> Say pretty, I kin tell you need lovin' by the way you wiggle your ass when you walk—and I'm jus' the guy what' kin put out yo' fire."
> "Let me rock you mamma, I kin satisfy your soul.
> Say, baby, give me the key to your pad. I want to play with your cat.
> Baby, you're fine enough to make me spend my rent money.
> Baby, I sho' dig your mellow action.

Rapping between men and women often is competitive and leads to a lively repartee, with the woman becoming as adept as the men. An example follows:

> A man coming from the bathroom forgot to zip his pants. An unescorted party of women kept watching him and laughing among themselves. The man's friends "hip" [inform] him to what's going on. He approaches one woman—"Hey baby, did you see that big black Cadillac with the full tires ready to roll in action just for you?" She answers—"No mother-fucker, but I saw a little gray Volkswagen with two flat tires."
> Everybody laughs. His rap was *capped* (excelled, topped).

When "whupping the game" on a "trick" or "lame" (trying to get goods or services from someone who looks like he can be swindled), rapping is often descriptive of the highly stylized verbal part of the maneuver. In well established "con games" the verbal component is carefully prepared and used with great skill in directing the course of the transaction. An excellent illustration of this kind of "rap" came from an adept hustler who was playing the "murphy" game on a white trick. The maneuvers in the "murphy" game are designed to get the *trick* to give his money to the hustler, who in this instance poses as a "steerer" (one who directs or steers customers to a brothel), to keep the whore from stealing it. The hustler then skips with the money (Iceberg Slim 1967:38).

> Look Buddy, I know a fabulous house not more than two blocks away. Brother you ain't never seen more beautiful, freakier broads than are in that house. One of them, the prettiest one, can do more with a swipe than a monkey can with a banana. She's like a rubber doll; she can take a hundred positions.
> At this point the sucker is wild to get to this place of pure joy. He entreats the con player to take him there, not just direct him to it.
> The "murphy" player will prat him (pretend rejection) to enhance his desire. He will say, "Man, don't be offended, but Aunt Kate, that runs the house don't have nothing but highclass white men coming to her place. ... you know, doctors, lawyers, big-shot politicians. You look like a clean-cut white man, but you ain't in that league are you?

After a few more exchanges of the "murphy" dialogue, "the mark is separated from his scratch."

An analysis of rapping indicates a number of things. For instance, it is revealing that one raps *to* rather than *with* a person, supporting the impression that rapping is to be regarded more as a performance than a verbal exchange. As with other performances, rapping projects the personality, physical appearance, and style of the performer. In each of the examples given above, in greater or lesser degree, the intrusive "I" of the speaker was instrumental in contributing to the total impression of the rap.

The relative degree of the personality-style component of rapping is generally highest when "asking for some pussy" (rapping 2) and lower when "whupping the game" on someone (rapping 3) or "running something down" (rapping 1). In each instance, however, the personality style component is higher than any other in producing the total effect on the listener.

In asking "for some pussy," for example, where personality and style might be projected through non-verbal means (stance, clothing, walking, looking), one can speak of a "silent rap" where the woman is won without the use of words, or rather, with the words being implied that would generally accompany the non-verbal components.

As a lively way of "running it down" the verbal element consists of two parts: the personality-style component and the information component. Someone *reading* my example of the gang member's narration might get the impression that the information component would be more influential in directing the audience response—that the youth worker would say "So that's how the gang got so big," in which case he would be responding to the information component, instead of saying "Man, that gang member is *bad* (strong, brave)," in which instance he would be responding to the personality-style component of the rap. However, if the reader would *listen* to the gang member on tape or could have been present (*watching-listening*) when the gang-member spoke, he more likely would have reacted more to the personality-style component, as my informants did.

Supporting this hypothesis is the fact that in attendance with the youth worker were members of the gang who *already knew* how the gang got started (e.g., "Am I right, Leroy? You was cribbin over there then"), and for whom the information component by itself would have little interest. Their attention was held by the *way* the information was presented—i.e., directed toward the personality-style component.

The verbal element in "whupping the game" on someone, in the above illustration, was an integral part of an overall deception in which the information component and the personality-style component were skillfully manipulated to control the "trick's" response. But again, greater weight must be given to the personality-style component. In the "murphy game," for example, it was this element which got the trick to *trust* the hustler and to leave his money with him for "safekeeping."

The function of rapping in each of the forms discussed above is *expressive*. By this I mean that the speaker raps to project his personality onto the scene or to evoke a generally favorable response from another person or group. In addition, when rapping is used to "ask for some pussy" (rapping 2) or to "whup the game" on someone (rapping 3), its function is *directive*. By this I mean that rapping here becomes the instrument used to manipulate and control people to get them to give up or do something. The difference between rapping to a *fox* (pretty girl) for the purpose of "getting inside her pants" and rapping to a *lame* to get something from him is operational rather than functional. The latter rap contains a concealed motivation whereas the former does not. A statement made by one of my high school informants illustrates this distinction. "If I wanted something from a guy I would try to *trick* him out of it. If I wanted something from a girl I would try to *talk* her out of it (emphasis mine)."

Shucking, shucking it, shucking and jiving, S-ing and J-ing or just *jiving*, are terms that refer to one form of language behavior practiced by the black when interacting with "the Man" (the white man, the establishment, or *any* authority figure), and to another form of language behavior practiced by blacks when interacting with each other on the peer group level.

When referring to the black's dealings with the white man and the power structure, the above terms are descriptive of the talk and accompanying physical movements of the black that are appropriate to some momentary guise, posture, or facade.

Originally in the South, and later in the North, the black learned that American society had assigned to him a restrictive role and status. Among whites his behavior had to conform to this imposed station and he was constantly reminded to "keep his place." He learned that before white people it was not acceptable to show feelings of indignation, frustration, discontent, pride, ambition, or desire; that real feelings had to be concealed behind a mask of innocence, ignorance, childishness, obedience, humility, and deference. The terms used by the black to describe the role he played before white folks in the South was "tomming" or "jeffing." Failure to accommodate the white southerner in this respect was almost certain to invite psychological and often physical brutality. The following description by black psychiatrist Alvin F. Poussaint (1967:53) is typical and revealing:

> Once last year as I was leaving my office in Jackson, Miss., with my Negro secretary, a white policeman yelled, "Hey, boy! Come here!" Somewhat bothered, I retorted: "I'm no boy!" He then rushed at me, inflamed and stood towering over me, snorting "What d'ja say, boy?" Quickly he frisked me and demanded "What's your name, boy?" Frightened, I replied, "Dr. Poussaint, I'm a physician." He angrily chuckled and hissed, "What's your first name, boy?" When I hesitated he assumed a threatening stance and clenched his fists. As my heart palpitated, I muttered in profound humiliation, "Alvin."
>
> He continued his psychological brutality, bellowing, "Alvin, the next time I call you, you come right away, you hear? You hear?" I hesitated. "You hear me, boy?" My voice trembling with helplessness, but *following my instincts of self-preservation*, I murmured, "Yes,

sir." *Now fully satisfied that I had performed and acquiesced to my "boy" status*, he dismissed me with, "Now boy, go on and get out of here or next time we'll take you for a little ride down to the station house! (emphasis mine)."

In northern cities the black encountered authority figures equivalent to the southern "crackers": policemen, judges, probation officers, truant officers, teachers, and "Mr. Charlies" (bosses), and soon learned that the way to get by and avoid difficulty was to *shuck*. Thus, he learned to accommodate "the Man," to use the total orchestration of speech, intonation, gesture, and facial expression to produce whatever appearance would be acceptable. It was a technique and ability that was developed from fear, a respect for power, and a will to survive. This type of accommodation is exemplified by the "Yes sir, Mr. Charlie," or "Anything you say, Mr. Charlie," "Uncle Tom" type "Negro" of the North. The language and behavior of accommodation was the prototype out of which other slightly modified forms of shucking evolved.

Through accommodation, many blacks became adept at concealing and controlling their emotions and at assuming a variety of postures. They became competent actors in the process. Many developed a keen perception of what affected, motivated, appeased, or satisfied the authority figures with whom they came into contact. What became an accomplished and effective coping mechanism for many blacks to "stay out of trouble" became for others a useful artifice for avoiding arrest or "getting out of trouble" when apprehended. *Shucking it* with a judge, for example, would be to feign repentance in the hope of receiving a lighter or suspended sentence, with a probation officer to give the impression of being serious and responsible so that if you violate probation, you would not be sent back to jail. Robert Conot reports an example of the latter in his book (1967:333):

> Joe was found guilty of possession of narcotics. But he did an excellent job of shucking it with the probation officer.

The probation officer interceded for Joe with the judge as follows:

> His own attitude toward the present offense appears to be serious and responsible and it is believed that the defendant is an excellent subject for probation.

Some field illustrations of *shucking* to get out of trouble after having been caught come from some seventh grade children from an inner city school in Chicago. The children were asked to "talk their way out of" a troublesome situation. Examples of the situation and their impromptu responses follow:

> **Situation:** You're cursing at this old man and your mother comes walking down the stairs. She hears you. Response to "talk your way out of this," "I'd tell her that I was studying a scene in school for a play."
> **Situation:** What if you were in a store and were stealing something and the manager caught you. Responses: "I would tell him that I was used to putting things in my pocket and then going to pay for them and show the cashier."
> "I'd tell him that some of my friends was outside and they wanted some candy so I was goin to put it in my pocket to see if it would fit before I bought it."
> "I would start stuttering. Then I would say, 'Oh, Oh, I forgot. Here the money is'."
> **Situation:** What do you do when you ditch school and you go to the beach and a truant officer walks up and says, "Are you having fun?" and you say, "Yeah," and you don't know he is a truant officer and then he says, "I'm a truant officer, what are you doing out of school?" Responses: "I'd tell him that I had been expelled from school, that I wasn't supposed to go back to school for seven days."

"I'd tell him that I had to go to the doctor to get a checkup and that my mother said I might as well stay out of school the whole day and so I came over here."

Situation: You're at the beach and they've got posted signs all over the beach and floating on the water and you go past the swimming mark and the sign says "Don't go past the mark!" How do you talk your way out of this to the lifeguard? Responses: "I'd tell him that I was having so much fun in the water that I didn't pay attention to the sign." "I'd say that I was swimming under water and when I came back up I was behind the sign."

One literary and one field example of shucking to avoid arrest follow. The literary example of shucking comes from Iceberg Slim's autobiography, already cited above (1967:294). Iceberg, a pimp, shucks before "two red-faced Swede rollers (detectives)" who catch him in a motel room with his whore. My underlining identifies which elements of the passage constitute the shuck.

> I put my shaking hands into the pajama pockets.... *I hoped I was keeping the fear out of my face. I gave them a wide toothy smile*. They came in and stood in the middle of the room. Their eyes were racing about the room. Stacy was open mouthed in the bed.
> I said, *"Yes gentlemen, what can I do for you?"* Lanky said, "We wanta see your I. D."
> I went to the closet and got the phony John Cato Fredrickson I. D. I put it in his palm. I felt cold sweat running down my back. They looked at it, then looked at each other.
> "Lanky said, "You are in violation of the law. You signed the motel register improperly. Why didn't you sign your full name? What are you trying to hide? What are you doing here in town? It says here you're a dancer. We don't have a club in town that books entertainers."
> I said, *Officers, my professional name is Johnny Cato. I've got nothing to hide. My full name had always been too long for the marquees. I've fallen into the habit of using the shorter version. My legs went out last year. I don't dance anymore. My wife and I decided to go into business. We are making a tour of this part of the country. We think that in your town we've found the ideal site for a southern fried chicken shack. My wife has a secret recipe that should make us rich here.*

The following example from the field was related to me by one of my colleagues. One Negro gang member was coming down the stairway from the club room with seven guns on him and encountered some policemen coming up the same stairs. If they stopped and frisked him, he and others would have been arrested. A paraphrase of his shuck follows: "Man, I gotta get away from up there. There's gonna be some trouble and I don't want no part of it." This shuck worked on the minds of the policemen. It anticipated their questions as to why he was leaving the club room, and why he would be in a hurry. He also gave *them* a reason for wanting to get up to the room fast.

It ought to be mentioned at this point that there was not uniform agreement among my informants in characterizing the above examples as shucking. One informant used shucking only in the sense in which it is used among the black peer group—viz., bullshitting—and characterized the above examples as *jiving or whupping game*. Others, however, identified the above examples as shucking and reserved *jiving and whupping game* for more offensive maneuvers. In fact, one of the apparent criterial features of shucking is that the posture of the black when interacting with members of the establishment be a *defensive* one. Some of my informants, for example, regarded the example of a domestic who changed into older clothing than she could afford before going to work in a white household as shucking, provided that she were doing it to keep her job. On the other hand, if she would be doing it to get a raise in pay, they regarded the example as *whupping the game*. Since the same guise and set of maneuvers are brought into play in working on the mind and feeling of the domestic's boss, the difference would seem to be whether the reason behind the pose were to protect oneself or to gain some advantage. Since this distinction is not always so clearly drawn, opinions are often divided. The following example is clearly ambiguous in this respect. Frederick Douglass (1968:57), in telling of how he taught himself to read, would challenge a white boy with whom he was playing by saying that he could write as well as the white boy, whereupon he would write down all the letters he knew. The white boy would then write down more letters than Douglass did. In this way, Douglass eventually learned all the letters of the alphabet. Some of my informants regarded the example as whupping game. Others regarded it as shucking. The former were perhaps focusing on the maneuver rather than the language used. The latter may have felt that any maneuvers designed to learn to read were justifiably defensive. One of my informants said Douglass was "shucking *in order to* whup the game." This latter response seems to be the most revealing. Just as one can *rap* to whup the game on someone, so one can *shuck* or *jive* for the same purpose—i.e., assume a guise or posture or perform some action in a certain way that is designed to work on someone's mind to get him to give up something. The following examples from Malcolm X (1965:87) illustrate the use of *shucking* and *jiving* in this context, though *jive* is the term used. Today, *whupping game* might also be the term used to describe the operation.

Whites who came at night got a better reception; the several Harlem nightclubs they patronized were geared to entertain and *jive* (flatter, cajole) the night white crowd to get their money.

The maneuvers involved here are clearly designed to obtain some benefit or advantage.

Freddy got on the stand and went to work on his own shoes. Brush, liquid polish, brush, paste wax, shine rag, lacquer sole dressing . . . step by step, Freddie showed me what to do. "But you got to get a whole lot faster. You can't waste time!" Freddie showed me how fast on my own shoes. Then because business was tapering off, he had time to give me a demonstration of how to make the shine rag pop like a firecracker. "Dig the action?" he asked. He did it in slow motion. I got down and tried it on his shoes. I had the principle of it. "Just got to do it faster," Freddie said. "*It's a jive noise, that's all. Cats tip better, they figure you're knocking yourself out!*" (Malcolm X 1965:48, emphasis mine).

I was involved in a field example in which an eight-year-old boy whupped the game on me as follows:

My colleague and I were sitting in a room listening to a tape. The door to the room was open and outside was a soda machine. Two boys came up in the elevator, stopped at the soda machine, and then came into the room and asked: "Do you have a dime for two nickels?" Presumably, the soda machine would not accept nickels. I took out the change in my pocket, found a dime and gave it to the boy for two nickels. After accepting the dime, he looked at the change in my hand and asked, "Can I have two cents? I need carfare to get home." I gave him the two cents.

At first I assumed the verbal component of the maneuver was the rather weak, transparently false reason for wanting the two cents. Actually, as was pointed out to me later, the maneuver began with the first question, which was designed to get me to show my money. He could then ask me for something that he knew I had, making my refusal more difficult. He apparently felt that the reason need not be more than plausible because the amount he wanted was small. Were the amount larger, he would no doubt have elaborated on the verbal element of the game. The form of the verbal element could be directed toward *rapping* or *shucking and jiving*. If he were to rap, the eight-year-old might say, "Man, you know a cat needs to have a little bread to keep the girls in line." Were he to shuck and jive he might make the reason for needing the money more compelling: look hungry, or something similar.

The function of shucking and jiving as it refers to transactions involving confrontation between blacks and "the Man" is both expressive and directive. It is language behavior designed to work on the mind and emotions of the authority figure to get him to feel a certain way or give up something that will be to the other's advantage. When viewed in its entirety, shucking must be regarded as a performance. Words and gestures become the instruments for promoting a certain image, or posture. In the absence of words, shucking would be descriptive of the *actions* which constitute the deception, as in the above example from Malcolm X, where the movement of the shine rag in creating the "jive noise" was the deceptive element. Similarly, in another example, a seventh grade boy recognized the value of stuttering before saying, "Oh, I forgot. Here the money is," knowing that stuttering would be an invaluable aid in presenting a picture of innocent intent. Iceberg showed a "toothy smile" which said to the detective, "I'm glad to see you" and "Would I be glad to see you if I had something to hide?"

When the maneuvers seem to be defensive, most of my informants regarded the language behavior as shucking. When the maneuvers were offensive, my informants tended to regard the behavior as "whupping the game." The difference in perception is culturally significant.

Also significant is the fact that the first form of shucking which I have described above, which developed out of accommodation, is becoming less frequently used today by many blacks, as a result of a new found self-assertiveness and pride, challenging the system "that is so brutally and unstintingly suppressive of self-assertion" (Poussaint 1967:52). The willingness on the part of many blacks to accept the psychological and physical brutality and general social consequences of not "keeping one's place" is indicative of the changing self-concept of the black man. Ironically, the shocked reaction of the white power structure to the present militancy of the black is partly due to the fact that the black has been so successful at "putting whitey on" via shucking in the past—i.e., compelling a belief in whatever posture the black chose to assume. The extent to which this attitude has penetrated the black community can be seen from a conversation I recently had with a shoe shine attendant at O'Hare airport in Chicago.

I was having my shoes shined and the black attendant was using a polishing machine instead of the rag that was generally used in the past. I asked whether the machine made his work any easier. He did not answer me until about ten seconds had passed and then responded in a loud voice that he "never had a job that was easy, that he would give me one hundred dollars for any *easy* job I could offer him, that the machine made his job 'faster' but not 'easier.'" I was startled at the response because it was so unexpected and I realized that here was a new "breed of cat" who was not going to *shuck* for a big tip or ingratiate himself with "whitey" anymore. A few years ago his response would have been different.

The contrast between this "shoe-shine" scene and the one illustrated earlier from Malcom X's autobiography, when "shucking whitey" was the common practice, is striking.

Shucking, jiving, shucking and jiving, or *S-ing and J-ing*, when referring to language behavior practiced by blacks when interacting with one another on the peer group level, is descriptive of the talk and gestures that are appropriate to "putting someone on" by creating a false impression, conveying false information, and the like. The terms seem to cover a range from simply telling a lie, to bull-shitting, to subtly playing with someone's mind. An important difference between this form of shucking and that described earlier is that the same talk and gestures that are deceptive to "the Man" are often transparent to those members of one's own group who are able practitioners at shucking themselves. As Robert Conot has pointed out (1967:161), "The Negro who often fools the white officer by 'shucking it' is much less likely to be successful with another Negro. . . ." Also, S-ing and J-ing within the group often has play overtones in which the person being "put on" is aware of the attempts being made and goes along with it for the enjoyment of it or in appreciation of the style involved. As example from Iceberg Slim illustrates this latter point (1967:162):

> He said, "Ain't you the little shit ball I chased outta the Roost?"
> I said, "Yeah, I'm one and the same. I want to beg your pardon for making you salty (angry) that night. Maybe I coulda gotten a pass if I had told you I'm your pal's nephew. I ain't got no sense, Mr. Jones. I took after my idiot father."

Mr. Jones, perceiving Iceberg's shuck, says,

> "Top, this punk ain't hopeless. He's silly as a bitch grinning all the time, but dig how he butters the con to keep his balls outta the fire."

Other citations showing the use of *shucking* and *jiving* to mean simply *lying* follow:

> It as a *jive* (false) tip but there were a lot of cats up there on humbles (framed up charges)" (Brown 1965:142).
> How would you like to have half a "G" ($500) in your slide (pocket)?
> I said, "All right, give me the poison and take me to the baby."
> He said, "I ain't *shucking* (lying). It's cream-puff work" (Iceberg Slim 1967:68).

Running it down is the term used by ghetto dwellers when they intend to communicate information, either in the form of an explanation, narrative, giving advice, and the like The information component in the field example cited under rapping (1) would constitute the "run down." In the following literary example, Sweet Mac is "running this Edith broad down" to his friends (King 1965:24):

> Edith is the "saved" broad who can't marry out of her religion . . . or do anything else out of her religion for that matter, especially what I wanted her to do. A bogue religion, man! So dig, for the last couple weeks I been quoting the Good Book and all that stuff to her; telling her I am now saved myself, you dig.

The following citation from Claude Brown (1965:390) uses the term with the additional sense of giving advice:

> If I saw him (Claude's brother) hanging out with cats I knew were weak, who might be

using drugs sooner or later, I'd *run it down* to him.

Iceberg Slim (1967:79) asks a bartender regarding a prospective whore:

> Sugar, *run her down* to me. Is the bitch qualified? Is she a whore? Does she have a man?

It seems clear that running it down has simply an informative function, telling somebody something that he doesn't already know.

Gripping is of fairly recent vintage, used by black high school students in Chicago to refer to the talk and facial expression that accompanies a *partial* loss of face or self-possession, or displaying of fear. Its appearance alongside *copping a plea*, which refers to a total loss of face, in which one begs one's adversary for mercy, is a significant new perception. Linking it with the street code which acclaims the ability to "look tough and inviolate, fearless, secure, 'cool'," (Horton 1967:11) suggests that even the slightest weakening of this posture will be held up to ridicule and contempt. There are always contemptuous overtones attached to the use of the term when applied to others' behavior. One is tempted to link it further with the degree of violence and level of toughness that is required to survive on the street. The intensity of both seems to be increasing. As one of my informants noted, "Today, you're *lucky* if you end up in the hospital" (i.e., are not killed).

Both *gripping* and *copping a plea* refer to behavior that stems from fear and a respect for superior power. An example of gripping comes from the record *Street and Gangland Rhythms* (Band 4, Dumb boy). Lennie meets Calvin and asks him what happened to his lip. Calvin tells Lennie that a boy named Pierre hit him for copying off him in school.

Lennie, pretending to be Calvin's brother, goes to confront Pierre. Their dialogue follows:

> Lennie: "Hey you! What you hit my little brother for?"
> Pierre: "Did he tell you what happen man?"
> Lennie: "Yeah, he told me what happen."
> Pierre: "But you ... but you ... but you should tell your people to teach him to go to school, man. (Pause) I ... I know ... I know I didn't have a right to hit him."

Pierre, anticipating a fight with Lennie if he continued to justify his hitting of Calvin, tried to avoid it by "gripping" with the last line.

Copping a plea, originally used to mean "to plead guilty to a lesser charge to save the state the cost of a trial," (Wentworth and Flexner 1960:123) (with the hope of receiving a lesser or suspended sentence), but is now generally used to mean "to beg, plead for mercy," as in the example "Please cop, don't hit me. I give" (*Street and Gangland Rhythms*, Band 1, Gang fight). This change of meaning can be seen from its use by Piri Thomas (1967:316) in *Down These Mean Streets*.

> The night before my hearing, I decided to make a prayer. It had to be on my knees, cause if I was gonna *cop a plea* to God, I couldn't play it cheap.

For the original meaning, Thomas (1967:245) uses "deal for a lower plea."

> I was three or four months in the Tombs, waiting for a trial, going to court, waiting for adjournments, trying to *deal for a lower plea*, and what not.

The function of gripping and copping a plea is obviously expressive. One evinces noticeable feelings of fear and insecurity which result in a loss of status among one's peers. At the same time one may arouse in one's adversary feelings of contempt.

An interesting point to consider with respect to copping a plea is whether the superficial features of the form may be borrowed to mitigate one's punishment, in which case it would have the same directive function as shucking, and would be used to arouse feelings of pity, mercy, and the like. The question whether one can arouse such feelings among one's street peers by copping a plea is unclear. In the example cited above from the record *Street and Gangland Rhythms*, which records the improvisations of eleven- and twelve-year-old boys, one of the boys convincingly *acts out* the form of language behavior, which was identified by all my informants as "copping a plea" with the police officer: "Please cop, don't hit me. I give." In this example it was clearly an artifice with a directive function and here we have the familiar dynamic opposition of black vs. authority figure discussed under shucking.

"Signifying" is the term used to describe the language behavior that, as Abrahams has defined it, attempts to "imply, goad, beg, boast by indirect verbal or gestural means' (1964:267). In Chicago it is also used as a synonym to describe a form of language behavior which is more generally known as "sounding" elsewhere and will be discussed under the latter heading below.

Some excellent examples of signifying as well as of other forms of language behavior discussed above come from the well known "toast" (narrative form) "The signifying monkey and the lion" which was collected by Abrahams from black street corner bards in Philadelphia. In the above toast the monkey is trying to get the lion involved in a fight with the elephant (Abrahams 1964:150 ff.):

> Now the lion came through the jungle one peaceful day,
> When the signifying monkey stopped him, and that is what he started to say:
> He said, "Mr. Lion," he said, "A bad-assed motherfucker down your way,"
> He said, "Yeah! The way he talks about your folks is a certain shame.
> "I've even heard him curse when he mentioned your grandmother's name."
> The lion's tail shot back like a forty-four
> When he went down that jungle in all uproar.

Thus the monkey has goaded the lion into a fight with the elephant by "signifying," indicating that the elephant has been "sounding on" (insulting) the lion. When the lion comes back, thoroughly beaten up, the monkey again "signifies" by making fun of the lion:

> . . . a lion came back through the jungle more dead than alive,
> When the monkey started some more of that signifying jive.
> He said, "Damn, Mr. Lion, you went through here yesterday, the jungle rung.
> "Now you come back today, damn near hung."

The monkey, of course, is delivering this taunt from a safe distance away on the limb of a tree when his foot slips and he falls to the ground, at which point

> Like a bolt of lightning, a stripe of white heat,
> The lion was on the monkey with all four feet.

In desperation the monkey quickly resorts to "copping a plea":

> The monkey looked up with a tear in his eyes.
> He said, "Please, Mr. Lion, I apologize."

His "plea," however, fails to move the lion

to any show of pity or mercy so the monkey tries another verbal ruse: "shucking:"

> He said, "You lemme get my head out of the sand
> Ass out of the grass, I'll fight you like a natural man."

In this he is more successful as

> The lion jumped back and squared for a fight.
> The motherfucking monkey jumped clear out of sight.

A safe distance away again, the monkey returns to "signifying":

> He said, "Yeah, you had me down, you had me at last.
> But you left me free, now you can still kiss my ass."

The above example illustrates the methods of provocation, goading, and taunting as artfully practiced by the signifier. Interestingly, when the *function* of signifying is *directive*, the *tactic* which is employed is one of *indirection*—i.e., the signifier reports or repeats what someone else has said about the listener; the "report" is couched in plausible language designed to compel belief and arouse feelings of anger and hostility. There is also the implication that if the listener fails to do anything about it—what has to be "done" is usually quite clear—his status will be seriously compromised. Thus the lion is compelled to vindicate the honor of his family by fighting or else leave the impression that he is afraid, and that he is not "king" of the jungle. When used to direct action, "signifying" is like "shucking" in also being deceptive and subtle in approach and depending for success on the naivete or gullibility of the person being "put on."

When the function of signifying is only expressive (i.e., to arouse feelings of embarrassment, shame, frustration or futility, for the purpose of diminishing someone's status, but without directive implication), the tactic employed is direct in the form of a taunt, as in the above example where the monkey is making fun of the lion. Signifying frequently occurs when things are dull and someone wishes to generate some excitement and interest within the group. This is shown in another version of the above toast:

> There hadn't been no disturbin in the jungle for quite a bit,
> For up jumped the monkey in the tree one day and laughed, "I guess I'll start some shit."

Sounding is the term which is today most widely known for the game of verbal insult known in the past as "playing the dozens," "the dirty dozens," or just "the dozens." Other current names for the game have regional distribution: *signifying* or "sigging" (Chicago), *joning* (Washington, D.C.), *screaming* (Harrisburg), and so on. In Chicago, the term "sounding" would be descriptive of the initial remarks which are designed to "sound" out the other person to see whether he will play the game. The verbal insult is also subdivided, the term "signifying" applying to insults which are hurled directly at the person and the "dozens" applying to insults which are hurled directly at the person and the "dozens" applying to insults hurled at your opponent's family, especially, the mother.

Sounding is often catalyzed by "signifying" remarks referred to earlier, such as "Are you going to let him say that about your mama?" in order to spur on an exchange between two (or more) other members of the group. It is begun on a relatively low key and built up by means of verbal exchanges.

Abrahams (1962b:209–10) describes the game:

> One insults a member of another's family; others in the group make disapproving sounds to spur on the coming exchange. The one who has been insulted feels at this point that he must reply with a slur on the protagonist's family which is clever enough to defend his honor (and therefore that of his family). This, of course, leads the other (once again, more due to pressure from the crowd than actual insult) to make further jabs. This can proceed until everyone is bored with the whole affair, until one hits the other (fairly rare), or until some other subject comes up that interrupts the proceedings (the usual state of affairs).

McCormick (1960:8) describes the dozens as a verbal contest

> ... in which the players strive to bury one another with vituperation. In the play, the opponent's mother is especially slandered ... then, in turn fathers are identified as queer and syphilitic. Sisters are whores, brothers are defective, cousins are "funny" and the opponent is himself diseased.

An example of the "game" collected by one of my students goes as follows:

> Frank looked up and saw Leroy enter the Outpost. Leroy walked past the room where Quinton, "Nap," "Pretty Black," "Cunny," Richard, Haywood, "Bull," and Reese sat playing cards. As Leroy neared the T. V. room, Frank shouted to him.
> Frank: "Hey, Leroy, your mama—calling you man."
> Leroy turned and walked toward the room where the sound came from. He stood in the door and looked at Frank.
> Leroy: "Look motherfuckers, I don't play that shit."
> Frank, signifying: "Man, I told you cats 'bout that mama jive" (as if he were concerned about how Leroy felt).
> Leroy: "That's all right Frank; you don't have to tell those funky motherfuckers nothing; I'll fuck me up somebody yet."

> Frank's face lit up as if he were ready to burst his side laughing. "Cunny" became pissed at Leroy.
> Cunny: "Leroy, you stupid bastard, you let Frank make a fool of you. *He* said that 'bout your mama."
> "Pretty Black": "Aw, fat ass head, 'Cunny' shut up."
> "Cunny": "Ain't that some shit. This black slick head motor flicker got nerve 'nough to call somebody 'fathead.' Boy, you so black, you sweat super Permalube Oil."

This eased the tension of the group as they burst into loud laughter.

> "Pretty Black": "What 'chu laughing 'bout 'Nap,' with your funky mouth smelling like dog shit.'

Even Leroy laughed at this.

> "Nap": "Your mama motherfucker."
> "Pretty Black": "Your funky mama too."
> "Nap" strongly: "It takes twelve barrels of water to make a steamboat run; it takes an elephant's dick to make your Grandmammy come; she been elephant fucked, camel fucked and hit side the head with your Grandpappy's nuts."
> Reese: "Goddor damn; go on and rap motherfucker."

Reese began slapping each boy in his hand, giving his positive approval of "Nap's" comment. "Pretty Black," in an effort not to be outdone but directing his verbal play elsewhere, stated:

> "Pretty Black": "Reese, what you laughing 'bout? You so square you shit bricked shit."
> Frank: "Whoooowee!"
> Reese sounded back: "Square huh, what about your nappy ass hair before it was stewed; that shit was so bad till, when you went to bed at night, it would leave your head and go on the corner and meddle."

The boys slapped each other in the hand and cracked up.

"Pretty Black": "On the streets meddling, bet Dinky didn't offer me no pussy and I turned it down."

Frank: "Reese scared of pussy."

"Pretty Black": "Hell yeah; the greasy mother rather fuck old, ugly, funky cock Sue Willie than get a piece of ass from a decent broad."

Frank: "Goddor damn! Not Sue Willie."

"Pretty Black": "Yeah ol' meat beating Reese rather screw that cross-eyed, clapsy bitch, who when she cry, tears drip down her ass."

Haywood: "Don't be so mean, Black."

Reese: "Aw shut up, you half-white bastard."

Frank: "Wait man, Haywood ain't gonna hear much more of that half-white shit; he's a brother too."

Reese: "Brother, my black ass; that white ass landlord gotta be this motherfucker's paw."

'Cunny': "Man, you better stop foolin with Haywood; he's turning red."

Haywood: "Fuck yall" (as he withdrew from the "sig" game).

Frank: "Yeah, fuck yall; let's go to the stick hall."

The above example of "sounding" is an excellent illustration of the "game" as played by fifteen-, sixteen-, and seventeen-year-old Negro boys, some of whom have already acquired the verbal skill which for them is often the basis for having a high "rep." Abrahams (1964:62) observed that "... the ability with words is as highly valued as physical strength." In the sense that the status of one of the participants in the game is diminished if he has to resort to fighting to answer a verbal attack, verbal ability may be even more highly regarded than physical ability. However, age within the peer group may be a factor in determining the relative value placed on verbal vis-à-vis physical ability.

Nevertheless, the relatively high value placed on verbal ability must be clear to most black boys at an early age in their cognitive development. Abrahams (1964:53) is probably correct in linking "sounding" to the taunt which is learned and practiced as a child and is part of "signifying," which has its origins in childlike behavior. The taunts of the "Signifying Monkey," illustrated above, are good examples of this.

Most boys begin their activity in "sounding" by compiling a repertoire of "one liners." When the game is played among this age group the one who has the greatest number of such remarks wins. Here are some examples of "one liners" collected from fifth and sixth grade black boys in Chicago:

Yo mama is so bowlegged, she looks like the bite out of a donut.

You mama sent her picture to the lonely hearts club, and they sent it back and said "We ain't that lonely"!

Your family is so poor the rats and roaches eat lunch out.

Your house is so small the roaches walk single file.

I walked in your house and your family was running around the table. I said, "Why you doin that?" Your mama say, "First one drops, we eat."

Real proficiency in the game comes to only a small percentage of those who play it, as might be expected. These players have the special skill in being able to turn what their opponents have said and attack them with it. Thus, when someone indifferently said "fuck you" to Concho, his retort was immediate and devastating: "Man, you haven't even kissed me yet."

The "best talkers" from this group often become the successful street-corner, barber shop, and pool hall story tellers who deliver the long, rhymed, witty narrative stories called "toasts." A portion of the toast "The Signifying Monkey and the Lion" was given above. However, it has also produced entertainers, such as Dick Gregory and Redd Foxx, who are virtuosos at repartee, and preachers, whose verbal power has been traditionally esteemed.

The function of the "dozens" or "sounding" is invariably self-assertive. The speaker borrows status from his opponent through an exercise of verbal power. The opponent feels compelled to regain his status by "sounding" back on the speaker or some other member of the group whom he regards as more vulnerable. The social interaction of the group at the Outpost, for example, demonstrated less an extended verbal barrage between two people than a "pecking order." Frank "sounds" on Leroy; "Cunny" "signifies" on Leroy; "Pretty Black" "sounds" on "Cunny"; "Cunny" "sounds" back on "Pretty Black" who (losing) turns on "Nap"; "Nap" "sounds" (winning) back on "Pretty Black"; "Pretty Black" finally borrows back his status by "sounding" on Reese. Reese "sounds" back on "Pretty Black" but gets the worst of the exchange and so borrows back his status from Haywood. "Cunny" also "sounds" on Haywood. Haywood defaults. Perhaps by being "half-white," Haywood feels himself to be the most vulnerable.

The presence of a group seems to be especially important in controlling the game. First of all, one does not "play" with just anyone since the subject matter is concerned with things that in reality one is quite sensitive about. It is precisely *because* "Pretty Black" has a "black slick head" that makes him vulnerable to "Cunny's" barb, especially now when the Afro-American "natural" hair style is in vogue. It is precisely *because* Reese's girl-friend *is* ugly that makes him vulnerable to "Pretty Black's" jibe that Reese can't get a "piece of ass from a decent broad." It is *because* the living conditions are so poor and intolerable that they can be used as subject matter for "sounding." Without the control of the group "sounding" will frequently lead to a fight. This was illustrated by a tragic epilogue concerning Haywood; when Haywood was being "sounded" on in the presence of two girls by his best friend (other members of the group were absent), he refused to tolerate it. He went home, got a rifle, came back, and shot and killed his friend. In the classroom from about the fourth grade on fights among black boys invariably are caused by someone "sounding" on the other person's mother.

Significantly, the subject matter of "sounding" is changing with the changing self-concept of the black with regard to those physical characteristics that are characteristically "Negro," and which in the past were vulnerable points in the black psyche: blackness and "nappy" hair.

They still occur, as in the above example: from the Outpost, and the change in the above illustration is notably more by what has been added than subtracted—viz., the attack on black *slick* hair and half-white color. With regard to the latter, however, it ought to be said that for many blacks, blackness was always highly esteemed and it might be more accurate to regard the present sentiment of the black community toward skin color as reflecting a shifted attitude for only a *portion* of the black community. This suggests that "sounding" on someone's light skin color is not new. Nevertheless, one can regard the previously favorable attitude toward light skin color and "good hair" as the prevailing one. "Other things being equal, the more closely a woman approached her white counterpart, the more attractive she was considered to be, by both men and women alike. 'Good hair' (hair that is long and soft) and light skin were the chief criteria" (Liebow 1966:138). Also, children's rhymes which before "black power" were

> If you like black
> Keep your black ass back

and

> If you like white
> You're all right

have respectively changed to

> If you like black
> You have a Cadillac

and

> If you like white
> You're looking for a fight.

Both Abrahams and McCormick link the "dozens" to the over-all psychosocial growth of the black male. McCormick has stated that a "single round of a dozen or so exchanges frees more pent-up aggressions than will a dose of sodium pentothal." The fact that one permits a kind of abuse within the rules of the game and within the confines of the group which would otherwise not be tolerated is filled with psychological importance, and this aspect is rather fully discussed by Abrahams. It also seems important, however, to view its function from the perspective of the non-participating members of the group. Its function for them may be directive: i.e., they incite and prod individual members of the group to combat for the purpose of energizing the elements, of simply relieving the boredom of just "hanging around" and the malaise of living in a static and restrictive environment. One of my informants remarked that he and other members of the group used to feed insults to one member to hurl back at another if they felt that the contest was too uneven, "to keep the game going." In my above illustration from the Outpost, for example, Frank seemed to be the precipitating agent as well as chorus for what was going on and "Bull" did not directly participate at all. For them the "dozens" may have had the social function of "having a little fun," or as Loubee said to Josh of just "passing the time" (Shorris 1966:65).

A summary analysis of the different forms of language behavior which have been discussed permit the following generalizations.

The prestige norms which influence black speech behavior are those which have been successful in manipulating and controlling people and situations. The function of all of the forms of language behavior discussed above, with the exception of "running it down," was either expressive or expressive-directive. Specifically, this means that language was used to project personality, assert oneself, or arouse emotion, frequently with the additional purpose of getting the person to give up or do something which will be of some benefit to the speaker. Only "running it down" has as its primary function to communicate information and often here, too, the personality and style of the speaker in the form of "rapping" is projected along with the information.

The purpose for which language is used suggests that the speaker views the social situations into which he moves as essentially agonistic, by which I mean that he sees his environment as consisting of a series of transactions which require that he be continually ready to take advantage of a person or situation or defend himself against being victimized. He has absorbed what Horton (1967:8) has called "street rationality." As one of Horton's respondents put it: "The good hustler ... conditions his mind and must never put his guard down too far, to relax, or he'll be taken."

I have carefully avoided, throughout this paper, delimiting the group within the black community of whom the language behavior and perspective of their environment is characteristic. While I have no doubt that it is true of those who are generally called "street people" I am not certain of the extent to which it is also true of a much larger portion of the black community, especially the male segment. My informants consisted of street people, high school students, and blacks, who by their occupation as community and youth workers possess what has been described as a "sharp sense of the streets." Yet is is difficult to find a black male in the community who has *not* witnessed or participated in the "dozens" or heard of "signifying," or "rapping," or "shucking and jiving" at some time while he was growing up. It would be equally difficult to imagine a high school student in a Chicago inner city school not being touched by what is generally regarded a "street culture" in some way.

In conclusion, by blending style and verbal power, through "rapping," "sounding," and "running it down," the black in the ghetto establishes his personality; through "shucking," "gripping," and "copping a plea" he shows his respect for power; through "jiving" and "signifying" he stirs up excitement. With all of the above, he hopes to manipulate and control people and situations to give himself a winning edge.

Eight

PATTERNS OF PERFORMANCE IN THE BRITISH WEST INDIES[1]

Roger Abrahams

In his survey of Negro folklore studies in 1943, Melville Herskovits pointed out that a number of immediate gaps in organizing and orienting field research needed filling: additional data, especially from certain key areas; a reconsideration of existing materials on the basis of underlying similarities and regional differences; fuller understanding of the social setting of the writings in the discipline (Herskovits 1943a). These gaps have not been filled, nor will they be; they are continuing problems for the investigator. However, the one gap pointed to by Herskovits that seems to have been most neglected is his call for a re-examination of materials in terms of similarities and differences on a regional basis. This comparative analysis has been carried out in convincing fashion by observers of religious practices, but not with the materials central to the study of expressive culture: tales, riddles, proverbs, modes of address and conversation, and so forth. There is an attitude toward words and word-usage in the performance context common to Negro communities in the United States and the British West Indies; this attitude shows up in a common pattern of performance. This pattern may be used both in defining a culture area and in pointing to important local and regional differences within that area. This pattern is not merely a configuration of cultural traits, most of which can be observed in any oral culture; rather it seems to be a deep structure that assumes many shapes in different regional environments.

MEN OF WORDS

Communities have devised only so many ways to organize themselves. Once a program or arrangement develops in one sector of life, it tends to repeat itelfs in other

A shorter version of this essay appeared in *Trans-Action*, Vol. 5, No. 8, (July–August, 1968), pp. 62–71.

areas. Principles of family organization in certain regards may be echoed in other structures of government, or of economics, and the same principles of order may also be seen in the structure of traditional performances. Folklore seems especially susceptible to this kind of analysis. As the expressive and aesthetic dimension of the culture of tradition-oriented groups, folklore is made up of items and performances which are self-consciously and artistically constructed. And because the performances are of a totally public nature, and therefore are conceived in terms understandable to all in the group, outlines of aesthetic organization are clearly stated. Folklore is constructed of conventional materials, and these conventions organize performance in the areas of form, content, imagined roles and role-relationships, and in relationships between participants in the aesthetic transaction. Because the performance is public and unrecorded, the audience must have a constant sense of orientation; that is, they must be aware at all times at what stage they are in the performance.

Conventions of performance therefore provide the kinds of markers the performer and the audience need to guarantee this constant sense of orientation. Virtually every scene of a folk play or a folk tale, for instance, must imply the totality of the composition, where it has been and where it is going. This is why convention must dominate folk performance. Since folk arts are so conventional, they provide few problems in describing their organization. However, though folk art is, by necessity, conventional, the typical forms and styles of performance differ from group to group. One may learn a great deal about a group from discerning what these stylistic abstractions are and therefore what its expectations are toward the performance situation.

In 1958 and 1959, while living in a predominantly Negro neighborhood in South Philadelphia, I observed a number of traditional performances and began to perceive a pattern of repeated traits in the roles played by the performer, his relation to his material and his audience, and in the audience's attitude toward the performer and his enactment. This pattern centered upon the acclaim given those individuals who were good at using words effectively—individuals I came to call "men-of-words." Significant in their performances was the way in which these artful narrators became closely identified with the style and action of the heroes they described. The audience seemed to identify with the enactment almost as fully as the speaker. An examination of how this situation was structured centered upon the relative lack of psychic distance (or removal) between performer and his enactment and between the audience and the described actions. A further trait inducing this strong sense of sympathetic involvement and vicarious identification was the repeated and insistent use of the first-person singular pronouns by the man-of-words. This was termed the "intrusive 'I'." Finally, it became clear that these performances almost always arose in contests between men-of-words, and that such contests were a community-accepted manner of demonstrating masculinity. Though other performance traits were discussed in my report on my Philadelphia findings (Abrahams 1964), these were the ones which seemed most characteristic.

My assumptions, while writing this book, were that this pattern was probably unique to urban Negro performers in the United States, and so I described them in terms of "oikotypicality" (local configuration of traits). Since then, field experience in the southern United States and in the British

West Indies has convinced me that this pattern is considerably more widespread and may be characteristic of performances in most New World Negro communities.[2]

This becomes clear, for instance, in a casual comparison of blues and calypso singers, for both build their art on personal identification, singing of what purports to be their own experiences or observations; and calypsonians perform most characteristically in the context situation. Furthermore, both types of performers are capable of achieving high status in their respective communities through practice of their art. (It is widely said throughout the West Indies, for instance, that the only man who might beat Dr. Eric Williams in a Trinidadian election is calypso master "Mighty Sparrow.")

The widespread nature of this performance pattern is even more forcefully demonstrated by one type of verbal contest observed in many Negro communities in the New World. This practice is often called "playing the dozens" or "sounding" in the United States, and in the West Indies is commonly called "rhyming" (Abrahams 1963; 1964). This adolescent verbal activity involves invective contests in which one youth will insult a member of another's family—usually mother—knowing that he will be answered in kind. The contest often begins with a simple curse, like "Fuck you," which may elicit the conventional response, "Fuck your mother." At this point the decision will be made whether to play or not. In "deep" sessions, subsequent insults will often be framed in rhyme, and will describe a sexual feat which the speaker purports to have committed himself, like:

I fucked your mother on a telephone wire,
And every jerk was a blaze of fire.

This battle is recognized simply as boasting, and though the contestants become deeply involved in the proceedings they seldom regard it as anything but entertainment. In many places in the West Indies the rules are actually spelled out by the boys before they begin to rhyme.

Most of the performance characteristics outlined above can be observed in this obscene verbal exchange: the constant insertion of the first-person pronouns, the close identification of the speaker with an imaginary situation, the achievement of sexual identity and (peer-group) status through good word-usage, and the word-contest structure of performance. Of course, the verbal effects are not as witty, as subtle, nor as complex as those of adult entertainments.

"Rhyming," unlike more complex verbal traditions, is practiced by most young men, though some are regarded as better talkers than others. In combination with the teasing and taunting also found as a well-developed verbal art among black children in many communities, this "rhyming" type of verbal interplay develops into two kinds of folklore activities and two kinds of men-of-words: good-talking and broad, or bad, talking.[3] Badinage remains an integral part of the expressive and communicative dimension of everyday life here. Almost any extended conversation can develop into an entertainment, especially a contest of wits. I have witnessed these impromptu performances at casual gatherings on the steps or at the pool hall in the big-city atmosphere of South Philadelphia, and at markets, rum-shops, and especially on buses and boats in the British West Indies. This kind of activity gives rise to the person adept at repartee, the broad-talker. Women are often as quick to enter such an on-the-spot contest of wits as men.

The good-talker, on the other hand, needs a more highly structured situation and more time to exhibit his talents. He commonly purveys a highly decorated and self-consciously artificial rhetoric; for these effects he must have a situation in which he can gain the complete attention of his audience. In the United States, the good-talker tends to hold forth at bars or pool halls, at private parties, or at religious meetings. In the West Indies, he may channel his talents exclusively into preaching, but more commonly he holds forth at special performances traditional in festivals, such as Carnival or Christmas, or at occasions like wakes or wedding feasts. In both the Islands and the mainland, some men-of-words have in the past specialized in writing friendship or love letters for other members of the community.

Though the ubiquity of the man-of-words has been emphasized here, the more interesting aspect of their presence is the way in which he develops his powers in different ways in the various Negro communities responding to different historical, geographical, and cultural conditions. And of equal importance is the way in which the man-of-words fits into the total picture of a community's traditions and institutions and how great a part he plays in the total range of expressive culture there. Two West Indian island communities, Tobago and Nevis, will be described to illustrate the varieties of this man-of-words tradition, how traditional expression harmonizes with the ethos in these communities, and what recent forces have effected changes in folklore, specifically in modifying the performance pattern.

TOBAGO

In Tobago there have been numerous traditional occasions for the man-of-words to exhibit this power: at *Bongos* (wakes), as storyteller or sermonizer, at Thanksgivings (parties commemorating the end of a trying experience), as speechmaker, and most notably, as a central performer in a Carnival *mas'*, as the touring groups of masqueraders are called there.[4] In these Carnival *mas'es* the stylistic traits of the man-of-words performance pattern are harmonized with certain Carnival characteristics. Most of the groups found on Trinidad and Tobago during Carnival exhibit the following traits: (1) they represent a community, or in the cities, a neighborhood; (2) traditional roles are played, and the roles are designated by traditional costumes and masks, and by a certain type of performance consonant with the role; (3) the roles (and costumes) usually portray power figures, either characters from the underworld (criminals, devils) or impersonations of hero-types (military figures, warriors); (4) individual performers usually take on stage names which are appropriate to the character being played; (5) they usually accumulate groups of followers who dress in similar style; and (6) the performer, while he may perform simply by interacting with the audience, nevertheless finds opportunity for the fullest statement of his abilities in competition with another performer playing the same type of role. The man-of-words pattern fits easily into this type of Carnival performance.

A *mas'* usually is organized around a virtuoso performer; a singer, a dancer, a stickfighter, or a speechmaker. He often performs alone, and especially in those roles in which money-making is the primary motivation. More often, he performs alone one day of Carnival and with his group the next. When he performs with his group, it is generally recognized that they represent the honor of their community, and they may use this factor in building up the dramatic interest in contests with other groups.

Most of these contests call for the performance of certain set pieces prepared by each virtuoso ahead of time, and then an improvised battle. This is true, for instance, in the *Caiso Mas'*, the ancestor of the modern calypso competitions, found on both Trinidad and Tobago. The various "chantwells"[5] or mastersingers would compose a song for the season and each would try to have it widely sung. Then when he met another calypsonian, he and his group would trade songs and the two chantwells would then generally engage in a "war," or contest of invective. As with most of these conflicts, they were for the amusement of the crowd; seldom was a winner declared.

Though Trinidad and Tobago share many of the same *mas'es*, Tobago has developed at least one, *Speech Band*, which seems to be unique to that island (Abrahams 1968a). This troupe for the most part follows the same kind of organization as the Trinidadian groups. They have one additional characteristic usually found at Carnival, but more often, in relation to the fancy costume *mas'es*: a fascination with exotic hierarchies. The members of the group form themselves in a very rigid status order, modeled after some British courtly hierarchy, rank depending primarily on speechmaking ability and experience. Characteristically, each performer takes on an appropriate name, the leader being "King George." When they march, the hierarchical arrangement is fully revealed. First comes the "Showboy," a clown figure who clears the way for the group. Then comes the apprentices, all called "Robins." Then come, in a cluster, the members of the King's Court, the knights such as "Hero, the Conqueror," "Duke of York," "Warrior Sealey," and many others. The King is immediately preceded by his "sons,"—"The Prince of Wales" and "The Duke of York." The King's organizer, called "Commander," will determine who speaks and in what order. As the names of the characters suggest, the speeches are properly heroic in tone and diction. They involve a wide range of subjects and themes, but they are always in rhyme, use inflated rhetoric, and are strongly hyperbolic:

Don't provoke Young Sealey until he gets set;
Nothing that I do I never forget.
Stretch forth your fingers to me and let us make a bet.
Words that I tell, you supposed to regret,
For I'm free and faithful, strong as deat'.
Here we are soldiers preparing for war.
Miracles to me are only like a cold drink of water.
These are the miracles, here they are:
Human bones I'll crush to make you thousand bags of Gibraltar's flour,
We'll preserve your bones into green pastures' butter.

There are significant differences between *Speech Mas'* and most of the groups in Trinidad. Most notably, in *Speech Mas'*, though the "King" is the acknowledged master at speechmaking, everyone in the group is given an opportunity to perform. This is ensured by "Commander." Furthermore, the unitary focus of the Trinidad groups on the virtuoso is further dissipated by providing for the training of future warriors, through the creation of the role of "Robin" for the younger men. Even the Robins may have a chance to speak and the more seasoned performers often help them to compose their recitations. This diffusion of performance, in the past, has enabled communities to feel more fully involved in the contest of wits which occurs on Carnival Tuesday when one *Speech Band* encounters another on the road. Furthermore, even then the pageantry of the costumes and the involved decorum involving the careful enunciation of the rules of battle will provide as much dramatic interest as the boasting and cursing contest itself. These performances of local men-of-words are, then, considerably more egalitarian in organization and less severely focused on the virtuoso abilities of the individual performer. A war-of-words in *Speech Mas'* is really a team affair.

This style of expressive organization in which dramatic focus is passed from performer to performer is characteristic of most entertainments on Tobago. Furthermore, recently this egalitarian approach to performance has become even more pronounced in certain Tobago communities, including Plymouth, the village investigated most extensively. This has brought about a number of changes in traditional enactments including what amounts to a rejection of even this modified virtuoso performance.

The reasons for this development are too complex and various to go into here, but a few of the most important facets may be outlined. Perhaps the most important negative force has been the identification of the virtuoso performance with Trinidad performers, and the stereo-typical association of the Trinidadian with self-centered and mercantilistic motives. Since Trinidad and Tobago achieved independence in 1957, Tobago has sensed that its second-class satellite status, present before nationhood, has become more pronounced. Though the islands are geographically close and have shared a great deal historically and culturally, they are different in many important respects. Trinidad is dominated by urban and semi-urban population centers and therefore has a predominantly mercantilistic wage-earning way of looking at life. Their economy is based, to a great extent, upon a surplus production of goods and a high degree of division of labor. They suffer from a complex cultural situation in which people from many different islands have been brought together in what has become a slum environment, and strong resentments have arisen between resident Negroes and East Indians. All of this has created tensions which are further exaggerated by the lack of employment and by overpopulation.

Problems of this sort are not so profound on Tobago, even in Scarborough, the seat of government and the center of population. In towns like Plymouth, because there has been such a steady migration from the town to Trinidad and elsewhere, there is little problem of providing enough food and employment for anyone who wishes to stay. Though half of the men in Plymouth work in the fields, life really centers on the beach where the men fish with seines. "Fishening," as they call it, not only provides them with their main source of protein but also with their major source of income when the catches are large enough to yield a surplus. In fact, life on the beach provides a model of all social and economic activities for the Plymouthian.

The most important value of beach life is cooperation. There are usually thirteen to fifteen seines in use, but only two can be cast at a given time because of the size of the beach. Therefore they must run by a system of "chances"—that is, they wait their turn. The two seines that are on their chance continue to throw until a reasonable catch is made (sometimes a week goes by without one). The three to six people who throw the seine are the principals in the catch, but everyone else on the beach at the time of the catch will get some fish for the pot that night if the size of the catch permits it. Furthermore, when repairs are to be made on a boat or seine, those who are best at such things will automatically help, and when a new seine is being "tied" nearly all of the men will do some knitting.

Existence of this sort calls for long periods in which no fishing is done, when the men "lime" (relax)—they drink and do repair work, sleep and talk. Those with more of a sense of initiative and individual enterprise can fish for themselves from a small one-, two-, or three-man boat. The men on the beach do not resent this because there is a ready market for all the fish caught, and at a high price.

Though there are dissident elements in life in Plymouth, even among the men on the beach, generally the spirit of cooperation reigns. When conflict does arise, it is commonly ascribed to outside influences, an ascription that is often substantially correct. When cooperation is threatened, the beach group and their families cohere and continue their life-ways in a self-conscious and stubborn fashion.

This ethos pervades all aspects of Plymouth life, especially in regard to concepts of family and community, property, and social and governmental status arrangements. In regard to this last, there *are* provisions for achieving status in Plymouth, and even on the beach. One man can become a net owner (who gets 40-75% of the take in good catches), or the "captain" of a net team (who gets two "shares"); nevertheless, these bestow no special social distinction. The men on the beach are consciously defensive about such subjects, insisting that anyone, even the Prime Minister, Dr. Eric Williams, when he comes to Plymouth, is just another "nyegar." And this is not a pious platitude; in a number of cases, men have left Plymouth and achieved some measure of status elsewhere, and then have returned to find their outside position of little account within the community.[6]

In one such case, that of a retired policeman, this resulted in a sense of frustration on his part which led him to attempt to "organize" the men on the beach under his leadership. The men acquiesced in his activities since they promised merely to add an element of formal organization to an already orderly existence. However, recently the government has attempted to get the men to organize a cooperative to provide more surplus fish at lower prices. Because the ex-policeman was not elected to the presidency of the cooperative, he then created a hostile ambience and developed an emotional argument that led the fishermen to refuse to join. Consequently, this cooperative fishing enterprise, encouraged and underwritten by the government, is now primarily made up of agricultural workers, shop-keepers, and retired civil servants. An atmosphere of conflict has arisen which is resented a great deal by members of both factions.

But the problem involves much more than just factions. Essentially, the government, and the cooperative as its agency, is asking the fishermen to break up their beach life and to reject beach values in favor of a fully capitalist and competitive world view. The fishermen feel that this would not only destroy their way of life but in its place would introduce the attitudes and values of the Trinidadians, who they feel are thieves and untrustworthy and, in personal relationships, dangerous and unpredictable They fear the incursion of big-city ways and values.

This reaction to Trinidadian ways seems to have affected performance patterns as well. In the last two decades there has been an unconscious drifting away from single-person performances involving men-of-words or men-of-action, and a contrary impulse emphasizing and elaborating those expressive traditions which are more communal. This is especially noticeable in the Carnival *mas'es*; such virtuoso performances as *Kalinda* (stick-fight dance), *Caiso Mas'*, and *Speech Band* have virtually disappeared as community encouraged activities (Elder 1966a; Crowley 1959). There are still performers of these *mas'es* living in Plymouth, but only one man bothers to perform at Carnival, and he isn't originally from Plymouth, feels himself a stranger in their midst (though he is from a town less than three miles away), and must go to another community to find a band with which to perform.

These virtuosos still bring gasps of admiration in Plymouth when they can be persuaded to perform. But they get no community support in the form of an active following and a set of apprentices, support which in the past has provided the life-blood of such performances. Instead, for Carnival, the town informally agrees on a theme for a *Fancy Costume Mas'* and they spend the two months before Carnival making appropriate costumes. This *mas'* is one in which all may participate. In doing this, they follow a recent trend in Trinidad (and indeed throughout the West Indies) but for very different reasons. Such groups have proliferated in Trinidad because they can be enjoyed by any audience; there is no chance that a foreigner will not understand their performance, as there is with many of the traditional virtuoso *mas'es*, and such visitors make up an important segment of the Carnival audience. Also, these virtuoso performances can only be played effectively before small groups, while the costume groups can be seen and appreciated by multitudes. Since there are fewer visitors on Tobago and their Carnival is primarily for their own amusement, the Trinidadian reasons for change do not operate as fully.

At least in the practice of the Plymouthian, the change in emphasis seems to have occurred because of his predilection toward community endeavors.

This cooperative pattern is reiterated in nearly all aspects of the lives of Plymouthians. It is reflected in the attitude toward making the family as extended as possible (each person has two godfathers and godmothers and everyone in the family refers to those individuals by this relationship); it is seen in the large number of savings groups or *susus*, sports clubs, and steel drum bands; but it is most fully seen in the traditional expressions which are still widely observed in the town. Most dramatically, the cooperative motive arises in times of crisis, such as when a member of the community dies.[7] Immediately, nearly all work in town stops and friends and family gather around the ones most affected. As many as forty or fifty men will then go about collecting wood, cutting it up, and putting together the coffin. The same is true of the digging of the grave; each male friend will take his turn with the shovel, while the others stand around watching. After the burial, a *Bongo* celebration will usually be held, the first night devoted to hymn-singing, but subsequent nights given over to games, dances, and riddling. Story-telling, once favored, is no longer often encountered, perhaps illustrating a further retreat from man-of-words performances. The games usually are organized on a circle arrangement; their accompanying song is performed in the chanter-response pattern usually associated with African practices, with the position of song-leader changing often. The dances are the same; they are performed in a circular arrangement, each dancer coordinating his movements with those on each side of him.

Other festival occasions reflect the same

communal preoccupation. Any new boat or seine calls for a fete, a christening, the appointment of godfathers and godmothers, and so on. Similarly, when someone has returned from a trip or recovered from an illness or had some other similar experience a "Thanksgiving" party is given. Finally, the most important holiday of the year is St. Peter's Day, Fisherman's Fete, in which not only Plymouthians but fishing folk from all over the island gather for games and the blessing of the boats. All of these call for the same kind of performance as those outlined in regard to the *Bongo* except that on St. Peter's Day all the local fishermen and many of their friends from other locales are called upon to improvise a speech or a song for the occasion, this being the last of the festivals to continue to encourage man-of-words performances.

But there is no sense of loss felt or expressed in Plymouth on the passing of these virtuoso traditions because the practices which have replaced them harmonize with the traditional orientation of the residents. Essentially, there is no sense of rejecting the ways of the past, as one finds in a number of other West Indian communities, but rather a selective emphasis on an alternative pattern of traditional performance, the group game or song or dance.

NEVIS

The island culture of Nevis contrasts dramatically with that of Tobago. Nevis, which has existed for over 300 years under British domination, has a style of performance and an accompanying ethos which emphasizes solo performance and an image of life as isolated and full of anxiety and conflict. There simply has not been a total acceptance by the Negro Nevisians of the British way of life and point of view, but they have espoused British performances and performance patterns because these facets of culture came closest to embodying the special Nevisian way of seeing and organizing life. Nevis folklore is the result of a syncretic coming together of African and European traditions. In terms of the actual items performed, Nevis folklore is predominantly British. But in terms of the context, the way in which a performance is organized, Nevis traditional expression is a development of the man-of-words pattern with its many African antecedents and analogues.

On Tobago there was always a balance between the two patterns of performance, the integrated and the virtuoso types, and recent developments away from the latter simply illustrate that a choice is being made. On Nevis, for very different reasons, there has also been a drifting away from the man-of-words pattern. Whereas on Tobago the situation develops because of a defensive shoring-up of the sense of community enterprise, on Nevis the only shoring-up and defensing done is that of individuals retreating into themselves. On Nevis there is very little community activity or feeling.

Nevis occupies a satellite status toward St. Kitts not unlike that between Tobago and Trinidad. It is one of the smaller of the British Leeward Islands. With St. Kitts, Antigua, and Barbados, it is one of the "Mother Colonies" in the British Caribbean. Tobago was never regarded as one of the great outposts of European power, never was a highly successful plantation enclave, and therefore has never been fully cultivated and over-populated. On the other hand, Nevis, settled in 1628, was one of the places in which West Indian sugar fortunes were made (Pares 1950; Merrill 1958) and therefore supported a large population of field slaves.

A hot springs system there was developed into a luxurious spa and became a favorite vacation spot for visiting British and for planter-residents of other West Indian islands. Consequently, Nevis has been dominated politically, economically, and culturally by Great Britain for over 300 years. Add this to the fact that the first field workers on the island were Scotch-Irish peasants transported for "political" crimes and the strongly British flavor of their traditional expressions is accounted for, to some extent.

The Scotch-Irish brought their countryside amusements with them, and many have been perpetuated by the Negroes who followed them. But these would not have become established were there not elements in the situation of Negroes on Nevis which made the British entertainments understandable and appropriate. One of the appropriate features was that the British amusements permitted a number of aesthetic features to be continued and elaborated, such as the use of topical satire for aggressive purposes and social control and, most important for the concerns of this study, the good-talker type of man-of-words performance. But the British and puritanical vision of the futility of love and any interpersonal involvement was also siezed upon by the Nevisian and related to the kinds of distrusts and divisions which are the pitfalls of the matrifocal family and institutionalized friendship network systems now in decay. This becomes especially evident in intersexual involvements. Not only are there many proverbs which argue that man and woman can't live together effectively (unless man uses force), but their songs and dialogues emphasize the same point of view. Perhaps the most dramatic example of this is the widely sung Nevisian adaptation of the English folksong "Johnny's So Long at the Fair," In English versions the maiden sings of Johnny who is late in returning from the fair and of the presents he has promised her. On Nevis the song has become a recitation of all the things Johnny has already given the maiden.

The ring on my finger is Johnny give me,
The ring on my finger is Johnny give me,
The ring on my finger is Johnny give me,
Johnny alone until morning.

Johnny also give her shoes, hat, and a number of other personal items. After all of these things are listed, she finally sings:

Johnny says that he love me, but I do not believe,
Johnny says that he love me, but I do not believe,
Johnny says that he love me, but I do not believe,
Johnny alone until morning.

This divisive and affect-less vision of life, in combination with a high degree of competition in economic, social, and aesthetic areas of life, is a reflection of the anomie observable on the island. Because the land has been misused, it is still owned primarily by the plantocracy or the government who often will not let it be planted, and because of the lack of any other means of livelihood, the island has been in an economically depressed state for nearly a century. But the anomic conditions are not only a result of economic factors, for in those instances in which a cooperative enterprise has been suggested which might lead them out of the spiral of economic stagnation, there has been no widespread move to act on the plan. On the largest and most populous side of the island, the peasants plant vegetable crops which are not highly suited to the land and which have a limited market. They are, however, crops which can be vended by individuals in market competition and thus fit into their competitive world view.

This bankrupt and anomic condition has led many residents of Nevis to envision themselves as living in a prison, quite dfferent from the image of the "tropical paradise" held by most of the visitors and part-time residents from Canada and the United States. Consequently, there have been a series of mass emigrations from Nevis to areas in which employment possibilities were better. Many went to New York and New Haven around World War I, others to the Dominican Republic in the 1930's, to Great Britain from 1945–1963, and presently there is a major exodus to the American Virgin Islands. Naturally the ones who leave are the more adventurous and often the more intelligent. Though the ones who have remained have often been severely tradition-oriented, they have not always been the best performers, and on Nevis only a charismatic speaker is capable of winning an audience.

As on Tobago, festivals provide the most important occasions for traditional performances on Nevis. The two most notable Nevisian occasions are Christmas and *Tea Meetings*. Both provide opportunities for the dramatic exercise of verbal dexterity in the framework of a context situation. But whereas Tobagonians have had an alternative of virtuoso or group performances, on Nevis the only type acceptable in this conflict-oriented community is the virtuoso contest. (Group-style performances on Nevis primarily are performed by children in their ring-games, and by small groups of chanteying men moving houses or boats.) Not only is the man-of-words given opportunity to display his powers in these festival performances, but almost the only kind of performance to which an audience will listen is when an individual arises and seizes attention by virtue of his entertainment abilities. Inevitably, such attempts are rewarded with verbal retorts and heckling, for the entertainment value of virtuoso performance relies strongly on the introduction of the contest element.

There are a number of occasions in which such contests are an integral part of the festivities. Wedding feasts, for instance, usually include a session in which toasts of an obscene, boasting, and comical nature are proposed by a succession of orators.

Here's to the girls that dress in black;
When they dress they never look slack.
When they kiss, they kiss so sweet,
Makes Tommy stand without feet.

Almost any other formal occasion will call forth speeches in contest of one sort or another.

During Christmas there are many different groups of strolling players who exist primarily to stage just such contests of wit, the most colorful being those who present the archaic folk dramas. These are of two types—first, domestic farces, which turn upon ribald seduction and courtship scenes which are primarily enacted in terms of an argument or contest of wits between the man and the woman or between the husband and his rival; and second, ritual-combat plays in which the dialogue between the combatants is rendered in elaborate language. The farces, in a sense, elevate the broad-talker to thespian status, while the combat-dramas bring good-talkers onto the stage.

In both categories, there are plays which have a long history of traditional dissemination. Of significance in this regard is the "Mummies" play, which is an extremely full rendering of the British "St. George and the Turk" play (Abrahams 1968b; Chambers 1933). Characteristically, there are a number of word and sword battles between various "champions": St. George and the Turk, St. George and the Black Prince of Paradise, and so on. The orations are not unlike those of the Tobago *Speech Band*. Similar plays are given about "Giant Despair and Christian," (taken from *The Pilgrim's Progress*) and "David and Goliath" (stemming, in part, from a homiletic play by Hannah More). A recent development on the pattern of serial combat of word and action is "The Cowboys and the Indians" plays. In these a whole set of characters introduce themselves, characters ultimately derived from Street and Smith pulp novels of the 1930's (with a big debt to Hollywood, as well). Then a situation is structured in which two of the cowboys, like "Bing Crosby from the Golden West" and "The Bar Bully" have a showdown. After a number of such confrontations, the Indians introduce themselves one by one (always as "black men") and there ensues a battle royal between the two groups—a fight not always won by the cowboys.

Troupes often know and perform two or three plays. The troupes are organized by a man-of-words who knows the plays by memory; he teaches the parts to the others by writing out "lessons" for them or by repeating the lines with them. The personnel changes from year to year, but organized as the troupes are around the "Captain," there is no threat of a break in the tradition. The captain usually has a "number-two man" who helps him put together the production every year. New troupes usually are formed when a number-two man goes off on his own. This is an apprentice system similar to that of the *Speech Band* on Tobago, but there are inherent weaknesses in this arrangement as developed on Nevis that have recently led to a breakdown in the performance of these Christmas "sports."

A certain amount of community cooperation is called for in organizing the troupe. In the past this was put into effect through the respect accorded the man-of-words; he usually was a highly regarded member of the community because of his verbal abilities. Emigration has carried away many of the best virtuosos. It has become more difficult for those remaining to attract personnel to their troupes, a situation aggravated by the increasing ego-involvement of the captains.

These factors have created a situation in which the position of captain is no longer one of such high status. The remaining captains react to this change by insisting that they be given their proper respect, especially by the younger members of the community who make up the potential additions to the troupe. The young find that they not only have to learn their parts from the captain but they also have to proclaim their respect for him over and over again. They react by refusing to join him. The only recruits, then, tend to come from the ranks of children of those players who have been with the captain in the past.

The Cowboy groups have less of a problem in this regard because of the number of status roles within the play itself, and because the role of the captain has devolved upon a number of players. The young players are anxious to graduate to important roles and the Cowboy Play allows them to do this because any number of combats can be added without altering its shape. One captain of an older play, "The Christmas Bull," found that the only way he could hold his troupe together was to rewrite the play. In the original there was one role for a bull who had a comic fight with an inept local plantation owner, but in the revision eight other bulls were added. Most of the captains are not willing to make such changes. If changes are made they are generally in the direction of enhancing the part played by the captain, already the longest and most heroic role.

The language of most of these plays is extremely ornate and hyperbolic, especially the hero-conflict dramas. A champion must, after all, excel in both words and deeds. The boasting speeches are not, however, quite so broad in style and outlandish in diction as the speeches made during the Tea Meeting.

The Nevis *Tea Meeting* is a remarkable combination of pageant, mock fertility ritual, variety show, and organized mayhem. The proceedings probably developed most immediately out of fund-raising church events introduced in the nineteenth century,[8] and are still to be encountered on a number of other islands in the British West Indies, but in many different forms (DeCamp 1967). Until recently, Tea Meetings were held often on Nevis on summer evenings during the full of the moon. A hall is engaged and a King and Queen and their court are chosen. Costumes are carefully prepared for the royalty and for the other performers. The night of the performance, the King and Queen are called for by a fife and drum (Big Drum) band. They go to the place of meeting where the rest of the community has gathered. Then they sit on the stage while members of the audience come up and perform some prepared routine—a song, poem, dialogue, speech, or dance, done by one or two performers, or a team song and dance such as *Japanese Fan Drill* or *Baby Drill*. The participants wear costumes appropriate to whatever role they are playing. In the middle of the evening tea (cocoa, or some other hot drink) is served, and some ceremonial cakes, fruit hanging from a *harbor* (sic), and kisses from the King and Queen are ritualistically auctioned. Then the King, the Queen, and members of the court make elaborate and ironic speeches. This is followed by other acts from the audience, which continue until dawn if the meeting is a good one. In the back sit the scoffers who make loud and often obscene comments about the performers and their routines.[9]

Organizing, or attempting to organize, the proceedings are two "chairmen." They are supposed to give a sense of continuity and order to the show and to determine who should perform at what time and when the tea should be served. One of them usually calls the meeting to order by making a plea for "decorum" and this speech announces the tone for the night.

> Ladies and gentlemen, this afternoon we stand here to accompany this company here, ladies and gentlemen, and I want to here, this afternoon, have decorum. Decorum. Remember the alphabet, ladies and gentlemen: A is for attention, B is for behavior, C is for conduct, and D is for DECORUM. And, ladies and gentlemen, as we march on further, we go to J is for justice and P is for peace that is Heaven for the flocks. I ask you to remember those few letters in the alphabet: A, B, C, D, P and J. Ladies and gentlemen, I won't procrastinate much more of the valuable time while I ask _____ to provide me with a piece.

As the chairmen continue to make their introductions and to comment on each act, it becomes clear that they are in fact the premier performers. They must not only make these interpolated speeches but they must also attempt to outshine the other performers, and most important, each chairman must prove himself the best speaker there. As they put it, each wants to be regarded as "the cock with the brightest comb." They preen their feathers by making long, inflated, macaronic speeches.

> That song reminded me of Moses standing on the banks of the Red Sea. It fills my heart

with *phil-long-losophy, entrong-losophy, joken* and *conomaltus. Impro, imperium, pompry, comilatus, allus comigotus,* which is to say I come here today without any study. *Dia Gratia,* by the grace of God, I have tried my best. Time is *tempus fugit.* The same. I will say a few words about Moses. His life he went into different parts; he spent forty years in Egypt, forty years in Medea, and forty years in the wilderness. I shall now, *sum bonum, malcum cum shalltum propendum peerum, desideratum, wōbiteratum attitaratin.* I shall now say *veedie, veedie, amrie,* which is to say, I came, I saw, and I conquered. And shall now leave my stand *backon-awalum, eloquent, precipitie, matic-matic, savong-savong.* For I'm well-known for this, a wild cannonball speaker. Who thinks they can come over harder than I? Why if anyone here come from the school, I come from the college. If they're from the college, I'm from the Temple Bar. If they are from the Temple Bar, I am from the House of Parliament. If they are from the House of Parliament, I am from the city of Cairo that is in Egypt.

Speeches of this sort simply proclaim the challenge that the other chairmen or some other performer felt called upon to accept. Meanwhile, each flourish of language causes the emotions of the audience to rise, including the hecklers in the back. As the noise mounts, the chairmen feel more of a need to assert their control, not only by becoming more eloquent but louder, and quite often, insulting. In one recent Tea Meeting reported to me, the only way one of the chairmen could reassert control was to grab his wife and to begin to do a highly obscene dance, but obscenity is not out of bounds on an occasion like this.

Most Nevisians will tell you they still love Tea Meetings. But recently there have been very few of them. The reasons are primarily the same as those that are causing the demise of some of the Christmas sports. The chairmen have become ego-involved all too often, and this is sensed by the audience, especially the hecklers. There is little attraction in placing oneself in such an assailable and potentially embarrassing position, and few young men are willing to learn the speechmaking craft. All of the chairmen, consequently, are middle aged or older, and therefore of the age which is becoming less respected and obeyed by the young. The brightest of the young, moreover, continue to leave the island. The competitive atmosphere in which the ceremony developed has now become overripe because of the insecurities felt by all; this is embarrassingly dramatized by the chairmen who fail to keep order. Whereas conflict or competition used to be the major form of communication and reaffirmation of community spirit, it now contributes to the feeling of anomie.

The breakdown of the traditional practices is, in other words, part of the larger degeneration of communication channels. People on Nevis in too many cases have retreated into themselves, lashing out at anyone who happens to come too close. In certain cases, this has resulted in a family banding together in the face of the threat from others in the community, but in other situations it is only the individual who becomes defensive and even paranoid.

THE SOCIAL USES OF THE PATTERN

In presenting Nevisian and Tobagonian man-of-words traditions in terms of their constituent elements and their recent changes, an attempt has been made to show that a variety of non-aesthetic forces may have important repercussions on aesthetic activities. But it has also been pointed out that these performances, as aesthetic entities, represent a model of interpersonal relations in the surrounding community. When forces within or outside the community bring about changes in these relations, these changes will be reflected within the structure of the traditional performance. The performance is, after all, a stylization.

The Nevisian Christmas plays are, as pointed out, very similar to the Carnival *Speech Mas'* on Tobago, especially in regard to the boasting rhetoric and the combative scene presented. But there is a wide divergence between the two islands in regard to the model of interpersonal relationships provided by these activities. These differences reflect a real divergence of world view. In the *Speech Mas'*, the band is organized on a double principle of status. The King is regarded as the finest speechmaker, but the Commander handles the business affairs—collecting the money, holding it, arranging with the Commander of the competing groups who should speak first and for how long. It is these two who must keep order throughout the contest. This dual responsibility, in addition to the provision for apprenticeship, diffuses attention away from a single performer. A sense of hierarchical order and decorum is built into such performances, bringing about a sense of control at all times in the proceedings. On the other hand, this very sense of order allows for greater flexibility in regard to the poetic orations. There are two kinds of speeches made by members of the Speech Band: set pieces written ahead of time, and improvised speeches which reply to one or another piece of the other team (usually the one just before the improvisation). The strength of the group therefore resides in part in the ability of the members in composition and memorization, and in part in their ability to improvise in proper style. The emphasis always is on coordination even in the contest atmosphere. Conflict becomes a positive mode of socialization.

On Nevis, the freedom to improvise is totally absent in the Christmas plays. One man knows the plays, teaches all the parts, takes the most important and heroic part himself, and it is his show from beginning to end. Such plays call for a high degree of coordination, and this coordination can only occur through community acquiescence in the charismatic leadership of the captain, and to some extent, his second man. It is up to these leaders to see that the players speak their lines as taught them, to work, in other words, from their position of superordination. This reliance on the compositions of the past seems to exist not so much as an aspect of the tradition-orientation of the community as a direct reflection on the insecurities of the captains, who must fall back on the patterns developed in the past.

The Nevis Tea Meeting, on the other hand, does call for ability to improvise on the part of the chairmen. But once again, there are significant differences between this technique and that of the members of *Speech Mas'*, for while the Nevisian man-of-words calls attention to himself through his improvisation. the Tobagonian speaks both for himself and for his team. Not only is there more occasion for improvisation on Tobago, but there is greater range of freedom in regard to topics the speaker may explore in his speech. The Tea Meeting chairman, to be sure, must "answer" the challenges hurled at him, and in the same terms as the challenge, but usually he merely uses the other speaker' theme to introduce his speech; and once the introduction is over he will fall back on set pieces he has used in the past. He may thus say, in answer to the speaker before him, "That magnificent, fantastico-fantastical rendition of that song of sorrowful parting brings to mind Ruth and Naomi standing 'midst the alien corn," and then he is free to give a speech learned in Sunday School about Ruth and Naomi, embellishing it with choice phrases from Greek and Latin. On Nevis, in other words, the man-of-words is just as restricted in his expressions as the community is in other aspects of life. The interpersonal contests which feature the performances are fraught with anxieties and tensions and are focused upon the individual performer; in throwing so much of himself into the performance he reflects, in a heightened fashion, the day-to-day interpersonal relations of most members of peasant groups on the island. Traditional contests, once a viable model of socialization, have become untenable to a group too strife-ridden; the order of the performance is dissipated, along with the importance of the man-of-words.

The juxtaposition of these two island cultures is instructive in a number of ways. First of all, it points to the wide range of responses to the plantation system and its decay which can be observed in the West Indies and shows that one gauge of diversity and change is to be found in the area of traditional performances. Second, it shows that though a pattern of organization may be observed in a number of communities, it may find very different uses and reflect almost diametrically opposed values. Furthermore, it suggests that such values can be clearly observed operating in the life of a traditional representation, and that such observation can lead to important insights that go far beyond purely folkloristic matters.

I have here shown in a tentative manner what might be done if we followed Herskovits' suggestion to work comparatively with the folkloristic data in hand to attempt to assess what is constant about the traditions in a culture area and what the important variables are. Here I have limited myself to a pattern of performance and to a discussion of that pattern on only two small islands. A similar study might profitably be made of problems such as the role of the scandalpiece, the libelous composition on local personages and events, in the maintenance of law and social control. In addition, study of the ways in which subordination has been handled in different Afro-American communities seems called for. Another fruitful study in the same realm would be a comparison of those New World Negro groups which encourage improvisation in their artforms, and those which discourage it, a topic only touched upon here. Such subjects, and others like them, might provide important insights into the value structure of communities and into the ways in which communications channels are established, used, maintained, changed, or eliminated.

NOTES

1. Material for this paper was gathered during a year in which I was a John Simon Guggenheim Fellow; I am, of course, much indebted to that foundation. I am also indebted to my colleague, David DeCamp, for valuable suggestions in regard to the operations of the man-of-words.

2. Recent ethnographic evidence indicates that the basis of the pattern comes from Africa. See, for instance, Messenger 1959; Blacking 1961; and Finnegan 1967. What Ethel M. Albert (1964:35) says of the Arunda seems typical of other African groups: "Eloquence is one of the central values of the cultural world view; and the way of life affords frequent opportunity for its exercise. Sensitivity to the variety and complexity of speech behavior is evident in a rich vocabulary for its description and evaluation and in a constant flow of speech about speech. Argument, debate, and negotiation, as well as elaborate literary forms are built into the organization of society as a means of gaining one's ends, as social status symbols, and as skills enjoyable in themselves."

3. I have elsewhere made this distinction, using the terms "good talker" and "good arguer." However, I have found this pair to be somewhat misleading, since arguing is an important weapon for both types. Consequently, I have developed upon the distinction in terms of level of diction, made by many West Indians between the art of "talking good" and that of "talking broad" or "talking bad," because "bad" talk means approximately the same thing in both the United States and the West Indies—being verbally facile, using a rapid-fire delivery, and a low but colorful diction.

4. Tobagonian *mas'es* are similar in organization and style to those described by Daniel J. Crowley, Andrew Carr and others, in the issue of *Caribbean Quarterly* (1956) devoted to Carnival on Trinidad.

5. "Chantwells" are also found connected with other *mas'es*.

6. One exception to this is that along with the teachers and trades-people in town, they are often picked to be godfathers, a position of some importance and responsibility in this community.

7. There is only a vestige of ancestor worship and very little fear of the walking (malevolent) dead in Plymouth.

8. A meeting of such a nature, under the name of *Tea Meeting*, is described on the neighboring island of Antigua in the early nineteenth century by Mrs. Lanigan (1844: Vol. 2, 171–74).

9. The importance of this organized chaos is strongly felt, in public performances, throughout English-speaking Afro-America (and probably elsewhere). Reisman has commented on its institutionalization in his article in this volume.

Nine

THE HOMOGENEITY OF AFRICAN–AFRO-AMERICAN MUSICAL STYLE

Alan Lomax

When Afro-American song style (so much in dispute among American folklorists and musicologists) is studied within a perspective of world song style, it can be seen as a typical member of one African style family, somewhat affected by European acculturation. In spite of the fact that blacks in the American colonies learned the various musical languages of their masters, they always adapted these novel musical devices to their ongoing black African stylistic practices. Such sweeping statements can only be supported or challenged in a context of comparison that includes data from Africa, Western Europe and the New World, both white and black. Here a report is made on such a study and one of its principal findings: Afro-American music, considered as a whole, is a sub-system of a continental Black African style tradition that seems to be one of the most ancient, consistent, and fertile of world musical families.

These conclusions were reached through the use of an empirical system for rating song performance called Cantometrics—the joint invention of Victor Grauer and myself. The Cantometric rating sheet enables trained judges to score a series of recorded song performances on the relative presence or absence of a number of pre-defined characteristics. (For a further explanation of Cantometrics the reader is referred to earlier sources—Lomax 1962, 1967 and Lomax *et al*. 1968, in which the Cantometric coding book appears.) This empirical rating scheme was applied to 2500-plus songs from 233 cultures for which information on social structure was available in George Murdock's *Ethnographic Atlas*. The cultures were assigned to culture areas in accordance with the Murdock culture-area system. The layout of the African sample appears in Table 9-1.

TABLE 9–1. *The Cantometric Sample for Africa*
N = 709 Songs

	No. of Songs		No. of Songs		No. of Songs		No. of Songs
WESTERN SUDAN		AFRICAN HUNTERS		Hehe	10	AFRO-AMERICAN	
Malinke	10	Dinga	10	Dasoga	10	Toco	13
Dogon	15	Mbuti	10			Carriacou	34
Diola-Fogny	10	Kung	10			Haiti	10
Bambara	10			MADAGASCAR		Jamaica	10
				Merina	10	Salvador	12
		SOUTH AFRICAN BANTU		Betsileo	10	Southern U.S.	11
EASTERN SUDAN		Chopi	10	Bara	10	Colombia-Ecuador Negro (Pacific Littoral)	10
Azande	11	Xhosa	10	Tanala	10		
Shilluk	10	Lozi	10	Sakalava	13		
Mayogo	10	Ndau	11	Tandroy	10		
Mamvu	10	Sotho	10			NORTH AFRICA	
		Shona	10			Egyptians	10
		Zulu	11	EQUATORIAL BANTU		Shluh	10
				Fut	10		
UPPER NILE				Bulu	14	SAHARA	
Luo	11			Ekonda	10	Kunta	10
Nandi	9	CENTRAL BANTU		Luba	12	Tuareg-Hoggar	10
Nuer	11	Bemba	10	Topoke	10		
Masai-Arusha	8	Lala	12			MOSLEM SUDAN	
Dinka	10	Luvale	10			Hausa	11
Pari	10					Wolof	8
				GUINEA COAST		Fulani	9
		NORTHEAST BANTU		Baule	10		
		Bahima	13	Fon	10	ETHIOPIA	
		Ruanda	9	Toma	10	Amhara	17
NIGERIAN PLATEAU		Unguja	10	Susu-Mende	6	Afar	8
No Sample.		Chagga	10	Yoruba	10	Galla	10

When each batch of Cantometric song style analyses is punched and computerized, the computer assembles areal profiles. These profiles are assumed to be statements about the most frequent musical behaviors likely to be encountered in a given area. The following display shows two such modal song performance profiles—one for *African Hunters* and one for *Sahara* (see Figures 9-1 and 9-2). The nature of the strong and evident contrasts between these two African sub-styles will become clear in what follows.

The two profiles represent the most extreme contrast to be found in Africa, indeed, in the world. It will be noted that the African Hunter profile runs mostly down the right side of the sheet where almost all the qualities that have to do with a highly integrated style are scored. If the reader will turn to pages 198–99, he will immediately note the similarity of this profile to those of Africa and Haiti. In fact, the computer programs for determining the level of similarity between such complex

AFRICAN–AFRO-AMERICAN MUSICAL STYLE   LOMAX

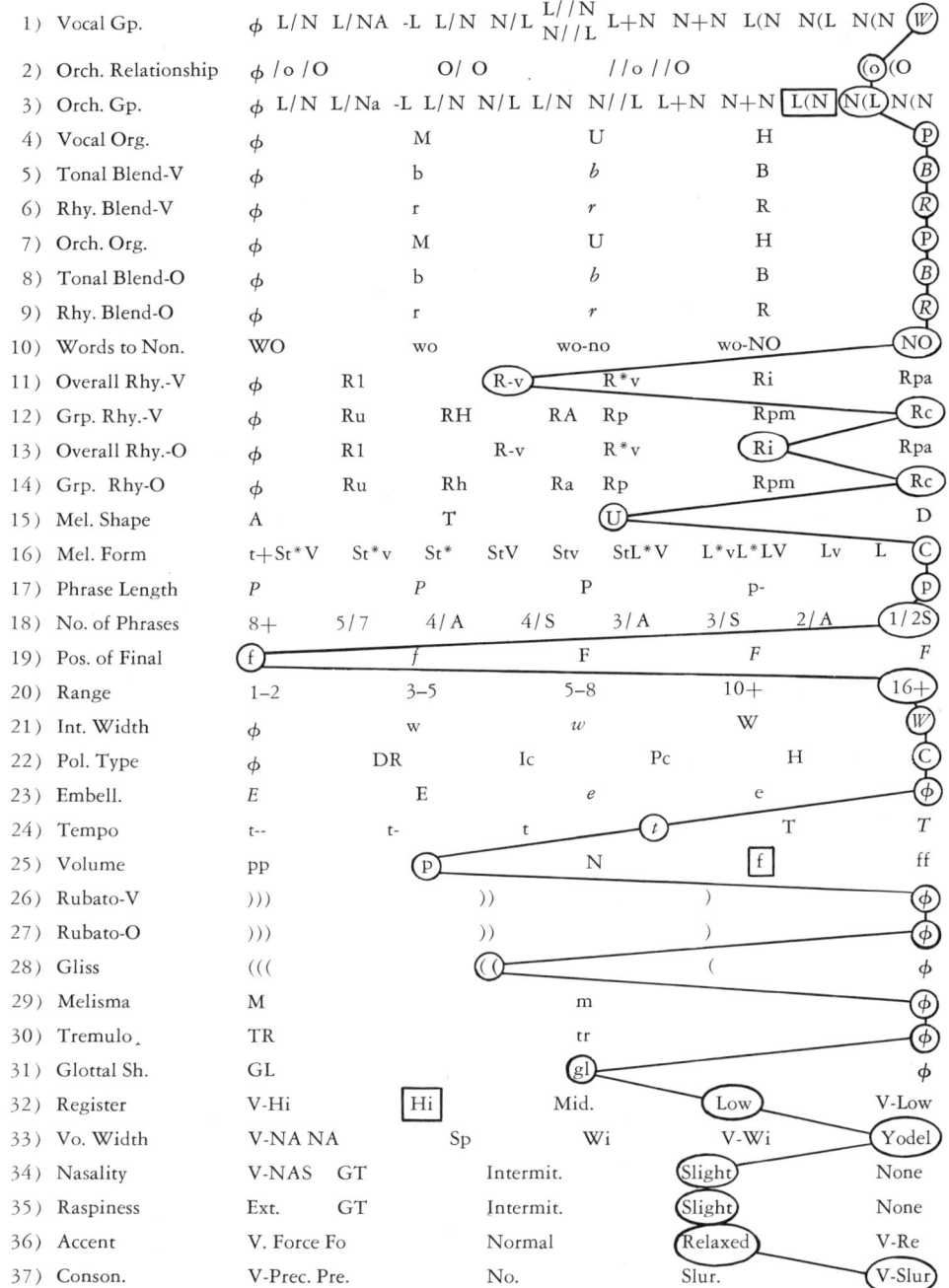

FIGURE 9-1. Cantometric Profile for African Hunters—30 Songs

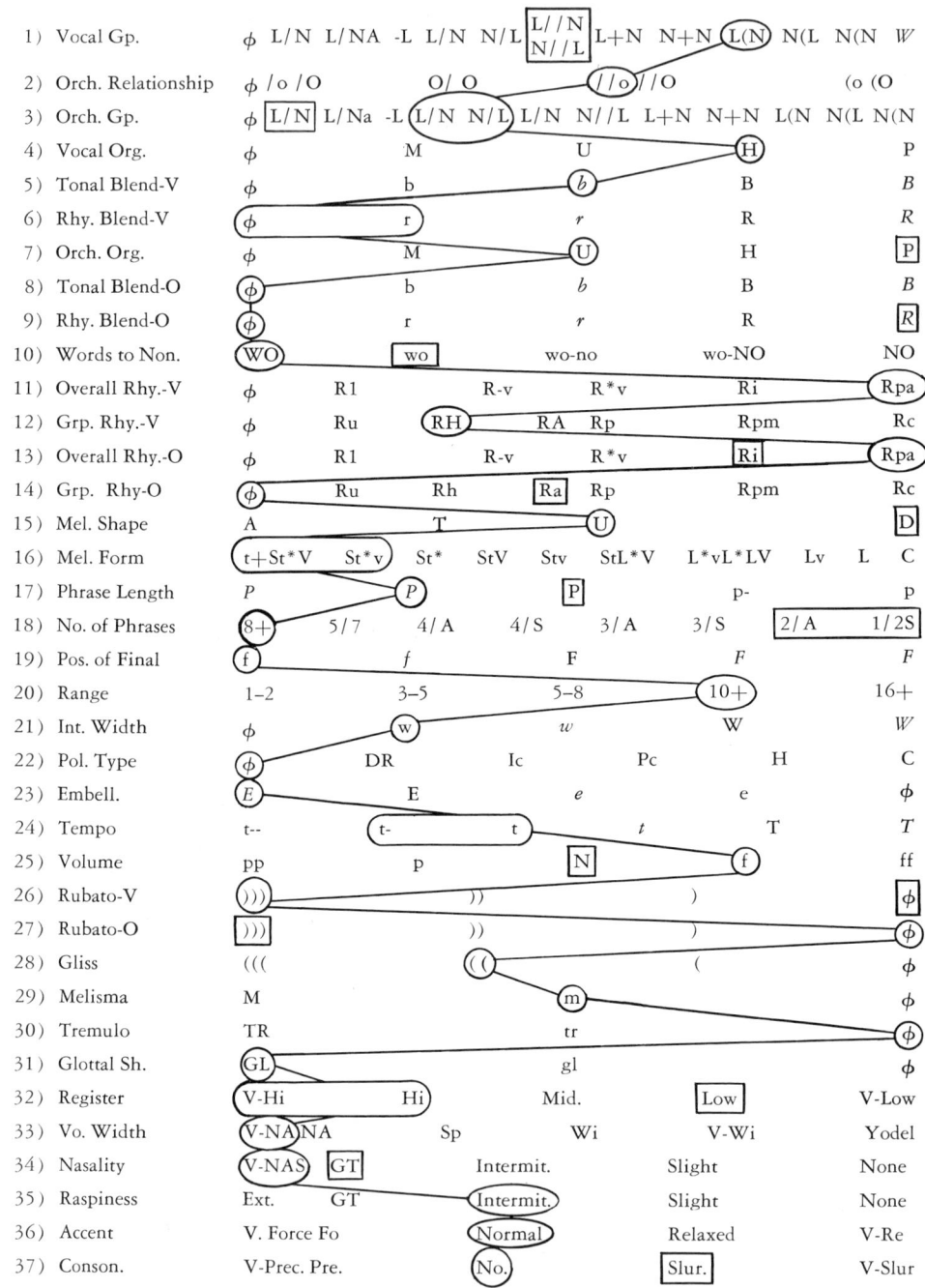

FIGURE 9-2. Cantometric Profile for Sahara—20 Songs

patterns would cluster these profiles in one family, along with all others from Black Africa and at a distance from the rest of the world. On the other hand, the Saharan profile, which runs largely down the left side and includes many of the traits we have come to associate with solo exclusive dominance in a performance, belongs to the stylistic type which is most common in the Orient.

The computer output has been considerably simplified in order to present the reader with profiles easier to inspect. Although there are generally several scores on every line, I have only indicated the most frequent point (enclosed in a circle) together with the next most frequent point (enclosed in a box)—if the two scores were fairly close. It must be realized that all the states or traits, represented by all the points on every one of the lines, probably occur with some frequency in every culture. In fact, however, most states are extremely infrequent, because song traditions confine the range of performance behavior within very narrow limits. After years of testing this scoring system, we are convinced that, when one characteristic occurs with a clearly major frequency on one line, this probably stands for a major tendency in the traditional music being studied. Each point singled out on these profiles, then, represents a song performance trait of extremely high frequency in its region. There now follows a running account of the two contrasting styles—African Hunter and Saharan.

1. *Vocal group: social organization.* African Hunter—interlocked; Saharan—overlapped; both very integrated, African Hunter—integrated and acephalous.
2. *Relation of orchestra to vocal group.* African Hunter—small, interlocked, and integrated; Saharan—heterophonic.
3. *Orchestral group organization.* African Hunter—overlapped, integrated; Saharan—unison, less integrated.
4. *Vocal group: musical organization.* African Hunter — polyphonic; Saharan — heterophonic.
5. *Chorus: tonal blend.* African Hunter—well blended; Saharan—moderately blended.
6. *Chorus: rhythmic blend.* African Hunter—well blended; Saharan—diffuse.
7. *Orchestral organization.* African Hunter—polyvoiced; Saharan—unison and polyvoiced.
8. *Orchestra: tonal blend.* African Hunter—well blended; Saharan—diffuse.
9. *Orchestra: rhythmic blend.* African hunter—well blended; Saharan—diffuse and well blended.
10. *Textual repetitiveness.* African Hunter—very repetitive; Saharan—nonrepetitive.
11. *Chorus: rhythmic type.* African Hunter—simple meters; Saharan—rubato parlando—free rhythm.
12. *Chorus: rhythmic organization.* African Hunter — contrapuntal; Saharan — heterophonic.
13. *Orchestra: rhythmic type.* African Hunter—irregular meters; Saharan—free or irregular meter.
14. *Orchestra: rhythmic organization.* African Hunter — contrapuntal; Saharan — accompanying or only one instrument.
15. *Melodic contour.* African Hunter — undulating; Saharan — undulating and descending.
16. *Melodic form.* African Hunter — canon; Saharan—through composed and complex strophe.
17. *Phrase length.* African Hunter—1 to 2 seconds; Saharan—5+ to 7+ seconds.
18. *Number of phrases.* African Hunter—1 to 2; Saharan—more than 1 or 2.
19. *Position of final.* African Hunter and Saharan—at the bottom of the sung scale.
20. *Average melodic range.* African Hunter—over two octaves; Saharan—more than a tenth.
21. *Interval width.* African Hunter—very wide octave skips frequent; Saharan—narrow minor seconds frequent.
22. *Polyphonic type.* African Hunter—counterpoint; Saharan—none.
23. *Embellishment.* African Hunter—very infrequent; Saharan—frequent and lavish.
24. *Tempo.* African Hunter — moderate; Saharan—slow and very slow.

25. *Volume*. African Hunter—soft and loud; Saharan—loud and moderate.
26. *Chorus: rhythmic freedom*. African Hunter—strict tempo; Saharan—rhythmically very free and some strict tempo.
27. *Orchestra: rhythmic freedom*. African Hunter—strict tempo; Saharan—strict tempo and some rhythmic freedom.
28. *Glissando*. African Hunter—frequent use; Saharan—frequent use.
29. *Melisma*. African Hunter—few or none; Saharan—frequent.
30. *Tremolo*. African Hunter—little or none; Saharan—little or none.
31. *Glottal shake*. African Hunter—frequent; Saharan—*very* frequent.
32. *Register*. African Hunter—low and some high; Saharan—very high or high with some low.
33. *Vocal width*. African Hunter—very wide with yodel; Saharan—very squeezed in, narrow.
34. *Nasality*. African Hunter—slight touches; Saharan—constant high nasalizing.
35. *Raspiness*. African Hunter — touches; Saharan—little or intermittent.
36. *Accent*. African Hunter—relaxed; Saharan—clear.
37. *Enunciation of consonants*. African Hunter—absent or very slurred; Saharan—clear or somewhat slurred.

The percentage similarity between the two profiles is 48%, far below the world average of 68% similarity for the 56 areas in the sample. Despite the overall dissimilarity of Saharan and African Hunter song profiles, however, the two share several traits that are universal and important throughout the continent—predominance of one phrase form, hot rhythm in the orchestra, and overlapped antiphony. These three traits together can give almost any music an African feel, forming a pattern that is both extremely old and uniquely African.

A second program computed the similarities between 56 such style profiles for the 56 culture areas covered by the Cantometric survey. Thereupon a factor analysis of the table of similarities, between each of the 56 areas and all others, produced clusters of the most closely linked areas. (For a further explanation of the statistical considerations involved, see Appendices 1 and 2, Lomax et al., 1968.) This factored musical style world is displayed in Table 9-2 which shows the findings of the factor analysis. The computer found six factors which grouped the areas together in the most efficient statistical classifications. This six-factor arrangement turned out to be the same system of cultural-geographic regions which we had discovered previously as the main style regions for song: (1) Black Africa, (2) Old High Culture (including North Africa), (3) Aboriginal North America, (4) Europe, (5) Insular Pacific, and (6) South America. (See Lomax et al., Ch. 4.)

Table 9-2 shows how the 56 areas were rank-ordered in terms of their loadings on each of the six factors. In the first four factors, each cluster is relatively pure of regional outliers. Thus, Equatorial Bantu stands at the head of #1, the Black African factor, and all areas of Black African culture lie above the 50% level in the rank order of loading on that factor. In the same way, the 40% level of loadings per factor clusters together musico-geographic areas that outline three other grand culture regions of continental dimensions—*Old High Culture, Aboriginal North America*, and *Europe*. In the case of the final two musico-geographic factors—Insular Pacific and South America—30% loading level gathers all the appropriate areas into the regional sets.

Thus a factor analysis of similarities of the areal song styles of the world shows that Black Africa, centering around the style of Equatorial Africa, is the most homogeneous of song style regions. The upper third of the African factor includes all of

TABLE 9-2. *Six World Style Regions Produced by Factor Analysis (27-Line Semi-P Similarity: Q-Factor Varimax)*

LOADINGS RANGE %	AFRICA	OLD HIGH CULTURE	NORTH AMERICA	EUROPE	INSULAR PACIFIC	SOUTH AMERICA
85–89	Equat. Bantu					
80–84	E. Sudan So. Afr. Bantu		S. W. Hunters			
75–79	Guinea Coast	Urban S.E. Asia Middle East	Arctic America			
70–74	Central Bantu Madagascar Afro-America	E. Asia Near East Village India	Plains Great Basin			
65–69	W. Sudan N.E. Bantu	Malay Indonesia	*Mato Grosso* Pueblos E. Woodlands N.W. Coast	W. Europe W. Eur. Overseas		
60–64	Upper Nile Moslem Sudan	Tribal S.E. Asia North Africa (A)	California	Old Europe Latin America	Melanesia	Andes
55–59	Ethiopia	Himalayas Sahara (A) *Medit. Europe*			Proto-Malay New Guinea	
50–54	*W. Polynesia* African Hunters		E. Brazil	*Central Asia* *Medit. Europe*	Micronesia	Interior Amazonia Guiana
50%						
45–49	E. Polynesia *Old Europe* Tribal India	Central Asia *Australia*	Mexico *Australia*			Caribbean Central America *Mexico* *Arctic Asia*
40–44		*N.E. Bantu* (A)	Patagonia *New Guinea* *Upper Nile* Guiana			
35–39	Melanesia Sahara Latin America	Micronesia Ethiopia (A)	*Interior Amazonia* Ethiopia (A)	Mexico	E. Brazil E. Polynesia	Patagonia
30–34	*E. Brazil* *Mexico* *E. Woodlands* *New Guinea* *W. Europe*	Central America	Andes Caribbean Moslem Sudan (A) *Tribal India* *Arctic Asia*	E. Polynesia W. Polynesia	W. Polynesia Tribal S.E. Asia	Arctic America Tribal S.E. Asia ---------- E. Brazil & Mato Grosso fall below .30 level

Note: Italicized cultures are out of region. (A) indicates out-of-region Africa.

Negritic Africa plus Madagascar and Afro-America. Half the spread of similarity includes all African areas south of the Sahara and only one out-of-Africa area—West Polynesia. Further down the list, below the level of in-region factor loading, Tribal India appears in its only major similarity occurrence in this comparison. All Cantometric style comparisons assert the strong trans-Indian Ocean links between the east coast of Africa, Tribal India, and the Maritime Pacific cultures. At the level of 35%, Sahara (which includes songs from Nubia and the Shluh) shows only a weak relation to the African pattern.

The next regional factor in order of importance and homogeneity is an enormous area, stretching right around the globe from Japan to Mauritania, including all those areas formed or touched by the development of early civilizations. This region, which we have called Old High Culture, embraces the urban-peasant cultures of the Mediterranean and takes in North Africa and the Sahara, above the 50% level of loading. *N.E. Bantu*, which encompasses the Interlacustrine kingdoms of the Watutsi and the Bahima, also shows an attachment to this factor.

The song style regions of Africa, then, seem to be arranged as follows:

1. A Negro heartland, including Madagascar and Afro-America.
2. A transition area between the Sahara and the Bantu heartland, including Western Sudan and N.E. Bantu, Upper Nile, Moslem Sudan, and Ethiopia (above 55%).
3. The African hunter-gatherer cultures—Pygmy and Bushman (above 50%).
4. The Saharan fringe to the North, strongly influencing N.E. Bantu (35%).

Black Africa (including Afro-America) is the most thoroughly recorded of all world regions. The Cantometric sample is drawn from every corner of this world. I feel it is rather unlikely that new field findings will drastically alter the broad outlines of this scheme.

The Cantometric system looks at song performance as a specialized act of communication whose principal function is to organize the response of human collectives in ritual or ritualized situations. It views all song performances in terms of three basic models:

1. Well-integrated and highly cohesive group performance in which the participants conform to an agreed-upon communication plan in a highly disciplined and orderly manner.
2. Moderately or poorly coordinated group performances, in which the participants follow the agreed-upon plan, but show a relative degree of independence from it.
3. Solo performance in which a skilled virtuoso dominates the communication space for a period, thus imposing his communication upon his more or less silent and passive listeners.

The extraordinary homogeneity of African song style is the result of the almost universal use by Africans of the first of these patterns—the highly cohesive, complexly integrated song model. Black Africans synchronize their motor and their vocal acts more tightly than the people of other culture regions. The set of song performance traits which facilitate vocal synchrony and produce unified choral performances are shown, in what follows, to link most Black African culture areas into a tight stylistic cluster. The vertical bars on the chart in Figure 9-3 stand for the full spread of this group of song traits in the whole world sample—from no occurrence to 100% at the top of the chart. Each horizontal line marks the position of an African culture area on one of these style definers.

The chart indicates that African areas tend to cluster in relation to most of the traits. Reading from left to right, one notes that when most Africans sing they are:

non-tense, vocally,
quite repetitious, textually,
rather slurred in enunciation,
lacking in embellishment and free rhythm,
low on exclusive leadership,
high on choral antiphony,
especially high on overlapped antiphony,
high on one-phrase melodies—the litany form,
very cohesive, tonally and rhythmically in chorus,
high on choral integration or part-singing,
high on relaxed vocalizing,
and highest on polyrhythmic (or hot) accompaniments.

This relaxed, repetitive, cohesive, multi-leveled, yet leader-oriented style is distinctively African. It dominates African song from the Cape of Good Hope to the Straits of Gibraltar and west into the American colonies. It is both a source and symbol of African cultural homogeneity.

Further study of the distributions on Figure 9-3 points to another important fact—that the African stylistic center lies between the two historic poles of African cultural history—Egypt and Mediterranean Civilization to the North, and the culture of the ancient African hunters in the south. These appositions can be traced all across the chart in Figure 9-3.

North Africa is represented by an arrow to the right, African Hunters by an arrow to the left, Equatorial Bantu (singled out as the proto-typical Black African area) by a bar to the left, and Afro-America by a bar to the right. Dots represent the remaining African areas. These symbols enable the reader to see how African culture areas group themselves on a series of Cantometric measures. In sum, the following patterns can be seen:

A. (1) *North Africa* is high on complexity factors—such as vocal tension, wordiness, precise enunciation, elaboration, and exclusivity.
(2) *African Hunters* are highest on simplicity factors—repetitiousness, slurred enunciation, absence of solo, acephalous choral organization. (Note: Elsewhere, strong and positive correlations have been established between level of productive and social complexity and degree of wordiness in song texts, precision of enunciation, exclusivity of leadership, use of elaboration in melodic and rhythmic factors. All these increase steadily with complexity (see Lomax et al., 1968).)
(3) *African Negro areas lie between these extremes.*
B. (1) *North Africa* is low on most integration factors—relaxed voice, cohesive, integrated, and interlocked chorus.
(2) *African Hunters* are high or highest on all these factors.
(3) *Negro Africa* is also very high on all these integration factors. Afro-American goes right along with other Black African areas in all these respects.

Several conclusions are indicated:

(1) That Black African song style is the product of two influences: (a) the leadership, dominance-oriented, information-heavy Old High Cultures to the north; (b) the acephalous, groupy, non-specifying African Hunter culture at the center and in the south.
(2) That the majority of Negro song styles are oriented more strongly toward groupiness, integration, and non-specificity than in the opposite direction. In other words, Negro song performance seems to be African Hunter or Pygmoid in type.
(3) Even the song styles of Northern Africa—Tuareg, Nubia, Shluh—retain characteristics which identify them as strongly African, perhaps Pygmoid, in character. Polyrhythm and leader-chorus overlap or interlock are frequent in most African song styles, including that of North Africa. However, these traits are more common

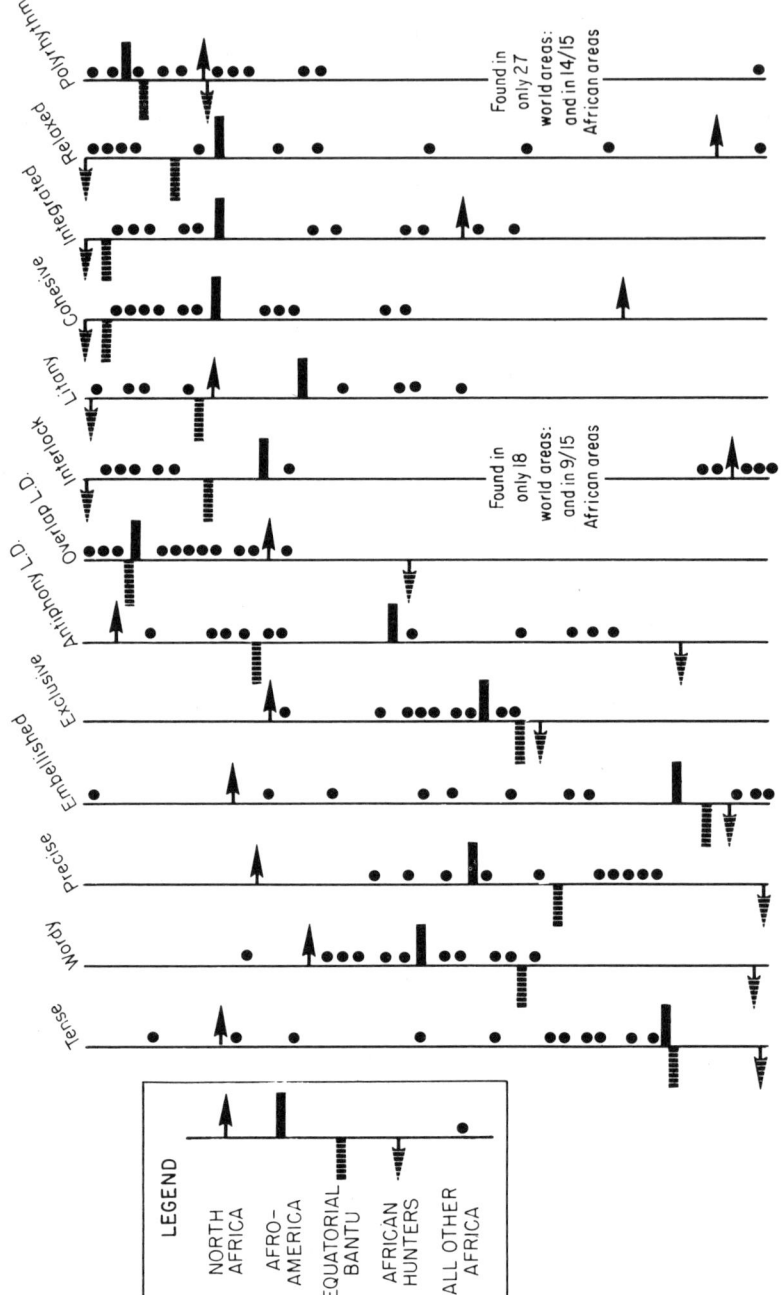

FIGURE 9-3. African Cultural Areas Rated on 13 Cantometric Traits

Note: The vertical lines represent scales of 13 Cantometric Traits from 0 per cent at the bottom to 100 per cent at the top. The position of each African culture area is represented on each scale by a symbol showing the importance of a trait in that particular area. By following the cross-hatched arrows, one can see that African Hunters are low on all complexity scales and high on all integration scales. The opposite condition holds true for North Africa, which is high on all complexity scales and low on all but two integration scales—litany and polyrhythm, which are basic traits of African song. The dots and bars standing for the rest of Africa generally fall between these two extremes with Afro-America (black bar) appearing in the middle of the African cluster.

in Bushman-Pygmy music than in that of any other of the world's peoples.

All integrative traits reach their peak of frequency among the Pygmy-Bushman remnants in Africa. Since the ancestors of these African gatherer-hunters have inhabited most of the African continent since the Paleolithic, it seems logical to attribute this style trace to them. Considered in this way, African Hunter song style is the most extreme form of the African group model. From it the music of the North African desert probably derives its polyrhythmic cast. Hunter style seems to dominate the musics of the black tribes south of the Sahara, and the reason for this is perhaps not far to seek, since the recent history of the African continent—the last 3000 years— is of its gradual occupation by black gardeners and pastoralists. As Negro tribes moved east and south into the jungle, they displaced, often absorbed, or established symbiotic relationships with the African Hunter bands, at the same time, apparently, acquiring their musical style. Evidence is everywhere at hand to support this notion.

(1) Many tribes sing in the hocketing, yodeling, contrapuntal Pygmy style. In all cases these are folk who have only recently replaced or still live in conjunction with the hunters.
(2) These Pygmoid songs are usually the most conservative in style—funeral songs, secret ritual songs.
(3) The tribes whose general style is most Pygmoid are close neighbors or show strong hunter culture influence—notably the South African Zulus, Xhosa, and others, who intermarried with the Bushmen and have Khoisan clicks in their language as well as Bushman traces in their music.
(4) Pygmoid style fades out and disappears among Berbers, Arabs, Cushites, and other peoples to the north and east.

The common stylistic thread which unites all Africa is repetitious, cohesive, overlapping or interlocked, multi-leveled, and hot. This style is primal in Africa, for our evidence points to the African gatherers as the inventors of counterpoint and hot rhythm. Certainly they are the most skillful practitioners of these arts among primitive peoples.

The ancient Pygmy-Bushman strain touches even the solo song styles of Africa. The female bards of the Tuareg, the poets along the Nile, the singing historians of the Watutsi, the praise singers of the Hausa, the court poets of the Zulu, the blues men and Calypsonians of the Americas—all practice a model of solo singing somewhat different from that of the rest of the world. In African solo singing voices tend to be more relaxed and playful—there is more verbal repetition and more slurred enunciation: orchestras are more frequently polyphonic and hot. The interplay between instruments and voice in African music is handled in a style special, among primitive orchestras, to the African Hunters. The Pygmy-Bushman signatures— interlock and overlap—cross talk between members of the orchestra, between the instruments and the singer, and sometimes even between a singer and a supporting solo voice—give African solo-accompanied style its distinctive flavor.

African stylistic unity may then be explained, at a first level, as the result of a unique and universal African experience— encounter with and absorption of the rhythmic traditions (song and dance) of the little people of Africa, famed for their abilities as dancers in the time of the Pharaohs. Since, however, the principal finding of Cantometrics is that song style functions as a suitable symbol for and reinforcement of social norms, we should expect to find that the Hunter style somehow suitably symbolizes the life style of

Black African gardeners. In terms of correlations, established at the $P<.001$ level, African hunter style signals:

(1) high complementarity between males and females
(2) social cohesiveness and solidarity
(3) delight in repetition
(4) an atmosphere of pleasurable eroticism.
(5) part interchangeability — multi-leveled integration.

(For details of these correlations see Lomax et al., 1968.)

This set of musical social traits is a distinctive base line for Black African music when it is compared to the musical styles of the rest of humanity. Within this pattern one finds distinctive differences between Black style on the one hand and Pygmy on the other. Black African style is more text-heavy, more precisely enunciated, and more leader-differentiated than Hunter singing. Cantometrics correlations show that these differential traits are clear indicators of a more complex productive and social system. Thus we have an explanation for the primary distinction between Black and Black Hunter style, even though both are high on all integration factors. In these terms, the Black style may be viewed as the variant of Hunter style, suitable to a culture tradition that was more complex both politically and productively. It is interesting to speculate how the blacks received this style and how they elaborated it, for this is perhaps the main event in the history of Black African music.

About 1500 years ago, as Murdock tells the story (Murdock 1959), Negro tribes in West Africa received the Malaysian crop complex, suitable for tropical agriculture. Thus they could expand south and east into the African jungle, displacing the hunter-gatherer peoples who had been the principal human inhabitants of this territory for thousands of years. The key components in this tropical gardening complex were yams and bananas, crops which generally involve large teams of males clearing and breaking the land and teams of females for the harvest. African yam gardening not only depends heavily on the involvement of women in agriculture, but on large, highly coordinated teams synchronously performing monotonous, simple tasks such as hoeing, weeding, paddling, transporting, hauling logs, and using the mortar and pestle. Without pleasure-giving synchrony in work, the everyday productive activities of tropical gardeners could not have been efficiently performed. The primary component of this work style is the mutual involvement of males and females in joint synchrony or in some symbolic representations of this situation.

The song style of tropical gardeners (notably in Oceania and Africa) reflects these essentials. This is one instance of a general Cantometrics discovery that song style performance varies cross-culturally by subsistence type and work team organization (see Lomax et al., 1968). African Hunter style evolved in a society primarily dependent on a feminine work team. It is feminine, playfully erotic, highly cohesive, and the most tightly and complexly synchronized of all styles. In these respects, it is suitable to the needs of the African Gardeners, since this productive system depends both upon the involvement of females and the operation of highly synchronic teams of agricultural labor performing repetitive tasks. The politically developed African Gardeners, however, usually replaced the acephalous and interlocked choral organization of the Hunters with a system of overlapped antiphony which singles out a strong, dominant leader.

In overlapped antiphony, we encounter a symbol of one of the universals of African life, the yea-saying, responsorial, and seldom silent village council or council of elders. In musical overlap, the chorus sings its part independendantly and responsorially during a portion of the song leader's section. Thus, there is a constant supportive and complementary vocal reaction to every new line the song leader produces.

The erotic nature of Pygmy style was also suitable to an expanding economy needing manpower for its growing lineages and its budding villages. Fertility and sexual prowess are central values in Black African life. Africans explain many of their dances as preparation of young people for their adult sexual roles in a polygynous world. In a world survey of dance we have found that African cultures lead all the rest in emphasis on bodily polyrhythm, where the shoulders and the pelvis erotically rotate and twist, often to two separate and conflicting meters. It looks as if this twisting pelvis style (and its reflection in hot rhythm) infuses African work and play with a steady feed of pleasurable erotic stimuli. These polyrhythms transform monotonous tasks into group amusements. Thus, the importance of full-blown and overt sexuality in the Black African culture pattern is again underlined.

The non-complex structure of text and tune and the multi-leveled structure of Pygmy-Negro performance style facilitate group participation, opening the door for anyone present to make a contrastive and complementary personal contribution to the song-dance performance. Thus in Africa, where large work teams are needed to accomplish heavy, monotonous hand labor in the tropical heat, we find a communication style maximally inviting, encouraging and eroticizing participation by all present. This Negro-Pygmy style was kept alive by the black slaves in America and now forms the baseline for the entire Afro-American tradition.

When the computer compares the similarities of the cultures in the African set analyzed by Cantometrics, the regional system previously presented is confirmed as well as refined. A seven-area classification of African song style emerges that reflects in a surprising measure the broad currents of African ethnography. Two criteria are brought to bear successively on each culture in order to find to which cluster it is most closely related.

(1) The world regional criterion. We rank-order all the similarities of the 66 cultures in the sample that lie within the African continent and split this rank order at the quartile. In order for a culture to be considered African, a larger percentage of its intercultural affiliations must lie above the quartile than in any other of the six world areas. All but nine of 66 African cultures passed this test. Eight of these belong to either Ethiopia, Sahara, or North Africa, territories whose musical style shows stronger areal affiliations to Old High Culture than to Africa.

(2) The areal criterion. In the same way, we looked above the quartile for the area shown to be most similar to each culture. The first-named area was considered the main areal classifier of each culture. In case two adjoining areas seemed to alternate at the peak of similarity for adjacent cultures (similar in other ways), either or both of these areas were used as areal classifiers. All the cultures in groups V, VI, and VII proclaimed their strong inter-similarity to most of the others in this way, but were classified into sets because of moderate tendencies in one direction or another. The cultures in group V were most similar to Central or Equatorial Bantu or to one of the other areas that included the cultures in this set.

In the classification in Table 9-3 a running title for each group appears as the heading for each of eight groups. The digit to the

TABLE 9-3. *66 African Cultures Clustered in Terms of Most Similar Areal Style.* (Indentured cultures are tied less strongly to cluster.)

I. *North African*
   3 Nubian Egypt—IR
   3 Amhara—PA
   7 Kunta—PC
   3 Shluh—IR
   7 Tuareg—PC
   4 Ruanda—CA
   9 Bahima—PC
   2 Fon—CA

   (related to)

II. *Cushitic*
   8 Afar—PC
   6 Galla—PA
   4 Dara—PC
   5 Tandroy—CA

   (tied to)

III. *Nilotic*
   5 Dinka—CA
   5 Nuer—CA
   (tied to Shilluk)

IV. *W. Sudanic*
   3 Wolof—CA
   1 Malinke (weak link)
   2 Bambara—CA
   1 Yoruba (weak link)
   2 Dogon—CA
   2 Hausa—CA
   2 Shilluk—CA
   4 Pari (weak)—CA
   2 Unguja—CA

V. *Gardener*
  (a) *Central*
   2 Luo—CA
   2 Lozi—CA
   0 Demba—CA
   1 Lala—CA
   0 Luvale—CA
   1 Luba—CA
   3 Basoga—CA

  (b) *Equatorial*
   1 Diola—CA
   1 Baule—CA
   1 Dulu—CA
   1 Toma—CA
   1 Mende—CA
   1 Yoruba—CA
   1 Malinke—CA
   0 Ekonda—CA
   3 Hehe—CA
   0 Azande—CA
   5 Nandi—CA
   2 Ndau—CA
   2 Chopi—CA
   2 Shona—CA
   2 Merina—CA
   2 Tanala—CA
   2 Betsileo—CA
   5 Sakalava—CA
   2 Jamaica—PA
   1 So. U.S.—PA
   2 Haiti—PA
   2 Salvador—PA
   1 Carriacou—PA
   1 Toco—PA
   2 Colombia-Ecuador—CA

VI. *South African*
   3 Sotho—CA
   4 Zulu—CA
   3 Xhosa—CA
   3 Chagga—CA

VII. *E. Sudanic* (Semi-Pygmy)
   1 Mayogo—CA
   1 Mamvu—CA
   8 Wodabe—PC
   – Masai-Arusha—CA
   1 Topeke—CA

VIII. *African Hunter*
   0 Kung—C
   0 Dinga—C
   0 Mbuti—C

The number to the left of each name indicates the percentage importance of animal husbandry in the culture on a 1–9 scale. Derived from the *Ethnographic Atlas*.

The letter codes to the right of each name designate the subsistence type on the following scale: C—collectors, G—hunter-fishers, IP—incipient producers, CA—gardeners with animal husbandry, HF—horticulturalists, PC—70% dependence on pastoralism, PA—plow agriculture, IR—irrigation.

left of each name represents the percentage importance of animal husbandry in the subsistence activities of that culture, as recorded in the *Ethnographic Atlas*. The letter code after the name gives the main subsistence type, according to an 8-point production scale developed by Arensberg and Lomax out of Murdock (Lomax *et al.*,

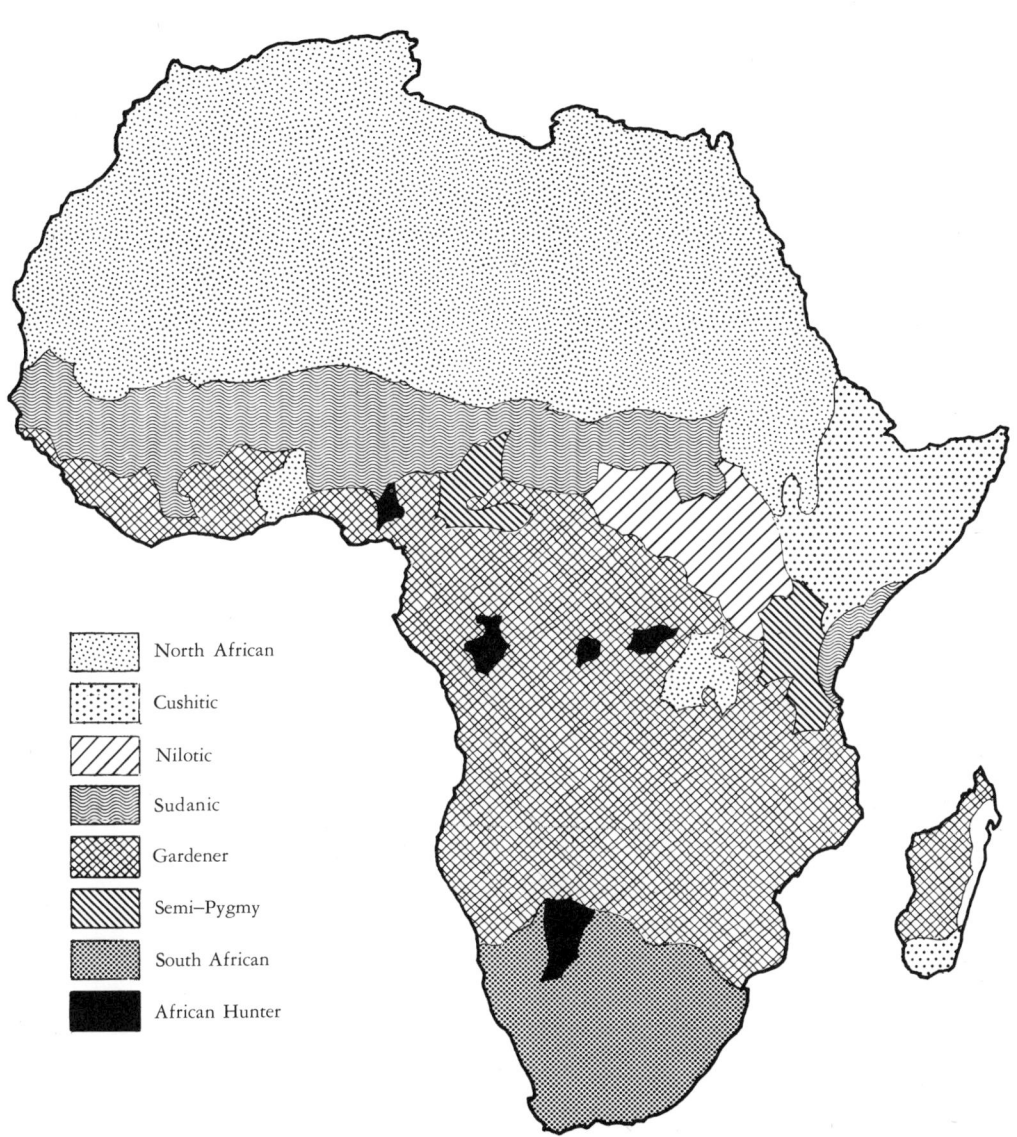

FIGURE 9-4. A Preliminary Sketch Map of African Song Style Areas

1968). It will be noted that the cultures in both the North African and Cushitic groups are more complex in subsistence practices and depend more upon animal husbandry than most members of the other five areal groups. The Nilotes and South Africans (sets III and IV) practice more animal husbandry than other African cultivators. The style of the simplest of African producers, the African Hunters, seems to have survived most clearly among the Eastern Sudanics.

The relevance of this scheme of classification to the cultural and historical geography of Africa becomes more apparent when it is used to map African culture areas. The seven song style areas might be summarily described as follows (see map, Figure 9-4):

1. *North African.* Wherever Old High Culture introduced animal husbandry, cereals, empire, and stratification, an exclusive, wordy, elaborate performance style is found. It dominates the Mediterranean coast, the Atlas, the desert, the Nile Valley, and turns up in the Interlacustrine kingdoms and in the empire of West Sudan and Dahomey.

2. *Cushitic.* Another and less complex aspect of Old High Culture that appears in parallel with style 1. Murdock believes that a Cushitic pastoralism came to Madagascar. Our similarity trace seems to confirm this suggestion.

3. *Nilotic.* Dinka and Nuer form a tight cluster, closely tied to Shilluk and Pari. It resembles West Sudanic in sharing traits with North Africa (importance of solo, solo accompaniment, strophic melodic form) but, in its use of one-beat meter and rhythmic unison resembles the style of the Circum-Pacific.

4. *West Sudanic.* Here, perhaps, is the trans-African sub-Saharan base from which Murdock believes agriculture and animal husbandry were diffused east from Sudan, then west from Azania. This style is still lower on complementarity and cohesiveness scales and higher in dominance and specificity measures than African Gardener styles.

5. *Gardener.* The style traces the spread of the yam gardener complex east into the forests of Nigeria, Equatorial, Lacustrine, and Central Africa, to the Indian Ocean and the Cape of Good Hope. This cluster is so tightly interlinked that, without adopting a new approach to style definition, Cantometric measures will not consistently and dependably subdivide it. This Black African style is found prominently in most of West and Equatorial Africa, in Madagascar and in Afro-America. One notes a general drop in the importance of animal husbandry in this cluster of culture. The Afro-American cultures form a sub-group with a more complex subsistence pattern. The Merina profile has characteristics that link it to Polynesian performance style. Both are text-laden, precise, well-blended, polyphonic, and performed by a simple choral organization—the principal model in Maritime Pacific.

6. *South African.* This style is closely tied to style 5. However, increased frequency of solo indicates complexity, at the same time that higher frequency of integration factors indicates absorption of Bushman influence.

7. *East Sudanic.* This style is tied to style 6. Use of specific African hunter traits such as hocketing, yodeling, interlock, and rhythmic counterpoint, show that these cultures indicate a strong and persistent hunter influence.

8. *African Hunter.* This style is found in pockets all across Black Africa.

Everything that we have learned from looking at clusters of African song style confirms these areal findings. Africa is an extremely homogeneous musical region, split along the southern Saharan border. This borderland looks in two directions: (1) to the complex pastoral or irrigation clusters of the north; (2) to the simpler gardening cultures with their African hunter center in the south. In this border area—among the Cushites, the Nilotes, and the Nubians—there are hints of old levels of Black African singing in which African Hunter influence is perceptible. Songs from this northeastern sector have much in common with the present-day singing of the Ethiopian pastoralists, of the Arabian Bedouins, of the tribes of India, and even of the people of far-distant Oceania. These connections direct our attention to the ancient and continuous ties of East Africa to Arabia, India, and Malaysia.

Meantime, we can perceive that the most familiar, *hot* African musical style developed in the melting pot of the West Sudan and West Africa, was touched with bardic influences from the North and acquired more and more African Hunter elements as the Negro tribes ranged east and south through the whole continent. Seen from this broad perspective, the song styles of Afro-America are, first and foremost, extensions of the cohesive tradition of African gardeners in the Western hemisphere.

A line-by-line Cantometric analysis points to one strong influence upon Negro singing in the West—that of European folk song. The most distinctive feature of West European song is the straightforward presentation of text-heavy, simple strophes. The Afro-American profile varies markedly from that of Africa only in relation to this West European features. Afro-America is: (1) the only African area in the first quartile for four-phrase strophes, where Europe leads the world; (2) the only African area below the median for complex litany (all African Bantu areas are in the first quartile here); (3) the only African area above the median on medium-length phrases (here West Europe leads the world); (4) the only area of African heartland in the first quartile for normal accent and above the median on wordiness, where Europe is in both respects outstanding; (5) the only African area below the median on fast tempo besides the Guinea Coast, which it strongly resembles; (6) the highest of all African areas in employing simple meter, an important trait of both West Europe and Africa.

In all other respects, Afro-American style is Cantrometrically identical with the core African gardener style. Its two closest congeners are Equatorial Bantu, at 85% similarity, and Guinea Coast, at 84% similarity. This conclusion contrasts strongly with that of most other older studies of the subject (Jackson 1943). Such analyses compare *printed* verions of the *melodies* and the *poetic texts* of Negro and white spirituals. If these two features are examined out of the context of their performance or a Cantometric analysis, many American Negro songs seem to be adaptations of white hymns or folk spirituals. Because of the accumulation of such evidence, George Pullen Jackson, who devoted a major part of his career to comparing printed versions of white and Negro sacred songs, concluded that there was not one shred of originality in the American Negro spirituals, that all were derived from white models. In the closing paragraph of his final study of the relation of black and white spirituals, he claimed defiantly that although others were "intent on finding the Ethiopian in the song-fuel heap," he hadn't found him yet!

Cantometric analysis points conclusively in another direction—that the main traditions of Afro-American song, especially those of the old-time congregational spiritual—are derived from the main African song style model. European song style did influence the African tradition in America in regard to melodic form and, of course, textual content. In most other respects, Afro-American song has hewed to the main dynamic line of the principal African tradition. This study of world song style strongly confirms the position taken by Herskovits in *Myth of the Negro Past* (1958:262–67). It is further illustrated by the similarity of an Afro-American performance profile, that of Haiti, to the general African profile (see Figures 9-5 and 9-6). As we have shown, this tradition is

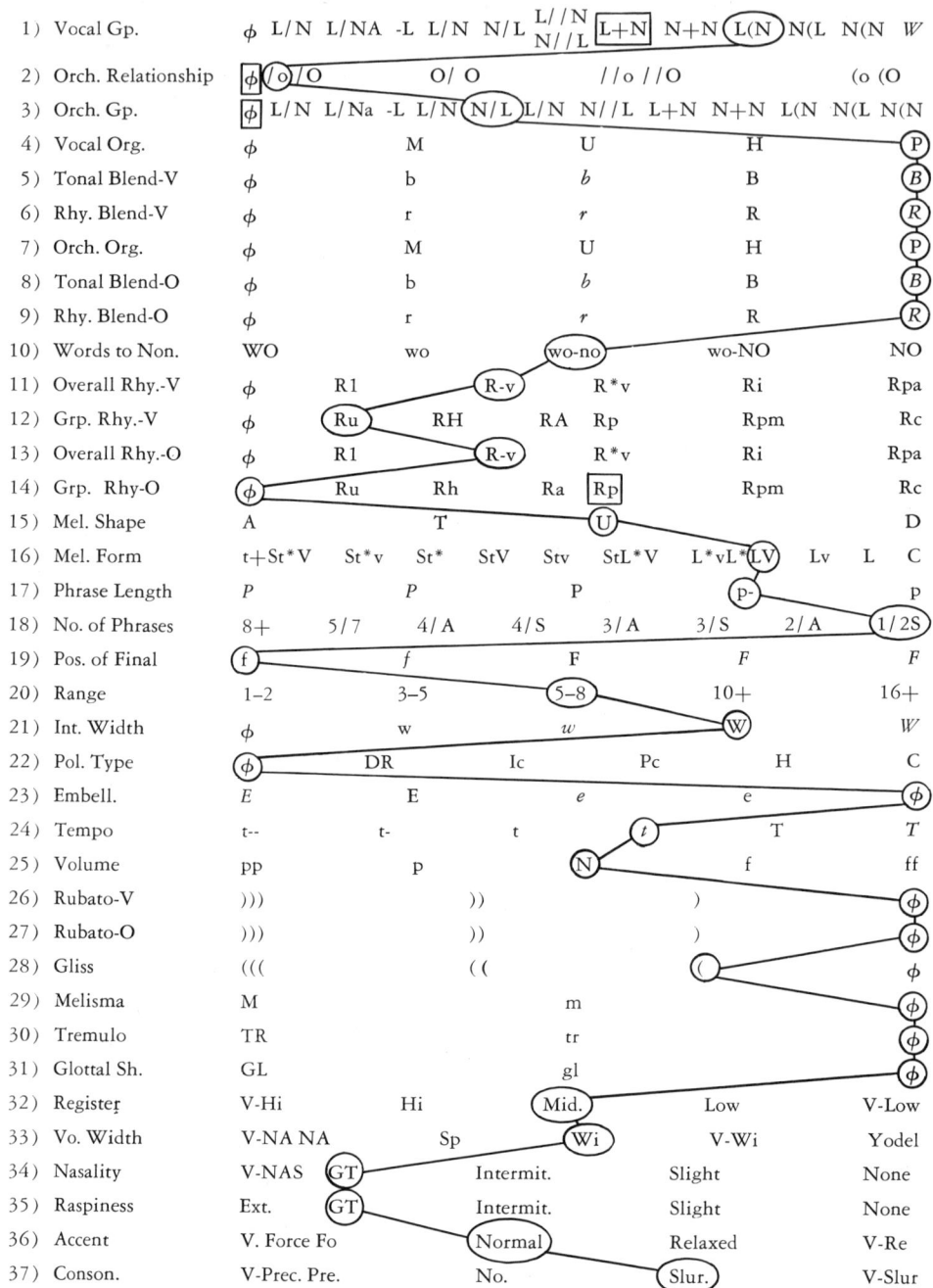

Figure 9-5. Cantometric Profile for Africa—666 Songs

AFRICAN–AFRO-AMERICAN MUSICAL STYLE   LOMAX

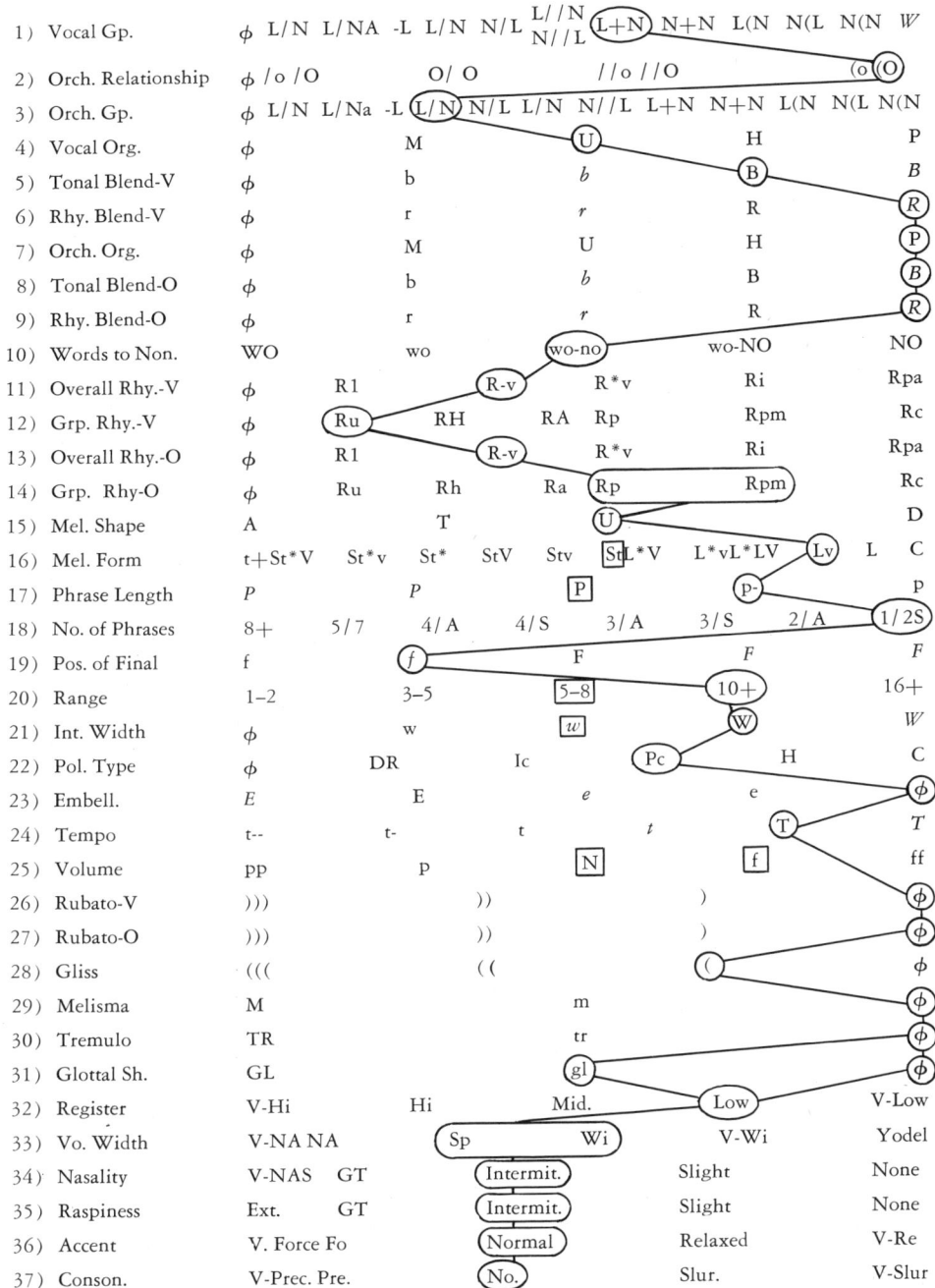

Figure 9-6. Cantometric Profile for Haiti—10 Songs

perhaps the most stable and the most ancient and, in many ways, the most highly developed of the musical languages of mankind.

There follows a brief summary of the main similarities and differences that show up in the comparison of the profiles for continental Africa (including the Cushitic and Arab north as well as Black Africa) and for Haiti. These two profiles show many scores on the right side of the line or in places that enhance highly integrated performance. The Haiti profile is notably less integrated in a number of key aspects. Overlap has diminished in importance. Vocal polyphony has all but disappeared. Choruses are less cohesive. Such a drop in choral solidarity is usually associated with an increase in the information load in the song—that is, with embellishment, with a heavier text load or sharper enunciation text, with more complex musical forms, or with a less wide vocal attack. Several of these traits appear in the Haitian profile.

1. *Vocal group: social organization.* Africa—overlapped antiphony—highly integrated, with some simple antiphony; Haiti—simple antiphony with some overlapped antiphony.
2. *Relation of orchestra to vocal group.* Africa—somewhat accompanying; Haiti—largely interlocked.
3. *Orchestral group organization.* Africa—social unison; Haiti—same.
4. *Vocal group: musical organization.* Africa—polyphony; Haiti—mostly unison.
5. *Chorus: tonal blend.* Africa—well blended; Haiti—moderately well blended.
6. *Chorus: rhythmic blend.* Africa—well blended; Haiti—same.
7. *Orchestral organization.* Africa—polyrhythm and polyphony; Haiti—same.
8. *Orchestra: tonal blend.* Africa—well blended; Haiti—same.
9. *Orchestra: rhythmic blend.* Africa — well blended; Haiti—same.
10. *Textual repetitiveness.* Africa — 50% repetitive; Haiti—same.
11. *Chorus: rhythmic tone.* Africa—simple regular meters; Haiti—same.
12. *Chorus: rhythmic organization.* Africa—rhythmic unison; Haiti—same.
13. *Orchestra: rhythmic type.* Africa—simple regular meters; Haiti—same.
14. *Orchestra: rhythmic organization.* Africa—no orchestra, some orchestral polyrhythm; Haiti—orchestral polyrhythm.
15. *Melodic contour.* Africa—undulating; Haiti—same.
16. *Melodic form.* Africa—litany; Haiti—litany with some simple strophe.
17. *Phrase length.* Africa—3 seconds; Haiti—3 seconds with some 5 to 7 seconds.
18. *Number of phrases.* Africa—1 to 2 phrases; Haiti—same.
19. *Position of final.* Africa—bottom note; Haiti—next to bottom note.
20. *Average melodic range.* Africa—a fifth to the octave; Haiti—a tenth with some fifth to octave.
21. *Interval width.* Africa—wide; Haiti—wide, some diatonic.
22. *Polyphonic type.* Africa—some of all types, types, but no dominant form; Haiti—mostly parallel chords.
23. *Embellishment.* Africa—little or no embellishment; Haiti—same.
24. *Tempo.* Africa—moderate; Haiti—fast.
25. *Volume.* Africa—moderate; Haiti—loud and moderate.
26. *Chorus: rhythmic freedom.* Africa — strict tempo; Haiti—same.
27. *Orchestra: rhythmic freedom.* Africa—strict tempo; Haiti—same.
28. *Glissando.* Africa—some glissandi; Haiti—same.
29. *Melisma.* Africa—infrequent; Haiti—same.
30. *Tremolo.* Africa—uncommon; Haiti—same.
31. *Glottal shake.* Africa—uncommon; Haiti—uncommon and frequent.
32. *Register.* Africa—mid; Haiti—low.
33. *Vocal width.* Africa—wide; Haiti—wide and some grating.
34. *Nasality.* Africa—much nasality; Haiti—intermittent nasality.
35. *Raspiness.* Africa—much vocal harshness; Haiti—intermittent vocal harshness.
36. *Accent.* Africa—moderate accents; Haiti—same.
37. *Enunciation of consonants.* Africa—slurred enunciation; Haiti—much clearer enunciation.

In the lines that have to do with melodic form, the Haitian style bears a clear European stamp, but upon an enduring African model. The similarity of the Haitian profile to that of the Guinea Coast is 69%.

The song styles of black communities in Brazil, Colombia, Venezuela, the United States, and many West Indian islands have been similarly studied Cantometrically. All adhere closely to the core Black African model, some even more closely than Haiti. The telltale stylistic pattern shown in Figure 9-3 is everywhere dynamically in evidence, not only in the musical folk communities, but also in the rich and varied black urban musical traditions. This is not merely a matter of survival of conformity to a blindly accepted heritage from the past. This is an ongoing, highly crystallized approach to communication and to interaction which has brought new music and new cultural developments to live in all American black communities. This core Black African style now affects and challenges, as an equal, the principal communication styles transported to the New World from Europe.

Ten

PERSONAL NETWORKS AND MUSICAL CONTEXTS IN THE PACIFIC LOWLANDS OF COLOMBIA AND ECUADOR[1]

Norman E. Whitten, Jr.

Reprinted with permission from *Man: The Journal of the Royal Anthropological Institute of Great Britain and Ireland* (1968), Vol. 3, No. 1.

This article seeks to analyze the symbolic expression of social relationships. I wish to demonstrate, with reference to a particular part-society, the way in which flexible interpersonal networks are expressed, and to some degree formed, through activities within musical contexts. The focus for analysis is the lower class Negro segment of the Pacific Littoral of Colombia and Ecuador. The Negro segment, consisting of a minimum estimated 250,000 persons, constitutes 90% of the population of the Pacific Littoral extending north from the Esmeraldas River in northern Ecuador to the San Juan River, Colombia, and including the Province of Esmeraldas, Ecuador and the coastal sectors of the Departments of Nariño, Cauca, and Valle, Colombia.[2] The Colombian Chocó is not included in this analysis.

Lower class Negroes in the Pacific lowlands must continually adjust their activities to the vicissitudes imposed by a fluctuating money economy, these fluctuations resulting from a sporadic exploitation of forest and sea resources. At any time, in any area, the money economy is best portrayed as a succession of boom and depression periods. For example, there have been booms in different places, at different periods, centering on gold, rubber, bananas, tagua, timber, fish, and shellfish, and sometimes on secondary booms such as those brought about by road, railroad, and port construction.

Social relationships considered to be adaptive to a fluctuating money economy are those which can be "activated" (Peranio 1961:95) in times of individual need, and in time of economic expansion, but which can remain "untapped" or dormant in time of relative depression. In the Pacific lowlands, activities establishing and reinforcing adaptable social relationships are most apparent in social contexts where music is the dominant mode of expression. For this reason, I will focus on adaptable social relationships which are portrayed through the activities of lower class Negroes in musical contexts.[3] Such activities are continually reinforced through community gossip. People gossip about the behavior of participants in recent musical events, and, through daily gossip, individuals assert strings of debts incurred by co-actors in various encounters within the context of musical occurrences.

The social relationships of the Pacific Littoral make up "quasi-groups" (Mayer 1966:97–102) which involve one internal "categorical relationship" (Mitchell 1966:52), apparently providing a social resource for the establishment of "personal networks." The categorical relationship, is female sexual solidarity. The personal network relationship, defined by Mitchell as "... the network of personal links which individuals have built up around themselves in towns" (1966:54), is adaptable to the money economy.

These concepts will be amplified and illustrated during the discussion of musical contexts in which the personal networks and the categorical relationship are symbolically portrayed, reinforced, and constructed. I will proceed by considering in turn five musical contexts: the *currulao*, or marimba dance; the *chigualo*, or *arrullo* (wake for a dead child); the *alabado* and *novenario* (which includes the wake and post-interment rites for a dead adult); the *arrullo* for a saint ("spiritual," or propitiation rites for a special saint); and the saloon and dance hall situation.

MUSIC AND SOCIAL RELATIONSHIPS

1. The currulao, or marimba dance, is held on most weekends and at special secular events. The music is produced by six or seven male musicians, two of whom play the marimba and the other four, drums; and two or three females shaking tube-rattles (called *guasás*). Most of the patterns of African music described by Waterman (1952:211–12), Merriam (1959:49–86), and Lomax (1962:433, 446–49) are clearly and strongly present.

The ambience of the marimba dance is tense, and the dancing stylized with an "advance-retreat" pattern between men and women being the prevalent style. A woman (or sometimes two women) takes the initiative in inviting the man to dance. The man and woman move toward each other, and then the man retreats and the woman pursues. She then turns her back and retreats, but as soon as he begins to follow she again turns toward him and he again retreats. This pattern is repeated again and again. The woman steadily advances, pivots, retreats, while the man becomes more and more excited, leaps into the air, stamps his feet in time with the drums, shouts, and waves his handkerchief or hat. He may even open his arms as if to grab the woman, but as she turns to him, he retreats (Whitten 1965:124–26; Whitten and Fuentes C. 1966).

Sometimes, when only the male singer performs and relates snatches of a stylized story about a journey, there is no dancing and people listen to the text.

The currulao is attended by a variety of persons from a community and sometimes from adjacent communities. Usually, husband and wife, or even lovers, do not attend the marimba dance at the same time. When couples do attend the same dance they do not dance with each other nor acknowledge each other's presence.

One of the most prominent themes taken from texts in the marimba dance refers to the freedom and necessity of men to move when they wish, to leave their women. The female counter-theme which matches that of the men (and which is sung in vigorous counterpoint to the male theme about travel and leaving women) is that of the ability to hold a particular man, while other men are moving on.

For example, the lead male singer, called *glosador*, always begins the singing with stylized shouts, which are followed by established and improvised verses. The female singers, *respondedoras*, harmonize with his long notes and sing set choruses to his verses. In the music's crescendo, the glosador and the respondedoras sing together. While the glosador improvises, yodels, and shouts, the respondedoras frequently sing choruses and verses like these:[4] "Good-bye, Berejú, good-bye, Berejú—I don't want, I don't want, I don't want to love; Because whenever I love, they will desert me." Or, the respondedoras may sing lines like these (indicating that a man is leaving his wife—usually related to an actual happening in the community): "Good-bye by the man, I now have my man;" or, "Ay, man, wait for me, man." While the respondedoras are singing, the glosador sings the following strophes (or similar strophes): "Those who are dancing, let them dance with care; For under the house, the Devil is standing; Don't arouse my desire to dance with you; Because when I dance, my belly hurts." Such strophes are variations on common themes in the marimba dance. In one very popular combination of these themes, the glosador sings this sequence in the course of about twenty minutes: "Come hear the marimba; It chases the Devil; I am the Devil; I am going on a trip; Do not dance with me, Because I might decide to stay with you." In response to this, or simultaneously with it, the respondedoras sing these lines: "The Devil is coming: Good-bye by a man; I now hold my man."

Elsewhere (Whitten and Fuentes C. 1966) it has been suggested that the marimba dance re-enacts potential problems between the sexes arising from the practice of serial polygyny. Such problems are re-enacted until dancers and musicians are too exhausted to continue. Unlike dancing in a saloon (discussed below), marimba dancing does not end in a night of new sexual alliances. Household structure is not rearranged afterwards, but the *normative portrayal* of rearrangement is expressed through the texts and activities in the currulao.

Although serial polygyny is normatively portrayed in the texts and activities, activities to implement the norm are prohibited in the context of the currulao. Dancers and musicians insist that the dance is a *baile de respeto* (dance symbolizing respect relationships). People are not supposed to touch one another during the currulao. They do, however, even dancing in a loose embrace in some dances (such as the *torbellino*). I suggest that the idea of respect and the insistence that people should not touch during the dance is a way of prohibiting sexual liaisons. People not only symbolically represent the existing prohibition against fulfilling the normative prerogative, they also explicitly state that the currulao is not the place to seek a new partner, and severely criticize outsiders (usually highlanders) who mistake the currulao activities for saloon activities and attempt sexual liaisons.

In terms of social relationships we can say that the *viability of attenuated affinal links*[5] is recognized and maintained in the context of the currulao. By symbolically emphasizing and portraying men's prerogative to change wives, together with an emphasis on women's attempt to hold men, a certain stability to the dynamic phases of the structure of serial polygyny (Freilich 1961:960–61) is given cultural expression, is symbolized and tolerated.

Figure 10-1 represents the idea of "attentuated affinity" as it functions in the broader system. Individuals *A* and *B* consider themselves "related" to each other through bond *X*. In the daily life of the people, attentuated affinal bonds provide major reference points around which a person builds his own network of obligations and responsibilities. Women, though "left" in the physical sense, are not "left" in the social sense. A man who has moved on and set up another household still cooperates, not only with his former wife in caring for children, but also with her relatives, and with his immediate kinsmen by involving them in a network of reciprocity.

In the Pacific lowlands the lattice of persons "related" by links of attenuated affinity ties together most people within a town, as well as those in the town and the rural hinterland. It is the currulao which gives the cultural expression and symbolic portrayal to such a lattice. The process of portrayal, together with cultural restriction in the context of portrayal, gives symbolic sanction to links of attenuated affinity, and in so doing culturally reinforces a loose but adaptable lattice of interpersonal ties. The lattice itself provides a broad foundation for cooperation between individuals in econmic and political pursuits (for an example see Whitten 1965:167–68, 183–94, and the paper "Strategies of Adaptive Mobility in the Colombian-Ecuadorian Littoral" in Part II of this volume).

2. The chigualo is a simple ceremony which expresses assurance that a dead child travels directly to heaven. Sometimes the term is used only for a stillborn, and "arrullo" for children who have lived for a few days to a few years, but there is no consensus about such usage. Texts from the spirituals (*arrullos*) sung during the wake are full of certainty that the "little angel"

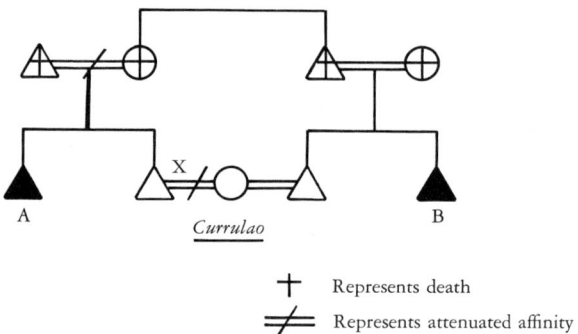

FIGURE 10-1. *A* and *B* consider themselves related through relationship *X*. The relationship is portrayed in the *currulao*.

(*angelito*) goes directly to heaven and will never return. The music is produced by between three and eight well known women singers (*cantadoras*) together with a number of male drummers related to the father of the child, to the mother, and/or to her husband. The cantadoras stand on one side of the table displaying the corpse, while a large chorus of young women sits on the other side. The singers and the chorus alternate in their songs, each group following a leader-response pattern. The singers are not paid but the mother and other close relatives obligate themselves to the singers—if they are served sufficient rum (*aguardiente*) at the wake the obligation is dissolved; if not, reciprocity in kind will be expected. The ambience is cordial, men may even flirt with the young women, provided that these are not recognized relatives or the mother of the child.

Two classes of people attend the chigualo: those who are considered to be significant kinsmen of the mother and father and/or mother's current husband, and others who simply wish to extend their sympathy. To those who are considered significant kinsmen, women in the kinship network of the mother serve aguardiente. Occasionally, one who wishes to reciprocate as a kinsman in the future asks for a drink, thereby expressing his willingness to cooperate with the network of kinsmen who are seen, in the context of the chigualo, as radiating from the couple. Those who make up, in effect, the localized segment of the personal kindred (Davenport 1959:563) of the mother and her husband and/or father of the child spend the entire night at the chigualo; others do not. Some close friends of the father of the child and/or of the mother's husband will stay all night, provided the father and/or the mother's husband themselves remain. Normally, such men alternate as drummers while the chigualo goes on.

It should be pointed out here that it is musical expression, as well as death, that establishes the meaningful context in which these social relationships develop and are maintained. I have seen people simply sit and look at the dead child for several hours (after dressing and arranging it) because the cantadoras had not yet arrived, or because a drummer could not control his beat. No aguardiente was passed, no conversations developed, no attempt to sort out important from residual visitors took place *until the music began*. Also, I have repeatedly noted that all the above relationships were activated without a dead child, when well-known cantadoras were paid by the ethnographer to "stage" a chigualo in a variety of towns and settings in western Colombia. Finally, in support of my contention that music, as well as death, is necessary for establishing a context portraying reciprocity within the personal kindred, Catholic priests report "confusion" over the symbolism attached to Baby Jesus. The Negroes interpret pictures of Baby Jesus wrapped in swaddling as being evidence of infant death, and hold ritual chigualos at Christmas time. During these chigualos the same patterns are manifest, except that the "mother" is replaced by the female head of the household (*jefe de la casa*), or the wife of the household head if there is a man in the position of husband-father.

The personal network which is reinforced during the chigualo is the localized segment of the personal kindred—particularly as this focuses on the mother of the child, but also as it involves kinsmen of her husband and/or the father of the child. Given the high infant mortality rate, most parents are assured several gatherings of significant kinsmen before they reach middle age.

Figure 10-2 represents the portrayal of

social relationships in the context of the chigualo. In this case *A* and *B* portray their kinship relationship to one another by reinforcing relationship *Y*. This relationship may be further reinforced through *compadrazgo* ties, either before the child dies, or, as is often the case, after the child dies. In the case where relationship *Y* is reinforced through a compadrazgo tie, the compadres *A* and *B* may assume responsibility for the performance of the chigualo. However, compadrazgo is not necessary for the portrayal and reinforcement of the relationship *Y*.

3. When an adult dies the wake and burial are more solemn affairs than when a child dies. Only local members of the deceased's kindred plus other friends and neighbors ordinarily attend the first wake, or alabado. Well-known cantadoras sing verses and choruses sometimes similar to those which are sung in the chigualo, but slowly, with a different rhythm, and with different inflections. No assurance is expressed at this time about where the ghost goes, and it is believed that it remains around the house and community. There is no drumming. The whole ambience is one of mourning. Aguardiente is passed by members of the deceased's household to the various members of the localized segment of the deceased's personal kindred.

After a week or nine days (custom varies) the dispersed members of the dead person's personal kindred join the local members at one of their homes (not necessarily the home of the deceased) to hold the most important rite, frequently referred to as *último alabado*, or *novenario*. People come to the house when the singing begins; and it is the beginning of singing in some household that defines the end of the ghost's sojourn on earth, and the beginning of his departure—whether or not the ghost likes it, and whether or not it is ready to leave.

At this second wake everyone sings dirges. The singing of these dirges is led by a well-known female singer, usually not related to the deceased, and continues for a matter of hours or up to several days, the

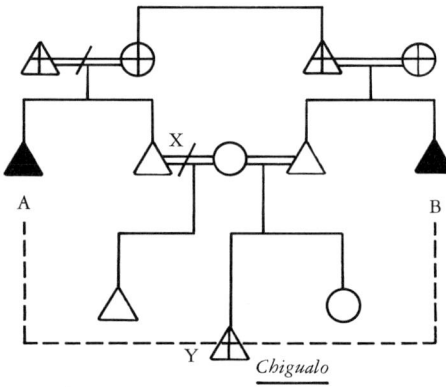

FIGURE 10-2. *A* and *B* consider themselves related through relationship *Y*. The relationship is portrayed in the *chigualo*.

length depending upon *how important the deceased was to his personal network of kinsmen.* Sometimes it is felt that the deceased's ghost is not leaving, and a special ceremony, *la tumba,* is performed to make certain of its departure. Importance of a person to his network of kinsmen refers to how central he was as a locus for economic and political cooperation and redistribution of surplus capital. As discussed in Part II, the rise of kindreds in the local class hierarchies of western Ecuador and Colombia begins with the localization of a siblingship and proceeds through a series of expanding ties to kinsmen as the siblingship solidifies its position in terms of upward socio-economic mobility. By transferring the centricity of ties from parents to some children, the upwardly mobile kindred tends to perpetuate itself, and takes on the character of a "stem kindred" (Davenport 1959:565) or "nodal kindred" (Goodenough 1962:10–11). Those individuals in any community who are in the central position of a dominant stem kindred (see Whitten 1965:155–61) are the most important. Normally, such persons are not only important to the recognized members of the stem kindred but also to others in the community, for they usually control certain crucial aspects of the community's political and economic resources.

The cantadora who leads the singing of dirges usually begins with the phrase "Good-bye first cousin, first cousin, good-bye," and is then joined by the chorus which sings "You go and leave me, alone with God." The ensuing dirge themes tell of demons coming for the deceased, the "Virgen Pura" mediating with Jesus so that the deceased may leave this world, the departure of the spirit, and the strength of saints and God to take the spirit from this world. The final dirge is usually this: "Holy spirit, powerful saint, Holy spirit, powerful and mortal." The emphasis in this singing is not on the intensification of ties but rather the *dismissal* of the dead person or his ghost, and the dismissal of the idea that he ever owned anything, or figured prominently in any network. In other words, Murdock's (1949:106) "criterion of decedence" is culturally recognized in the Pacific lowlands.

It seems to me that more than anything else the último alabado asserts the necessity for a living individual to be a locus for a network of kinsmen. People are very concerned that the ghost be dismissed, for if he returns he may well be displeased with the conduct of the young—particularly those in the process of establishing sexual liaisons—and with the disposal of property (e.g., house, canoe, clothes, machete, axe, net) which normally takes place on a consensus basis wherein the occupant of the house is regarded as owner of everything in the house, and where those who normally worked with the deceased "own" the implements with which they worked (axe, machete, canoe, net).

Just as individuals are concerned with dismissing the ghost, and the idea that the deceased was ever important in maintaining a network of individuals, so are they equally concerned with maintaining the network itself. The alabado provides a mechanism for efficiently re-sorting network ties. Some individuals at the último alabado do break links of reciprocity by saying that they are not really kinsmen to other participants for the link has gone. But most individuals exchange aguardiente and compliments, and talk about the dismissal of the ghost (e.g., by discussing how the ghost must now be gone, how difficult it will be for him to return, and by symbolically "forgetting" who the person was). During such discussions the importance of various individuals in the economic and political life of the community is discussed and people stress whatever socially recognized bonds they may have to important living individuals. In some cases the important people are the children, or some of the children, of the deceased; in other cases, not. But in asserting new relationships to important individuals, people *do not refer to any bond requiring reference to a dead person.*

discouraged. Because it is fairly easy to rearrange one's personal network to meet new contingencies, it seems to me that a flexible, adaptable kinship system is maintained on a personal network basis.

Figure 10-3 represents the process in simplified form. A and B, in the context of the alabado, dismiss relationship Z at the death of either of their parents. In seeking a socially recognizable relationship through

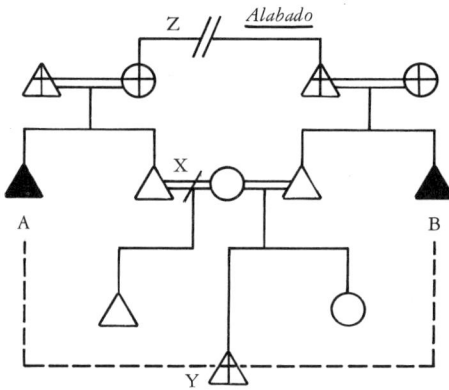

FIGURE 10-3. In the context of the *alabado*, A and B, who were once related through relationship Z, break the genealogical bond between them and seek a new bond, which is normally bond X, often supported by relationship Y.

In asserting relationship to an important person, individuals within any town are forced to find a series of links which connect them through living people. The most frequently discussed links are those developed through attenuated affinity. By denying genealogical links necessitating reference to a dead person, and by asserting "relationship" through past sexual and sexual-plus-economic alliances and liaisons, the *viability of networks maintained through attenuated affinity is reinforced*, and any network which might be based on a concept of descent is

which to continue patterned cooperation they recognize the viability of relationship X. This relationship may also be reflected in relationship Y and might even be supported through a compadrazgo tie. However, if A and B did not have relationship X, then there would not normally be reason to continue a compadrazgo tie.

The context of music relating to final dirges dismisses the individual who might represent the continuation of property and network loci. By stressing dismissal, persons may remain in networks but must find support from other individuals involved in contemporary economic pursuits. The immediacy of life is apparent; and the other world and members of it are not to be involved in the practical day-to-day contingencies of reciprocating with kinsmen or other community members.

4. The fourth context of musical expression is defined by a special day devoted to the propitiation of a saint. Such saints' days occur irregularly in the Pacific Littoral and the degree and intensity of musical expression also varies.[6]

Organizing and performing the music for a saint's day (sometimes called a *velorio*) and indeed remembering just when the day is to be, is strictly a female responsibility. In communities where clergymen object to holding saints' arrullos, women hold a secret arrullo well away from the center of town, and away from the Catholic Church.

Essentially, the music is made by a group of women with *maracas* and/or tubeshakers who sing in a rotating leader-response pattern and move in rhythm, clapping their hands for added rhythm. They normally get one or two of their male relatives, perhaps their sons, to play one or two drums, but may sometimes supply their own rhythm and dispense with the drums. They may be accompanied by a marimba, over whose playing they keep close supervision. The older women are in turn the leaders; the younger are always respondents.

In general, older women are in charge of the arrullo, although most women in a community or in a neighborhood participate at some time or another during the day. Normally no aguardiente is passed around, and men are discouraged from turning the saint's day into a fiesta with national music and aguardiente, though this sometimes happens. If it does, however, groups of women still hold their own arrullos semi-privately.

The social relationships portrayed in the activities and sentiments stress, above all else, "womanness." They relate to the solidarity and intra-sexual cooperation among women and they reinforce patterns of female authority. They may be termed *categorical*. No particular networks are portrayed, or reinforced, and cooperation at an arrullo does not seem to ally particular networks of participants in other contexts of life; nor are enduring groups reinforced or established. This is a time when women decide on the musical event, design the context, and withdraw to continue their own musical context if the situation begins to take on the character of saloon-dance hall interaction.

5. Our final context of musical expression is that of the saloon or dance hall. Here we find either a dance band or gramophone playing popular national music.[7] Although people go to saloons to drink and to dance at any time, I shall discuss only the weekend or fiesta pattern where a large segment of lower class Negroes of both sexes gathers.

In the context of saloon music Negro men of the Pacific Littoral further solidify relationships within an actual cash-labor group (e.g., a dock gang, steady saw-mill employees, a group of railway workers) by sitting together, spending the same amount of money on one another, by passing drinks nearly exclusively within the circle of cooperating men, and by letting others know that it is the cash which they make at the same job which is important, not other ties to community members not engaged in steady wage-work. Other men drain off the economic capital of a head of a traditional work group, or the focus of a politically or economically important kindred, by insisting that he buy something for everyone since he has more money than the rest.

Besides solidifying relationships within an actual cash-labor work group and "leveling" the head of a traditional work group or focus for an important kindred, men also establish and intensify dyadic contracts by exchanging aguardiente and dancing partners.[8] By so doing, they also set up a situation which facilitates household fission. In this article I want to focus on this third social relationship—the establishment of relatively brittle symmetrical dyadic contracts (Foster 1961:1174) through the ritualized exchange of aguardiente and female dancing partners. I will also illustrate the process whereby household composition can be tactically rearranged in the context of saloon activities.

Men with some money enter the saloon and sit alone or in small groups. Men with no money sit within the saloon, but rather bring a woman in to dance. Men with money give a drink to friends and relatives sitting in the saloon and to those entering to dance. The drink is handed; neither man looks at the other—the recipient gulps it, shakes the last drop or two out, spits on the floor, and hands the glass back without offering thanks. Should he offer his thanks, equal exchange is made, thereby eliminating a basis for continuing an exchange pattern. The dyadic contract is closed by verbally expressing thanks. If the man is sitting within the saloon he returns to his table; if entering to dance he dances with the woman and then goes back outside, or stands against the door or wall. The woman leaves the saloon after the dance.

Sometimes, the recipient becomes a donor by giving the drink he accepts from one man to yet another man. If a woman asks her dancing partner for a drink he indicates that the man offering him a drink should give it to her. Rarely does a man take a drink from another man and then give it to the woman with whom he is about to dance, or with whom he is dancing. In this context women may receive a drink *for* a man, but not directly (symbolically) *from* a person—it is not up to the woman to receive a prestation (a gift with implied contingency) and thereby be in the position of agreeing to reciprocate (by not thanking the one who proffers the drink) or refusing to do so (by thanking the man and thereby making immediate exchange). Rather, she must symbolize a prestation *to* a man, and this is normally the man with whom she is dancing at the moment. The gift to the woman is regarded by the giver as prestation to the man with whom she is dancing.

Women, except for a few being courted, or for a few prostitutes working within the saloon, remain outside during the earlier part of the night, where they wait for a man to take them inside to dance. They usually accept all invitations to dance, but normally do not dance with their husbands, even on the rare occasions when they attend the saloon together.

While dancing, a man may suggest that he and the woman spend the night together; she will frequently consent, especially if she has no husband in residence. It is common for the couple to continue residing together. In this sense, sexual associations in saloon contexts, unlike those in the currulao, serve to change the structure of particular households. Ordinarily, before a man asks a woman, he is aware of her current situation and will not attempt to "steal" her from another man—for such an attempt will normally result in violence.

A man frequently takes a woman by the hand and leads her to another man; he offers her hand, none of the people look at one another, and the woman and man dance. At the end of the dance the man walks the woman back outside or back to the giver.

Offering a woman to another man as a dancing partner is not an offer of the woman herself. The man who accepts the invitation to dance is not expected to make sexual overtures of his own.

In the context of the saloon, a dance and a drink are equivalent tokens of exchange. Verbal personal compliments and proffered thanks are also tokens equivalent to a drink and a dance, but the quality is different. A drink and a dance carry implied contingencies for reciprocity, while verbal personal compliments and proffered thanks for a drink and a dance are terminal (closed) exchanges. By accepting a shot of aguardiente (or a glass of beer when affluence is particularly high) and/or by dancing with a proffered woman *without returning thanks*, the recipient indebts himself to the donor. Payment can easily be made by immediately reciprocating, or it can be withheld and made in other ways in contexts involving economic return for those reciprocating.

Such loaning of dance partners and tendering of alcohol continues throughout the night in a saloon, and people are careful to remember what is given to whom (though not necessarily what is received from whom). In daily gossip people frequently remind individuals to whom they have given something how much they are doing for them; not uncommonly, one not reminded "forgets" what he has received, though he remembers his own generosity to individuals from whom he wants something.

The network of personal ties established in saloons is apparent primarily when there is economic gain to be had for group labor on a short-term basis. The social relationships themselves are long term, but they are activated only on the basis of short-term group labor. Particular groups organized to exploit a situation for economic profit (e.g., a labor gang, political party, temporary dock gang) vary in composition through time, but the broader networks vary little through time, except by actual migration. The network of reciprocating men bound through the mutual exchange of a drink and a dance can be activated by individuals to whom a number of people owe favors. To stimulate such networks lumber buyers, budding politicians and traders, among others, make it a point to buy a whole bottle of aguardiente for an interacting group of men. The buyer of the bottle, however, does not sit with the men or speak to them if he wishes to obligate them—for if they have a chance to thank him profusely and to pour for him, or in other ways to express subservience, the incipient asymmetrical contract (Foster 1961:1174; 1963:1281) can be closed, or terminated.[9]

In the context of saloon music it can be said that the social components of household structure may realign as men seek new partners and women accept new overtures, and that men intensify the potential for cooperation among themselves by the exchange of dance partners and aguardiente as tokens for future economic cooperation.

SUMMARY AND DISCUSSION

In summary, this article may be taken as a preliminary attempt to go a bit beyond the point well expressed by Merriam (1964b:226) in his discussion of the functions of music "... it is clear that in providing a solidarity point around which members of society congregate, music does indeed function to integrate society." Merriam is talking about the function of music in terms of general intrasocietal integration; I am attempting to speak about musical contexts within a particular marginal social system as they support the development of personal networks, adaptable to economic fluctuations in a larger money economy.

Women express their sexual solidarity through the various arrullos to saints, by playing leading roles in chigualos and alabados, and by serving as constant "antagonists" in their role during the currulao in which the singers collectively express their particular ability to hold particular men. Such female solidarity seems to provide a basis from which men move, manipulate, and strive to involve themselves in personal networks which are strategic to the larger money economy.

The chigualo helps to establish the relative boundaries of the local personal kindred and reinforces networks of kinsmen around the bereaved parents of a dead child. At the same time, however, it becomes apparent that networks are shifting and overlapping as the central actors for one chigualo become more peripheral participants in the next. The idea of a living, tangible locus for personal networks is strongly expressed in the dismissal of the dead in the last alabado for the deceased adult.

We can regard the currulao and saloon musical contexts as being in symbolic opposition, and regard the other three contexts as supporting social relationships which form the basis for symbolic strategies portrayed in the currulao and saloon contexts. The currulao provides an expressive context which permits household and marital structure to be realigned when necessity demands it, but also provides stability for the particular structure at the time of the currulao. The saloon, on the other hand, provides the instrumental context of actual facile fission in domestic units, and at the same time establishes an expressive context in which economically feasible reciprocity can be established, or portrayed, through the exchange of acceptable tokens.

Symbolic opposition seems to be increasing with developing urbanism, and with incipient urbanization. In the large towns of the Pacific lowlands (Esmeraldas, Limones, San Lorenzo, Tumaco, and Buenaventura) where race lines appear to be stiffening, the intensity of saloon dancing is matched by the growth of marimba houses.[10] On Saturday night individuals may choose to attend one or the other. In the saloon there is the potential for future cooperation, and for household fission, but there is also a certain cost in reciprocity, and the potential risk of an unsatisfactory new spouse. In the marimba house, on the other hand, stability of the particular structure is guaranteed, but the gain in terms of the future is nonexistent.

Interestingly enough, although men and women make this choice week by week (that is, choose to attend the curralao or the saloon) they are not consistent in their choices. It is generally difficult, and in some places impossible, to differentiate aggregates in terms of attendance. While they are acting in one context they deride the other. In towns, it appears that the instrumental and expressive contexts for household fission and fusion are regarded as being in symbolic opposition; the choice made in favor of one context generates a negative sentiment toward the opposite alternative.

In the rural hinterland, there seems to be either a marimba or a saloon context on a given weekend. People either play national music and engage in activities described above for the saloon context, or they go to the marimba house and hold a currulao. When acting in one context hinterland Negroes usually deny that they *ever* act in the other. They say, for example, when engaging in saloon activities, that "no one ever holds a currulao on this particular river." But the same people, when holding a currulao, deny that anyone knows how to play national music.

This suggests that the musical patterns in hinterland and town parallel one another, but that the greater diversity within a town exerts a pressure toward individual choice in terms of musical context. In the Pacific lowlands, musical contexts, whatever the settlement pattern and proximity to the cash economic loci, do seem central in reinforcing and maintaining adaptable social relationships through a process of symbolic portrayal.

It is within contexts dominated by musical expression that one finds the greatest evidence for the reinforcement and maintenance of flexible personal networks within the Pacific Littoral of southwest Colombia and northwest Ecuador. These personal networks can serve an individual in time of personal need or can be activated for general economic return during boom periods. During times of relative depression the manipulations within musical contexts continue as men establish and break links in networks of kinsmen and friends, fortifying a system of links to individual persons which may be strategic as opportunities for economic gain develop.

NOTES

1. Data for this article were gathered in northwest Ecuador during the summer of 1961 and the winter and summer of 1963 under the auspices of two supplemental NIMH grants to Fellowship No. 14,333. The Colombian data were collected under the auspices of Tulane University and the Universidad del Valle while I was at the International Center for Medical Research and Training, Cali, Colombia, during 1964–65. Grateful acknowledgment is made to these sources of funds. Parts of the article, which is slightly modified from a version appearing in *Man*, are presented in a different manner and with different emphasis in the author's book (1965). Permission to reprint such portions, and to discuss the material in a new light, is granted by Stanford University Press and by the Royal Anthropological Institute of Great Britain and Ireland.

This article has benefitted from several critical readings by Dorothea Scott Whitten. Lee Rainwater, Charles A. Valentine, and Robert C. Hunt made critical and perceptive comments, without which the article would have suffered. I also wish to thank Jerome Stromberg and Kenneth Little for their comments. No faults, of course, can be attributed to anyone other than the author.

2. For an analysis of the material culture and ecology of the region see West (1957). Illustrative studies of two particular towns are given in Whitten (1965) and Price (1955). General historical sources include King (1945), West (1952), Hudson (1964), Merizalde del Carmen (1921), Paredes Borja (1963), and Hernández de Alba (1946). Pavy (1967) has recently tried to work out some of the tribal origins of Negroes entering the region.

3. The music of the Pacific lowlands is, to the outsider, the most striking complex of the culture area, and in some respects, aspects of the music are strikingly African. I wish to note in passing that the greatest complex of African musical traits exists in a *secular context* (in the currulao, or marimba dance), discussed below. This is offered as a striking exception to the point most recently propounded by Nettl (1965:174) that African styles tend to be retained in sacred contexts, in association with African cults. In the Pacific lowlands, at least, African musical styles have not been "retained"—that is, have not "survived" in the face of change in other parts of the system—but rather have been adapted to function in secular contexts. By symbolically portraying relationships which are adaptive, the style of portrayal has continued. Although the style of music is often African in rhythm and melody, a Spanish content endures throughout (cf. texts in Whitten 1967 and in Whitten and Fuentes C. 1966).

4. The actual transcriptions are published in Whitten (1967) and Whitten and Fuentes C. (1966).

5. Briefly, attenuated affinity refers to a broken marital bond which is used as a decisive reference point in the establishment of meaningful relationships among members in a kindred network. The attenuated affinal bond functions just as an affinal or consanguineal bond in allying individuals, or networks of individuals.

6. Prominent saints (apart from Mary, Joseph, and Jesus) include San Antonio, the Virgen de Carmen, the Virgen de La Laja, the Virgen de Atocha and the Virgen de Belén (who is not the same as María, "La Virgen Pura").

7. E.g., *cumbia, gaita, merecumbea, guaracha,* etc.

8. For a full sociopsychological and sociological treatment of processes of exchange see Thibault and Kelley (1959) and Blau (1964). These dyadic contracts may strengthen existing kinship and compadrazgo ties, or lead to the establishment of new ties which may eventually lead to kinship or compadrazgo relations. For an analysis of compadrazgo see Whitten (1965:69-74).

9. For a discussion of the labor groups which are activated by economic middlemen see Whitten (1965:69-74; 105-07; 148-54; 157-58; 164-65; 185-86).

10. In 1963 San Lorenzo seemed atypical of this pattern. The marimba appeared to be in decline both in this port town and in the rural hinterland. However, this was a time in which a potential advantage in upward socio-economic mobility was perceived by most people in the town and, in the context of potential upward mobility, the marimba dance is negatively valued. However, by 1965 the currulao in San Lorenzo again manifested the characteristics and fitted the generalizations here offered. It seems that with a stiffening of race lines in the process of expanding capital resources, an adaptive mode is strengthened instead of a direct competitive mode of interaction in a money economy. This point will be elaborated in Whitten (n.d.), "The ecology of race relations in northwest Ecuador" (paper read at the 1969 American Anthropological Association meetings, New Orleans).

Eleven

AFRO-AMERICAN MUSICAL ADAPTATION

John F. Szwed

Reprinted with permission from *Journal of American Folklore* (1969), forthcoming.

The earliest Afro-American studies were devoted to the music of African slaves. Nothing about Negro aggregates seemed more fascinating than the mystery of the origins of his music. Was it an African product, reshaped to fit the New World? Or was it Anglo-American music, refashioned by African sensibilities? As basic questions, these were appropriate, but instead of leading to deeper understanding they led to a dead end. This passion to illuminate origins resulted in explanations that were frequently short-sighted and territorially limited. Although Melville J. Herskovits' own work pursued the same interests, Herskovits (1958:261–69) clearly warned that such efforts suffered from a severe lack of knowledge of African music, and from a startling shortage of information on the secular music of Negroes. Perhaps if students of Afro-America had been more interested in United States Negroes they would have noted that in some areas of expressive culture—notably music, dance, and oral narrative—"Africanisms" have varied in intensity over time, rising and falling with specific conditions.[1] For example, one still reads in such authoritative sources as Nettl (1965:172) statements that African musical influences persist most strongly in sacred contexts, a point belied by even a casual acquaintance with Negro popular music today.

Part of the problem, then, with studies of Afro-American expressive culture has been poor observation and selective neglect; the rest is simply a matter of inadequate conceptualization. Since anthropologists have chosen to reject biological-instinctual explanations of musical behavior in favor of cultural explanations, they must offer statements in social-cultural terms that realistically explain long-persisting patterns of musical behavior. Once we move beyond questions of origin and move on to problems of persistence and change, we need answers to questions such as the following: What is the relation between normative musical traditions and those that challenge them? How do individual learning experiences relate to normative patterns? Is there some direction or drift in the change of musical models? Do models rise and fall in popularity? What variability from normative models is permitted? These questions remain unanswered in the present state of ethnomusicology.

Recently, several significant contributions to the study of Afro-American music seem to point the way toward the broader understanding needed. Alan Lomax' (1962; 1967b; 1968) cantometric analysis, for example, has richly illuminated the cultural dimensions of music and raised the essential issue of the adaptational nature of song styles. Norman Whitten's (1968) recent work on Colombian and Ecuadorian Negroes reveals suggestive directions for studying social change through symbolic musical behavior. What is needed now is a conceptual framework in which changes and retentions of musical style and context can be understood within a synthesis of social and cultural change. Such a framework would take into account not only the social and cultural facts of a musical society, but would also integrate a people's musical forms and their associated performance roles and styles. It is to this central point that this paper is directed: that *song forms and performances are themselves models of social behavior that reflect strategies of adaptation to human and natural environments.* For Afro-America, then, the problem becomes one of defining the environing situations, establishing parameters of adaptation for "black aggregates," and of relating the musical conceptions of such black aggregates to their common experience.

THE PREACHER VS. THE BLUESMAN

The distinction between sacred and secular music—the most significant native musical categories of the Negroes in the United States—was probably set by the middle of the 1800's, and certainly before 1900.[2] Although Calvinist notions contributed to the dichotomy, reformulated African religions were also important in defining the differences between sacred texts and the "devil's music." Alan Lomax (1960:226; 1966:106–09) has remarked on the widespread belief that skill on the fiddle required a pact with the devil (in a churchyard or at a crossroads). Later, a similar pact was required of the blues singer (Lomax 1960:xxiv [Lomax is probably quoting Zora Neale Hurston]):

> As part of his initiation into the vaudou cult, the Negro novice must learn to play the guitar. He goes to the cross-roads at midnight armed with a black cat bone, and as he sits in the dark playing the blues, the Devil approaches, cuts the player's nails to the quick, and swaps guitars. Thus the vaudouist sells his soul to the Devil and in return receives the gift of invisibility and the mastery of his instrument. These practices may explain why the religious often call an expert Negro folk musician "a child of the Devil" or "the Devil's son-in-law."

The significance of the sacred-secular distinction lies not just in their perceived differences as music, but also in their mutual exclusiveness: it was felt that performance of one or the other implied the social character of an individual. The literature of American Negro music abounds with this musical distinction, the nature of the persons who perform them, and the motivations that underlie the songs (Charters 1965:35;

Klatzko n.d.; Oliver 1965:17–18; Parrish 1942:93; Scarborough 1925:97–98; Strachwitz 1954:16–17). For example, in an interview with the Rev. Robert Wilkins (a former blues singer) the two musical forms are summarized by Pete Welding as follows (1967:55):

> Distinguishing between spirituals and blues, Rev. Wilkins remarked that he performs only the former currently because of his conviction that the "body is the temple of the spirit of God" and that only one spirit can dwell in that body at any time. Blues, he feels, are songs associated with the devil spirit, that the feeling blues expresses is not spiritual but sorrowful. It is true that blues help to relieve the "natural soul" of the singer but they fail to provide the sufferer any real spiritual solace; this can come only of praising the Lord and giving Him thanks for all things, good and bad alike.... The blues, he said, describe and relieve emotional troubles one might experience during life. The blues singer composes his songs primarily for himself but always is conscious of other potential listeners who might "be happy and enjoy it as I sing it."

There is no question that the two forms were felt to be mutually exclusive. It is common, even today, for religious leaders to exhort their followers "to give up blues singing and join the church." Zora Neale Hurston quotes a sermon in *Jonah's Gourd Vine* (1934): "The blues we play in our homes is a club to beat up Jesus." Even the practicing bluesman may hold this view. Harriet J. Ottenheimer (1965) comments on New Orleans blues singer Babe Stovall:

> He calls his talent a God-given gift and explains that because talent comes from God, it should be used for the playing of spirituals only, as a way of thanks for the gift. He styles himself as a sinner, however, and so plays other music, especially blues, besides spirituals. He plans to repent someday, and cease playing blues altogether, sinful music, in his opinion.

And the mother of infamous Mississippi bluesman Robert Johnson claimed that on his death-bed her son hung up his guitar and renounced his blues life, thus dying in glory (Lomax: personal communication).

As the examples reveal, the sacred-secular dichotomy is not as clear as it might first appear. Secular function and text are not enough to place a form of music into opposition to church songs. Writings on the Afro-American folk song show, for example, that committed church members and religious leaders do not object to work songs and field hollers. Rather, it is the blues and bluesmen that represent the essence of the anti-sacred. The basic issue as American blacks have seen it, then, is one of a sacred-blues dichotomy.

The importance of this song dichotomy has not gone unnoticed. Roger Abrahams, for example, in his rhetorical analysis of urban Negro folklore sees this as another example of the distinction between two types of "men-of-words" or "good-talkers" in the Negro community: the street-corner bard and the preacher. Abrahams conceives of this as a context for verbal power, the street talker addressing himself to the "homosexual, anti-feminine world of the early adolescent," the preacher directing his words "to women as well as men" (Abrahams 1964:62–63). But in *Urban Blues*, Charles Keil devotes himself to an intensive discussion of the sociological *similarities* underlying the two performance roles, commenting on the fact that many blues singers have become preachers (although, as he suggests, the process is not reversible). Common role characteristics, then, apparently are what makes the perceived differences in behavior so necessary, for as he points out, "Bluesman and preacher may be considered Negro prototypes of the no-good and the good man respectively" (Keil 1966:148).

Abrahams and Keil point to a very real opposition—that of the character of roles—but it appears that these roles exist in relation to the structure of what they perform and how they perform, as well as in the function of their performance. To illustrate, then, let me discuss these opposed forms—the church song and the blues.

The church songs and spirituals of Negroes in the southern United States closely resemble West African song style, particularly in their strong call-and-response pattern. An 1867 description of this pattern still remains one of the most succinct (Allen *et al.*, 1867):

> There is no singing in parts, as we understand it, and yet no two appear to be singing the same thing—the leading singer starts the words of each verse, often improvising, and the others who "base" him as it is called, strike in with the refrain, or even join in the solo, when the words are familiar.
>
> When the "base" begins, the leader often stops, leaving the rest of his words to be guessed at, or it may be that they are taken up by one of the other singers. And the "basers" themselves seem to follow their own whims, beginning when they please, striking an octave above or below (in case they have pitched the tune too low or too high), or hitting some other note that chords, so as to produce the effect of a marvelous complication and variety, and yet with the most perfect time, and rarely with any discord. . . . they seem not infrequently to strike sounds that cannot be precisely represented . . . slides from one note to another, and turns and cadences not in articulated notes.

This early description accurately notes the tightly woven interplay between members of the singing group, where a leader sets the pattern for the song, but the group shapes its response independently. The nature of the group song-response was such that the song was participatory in nature: it invited the participation of all church members by leaving melodic and harmonic "holes" in the song that could be filled or left empty as the choice was made. At the same time, it was redundant enough to allow easy entrance into the message at any point. The church-song was a group phenomenon, hinged loosely on a leadership pattern, and in this sense, the traditional spiritual (or for that matter the shout, and other religious forms) perfectly paralleled the organizational structure of the American Negro Church and the cooperative work team.

The blues, on the other hand, are almost unique among traditional American Negro folk-song forms. First, they are sung solo, without the typical vocal call and response pattern so well known in other song forms. (Of course, other songs than blues are sung solo—for example, the field holler and the lullaby—but these are forms that imply physical or social distance. In the case of the holler, the singers are separated from one another in the field; the lullaby is addressed to an infant, itself not able to reply in song.) Since the blues are sung solo, the form itself implies authority as much as does the classic Western European ballad: although the audience or the guitar may comment supportively, there is no *song space* for group participation. But as the blues are completely personalized (what Abrahams called the "intrusive 'I'"), there is an absence of the "objectivity" so widely commented upon in the ballad form.

Second, the blues are the least redundant of all American Negro forms. Thus, there is greater concern for textual message and meaning: the blues are information-oriented.

At the first look, of course, the blues

appear wholly distinct from Western European song forms, and thus, commentators have always pointed to the "blues scale" and the improvisatory character of the song as marks of its African character. But this is deceptive. The blues performance is in many ways closer to white American folk music than to most other Afro-American song forms. When compared to Lomax' (1962) white American and African cantometric song profiles—particularly in the parameters of vocal group organization, wordiness of text, embellishment, melisma, and raspiness of voice—the blues fall between the two culture areas' musical orientations. Lomax' (1967a; 1968) analysis is also helpful in suggesting the kinds of "normative messages" carried by the blues. As they are solo, rather than the more familiar interlocked leader-group song, they suggest a tendency toward authoritarian leadership patterns. The lesser use of nonsense words and redundancy in the blues is another indicator of complexity typical of the music of complex societies. By the same token, solo singing characterizes individualized work patterns, as opposed to the more complex work groups of West Africa and American slavery. Since blues were usually sung by men (in the rural setting) as opposed to the mixed female-male singing of the churches, blues suggest that men are being presented as musical models in a shifting social order.

Blues, like religious behaviour, are highly ritualized, with an apparent intention of easing or blocking "transformation of state in human being or nature" (Wallace 1966:106), rather than merely 'entertaining": ritual events attempt to restore social equilibrium, change organizational structures, or ease personal conditions of stress. Thus, singers speak of the blues as "relaxing the nerves," "giving relief," and "kinda helpin' somehow." Gospel singer Mahalia Jackson makes the point (Feather 1964:46):

> But he [the Negro] created his songs to lift his burden ... so those that did not believe in God, they created the blues in the same vein that almost they wrote their spirituals.

The blues allow some things to be sung that could not otherwise be expressed. Henry Townsend of St. Louis, for example, says (Oliver 1965:164-65):

> There's several types of blues—there's blues that connects *you* with personal life—I mean you can tell it to the public as a song, *in* a song. But I mean, they don't take it seriously which you are tellin' the truth about. They don't always think seriously that it's exactly *you* that you talkin' about. At the same time it could be you, more or less it *would* be you for you to have the feelin'. You express yourself in a song like that. Now this particular thing reach others because they have experienced the same condition in life so naturally they feel what you are sayin' because it happened to them. It's a sort of thing that you kinda like to hold to yourself, yet you want somebody to know it. . . . Now I've had the feelin' which I have disposed it in a song, but there's some things that have happened to me that I wouldn't dare tell, not to tell—but I would *sing* about them. Because people in general they takes the song as an explanation for *themselves*—they believe this song is expressing *their* feelings instead of the one that singin' it.

The blues singer is by no means a shaman, but he performs in many of a shaman's capacities. He presents difficult experiences for the group, and the effectiveness of his performance depends upon a mutual sharing of experience.[3] Another former blues singer, now turned religious singer, L'il Son Jackson, makes the point this way (Oliver 1965:165):

> You see it's two different things—the blues and church songs is two different things. If a

man feel hurt with inside and he sing a church song then he's askin' God for help. It's a horse of a different color but I think if a man sing the blues it's more or less out of himself. ... He's not askin' no one for help. ... But he's expressin' how he feel. He's expressin' it to someone and that fact makes it a sin, you know, because it make another man sin ... you're tryin' to get your feelin's over to the *next* person through the blues, and *that's* what makes it sin.

The essential difference between the two means of psychological release focuses on the "direction" of the song: church music is directed *collectively* to God; blues are directed *individually* to the *collective*. Both forms perform similar cathartic functions, but within different frameworks. There is potential in the song for individual and group expiation, as the singers themselves testify. At the same time, there is a means by which both the singers' and the listening individuals' personal conditions may be rendered social, even under large-scale pressures that threaten to change individual or group identity.

SINGING THE CHANGES

I have briefly described the structure of these opposed musical forms in order to arrive at my central point: that musical forms and their associated performance roles and styles reflect alternative adaptational strategies, and that styles and counterstyles can and usually do co-exist in a single society.

As a popular music form, blues arose in the early 1900's, the period of the first great Negro migrations north to the cities. The blues were a form of secularized ritual—a breakaway from sacred forms (the spiritual or the gospel song) performing parallel functions. As such, the formal and stylistic elements of the blues seem to symbolize newly emerging social patterns during the crisis period of urbanization. As opposed to the group-conservative orientation of the sacred songs, the blues were authoritarian, aggressive, offering a secular-personalized view of the world, they were a "toughminded" solution to social problems. Lomax quotes an anonymous informant (Lomax 1959:7–8):

The blues is just *revenge*. Like you'll be mad at the boss and you can't say anything. You out behind the wagon and you pretend that a mule stepped on your foot and you say, "Get offa my foot, god-damn sonofabitch!" You won't be talkin' to the mule, you'll be referrin' to the white boss. ... That's the way with the blues: you sing those things in a song when you can't speak out.

By replacing the functions served by sacred music, the blues eased a transition from a land-based agrarian society to one based on mobile, wage-labor urbanism. This is all the more apparent from the standpoint of the characteristics of the blues singer's role: unlike the stable, other-worldly, community-based image of the preacher (approved by Negro and white communities alike), the bluesman was seen as a shadowy, sinful, aggressive, footloose wanderer, free to move between sexual partners and to pull up stakes as conditions dictated (Melnick 1967:139–49). Keil makes this point (1966:152):

The bluesman is in a sense every man: the country bluesman is an archetype of the migrant laborer; the city bluesman, a stereotype of the stud, the hustler; the urban blues artist, something of an ideal man or prototype for his generation as well.

The bluesman, for example, formalizes weak familial ties by making them appear culturally normative rather than just a "problem" for individuals. To paraphrase a gospel song (although I am inverting its meaning), he "lives the life he sings about in his songs."

Finally, as a stylistic mode, the blues mediate between the African and North American white musical sensibilities and thus provide an aesthetically satisfying musical statement of social reality, one most adaptive in aiding the transition from African slave to Afro-American.

These stylistic models are more than just descriptive manipulations. In the fullest sense, they symbolize and reinforce social behavior. When Martin Luther King and the southern leaders of the civil rights movement sought to collectivize group action, they returned to the older and more stable group orientation of the spiritual to coordinate activity. But when northern black power leaders (such as Stokely Carmichael) operate, they surround themselves with jazzmen (the instrumental analogue of the blues singer) and singers of updated secular folk songs.

In the last few years, however, there has been a conscious rejection of both spirituals and blues by urban Negroes. Spirituals and their traditional performance styles have almost disappeared and are now replaced by the more complicated, professionally oriented "gospel music," which Arna Bontemps calls a compound of "elements found in the old tabernacle songs, the Negro Spirituals and the blues" (Bontemps 1944:431). A strong rhythmic structure with hand-clapping, shouting, and aggressive interplay characterizes this new church song. Gospel music is often not performed by the church members themselves, but by choirs who train for the performances. As they see themselves as professionals, they often perform outside of the church at quite secular functions. E. Franklin Frazier (1963:75) saw this change in musical style as a change in Negro religious life-style:

> The Gospel Singers ... do not represent a complete break with the religious traditions of the Negro. They represent or symbolize the attempt of the Negro to utilize his religious heritage in order to come to terms with changes in his own institutions as well as the problems of the world of which he is a part.

Today blues—even of the electrified, city variety—are characterized by many urban Negroes as "dirty," "down-home," and "old-time." What has risen to replace both the blues and spiritual is the broad category of music known as "soul," a popular secular music, markedly similar to gospel music in every way but its verbal content.[4] Soul-singing—typified by such as Sam Cooke, Aretha Franklin, and Otis Redding (all of them former church singers)—is a polished, arranged blending of European *bel canto* tradition and African call and response that allows for formalized group interplay with highly developed solo passages. Although it may be premature to regard it as such, it appears that soul music has drawn from the older model of spirituals and the blues model and, unifying the sacred-secular dichotomy, produced a stylistic mode that is adaptive to a situation in which urban Negroes are stabilizing within self-contained ghetto sub-cultures upon the mixed base of mutual aid and individualism best captured in the concept of black power.

Soul music thus appears to exhibit a revival of "Africanisms" (really older Afro-American style features), particularly in its rhythmic characteristics and call and response features. This borrowing of older musical patterns has been made possible only because some members of the community have continued to operate with former musical-social models. Although these older patterns have not been popular in the mass media, they have remained influential through critical and slow-changing social institutions in the Negro community: the store-front church and the neighborhood bar, as well as grandmother's rocking chair and children's schoolyard games. Earlier musical forms have continued to exist in older members of the community, who act as repositories of past traditions and out-dated adaptational features. In short, although there are at any given time in a society a normative performance style and performance role, there are also counter-styles and roles, surviving from the past and available to be reworked to form new styles.

OTHER AFRO-AMERICAN COUNTER-STYLES

It remains to be seen whether the particular dichotomous model of musical adaptation here presented for the United States will hold for other parts of Afro-America. At first glance, it would appear that those areas of slavery that lacked a strong Protestant reinforcement for sacred-secular music might not fit the case. Tentatively, however, it appears to apply at least in the West Indies and in Colombia and Ecuador, areas under varying degrees of Catholic and Protestant influence.

In Trinidad, calypso, a form often compared with the blues, holds a parallel position in relation to the songs of the cults and organized churches (Elder 1966b). Like the blues, calypso developed after slavery, during the period of urbanization on the island, and seems to have a similar behavioral and stylistic base. Calypso is sung solo, is minimally redundant, and is highly personalized. Certainly calypso is authoritarian in performance pattern and text, and the combative nature of calypsonians during (and out of) performance is widely noted. It is also clear that the exponents of calypso are drawn from the most independent, "rootless," and aggressive strata of Trinidad society.[5]

Unlike the blues, calypso continues to dominate the urban musical landscape long after its nineteenth-century origins, functioning with immense popular support. The difference seems to lie in the fact that the middle class (of all colors) has chosen to adopt the calypso as a musical-social model of emerging Trinidadian-Tobagonian nationalism, making it the focus of its most important public ritual (Carnival) and one of its most successful aesthetic exports. To be sure, calypso song is a veritable statement of national character to Trinidadian residents and to the other islands in the West Indies as well, where Trinidad is identified as the epitome of urbanization and aggressive independence (Crowley 1967).

In Colombia and Ecuador there is again a dichotomous and opposed conception of music, but Norman Whitten's analysis (1966; 1968) suggests that Euro-American sacred-secular distinctions appear to be absent or irrelevant. Instead, musical forms and roles are pure statements of alternative behavioral strategies. Here, the marimba dance (*currulao*) and the saloon dance (popular "national" music) are in contrast. In the marimba song male and female singers and musicians are divided both in terms of what they sing and how they perform: in call and response style the two sexes' views of household and sexual realignment are expressed, and in so doing, provide stability to existing structures. In saloon dances, on the other hand, bands or phonographs provide the musical setting for token exchange of drinks and dancing partners between males which leads to new sexual partnerships and to solidification of interpersonal networks which in turn crystallize into cooperative men's groups during times of economic gain. In both musical events dancers also symbolically express contrasting notions of sexual alignment.

In urbanized areas these musical performances grow more intense and they are staged on the same nights so that a choice of attending one or the other must be made. In fact, individuals *do* attend one and then the other on different occasions. Yet, in doing so, they deny their participation in the other events, and even their existence.

Whitten's observation (1968:61) that individuals do participate in different musical events, even though they see them as mutually exclusive, serves as a warning that our present understanding of Afro-American (or any other) musical categories may be incomplete and even superficial. Further inquiry may reveal that alternative music forms not only exist simultaneously, but may also be more available to individual option than we have so far been led to believe. This may indeed be part of what Lerone Bennett, Jr., means when he warns against Euro-American interpretations of the Negro tradition (1964:85–86):

> The essence of the tradition is the extraordinary tension between the poles of pain and joy, agony and ecstasy, good and bad, Sunday and Saturday. One can, for convenience, separate the tradition into Saturdays (blues) and Sundays (spirituals). But it is necessary to remember that the blues and the spirituals are not two different things. They are two sides of the same coin, two banks, as it were, defining the same stream.

But whether or not a dichotomous model of musical social reality is fully applicable to Afro-America, a unified musical form and performance role analysis appears necessary. An awareness of styles and counter-styles in all aspects of expressive culture should offer us a richer and more realistic picture of the New World Negro experience.

NOTES

1. A slightly different version of this paper was read at the 66th annual meetings of the American Anthropological Association in Washington, D. C., December 1.
2. Jeanette Robinson Murphy spoke of the opposition between church songs and "fiddle" songs in 1899 (see Murphy 1899).
3. For similar points concerning Negro song in general, see Jahn 1961:224–25; and Dauer 1958:74.
4. Soul music is so very close to gospel music that it often draws criticism from older followers of the sacred-secular distinction. Bluesman Big Bill Broonzy criticized Ray Charles thus: "He's got the blues he's cryin' sanctified. He's mixin' the blues with the spirituals. I known that's wrong" (Karpe n.d.). See also Szwed (1966, 1968).
5. For a discussion of the aggressive roots of calypso, see Pearse 1956; Crowley 1959; and Elder 1966a.

Part two

SOCIO-ECONOMIC ADAPTATIONS

Twelve

TOWARD A DEFINITION OF MATRIFOCALITY

Nancie L. González

The term "matrifocality," or women-centered, has now clearly become an accepted part of the anthropological vocabulary. It has been found useful by ethnographers and sociologists working in widely scattered parts of the world. Since it was first used in reference to societies of poor blacks—especially in the West Indies—it is often associated more with the Afro-American areas of culture than with others. Indeed, it has even been suggested that matrifocality is a survival of African culture, or that it is a direct result of conditions imposed upon the slave societies in the New World. Neither of these views has much currency today—especially since matrifocality has been attributed to peoples as diverse as the Javanese, the Mescalero Apache, and the inhabitants of East London. If matrifocality as a conceptual tool is to become useful, there must be some agreement about what it is. However, not only is it extremely difficult to find explicitly stated definitions of matrifocality, but there is much variance in its meaning as implied by the diverse usage of the term. In some cases matrifocality seems to imply that women are somehow more important than the observer had expected to find; in other words, that the general status of women in the society is "rather good." This, of course, implies that the observer had certain ideas concerning the usual or proper balance of status between the sexes before he made the study. Without knowing the individual scientist's value position, then, it becomes difficult to evaluate qualitative statements concerning the "importance of women."

In other cases the anthropologist has seemed to mean that women have a great deal to say about how the money or income is spent, which in fact says quite a lot about the culture in general. But for still others the term is taken to mean those households in which the woman is the primary *source* of income. At times, as in US census materials, for example, the term "woman-headed" means that there is no resident male in the household. Yet there are many societies which have been characterized as matrifocal in which men were indeed members of the households. And, of course, there are also instances where the household is "woman-headed," while the men, the society leaders, live in men's houses, as in highland New Guinea (Rowley 1966).

Here I would like to discuss the concept of matrifocality, first in structural, and then in functional terms. The purpose is not so much to review writings on the subject as it is to try to lay bare some of the features which seem to arise over and over again in using this concept, with a view toward explaining the distribution of the form in adaptive, evolutionary terms.

In relevant publications, discussion often starts with descriptions of the "matrifocal family," often used synonymously with another social structure which I have labeled the "consanguineal household" (González 1965). For the purposes of this paper, I would prefer to use the concept "matrifocality" since the term "family" leads to an unnecessary confusion between the domestic units and kinship networks. To elaborate, it is possible to have dispersed families in which the members do not actually reside in the same place. For example, the husband-father may reside in the rear of a tavern where he is the proprietor. His meals may be brought to him daily by an adult daughter, while his wife may be "living in" as a maid in a middle-class household. Their minor children may be parceled out among various relatives, to whom the parents may pay a small sum for their keep. Nevertheless, a good deal of affective cohesion may remain, in which case the structure of the family as a *kinship network* is preserved through mutual concern frequent visiting, and patterned reciprocity.

Households, on the other hand, may also exhibit multiple and shifting membership so that these too are not the simple concrete units which we once assumed them to be. Thus a particular individual may take his meals in one household, sleep in another, and yet contribute financially to these plus still another. Of which, then, is he a member? Or conversely, what is the composition of households A, B, and C above? Is our exemplar individual to be considered a member of each or of none? Furthermore, what is the "family" or "families" of which he is a member? Clearly, the concepts "family" and "household" must be kept distinct in the light of contemporary ethnographic data, particularly from the Afro-American culture area.

I suggest that we reserve the term "household" for the cooperative group which maintains and participates in a given *residential* structure, even though the contribution of any one individual may be only part-time. In this case, the concept that households are closed, bounded units must be modified. Indeed, the fact that individuals have simultaneous loyalties to more than one such grouping may be important in understanding the social structure as a whole. I furthermore suggest that men, particularly, tend to be placed in positions in which potential conflict between households devolves upon them, thus putting strain upon the individual in his role in one or both units. I shall illustrate this situation below with materials from my own and other's fieldwork.

"Family" seems most usefully defined in terms of kinship networks; that is, the different types of families can be described in terms of the kinds of kinship bonds among the different individuals considered to be members of the unit. In this sense the family grouping may be considered a concrete unit but is not necessarily a co-residential unit. Neither can we say, structurally speaking, that families are mutually exclusive, bounded units. Quite clearly there may be overlapping membership at all levels and in all types of families. This may manifest itself in an individual's continued participation in his natal family after marriage, and also, as in much of the West Indies, in cases wherein one male occupies the position of "husband-father" in two (or more) nuclear families. One problem faced by the anthropologist is to determine the ways of describing structures such as these. Another is how to measure and analyze the effect upon the society of the overlapping and possibly conflicting roles of the male.

Meyer Fortes (1958:9) has suggested a way of analyzing domestic groups using internal, functional differentiation as his base. He starts with what he calls the matricentral cell consisting of the mother and her immature children. The next unit is the nuclear family, composed of the matricentral cell plus a protective male in the role of "husband-father." Although Fortes did not consider this possibility, it is necessary to point out here that the matricentral cell may also be under the protection of a male filling *none* of these roles, but who rather stands to the matricentral cell as "brother-uncle" or even "son-brother." Few would label the latter examples "nuclear families."

The unit described by Fortes is the domestic group itself, by which he apparently means household. This includes the nuclear family plus any other relatives who may be co-residing in the same house. At this point the distinction between "family" and "household" is crucial.

For some purposes it may be useful to consider the interpersonal relationships involved rather than the group composition, as Fortes has done. Thus, instead of matricentral cell I suggest we examine the "mother-child dyad," which emphasizes the salient *bonds* between mother and child rather than the group of people. In matrifocality the other relationships among family members tend to be defined in terms of this original mother-child relationship. Thus, ties are stronger among uterine siblings than among those sharing only a father. The protective male, if present at all, may be important to ego primarily as "mother's husband," whether he is ego's father or not. Other relationships will also be defined in terms of the mother (mother's father, mother's sibling, or even something as non-specific as "one of my mother's relatives"). It may be further enlightening to consider the total agglomeration of interpersonal relationships as the concrete structure we call "household," from which we abstract *only* those relationships which pertain to the central females or which derive from them. We can then call this analytic structure "matrifocality."

Let us turn now to a consideration of how one may *recognize* matrifocality—i.e., what does a matrifocal society look like from a structural point of view? Within the domestic context, the mother-figure would be least likely to have multiple or shifting allegiances to different households and or families. Rather, the female (or females) who fills the role of mother would tend to be the stable figure around whom other members cluster, whether or not they are physically present. In a matrifocal society one would normally expect to find that when members of the extended family are included in the household, these are more likely to be relatives of the mother than of the father. Similarly, one would expect to find that personal contacts occurred more frequently with mother's kin that with father's kin. In terms of decision-making or patterns of authority, here again one would expect that in societies labeled "matrifocal" women would be free to make decisions concerning the household and to discipline children, although this is not to suggest that they never call upon males for assistance or guidance in these matters. The crucial issue would be the possibility, given the value system of the society, for women to even consider making decisions without calling in a male authority figure. The *degree* of matrifocality (for I do not consider this an either-or phenomenon) is the issue at stake here. Indeed, one may wish to distinguish one society *or* sector of it as relatively more matrifocal than another society or sector.

Finally, in our hypothetical matrifocal society, one might expect that in the eyes of the children the maternal figures would be strongest, most stable, and most dominant; they would see their mothers as being not only nurturing, but disciplinary figures. Quite possibly the degree to which these impressions are felt could be determined through the use of projective tests among the children in the society.

When we consider not only the internal relationships within the domestic grouping, but the relationships between such units and between them and the society at large, an idealized matrifocal society would be one in which the central female figure of each domestic group represents it in jural matters at other levels. Although it is clear that the position of women in this latter sense varies tremendously from one society to another, we know of no society which delegates the woman as *primary* representative at the highest levels of integration. On the other hand, it is clear that women do participate in jural affairs in some societies, and perhaps in this sense we could label those societies which grant women a larger or more important role as more strongly matrifocal. It should also be pointed out, however, that it is possible to have matrifocal family organization without having matrifocal societal organization.

A word of warning here for investigators—just because no concrete or formalized female-dominated structures are found does not exclude the possibility that women may be a very real force in the operation of the society at jural levels. The value system may explicitly reject women as a political or a jural force, yet it is well known that women may operate either through informal pressure groups or as individuals to get things done. If they control the domestic purse strings, this implies that they are an economic force to be reckoned with in terms of the society as a whole.

Let us consider briefly some other kinds of structures, institutions, or circumstances which have been thought to coincide with or induce matrifocality cross-culturally. These include (a) African origin and/or slavery, (b) unstable marriages, and where the concept applies, free unions and consequent illegitimacy of children, (c) consanguineal households, in which the adult cooperating unit is composed of consanguineally related kin, rather than a marital couple, (d) bilateral kinship systems with either bilateral kindreds, nonunilineal descent groups or both, and (e) a numerical shortage of males caused either by the frequent migration or absence of men performing wage labor, waging war, or experiencing higher death rates.

Now let us consider the validity and utility of each of the above so-called social factors. (a) The distribution shown by anthropologists for matrifocality is broad enough to indicate that African origin in and of itself is not significant. It is very likely important that the African migration to the New World under slavery was one of the first instances in the world in which the conditions for the development of matrifocality arose, and it is perhaps for this reason that social scientists first became aware of the form in the West Indies and in the United States South among persons of African origin. However, today we have reports of matrifocality not only from the West Indies, but also from various parts of Latin America (Hammel 1964; Lewis 1966a; Mintz 1956), Java (Geertz 1959), East London (Young and Wilmott 1957), Scotland (Smith 1956), South Italian peasants (Lopreato 1965), the Mescalero Apache (Boyer 1964), and some places in the Pacific (Calley 1956; Kay 1963).

(b) Frequently it is assumed that a high rate of marital instability coincides with culturally defined weak conjugal ties. In such cases, the mutual affective bonds between husband and wife never develop strength sufficient to replace those between each spouse and his consanguineal kin. This is certainly the case in the West Indies, among United States southern blacks, and perhaps elsewhere. However, the fact that the two are not necessarily related is shown by Hildred Geertz's material from Java in which the conjugal tie is strong and yet marriage is unstable. In London, Scotland, and very possibly European peasant society, there is not only considerable stability in marriage but also a strong conjugal tie. The final and fourth logical possibility is that in which there is stable marriage with a weak conjugal tie. This last situation seems to exist in many tribal situations with strong patrilineages, but matrifocality seems not to exist under such circumstances. We will therefore exclude this from the present analysis. In fact, elsewhere I have used this as an explanation of why matrifocal families are not found in tribal areas of Africa (Solien 1959).[1]

For all but the last of these situations there are cases in which the society and/or the family system has been characterized by investigators as matrifocal. If we take

	Weak Conjugal Tie	Strong Conjugal Tie
Unstable Marriage	West Indies (Matrifocal)	Java (Matrifocal)
Stable Marriage	Kachin Nuer	East London (Matrifocal)

FIGURE 12-1

marital instability and/or a weak conjugal tie as being crucial for the present definition of matrifocality, then, as shown in Figure 12-1, we are faced with the dilemma of deciding *which* of the three types *said* to be matrifocal should be excluded from the category I am so designating here. My decision not to exclude any, but rather to reject marital stability and strength of conjugal tie as important indicators of the existence of matrifocality is related to the *definition* of that concept, which I think *must* involve the question of female roles.

(c) In a 1963 survey of what he called the consanguine or matrifocal family, Kunstadter used a definition for the matrifocal family which he said he took from my doctoral dissertation. In fact, this definition pertained to the consanguineal household, which as I have indicated, is quite a different thing. I defined the consanguineal household as a "co-residential kinship group which includes no regularly present male in the role of husband-father. Rather, the effective and enduring relationships within the group are those existing between consanguineal kin" (Solien 1959). The consanguineal kinfolk may be male or female in any combination. A consanguineal household may or may not be matrifocal. Conversely, a matrifocal family may quite well include a regularly present person in the role of husband-father.

To illustrate further the difference between these two concepts, let us consider the traditional Nayar of the Malabar coast, a group which Kunstadter felt exemplified one extreme in a hypothetical continuum of matrifocality. I would say that the Nayar were *less* matrifocal than other groups that have been studied even though the consanguineal household existed among them not only as the ideal type but as the most frequent form. To my knowledge, at least, there has been no society except the matrilinear Nayar that maintains the consanguineal household as its only form. Affinal households or those containing at least one conjugal pair are always found as alternate structures. Indeed, an important characteristic of the type of society which has consanguineal households is the fact that other kinds of households simultaneously exist, and that they may change from one kind to another under different types or even combinations of stimuli. It should be emphasized again that virtually all households among the Nayar were consanguineal, being composed of a group of women related through the maternal line, their children, and brothers of the women, the latter being present only part of the time (Gough 1952:85).

Among the Black Carib, with whom I have worked, consanguineal households of all types made up only 45% of the total households within the society. Furthermore, the composition of the consanguineal households varied. Fifty per cent of them were actually made up of a single woman plus her children. In many cases the households in this category included older children who were employed sometimes as fishermen or errand boys, or who stayed home and took care of the younger children while the mother went to work. About 25% of the consanguineal households consisted of two or more related women plus their children and another 25% included two or more related women plus their children plus males consanguineally related to the adult women. There might be males who, although not regularly present, nevertheless dropped in upon the women occasionally, either for purposes of sexual contact or because they had children within the household whom they wished to visit. In some cases these households depended upon contributions, both in money and in goods, from several such males, either in a series or simultaneously. However, and this is the crucial point in identifying the consanguineal household, *the effective and enduring relationships are those existing between consanguineal kin.* There were frequently several individuals who shared authority within these consanguineal households. The oldest female in the group frequently made formal decisions, and the most active, vociferous female was often the representative of the household vis-à-vis other households and the society. Yet men, in their roles as brothers, uncles, sons, or cousins, were called upon by the women when they needed any type of assistance, whether moral, financial, legal, or physical.

Since men frequently were related to several households and families in their different role capacities, their loyalties tended to be divided. In such cases there were sometimes conflicts over which household deserved more of a man's attention, time, and money. Here again, I would say that it is one of the structural features of matrifocality that, given a conflict in loyalties, a man is more likely to turn first to his mother and secondarily to his sister rather than to his wife, or for that matter, to any woman who is the mother of his children.

It is true that among both the Nayar and the Black Carib men were absent from the home villages intermittently—for carrying on warfare in the case of the Nayar, and for wage labor among the Carib. If we take only this factor into consideration there might appear to be a structural similarity between the two groups. However, if we consider the supra-domestic elements of the two sociocultural systems, important differences appear, suggesting that we are not dealing with comparable units. A Nayar male gained status in the society at large through his participation in ritual, jural, and economic activities, all of which were intimately connected with the matrilineage. Conversely, the matrilineage or segment of a lineage could not afford to lose males who performed many functions necessary for the maintenance of the group as a whole. Therefore, the consanguineal household among the Nayar can be understood only in relation to the matrilineal organization of the entire society in which this particular type of dwelling unit was highly valued. Presumably it was highly valued because it enhanced the stability of the matrilineage. It might be said that within such a society, where the men must be absent a good portion of the time, it was necessary for the preservation of the matrilineal organization to have them associated with members of their matrilineage during the time they were at home rather than dispersed, as they would have been if they lived with their wives. This type of residence was also important in relation to the prevailing customary law in regard to inheritance and division of property rights.

In Black Carib society, on the other hand, several different household types exist, each of which appears to be functional under different circumstances. The consanguineal type tends to be one of the most common, yet cannot be considered the ideal form. In spite of the fact that the nuclear family household is the preferred form, not only in terms of expressed ideals, but also in the sense that it is the single most common form (28% of total households), it appears that the economic base of Carib society is such that this ideal is difficult to achieve and maintain by the majority of the members of the society. As Sahlins (1965b) has so skillfully reminded us, ideology and composition of social structures are not necessarily (or perhaps even usually) congruent. In speaking of descent, he says, "Modes of recruitment and affiliation at the lowest level may merely reflect higher level structural imperatives, thus injecting into everyday household and community life the relations appropriate to the working of the larger polity" (*ibid.*: 106). The converse may also be true. That is, the *idiom* at the lowest levels may reflect a value system appropriate to the larger society, yet group composition may yield to more immediate pressures. The consanguineal household seems then to be formed by default rather than as a positive mechanism oriented toward reinforcing solidarity among members of a matrilineage in which the loss of males would be fatal to the system, as among the traditional Nayar. Males are, of course, important in many ways to a Black Carib household, but it matters little to the unit as a whole whether they occupy the role of brother, uncle, husband-father, or son.[2]

It is interesting to note that as traditional Nayar society breaks down, affinal bonds tend to replace consanguineal ties as the basis of household membership. According to Mencher (1962:232), there has been a recent tendency for males to live with their wives, even though they may still leave the village periodically in search of work in the towns. In such cases, they send money home not only to their wives, but *also* to their mothers and sisters. It may be that this newer situation will tend to mold Nayar society into a form more like that of the Black Carib and other similar groups. That is, the consanguineal household may cease to be the ideal and preferred form, yet persist as an *alternate* type, formed when for one reason or another the persons fulfilling the husband-father role(s) drop out, leaving behind the consanguineal core of women plus whatever male kinsmen the women can recruit for assistance of various kinds.

The consanguineal household exists, then, both among the classical and modern Nayar and among the Black Carib, but matrifocality is possibly characteristic only of the latter, although it may be developing among the modern Nayar concomitantly with the breakdown of the matrilineages themselves.

Consanguineal households, then, are frequently matrifocal, but they are not necessarily so. Conversely, affinal households may or may not be matrifocal. Although 55% of the Black Carib households in Livingston in 1956 contained a husband-wife pair, some of these were also matrifocal, as measured by female stability, role dominance, and authority patterns. One way of measuring the degree of matrifocality in affinal households might be to check the number and kinds of kin-linkages within them. That is, if we take the marital couple as the core, we may then note whether other members are included in this household by virtue of their kinship bonds with the man or with the woman. Here we would be concerned not only with adults, but very importantly, with the children. We must know *whose* children they actually are, who maintains them, and who has ultimate authority over them. If they are children of the woman by a former spouse, does her present husband become a father-figure to them, or does he relate to them only as their mother's husband? Only with information of this sort can we assess the degree of matrifocality within a household. I should stress again that matrifocality has nothing to do *per se* with the consanguineal household, although it is probably true, for reasons to be brought out below, that *most* consanguineal households also tend to be matrifocal.

(d) If we examine the publications cited, we find that the only one of these characteristics which seems always to be associated with matrifocality is bilateral kinship. It may be that these two elements co-vary because they are not in fact independent variables and that both are reflective of some other determining factor. Bilateral kinship systems are, in fact, *unmarked*, and therefore provide more flexibility in the structuring of kinship-based groups. In this sense the apparent correlation between bilaterality and modern mass society is not surprising.

(e) The available writings also show that relative absence of men in the system does not in and of itself bring about matrifocality. That is, matrifocal systems coincide with both presence and absence of regularly resident men, and non-matrifocal families coincide with both the presence and absence of males.

By "absence of males" we usually understand *physical* absence and along with this, assume that they are absent from the locale —that is, they are not only absent from the household, but from the village or the community as well. In other words, they are not physically present as residents in this household. Here again, "absence of males" is not a unitary descriptive phrase. What I mean by this is that the "husbands" may be absent from a particular household but present in the village, actually living or sleeping in some other woman's household. This other woman may be a second spouse, or she may be the man's mother, sister or other relative. Virtually all monographs dealing with family structure in the Caribbean document this phenomenon, some handling it under the rubric "polygyny" (Freilich 1961; Whitten 1965:126), others under "extra-residential" mating (Otterbein 1966:67; M. G. Smith 1962b). Another type of absence involves absence from the village itself. Elsewhere I have tried to show that when males migrate to find jobs, the length of time they are absent and the patterns of their migration are themselves important factors in understanding the kinds of social structures which arise to cope with their absence (Solien de González 1961).

But there is still a different kind of absence which I think we should consider if we wish to understand matrifocality cross-culturally. In many cultures, particularly the United States modern middle class, the male may be physically present during the evenings and the nights, but physically absent during a great deal, if not most, of the day. It might be added that he is "psychologically absent" a great deal more than this. It would seem that the more removed the economy from agricultural and handicraft pursuits, both of which are clearly types of economic activities involving the entire household, the more male roles focus on non-domestic matters. Not only is the male required to leave the household daily in order to work, but it could be said that the domestic and jural domains have become concretely, as well as analytically, differentiated from each other as a result of the rise of the industrial system.

In regard to the domestic domain, not only has it become further removed from the jural domain, but it has expanded considerably to include much more than it did in primitive, pre-industrial society. Thus the domestic domain today, as always, includes concern with socialization of the young, nutrition, protection and nurturing of group members, health and disease, and so on. In primitive society there were few functionally specific non-domestic institutions to cope with these needs as there are in modern states. Today the domestic domain embraces *not only* those functions which continue to occur within the household, but it also must deal somehow with those higher level structures and institutions which directly affect the domestic unit, but which are beyond its immediate control. Such areas as schools, public health, civic improvement, consumer buying, and the like, are included here. At this point, relations *between* households, as well as between the household and higher levels, become relevant. In primitive society the relationships between households were most often cast in terms of kin relations and were thus assigned to the appropriate linking kinsmen, depending upon the type of systems involved and the individual case. In modern mass society these matters have been increasingly removed from the lower-level household or domestic domain and are manipulated through a relatively new set of institutions and concrete structures which serve to relate one household to another, and the entire domestic domain to the jural. We might call this intermediate domain the supra-domestic.

Since males are increasingly absent in both a physical and psychological sense from the domestic scene, a growing emphasis upon the role of the woman both in the domestic and the supra-domestic domain is not surprising. As such, the patterns of behavior and their institutionalized structures could be considered forms of adaptive response to the exigencies of the modern economic system.

Although it is true that in many countries today women also play a certain role in the jural domain proper, there are two points which I would like to stress in regard to this point. The first is that women are still in a minority in the jural domain both in terms of numbers and in terms of the amount of authority and power they exercise as a class. This situation is, nevertheless, changing rapidly in many countries. The second point which must be emphasized is that even though women are moving into this area, this does not imply that the system is matrifocal. What it does seem to imply is that as societies develop, the sexual division of labor becomes less rigid, and roles are structured more on the basis of ability, training, and personality than on sex. Therefore just because a woman happens to be the prime minister of India does not suggest that she is behaving as a woman or representing women in that role. The fact that she is a woman in this sense is merely coincidental and has nothing to do with matrifocality. Women as *a class* may carry some weight in the jural domain, but is most likely to be concentrated in those areas which articulate directly with the domestic domain, as suggested above.

I have never seen in the discussions of matrifocality any consideration of its opposite—patrifocality. It might be wondered why we should be so startled by observations concerning the position of women in some societies that we devote tremendous time and attention to an understanding of these patterns. Could there be an element of ethnocentric bias in this?

The answer to this lies, I think, in the fact that the bulk of the anthropological studies made before the first quarter of this century dealt with primitive sociocultural systems. In these, the major economic base was one in which the domestic group as a whole was intimately related to the actual subsistence quest. Furthermore, populations were small, not too densely settled, and political systems were fairly simple and "close to home." Division of labor by sex and age was basic, and roles were well-defined. Furthermore, the number and variety of roles fulfilled by any one person were limited, as were the roles assigned to either sex. In societies such as these, where the domestic and jural domains were in fact quite close, it has never been surprising to anthropologists to find patrifocality as an important organizing principle. On the other hand, if we agree that changes in economy, technology, and general energy utilization are associated with changes in social structure, we should not necessarily expect to find patrilocality in all types of sociocultural systems. It is precisely in those where the domestic and jural domains tend to be separated the farthest that we might *expect* to find the complex of phenomena that we are calling matrifocality—*but not necessarily equally in all segments or classes or at all levels of the total society,*

I suggest that there are certain kinds of societies or sub-societies in existence in the world at the present time in which the jural domain has not only been increasingly removed from the domestic domain, but in fact has been taken almost completely out of the particular sub-society itself. What I mean here, more precisely, is that the members of such societies are not granted full admission to the society as a whole either as individuals or as a social segment. Rather, the sub-society becomes the equivalent of what we call in other contexts the lower classes or minority groups. The males in such a society will probably not only have low earning power, which is relevant to the domestic domain, but they will have very little, if any, jural power with regard to the larger society. Men are effectively cut off from the domestic scene since they tend to be funneled away from the local area in their pursuit of employment. Most are even excluded from labor unions due to the nature of their jobs, which are generally unskilled and impermanent. Thus, they have no opportunities to become involved in active participation in jural affairs of the society at large even in the work sphere. As such, the male role assemblage for such social segments might be termed denuded, and it may be that what we are calling matrifocality is simply a recognition of a situation in which male roles are not as complete as those filled by females.

In support of this idea, I might mention the oft-cited comment that there are differences between the upper and lower classes in terms of matrifocality. For Latin America, it has been pointed out that the patriarchal authoritarian patterns typical of the upper classes are not characteristic of the lower, and that the woman in the lower sectors has power, dominance, and independence not granted her upper-class counterpart (Goldkind 1961:376; Morse 1962:334). This also seems to be true in many West Indian societies (Clarke 1957; Henriques 1953; R. Smith 1956; and many others) and among black Americans in the United States (compare Frazier 1957a with Stack in this volume). Indeed, Oscar Lewis points to matrifocality as one of the characteristics of his "culture of poverty," which he claims has cross-cultural validity. Geertz (1961) specifically makes the same point when he says that the matrifocal family" . . . indeed seems characteristic of those groups which form *dependent* (my emphasis) parts of a wider, more complex society" (Geertz 1961:23). He goes on to point out that this pattern is also found among rural wage-laborers, but *not* in a situation where ". . . ownership, control, and the use of real property is the sole basis of family economy as it is in a true peasant society" (Geertz 1961:24).

I think that most observers would agree to the correlation between lower class sectors in an industrial system and matrifocality, but the explanatory factors behind this relationship are generally left obscure. R. Smith (1956:128) has argued that it results from the subordinate and economically insecure status of the adult male within the broader socio-economic sphere. I thoroughly agree with this conclusion, but I feel it focuses too narrowly on the importance of cash income to the household and upon the psychological effects of his inability to so provide upon the male.

Instead of concentrating upon the negative aspects of matrifocality I suggest that we look to the possibility of its offering a selective advantage for the sub-society under certain conditions of strain in the adaptation of the latter to the industrial system. I suggest that the consanguineal household offers financial and psychological security to the female *and* to the male and thus, to the maintenance of a fairly stable home environment even when jobs are hard to find and remuneration low. I have documented for the Black Carib the pressures placed on a man to be a good provider for the woman and children dependent upon him. When he fails to bring cash into the system, he may be rejected by his spouse, but *never* by his mother, sisters, or other consanguineal kin. Conversely, a woman can ill afford to cleave only unto one man, cutting herself off from other conjugal or extra-conjugal unions or from male kinsmen, for in such systems the chances that any one man may fail are high. Should her husband disappear or fail to provide regularly, a woman needs the support of other males. By dispersing her loyalties and by clinging especially to the unbreakable sibling ties with her brothers, a woman increases her chances of maintaining her children and household even when any one attached male is incapable of helping her.

Second, it may be that matrifocality in certain domains is adaptive in what I have elsewhere termed *neoteric societies*[3] (1969), because it succeeds in "keeping the home fires burning" even in the recurrent absence of men, thus enhancing the survival chances of the sub-society on the one hand and the existing relationship between this and the whole.

Matrifocality not only serves to maintain the individual household units, but also encourages the development of new concrete structures which, operating on the supra-domestic level, function to enhance neighbourhood or community solidarity by relating one household to another. Thus, women's clubs of one sort or another may be observed even in what we might think of as "incipient matrifocality." A further step would be the emergence of women's pressure or action groups which articulate with the national (or international) power structures in such a way as to improve conditions in the domestic domain for the sub-society concerned. I offer the above analysis as a further attempt to explain matrifocality—how it comes about, how it is perpetuated, and what functions it serves in relation both to the society as a whole and to the smaller sub-sector.

It may be that in industrial society, in those sectors which occupy a low status position within the society as a whole, the domestic and supra-domestic domains are the only ones which may be said to exist as outlined above. Therefore, since these tend to be dominated by women, we may refer to the sub-society as being matrifocal in organization.

However, there is recent evidence to indicate that new types of organization and structures by means of which the sub-society deals with the larger society are developing in some areas. Among others, I might mention the squatters' organizations in some Latin American cities (Mangin 1967b), black power and other civil rights groups in the U.S., and techniques such as the hunger-strike, newspaper denunciations, and sit-ins, which have been used so effectively in recent years in many parts of the world. Although not all of the new structures and mechanisms will survive and become institutionalized, it seems likely that the present relationships between the dominant and under-privileged sectors in modern industrial society will not long endure. Change in this structure can and has come about in different ways, but it does not seem likely that it will be spearheaded by the matrifocal elements of this local social organization. In other words, it may well be that there is a heretofore unrecognized, or a newly developing jural domain within these neoteric societies. I expect that when more is known about them, we will discover that there are domains which are in fact dominated by men rather than women. The whole problem of matrifocality then becomes a matter of perspective.

In conclusion, it is my view that the term "matrifocality," as it has been used by anthropologists and sociologists, refers to female role dominance in concrete social structures such as families, households, neighborhoods, communities, voluntary associations, and so on. It has been shown to occur almost exclusively in certain sectors of modern mass society, and I suggest that it may be better understood by casting it against the analytic framework of domestic, supra-domestic, and jural domains. These domains are not equally represented in all types of societies or sub-societies—the supra-domestic domain seemingly being a product of industrial civilization, and the jural domain being under-represented in neoteric societies. Matrifocality appears as an *organizing principle* only in the first two of these domains, and it seems directly related to the increasing complexity of society with the development of industrialization. With increasing separation of the domestic and the jural domains and with the rise of the supra-domestic domain, it becomes more difficult for males to carry on in all of these areas at the same time. This type of role allocation seems to function positively from the point of view of the sub-segment of the society in that vital functions continue even in the absence of the husband-father figure, and as such, of course, this also contributes to the maintenance of the total social system in which males of a certain social class or ethnic background may be channeled into particular types of jobs which are considered generally undesirable but which nevertheless are essential from the point of view of the total economy. However, new concrete structures may arise within the sub-society aimed at restructuring the relationships with the larger whole. These may be seen as falling into the jural domain, and dominated by males. Matrifocality, then, always seems to be restricted to the domestic and supra-domestic domains.

NOTES

1. At the time I was carrying out the fieldwork, I viewed the subjects of household and family differently from the way I view them now. Therefore, in making tabulations from the original census sheets, I failed to test for certain correlations which would have been useful. Thus, I should have included many of the households I placed in the category "one woman plus children" into the category "one or more women plus children plus consanguineally related males." This would have been more appropriate in view of the fact that many of the women living alone with their children in fact had near-adult sons who were capable of making household repairs, earning money, and in general behaving as protective and supporting males. Another series of calculations which I wish I had were the number of linkages through the maternal line versus number of linkages through the paternal line in the extended affinal households. As can be seen in my original *Table 3* (1959:87), I did not separate extended family households from nuclear family households if they contained at least one marital couple. I have gone on in that table to tabulate the couples and the types of bonds they had with the children in the unit. Thus I have categories for the following: "one couple plus children, at least one of which is the child of both," "one couple—no children," "one couple plus children of the women only," and "one couple plus children belonging to neither." I have frequently been asked about the affinal households which included these people plus other relatives of the conjugal pair. Unfortunately, since my emphasis at that time was somewhat different from what it is now, I did not include these items in my early reports, and even more unfortunately, the original census sheets from which these data were taken disappeared in the shipping of my materials from Guatemala in 1964. Therefore, I have only the quantitative materials already reported plus qualitative data concerning those kinds of relationships with which we are now concerned.

2. This is not negated by the fact that Skinner (1955) found matrifocality developing among patrilineal East Indians in British Guiana, since he also notes that extant acculturative forces were pushing them toward a bilineal or nonlineal state at the same time. Matrifocality seems not to develop as long as the patrilineages remain ideologically strong and functionally operative.

3. By this I mean societies which are neither primitive nor peasant and which are living on the fringes of industrial civilization. Such societies are locally distinguished from the larger societies of which they form a part; existing as a small in-group with some distinctive customs and traditions although economically and politically dependent upon the larger society.

Thirteen

BLACK TRADERS OF NORTH HIGHLAND ECUADOR[1]

Kathleen Klumpp

The manner in which the various social segments of the peasant population of highland Ecuador are linked to the national economy is related to the degree of dependency on the sale of something for a livelihood and to the nature of the channels through which distributive activities take place. The sale of agricultural produce within a market place organization is the primary means by which the rural Chota Valley Negro population of the northern Ecuadorian Andes is tied to and integrated into the national economy. This article will focus on the internal marketing system in which the highland Negro peasants of Ecuador are involved and on the nature of the interpersonal relationships which are initiated through trading activities.

While providing the primary means for the exchange of material goods, an internal market system is also an important mechanism through which the relationships between various social and ethnic categories may be expressed. Sidney Mintz (1959a:20) has discussed an internal market system as a "mechanism of social articulation" suggesting that it may be viewed as a basic set of economic processes in which societal segments intersect. Ecuador is an ethnically plural society and production and distribution for money constitutes an important focus for interpersonal and structural relationships between various ethnic segments. Though an inquiry into the interactive situations of the marketing process one may be provided with knowledge of the economic roles of these ethnic segments and, in addition, with important insights about how members of these segments perceive themselves and one another. In the north highlands, the three ethnic groups which interact in the internal marketing system are Negro, mestizo, and Indian, each being represented by different economic capacities. The concept of "social race" as used by Wagley (1965) parallels my usage of the term "ethnic".

An internal marketing system will refer to the processes and activities involved in getting material goods from the producer to the ultimate consumer, and not to a network of market place sites or centers of exchange as the term has been previously employed (Mintz 1959a). It is important to keep this distinction in mind because the unit of analysis will be the nature of the relationships initiated in the process of cash-oriented exchange, whether or not this exchange takes place within actual market places. It will be demonstrated that the nature of highland Negro peasant marketing behavior is characterized by varying patterns of action and circumscribed by quite different sets of restraints at the local level of intracommunity exchange than at the national level of market place trade.

Market place studies by virtue of the unit chosen have viewed the relationships of participants within the arena of the market place site as the basis for statements characterizing peasant marketing behavior and the extent to which it may be set forth through reference to the market model. Several difficulties emerge in this approach. First, concentrating on the market place obscures the importance of alternative exchange channels through which distributive activities take place and in which the economic relations between the participants may be influenced by other social considerations. Ortiz's (1967) article on Colombian peasant marketing behavior is an illuminating example of the differences which emerge in interactions in the market place and in stores. Second, marketing studies have neglected a consideration of the peasant productive sector as a fundamental part of an internal market system. Statements describing the extent to which marketing behavior is similar or dissimilar to that postulated by the market model cannot be convincingly made without considering the behavioral patterns of the producers at local levels of exchange. The market place site cannot be considered as if it were a closed microcosmic unit in which the applicability of formal economic theory to peasant exchange may be tested without reference to the total range of patterning of market behavior in the exchange network.

The first part of this article will deal with the ecological and ethnic contexts of trading in the Chota Valley and on a national scale and will consider the nature of the marketing system at the local level of intracommunity exchange. The second part will focus on the interpersonal relations between buyers and sellers within the context of a large urban market place site in Quito, Ecuador's capital city, and consider the relative influence of ethnic identity in shaping these relations. Throughout both sections, the influence of social and economic considerations in price formation will be discussed.

ECOLOGICAL CONTEXT OF MARKETING

The Chota Valley is located in the northern highlands of Ecuador in the provinces of Imbabura and Carchi, approximately 105 miles by road north of the nation's capital, Quito, and 21 miles northeast of Ibarra, the provincial capital of Imbabura. The valley is divided by the Chota River which provides both the natural and the political boundary between the two provinces. Along the river, in the valley floor, runs the Pan American Highway, which is the only highland thruway connecting northern and southern Ecuador. All traffic from Colombia and the north highlands must pass through the Chota Valley by means of this cobble-stoned road in order to reach Quito and points further south. The Negro settlements, which are located on the valley floor either directly on or very near to the highway, thus have ready access to transportation facilities going in either direction at almost every hour of the day and night. There are more than eight commercial bus lines in addition to many trucks which are willing to pick up passengers and their cargo. By bus the trip to Quito, traveling by night as the traders must do, takes about 9 hours. The excellent transportation facilities possessed by the Negro population of the Chota Valley is a very important factor in understanding why these cultivators are able to market their own produce directly in the largest urban centers of the highlands. They do not have to organize special transport facilities, although the members of some settlements have done so, nor do they have to rely on outside intermediaries to market their produce. A few non-local middlemen do buy in the valley. However, the Chota peasants are in no way dependent upon them as a means of distributing their produce.

Between the Colombian-Ecuadorian border and Quito there are only two highland river basins which at their depths are characterized by a tropical climate (Teran 1966:185). From north to south respectively these are the Chota and the Guayllabamba River basins. The two basins are remarkably similar in crop production, cultivating many of the same fruits and vegetables. Most important is that these basins are the only north highland source of the avocado. The activities of the individual traders from these two valleys is essential to the task of leveling out regional differences in climate, altitude, and crop specialization. From the Chota Valley, produce moves north to the regional market centers of San Gabriel and Tulcán and reaches many of the smaller outlying towns and villages. The southern destinations of produce originating in both the Chota and the Guayllabamba valleys is Quito, Latacunga, Ambato, and Riobamba.

The Chota Valley is characterized by a semi-arid, warm climate with a mean annual rainfall at the base of only 293.5 mm. (Teran 1966:193). The area of most extensive cultivation is at the base of the valley along the River Chota where irrigation canals are run into the fields. This is also the area of the densest Negro population, with the smallest plots of land, and with the heaviest emphasis on a wide variety of cash crops. The size of the average family plot is between 2 1/2 to 5 acres. Although there is variation from one village to another in crop production, the inventory for the settlements located on the valley floor includes the tomato, sweet manioc, bean, sweet potato, anise, sugar cane, avocado, cotton, cucumber, papaya, lemon, orange, plantain, cabuya, melon, and carrot. The settlements located directly on the Pan American Highway devote approximately three-fourths of the family plot to cash crops of a rapidly perishable nature which are not subsistence staples. The settlements located off the main highway, however, grow a larger proportion of crops intended primarily for self-consumption such as the bean, sweet potato, sweet manioc, and the plantain, although small amounts of these products and cotton and sugar cane are sold. Sugar cane is marketed directly at a mill in the valley. Two settlements in the valley are national custom control points where all vehicles are inspected for contraband goods from Colombia. The existence of these stops has resulted in an important internal market for immediately consumable foods. With the exception of sugar cane and the produce sold in these two settlements, all other produce is taken to market places, the most important of which are located outside the Chota Valley itself.

Until 1964 most of the Negro small holdings pertained to one of the *haciendas* in the valley. Before the Agrarian Reform Law of 1964, the majority of the Negro agriculturalists were *huasipungueros*; that is, serfs tied to a particular *hacienda* through usufruct rights to a plot of land (the right to use the property of another without changing or damaging its substance) in return for three to four days weekly labor cultivating the *hacienda* lands plus a small monetary remuneration of approximately $.05 daily. The Agrarian Reform Law has meant the rupture of all traditional obligations between the *huasipungueros* and *hacienda*. A man is now free to sell his labor to any contractor and the *hacienda* is not under any obligation, as it was preceding the Reform, to continue to utilize the resident population as its labor source. The Agrarian Reform has not as yet affected the patterns of marketing. Although the agriculturist now owns the plot of land from which produce is sold, ownership was not a prerequisite before the Reform to engage in trading activities. The marketing patterns of today developed with the use of motorized transport.

The large market centers in the Ecuadorian highlands are located in the municipal townships and are under the legal jurisdiction of the city government which imposes taxes and other regulations. Throughout Ecuador, most of the trading activities are dominated by mestizos, although Indians may be found who are both retail sellers and wholesale intermediaries especially in certain specializations such as cattle-raising, textiles, and meat-slaughtering. However, mestizos form the large body of non-agricultural specialist intermediaries who dominate the main arteries of trade, both to the rural areas and away from them, and in the distribution from the producer to the consumer. It is the mestizos who are most often the country buyers, the truckers, the wholesale distributors, the processors, and the retailers. Whereas the mestizo is important in the internal marketing system in his role as a middleman, retail seller, and consumer, the Indian participates in the market system primarily in the economic capacity of original producer and consumer, although, of course, not all Indians gain their livelihood in agricultural pursuits. The position of highland Negroes will presently be made clear.

THE PROCESS OF TRADING

The combined roles of cultivator and country wholesale buyer occupied by the Negro peasants from the Chota Valley is an unusual pattern in highland Ecuador and must in part be understood by ecological factors of readily available market places and a high demand for sub-tropical produce, especially the avocado, in the highlands.

In order to understand that aspect of the internal marketing system in which the Chota producer and producer-trader take part, the exchange of the avocado will be taken as the starting point. It is one of the most important cash crops upon which most of the trading activities are concentrated. The category of trader will be defined to include only those who buy produce from the plots of others to resell. It will not include those peasants who occasionally take small amounts of produce from their own plots to market without initially buying.

During the months of June, July, and August, between 50 to 65 individuals, the large majority women, buy avocados weekly to sell either in Ibarra or in Quito. Over 90% of the traders have access to land from which a minimal supply of avocados is obtained. Those who do not own a small plot are usually able to obtain a basic supply through sharecropping. Paying a yearly land rent does occur, but infrequently.

The process of marketing begins with the initial buying of avocados from other members of the same community. The traders living in the various settlements are not identified primarily by their occupation by either nontraders or themselves—that is, traders are thought of as primarily agriculturists who have taken up trading activities as one of several alternative ways of obtaining enough cash to buy food staples and other household necessities. However, there is a relative ease of movement in and out of trading activities. Other alternative sources of income are derived through fattening pigs and raising chickens to resell, carrying contraband, or selling avocados in the orchard. During the harvest season when market prices for avocados are extremely low, there is a tendency for some traders to switch from buying avocados to selling them in their own settlements until prices rise again. There are two sorts of traders who decide to switch from buying to selling: (1) those with small-scale operations who cannot survive three or more months of trading with accumulating decreases in the amount of capital available for weekly expenditures on avocados, and (2) those who do not lack sufficient capital with which to buy avocados, but feel that the effort expended is not worth the resultant cash income. The latter category includes those who have relatively larger plots of land from which they derive a substantial amount of avocados. Moreover, the selling prices in the orchard are often not much below those received in the market place in the same week. It is evident that the point at which the rewards are less than the effort required is necessarily a subjective evaluation subject to the intensity of the need for the small amount of cash received through selling in the market.[3] In addition to the economic factors mentioned in the decision to trade in the market place or not, a crucial element seems to be whether the individual enjoys the activity. Many women say that they are easily bored spending long periods of time in the home, and that they enjoy the freedom entailed in trading along with the hustle and bustle of the cities.

In the various Negro settlements, both the buyers and the sellers are rural cultivators who share not only a similar socio-economic position and cultural heritage but, more importantly, are linked by kinship, friendship, and *compadrazgo* (ritual co-parenthood) ties. Although the interactive patterns of the Chota buyers and sellers are necessarily founded in mutual economic need, they are strongly influenced by these enduring and often multiple social ties. The expectation of mutual favors entailed in these social relationships not only structure the buyer-seller interactive performance, but restrict the sorts of economic choices available to the Chota trader as well. It is to intracommunity buyer-seller relationships that we now turn.

Buying and selling avocados in the valley is carried out in a casual and relaxed atmosphere, in sharp contrast to the tenseness characterizing the market place exchange. The traders leave their households early in the morning to meet the sellers in the orchards. The sellers gather up the avocados and then pack them into large sacks which are carried to a clearing near the orchard entrance where the buyers are waiting. Although avocados are bought through bargaining both in the Chota Valley and in the market place, intracommunity bargaining differs significantly from that observed in the market place. Both parties to the transaction in the Chota Valley accede more easily to the other's terms. Attempts are made to bargain in mild and subdued tones in order to avoid the possibility of offending one's partner. The elements of antagonism, with buyer and seller pairs aggressively vying with each other, is minimized in bargaining within the valley. Buyer-seller quarrels are likely not only to terminate an incomplete transaction but also to create social tensions outside of the buyer-seller situation itself, especially with kin, friends, and *compadres*. Market place transactions as well may not be completed when one of the bargaining pairs is offended. There are, however, two different conceptions of what constitutes an offense. Aggressiveness with harsh verbal bantering manifested while bargaining in the market place is not sufficient cause for offense, although in the Chota Valley communities similar bargaining behavior closely approximates what Sahlins (1965a: 148–49) terms "negative reciprocity" and is considered by the participants as unsociable and conflict-laden. Thus, while interactive relationships in the country exist in order to exchange material goods they also take place within a personal network and are greatly influenced by social evaluations exterior to the actual social situation.

Although dissembling about selling price is a bargaining strategy employed by the mestizo intermediaries in the market place, it is not commonly practiced by the buyers in the Chota Valley because both the traders and the sellers are well aware of last week's market prices. Equal access to market knowledge results from country producers and their buyers living in the same settlements, which also facilitates discussion of the state of the market. The Chota producer-seller is at no disadvantage at the local level due to the effective network of communication.

The Negro trader selling in Quito, at the national level, is at a greater disadvantage in acquiring market information than her mestizo client who remains in the city during the week. Because of rapidly fluctuating prices and the lack of a means by which rapid assessment of marketing conditions may be made, being physically present in the market place is the *only* way that knowledge of a particular supply-demand situation may be gained. Therefore both the traders and their suppliers are equally ignorant of market conditions at the time when such information is needed—that is, while transacting in the countryside.

Although both the producers and the traders agree that the latter should make some "profit," expressed in terms of the difference between the purchase price of the avocados and the price at which they are sold,[4] there is no concept of a customary or "just" profit margin regulating price determination, as exists among Jamaican traders (Katzin 1960:310). In fact, the notion of a profit margin in itself is not operative. Because avocados are generally bought in non-assorted size lots, classified, and then sold according to size, a direct ratio between the prices paid per hundred while buying and those received in the market place may not exist. Nevertheless, the trader does make a general overview of the spread between per hundred buying and selling prices. The price of avocados which the traders are willing to pay depends only in part upon the selling price in the market the previous week. It also depends upon expected long-range price levels for the time of year and on the expectation of receiving a certain price at the market the following week. A sudden drop in market prices (which is a common occurrence) does not necessarily influence the next week's buying prices unless such drops become continuous over time as in seasonal fluctuations. Whether or not the wife of the cultivator is receiving enough for the sale of avocados depends on (1) what she previously has sold for during this time of year, (2) what others are selling for that particular day, and (3) her subjective estimate of what she thinks the trader can sell for the next day.

A large part of the Chota traders' possibility of making a profit lies in their ability to estimate proportions in an unassorted lot. There is a fairly precise estimation on the part of the transacting pair of the various proportions of each size present. If it appears to contain more "thirds" than "regulars" or "large" then the lot will be bought cheaply, at about S/8 or S/11 per 100. The larger, preferred avocados will be bought at about S/15 to S/18. The proportion of sorted avocados carried to market is usually three-fourths of the medium and small sizes and one-fourth of the large. Although transportation costs are greater for the larger sizes because the charge is per sack, the largest proportion of the total income per sack is derived from sale of the large sizes. In fact, the traders usually make very little profit and at times actually lose on the smaller sizes if the cost of a mixed lot exceeds the total income from the separate sale of different sizes. Although the Chota traders recognize this, a particular loss does not seem to affect the next week's decision about what sizes to buy. Choosing to continue to buy the smaller sizes is not "irrational," though; rather, it must be understood through a consideration of the nature of the restrictions on alternatives, for it would be inconceivable for the trader to refuse to buy anything except the larger sizes from a seller with whom she shares strong social ties. To do so would involve both a social and an eventual economic cost which the trader could not bear. Traders rely primarily on their relatives, friends, *compadres*, and neighbors to sell them avocados and to extend essential services. Only the mestizo traders who buy in the local settlements are free from these social expectations and buy in proportions of three-fourths large and one-fourth medium and small. By continuing to buy the poorer avocados, one may argue, the Negro traders obviate social conflicts and thereby not only insure their source of supply but their continuity as traders as well. However, the traders themselves do not engage in a conscious strategy of decision-making in which all the possible consequences of different courses of action are explored nor do they verbalize any of these functional ends. "We buy the smaller avocados because they are selling them," people say. The fact that alternatives are foregone through the fulfillment of buyer-seller behavioral expectations should not be confused with a process of conscious maximization.[5]

During the months when prices in the market place drop, the Chota traders must rely heavily on their ability to secure credit or cash loans. The sellers themselves are usually willing to give the trader avocados on credit. The value of credit may extend up to S/300 (U.S. $15.00), but the specific amount will be influenced by the seller's estimation of the buyer's ability to pay for the goods the day after the buyer returns from the market. There is an expressed sense of pride in having and maintaining good credit relationships because it reflects on one's ability to manage successfully in trading activities. This ability is not only dependent on the skill of the trader within the market place, but also on the way cash is managed within the family. Women generally handle family finances, apportioning money as they wish, but with the tacit consent of the male head of the household. In families in which the wife does not market, the husbands tend to have more direct control over money uses.

Cash loans are extended by friends, relatives, *compadres,* fellow traders from one's own settlement, and occasionally by the mestizo traders who buy in that settlement. Those who extend the loans are themselves frequently indebted to others. Many prefer not to ask relatives for a loan because "one should not so inconvenience relatives," but in fact they *do* ask for help. With the exceptions noted above, borrowing within the community is normally done with extreme reluctance. "Those who loan you money will gossip, telling everyone that you are poor, that you have nothing because you are wasteful. A poor person is despicable!" Retail shopkeepers who are patronized by Chota traders and non-Negro *compadres* who live in the towns are also potential outside sources of loans.

SOCIAL RELATIONS WITHIN THE MARKET PLACE

The market place of San Roque is only one of several large municipal market places in Quito. Like most municipal markets located in large regional centers, it is highly regulated by the city government on both the retail and wholesale levels. There is a complex system for obtaining retail stall space, monthly taxes on the stalls, vending taxes for those categorized as *ambulantes* (non-permanent mobile sellers, country wholesalers), fines, sanitation and food quality controls, officials to maintain peace and order, distinct wholesale and retail sections, and price controls. Price controls consist of the establishment of retail ceilings on all agricultural produce sold in the market place. Price ceilings are usually set to accommodate seasonal fluctuations in supply of agricultural produce, especially for perishables, but also for non-perishables, since storage facilities for all produce are seriously lacking. In San Roque, if the scarcity of avocados pushes the price up along the chain of intermediaries, forcing the retailer to exceed the fixed upper level, the market *control* will force the price down to the level of the country wholesale trader.

Most of the city buyers live and work in Quito as retailers and as secondary wholesalers of perishable produce. Many have permanent stalls in the market place. Other buyers come from the nearest large cities to the south of Quito.

The close spatial arrangement of the Chota traders into village clusters in the wholesale section of the market place facilitates the flow of price information. Bargaining is loudly carried out so that when one buyer is advancing bids, the others can overhear the transaction. Thus, no one seller is at a disadvantage through lack of access to information. Moreover, the spatial distribution also encourages animated verbal exchange among the Chota sellers. In contrast, the mestizo buyers rarely interact verbally—each goes about the business of acquiring stock quite independently. The buyers, although acting as autonomous units, do tacitly cooperate. Each adheres to the rule of separate bidding and buying, each completing a round of bargaining with the potential seller before the next buyer approaches. The practice of completing the round of price negotiations regardless of whether it results in an impasse or a sale is an obvious means of avoiding disagreements between buyers over potential sellers. This system, of course, can only function in conjunction with the sellers who do not compete overtly with one another for potential buyers.

The overall framework and rhythm of bargaining in San Roque varies with the seasonal fluctuations of sub-tropical produce. Depending on the ratio of the buyers to the sellers, the amounts which each seller has to offer, and the amounts which the buyers are able to purchase, either the buyers or their sellers will have more influence in shaping the course of the transaction. At no time, however, does either member of the transacting pair have the power to dictate the terms under which she is willing to buy or sell, although the mestizo buyers, during the harvest season, approach this state more than the Chota sellers. Although the perceived conditions of supply and demand operating at any day in the market place will set the upper limits to which a partner will have the advantage in bargaining power, such factors as skills in marketing and the nature of the buyer-seller relationship will affect the actual price reached.

There are three stages in bargaining: (1) initial probes in which the buyers and the sellers obtain an idea of each other's perception of the supply-demand conditions that particular day; (2) serious haggling in which the range of buyer-seller bids are narrowed down; and (3) completion of the transaction. The patterns of buyer-seller interaction during the second stage differ significantly according to whether the Chota traders' desire to sell is greater than the buyers' apparent interest in their avocados, giving rise in both cases to an imbalance in perceived power. When the plaza is slow for the Chota traders, they actively seek out buyers. Buyers, moreover, effectively employ words and gestures indicating indifference and self-confidence as a strategy geared to impress upon the seller her defensive position. When avocados are scarce, the performers of the defensive-offensive positions are reversed.

The final stage in completing the transaction is the most interesting because it is during this time that personalistic elements in the buyer-seller relationship manifest themselves. If the seller feels that she has less bargaining strength than the buyer, she will initiate the final interaction, calling the buyer back with a plea of "How much will you pay me for them?" However, when the advantage lies with the seller, it is the buyer who returns and asks for a quotation of the "last price" (*el último*) below which the seller supposedly will not go. Both these requests, by either the buyer or the seller, are different from past bids in that the solicitor is asking for a realistic and serious evaluation of the price she thinks would be fair, considering the general market conditions that day. Concessions below the statement of the "last price" are made according to an estimation of one's partner as a "good customer" (*buen cliente*). The buyer will consider primarily whether her client has consistently supplied her with avocados during the seasons of scarcity, giving her preference over other buyers, whereas the seller will take into consideration the regularity of the buyer in glut seasons and whether she has been willing to extend other important services to be discussed below.

Both buyer and seller consider whether they have had any previous disagreements over suspected dishonesty in handling money or over the sacks owned by both. Often, in the hopes of encouraging a good price concession, one of the transacting partners will explicitly remind the other of favors extended in the past. Although the reciprocal obligations which develop in the market place between the Chota traders and their clients endure over time, they are not fulfilled through a structure as rigid as that entailed in a trading partnership. There is no need for unvarying weekly attendance on the part of either the sellers or the buyers nor an agreement, tacit or overt, that transactions will be made with the same individuals each week. The Chota traders complete final sales with usually from 2 to 4 buyers each. Most of these buyers are considered to be "good customers," but some share a more personalized relationship than others and are therefore able to obtain a price below the "last price" with greater ease. If the Chota trader does not share a sense of amicability and cooperation with the buyer, she will refuse to make further price concessions below either her first or second statement of the "last price."

SOURCES OF CONFLICT AND CO-OPERATION IN MARKET PLACE BUYER-SELLER RELATIONSHIPS

There are two major sources of conflict in the buyer-seller relationship: one of which is embodied in the rules of bargaining behavior, and the other which is inherent in any marketing system lacking an effective and standardized means for identifying goods. The sources of cooperation lie in the participants' attempts to buffer the otherwise shattering effects of seasonal fluctuations in supply through the establishment of personalized exchange relationships involving a set of long-term reciprocal obligations.

The nature of these personalized economic relationships corresponds in many ways to what is known as "pratik" among Haitian market women (Mintz 1961). However, in Ecuador, the personal elements in market place buyer-seller relationships do not appear to be as extensively developed as among Haitian market women, although their basic functions appear to be similar.

Stealing and lying are not only allowable but expected bargaining behavior, within limits, in the market place. Both parties to the transaction must look out for their own interests and, therefore, if one is deceived, the fault lies not with the offender, but with the recipient. Distrust is especially prevalent in buyer-seller relationships which are irregular, but even among preferred customers a participant may attempt to deceive her partner if she thinks that she will succeed. However, one of the most important functions of the "good client" relationship is to introduce an element of reliability and trust. If blatant dishonesty occurs, the relationship will most likely terminate.

The ownership of avocado sacks is one of the most frequent focal points of quarrels between buyers and sellers. These disagreements are not only related directly to the expectation of deception, but also to an imprecise system of ownership identification which allows the deception to occur. If an argument over a missing sack arises between a buyer and seller who have built up a relationship of relative trust and confidence, it is usually resolved through a mutual count without violent and harsh verbal displays. When serious arguments do arise, it is most often, but not always, with buyers with whom the seller has not regularly transacted and involves direct accusations of dishonesty. Each shouts charges that the other is a "thief" and "without shame." A buyer with a reputation for frequent and serious attempts at deception will simply be refused as a client by some of the Chota sellers even though he may not have previously transacted with this individual. Another important source of conflict is over money. It arises most frequently in the payment stage of the transaction when, after a mutual agreement on a certain price, the buyer short-changes the seller. Such occurrences are commonplace. Far from outraging the seller, they are regarded as little more than necessary and expected annoyances even though the seller suspects that the error was intentional.

Among Chota market women, the existence of a personal economic relationship is entailed in the statement that a particular buyer is a "good customer." A good customer shows a willingness to grant priorities in the market place. However, as already pointed out, quarreling is not absent even among those who consider one another "good customers." Nevertheless, even when arguments do occur between regular customers, the cause is more readily attributed to an unintentional mistake and quietly solved. There is the mutual expectation that each deal honestly with the other, and if a flagrant violation of this trust occurs, the relationship is permanently shattered.

Between customers, the term *comadre* or *compadre* is the accepted form of address, and between good customers, the first name is added. The Negro Chota sellers, however, do *not* share in *compadrazgo* relationships with their mestizo buyers, though they *do* extend the *compadrazgo* terminology across ethnic lines. The extension of such terms to include casual acquaintances is particularly prevalent in highland Ecuador when the social relationship is between members of two distinct ethnic groups such as between Indian and mestizo, Indian and Negro, and Negro and mestizo. This broadening of the usage of *compadre* terms is especially developed in market place trading (which has a high frequency of inter-ethnic and stranger relationships) and appears to introduce a personal tone into an essentially impersonal activity. Moreover, between "good customers" the diminutive is added to the first name, thereby stressing the element of friendliness in the relationship. When some of the Chota traders were asked why they addressed the buyers as *compadres* and vice versa, one perceptive informant answered "to put one in a mood of greater trust."

Having and maintaining good customers is exceedingly important both from the point of view of the buyer and the seller. The buyer in times of scarcity is assured that her good customers will sell to her during these times. The Chota seller, likewise, during times of glut must depend upon her good customers not only to buy from her but also to extend other types of favors.

During peak productivity, the seller risks the danger of not being able to dispose of all her produce even when her customers buy from her. It would be unheard of to pay the transportation costs to haul the produce back to the Chota Valley or to Ibarra to sell. The perishability of avocados necessitates that she dispose of them that day. There are two alternatives open to the seller when faced with this situation: first, she may trust the avocados to a buyer; and second, she may face the humiliation of selling very cheaply in the wholesale warehouse of the market place. The second alternative is taken only when the first fails.

The system of entrustment (*defar fiado*) consists of leaving the avocados with a trustworthy buyer to sell during the Chota trader's absence. If the buyer, already supplied with her necessary stock for the week, decides to extend this assistance to the seller, the worth of the avocados is determined that day by both participants. The buyer usually attempts to be just and establishes the value according to the average prices being paid that day in the plaza for the same size category. During the intervening week, she will sell the avocados and pay the predetermined amount of money the following week to the seller. The entrustment system functions to the advantage of both buyer and seller. The direct advantages to the buyer lie in the possibility of making a greater profit than normal in the event that prices rise during the intervening week and in selling without having had to secure the necessary capital with which to buy. An indirect, but nonetheless important advantage is in reinforcing the set of reciprocal obligations between the buyer and the seller. The buyer is thus securing a future supply of stock during the scarcity season, and in addition, will be able to manipulate this favor in obtaining a good price concession. If the seller were not able to entrust her goods, she might be forced to discontinue as a trader. The entrustment system may be viewed as a means by which the seller is shielded from the full force of sudden price drops. The Chota trader, however, is not protected from paying extremely low prices when selling her avocados in the warehouse. During the months of peak productivity, with many of the Chota traders operating largely on credit anyway, such a loss weighs heavily and is especially difficult to recover from.

Other forms of cooperation and mutual assistance expressed through the giving of priorities include the giving of an "extra bit" (*napa*) of produce to the buyer, and the occasional granting of a cash loan to the seller. The extension of loans to sellers is infrequent, but when it does occur, is interest free.

Friendliness among buyers and sellers is better manifested in inter-active patterns during non-bargaining interludes. During these periods of time, the occupational role identity of "buyer" and "seller" is not sustained. Rather, other identities such as age mates, friends, or members of the opposite sex predominate and define the interaction situation. While the particular pair is engaged in serious bargaining, the dominant interaction element is conflict and opposition in which each participant is attempting to maximize her profit. Although the object of the bargaining is to outmaneuver the other, the relationship is not completely anonymous for the identities of the participants as market place friends is still operative. By definition, however, these identities cannot predominate. The personal relationships shared by the participants in market place exchange is one of the basic resources to be manipulated in bargaining. After the completion of a sale, though, the two are no longer contenders, and their identities as friends comes to the fore through patterns of joking and teasing.

ETHNIC IDENTITY AND MONETIZED EXCHANGE

The nature and extent to which ethnic identity shapes interpersonal behavior in the market place must now be examined. The relations between Negro sellers and *mestizo* buyers who belong to different ethnic groups will serve to initiate a discussion of some significant variables in the role of ethnic identity in monetized exchange throughout highland Ecuador.

Both the mestizo and the Chota Negro traders fall within the lower limits of a hierarchial scale of social status. However, within these limits, the mestizos identify themselves and are identified by all other ethnic groups as higher on the scale of prestige evaluation than either the highland Negro or the Indian. Depending on the region of Ecuador and who is doing the evaluating, the Negro may be placed socially above the Indian, below the Indian, or at the same level. Trading relationships between the Chota sellers and their buyers should, therefore, reflect the asymmetry of ethnic status inequality.

The ethnic identity of each participant in a monetized transaction may be considered to form the setting or the stage for performing buyer-seller roles. The expectations comprising the roles of buyer-seller are well defined and serve quite adequately as guides to action in most situations, whereas the behavioral expectations of ethnic identity are far too generalized to serve as concrete guides to behavior. Monetized exchange in itself does not preclude the entry of ethnic factors, however. There is a set of prescriptive behavior entailed in buyer-seller roles which must be performed in order that the transaction be completed, but within these limits there are differential possibilities for ethnic identity to shape the actual exchange. It is suggested that these possibilities vary with the degree to which the buyer-seller relationship is personalized—whether the exchange is through bargaining or non-bargaining—and the presentation of self by the parties in bargaining encounters.

During the process of reaching a mutually satisfactory price, the relative status positions accorded to the Chota Negroes and their buyers do not appear to be especially significant for understanding the content of the actual interactive performance. Although ethnic identity rarely appears in the content of verbal exchange, this is not to say that it is not significant or that its influence is not felt in bargaining. The individual's self-image as *Negro* or as mestizo and the other's perception of him seem rather to set the broad limits on the sorts of behavior which will be regarded tolerable or acceptable.

It is precisely through instances of an infraction of the parameters of acceptable behavior that the limits themselves become manifest. Such instances occasionally occur in the market place if the transaction process is unusually stressful, as for example when a serious imbalance in supply and demand is perceived. When the market conditions are very unfavorable to either member of the bargaining pair, serious disagreements easily arise between participants who do not share a personalized exchange relationship.

It is in situations of tension that ethnic identity may be brought into play in the interaction. For example, a Chota trader was quarreling bitterly with a non-regular mestiza buyer over the ownership of a sack. The potential buyer, in the heat of the argument, called the Chota trader a "thief," and said disgustedly as she began to walk away, "What an ugly nigger!" (¡Que negra tan fea!), the Spanish term for "ugly" having the denotation of being unpleasing both in personal conduct and appearance. The trader shouted angrily back to her, "I am not just anybody, I am a lady! Because I am black, you think you can treat me this way?" The trader's sarcastic retort to inform the buyer that she had clearly exceeded acceptable behavior. This example is also significant because it summarizes in an interactive context statements by both mestizo buyers and Negro sellers of an ideal that ethnic identity be irrelevant in buyer-seller relations. As Goffman (1959:9-10) has well pointed out, attempts are made to reach an interactional *modus vivendi*: "Together the participants contribute to a single over-all definition of the situation which involves not so much a real agreement as to what exists but rather a real agreement as to whose claims concerning what issues will be temporarily honored."

It is suggested then, that status evaluations based on ethnic identity will be suppressed by the superordinate member of an interaction if expression of asymmetrical evaluation easily leads to open conflict. For those who share an enduring exchange relationship, the consequences of an ethnic offense weigh heavily both in terms of the psychological satisfactions of a market place friendship and mutual economic benefits. The attributes of ethnic membership thus figure as elements in the interaction between "good customers" if only as a determinant of what actions or tactics should not be employed. Ethnic identity, then, proscriptively structures personalized buyer-seller relations by prohibiting the entry of status considerations.

In impersonal buyer-seller relations involving bargaining, the manner in which the ethnically subordinate individual presents himself bears centrally on how ethnic identity structures the interaction. The self image presented by the individual is less important in fixed price transactions than the actual social status accorded to the ethnic group. In bargaining, however, in contrast to fixed price transactions (discussed below), the interplay of presented self image and ethnic group status is very important in determining whether ethnicity enters or is excluded from the transaction.

There are stereotyped expectations in highland Ecuador about how members of different ethnic groups behave in interpersonal relations. These expectations constitute the initial information possessed by the participants about each other. The manner in which the individual presents himself—submissively or assertively—offers additional information which either reaffirms or contradicts the ethnic group stereotype. The Chota Negroes are characterized as being assertive in their relations with members of a dominant status group and "volatile" (*impetuosos*) when offended.

Such characterization suggests an incongruence between an inferior social status and non-subservient interethnic behavioral patterns. With the exception of certain regional groups, Indians (unlike Negroes) are expected to behave with deference in the presence of status superiors. These stereotypes are significant in all social relationships but especially so in negotiated price-making.

Bargaining requires that the participants manage an impression of strength, both verbally and through posture or stance. Any signs of submissiveness, even if it simply be a hunched over stance with the head bowed, will be taken advantage of in bargaining. It is not uncommon that sales with Indians be completed in spite of verbal and/or non-verbal ethnic abuse. Examples seen within market places occur most frequently between Indian sellers vis-à-vis aggressive mestizo buyers. Verbal abuse in such transactions stresses the Indian's status inferiority. For example, he may be called a "dirty, piglike Indian" (*indio sucio, puerco*). A bargaining strategy of intimidating one into a hurried unprofitable sale is the frequent result.

Such tactics are only attempted by the dominant partner when there is a good possibility of coercing a sale or when an otherwise silent and submissive Indian has refused to meet the mestizo's price demands. An Indian who does not convey a self image of inferiority is more likely to be treated with respect in bargaining.

When the image conveyed about the individual reaffirms an ethnic stereotype of assertiveness, ethnic status infrequently enters into the exchange. Assertiveness to the point of aggression in bargaining informs the status dominant partner that the Chota traders' concept of acceptable behavior must be honored or no sale will result.

Different from bargaining is the system of fixed price transactions. Impersonal transactions in which some good or service is purchased at a fixed price are interpreted by the Chota Negroes as those situations in which ethnic discrimination most readily appears. One of the most frequent sources of complaint is to be assigned to the last row of seats on a bus after having purchased one's ticket before any of the passengers sitting up front. Buses in highland Ecuador are a symbolic representation of the status differentiations accorded to the various ethnic categories: "whites" sit in the very first rows; a variety of mestizo types are found up toward the front, middle, and back; and Indians and Negroes occupy the last rows of seats.

One Chota Negro, not being able to obtain a seat, volunteered the perceptive comment that "the money of the poor Negro is worthless!". In fact, it is not effective in securing for him adherence to the ideal expressed by the bus personnel of "first come, first serve." Other common complaints are directed toward those who make them wait until last when buying in a store, while mestizos and "whites" who had arrived later are attended to first. Similar differential treatment is found in post-offices and other governmental establishments.

Interestingly enough, when ethnic discrimination is perceived, the Chota Negroes, unlike many Indians accorded similar treatment, do not remain silent. It is because of their candid and forthright public expression of resentment that they share the reputation among Ecuadorian non-Negroes, especially the mestizos, with whom they interact the most, as being aggressive and rude (*mal educados*).

Usually a common element in fixed price transactions is differential treatment symbolized by status ranking. The Chota Negro comes last because there are others of higher social status. Here the status ranking is more important than the self-image which is projected. Fear of losing the Chota traders' business does not appear to be an important sanction in part because ticket salesmen and office personnel are not infrequently salaried petty bureaucratic officials. However, even when there is the possibility of losing the Chota Negroes' business, more business may be lost by not serving the higher status people first. Regardless of economic interest, ethnic discrimination may result through the superordinates' attempts to maintain their ego status and the self-image of other customers.

As has been suggested, these forms of discrimination result from the widespread attitudes of prejudice towards Negroes in the social race sense—i.e., by virtue of being at the bottom of the socio-economic system along with the Indians, and perhaps in some cases to simply being biologically Negro. In any case, at this point in time, the Chota traders' own perceptions of the determining factors do not involve a separation of the biological and the social.

SUMMARY

This paper has attempted to demonstrate that the study of trading is a useful means of gaining insight not only into the position of the Chota Valley Negroes within the larger context of an ethnically plural society, but also into the patterning of peasant marketing behavior in highland Ecuador. By viewing an internal marketing system as a distributive process, it has been shown that the marketing behavior of the Chota traders cannot be understood with reference only to the patterns which predominate in the arena of the market place. Equally important is the nature of mutual behavioral expectations of buyers and sellers at the level of intracommunity exchange. It is apparent that two sets of behavioral patterns are in operation, each with a different set of rules, but both embracing bargaining activity and personal relationships. Interpersonal relationships in both the rural villages and in the market place are instrumental in that they arise out of a mutual economic need which the exchange of cash for goods may fulfill. However, there are important differences in the nature of this exchange. The ties linking the Chota trader to the producer are enduring and often multiple, exist extrinsically to the exchange relationship itself, and strongly channel the participants' perception of the alternative courses of action which may be pursued. The influence of social ties in decision-making is especially apparent in buying patterns. Although the greatest demand in the market place is for the large avocados, the traders buy all sizes. The mestizo buyers in the valley, free from these restrictions, can directly economize, refusing to buy other than their size preference. The basis for granting priorities (credit, price and quantity concessions, and time extension on payment) arises out of the obligations and expectations, both of an economic and social nature, entailed in the formal ties of kinship, fictive kinship, and the informal ties of friendship and neighborliness. These priorities may be considered part of a wider network of favors and debts of gratitude permeating the social life of the community. Both the traders and the producers from a single village see themselves as sharing a common cultural identity, inevitably interacting with and dependent upon one another. The village is the main point of identification among the Chota peasants, and its separateness from other communities is symbolized in the market place by the village cluster spatial arrangement of the Negro traders.

The interaction patterns in the market place are shaped by both recurrent and non-enduring "stranger" relationships. The former are personalistic ties which introduce an element of trust and minimize conflict. The origin of the buyer-seller personal bonds is occupational in nature and market place friendships are considered to be a major resource to be manipulated in achieving price concessions and other services. The benefits of giving and receiving priorities are mutual for they not only protect the seller from the impact of sudden price fluctuations, but also guarantee the continuity and security of the relationship by cementing the sets of reciprocal obligations. Relationships between non-regular buyers and sellers do not exhibit the personal factors, price concessions are not necessarily given, and it is expected that forms of dishonesty will be attempted. Serious quarrels are prevalent and are not so readily attributed to a possible "mistake" as they are among "good clients."

It is evident that both the buyers and the sellers are influenced by the forces of supply and demand operating in the market place, although neither the price nor the quantity of produce brought to the market is entirely determined by these impersonal forces. Incorporated within the internal marketing system are price concessions and other priorities which introduce "non-economic" factors into the determination of price. Through the system of entrustment the city traders help the sellers receive a price for their avocados above that which they would have received in the market place had they been forced to sell. Moreover, there are attempts by the municipal government to enforce retail price ceilings on produce, thus interfering with the forces of supply and demand that are operating.

Wolf (1966:43) and others point out that there are limitations which are inherent in the peasant type of life inhibiting a capacity to participate flexibly in that part of the economy operating largely through supply and demand. These limitations can be clearly seen in the case of the Chota cultivators who cannot quickly modify production patterns to meet changes in the market price of avocados. However, the personalized economic relationships present at all levels of the marketing process in addition to the alternative occupational role of seller establish a certain resiliency whereby the economic shocks of a monetized market system maybe more readily absorbed.

NOTES

1. The writer is grateful to the University of Illinois Department of Anthropology for funds which made the field research for this paper possible and especially to Joseph B. Casagrande of the Department of Anthropology, University of Illinois, for valuable criticism and guidance.

2. The term "mestizo" refers to an ethnic category. It refers to someone who is not recognizable in terms of dress or speech as an Indian, but yet does not belong to the highest socio-economic stratum of "white." Mestizos may be rural cultivators and non-agricultural specialists. The majority live in urban centers and small villages and are to be distinguished sharply from the Indian in cultural outlook and self-identity.

3. On this point, see A. V. Chayanov 1966. The Russian economist postulates that the key to understanding peasant economic behavior lies in the factors which determine the balance between the urgency of family needs and the drudgery of labor.

4. The value of all other resources used in production, such as the trader's labor, land, and materials, is not considered in his "cost" as quantifiable entities. The labor involved in buying and selling in the orchards, in sorting and packing avocados, and in the long trip to the market is not hired, and therefore not allocated by price. There is very little productive equipment which has to be bought and even that which is, is simply not deducted from the total income. Furthermore, the value of land does not affect "cost" considerations. The Chota peasant does not think of his land in terms of a monetary value recently imputed to it by the Agrarian Reform Institute. It is now possible for the Chota small-holder to mortgage his land to a national credit and development bank for a cash loan, although he still cannot sell his plot on an open land market. However, land was not and is not today viewed as a productive factor in the capitalistic sense; that is, whether or not the selling of avocados is "profitable" to the cultivator and trader has no relation to the market value of his own piece of land. This is not the case with peasants, however, who are paying rent on the land from which they derive produce to be marketed. That owned land is not viewed as a factor of production can be seen by the fact that the trader does not include the value of the produce taken from his land to be sold in the market place in his "cost." Thus, "cost" for the trader is reduced to the amount spent on buying avocados from the plots of other peasants.

5. For a discussion of the assumption of maximizing behavior and its relationship to the processes of decision-making see Joy 1967.

Fourteen

DIFFERENTIAL ADAPTATIONS AND MICRO-CULTURAL EVOLUTION IN GUYANA[1]

Leo A. Despres

Reprinted with permission from *The Southwestern Journal of Anthropology* (1969).

This paper presents a case study of social adaptation and micro-cultural evolution in Guyana. Its purpose is theoretical as well as substantive. Guyana belongs to a class of societies that many writers have described as pluralistic (Coleman 1960; Geertz 1963). Societies of this type are of considerable interest to social scientists not only because they are widely represented among the new nations but also because they bring into unusual focus the processes of cultural continuity and change. In addition, while these societies are inherently unstable under conditions of change, they also disclose the characteristics of well-organized social systems. It is the point of view of this paper that the conditions of pluralism are best revealed in terms of their evolutionary development. The ecology of these systems discloses that their characteristic patterning derives from the differential adaptation of culturally dissimilar populations to selective environmental forces. The analysis of the Guyanese data may proceed more meaningfully if it is prefaced with a brief discussion of relevant theoretical considerations.

THEORETICAL CONSIDERATIONS

The interdependent units of plural societies comprise culturally differentiated sections of unequal status and power rather than socially differentiated persons (Despres 1964, 1967). These cultural sections may persist as corporate categories; in which case they are made up of relatively unorganized population aggregates. These population aggregates are categorically distinguished by their different cultural and, in some instances, racial features. When these aggregates disclose autonomous sectional organizations that correspond to sectionally specific institutional structures, they assume the characteristics of corporate groups. Ultimately, the plural society depends for its maintenance on the regulation of intersectional relationships by a dominant section organized as a corporate group.

Considering that in most instances the populations making up the societies of this type have been subjected to what appears to be the same environmental forces for prolonged periods of time, interesting questions of a cultural evolutionary nature may be raised. How is it that these populations did not develop institutional structures expressive of a common culture? What factors have contributed to the persistence of differentiated cultural systems when populations are incorporated within a politically unified territorial framework? What adaptive processes have precluded the modification of cultural differences under these circumstances? In short, how do plural societies evolve and how do they persist?

The problem of cultural continuity and change has been a major focus of anthropological research in the Caribbean since Herskovits' pioneer work on the bush Negroes of Surinam (M. and F. Herskovits 1934) and his subsequent studies in Haiti (1937b) and Trinidad (M. and F. Herskovits 1947b). We need not dwell upon the validity of Herskovits' "Africanism" thesis other than to note that he did not explore the extent to which deeply rooted sub-cultural patterns constituted differential modes of adaptation to selective environmental influences (M. G. Smith 1965: 24–37). Nor did he consider in any systematic way the implications of these sub-cultural patterns for the structure and organization of plural societies.

The idea that sub-cultural patterns may be viewed as adaptations to relatively specific environmental conditions predates modern anthropological research (Helm 1962). With respect to Caribbean studies, Julian Steward and his co-workers (1956) seem to have been the first to give this idea systematic treatment, delineating the regional sub-cultures of Puerto Rico and establishing their interrelationships within the national society.

The ecological framework developed by Steward (1938) has been used with some success in studying peoples with simple technologies and whose dependence on their physical environment is both direct and compelling. However, with respect to the analysis of more complicated ecosystems, Steward's framework is severely limited in its formulation. Thus, the model I shall use in analyzing differential social adaptation and micro-cultural evolution in Guyana derives essentially from the work of Alland (1967) and others (Mayr 1963; Vayda and Rappaport 1968; Wolpoff 1968).

Following Alland (1967: 143–238), behavioral evolution is considered to have the same restrictions as somatic or biological, evolution; i.e., all adaptations are environment specific. Two major types of adaptive behavior have evolved in the animal kingdom: innate responses and learning. In the case of man, culture is a learned behavioral code which evolves in response to selective environmental forces. The environmental forces that primarily affect the evolution of culture are physical and biotic and the latter includes culture.

Selective influences on biological as well as behavioral forms are exerted within ecosystems. While biological and behavioral forms are clearly related from the point of view of human evolution, it is the latter which are the object of the present study. Adaptation refers to the ways in which individuals socially adjust their behavior to environmental influences and changes. In the case of social adaptation, some individuals will succeed more than others and some will not succeed at all. In any event, the the adaptive responses of individuals provide models for learning behavioral codes. These behavioral codes form cultures. Adaptation, thus, may be viewed as a temporal process in terms of which transgenerational changes in behavioral codes are directed by selective environmental forces. The sum effect of these transgenerational changes is cultural evolution.

Applying this particular model to Guyana, I will focus primarily on its African and East Indian populations. First, the different types of environments in which these two populations compete, or have competed, with one another for scarce resources will be described. And an outline will then be presented of the strategies with which Africans and East Indians have socially adapted to the environmental forces affecting their competition for resources. And, finally, the transgenerational changes in behavioral codes resulting in the plural organization of Guyanese society will be delineated.[2]

ENVIRONMENTAL ZONES

Guyana is a small country with a total land area of approximately 83,000 square miles. As of 1960, this territory was inhabited by 600,000 people. According to census classification, they are divided as follows: Amerindians (American Indians), 4.0%; Europeans, 0.9%; Portuguese, 1.4%; Chinese, 0.6%; "Mixed" or "Colored," 11.3%; Africans, 33.5%; and East Indians, 48.2%. The Amerindians are the only indigenous population. All others were brought to Guyana as a result of European colonial expansion. The Africans were imported as slaves. With the termination of slavery, indentured workers were imported—first the Portuguese, then the Chinese, and finally the East Indians from India.

Land, resources, and people are facts of considerable importance in any ecological discussion. With respect to land, Guyana can be divided into three major environmental zones. First, deep in the interior, there is a belt of grassy plateaus known as the Rupununi Savannahs. About 2.5 million acres of these savannahs are used by a few cattle ranchers of European descent. The cultivable lands in the Rupununi are limited to the foothills of the Kanuku Mountains. These lands are occupied by Amerindians who continue to practice shifting agriculture. An unknown number of the Amerindians in the Rupununi also work for ranchers.

East and north of the Rupununi is a broad belt of equatorial rain forest which makes up approximately 77% of Guyana's total land area. This region contains most of the country's timber and mineral resources. It also contains two major bauxite mining complexes, one located at Mackenzie on the Demerara River and the other located on the Berbice River at Kwakwani. Outside of these mining towns, the forest region is sparsely inhabited by Amerindian populations whose settlements are usually located along major rivers. Most of these Amerindians either practice shifting cultivation or they are employed by timber contractors.

The third environmental zone is located along the Atlantic seaboard. It stretches for approximately 270 miles between the Orinoco Delta in the west and the Courantyne River in the east. In the same direction, the depth of this coastal strip varies from about 10 to 40 miles. For the most part, this area is a low-lying, flat, and swampy strip of marine alluvium running parallel to the ocean. It is slightly below the level of spring tides but

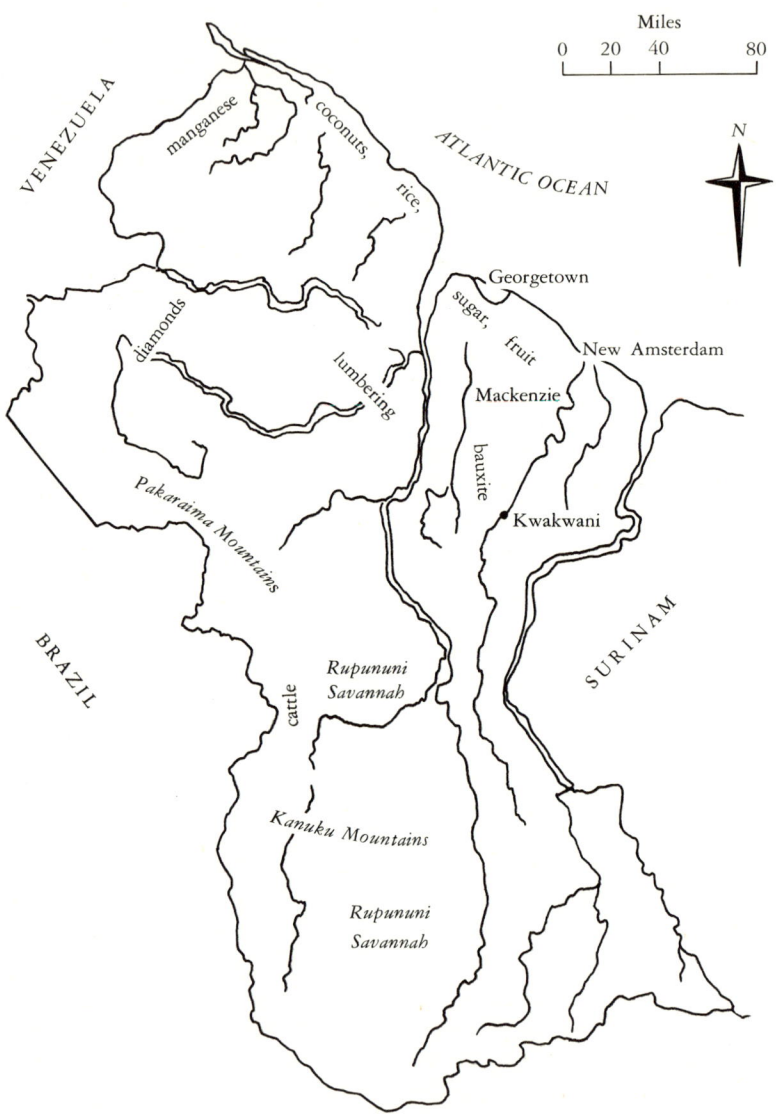

Figure 14-1. Guyana.

inland it rises to a level of about twelve feet. A dual problem stems from this condition: preventing flooding by seawater and disposing of the water that flows from the hinterland and accumulates in the coastal lowlands. The solution to this problem has necessitated an elaborate system of drainage ditches, dams, sea walls, and water sluices or kokers.

The general ecology of Guyana is reflected in its present economy. Guyana's principal income derives from two resources, sugar and bauxite. Currently, there are nineteen sugar estates. Fifteen of these are owned by Booker Brothers, McConnell and Company, a London-based firm. In 1958, sugar and sugar products made up 62% of the f.o.b. value of exports (Sessional Paper No. 5/1959). Forty-five percent of the country's revenue from income taxes and excise duties derives from sugar. An officer of Bookers has estimated that sugar, directly or indirectly, supports nearly 80% of the population (Haynes 1954:18–20).

Next to sugar, bauxite mining is the largest source of national income. Guyana is the third largest producer of bauxite ore in the world. In 1959, more than 1.6 million tons were exported, mainly to Canada and the United States. Two companies extract this ore, Aluminium Ltd. of Canada and Reynolds Metals of the United States. In 1958, they produced 21% of the total f.o.b. value of exports. Of the two companies, Aluminium Ltd. of Canada holds the largest investment in Guyanese bauxite. In addition to bauxite, diamonds and gold also are mined. As a source of national income, however, they have not fulfilled their early promise.

Apart from sugar and bauxite, the only other major source of income is rice, a crop grown primarily by peasants on small family farms. More than half of the rice produced is consumed in Guyana, but increasing amounts are being exported to the Caribbean. While the export value of rice is not yet great, rice agriculture provides the second largest source of employment in the country.

Thus, the coastal zone is of principal interest to the present study. Although it represents only 7% of the total land area, it contains 90% of Guyana's population and practically all of its important agricultural and commercial activities with the exception of bauxite mining. From an ecological point of view, the coastal zone may be divided into three related but relatively different types of environments: plantations, rural villages, and cities.

PLANTATION ENVIRONMENTS

Mintz (1959b) has suggested that a plantation is a capitalistic type of agricultural organization in which a considerable number of laborers are employed under unified direction and control in the production of a staple crop. In the case of Guyana, plantations are also territorial units with resident populations. Thus, in addition to representing a type of agricultural organization, plantations also disclose distinguishable environments within which populations adapt.

The social and physical resources necessary for the operation of a plantation system of production include land, labor, capital, technology, and markets. The relationship of these parameters serve to define the particular dimensions of plantation environments. In addition, with reference to the African and Indian populations, variation in these parameters has significantly influenced their differential adaptation.

It has already been noted that the coastal lands of Guyana comprise a low-lying strip of marine alluvium which is subject to flooding and that the utilization of these lands for plantation agriculture presents a continuous problem of water control. Except for changes in technology, the solution to this problem is essentially that which was worked out by the early Dutch settlers and it has left a permanent imprint on the physical layout of plantations as well as coastal villages. Briefly, on application to the Dutch authorities, each settler was granted a rectangular tract of land with an average inland depth of 750 Rhynland roods from the sea and a facade of 100 roods—an area of approximately 250 acres (Young 1958:2). The first step in putting this land under cultivation involved the construction of dams and drainage canals at the front and back and along each of its lateral sides, and the construction of an irrigation canal along the center line. After these canals were completed, water sluices had to be conconstructed on both ends of the sideline trenches and usually smaller canals had to be dug from sideline to sideline in order to irrigate cultivation beds. When all this was accomplished and the land was put under cultivation, the owner was entitled to claim an additional 250 acres to the rear of the first and the land behind this "seconddepth," usually savannah, could also be used.

Thus, under the Dutch, the typical plantation was a narrow strip of empoldered or reclaimed land (about 3 miles in depth and .23 miles in width) containing approximately 500 acres. Reclaiming this land required the construction of dams, sluices, and more than 10 miles of drainage and irrigation ditches. However, empoldering did not entirely solve the problem of water control. The crux of this problem lies in the fact that earth movement is continually taking place along the entire shoreline, consisting of alternating periods of severe erosion and accretion, and this creates the need for continuously rebuilding sea defenses and clearing drainage and irrigation canals of plant life and soil deposits. Needless to say, all of this requires a very large amount of relatively cheap labor. Under the Dutch, and subsequently the British, labor was provided by the importation of thousands upon thousands of African slaves.[3]

By 1803, when the British finally assumed control of Essequibo, Demerara, and Berbice, a plantation economy based on the institution of chattel slavery was firmly established. In 1828, the population of Guyana included approximately 100,000 slaves, a few thousand Amerindians (perhaps less than 15,000) and 3,529 Europeans. Of the total population, approximately 20,000 slaves and perhaps 2,500 Europeans resided in the port towns of Georgetown and new Amsterdam (only two villages existed on the entire coast). More than 80,000 slaves were allocated to a few hundred Europeans who owned, or managed, 404 plantations of the type described. Of these plantations, 230 cultivated sugar and 174 cultivated cotton and coffee. Private capital maintained the plantations and was derived primarily from the favorable European markets that existed for the products of tropical agriculture, particularly sugar.

The political adjunct to this system involved a form of colonial government that was completely dominated by the plantocracy. By virtue of the Articles of Capitulation under which the British took possession of the Guyanese colonies, Dutch governmental and legal institutions were preserved. Roman-Dutch law, rather than British common law, became the law of the land. This favored the plantocracy in two very important respects. First, it protected the right of absolute ownership of property, making it possible to withdraw huge tracts of land from the public domain. Second, it withheld fiscal powers from the Crown and vested these powers in an elected body that was completely controlled by the planters. In short, until 1928, the plantocracy in Guyana had a constitutional charter by which it could, and did, effectively control the government.

Nevertheless, the parameters that serve to define plantation environments have been highly unstable. Let us begin with labor. Over the opposition of the planters, the British Parliament terminated slavery in 1833.[4] This was followed by a period during which the freed slaves were bound as paid apprentices to their estates, but this system of forced labor too was ended in 1838. Emancipation set into motion a series of changes that altered the entire ecology of the plantations.

The immediate effect of emancipation was disastrous for a great many planters. Because of market conditions and the low productivity of Guyanese soils, coffee and cotton planters were the first to go bankrupt under the impact of wage labor. Of the 174 plantations growing these crops in 1828, only 16 coffee plantations remained in 1849. Subsequently, these also failed.

The value of sugar plantations declined precipitously. Although the price of sugar remained relatively stable in the European market, between 1835 and 1846, its production in Guyana fell off from 68,803 to 26,211 hogsheads. This drop in production was due mainly to the migration of African workers from the estates. By 1849, the African population on the sugar plantations had declined to 19,939 (Young 1958:23). Many plantations were abandoned by their owners. A great many more were sold to absentee speculators or to groups of ex-slaves for less than half their original value (Nath 1950:40–49). Practically the entire old proprietary class of planters (i.e., owners who resided in the colony) was wiped out.

The ultimate effect of these changes with respect to the plantations may be summarized as follows:

Land

Since emancipation, the number of sugar plantations has continued to decline but, by a process of consolidation and the substitution of corporate ownership for proprietary ownership, the overall size of plantations has increased. For example, of the 230 plantations that existed in 1834, only 24 remained in 1948. The typical plantation of 1834 occupied 500 acres of land. In 1954, twenty-one plantations occupied approximately 155,000 acres, an average of 7,380 acres per plantation.

Of equal significance is the fact that between 1841 and 1948, the total number of acres under sugar cane cultivation increased from 24,850 to 67,372. In 1954, the number of acres under cane cultivation represented 26% of the land under cultivation in the entire country. Also during this period, the per acre yield of sugar increased from approximately 1.5 to 3.1 tons and, needless to say, the quantity of sugar exported increased accordingly.

Labor

Prior to 1834, the typical plantation population included a proprietor or his manager, perhaps their families, a small cadre of European overseers and, depending upon the capital available, approximately 200 slaves. After 1838, when many of the freed slaves gave evidence of wanting to quit the plantations to work land of their own, the planters organized a program by which indentured workers could be imported in sufficient numbers to provide a steady supply of cheap labor. Between 1835 and 1918, when the indenture system was terminated, 341,600 workers were imported. Of these, 70% were imported from India; 12% from the West Indies; 9% from Madeira; and most of the rest from Africa, the East Indies, and China. In 1946, the population residing on sugar plantations totaled 71,480. The median population for all plantations was 2,845 (Giglioli n.d.: 5–8). Thus, between 1834 and 1946, the population available for labor on sugar plantations remained relatively constant (80,000 compared to 71,480).

Capital

In theory, the capital available for investment in the plantations is private and closely tied with profit-taking in the sugar market. This seems to have been the practice prior to emancipation but after 1838 it was no longer the case. Following emancipation, as proprietary planters went bankrupt, a new plantocracy came into being. It consisted primarily of managers who represented the corporate interests of large companies. The almost complete economic ascendancy of this group is particularly evident in the period between 1891 and 1911 when the number of plantations declined from 101 to 44. Their political ascendancy was assured by the same constitution which had permitted the old proprietary class of planters to completely dominate the government.

By virtue of their control of public funds, the planters were able to support capital formation by diverting substantial amounts of the colony's general revenue into projects that were directly beneficial to their own interests. Representatives of the sugar oligarchy occupied positions of influence and power on such statutory boards as Drainage, the Central Board of Health, Transport and Harbours, the Civil Service Board, Public Works, Lands and Mines, and the Department of Agriculture. Public works projects involving roads, railways, drainage schemes, sea defenses, and water conservation were designed and developed primarily to benefit the plantations. The Department of Agriculture devoted most of its attention to experimental programs designed to develop new and better varieties of sugar cane.

More specifically, by placing immigration under state control, the entire program of importing indentured workers for the plantations was financed largely with funds drawn from the general revenue. In 1894–95, for example, the newly developing gold industry was required to pay direct taxes on the total value of its production in a ratio of 20 to 1 as compared to the sugar industry. This money went into the colony's general revenue and was used to support the normal functions of government. At the same time, almost all of the taxes paid by the sugar industry before 1918 were diverted from the general revenue and used by the government to subsidize the immigration of indentured workers.

In short, after 1838, the capital available for investment in the plantation production of sugar derived not only from profit-taking in the market but also from public subventions, or grants. This not only promoted the development of corporate ownership but it served to stabilize the plantation environment under the control of a European managerial elite.

Technology

The plantation production of sugar in Guyana has always been a labor-intensive operation. In part, this is a consequence of those physical environmental factors which have necessitated the construction and maintenance of a vast and complicated system of water control. Nevertheless, the plantation environments have been affected by the technological developments that have taken place.

During the century that followed emancipation, most technological developments were related to milling processes, cane improvement, and pest control. Developments in none of these areas seriously altered the need for a large quantity of cheap labor. However, since the 1930's, operations having to do with tillage and with the maintenance of drainage and irrigation systems have been increasingly mechanized. Also, with the introduction of mechanical loaders and with improvements in transportation, it has been possible to centralize milling processes in the larger and more efficient factories (in 1948 only 16 of the remaining 24 plantations had factories). All of these more recent changes in technology have contributed to the growth of a surplus labor force on the estates. Thus, in 1946, about 23% of the adult population residing on plantations had never been employed as sugar workers.

Markets

Over the past hundred years, the prices paid for Guyanese sugar have fluctuated extensively. Apart from minor recoveries, the secular trend in prices has been downward (Nath 1950:229). The price obtained for Guyanese sugar in 1941 was only 28% of the price obtained in 1841. However, these changes in market conditions seem not to have directly affected plantation environments.

There are several reasons for this development. For one thing, except on one or two brief occasions, Guyanese sugar has enjoyed considerable protection in the United Kingdom. This has permitted planters to respond to fluctuating prices by adjusting the acreage under cultivation. Second, as prices have generally declined, the cost of production has also declined. In part, this has been due to the benefits which planters have derived from public funds. It is also due to technological improvements and industrial reorganization. And finally, under the indenture system wages and benefits remained relatively stable at low levels and did not respond to increased productivity. Thus, except under conditions of severe depression, as was the case during the 1930's, planters have been able to absorb falling prices without critically cutting their margin of profit.

VILLAGES AS ENVIRONMENTS

The village and riverine settlements comprise a type of environment which is quite different from the sugar plantation. The greatest contrast is between a capitalistic and a peasant organization of agricultural production. By the use of commercial labor, plantation owners or managers completely alienated subsistence from the production of cash crops. Thus, they have been able to exercise considerable control over internal (e.g., acreage under cultivation) and external (e.g., markets) environmental influences. Peasant agriculturalists, on the other hand, neither utilize much by way of wage labor nor do they separate subsistence from the production of cash crops. Unlike the planters, peasants exercise relatively little control over internal and external environmental factors.

Apart from the organization of agricultural production, the parameters that disclose village environments are much the same as those that serve to define plantation environments: these include land, population, capital, technology, and markets. The difference between villages and plantations with respect to these parameters may be briefly summarized as follows:

Land

Except for recently developed land-settlement schemes, almost all the coastal villages were originally laid out as plantations. Typically, these villages incorporate approximately 500 acres of land. Where "third-depth" Crown lands are available and sufficiently drained to be used, village lands may be extended as much as 250 acres. However, soils and the amount of cultivable land available varies from one village to another. Where sea defenses have not been erected, large sections of villages are too salified to be cultivable. Even where sea defenses do exist, considerable land may be taken up by drainage and irrigation works, roads, and residential occupation. Apart from variations of this type, the physical dimensions of these village-plantations have remained relatively the same as when they were first established.

The same problem of water control exists for the villages as for the sugar plantations. In the case of the villages, however, the problem is much more acute. One reason for this has to do with the extent of village lands: it is too limited to allow for the development of effective systems of water control. Even the maintenance of internal drainage systems has generally overtaxed the resources available in most villages. Moreover, many villages are sufficiently removed from sugar plantations so that they have never been protected by the construction of permanent sea defenses and water conservancies. The frontlands in these villages are continuously inundated by high tides. Beyond the tidelands, soils may be useful but, without water conservancies, there is a risk of crop destruction because of excessive rain or drought.

Population

The growth of Guyana's village population between 1831 and 1954 shows a remarkable shift in percentage distribution. In 1831, there were no coastal villages to speak of and 85% of the total population (100,536) resided on plantations. By 1954, only 20% of the coastal population (420,920) resided on plantations; 32% lived in urban environments; and 48% lived in more than 400 rural villages and land settlements (Marshall 1955:105).

Capital

In recent years, the central government has become an extremely important source of capital for peasants. Still, the major source of capital continues to be wage employment (typically in the sugar industry); private moneylenders (usually shopkeepers and rice mill owners); and the sale of cash crops. Of these, wage employment has perhaps been the most important. The village movement, for example, was made possible by the savings which freed slaves were able to accumulate from the wages they received during the period of apprenticeship that followed their emancipation (Young 1958:12–23). Similarly, the acquisition of village lands by indentured workers involved an expenditure of the savings they accumulated from wages (Nath 1950:61–65).

Thus, capital formation among peasants has been extremely difficult. Although some peasants have been able to expand their capital resources and diversify their investments, usually by combining wage employment with the cultivation of cash crops, the amount of capital available to most has never been sufficient to generate significant economic development in village environments.

Technology

There has been very little by way of technological change in the villages. There has been practically no controlled experimentation with the various kinds of crops that peasants cultivate or with the poultry, pigs, goats, and cattle that some of them keep. There have been no technological developments with respect to pest control. Drainage and irrigation systems, where they exist, have been maintained almost entirely by manual labor. Inefficient, single-stage rice mills still exist in most areas. And, until the post World War II period, very few peasants have been able to acquire tractors, and other types of farm machinery.

Markets

The major crop cultivated by peasants is rice. Other crops include coconuts, coffee, cocoa, fruit (citrus, bananas, mangoes, pineapples, avocado pears, guavas, and papaws), ground provisions (cassava, plantains, eddoes, yams, and sweet potatoes), and garden vegetables. Except for rice and coconuts, none of these crops has ever enjoyed an export market of any significance. For approximately sixty years, rice has been second only to sugar among agricultural exports and copra has been third. Also, rice is the most important domestic food and it enjoys a relatively profitable local market. Thus, between 1903 and 1959, rice cultivation expanded from 17,500 to 179,200 acres. Except for coconuts, which occupied 34,000 acres in 1959, all other crops combined occupy less than 50,000 acres. In terms of marketing, rice was put under government control in 1939. Only since 1945 has the government extended market assistance to peasants growing crops other than rice.

URBAN ENVIRONMENTS

Urban environments in Guyana exist in two port cities, Georgetown and New Amsterdam. Both were established in the late eighteenth century. While Georgetown has grown steadily as the country's principal port and capital city, New Amsterdam has declined in importance both as a port and an urban center. In 1946, New Amsterdam (an area of 1.1 square miles) had a population of 9,576. By way of contrast, Georgetown and its suburbs contained a population of 94,035 in an area of 5.5 square miles. Although the urban population tripled during the nineteenth century, Guyana did not become very urbanized. In fact, between 1841 and 1921, the urban proportion of the total population remained relatively constant at approximately 22%. Since 1921, the urban proportion has increased to almost 28%. However, practically all of this increase may be attributed to the growth of Georgetown and its suburban environs.

As in other parts of the world, urban environments in Guyana are extremely complex. By way of contrast to plantations and villages, they disclose a great number of niches within which individuals and groups may exact livelihoods. Thus, the parameters of the urban environments differ somewhat from those that are functional with respect to plantations and villages. In the case of urban niches, the most relevant parameters are population composition, employment opportunities, education, capital and power structure. While these variables are obviously interrelated it will contribute to clarity to consider them separately.

Population Composition

Of the various racial groups that make up the Guyanese population, the majority of Europeans, Portuguese, Chinese, and the Mixed (most of whom are of African and European descent) are urban. Africans and East Indians are predominantly rural. However, only 61% of the Africans live in rural areas compared to 90% of the East Indians. With respect to urban environments, the racial composition of the population is more important than the rural-urban distribution of racial groups. This is summarized in Table 14-1 for 1946, the last census for which data of this type were available.

As Table 14-1 indicates, East Indians comprise 43.5% of the total population but only 15.7% of the urban population. Africans, on the other hand, are only 38.2% of the total but 54.4% of the urban population. If the Mixed population is added to these figures because of its tendency to identify itself and to be identified as African, then clearly the urban population is predominantly (75%) made up of Africans or persons of African descent.

Employment Opportunities

Employment opportunities are an important parameter of most urban environments. They serve to identify the niches in which individuals and groups may adapt. In addition, the number and variety of opportunities available are principal attractions to rural migrants and migration to the cities is one of the chief factors in urban growth and development.

In Guyana, urban environments are conditioned by the fact that employment opportunities are limited in number. Unemployment is considerably higher in the cities than in the rural areas. In 1956, the labor force numbered 164,000 persons of whom 33% were classified as urban and 67% as rural (McGale 1957). Of the total labor force, 29,600 were unemployed. However, only

TABLE 14-1. *Composition of Urban Population, 1946*

RACIAL GROUP	URBAN	TOTAL	PERCENTAGE OF TOTAL POPULATION	PERCENTAGE OF URBAN POPULATION
Amerindians	205	16,322	4.3	0.2
Portuguese	6,258	8,543	2.3	6.0
Europeans	1,745	2,480	0.7	1.7
Chinese	2,284	3,567	0.9	2.2
Mixed	20,273	37,685	10.0	19.6
African	56,390	143,385	38.2	54.4
East Indian	16,241	163,434	43.5	15.7
Other	206	285	0.1	0.2
Total	103,602	375,701	100	100

16% of the rural labor force was unemployed compared to 22% of the urban labor force. Thus, the urban environments presented more opportunities for unemployment than rural environments.

On the other hand, in 1956, urban environments also provided more jobs of a greater variety than did the rural sector. For example, if employment is considered in reference to type of industry, the agricultural industry alone provided jobs for 61% of the employed labor force in rural areas. By way of contrast, three very different industries were required to provide an equal percentage of jobs for the employed labor force in urban environments: i.e., manufacturing, wholesale and retail trade and public administration and professional services. In terms of occupational groupings, 50% of all managers and executives; 52% of sales workers; 53% of professionals; 67% of domestic workers; and 72% of all clerical workers were employed in urban environments. In sum, although unemployment makes the competition for jobs more intense in the urban sector, it does not detract from the variety of employment opportunities.

Education

Education also is an important parameter in the urban areas. In 1946, only 5% of the urban population over the age of ten were illiterate. The proportion for the rural population was 28%. Although a direct correlation cannot be provided from the data available, it appears that employment opportunities in urban environments favor the better educated. For example, in 1956, clerical workers, transport workers, professionals, managers, and executives comprised 43% of the urban employed labor force and only 15% of the rural employed labor force. All these occupations require considerably more education than the predominantly agricultural occupations in rural areas.

Capital Formation

Capital is an extremely consequential parameter with respect to large business establishments regardless of the environments in which they may be located. However, capital formation is also important with respect to the self-employed. This category makes up 27% of the urban and 34% of the rural employed. In rural areas the self-employed may be small shopkeepers, vendors, or artisans, but the vast majority are farm operators, particularly of the peasant variety (96% of all farm operators have less than ten acres). In urban areas, practically all the self-employed are shopkeepers, artisans, vendors, taxi operators, home laundresses, odd-jobbers, and the like. In both urban and rural areas, the ability of the self-employed to generate capital determines whether or not they can succeed in pursuing their enterprises independently.

It is evident from available data that capital formation is not, on the whole, particularly impressive among the self-employed. Still, the potential for capital formation is considerably greater for the urban than the rural self-employed. Even if we exclude females and thereby omit persons whose earning capacity is extremely low, approximately 55% of all self-employed males reported earnings below the $15/week minimum rate for daily-paid manual workers in government employment in 1956. Nevertheless, 64% of the urban compared to 37% of the rural self-employed males reported earnings in excess of $15/week. More significantly, 35% of the urban compared to only 10% of rural self-employed males reported earnings in excess of $25/week.

This differential is not diminished by the urban cost of living because in 1956 the average weekly expenditures of all urban families was slightly lower than that for families living in plantation districts (Paro 1957).

In sum, self-employment opportunities are greater in rural than in urban areas but, on the other hand, urban opportunities are much more rewarding for those who can take advantage of them. Thus, over the years, an unknown number of penny capitalists have been attracted to the cities. These are individuals who have accumulated capital in rural areas, or who have the ability to generate capital once they have established themselves in urban environments.

Power Structure

The power structure of any society is defined by the differential command that individuals and groups are able to exercise over the actions of others and over the allocation and use of scarce resources. In Guyana, the power structure is urban-based. In fact, it is not too much of an exaggeration to say that the urban power structure is the national power structure. Until 1966, this power structure was of the colonial type. As a British colony, both political and economic control were vested almost entirely in the European community. Thus, colonial policies and practices comprised a complex of environmental factors to which individuals and groups in all environments had to adjust.

The overall character of Guyana's power structure has been described elsewhere (Despres 1967). Here, it suffices to point out that this power structure has special implications for urban environments. Briefly, because the colonial establishment (including those groups that implement the decisions of the establishment) is urban-based, it follows that the more urbanized populations are less removed from the sources of power than the rural populations. Thus, the Portuguese, Chinese, Mixed, and Africans tend to occupy a higher position in the power structure of the society than the East Indians. This is most immediately evident with reference to the positions of authority that members of these groups tend to occupy within business, industry, and public administration. In numerous ways, and to varying degrees, this stratification structure has to be contended with and the manner in which one deals with it may ultimately determine the niche that one occupies in urban environments.

Having described the physical and social environmental forces that are operative with respect to the principal coastal environments, we may now turn our attention to the adaptive strategies that Africans and East Indians have developed with respect to both coastal and plantation environments.

ADAPTIVE STRATEGIES: PLANTATION ENVIRONMENTS

Since 1838, East Indians have almost completely displaced Africans from plantation environments. In 1838, except for Europeans and a few indentured Madeirans (Portuguese) and West Indians, the entire plantation population was comprised of Africans. By 1911, the proportions of Africans and East Indians in the plantation population were, respectively, 10 and 86%. Since 1911, the African proportion has stabilized at about 15 % and the East Indian proportion at approximately 82%. The history of this demographic change discloses the differential strategies by which each of these groups has stabilized its relationship to these particular environments.

First, the 44,456 Africans who gravitated away from the plantations in the 1840's did not do so simply because they wanted to flee from the source of their former bondage. On the contrary, the first migratory wave from the estates was created by a general strike in 1842. The strike developed when, among other things, the planters attempted to reduce wages of African workers to the pre-emancipation level in order to help defray the costs of importing more than 50,000 indentured workers. Strikers, it seems, were summarily ejected from estate lands. A more severe strike developed in 1847, when the planters again attempted to reduce wages (Young 1958:15–21). By 1850, only 19,939 Africans remained on the plantations.

It is evident that the majority of Africans could not, or would not compete with East Indian sugar workers. However, this was not the case for a sizeable minority. In 1946, more than 10,000 continued to live on the estates. In addition to them, there were many more who did not live on the estates but who continued to work on them. In other words, some Africans have developed strategies adaptive to plantation environments. Specifically, there are several major niches in plantation environments that Africans have been able to occupy in relative isolation from the economically depressing effect of cheap East Indian labor. These niches include highly skilled or heavy-duty jobs such as pan-boiling, portering, and cane cutting; certain security jobs such as watchmen; and domestic jobs in the homes of European senior-staff.

There are specific reasons why these positions have favored the employment of Africans. Pan-boiling, for example, is a highly skilled and well-paid factory operation. Since Indian indentures were viewed as temporary workers, the planters did not want to assume the costs of training them for a task that was as critical to the production of sugar as pan-boiling. Thus, pan-boiling came to be an African occupation from which East Indians were excluded by virtue of the fact that Africans generally would teach the required skills only to other Africans.

Cane cutting is a seasonal task for which piecework rates are paid in order to expedite the removal of canes from the fields before their sucrose content deteriorates. Because of the relatively high rates paid to canecutters, the task has attracted Africans who are not otherwise interested in estate employment. At the same time, the planters have always believed that Africans make more efficient cane-cutters than East Indians because of their physique and stamina. While most cane cutters are East Indians, planters whenever possible will recruit gangs of Africans from the coastal villages. In 1946, for example, approximately 40% of all piecework in the cane fields was performed by migrant workers and most of these were Africans. For similar reasons, Africans have also been preferred as porters.

The planters have preferred to employ Africans in security positions for reasons other than their physique and stamina. Since the introduction of the indenture system, most of the difficulties on the estates have involved East Indian opposition to the estate managers. Because there has been little love lost between Africans and East Indians, the plantation managers have felt somewhat more secure by investing Africans with the responsibility for protecting estate property. Typically, it has been Africans who have put down most East Indian strikes on the estates.

In the case of domestics, Europeans prefer Africans, who, compared with Indians, have been significantly acculturated to European food habits, customs, and traditions. Moreover, Africans in Guyana have been domestics for Europeans since the days of slavery. East Indian women are rarely domestics.

The question remains, Why have Indians rather than Africans adapted to the other available niches? The response to this question must underscore two sets of factors. First, the indenture system itself provided East Indians with a competitive advantage. And second, the social and cultural resources that Indians drew upon enabled them to develop strategies that were much more suitable to the conditions which plantation environments imposed.

To suggest that the indenture system gave East Indians a competitive advantage is not to deny that their life was harsh; rather, it is to recognize that under the immigration and labor laws indentured workers were provided with more security than non-indentured workers. For example, their jobs were secured by contract. They could be fined for not doing their work satisfactorily but because of their immigrant status they could not be easily discharged. Indentured workers could accumulate leave at the rate of one day for every two consecutive weeks of work and in the amount of 26 days in any one year. In their free time they could sell their labor to others or they could work for their own profit whatever land the planters allowed them to use. And finally, by law, the planters were required to provide indentured workers with minimum housing, clothing, food, and medical care. All these entitlements did not compensate for the low wages that were paid but they were generally unavailable to non-indentured workers.

Some of the social and cultural resources that Indians introduced to the plantation environments were as important as these incremental benefits. Particularly important were those customs that pertained to family and kinship organization. Most of the traditional Indian kinship system has been retained. Inheritance is patrilineal and tends to follow the principle of ultimogeniture, to the youngest son. Marriages are arranged with traditional ceremony (R. T. Smith and Jayawardena 1958; 1959). In the marriage of daughters, the rule of village exogamy is normally followed. When sons marry, residence tends to be patrilocal from a few months to a few years, the time depending upon the number of sons, their ages, and how rapidly they marry.

Patrilocal residence provides a basis for the extended family to function as a corporate economic group among Indians. The father and sons work together. When the oldest son marries, he lives with his father who, as the head of the household, continues to manage the family income. After the father dies, brothers frequently continue to work cooperatively. Subsequently, when their own sons marry, the family estate is divided and the youngest brother's share is usually the father's original estate, including land and house.

Drawing upon these elements of kinship organization, Indians were able to secure economic resources by a strategy of family employment. While the adult males of a household worked in a variety of occupations (e.g., cane-cutting, cultivation, drainage and irrigation gangs, and so on), the females worked in occupations that involved lighter tasks (e.g., weeding gangs, planting gangs). Young boys also supplemented the family income by working in boys' gangs. These were assigned such tasks as caring for animals, cleaning stables, carrying water, or weeding cane fields. The contribution that young boys made to family incomes on the one hand, and to estate work on the other, was important enough that parents as well as planters persuaded the colonial government to exempt East Indian children from Guyana's Compulsory Education Ordinance (passed in 1876).

Another way in which the Indian family structure facilitated their adaptation has to do with the cultivation of rice. As a reward for loyal service, many families were loaned small parcels of land to cultivate rice. Families with sufficient resources rented land for this purpose. This did not seriously interfere with estate employment because the crop seasons for sugar and rice do not entirely overlap. Moreover, when some members of a family are needed to harvest cane, others are available to harvest rice. Thus, rice lands were worked cooperatively by members of the family in order to supplement wages. Even as wages improved in the sugar industry, the cultivation of rice continued to be a major pre-occupation for those Indian sugar workers who desired to accumulate capital and thereby eventually terminate their wage employment. In 1961, at Plantation Skeldon, more than 20% of the Indian sugar workers cultivated an average of five acres of rice as a family enterprise.

ADAPTIVE STRATEGIES: VILLAGE ENVIRONMENTS

The history of Guyana's village movement is one of migration from the plantations, first of Africans and then of East Indians. It is also a history of the competition between these two groups for village lands. Africans have not been particularly successful in this competition. In 1881, for example, they comprised 65% of the village population while East Indians and Chinese, together, made up only 13%. By 1955, East Indians alone comprised 54% of the village population and the African proportion had declined to 37%. Today, in some districts, very few villages remain in which Africans form even a noticeable minority. Nevertheless, more than 90,000 Africans continue to reside in villages. The niches they occupy, contrasted to those occupied by East Indians, disclose their differential adaptation to these particular environments.

The African peasantry that emerged in the 1840's and 1850's lacked the resources necessary to develop a viable cash crop economy. For one thing, most of the plantations that they purchased had been abandoned estates in very poor repair. The buildings were deteriorated; the roads had been neglected; drainage systems were clogged with vegetation; dams had to be built anew; and much of the farmland had returned to bush. These necessary improvements required capital, but having used their capital to purchase land, most Africans had nothing left for development or operating costs. Moreover, ex-slaves could not secure capital other than in the form of wages.

Added to these difficulties were the problems of land fragmentation. To appreciate the complexities of these problems, one must first consider the two types of villages that Africans established. Young (1958:10–13) has called these "proprietary" and "communal" villages. The former were settled by individuals who had sufficient capital to purchase land separately. Thus, in proprietary villages, each proprietor held a title describing the land he purchased. However when individuals did not have sufficient capital to buy land in this way, they pooled their resources and purchased land collectively. By way of a single deed, land titles in communal villages were vested in the names of representatives of a group of purchasers, and individual members of the group were listed on the deed as owning a specified number of shares (or fractions thereof) of undivided land.

Communal villages became the dominant form of African rural settlement and they provided the basis for land fragmentation problems that have never been solved. The first type of fragmentation engendered by collective purchases was physical. When shares were divided, care was taken to provide each shareholder with a proportionate amount of good and poor soils. To achieve this equity, agricultural lands were divided either into widely separated plots or parallel strips varying from 10 to 80 feet in width and four to five miles in depth, depending upon the number of shares owned. Both procedures made cultivation extremely inefficient.

Land fragmentation was further augmented by what Africans call "children's property." Under the Roman-Dutch law, in the event of intestacy, the widow and children of a proprietor inherited specific but undivided shares of his or her land. This is called children's property because it belongs to successive generations of a proprietor's descendants as a group. Rights to such property cannot be alienated unless all the living descendants agree to alienate them. In the meantime, any person who can validate a claim to children's property must be given access to some portion of it and he may use whatever is his share as he sees fit.

In addition to children's property, the division of proprietary and occupation rights progressed quite rapidly because of the African pattern of kinship. Under slavery the traditional patterns of African kinship were destroyed. Whatever these patterns might have been, they were replaced with a bilateral structure that is extended by regular marriages as well as the practice of serial polygyny (R. T. Smith 1956). The equal division of property among offspring transformed this bilateral structure into one that is multilineal. In other words, in each generation, ego's legitimate children inherited along with his illegitimate offspring, and his sons inherited as well as his daughters. Therefore, it was not very long before the land available in most African villages became children's property. Proprietary and occupation rights were so fragmented that it was impossible to know precisely who owned what or who was responsible for what was owned.

In view of these circumstances, the problem of land management became a serious obstacle to the development of a cash crop economy among Africans. For example, if one shareholder allowed his dams and ditches to deteriorate, it affected the production of all his neighbors. Needless to say, the solution to this problem required tremendous cooperative effort not only on the part of kinsmen but also on a community-wide scale. However, African peasants had no traditions of social organization to meet this need. The kindreds associated with the inheritance of children's property did not constitute corporate economic units and, at the same time, there was no tradition of village organization capable of allocating rights and responsibilities with respect to property on a community-wide basis.

Subsequently, as the villages deteriorated and became a serious health problem to the entire country, various forms of local governments were imposed by the central government. Many of the communal villages were partitioned for tax purposes. However, this too failed to solve the problems of land management. Most of the taxes collected were used to maintain public roads and sea defenses that were primarily important to the plantations, and there was seldom enough tax surplus to put village lands in repair. Moreover, as village lands became less productive, villagers had to seek outside employment in order to raise money for the payment of taxes. And finally, partitioning provided only a temporary clarification of land relationships by the distribution of new titles. As soon as these proprietors died, the titles once again devolved upon the children, and land relationships were as confused as before.

From the point of view of social adaptation, the effects of these difficulties on the African village population may be summarized as follows:

First, although precise data are not available, it is evident that between 1881 and 1955 a considerable amount of land that was once owned by Africans had been either abandoned or sold to East Indians. Also during this period, there has been a continuous migration of village Africans in search of non-agricultural employment.

Second, agriculture among Africans tends to be primarily for purposes of subsistence (Despres 1967:86–94). Ground provisions, unproductive both in terms of market and food values, are grown mainly for home consumption. The produce from coconut and fruit trees are also picked for home consumption. Small amounts of surplus are sometimes marketed.

Finally, since income from agricultural production is insufficient to buy necessities or to pay taxes on children's property, most African peasants are directly or indirectly independent upon some type of wage employment. Relatives (typically husbands and sons) who are employed in urban occupations, bauxite mining, the diamond and gold fields, or in cane-cutting, are the major sources of income. As a consequence, African village populations tend to be comprised of women, children, men over fifty years of age, and temporarily unemployed males in their productive years. All these draw upon the subsistence value of children's property in times of need. Because of the availability of children's property, Africans continue to represent a sizeable proportion of the population in village environments.

By way of contrast to Africans, East Indian peasants contrast with Africans in their development of a viable cash crop economy based on the cultivation of rice. In 1955, when they comprised 54% of the village population, Indian peasants made up 71% of all farm operators. There are several reasons why Indians have been more successful than Africans in adapting themselves to cash crop agriculture in village environments.

First, the migration of Indians from the plantations developed under circumstances that were very different from those affecting the movement of Africans (Nath 1950:84–110). Under the indenture system, the repatriation of workers to India not only entailed a loss of plantation labor but it also constituted an unproductive drain on the government's general revenue. As early as 1863, it was suggested that the government encourage Indian immigrants to surrender their return passage rights in partial exchange for grants of land. Subsequently, Crown lands were made available for this purpose. To further assist Indian settlement, between 1871 and 1950, the government purchased privately owned plantations and converted them into land settlement schemes.

Second, these land settlement schemes were provided with government aid and supervision. Unlike the plantations purchased by Africans, they had been kept in fairly good repair. Land in the schemes was divided into uniform lots and these, in turn, were not allowed to be sub-divided into less than half-acre plots. Tenure was secured by individual title and Indians were instructed by various governmental agencies about the importance of preventing these titles from lapsing into children's property.

Third, property titles in Indian villages serve to differentiate between productive land, on the one hand, and real estate or housing on the other. By way of contrast to African villages, only land used for cultivation purposes is taxed. This strategy has had several advantages. It has provided a more rational basis for the allocation of responsibilities with respect to the maintenance of water control systems. It has facilitated the development of more efficient local government. It has enabled East Indian proprietors to aggregate productive land for sons who may construct dwelling units in the village without assuming the burden of taxation until they have acquired productive land. And finally, it has made it easier for landless sugar workers to settle in village environments by renting or working the land of others.

Fourth, the kinship patterns described for Indians in the preceding section also facilitated their adaptation to village environments. As corporate economic units, patrilocally extended households provided a relatively efficient basis for capital formation under the circumstances of peasant agriculture. In recent years, this method of operation has not only enabled Indian families to expand their holdings by renting or buying land from less efficient users, but it has also made it possible for them to acquire tractors and other types of modern farm machinery.

Finally, the cultivation of rice also provided Indians with an adaptive advantage. Compared to ground provisions, rice is an extremely productive crop both in terms of market and food values. Rice has always enjoyed a good local market. The First World War provided an export market in which relatively attractive profits were made. Although a depression set in following the war, it disappeared with the outbreak of the Second World War. In order to stabilize the rice economy in keeping with the war effort, the central government established a single buying and selling agency for both local and export markets. Since 1939, the rice economy has remained protected, and, as a result, Indian peasants have been provided a degree of economic security which was never available to Africans who cultivated ground provisions.

ADAPTIVE STRATEGIES: URBAN ENVIRONMENTS

Pushed out of their jobs on plantations by low wages and indentured labor, unable to develop anything but a subsistence economy in the villages, Africans increasingly turned to urban sources of employment. Census figures, summarized in Table 14-2, provide evidence for the rapidity and magnitude of this change. Between 1891 and 1946, the proportion of the African population living in urban environments increased from 20.5 to 39.3%. At the same time, the African proportion of the urban population increased from 35.9 to 54.5%.

When these figures are compared to those for East Indians, it would appear that the East Indians are becoming urbanized just as rapidly as Africans. However, this is not the case. Between 1891 and 1946, the ratio of urban increase to increase in total population among Africans was 4.8 compared to 3.6 for East Indians. To state the matter differently, with respect to most urban niches, Africans have had a competitive advantage over East Indians. There are many reasons for this but it will suffice to consider four: education, skills, kinship, and power structure.

Africans, more than any other group, have taken advantage of developments in education. Perhaps one reason for this has been their desire to live as Europeans live. Another consideration involves the controlling leadership which African teachers have exercised in the field of education. In the village, the headmaster occupied a position of pervasive influence and trust and the young as well as the old sought his advice on matters of importance. Also, education in Guyana has been primarily under the control

many employment opportunities in urban environments. Since 1891, Africans have almost completely dominated the teaching profession. As early as 1900, they comprised an overwhelming majority of the unpensionable staff in practically every department of the public service. In 1940, Africans represented 67% of all pensionable public servants. By 1960, they ranked second only to Europeans among departmental heads in the public service. By way of contrast, in 1931, only 12% of all Guyanese professionals and public servants (6,202) were East Indians. Also in 1931, only 7.2% of all Guyanese in the teaching profession (1,397)

TABLE 14-2. *Africans and East Indians in Urban Population, 1891–1946*

PERIOD	PERCENTAGE OF AFRICANS IN URBAN AREAS	PERCENTAGE OF INDIANS IN URBAN AREAS	AFRICAN PROPORTION OF URBAN POPULATION	INDIAN PROPORTION OF URBAN POPULATION
1891	20.5	5.0	35.9	8.4
1911	28.2	5.8	42.2	11.0
1921	29.4	6.2	50.6	11.3
1931	33.5	7.1	53.6	12.0
1946	39.3	9.9	54.4	15.7

of Christian denominational bodies and these have been a well-organized influence in the lives of most Africans. Finally, until 1933 Indian children, unlike African children, were exempted from the Compulsory Education Ordinance of 1876. Whatever the reason, formal education has touched the lives of most Africans to a considerable degree. Thus, in 1946, only 2.7% of the African population over ten years of age was illiterate compared to 44% among East Indians of the same age group.

Although precise data are not available, there can be little doubt that education has opened the door for Africans to a great

were East Indians. As late as 1960, East Indians comprised but 16% of all pensionable civil servants and only 6 Indians, compared to 26 Africans, could be counted among 57 departmental heads. In sum, education has given Africans a considerable advantage with respect to the higher status occupations.

Second, the early development of certain marketable skills has also provided Africans with a competitive edge in urban environments. Even during slavery there existed a relatively large pool of skilled African workers in Georgetown and New Amsterdam, including construction workers, carpenters, woodcutters, porters, dockworkers, shipbuilders, and the like. Then between 1871 and 1914, several new industries emerged which immediately attracted large numbers of village Africans. These industries included gold and diamonds, balata, lumber, and bauxite. By 1891, approximately 30,000 Africans were employed as diamond- and gold-seekers, balata-bleeders, and woodcutters. When the bauxite industry was organized, in 1914, its labor force was almost completely African and it has remained so ever since. Although these industries operated in the interior, the workers they employed were drawn primarily from the villages and, subsequently, many of them settled their families in Georgetown where they could visit them more often and more easily.

In any event, Africans have dominated the skilled trades in Georgetown and New Amsterdam. By 1960, they formed a substantial majority in amost every urban-based labor union. For the most part, this included unions catering to the interests of dockworkers, transport workers, postal and communications workers, postmasters, teachers, construction workers, civil servants, mine workers, printers, medical workers, seamen, and general (unskilled and semiskilled) workers. These, then, are the niches that rural Africans tend to fill when they move into urban environments.

Kinship is a third factor which has undoubtedly contributed to the adaptation of Africans in urban environments. Compared to Indians, Africans have a loosely structured bilateral kinship system. This system does not provide for well-integrated corporate groups and that has been to their disadvantage in village environments. However, it is supportive of widely extended personal kindreds. For example, in a 1961 survey of two African villages, 74% of all married sons and 36% of married daughters lived outside of the village district. (The comparable figures for two Indian villages were 11 and 69%.) The affective ties which individuals may develop within this extended network facilitates their movement to and from urban environments. When jobs are available in cities, village Africans frequently move in with urban relatives. When employment cannot be found, or when jobs are lost, the same individuals may easily return to the villages where they can live with other relatives who occupy children's property. Because of the nature of their kinship system, East Indians are considerably less responsive to urban opportunities.

A final factor which has been worked to the advantage of Africans in urban environments is the power structure. Under colonial rule, and because of their education and skills, large numbers of Africans were recruited to fill positions in the public service bureaucracy, in business houses, in the communications media, and in industry. These positions, for the most part, have not been sources of ultimate power with respect to policy. However, they have provided Africans with considerable influence and control with respect to the implementation of policy. Inevitably, this influence and control has been utilized to promote the interests of friends, relatives, and other Africans. Thus, it has not been easy for many Indians to secure various kinds of urban employment even when qualified.

Until 1953, when they began to assert themselves politically, East Indians did not migrate to urban areas in large numbers. As Table 2 reveals, the East Indian proportion of the urban population increased only 4.7% between 1911 and 1946. In 1946, the total East Indian urban population was 16,241. Thirty-six percent of this total was under 15 years of age. In addition, almost half of it was female. When it is considered that self-employment for East Indian females is lower than for any other group, a substantial number of the East Indian urban population may be effectively discounted from the urban labor force.

Unlike Africans, East Indians who migrate to cities tend to be small shopkeepers, vendors, unskilled workers, and farm operators. The latter, numbering over 500, cultivate vegetable gardens on small plots of land which are available for rent or purchase in various parts of urban environments. Unskilled East Indian workers are most noticeably employed by the Rice Marketing Board, the Public Works Department, and by several Indian-owned business establishments. Many unskilled workers are also employed as groundskeepers by Europeans and Portuguese. Vending and shopkeeping are generally family-operated enterprises established on the basis of capital that has been accumulated in rural areas. Many Indian shopkeepers in Georgetown and New Amsterdam maintain corporate ties with relatives who continue to operate shops, rice farms, and, in some cases, rice mills in village environments. In fact, the capitalization of urban businesses on the basis of rural enterprises has been a major avenue of vertical mobility for a great many East Indian peasants and this particular pattern of mobility is rarely in evidence among African peasants.

DIFFERENTIAL ADAPTATIONS: THE PLURAL SOCIETY

The stable ecological adaptations of Africans and East Indians, cross-cutting different environments, have ordered different sub-cultural systems. Some of the differences between these systems are historical, e.g., the Indian pattern of kinship. On the other hand, other differences derive from the dissimilar conditions that Africans and East Indians, respectively, experienced as slaves and as indentured workers: e.g., the destruction of African patterns of kinship. The constraints that these conditions imposed were such that had Indians been imported as slaves, and Africans as indentured workers, the former might very well have traversed a course of micro-cultural evolution similar to that which has been described for the latter. The differential adaptations that these sub-cultural systems disclose form the plural society.

In view of the data presented, it clearly emerges that, contrary to widely held opinion, the *selective advantage of the plural society is the reduction of competition between culturally distinctive groups*. If plantations, villages and cities are considered separately, there is abundant evidence of competition between Africans and East Indians. However, when these environments are viewed as functional parameters of an overall ecosystem, it is equally evident that the process of differential adaptation, both within and across environments, has resulted in the reduction of subsequent competition. Within each environment Africans and East Indians fill different niches and, thus, they tend not to compete with one another on a day-to-day basis for the same resources. Of equal significance is the fact that the same process which serves to reduce competition also serves to maintain cultural differentiation. In short, the cultural characteristics that serve to separate various subgroups in Guyanese society are primarily adaptive.

These findings suggest considerations of a more general nature. Although obvious, the point needs emphasis: societies are very complex ecosystems. The plural society is a particular type of ecosystem. Specifically, it is an ecosystem formed by the encapsulation of culturally distinct groups within a territory that is relatively closed by political boundaries. Assuming that such a territory has limited physical resources, one would expect competition for these resources to exist.

Given these circumstances, Gause's competitive exclusion principle is relevant.[5] Whenever two species—culturally differentiated populations—are in competition for the same resources, one of three alternative resolutions is possible: (a) one population may migrate (leave the country); (b) one or both populations may become culturally extinct; or (c) one or both populations may re-adapt their cultural system. All three of these possibilities are in evidence in different parts of the world today. However, which of these resolutions will develop and under what circumstances cannot be predicted until much more is known about societies as ecosystems and about the processes of microcultural evolution.

In the case of Guyana, the effect of ecological competition is quite obvious: Africans and East Indians have re-adapted their cultural systems. The reasons why re-adaptation has been possible are also obvious. The overall ecosystem has provided three relatively distinct environments and each contains a range of niches. Africans have been comparatively successful in one of these environments. This has allowed them to adapt within the other two environments by occupying more specialized and less competitive niches.

A final point with respect to plural societies: *any change which reduces the number of distinguishable environments will inevitably re-establish or increase competition throughout the entire ecosystem*. However, it appears that the only type of change capable of reducing the number of environments to the point where a plural adaptation is no longer possible is the development of a modern industrial economy. Under these circumstances, it seems, cultural sections must inevitably become extinct.

NOTES

1. I wish to acknowledge the insightful comments of my colleagues, Milford H. Wolpoff and Melvyn C. Goldstein, in preparing this paper.
2. The data used in this paper were collected in 1960–61 for an entirely different type of study. Thus, for the purpose of ecological analysis, they are not well balanced in quantity or uniform in authority. The application of Alland's model to these data can be followed only in general outline.
3. The importance of Dutch influence in British Guiana is described in Despres (1967: 30–67).
4. The act to abolish slavery was passed by Parliament in August, 1833, and it became effective on August 1, 1834.
5. For a discussion of Gause's exclusion principle, see Ernst Mayr (1963: 66–72).

Fifteen

A RESPONSE TO MARGINALITY: THE CASE OF BLACK MIGRANT FARM WORKERS[1]

Dorothy Nelkin

Reprinted with permission from *British Journal of Sociology* (December 1969), London: Routledge & Kegan Paul Ltd.

This paper will explore aspects of the social organization of migrant farm labor crews and argue that these crews constitute a distinctive type of sociocultural organization. Many of the characteristics of migrant labor crews have developed, however, not as a reflection of internal cultural values, but as an adaptive response to their marginal position in American society. The marginality of the migrant worker is not adequately reflected in the classic definition of the marginal man "who through migration, education, marriage, or some other influence leaves one social group or culture without making a satisfactory adjustment to another and finds himself on the margins of each but a member of neither" (Stonequist 1937:2–3). This definition stresses the personal ambivalence of the individual poised between two distinct cultures who experiences problems to the extent that these cultures conflict. Some of the qualifications and redefinitions stimulated by Stonequist seem somewhat more relevant.[2] In particular, Antonovski (1956:57) included in his definition of a marginal situation, examples "where some of the members of one group for one reason or another come under the influence of another group ... and where cultural and/or racial barriers serve to block full and legitimate membership within another group."

In the situation considered in this paper, the relevant issue is not "culture conflict" experienced by mobile individuals, but rather group isolation and the relatively impermeable barriers established by the dominant society. The migrant community is marginal in that it is situated on the fringes of a larger society. Economically and legally, migrants must cope with the realities of this society and they are expected to share its values. They are not accepted as belonging to a distinct and viable sub-culture, nor are they fully accepted as a part of the larger society. In this sense, marginality is a situational context in which the migrant community must minimize internal disruptions while, at the same time, maximizing adaptive advantage to the larger society, on which it depends.

The demands which these needs impose on the community are not necessarily consonant. To maintain internal stability there is a striking tendency to minimize the existing differences between participants, to encourage homogeneity, and to restrict the development of prestige distinctions. This tendency is, in fact, fostered by the larger society which has established isolated and undifferentiated conditions for a group which it regards as homogeneous. Yet, the values and demands of the larger society tend to emphasize competition and encourage status differentiation. These contrasting tendencies coexist with significant implications for social interaction in most labor crews.

I would like to stress at this point the considerable variation that exists between one crew and another. The style of social behavior within a crew depends on many variables such as its composition, the technology of the work, the character of the crew leader, the size of the camp. I am contending here that marginal status is shared by all migrant crews. The social patterns which make life viable under the routine circumstances in which migrants live from day to day contrast with the expectations of the larger society. The resulting contradictions tend to generate a certain style of adjustment manifest to a greater or lesser degree in different crews.

I will first describe relevant aspects of the migrant labor system as it operates in the eastern United States. The marginal situation of migrant workers will be described followed by a discussion of the leveling tendency as a basic normative pattern. The final section will deal with conflicting tendencies and mechanisms which migrants use to resolve the dissonance characteristic of existence as a marginal group.

THE MIGRANT LABOR SYSTEM

The migrant crews of concern in this paper are groups of southern Negroes who leave their home base in the South in the spring and settle in a northern agricultural community for three to five months during the harvest season. Upon arriving, a migrant is likely to live in a camp housing from thirty to eighty people.[3] Some migrants make their own arrangements with a grower and travel with family or friends in a private car. They will then settle in a camp with a number of other people, and this group will live together for the summer as a work crew. In the eastern United States, however, most migrants are brought north in a bus by a crew leader who has contracted with a grower to hire a specific number of people for the harvest. A crew leader recruits his people according to his personal predilection, and the composition of the crew depends entirely on his style of recruitment. The social configuration of migrant labor crews, therefore, varies considerably. At one extreme are crews composed largely of kin. In one case, for example, the crew included the six children of the crew leader and their spouses and children. There were also several unrelated persons in this crew, all of whom left after several weeks. In another crew, 36 of the 58 people belonged to three separate sibling groups related through marriage. At the other extreme are crews of single males picked up from many different places enroute from the South. Most crews are a mixture of families and single men and women, some who have known each other previously, some who are total strangers.[4]

People enter the migrant labor stream for a number of reasons. Some fit a common stereotype, being winos unable to hold any other job. Some of the younger men are in the stream because of personal problems compelling them to leave home temporarily. There are a number of people who have legal problems and feel they can effectively disappear in the migrant labor stream. Some are old or sick and are unable to find other work. Some of the younger people left unsatisfactory jobs in the South, lured by extravagant promises of lucrative possibilities. Most people claim to prefer a job where there is little structure and responsibility and few demands to be on time or to follow a rigid set of expectations.

The variety in crew structure can be briefly illustrated by two contrasting cases (Friedland and Nelkin 1967) (see Table 15-1).

Two points must be emphasized. First, except for a few highly skilled pickers, the migrant labor stream seems to represent a respite from the demands of society, sometimes by choice, but usually through lack of alternatives. A camp is, in this sense, a sanctuary. Second, a crew consists of people who are often strangers, but who must live together in the closest proximity for a temporary period. Migrants in a given camp interact closely in a wide range of work and non-work activity, sharing common conditions in the camp and in the fields.

SOCIAL CONDITIONS

The physical setting shared by the crew is often squalid. Most camps consist of barracks or shacks with tiny, identical rooms.

TABLE 15-1. *Two Contrasting Crews*

CREW	SIZE*	AGE STRUCTURE	% SINGLES**	NUMBERS OF TRIPS NORTH	PERCENTAGE FROM SAME HOME STATE (FLA.)
x	100	50% under 25 yrs. 25% over 40 yrs.	93%	47% first trippers 10% 10 trips or more	28%
y	61	30% under 25 yrs. 28% over 40 yrs.	32%	4.9% first trippers 41% 10 trips or more	86.9%

* Over age 14.   ** No attachments in camp.

Occasionally a larger room serves as a "bull pen" or dormitory. There is a center, called a "juke," where people cook, eat, gamble, and drink together. The migrant has few alternatives in his social activities. He is essentially forced into a pattern of twenty-four hour interaction within a limited physical setting with the same people. Boredom is a common complaint.

> We were sitting around the yard doing nothing and trying to find something to do. Someone suggested we go to the drive in, but we didn't have any way to get there ... so there we were, sitting around the place with nothing to do, and it was very lone-

some. Nobody was talking to anyone, nobody had anything to do because everyone wanted to go somewhere and couldn't go. After a few games of checkers in the juke we decided that we wouldn't be going anywhere that night and there was nothing better to do than to go to sleep.

WORK CONDITIONS

The people in the camp also work together under common conditions. The formal structure of the work in most situations requires few distinct occupational roles and there are limited possibilities for mobility.[5] Migrants, as a rule, work on farms where there is a minimal technology, and in any case members of the group are seldom trained to operate complicated equipment. There is, however, some degree of occupational differentiation. There are people who drive the trucks, check the quality and condition of the produce, and weigh and grade the produce when it arrives on the truck. There are field walkers who supervise the picking to ensure that the fields are picked clean. While these are distinct social roles, they may be handled conjointly by one or more persons and they are often temporary. It is not unusual to find a person who is a grader on one day picking with the rest of the crew on the next. This absence of permanent occupational roles eliminates the possibility of upward mobility within the system.

The method of wage payment, however, does allow for economic differences within the crew. For most tasks, the migrant is paid on a piece-work basis. And except for certain crops which are partly mechanized, such as celery, the work is highly individualized. The productivity of one person is totally independent of the productivity of others. Thus, there exists the possibility of considerable variation in income according to skill, physical strength, or stamina. Actually, variation is minimized since a crew works the same field under similar conditions. If the weather is bad or the crop is thin, the productivity of all workers is affected equally. Furthermore, and this must be stressed, the group as a whole and individuals within it have little control over the conditions or decisions which affect work. These are determined by the weather or "the man" and both are perceived as equally arbitrary and unpredictable. With this brief factual background I turn to the question of the group's position with respect to the wider society.

THE MARGINALITY OF MIGRANT WORKERS

The migrant labor crew is not a permanent or continuing social unit. It is formed for part of the year, disbanding in the South where the people, if they continue in agricultural work, usually do so on a day-haul basis. While in some cases the core of a crew returns to the same camp in the North each summer, there is a heavy turnover, particularly in crews with many single men. Thus, the social unit is an intermittent one. Groups form and live together in the closest proximity only temporarily. In addition, during the brief period in which the crew exists as a social unit, membership is fluid: people come and go during the course of a season.

This intermittency, this lack of permanence, is important in understanding the status of migrants relative to the larger society. In a society where stability, permanent employment, and regularity are highly valued, migrant labor has pejorative connotations. It is assumed that only the dregs of society would "work the seasons."

Migrants are stereotyped as unreliable, nonproductive, unteachable, and seldom to be trusted.

At the same time, it is often assumed that migrants are satisfied with the circumstances in which they live. Community officials were genuinely shocked by a protest among migrants in one agricultural community.

> "Why," said the Mayor, "they walked by here on the road and I waved to them and they laughed and smiled ... real happy you know."
> "This place is a paradise compared to what they are used to living in," said the wife of a police chief. "Of course, you or I wouldn't want to live that way, but I believe they like it fine." (New York Times, July 17, 1966.)

In the face of increasing public concern over the conditions of the migrant labor situation, these stereotypes persist. The feeling is that individuals who do not fit this stereotype would not continue to be migrants.

These attitudes are manifest in the carefully maintained social isolation of crews. Migrants are set apart from the larger society in the North by several factors. First, the group is racially distinct. Most migrants in New York State are black except for some 5,000 Puerto Ricans.[6] With the exception of small clusters of ex-migrants who have remained permanently in the rural North, there are few nonwhite persons in northern agricultural communities. Second, the group is economically distinct from most of the population in its obvious poverty and in the low status of its employment. Third, the migrants are marked off from the community geographically. Labor camps are generally located a number of miles outside of town in isolated spots often invisible from the highway. Access to town is difficult due to lack of transportation. Where migrants have reason to use the facilities of the local community there is every effort to keep them apart, to maintain invisibility. The illegal sale of alcohol in camps, for example, is openly sanctioned in order to discourage the use of bars in town. Finally, migrants are isolated socially. There is little communication between most migrant labor camps and the larger society except via agencies specifically designated to deal with the migrants as *problems*. These include social workers, law enforcement officers, and the like.

The migrant labor camp is also far removed from the main stream of civil rights activities. Those migrants who know about race riots or other urban-centered events tend not to associate the implications of these events with their lives. Much of the turbulence which characterizes life in the urban ghettos has not yet reached the labor camps, a fact which suggests its greater social distance from the predominant social order.

Migrants tend to perceive moving out of the system as nearly impossible. Conversations reflect low self-esteem and a sense of personal inefficacy. "They can always get someone to work: there must be a million niggers around here out of work who need a job." Many often express the desire to get out, but few have concrete plans or actually expect to take the step.

> Everyone was talking about how glad they would be when they could leave and that they would never come back again. One cynic said, "Look, you fellas will all be back next year. Look what happened to Sam. Sam said the same thing last year, that he'd never come back, but where is he? He's right here with us. I've been here on the season on and off for seven years and I've been saying the same thing also, that I would never come back. So I am looking forward to seeing all of you fellas back here next year."

There is a tendency to become trapped by the system, and this is verbally recognized and disdained. It is often expressed by disparaging the aspirations of others. "You better get used to picking because you're never going to be a school teacher or any other kind of lady. You'll be in the fields for the rest of your life." This kind of response to relative status, a response which assumes that the system is closed, bears significantly on social relationships within the system.

LEVELING TENDENCY IN MIGRANT CAMPS

The reciprocal expectations which regulate relationships within migrant labor camps have developed as an accommodation to the conditions described above. Regulating social relationships in the camps, however, poses unique problems because of the intermittent quality of the social organization. In permanent communities relationships are developed and stabilized slowly over a period of time. Complex systems of norms are understood by all participants. While the migrants bring with them many of the values, norms, and attitudes of southern Negro sub-cultures, the migrant labor camp evokes its own set of norms which has to do with relationships within the temporary and marginal setting in the North.

To be effective in an intermittent situation, norms must be simple and easily and rapidly assimilated. There are, in fact, relatively few norms, and these change or must be reasserted as new groups enter the camp and new relationships must be defined. While social definitions are unstable, there are few opportunities for social avoidance because of the limited and isolated physical setting. To reduce the potentialities for misunderstandings under these circumstances, there is a tendency in the camps to minimize the differences between participants; to bring people to a common level.[7]

Social status "leveling" must be understood within the context of marginal status. Where people feel threatened by the outside society, the anonymity afforded by a homogeneous social structure is protective. Moreover, innovative or assertive behavior is non-functional in a group sharing common conditions within a system permitting little upward mobility. Where the basic decisions affecting a group are made from outside, hierarchy or power within the group has relatively little meaning. Migrants perceive little possibility of moving out of the system. They are aware of the opportunities which exist, but more aware of their inability to attain them. Thus, there exists a phenomenon which Erasmus (1967) calls the "rate buster model." "The rate buster incurs emnity by establishing new standards of performance which become an index for measuring the inadequacy of his fellow workers . . . where social mobility is relatively limited they may act together in bringing sanctions against the mobile individual as a means of protecting their own self image" (Erasmus 1967:378–79)

Sanctions against individual assertiveness are first manifest during the socialization period when the crew shapes up early in the season. The leveling tendency is evident in the patterns of social interaction in the camps and, to some extent, in the work place.

THE SOCIALIZATION PERIOD

Any person can walk into a camp and become part of the labor crew. In recruiting migrants, few questions are asked about background or experience. Social security regulations require that the grower or crew leader have the full name of each worker, but many crew members know each other only by first name or nickname. This is quite apparent to many of the outsiders who enter the camp for one reason or another. If a policeman or inspector, for example, inquires about an individual, he will usually be confronted by a total blank. While much of this ignorance is contrived, in fact people know very little about one another and curiosity in this direction is not encouraged. A person's background is understood to be his own business. In this way, prior social distinctions are minimized. A migrant in entering the camp is essentially divested of status and begins his stay at a level with other participants.

SOCIAL INTERACTION IN THE CAMP

Erving Goffman has suggested that "informal social participation is an ultimate validation of relationships of intimacy and equality with those with whom one shares this activity. A party then is by way of being a status blood bath, a leveling up and a leveling down of all present, a mutual contamination and sacrilization" (Goffman 1961). Drinking, gambling, and similar forms of convivial activities are predominant features of migrant life.[8] Their prevalence is often interpreted by the external community as proof of irresponsibility. In fact, such activities are highly functional and all people in the camps are expected to participate.

People drink together in the jukes where the piccolo (juke box), inevitably turned up to full volume, precludes conversation. It is common in many camps for most people, including women, to be drunk to the point of incoherence on weekends, but relatively few people drink heavily during the week or drink alone. Those who do are called "winos," a label with derogatory connotations. Drinking is a leveler. Aside from the common physical effect of alcohol, drinking skims the excess cash that any individual might have earned.[9] It is expected that those with money buy the booze and share it. No accounts are kept and reciprocation may take other forms.

Patterns of friendship reflect the tendency to minimize distinctions. Friendships form quickly and need not be based on long-term association. A high value is placed on reciprocity and liberality among friends. No records are kept of exchanges; there is little sense of "tit for tat," but rather a mutual sense of obligation which can be fulfilled by either social or economic means. The expectation of liberality is inconsistent with the desire of some individuals to save and occasionally creates problems. "Here I am trying to save money and all he does is borrow money from me and get on that card table and lose it all. I can't save at all. All that I've saved I've given him to gamble because he's done so much for me and I couldn't really turn him down."

Gambling itself has a leveling effect and is a major social activity. While there are skill differences in gambling, its basic aspect is, of course, chance, a commodity equally available to all participants. It is interesting in this respect to note the important role of superstition among gamblers who talk of "rootmen" in the South providing charms or magic beans, who recite good-luck jingles and use the contents of dreams to guide their fortunes. Gambling and other activities where chance is a major component are socially relevant in a group which has little control or determination over its destiny. It is only by chance of fate that things go well; therefore, behavior tends to maximize the possibility of a lucky break.

INTERACTION AT WORK

The leveling tendency extends to the work place. It is not surprising that in work paid by the hour, those who work fast are criticized for jeopardizing the group. However, those who pick slowly are also encouraged to keep up. "You've got to keep up. You don't have to work too hard because you are working by the hour and nobody is watching over us, but we just like to stay together so we can talk to each other." Those who complete their rows often wait or help others complete theirs.

The extent to which payment by piece work encourages individuality in picking depends to a large extent on the physical conditions of the field. On a bad day with limited possibility of high productivity, people tend to work slowly and to help one another. On a day with potential for all, however, people work quite hard, often competing with one another. The individual incentives intrinsic to a piece-work system are a source of dissension. For example, in picking fruit trees it is normatively understood that people are not to skip around to get the best trees but to take their chances in turn. Moreover, one is not to pick only the bottom or easily accessible part of the tree, but to finish the whole tree, including the hard-to-pick areas, before moving on. However, since payment is by the unit picked, there is a tendency to avoid scrawny trees, or to leave the tops. This leads to resentment and conflict within the group.

The earnings of migrants vary in different camps, but expectations are generally pessimistic, an attitude which is reflected in the relatively low level of goal-directed behavior. Most people are concerned with the present, the here and now. A striking illustration is the relation between productivity and the time of wage payment. Sometimes weekly wages were paid on Thursday instead of Friday. Work done on Friday was to be compensated the following week. When this happened, people were unable to see the relevance of working on Friday and productivity declined. Similar reasoning accounts for a sizeable number of "$3 a day men" or "target workers," who produce only enough to provide sustenance for the day.

> The people seem to live from day to day with the exception of a family from Alabama. No one is saving money to buy any particular thing. When the people first came to the camp they generally said, "Well, I just want to make enough money to get out of debt." Now it seems to be "I just want to get a man" (a bottle of wine).

Immediate and arbitrary circumstances seem to determine many aspects of the system, including the pattern of leadership. A crew leader must be able to transport his workers and find them jobs, but actually getting people to join his crew can depend less on his ability to fulfill the goals of the work than on a number of irrational factors or situational events at a particular time. In one camp a crew leader was hospitalized for several weeks early in the season. During his absence another man temporarily assumed leadership. By the time the original crew leader got back to work it became apparent that he no longer had a crew. He tried to regain the loyalty of the group using rational goal-related arguments. He noted that he had the truck and contracts with a number of farmers. In contrast, the replacement, a glib talker and popular story teller criticized the crew leader largely on the basis of his weight. "That guy is so fat he needs two toilets side by side to sit on." The crew sided with the replacement, attracted by his personal appeal, his charismatic quality. The personal skills of a crew leader and his verbal facility seem to be at least as important as efficiency in finding jobs.

Most people tend to avoid leadership or supervisory roles. "If I was in the army, I would want to be a private. I don't want to have anyone's lives on my hands." When asked in an interview "What sort of jobs would you like to have in this crew?" the answer was usually "a picker." This is buttressed by the experience of growers who find that people hesitate to accept the responsibility of supervision even when opportunities are available. Growers who seek alternatives to the crew leader system find that supervisory authority must be exercized from outside the structure, that individuals selected from within the crew are resented. Crew leaders express similar opinions. One was having problems keeping his crew after he had selected a foreman. He explained his difficulties as follows:

> I try to give them something better than anyone else and they don't appreciate it.... Negroes just don't like to have other Negroes as their superior, they just don't like to see anyone elevated above the level of anyone else. They all feel they are capable of doing the same thing and ... will try to get the person fired.

For those in supervisory positions, a personalistic style is the most viable one. Field walkers project themselves as "one of the boys" and when they must assert authority, do so by referring back to the authority of the crew leader.

While the leveling process pervades most aspects of social relationships, it merely discourages but does not preclude the development of informal prestige distinctions within the camp. A pecking order does in fact assert itself with significant implications for the system.

CONFLICTING TENDENCIES AND THEIR RESOLUTION

Informal distinctions are formed on a somewhat different basis than in the larger society where status is compartmentalized and is associated with particular activities. In the labor camp, because all activities are performed within the same group, status criteria are more generalized. The most respected people in the camps seem to possess several related qualities. They have a relatively stable marriage, are good pickers, knowledgeable about local environment, physically strong, relatively well-educated, and have a number of social skills, particularly verbal facility. Note that many of these qualities are those emphasized in middle class society. Television programs reinforce middle class values which are voiced in several contexts.[10] People will discuss the evils of alcohol while they continue to drink. Common law marriages are labeled with derogatory terms such as "muck" or "tramp marriages," but the lack of privacy and the fact that many families are separated for the season are incompatible with stable marital relationships, and many common law marriages are formed for convenience during the summer season. Similarly, there are those who praise the virtues of steady work, but weather and other uncontrollable circumstances often preclude its possibility. And there are occasional attempts by individuals to clean up the common bathroom or cooking facilities, but with overcrowding they are soon neglected again. Thus, while the values of the larger society are received and understood, conditions tend to preclude their realization.

Status distinctions are encouraged, however, primarily by the individualization of work. The formal structure of work, which is the very basis for the existence of the group, puts little priority on group identification and provides formal and direct incentive for the development of individual skill and competition. Verbal facility, skill in games, and success with women are also sources of prestige. However, these same abilities are sources of friction and violence. For status distinctions, once formed, are seldom crystallized. The pecking order is extremely fluid and fragile.

Take the case of Willy. At the beginning of the season Willy stood out as a popular and well respected figure. He was strong, productive, and bright. As he became more sure of himself he became conspicuous. People objected to his growing independence and put him down. One of the main causes of Willy's downfall was his tendency to "mouth off," to assert his position. He was highly criticized, for example, for displaying knowledge. "Just because he had a little knowledge he thought he knew everything. Knowledge isn't everything." In another instance, "You are always trying to make somebody look small. That's why I'll never tell you nothin'."

A number of mechanisms are used to deal with the pecking order. Perhaps the most interesting one is a verbal game called "playing the dozens." The "dozens" is a game in which a series of aggressive insults usually directed to a person's mother are exchanged by two protagonists.[11] The initial victim is scorned or criticized. If he responds, the game begins.

> "You know, Shakespeare said 'all good things come to those who wait.'"
> "Well, I've been waiting a God-damned long time and nothing's come."
> "All the damn wine you drink, if something did come you wouldn't see it."
> "I'm sorry sir, I don't allow myself to engage in conversation with a white man."
> "Oh, your mammy works in the packing house on the muck and you know the salesmen, they're white.... How do you think your mammy pays the bills?"
> "For all I know, I could be your daddy."
> "Your mammy sold herself in the corn fields for a shot of corn whiskey."

The game has a collective aspect which is crucial. It is always played for an audience which acts as a sounding board, the group response determining the subsequent pattern of expression, and the eventual winner. A good player gains prestige but runs the risk of having to fight, for many verbal exchanges develop further.

The dynamics of a camp can in a sense be regarded as a dialectic between two contradictory dispositions; the tendency toward homogeneity, on the one hand, and the continual reassertion of a pecking order, on the other. This dialectic has dysfunctional implications. For one thing, it leads to a great deal of physical violence. There is an atmosphere of tension, and fights occur with little provocation—over cards, women, or merely verbal disagreements. Most people carry knives and there are frequent threats and occasional slashings, though relatively few which lead to hospitalization and public interference. It also has important implications for the cohesion of the group and for the potential for social change. Despite common pressures and conditions, there is very little solidarity among migrant workers. The system is atomistic; there is little trust among individuals.

The atomistic quality of the system is sustained by the normative barriers to the development of leadership and hierarchy. The absence of status distinctions does not in any way imply cohesion. There are cases where equalitarian norms evoke solidarity vis-à-vis the dominant society, as among Guianese plantation workers studied by

Jayawardena (1967) but in the case of migrant workers there is no sense of organization to meet specific needs or goals. It was suggested one day in the fields that if everyone would just walk off, the "man" would have to raise the price. Everyone agreed, but everyone continued to work, including the person who suggested the walkoff. Few people trust one another sufficiently to support a protest action and fear that they would lose out by initiating such action. Organization for the purposes of exerting pressure to meet common needs is not a meaningful idea. Migrants have had no experience in the efficacy of organization and lack the necessary leadership and differentiation. The response to marginality rarely takes the form of protest. The response is rather an adaptive one. In many cases, it consists of apathy and accommodation.

Aggression toward the dominant society is seldom expressed directly. However, various accommodating mechanisms serve to relieve tensions arising from relationships with white society. Humor is an important mechanism of accommodation. Structurally, jokes assume several forms. The more popular jokes construct situations in which the white man's actions against a Negro backfire. Through cleverness and earthiness rather than status or power, the Negro or the underdog wins out in the end and the white man or the dominant figure becomes a fool. The Aesopian structure of the following joke is a common one.

> A rat fell into a whiskey barrel and was swimming around until a cat spotted him. "Hey brother cat, get me out of here." The cat said, "Why should I get you out? I don't have time." "Look, brother cat, you get me out of this whiskey and I'll let you eat me up." The cat agreed, got him out of the barrel and put him aside to get the whiskey out of him. Finally, the cat said, "Okay, come over and live up to your promise to let me eat you up." Brother rat said, "You must be kidding." "Brother rat, aren't you a man of your word, you said you'd let me eat you up?" The rat responded, "Brother cat, a man might say anything when he's in whiskey."

In some jokes, roles are reversed; Negro migrants assume the attributes of the structurally dominant and many of the stereotypes characteristically attributed to migrants are projected upon white people. In others, the actual structure of dominance and subordination is maintained, the Negroes taking abuse but subtly outsmarting the white man. In all cases, a dichotomy is established between "we" and "they," the oppressed and the oppressor. Jokes and stories deal directly with the elementary preoccupations of the people and are warmly appreciated. They serve not so much to reinforce common goals but rather to resolve some of the tensions and the conflicts flowing from difficult relationships. The following joke illustrates how an absurd context is used to transfer a painful relationship to humorous expression.

> There was this nigger out on the front of this white woman's house down in Georgia. He was starved; hadn't had anything to eat in three days. He was trying to think of a way to get something to eat. He saw the woman come out on her porch so he said to himself, "I'll bet if I go up there and start eating the grass she'll give me something to eat." So he ran to the lawn and started chomping on the grass. The woman looked at him and said, "Oh my God, look at that poor nigger out there eating the grass." She said, "Sir, sir!" The man looked up, "Ma'am?" "When you finish with that short grass there, there is some longer grass in the back if you want it."

By representing a shared reality through humorous symbols, a good story teller can dissolve tension and prevent conflict from becoming unmanageable. The common practice of using the names of people in the camp in jokes and stories enhances the dynamic relationship of the humor to the situation. Story-telling sessions are an important part of life: popular jokes are reiterated again and again with a mere phrase evoking laughter for days. Common strains and tensions are thus dissolved and difficult situations are accommodated.

To conclude briefly, I have focused on some of the characteristics that have developed within a group in response to the conditions imposed by marginal status. The norms which are emphasized within a labor camp reflect the need for support and gratification not forthcoming from a society to which the group is marginal: the migrant labor crew is, in a sense, more a cocoon than a structured community. The tendency to minimize individual distinctions within the camp is predominant, but it coexists with conflicting hierarchical tendencies. The patterns of social relationships in these circumstances are atomistic, contentious, and discouraging to the development of leadership, structure, and organization. In the highly structured dominant society, these patterns are dysfunctional and serve only to reinforce and perpetuate the marginality of the migrant worker.

NOTES

1. Material for this paper was developed as part of a project on the social organization of migrant labor directed by William H. Friedland, New York State School of Industrial and Labor Relations, Cornell University. The research has been supported by grants from the Manpower Administration of the U. S. Department of Labor, the Cornell Experiment Station, and the Ford Foundation. In the writing of this paper, comments by Victor Turner and Norman Whitten were most useful. The research, utilizing participant observation and interview techniques, has been a part of a teaching/research program and has been assisted by students from Cornell University and Tuskeegee Institute. The study has concentrated on migrants in New York State. According to crude census data, there are approximately 15,000 southern Negro migrant workers in New York State during the peak harvest season, plus about 6,000 Puerto Ricans. Our study has been limited to Negro crews.

2. See for example, Goldberg 1941; Green 1947; Antonovsky 1956; Mann 1957; and Dickie-Clark 1966.

3. Out of 171 crews recruited for New York State during April 1967, 36.2% contained from 5 to 30 workers; 56.1% had 31 to 80 workers; and 7.6% had more than 80 workers. Generally one crew will occupy an entire camp, but there are also several large multi-crew facilities.

4. Details on crew composition are available in a report to the United States Department of Labor by Friedland and Nelkin (1967).

5. This, of course, varies with the level of technology. Farms with harvesting machinery require a number of people with specialized occupational skills. However, these farms employ a permanent labor force which handles skilled tasks.

6. There are also several small groups of derelict whites who are recruited into separate camps by "bar-sweeping" in local cities. There are several hundred Mexican families who enter the state for short periods of time as farm workers.

7. A leveling tendency fostered by similar conditions is a theme which runs through some of the writings on peasant culture. See Wolf 1957 and Nash 1963.

8. Jayawardena (1967) has described the "high expenditure on conviviality" among Guianese plantation workers in a similar framework. It reinforces "mati," which is the norm of equality in social status within the group. However, "mati" suggests not only egalitarian norms but solidarity and cohesion as well.

9. This is similar in a way to the heavy expenditure on religious ceremonies which function to siphon off excess wealth in many Meso-American societies. See Wolf 1955.

10. Television, of course, also offers information on race riots. However, news programs are usually avoided, and probing concerning attitudes toward riots suggest that with the exception of some of the younger men, few people seem to identify with events in the urban ghettos.

11. The dynamics of the game have been dealt with by Dollard 1939.

Sixteen

THE KINDRED OF VIOLA JACKSON: RESIDENCE AND FAMILY ORGANIZATION OF AN URBAN BLACK AMERICAN FAMILY[1]

Carol B. Stack

INTRODUCTION

Concepts can become so widely accepted and seem so obvious that they block the way to further understanding. Descriptions of black American domestic life (Frazier 1939; Drake and Cayton 1945; Abrahams 1964; Moynihan 1965; Rainwater 1966a) are almost always couched in terms of the nuclear family and in terms of the fashionable notion of a matrifocal complex. But in many societies the nuclear family is not always a unit of domestic cooperation, and the "universal functions" of family life can be provided by other social units (Spiro 1954; Gough 1959; Levy and Fallers 1959; Reiss 1965). And matrifocal thinking, while it may bring out the importance of women in family life, fails to account for the great variety of domestic strategies one can find on the scene in urban black America. The following study suggests that if we shed concepts such as matrifocality we can see that black Americans have evolved a repertoire of domestic units that serve as flexible adaptive strategies for coping with the everyday human demands of ghetto life.

In the fall of 1966 I began to investigate black family organization in midwestern cities. I concentrated upon one domestic family unit—the household of Viola and Leo Jackson—and their network of kinsmen, which proved to number over 100 persons.[2] My immediate aim was to discover when and why each of these people had changed residence, and what kind of domestic unit they joined during the half-century since they had begun moving north from Arkansas.

The data show that during the process of migration and the adjustment of individuals to urban living, clusters of kin align together for various domestic purposes. It soon became clear that matrifocal thinking provided little insight into the organization of domestic units of cooperation, for example, those groups of kin and non-kin which carry out domestic functions but do not always reside together (Bender 1967). In certain situations such as the death or desertion of a parent, the loss of a job, or in the process of migration it was found that an individual almost always changed residence. But matrifocality proved to be a poor predictor of the kind of domestc unit the individual might subsequently enter. Among Mrs. Jackson's kin one can find various assortments of adults and children cooperating in domestic units: children living with relatives other than their parents, and also clusters of kin (often involving the father) who do not reside together but who provide some of the domestic functions for a mother-and-child unit in another location. Not only does matrifocal thinking fail here, but also little or nothing in the current writing on black American family life helps deal with questions such as the following that arise when we examine Mrs. Jackson's kin: Which relatives can a person expect will help him? Which relatives will care for parentless or abandoned children? And who will look after the ill and elderly? I will discuss these questions, and the challenge that Mrs. Jackson's kin and their lifeways put to our powers of explanation. First, however, I will deal briefly with the nature of matrifocal thinking.

THE MATRIFOCAL COMPLEX

Matrifocality has become a popular replacement for the discarded nineteenth-century concept of matriarchy. Some would argue that matrifocality is more sophisticated, but I suggest that it is no more useful than matriarchy for characterizing urban Negro households.

When the rules for reckoning kinship are not explicit, then it is difficult to determine the basis upon which households are formed. As so, as M. G. Smith (1962b:7) has pointed out, by necessity the anthropologist then must rely on data on household composition. It is in this context that the term "matrifocality" is most widely used. However, it also has been used to refer to at least three units of information: (1) the composition of a household, (2) the type of kinship bond linking its members, and (3) the relationship between males and females in the household. In fact, matrifocality tells us little about the actual composition of the household, and the relational link upon which the household is formed. Schneider (1961) points out that in the past the terms "matrilocal marriage" and "matriliny" were used interchangeably (see Bachofen 1861) and that the matriarchal complex referred to a household which did not include the husband or father. Both González (1965) and Smith (1962b) use matrifocality to refer to the composition of households. These and similar formulations ignore the developmental history of domestic groups (Goody 1958). In addition, they supply no information on the age and circumstances in which individuals join households, the alternatives open to them, the relational links they have with other members, or who the members are. *Matrifocality is not a residence rule, and in particular, it is not a rule for post-marital residence.* Residence, one of the dynamics of social organization, can be understood only if the basis for the active formation of households is known.

A further complication is that notions such as matrifocality, maternal family (C. King 1945), and matriarchy inadvertently are associated with unilineal descent. It was Bachofen's contention (1861) that matriliny (descent through women) and matriarchy (rule by women) were but two aspects of the same institution (Schneider 1961; Lowie 1947). This claim had to be discarded when observers failed to find any generalized authority of women over men in matrilineal societies. This controversy is well known. What is less widely appreciated is that there is a close parallel between matriarchal and matrifocal thinking, in that both imply descent through women. For example, M. G. Smith (1962b) defines Caribbean matrifocal households as ones which are composed of blood-related women plus all their unmarried children. González (1965:1542) defines consanguineal households in terms of the type of kinship bond linking adult men and women in the households such that no two members are bound together in an affinal relationship. She suggests that consanguineal households may also be matrifocal (1965:1548) and that there is evidence that consanguinal households exist among lower class Negro American groups (DuBois 1908; Frazier 1939; C. King 1945). The tentative classification that emerges from studies of black American households as consanguineal or as both consanguineal and matrifocal is confusing. In this confusion the use of the notion of matrifocality roughly coincides with Schneider's (1961:3) definition of matrilineal descent units in which he states that the "individual's initial relationship is to his mother and through her to other kinsmen, both male and female, but continuing only through females." *Matrifocality is not necessarily a correlate of matrilineal descent, nor does it imply a structure for linking families in the same community.*

The term "matrifocality" may have value as an indication of the woman's role within the domestic group, but it tells us little about authority, decision-making, and male-female relationships within the household, among extended kin, and in the community. Used in this context to refer to a dominant female role, and as a designate of residence classification, reference to the matrifocal household may lead to confusion between residence and role behavior. Analysis of role relationships and interactional patterns which is limited to their classification as matrifocal is at best uninteresting. The role organization of urban Negro households exists in a dynamic system which can be illustrated by the life histories of individuals in households as they adapt to the urban environment. This adaptation comes out dramatically when one examine's Viola Jackson's kin and their many ways of forming a domestic unit.

Frequently, discussions of matrifocality and consanguineal households ignore crucial aspects of family organization. Some of the matrifocal thinkers seem to assume that children derive nothing of sociological importance from their father, that households are equivalent to the nuclear family, and that resident husband-fathers are marginal members of their own homes (M. G. Smith 1957b). A look at Viola Jackson's kindred raises doubts about many of these assumptions.

URBAN FAMILY ORGANIZATION

Clusters of Kin

The past fifty years have witnessed a massive migration of rural, southern blacks to urban centers in the United States. The kindred of Viola Jackson are a part of this movement. Ninety-six of them left the South between 1916 and 1967. Some of them first moved from rural Arkansas to live and work harvesting fruit in areas around Grand Rapids and Benton Harbor, Michigan, and

Racine, Wisconsin; eventually they settled in the urban North. Two major patterns emerge from their life histories: (1) relatives tend to cluster in the same areas during similar periods: and (2) the most frequent and consistent alignment and cooperation appears to occur between siblings.

During the process of moving, Viola Jackson's kin maintained communication with relatives in the South. They frequently moved back to the South for short periods, or from Chicago and other midwestern cities to fruit harvesting areas on a seasonal basis. Therefore it is difficult to separate the data in terms of phases such as "migration" and subsequent "urban adaptation." During some seasons bus loads of rural blacks were brought to the North to harvest fruit. Many families worked their way back South only to repeat the process in order to avoid the poverty and unemployment there. This circulatory migration mainly involved the younger families and individuals.

Frequently, migrant workers follow their relatives and large urban neighborhoods reflect the geographical boundaries of the hinterland. Once these facts are established it is important to find out who made the original move, his age at the time of the move, which relatives joined one another to form households, and the context of each move.

Between 1916 and 1967 Mrs. Jackson's kin lived in five states, and groups of 10 to 15 individuals tended to cluster in the same areas during the same time periods. An example of this can be seen in Table 16-1, which shows where Viola's mother and siblings were living during that time period.

The basis for the active formation of households during migration and urban settlement can only be understood if material developing out of life histories is related to the realities of kinship and non-kinship factors. During this period of migratory wage labor in the young adult's life, the data show that the strongest alignment is of co-operation and mutual aid among siblings of both sexes (after the age of thirteen). Siblings left the South together, or shortly followed one another, for seasonal jobs. They often lived together in the North with their dependents and spouses, or lived near one another, providing mutual aid such as cooking and child care.

Domestic Arrangements

CASE 1

In 1945 *C* left her husband and daughter in the South with his parents and moved to Racine, Wisconsin, to harvest fruit. At the same time *C's* brother's wife died leaving him, *J*, with two young sons. *J* decided to move north and join *C* in Racine. He and his two sons took a bus to Racine where he got a job in a catsup factory. The company furnished trailers which *C* and *J* placed next to each other. *C* cooked for *J* and his two sons and cared for the children. They were cooperating as a single domestic unit. This situation continued for about a year and a half and then they all returned to the South.

CASE 2

By 1946 Viola and Leo had four children and Leo was picking cotton. They were anxious to leave the South in order to find better wages and living conditions. Viola, Leo, and their children joined a bus load of people and moved to join Viola's brother, *L,* in Benton Harbor, Michigan. In Benton Harbor all the adults and the older children worked harvesting fruit. At the same time Leo's twin brother and Viola's brother, *J*, and his two sons moved to Benton Harbor. Leo's twin brother moved into Viola's and Leo's household. *J* and his sons moved into

TABLE 16-1.
Residence and Kin Clusters

Area and Time Period	Ego's Mother (Magnolia)	Ego (Viola)	B	Z	Z	Z	B
Arkansas 1916–1917	X	X	X				
Arkansas 1928–1944	X	X		X	X	X	X
Blythe, Calif. 1927–1928	X	X	X				
Grand Rapids, Mich. 1944–1946			X		X		
Racine, Wisc. 1947–1948		X		X			X
Benton Harbor, Mich. 1946–1948		X	X	X			X
Decatur, Ark. 1948–1952	X	X			X		X
Chicago, Ill. 1950–1953				X			
Champaign, Ill. 1952–1954	X	X	X				
Gary, Ind. 1954–1955			X				
Champaign, Ill. 1955–1967	X	X	X		X	X	X
Chicago Heights, Ill. 1959–1967				X			
Chicago, Ill. 1965–1967			X				

the household of *J's* brother, *L,* and *L's* wife.

CASE 3

In 1948 *C* decided to move north again. This time she took her daughter with her. She moved to Benton Harbor where Viola and her family, their two brothers, *L* and *J,* and Leo's twin brother were all living. *C* and *J* and their children began cooperating as a single domestic unit as they had in Racine.

The pattern described above of cooperation and mutual aid among siblings becomes even more apparent as these individuals move to urban areas. Sibling alignment in the urban context will be discussed in the next section.

SIBLING ALIGNMENT AND KIN CO-OPERATION IN URBAN AREAS

Understanding residence and family organization for people whose economic situation is constantly changing, and who therefore frequently change households, is not easy. Aside from the common observations of household composition based upon where people sleep, there are many other important patterns to be observed, such as which situations lead to a change in residence, which adults share households, and with which adult relatives are children frequently living.

One pattern, a continuation of a pattern formed during the early stages of migratory labor, is the cooperative alignment of siblings. By the time the majority of Viola Jackson's relatives had established permanent residence and jobs in the North there were numerous examples of siblings forming co-residential and/or domestic units of cooperation. These sibling-based units, apparently motivated by situations such as death, sickness, desertion, abandonment, and unemployment, most often focused around the need for child-care arrangements. Here are two examples:

1. SISTER/BROTHER

In 1956 Viola and Leo were living in Champaign, Illinois. Viola's brother, *J*, took the train from the South to visit them. After the visit he decided to move to Champaign with his two sons and look for work. *J* rented a house near Viola's and got a construction job. When he brought his sons to Champaign Viola cooked for them and cared for them during the day.

2. SISTER/SISTER

In 1959 Viola's sister, *E*, was suffering from a nervous breakdown. *E's* husband took their four youngest children to his mother in Arkansas. *E's* sister, *C*, was living in Chicago and she cared for *E's* oldest daughter. After *E's* husband deserted her, *E's* twin sister, *M*, moved into *E's* house. The household was composed of *E*, her oldest daughter who had been in Chicago, *M*, and *M's* two youngest daughters.

These alignments may be largely attributed to adaptation to urban socio-economic conditions. One such urban pattern is a minimum of emphasis on the inheritance of property. For obvious social and economic reasons, poor and highly mobile urban apartment dwellers do not develop strong ties to a homestead or a particular piece of land, even though they may express strong regional and even neighborhood loyalty or identification. This contrasts with the rural South and with Young's and Willmott's (1957) observations that apartments in Bethnal Green were kept in the family. The high frequency of moving from one apartment to another in economically depressed urban areas is related to the degree of overcrowding, the shortage of apartments, urban renewal, and the changing employment situation. Another situation causing these alignments to form is the arrival of a new migrant to the urban area wherein he lives with siblings. With time, if he successfully establishes himself in a job in the urban area he may move out of his sibling's household.

CRISIS SITUATIONS AND THE RESIDENCE OF CHILDREN

It has already been pointed out that migration, unemployment, sickness, and desertion by necessity often lead to a change in residence. Most often these changes are closely related to the need for child-care arrangements. The choices and expectations involved in placing children in a relative's home largely focus around which adult female relatives are available. In selecting the specific relative, the following criteria are considered: the geographical locations of these adult female relatives; their source of financial support, their age, their marital status, the composition of their household, and the ability of the people making the decision to get along with these females. At the same time, due to the flexibility and mobility or urban individuals, decisions frequently center around the relational link the child has with female members of a particular household. This means that the distance and location of a household, for example, are not a great deterrent, and that in fact the economic, distance, and other decisions are made after the kin criteria are met.

Children in the extended kin network of Viola Jackson frequently live with relatives other than their biological parents. The child-female links which most often are the basis of new or expanded households are clearly those links with close adult females such as the child's mother, mother's mother, mother's sister, mother's brother's wife, father's mother, father's sister, father's brother's wife.

Here are some examples.

RELATIONAL LINK	DOMESTIC UNIT
Mother	Viola's brother married his first wife when he was sixteen. When *she* left him, she kept her daughter.
Mother's mother	Viola's sister, M, never was able to care for her children. In between husbands, her mother kept her two oldest children, and after M's death, her mother kept all three of the children. Her brother offered to keep the oldest girl.
Mother's mother	Viola's daughter (age 20) was living at home and gave birth to a son. The daughter and her son remained in the Jackson household. The daughter expressed the desire to set up a separate household.
Mother's sister	M moved to Chicago into her sister's household. The household consisted of the two sisters and four of their children.
Father's mother	Viola's sister, E, had four daughters and one son. When E was suffering from a nervous breakdown her husband took three daughters and his son to live with his mother in Arkansas. After his wife's death he also took the oldest daughter to his mother's household in Arkansas.
Father's mother	When Viola's younger sister, C, left her husband in order to harvest fruit in Wisconsin she left her two daughters with his mother in Arkansas.
Father's sister	When Viola's brother's wife died, he decided to raise his two sons himself. He kept the two boys and never remarried. His residence has consistently been close to one or another of his sisters who have fed and cared for his two sons.

These examples do indeed indicate the important role of the black female. But the difference between matrifocal thinking and thinking about household composition in terms of where children live is that the latter can bring to light the dynamics of household formation, and the criteria, rules, and decisions that the process entails.

The summaries of the social context in which children changed households indicates which adult female relatives are frequently called upon for service. The alignment and cooperation between siblings, such as mother's sister and father's sister, has already been noted. This has been underestimated by workers who select the grandmother household (especially mother's mother) as the only significant domestic unit. It must be noted that the crucial role which paternal as well as maternal grandmothers assume in socialization is a frequent, but definitely not a unique, alternative.

Since social scientists have stressed the existence of female-centered, woman-headed, matrifocal black families, it is of particular interest to look at the formation of grandmother households in Viola's kin. Here is a summary of the households in which Viola's mother, Magnolia, has lived.

MAGNOLIA

AGE	CONTEXT OF DOMESTIC UNIT OR HOUSEHOLD
60	In 1958 Magnolia's second husband died and she was left alone with her daughter's (*M*) two oldest children. Viola sent her two oldest sons to care for Magnolia and the two children.
62	In 1960 Magnolia moved to Champaign and joined the household of her twin daughters, *E* and *M*, bringing *M's* children with her.
65	After *E's* death, Magnolia and her daughter moved to Danville, Illinois, with *M's* two children, who Magnolia raised in the South, and *M's* two youngest children.
67	After *M's* death, Magnolia joined her daughter Viola's household for a short time.
67	Soon afterward, Viola and her husband rented a nearby house for Magnolia and the four grandchildren. Magnolia is on welfare, cares for the four children, and constantly receives help from the Jacksons and from her children living in Chicago.

When a grandmother household is characterized as matrifocal we get little insight into the dynamics of its formation. At best, it suggests a mother hen who gathers her chicks about her. After age sixty, Magnolia's residence was determined by her children, who decided to bring her to the urban North to care for her. Her move North was prompted by her children's concern for her health and well-being.

We find that Magnolia has frequently shared households with her children and grandchildren. In fact, she has consistently moved to join her daughter's households to be cared for, or to care for her grand-children. Instead of simply gathering her flock, each move and new household in which Magnolia lived after age sixty was formed on a different basis.

By the time Magnolia was elderly she was living in the urban North in a grandmother household caring for her grandchildren. This was the result of the illness and subsequent death of one of her daughters. At this time a house was rented and maintained for Magnolia and the four grandchildren by Viola and her husband, Leo. The rented house was one block from Viola's home and the two households functioned primarily as a single domestic unit of cooperation. The cluster of relatives consisted of four generations: Magnolia, the four grandchildren, Viola and Leo Jackson, ten of their children, and their grandchild, the son of Viola Jackson's oldest daughter.

This four-generational kin cluster is not a co-residential unit, but a domestic unit of cooperation. The main source of financial support consisted of Leo's seasonal construction work, welfare payments to both Magnolia and Viola's daughter (for her son), and the part-time jobs of some of the teenage children. These individuals used Viola's house as home base where they shared the evening meal, cared for all the small children, and exchanged special skills and services. Frequently, Viola's brother (whose wife had died) ate with the group and participated in the exchange of money, food, care for the sick, and household duties. The exchange of clothes, appliances, and services in crisis situations extended beyond this kin cluster to relatives in Chicago and St. Louis. This group is an example of an urban kinship based domestic unit which formed to handle the basic family functions.

CONCLUDING REMARKS

The examples from the preceding sections support the suggestion that domestic functions are carried out for urban blacks by clusters of kin who may or may not reside together. Individuals who are members of households and domestic units of cooperation align to provide the basic functions often attributed to nuclear family units. The flexibility of the blacks' adaptation to the daily social and economic problems of urban living is evidenced in these kinship-based units which form to handle the daily demands of urban life. In particular, new or expanded households and/or domestic units are created to care for children. The basis of these cooperative units is co-generational sibling alignment, the domestic cooperation of close adult females, and the exchange of goods and services between the male and female relatives of these females. To conclude, it is suggested that these households and domestic units provide the assurance that all the children will be cared for.

NOTES

1. The author would like to thank Professors E. Bruner, D. Shimkin, F. K. Lehman, D. Plath, and O. Lewis, and Mr. W. Ringle, for their interest in this work and helpful comments.
2. Names throughout the paper are pseudonyms.

Seventeen

WHAT GHETTO MALES ARE LIKE: ANOTHER LOOK[1]

Ulf Hannerz

Ever since the beginnings of the study of black people in the Americas investigators have commented on the ways in which black men and women—in particular some men and women—differ in their behavior from their white counterparts.[2] Most of these comments have focused on the nature of the black family, and especially on female dominance. Herskovits saw the close bond between mother and children, and the peripheral status of the father, as an African vestige, typical of polygynous marriage where every woman with her offspring formed a separate unit. Yet he was aware that this pattern was changed and adapted to New World slavery (Herskovits 1941:181). Frazier is generally regarded as the pioneer among those who have ascribed to American slavery itself the strongest influence in undermining the stability of marital unions (Frazier 1932, 1934, 1939, 1949). But Frazier also saw a strengthening of the marriage institution among rural freedmen in southern states, and another weakening following migration and urbanization. He makes relatively clear that economic insecurity was one characteristic of city life, but this point is frequently dimmed by his imagery of other urban evils: anonymity, disorganization, lack of social supports and controls. Undoubtedly, he was influenced by his contemporaries in the Chicago school of sociology, who saw the city primarily in such terms. Under those conditions, the lower class black family allegedly reverted, with matrifocality, to a primitive evolutionary stage (Frazier 1934:198). Obviously, Frazier found practically only weaknesses in the matrifocal family arrangement. His studies contain an abundance of comments on the evils of "broken" families but are quite deficient in social and cultural analysis of a more intensive sort.[3]

The emphasis on the socio-economic

matrix of family life which Frazier's work foreshadowed has emerged as the third major perspective in black American family studies, and this point of view is now probably dominant. It relates the absence or marginality of the husband-father in many black households to the low occupational status, poor income, job insecurity, and unemployment of many black males. Of little importance as a provider and in the articulation of the household with the wider structure of the society, the male is deprived of some of the most important features of the male role as defined in the dominant high-status cultures of New World societies. Consequently, his position in the household is undermined, and the female becomes dominant.

This synchronic explanation, like the Africanist and slavery explanations, applies to many black groups in the New World. An important statement in this vein is R. T. Smith's *The Negro Family in British Guiana* (1956), but it is also voiced frequently by scholars concerned with black ghetto families in the United States. The famous "Moynihan report," although in some ways a curiously ambiguous document, points to the correlation between household form and economic-occupational factors (United States Department of Labor 1965:19–25). In some of the comments on the "Moynihan report," and in other studies which were more or less part of the ensuing debate about the black family, the same point is made more clearly (Gans 1967; Herzog 1967; H. Lewis 1967).

Most of what has been said about the sex roles of New World black people can find its place in one of these three perspectives. However, this means that the studies only marginally involve the discussion of sex roles *per se*, as they are first of all studies of the family or household as an institution. This may still provide a reasonably clear view of the female role, since it is clearly enacted to a great extent within the matrifocal household. It is the man's life, then, which tends to occur somehow "out there, somewhere," away from studies of black domestic life, because his major characteristic as far as the household is concerned is absence or marginality.

Under such conditions, what is the male role, and how is it replicated in generation after generation? To what are those boys socialized who again and again grow up to exist on the periphery of households, and how is their role handled in adult life? What we need in order to answer such questions is micro-sociological data concerning cultural management and transmission pertaining to the male role. Such data are seldom offered. Yet it is possible to piece together some kind of a picture of the lower class black male. In the United States, his popular image was summed up by Norman Mailer in his essay on *The White Negro*: the black male lives in the present, subsists for the kicks of Saturday night, gives up the pleasures of the mind for the pleasures of the body, and gives voice to the character and quality of his existence in his music (Mailer n.d.).

Certainly there is some poetic exaggeration in Mailer's picture, and a great deal of stereotyping in the general public's imagery concerning the people of the black ghetto. But hardly anyone acquainted with life in the ghetto can fail to see that there is also much of reality involved. Rainwater's sketch of the "expressive life style" shows a trained social scientist's picture which is remarkably similar to Mailer's (Rainwater 1966b:113 ff.).[4] Undoubtedly there is a sizeable segment of the male population which is strongly concerned with sex, drinking, sharp clothes, and "trouble," and among these men we find many of those only marginally involved with married life. Of course, a great many men in the ghetto live largely according to the mainstream styles of life, and in stable marriages; there is much heterogeneity in ghetto life styles. But to a considerable extent, it is to the former that we should turn our attention to see what pattern of maleness goes with matrifocality.

We may note, too, that some features of this life style are noticeably recurrent in lower class black communities in the New World. Clarke, for instance (1957:91), writes that in Sugartown, a proletarian Jamaican township,

> ... sex was a favorite subject of conversation with both men and women. Men enjoyed talking about their sexual prowess, the number of children they had fathered and the number of their conquests, referring with especial pride to any relationship with a virgin. Both men and women regarded sexual activity as a normal part of adult and adolescent life, and there was never any attempt to temper the discussion if children were present. Childish and adolescent precocity was, on the contrary, regarded with tolerant amusement and, in the case of boys, with admiration.

Otterbein (1966:67), in describing the mating system of the Andros Islanders of the Bahamas, writes that the Islanders

> ... believe that the biological nature of the male compels him to have sexual intercourse with as many women as possible. This drive is expected to manifest itself in adolescent males. If a boy does not begin to have coitus by his late teens, people will begin to wonder if he is a "sissy" (homosexual). Most young men, however, live up to community expectations—behavior which is expressed in the saying: "Boys are like dogs."

There is also Freilich's (1961:965) description of the focal concerns of the black peasants of Anamat, Trinidad:

> The Anamatian Negro feels best, most alive, when he is in a fête. This is making the most complete use of the "now." The basic ingredients that go into making a really good fête are people, rum, music, and sexual play. Frequently, the Negro does not get a chance to have all these ingredients present at one function, but if any two of them are present he still considers himself to be in a fête.
>
> A rendezvous with a girl friend is considered one of the more popular fêtes. Here it is possible to drink, dance, have sexual play, and receive the acclaim of the community.
>
> A man who has many affairs gets what the local people call "fame," that is a sort of renown for being a real man. He is then referred to as a "hot boy." One tries to remain a "hot boy" for as long as possible and a Negro farmer in his sixties was still going strong as of July 1958. Those who do not appear to be "hot boys" on the other hand, are looked on as rather strange individuals.

This essay is an attempt to outline the social processes within the ghetto communities of the northern United States whereby the identity of streetcorner males is established and maintained.[5] Although based on fieldwork in but one North American urban community, the analysis is probably applicable to some extent also to other black communities in the New World where males grow up and exist in similar socio-economic conditions, a similar matrix of interpersonal relationships and, as the quotations above seem to tell us, into a similar complex of cultural values and definitions. As a role analysis, it involves an attempt to consider all significant relationships of the male in which socially induced sex-specific behavior occurs or is commented upon within the black community. In employing such a framework, it tends to differ from the institutional family analysis which has been strong in the social anthropology of New World black life, and stands closer to the kind of network conceptualization which has only recently become generally recognized as an analytical tool in social anthropology (Barnes 1954; Bott 1957; Epstein 1961; Mitchell 1966; Mayer 1966).[6]

To set the stage and state the issues involved in such an analysis, we may look at the views expressed by two predecessors in the study of the ghetto male role. One of the two is Charles Keil, whose *Urban Blues* (1966) is a study of the bluesman as a "culture hero"—according to Keil, the urban blues singer, with his emphasis on sexuality, "trouble," and flashy clothes, gives expression to a cultural model of maleness which is highly valued by the ghetto dwellers and relatively independent of the mainstream cultural tradition. Keil (1966:28) criticizes a number of writings which tend to see this conception of the male role as rooted in the individual's anxiety about his maleness, finding them unacceptably ethnocentric:

> Any sound analysis of Negro masculinity should first deal with the statements and responses of Negro women, the conscious motives of the men themselves, and the Negro cultural tradition. Applied in this setting, psychological theory may then be able to provide important new insights in place of basic and unfortunate distortions.

Keil, then, comes out clearly for a cultural interpretation of the male role we are interested in here. But Elliot Liebow, in *Tally's Corner* (1967:223), a study resulting from the author's participation in a research project which definitely considered ghetto life more in terms of social problems than as a culture, reaches conclusions which, in some of their most succinct formulations, quite clearly contradict Keil's:

> Similarities between the lower-class Negro father and son ... do not result from "cultural transmission" but from the fact that the son goes out and independently experiences the same failures, in the same areas, and for much the same reasons as his father.

Thus father and son are "independently produced look-alikes" (*ibid.*). With this goes the view that the emphasis on sexual ability, drinking, and the like, is a set of compensatory self-deceptions which can only veil unsuccessfully the streetcorner male's awareness of his failure.

Keil and Liebow, as reviewed here, may be taken as representatives of the differing opinions on why black people in the ghettos, and in particular the males, behave differently from other Americans. One involves a cultural determinism internal to the ghetto, the other an economic determinism involving the links between the ghetto and the wider society.[7] It is easy to see how the two views relate to the perspectives on determinants of domestic structure. As we have said, it seems that the socio-economic determinism (as represented by Liebow) is at present the majority point of view among social scientists engaged in this field of study. Admittedly, the present opportunity structures places serious obstacles in the way of many ghetto dwellers, making a mainstream life style difficult to accomplish. Thus, if research is to influence public policy, it is particularly important to point to the wider structural influences which can be changed in order to give equal opportunity to ghetto dwellers. Yet some of the studies emphasizing such macro-structural determinants involve somewhat crude conceptualizations which are hardly warranted by data and which in the light of anthropological theory quickly appear oversimplified.

First of all, let us dispose of some of the opposition between the two points of view cited above. There is not necessarily any direct conflict between ecological-economic and cultural explanations, and the tendency to create such a conflict in much of the current writings on poverty involves a false dichotomy. Anthropologists assume that culture is transferred from generation to generation, and also that it is influenced by the community's relationship to its environment. (The fact that the environment in this case is social rather than natural does not make a great difference—besides, contemporary ecological anthropology tends to take the social environment into consideration as well.) Economic determinism and cultural determinism can thus go hand in hand in a stable environment. Since the ecological niche of ghetto dwellers has long remained relatively unchanged, there seems to be no reason why their adaptation should not have become in some ways cultural. It is possible, of course, that the first stage in the evolution of the ghetto-specific life style consisted of a multiplicity of identical but largely independent adaptations from the existing cultural background—main-stream or otherwise—to the given opportunity structure, as Liebow suggests, thus creating a statistical norm of behavior which is not truly a cultural norm. But the second stage of adaptation—by the following generations—involves the perception of the first-stage adaptation as a normal condition, a state of affairs which from then on can be expected. What was at first independent adaptation becomes transformed into a ghetto heritage of assumptions about the nature of man and society.

Yet Liebow implies that father and son are independently produced as streetcorner men and that transmission of a ghetto-specific culture has a negligible influence. To those adhering to such a standpoint, strong evidence in its favor is seen in the fact that ghetto dwellers—both men and women—often express mainstream sentiments about sex roles. Most ghetto dwellers would certainly agree, at times at least, that education is a good thing, that gambling and drinking are bad, if not sinful, and that a man and a woman should be true to each other. Finding such opinions, and considering Keil's statement quoted above about deriving the ghetto cultural interpretation from statements and responses of the black people themselves, one may be led to doubt that there is much of a specific ghetto culture. Noting the behavior which contradicts the stated values, then, one arrives at two questions: "Is there any reason to believe that ghetto-specific behavior is cultural?" And, if that should be the case, "What is the nature of the co-existence between mainstream culture and ghetto-specific culture in the black ghetto?"

To answer the first question, one might look again at the communications about behavior related to the male identity in the ghetto. This is where we should trace all significant relationships in the typical streetcorner male network. One set of relationships in which such communications occur frequently is the family; another is the male peer group.

Much has been made of the notion that young boys in the ghetto, growing up in matrifocal households, are somehow deficient in masculinity, or uncertain about masculinity, because their fathers are absent or peripheral in household affairs.[8] It is said that they lack the role models necessary for learning male behavior, the kind of information about the nature of masculinity which a father would transmit unintentionally merely by going about his life at home is missing. The boys therefore supposedly experience a great deal of sex role anxiety, as a result of this cultural vacuum. (Writings in this vein include Miller 1958; Rohrer and Edmonson 1960; Derbyshire *et al.* 1963; Pettigrew

1964). It is possible that such a view contains more than a grain of truth in the case of some quite isolated female-headed households. Evidence from studies of such households in other social contexts point in this direction (Burton and Whiting 1961; Pettigrew 1964). In the ghetto situation, however, there may be less to this than meets the eye.[9] First of all, a female-headed household without an adult male in residence but where young children are growing up—and where it is thus likely that the mother is still rather young—is seldom one where adult males are forever absent. More or less steady boyfriends (sometimes including the separated father, on visits which may or may not result in a marital reunion) pass in and out. Even if these men do not assume a central household role, the boys can obviously use them as source material for identifying male behavior. To be sure, this male role model is not a mainstream role model, but it still shows what males are like.

Furthermore, not only males can teach males about masculinity. Although role-modeling is probably essential, other social processes can contribute to identity formation. Mothers, grandmothers, aunts, and sisters who have observed men at close range have adopted expectations about the typical behavior of men which they express and which influence the boys in the household. The boys will come to share in the imagery of the women concerning men as they are exposed to women's conversations, and often they will find that men who are not regarded as good household partners (that is, in the mainstream male role) are still held to be attractive social companions. Thus the view is easily imparted that the hard men, good talkers, clothes-horses and all, are not altogether unsuccessful as males. The women also act more directly toward the boys in these terms—they have expectations of what men will do, and whether they wish the boys to follow in these steps or not, they instruct them in the model. Boys are advised not to "mess with" girls, which is at the same time emphasized as the natural thing which they will otherwise go out and do— and when the boys start their early adventures with the other sex, the older women may scold them but at the same time point out, not without satisfaction, that "boys will be boys." This kind of maternal (or at least adult female) instruction of young males, also noted by Abrahams (1964:28) and Keil (1966:23), is obviously a kind of altercasting (Weinstein and Deutschberger 1963), or more exactly, socialization to an alter role—that is, women cast boys in the role complementary to their own according to their experience of man-woman relationships. One single mother of three boys and two girls put it this way:

> You know, you just got to act a little bit tougher with boys than with girls, 'cause they just ain't the same. Girls do what you tell them to do and don't get into no trouble, but you just can't be sure about the boys. I mean, you think they're OK and next thing you find out they're playing hookey and drinking wine and maybe stealing things from cars and what not. There's just something bad about boys here, you know. But what can you say when many of them are just like their daddies? That's the man in them coming out. You can't really fight it, you know that's the way it is. They know, too. But you just got to be tougher.

This is some ways an antagonistic socialization, but it is built upon an expectation that it would be unnatural for men not to turn out to be in some ways bad—that is fighters, drinkers, lady killers, and so forth. There is one thing which is worse than a no-good man—the sissy, who is his opposite. A boy who seems weak is often reprimanded and ridiculed not only by peers but also by adults, including his mother and older sisters. The combination of role-modeling by peripheral fathers or temporary boyfriends with altercasting by adult women certainly provides for a measure of male role socialization within the family.

However, when I said that the view of the lack of models in the family was too narrow, I did not refer to the lack of insight into social processes in many matrifocal ghetto families so much as to the emphasis on the family as *the* information storage unit of a community's culture.[10] I believe it is an ethnocentrism on the part of middle class commentators to take it for granted that if information about sex roles is not transmitted from father to son within the family, it is not transmitted from generation to generation at all. There exists in American sociology, as well as in the popular mind, what Birdwhistell (1966) has termed a "sentimental model" of family life, according to which the family is an inward-turning isolate, meeting most of the needs of its members, and certainly the needs for sociability. The "sentimental model" is hardly ever realistic even as far as mainstream American families are concerned, and it has even less relevance for black ghetto life. Ghetto children live and learn out on the streets just about as much as within the confines of the home. Even if mothers, aunts, and sisters would not have streetcorner men as partners, there is an ample supply of them on the front staircase or down at the corner. Many of them have such a regular attendance record as to become quite familiar to children and are frequently very friendly with them. Thus again, there is no lack of adult men showing what adult men are like. It seems rather unlikely that one can deny all the role-modeling effect of these men on their young neighbors. Some of these men may be missing in the U.S. census records, but they are not missing in the ghetto community.

Much of the information gained about sex roles outside the family comes not from adult to child, however, but from persons in the same age bracket or only slightly higher. The idea of culture stored in lower age grades must be taken seriously. Many ghetto children start participating in the peer groups of the neighbourhood at an early age, often under the watchful eye of an elder sibling. In this way they are initiated into the culture of the peer group by interacting with children—predominantly of the same sex—who are only a little older than they are. And in the peer group culture of the boys, expressions of the male sex role are a highly salient feature. Some observers have felt that this is a consequence of the alleged sex role anxiety discussed briefly above. This may be true, of course, and it may have had an important part in the development of male peer group life as a dominant element of ghetto social structure. In the present situation, however, there is not necessarily such a simple psycho-social relationship. Most ghetto boys can hardly avoid getting into peer groups, and once they are in them they are efficiently socialized into a high degree of concern with their sex role. Much of the joking, the verbal contests, and more or less obscene singing among small ghetto boys—obligatory forms of interaction among them—serve to alienate them from dependence on mother figures and train them to the exploitative, somewhat antagonistic attitude toward women which is typical of streetcorner men. This is not to say the cultural situation is always very neat and clear-cut, and this is particularly obvious in the case of the kind of insult contest called "playing the dozens," "sounding," or in Washington, D.C., "joning," a form of ritualized interaction which is particularly common among boys in the early teens (for descriptions see Kochman in this book. See also Dollard 1939; Berdie 1947; Abrahams 1962b). When one boy says something unfavorable about another's mother, the other boy is expected either to answer in kind or fight, in a kind of defense of his honor (on which apparently that of his mother reflects). But the lasting impression is that there is something wrong about mothers—they are not as good as they ought to be ("Anybody can get pussy from your mother"), they take over male items of behavior and by implication too much of the male role ("Your mother smokes a pipe"). If standing up for one's family is the manifest expected consequence of "the dozens," then, it can apparently hardly be avoided that a latent function is a strengthening of the belief that ghetto women are not what they ought to be.[11] The other point of significance is that the criteria of judgment about what a good woman should be like are apparently mainstream-like. She should not be promiscuous, and she should stick to the mainstream-like female role and not be too dominant. The boys, then, are learning and strengthening a cultural ambivalence involving contradictions between ideal and reality in female behavior. We will return to a discussion of such cultural ambivalence later. But the point remains that even this game involves continuous learning and strengthening of a cultural definition of what women are like which is in some ways complementary to the definition of what men are like. And much of the songs, the talk, and the action—fighting, sneaking away with girls into a park or an alley, or drinking out of half-empty wine bottles stolen from or given away by adult men—are quite clearly preparations for the streetcorner male role. If boys and men show anxiety about their masculinity, one may suspect that this is induced as much by existing cultural standards as by the alleged nonexistence of models.[12]

This socialization within the male peer group is a continuing process; the talk that goes on, continuously or intermittently, in the sociable sessions of adult men at the street corner or on the front steps may deal occasionally with a football game or a human-interest story from the afternoon newspaper, but more often there are tales from personal experience about drinking adventures (often involving the police), about women won and lost, about feminine fickleness and the masculine guile which sometimes triumphs over it, about clothing or there may simply be comments on the women passing down the street: "Hi ugly ... don't try to swing what you ain't got."

This sociability within the male peer group, then, like much other sociability seems to be a culture-building process (Watson 1958). Shared definitions of reality are created out of the selected experiences of the participants. Women are nagging and hypocritical; you can't expect a union with one of them to last forever. Men are dogs; they have to run after many women. There is something between men and liquor; liquor makes hair grow on your chest. The regularity with which the same topics appear in peer group sociable conversation indicates that they have been established as the expected and appropriate subjects in this situation, to the exclusion of other topics.

> Mack asked me did I screw his daughter, so I asked, "I don't know, what's her name?" And then when I heard that gal was his daughter all right, I says, "Well, Mack, I didn't really have to take it, 'cause it was given to me." I thought Mack sounded like his daughter was some goddam white gal. But Mack says, "Well, I just wanted to hear it from you." Of course, I didn't know that was Mack's gal, 'cause she was married and had a kid, and so she had a different name.

But then you know the day after when I was out there a car drove by, and somebody called my name from it, you know, "hi darling," and that was her right there. So the fellow I was with says, "Watch out, Buddy will shoot your ass off." Buddy, that's her husband. So I says, "Yeah, but he got to find me first!"

Let me tell you fellows, I've been arrested for drunkenness more than two hundred times over the last few years, and I've used every name in the book. I remember once I told them I was Jasper Gonzales, and then I forgot what I had told them, you know. So I was sitting there waiting, and they came in and called Jasper Gonzales, and nobody answered. I had forgotten that's what I said, and to tell you the truth, I didn't know how to spell it. So anyway, nobody answered, and there they were calling "Jasper Gonzales! Jasper Gonzales!" So I thought that must be me, so I answered. But they had been calling a lot of times before that. So the judge said, "Mr. Gonzales, are you of Spanish descent?" And I said, "Yes, your honor, I came to this country thirty-four years ago." And of course I was only thirty-five, but you see I had this beard then, and I looked pretty bad, dirty and everything, you know, so I looked like sixty. And so he said, "We don't have a record on you. This is the first time you have been arrested?" So I said, "Yes, your honor, nothing like this happened to me before. But my wife was sick, and then I lost my job you know, and I felt kind of bad. But it's the first time I ever got drunk." So he said, "Well, Mr. Gonzales, I'll let you go, 'cause you are not like the rest of them here. But let this be a warning to you." So I said, "Yes, your honor." And then I went out, and so I said to myself "I'll have to celebrate this." So I went across the street from the court, and you know there are four liquor stores there, and I got a pint of wine and next thing I was drunk as a pig.

Were you here that time a couple of weeks ago when these three chicks from North Carolina were up here visiting Miss Gladys? They were really gorgeous, about 30–35. So Charlie says why don't we stop by the house and he and Jimmy and Deekay can go out and buy them a drink. So they say they have to go and see this cousin first, but then they'll be back. But then Brenda [Charlie's wife] comes back before they do, and so these girls walk back and forth in front of the house, and Charlie can't do a thing about it, except hope they won't knock on his door. And then Jimmy and Deekay come and pick them up, and Fats is also there, and the three of them go off with these chicks, and there is Charlie looking through his window, and there is Brenda looking at them too, and asking Charlie does he know who the chicks are.

Peer groups thus give some stability and social sanction to the meanings which street-corner men attach to their experiences—meanings which may themselves have been learned in the same or preceding peer groups. They, probably more than families, are information storage units for the ghetto-specific male role. At the same time, they are self-perpetuating because they provide the most satisfactory contexts for legitimizing the realities involved. In other words, they suggest a program for maleness, but they also offer a haven of understanding for those who follow that program and are criticized for it or feel doubts about it—and of course, all streetcorner males are more or less constantly exposed to the definitions and values of the mainstream cultural apparatus, so some cultural ambivalence can hardly be avoided. So if a man is a dog for running after women—as he is often said to be, among ghetto dwellers as among Otterbein's Andros Islanders, as quoted above—he wants to talk about it with other dogs who appreciate that this is a fact of life. If it is natural for men to drink, let it happen among other people who understand the nature of masculinity. Thus the group maintains constructions of reality, and life according to this reality maintains the group.[13]

It is hard to avoid the conclusion, then, that there is a cultural element involved in the sex role of streetcorner males, because expectations about it are manifestly shared and transmitted rather than individually evolved. (If the latter had been the case, of course, it would have been less accurate to speak of these as roles, since roles are by definition cultural.) This turns us to the second question stated above, about the co-existence of mainstream and ghetto-specific cultures. Streetcorner men certainly are aware of the ideal of mainstream male role performance—providing well for one's family, remaining faithful to one's spouse, staying out of trouble, and so on—and now and then everyone of them states it as his own ideal. What we find here, then, may be seen as a bi-cultural situation. Mainstream culture and ghetto-specific culture provide different models for living, models familiar to everyone in the ghetto. Actual behavior may lean more toward one model or more toward the other, or it may be some kind of mixture, at one point or over time. The ghetto-specific culture, including the streetcorner male role, is adapted to the situation and the experience of the ghetto dweller; it tends to involve relatively little idealization but offers shared expectations concerning self, others, and the environment. The mainstream culture, from the ghetto dweller's point of view, often involves idealization, but there is less real expectation that life will actually follow the paths suggested by it. This is not to say that the ghetto-specific culture offers no values at all of its own, or that nothing of mainstream culture ever appears realistic in the ghetto; but in those areas of life where the two cultures exist side by side as alternative guides to action (for naturally, the ghetto-specific culture, as distinct from mainstream culture, is not a "complete" culture covering all areas of life),[14] the ghetto-specific culture is often taken to forecast what one can actually expect from life, while the mainstream norms are held up as perhaps ultimately more valid but less attainable under the given situational constraints. "Sure it would be good to have a good job and a good home and your kids in college and all that, but you got to be yourself and do what you know." Of course, this often makes the ghetto-specific cultural expectations into self-fulfilling prophecies, as ghetto dwellers try to attain what they believe they can attain. (To be sure, self-fulfilling prophecies and realistic assessments may well coincide.)

On the whole, one may say that both mainstream culture and ghetto-specific culture are transmitted within many ghetto families. We have noted how socialization into the ghetto-specific male role within the household is largely an informal process, in which young boys may pick up bits and pieces of information about masculinity from the women in the house as well as from males who may make their entrances and exits in it. On the other hand, when adult women—usually mothers or grandmothers—really "tell the boys how to behave," they often try to instill in them mainstream, not to say puritan norms—drinking is bad, sex is dirty, and so forth. The male peer groups, as we have seen, are the strongholds of streetcorner maleness, although there are times when men cuss each other out for being "no good." Finally, of course, mainstream culture is transmitted in contacts with the outside world, such as in school or through the mass media. It should be added, though, that the latter may be used selectively to strengthen some elements of the streetcorner male role; ghetto men are drawn to Westerns, war movies, and crime stories both in the movie house and on their TV sets.

As mentioned above, even if the nature of

men's allegiance to the two cultures makes it reasonably possible to adhere, after a fashion, to both at the same time, as in the last statement quoted, the bi-cultural situation of streetcorner males involves some ambivalence. The rejection of mainstream culture as a guide to action rather than only a lofty ideal is less than complete. Of course, acting according to one or the other of the two cultures to a great extent involves bowing to the demands of the social context, so that situational selectivity from the point of view of the actor plays a part in guiding his behavior. A man whose concerns in the peer group milieu are drinking and philandering will try to be "good" in the company of his mother or his wife and children, even if a complete switch is hard to bring about. There also are peer groups, of course, which are more mainstream-oriented than others, although even the members of these groups are affected by streetcorner definitions of maleness. To some extent, then, the varying allegiance of different peer groups to the two cultures is largely a difference of degree, as the following statement by a young man implies.

> Those fellows down at the corner there just keep drinking and drinking. You know, I think it's pretty natural for a man to drink, but they don't try to do nothing about it, they just drink every hour of the day, every day of the week. My crowd, we drink during the weekend, but we can be on our jobs again when Monday comes.

Contextual culture change on the part of a man can then also be brought about by a change of peers—and there are men who move from one group to another with concomitant changes of behavior.

However, although situational selectivity brings some order into the picture of this bi-cultural situation, it is still one of less than perfect stability. The drift between contexts is itself not something to which men are comitted by demands somehow inherent in the social structure. Ghetto men may spend more time with the family, or more time with the peer group, and the extent to which they choose one or the other, and make a concomitant cultural selection, still appears to depend considerably on personal attachment to roles, and to changes in it.[15] The social alignments of a few men may illustrate this. One man, Norman Hawkins, a construction laborer, spends practically all his leisure time at home with his family, only occasionally joining in the streetcorner conversations and behavior of the peer group to which his neighbor, Harry Jones, belongs. Harry Jones, also a construction worker, is also married and has a family but stays on the periphery of household life, although he lives with his wife and children. Some of the other men in the group are unmarried or separated and so seldom play the "family man" role which Harry Jones takes on now and then. Harry's younger brother, Carl, also with a family, used to participate intensively in peer group life until his drinking led to a serious ailment, and after he recuperated from this he started spending much less time with his male friends and more with his family. Bee Jay, a middle-aged bachelor who was raised by his grandmother, had a job at the post office and had little to do with street life until she died. Since then, he has become intensively involved with a tough, hard-drinking group and now suffers from chronic health problems connected with his alcoholism. Thus we can see how the life careers of some ghetto men take them through many and partly unpredictable shifts and drifts between mainstream and ghetto-specific cultures, while others remain quite stable in one allegiance or other.

The sociocultural situation in the black ghetto is clearly complicated. The community shows a great heterogeneity of life styles; individuals become committed to some degree to different ways of being by the impersonally enforced structural arrangements to which they are subjected, but unpredictable contingencies have an influence, and their personal attachments to life styles also vary. The socio-economic conditions impose limits on the kinds of life ghetto dwellers may have, but these kinds of life are culturally transmitted and shared as many individuals in the present, and many in the past, live or have lived under the same premises. When the latter is the case, it is hardly possible to invent new adaptations again and again, as men are always observing one another and interacting with one another. The implication of some of Frazier's writings, that ghetto dwellers create their way of life in a cultural limbo—an idea which has had more modern expressions— appears as unacceptable in this case as in any other situation where people live together, and in particular where generations live together. The behavior of the streetcorner male is easily experienced as a natural pattern of masculinity with which ghetto dwellers grow up and which to some extent they grow into. To see it only as a complex of unsuccessful attempts at hiding failures by self-deception seems, for many of the men involved, to be too much psychologizing and too little sociology. But this does not mean that the attachment to the ghetto-specific culture is very strong among its bearers. Rodman's concept of a lower class value stretch is a realistic statement of many ghetto dwellers' cultural involvement:[16]

> Lower-class persons in close interaction with each other and faced with similar problems do not long remain in a state of mutual ignorance. They do not maintain a strong commitment to middle-class values that they cannot attain, and they do not continue to respond to others in a rewarding or punishing way simply on the basis of whether these others are living up to the middle-class values. A change takes place. They come to tolerate and eventually to evaluate favorably certain deviations from the middle-class values. In this way, they need not be continually frustrated by their failure to live up to unattainable values. The resultant is a stretched value system with a low degree of commitment to all the values within the range, including the dominant, middle-class values" (Rodman 1963:209).

The question of whether streetcorner males have mainstream culture or a specific-ghetto culture, then, is best answered by saying that they have both, in different ways. There can be little doubt that this is the understanding most in line with that contemporary trend in anthropological thought which emphasizes the sharing of cultural imagery, of expectations and definitions of reality, as the medium whereby individuals in a community interact. It is noteworthy that many of the commentators who have been most skeptical of the idea of a ghetto-specific culture, or more generally a "culture of poverty," have been those who have taken a more narrow view of culture as a set of values about which an older generation consciously instructs the younger ones in the community. Thus Valentine (1968:113) hypothesizes that

> "... lower-class life does not actually constitute a distinct sub-culture in the sense often used by poverty analysts, because it does not embody any design for living to which people give sufficient allegiance or emotional involvement to pass it on to their children."

Roach and Gursslin (1967:387–88) too, in their critique of the "culture of poverty" concept, imply that cultural transmission invariably involves a strong normative system. Obviously, the answer to whether there is a ghetto-specific culture or not will depend to some extent on what we shall mean by culture. Perhaps this is too important a question to be affected by a mere terminological quibble, and perhaps social policy, in some areas, may well proceed unaffected by the questions raised by a ghetto-specific culture. On the other hand, in an anthropological study of community life, the wider view of cultural sharing and transmission which has been used here will have to play a part in our picture of the ghetto, including that of what ghetto males are like.

NOTES

1. This paper is based on fieldwork in a black low-income neighborhood in Washington, D.C., between 1966 and 1968. The study was made possible by a grant from the Carnegie Corporation to the Urban Language Study of the Center for Applied Linguistics. An earlier version was presented at the 66th annual meeting of the American Anthropological Association, Washington, D.C., December 3, 1967. The subject of ghetto sex roles will be dealt with more extensively in the author's forthcoming book, *Soulside: Inquiries into Ghetto Culture and Community*.

Those portions which are quotations of ghetto dwellers derive from notes made as soon as possible after the statements were made. They are probably quite accurate in terms of content and vocabulary but should not be taken to give any indication of the phonology and the syntax of the actual speech.

2. The term "black" will generally be used here for ethnic identification, in line with the current trend of preference among at least younger and more politically aware Negroes in the U. S.

3. For a recent criticism of pejorative elements in the Frazier tradition of family studies see Valentine (1968).

4. Rainwater's essay offers a social-psychological functional interpretation of the "expressive life style" which largely complements the perspective of cultural dynamics offered here.

5. The apt term "streetcorner men" is used by Liebow (1967), who may have derived it from Whyte (1943).

6. The network, as the term is used here, is an "ego-centric" social structure—that is, one takes as a point of departure one person and traces his relationships. The definitions in the works quoted are somewhat variable, but this seems to be the general use of the concept.

7. Admittedly, to some extent both Keil and Liebow introduce qualifications. Keil points to the influence of long-lasting poverty and oppression in shaping black culture, but he implies that at the present point of cultural development the ghetto dweller's culture is quite independent of mainstream culture. Liebow (1967: 223) writes: "No doubt, each generation does provide role models for each succeeding one." Immediately thereafter, however, he dismisses the point as unimportant.

8. Matrifocality is defined here in behavioral rather than compositional terms—if the household affairs are female-dominated, it is a matrifocal household even if a marginal husband-father resides in it. Viewed this way, of course, matrifocality becomes a matter of degree.

9. Another aspect of the impact of matrifocality on children in a black community was discussed from an anthropological vantage point by Powdermaker (1939:197), where she also pointed to the difficulties with cross-cultural psychological inferences: "There is little if any indication that the fatherless household among these Negroes tends to result in the kind of psychological complications which clinical workers have come to associate with middle-class white households where there is no father. The economic situation is one guard against this. The Negro mother usually works out during the day, or, if she is home, she is extremely busy doing her own work or the washing she takes in from outside. She lacks time, opportunity and energy to lavish on her children the over-protection which leads to those emotional difficulties characteristic of certain fatherless white families. Equally important is the circumstance that most mothers, even in households which lack a man, do not want for sexual outlet, and therefore are not impelled to seek from their children some substitute for the satisfaction normally derived from a mate."

10. The notion of social groupings as information storage units of culture has been introduced and explored by Roberts (1964).

11. The distinction between manifest and latent functions is, of course, that suggested by Merton (1957:19 ff.).

12. This means that even if peer groups and their culture meet a need for some anxious males, as is generally suggested, they are a part of the ghetto scene which demands adjustment to its standards also by males without such prior anxiety, as a price of a membership which may be difficult to avoid. Whether fathers are present or not, the peer group sets its own model of masculinity for members. Some writers, such as Rohrer and Edmonson (1960), seem to be on the verge of recognizing the peer group as a reality *sui generis* in the socialization of boys, but they are still reluctant to admit that sexual identity anxiety is not necessarily the first-order determinant. In their picture, peer group life seems forever invented anew as an answer to this psychological need. Yet the rituals of this life shows that there is a lively cultural tradition.

13. A relevant statement on conversation as an instrument for the maintenance of social reality is that by Berger and Luckmann (1966:140 ff.).

14. One may, of course, prefer to speak of the ghetto-specific sub-culture. The amount of analytical sharpening which the sub-culture concept has brought to sociology and anthropology has not been impressive, however, so using it consistently here may not have balanced the clumsiness of expression which it would have added. It should be clear, however, that ghetto-specific culture consists only of a relatively small number of cultural items and complexes compared to the amount of general American culture which ghetto dwellers and others share.

15. In adherence to Goffman's definitions (1961:88–9), *commitment* to a role refers here to impersonal structural arrangements which force an individual to certain lines of action, while *attachment* refers to a person's being "affectively and cognitively enamored, desiring and expecting to see himself in terms of the enactment of the role and the self-identification emerging from this enactment."

16. Rodman's "commitment" seems to equal Goffman's "attachment;" cf. note 15.

Eighteen

STRATEGIES OF ADAPTIVE MOBILITY IN THE COLOMBIAN-ECUADORIAN LITTORAL[1]

Norman E. Whitten, Jr.

Reproduced by permission of the American Anthropological Association from the *American Anthropologist* (1969), Vol. 71, No. 2.

THEORETICAL AND METHODICAL INTRODUCTION

Since the publication of Andrew Whiteford's (1960) book on class in Popayán, Colombia, and Querétaro, Mexico, there has been an increasing cry for more studies of Latin American stratification (cf. Erasmus 1961b: 843–45). Standing against the tide to delineate the social strata is Richard N. Adams with his contention that, essentially, there is no class conscious middle sector in most of Latin America (1967:47–53). Adams overstates his point to make an important contribution; namely, that the study of strata themselves tells us little about a society without a self-conscious perpetuating, stable, middle sector. Social mobility, the exercise of power, and the tactics adopted to support survival and to advance define the daily machinations of Latin Americans, not the socio-economic "class" within which they fall. The purpose of this paper is to analyze aspects of socio-economic mobility in the Pacific Littoral of Colombia and Ecuador in such a way as to refine perspectives on social organizational features of people at the bottom of an economic hierarchy. A refinement of perspectives, which should supplement a stratification model, is necessary if anthropologists are to describe effectively lower strata in national class systems, for it seems that it is among the lower strata of such systems that models focusing on the class hierarchy have the least explanatory value.

In general, a stratification model groups families in a hierarchal arrangement according to a set of variables (cf. Kahl 1957; 1965; Young and Young n.d.; Ossowski 1963; 121–44) and regards mobility as gaining power over the control of chances in certain spheres of activity (Lenski 1966:74–75). To supplement such a model, I shall focus on a sequence of strategies for coping with the coping with the socio-economic environment, suggesting that by understanding the *probable sequence of successful* strategies, we should be better able to portray relationships and linkages among complementary groupings within a particular socio-economic environment.

I will focus on strategies of socio-economic mobility of people who, by national standards of Colombia and Ecuador, fall into the "lower class." The stratification model implies that the power of lower class persons over events influencing their well-being is minimal vis-à-vis other groups. The stratification model is convenient and efficient, but it is not productive because within any particular residential community in the Pacific Littoral lower class people view their system as internally differentiated. This differentiation can be described in terms of the social strategies which people adopt in the process of mobility. These strategies often appear to contradict one another within a community, and the apparent contradictions define three sectors made up of aggregates of people differentiated by the means by which they cope with national economic, social, and political orders. The three sectors are: the lower class peasants, the lower class proletariat, and the *local* entrepreneurial middle class. Again, it must be stressed that "middle class" refers to an *intra-community perspective*. It is a cultural category which is necessarily labeled in order to understand upward striving and emulation, but should not be confused with *national* socio-economic strata. The three sectors are bound by the strategies used by particular groupings of people passing through a social mobility sequence in which "peasant organization" transforms to "proletariat organization" and "proletariat organization" becomes realized in the activi-

ties of the local entrepreneurs. The various organizations are seen as parts of the same social structure (Firth 1951:35–40), and the mobility sequence is viewed as a developmental cycle.

At this point it is necessary to be clear on the use of terminology. I use *strategy* in the Webster's Third sense of "skill in managing and planning." Skill does not necessarily imply a conscious long-range plan. The game style of a people at a given time may be judged strategic, or not strategic. One can determine, for example, that at a certain time, kinsmen are an economic drag and it is strategic to dispose of them; at another time the same kinsmen could provide economic security and it would be judged strategic to cultivate them. The general strategy could be stated in terms of the skill and planning needed to tap kinsmen when needed, but to withhold from them when they are a burden. *Tactics* are skillful methods used to gain an end. The way in which an individual either mobilizes his kinsmen for security, or gets rid of them when they respresent a burden, would be tactical.

A *developmental cycle* is, essentially, a model of social structure, or an aspect of social structure, built out of phases; one phase is conceived of as developing out of another, the whole replicating cycle representing the structure. A *phase* is a particular organization, at a particular time, perceived as deriving from a prior phase and being in the process of evolving into a subsequent phase. To date, the concept of developmental cycle has been used to describe household and family structure (Fortes 1958; Goody 1958; Smith 1956), to understand hamlet and kindred structure (Goodenough 1962; Whitten 1965), and to present the development of family business (Hunt 1965). Recently, Gluckman (1965:277) suggests that political process should be conceived of as sequences of developmental cycles within "structural time" (see also Evans-Pritchard 1940; Leach 1954).

By understanding a developmental cycle of successful movement through a succession of strategies, one can understand more clearly what the structure of power and economic competition is within any community. Without a developmental cycle model of successful strategies, a distorted idea of social disorganization at the community level would probably be presented by any observer seeking regularities within a "lower stratum." An example of such a negative explanatory device in the Pacific lowlands is Mallol de Recassens (1963); Judith Blake's approach to the Jamaican family (1961) also suffers from this approach.

Probably one of the great problems of research within a lower stratum is that people at the bottom have a sequence of strategies to play to move out of the stratum. When strategies appear to contrast, or to contradict one another, the data puzzle investigators. Investigators all too often confuse developmental cycle phases with hierarchical stages and fail to ask the crucial methodological question: "To what phases of a cycle do the contrasting strategies belong?" Frequently, the label "disorganized" or "random" is given to lower class strivers in a frustrated effort to "explain" their lifeways (see Blake 1961; Henry 1965).

The study of strategy implies the study of power, for according to Richard N. Adams (1965:268), "Power lies in the ability to manipulate events and people so that things turn up to your advantage." As Gerhard Lenski (1965) points out, it is crucial to have a concept of power if one is to understand any stratified system, *as a system*. In this paper I wish to distinguish processes that involve economic power, social power, and political power, and so I will adopt Max Weber's analytical terminology and regard "class" as the life chances of people as the result of their objective economic situation, "status" as the shared style of life determined by the amount of "social honor" people have attained, and "party" as actual groups whose action "is oriented toward the acquisition of power . . . toward influencing communal action" (Weber 1958:180–85).

ETHNOGRAPHIC INTRODUCTION

Before moving to the model of successful strategies which contribute to the process of adaptive mobility, a brief ethnographic introduction is necessary. Although Thomas J. Price (1966:1548) notes that my earlier discussion (Whitten 1965) can be applied to the Chocó of Colombia, I am unsure of such an extension. My data will include the large and small towns, and some of the hinterland from the San Juan River, Colombia, south to the Esmeraldas River, Ecuador. The major port towns include Guapi, Iscuandé, San Lorenzo, and Limones. Larger river towns, Timbiquí and Barbacoas, and smaller river towns such as Naya, Mitay, Borbón, and Maldonaldo fit the model, while the only hinterland areas in which I have had sufficient experience to generalize my model with a degree of moderate certainty are the areas drained by the Raposo, Telembí, Santiago, and Cayapas rivers, and the island of Gallo north of Tumaco.

The economic structure of the Pacific Littoral is based on the exploitation of forest and sea resources. Such exploitation is sporadic, best portrayed in any area, at any period of time, as a succession of boom and depression periods. For example, in different areas, at different times, there have been booms centering on gold, rubber, bananas, tagua, timber, fish, and shellfish, and sometimes on secondary booms such as those brought about by road, railroad, and port construction, and by shipping and heightened commercial activity. *Within any phase of a life cycle of an individual, or developmental cycle of a group, the only constant to which individual or organization must adapt is economic fluctuation.* In order to set the developmental cycle of adaptive mobility in its sociopolitical as well as geographic and economic context, I will very briefly sketch the sociocultural sectors within which people cope with Pacific lowlands economy, using a standard stratification model.

First, there is the absentee elite, whom I shall mention only to say that I know very little about them. They are Europeans and mestizos who do not live in the rainforest or on the rainforest coast, and seldom visit the region. They live in such cities as Cali, Bogotá, Quito, and Guayaquil. Their involvement in coastal affairs is large-scale and long-range. Normally, they own major interests in logging or shipping and use political advantage for economic gain. Fluctuation itself at the local level would not affect the local elite.

Second, the managerial and entrepreneurial white and mestizo upper class are the *local* elite of any community, although at any given time particular communities may not have such a local elite. They are politically flexible and are the *apparent* loci of coastal economic and political power. They are totally involved in the fluctuating money economy, for they are the ones who make large immediate gains, and also fall victim to depression periods, always running the risk of large-scale failure, through either direct economic loss or loss of political control. Such a managerial and entrepreneurial upper class ranges from political appointees to speculators in lumber and shipping. Ethnically they are European and mestizo.

There are also some Negroes and what I call "light Costeños" in this sector. In the Pacific lowlands color is significant from the standpoint of the highlanders and Europeans, but it is not part of the ethnic perspective of the Negro Costeños. People whom I label "light Costeños" often regard themselves as ethnically "mulato" or "blanco" vis-à-vis highlanders, but ethnically "moreno"(Negro) vis-à-vis Negro Costeños. I will return to the Negro and light Costeño division of this sector below, since it represents an intriguing organizational adaptation.

Third, the professional "middle class," to be found in any community, includes engineers, medical doctors and assistants, and lawyers; normally those who failed in the interior because of professional inability, political conflicts, or lack of economic capital to begin a profitable practice. Occasionally they are only temporarily engaged in a coastal project and are transient. The salary paid such individuals is sufficient to maintain respectability and moderate security in the interior and on the coast, but is insufficient for investment in coastal life, unless socio-economic attachment to highland life is severed. Ethnically mestizo, and occasionally European, the majority of people in this class retain a home in the interior, usually visiting with their families only on special holidays and vacations.

Fourth, the entrepreneurial middle class includes local middlemen for forest products, cash farmers, local businessmen, and middlemen bridging political parties. The entrepreneurial middle class deals heavily in "social capital"[2] to cement their positions and continue in a middle-range sector during times of relative depression. Most of the entrepreneurial middle class are Negro and light Costeño, although increasing numbers of highland and coastal mestizos and an occasional European can be found in this position. Socially, however, until very recently, such people became involved by affinity in the Negro-light Costeño way of life.

Fifth and sixth, the proletariat poor is made up of those dependent on money for their survival, while the peasant poor include the mass of people who engage in activities bringing a direct cash gain only insofar as such activities complement and do not impinge upon continuing subsistence work such as fishing and farming.

Seventh, the tribal poor are the Cayapa, Chocó, Noanamá Indians who, except for culture content, live a life similar to, but more closed than, that of the Negro peasants.[3]

STRATEGIES OF ADAPTIVE MOBILITY

Direct power over economic resources is impossible for the mass of Costeños. Survival for peasant, proletariat, and middle-class entrepreneur is contingent upon mobility. At any place, at any time, inputs from the externally generated money economy may rapidly dwindle, becoming insufficient to support a population, or a given organization within a population. There are three "types" of mobility that permit individuals, families, and larger groupings to survive: *spatial mobility* where people move either to establish a new farm, seek a better fishing ground, or a better short run job; *horizontal mobility* where individuals gather around a traditional work group head, support his drive to high social status while leveling his economic income; and *vertical mobility* through which individuals and aggregates move upward within a community by consolidating social capital to exploit economic and political opportunities. All three forms of mobility are complementary, and each is defined by differential usage of social capital during a developmental cycle.

All the strategies employed by Negroes and light Costeños can be described in terms of their tactical opening, closing, and breaking of dyadic contracts, usually within a network of real, ritual, or fictive kinsmen. Dyadic contracts, according to George Foster (1961:1174) are "informal, or implicit, since they lack ritual or legal basis." In the Pacific Littoral dyadic contracts are established when ego proffers a prestation— a gift, an offer to give, or a token such as a shot of aguardiente—and alter withholds thanks thereby implicitly establishing an open contract for future reciprocity. Should alter thank ego, the contact is regarded as closed by ego: only when alter refuses the prestation, or when ego asks alter for help and alter refuses is the contract broken (see Whitten 1968). Implicit contracts are made explicit through networks of gossip by the ego proffering the prestation.

Open contracts in the Pacific lowlands take on a serial character If a man cannot repay a debt when his assistance is needed, but wants to keep his dyadic contract open, he asks others to help; if they agree, all parties to the agreement enter into a relationship that amounts to a series of open contracts.

The adaptive significance of kinship among Negro peasants and proletariat is bound to the ability of kinsmen to manipulate dyadic relationships. The dispersed lower class kindred makes possible spatial mobility which is essential in a subsistence economy with shifting cultivation and a marginal, fluctuating money economy. When traveling, a Negro peasant or proletariat ordinarily chooses a route that takes him from relative to relative. Travel is hard and travelers always press on strongly, sometimes moving for 16 or 24 hours at a time with little rest. Arriving at a kinsman's home, they move in with scant greeting, usually expecting a drink and then a long sleep. There is no opportunity for host to refuse the host role, and the guest is too tired to haggle over time and obligation. By the time the guest awakens, the host has made it known to neighbors that the guest has moved in with him and that he has had to sacrifice much to accommodate his kinsman. The ensuing sentiments are that the guest has placed himself in debt to his host.

During such travel, a Costeño will be fed and housed for as long as he cares to stay. He reciprocates directly by contributing to the household, and indirectly by obligating himself to extend similar courtesies to his host and to persons to whom his hosts are obligated. Incidentally, the traveler is also in a good position to help the host work out his animosities. Since he is not a permanent resident of the village, town, or settlement, he is not under any residential obligation to respect the property of others and so may steal from an enemy of the host. Also, as a stranger he is regarded as fair game by others of the community, especially on the eve of his departure. A guest must reciprocate when called upon, either personally or through friends and relatives who owe him something. There is really no closed contract for dispersed contractants—one either leaves the contract open, or breaks it.

Within a community, however, closure is an alternative. Reciprocal obligations can be closed on good faith only by cash payments for labor. Negro peasants and proletariat do not expect cash payment from recognized members of a personal kindred. A man in need of something will first approach a member of his personal kindred. Series of reciprocal obligations bind the localized segment of the personal kindred together, just as a series of reciprocal obligations incurred through spatial mobility bind the dispersed segments. It is by economic reciprocity and the serial nature of such reciprocity that the kindred is most readily definable at a given time. A Costeño would feel that he "had to" house members of his personal kindred if he were asked, and that he would "want to" help them if help were needed.

For relatively localized peasants and proletariat the strategy is normally to close local contracts that press on a household and to open as many contracts as possible that provide for spatial mobility. This strategy, in turn, may produce a "bind," for a strategy oriented toward maintaining spatial dispersion functions to economically drain reciprocating kinsmen if spatial mobility is provided for, but not actualized. With all one's energies oriented toward exploitation of the local resources, the time and motivation to move may be weakened. This weakening, plus the exploitation by dispersed relatives of the localized person's household resources (which reflect his ability to exploit the local situation) serve as a constant drain and provide an unsatisfactory insurance policy. What good are dispersed relatives providing for spatial mobility if the townsman does not want to relocate, and feels he can do well to remain settled?

There is a solution to the necessity to move within a fluctuating money economy, and to remain in one's residential community where specific techniques for the exploitation of varied resources may be developed through a long period of time. The solution is to move upward by extending power over the resources themselves. To understand the process of vertical socio-economic mobility, it is helpful to recognize another kind of contract, the asymmetrical, referring to socio-economic exchange patterns between people of different socio-economic statuses. These are characterized by the contractants' owing different kinds of things (Foster 1961:1174; Fallers 1965:135–37). For the Negroes and other Costeños of the Pacific Littoral, it is a matter of social honor that contracts operate assymetrically between persons of different economic standing. Negroes and light Costeños expect one another to reciprocate according to their *apparent* means. *A man who has more is supposed to give proportionately more than a man who has less.* What this may mean is that as social power increases, conspicuous giving also increases, the net effect being horizontal, not vertical, mobility.

An excellent illustration of this leveling process (which I characterize as a process of horizontal mobility) is that of the timber *minga* of northwest Ecuador and parts of western Colombia (also known as *Winúl* in southwest Colombia). Essentially, the minga party is composed of from 8 to 20 men, all of whom claim that they are working with one leader (*jefe de la minga*) only for the duration of one, short-range (a week to three weeks) work party. The work rationale is that there is a rotation of leaders within the party each of whom will, in turn, organize a party and take all the profit. In actual practice, there are few minga heads within any community or area. The same heads organize parties again and again, and generally the same men work for them. The minga head *always* takes the profit for himself; the men *always* say that they work for him because he will one day go on their minga (see Whitten 1965:69–74; Erasmus 1956:449).

Although momentary profit may be his, sustained economic advantage is lost. To keep his prestige position and power over his workmen, the minga head must be characterized by his *conspicuous giving* (Erasmus 1961a:101–34) which keeps him solidly in the lower proletariat sector despite entrepreneurial activities and occasional large earnings. His social status does not establish an avenue for economic mobility. The minga head, after a minga, owes favors to workers' families and members of their personal kindreds. He "loans" money, and buys liquor as a gift to groups of men; the men in turn distribute the shots of their aguardiente to kinsmen as tokens of reciprocity. The minga host converts his economic resources into power and prestige over those who work on the mingas he organizes. He is the center of an interesting network functioning in an economic context. The highest expressions of network interaction are the occasional money-earning mingas undertaken by the core group led by the minga head.

It seems that the ideal of rotating hosts cannot exist given economic fluctuations— any such system could not continue through depression periods. One or another host would be constantly left, on the one hand, with a series of obligations which he could not meet and, on the other hand, with a string of credits which he could not realize. By holding one man perpetually responsible, and by rewarding him with high status while at the same time draining his economic capital so as to thwart the development of paternalism, a viable adaptation in the area of group organization and labor recruitment is made to a fluctuating economic situation in the Pacific lowlands.[5]

From the illustration drawn from data on the lumber minga, it should be clear that conspicuous display of material possessions by the upward-mobile or middle class man should result in economic leveling. This actual economic threat imposed by cultural expectations of assymetrical redistribution necessitates an examination of the strategies employed by the successful. The process which I shall now describe is that of vertical mobility in which people move upward through a sequence of strategies to gain increasingly direct power over local sociopolitical resources, and use such power to gain indirect control over economic activities.

In the following model of the developmental cycle of successful strategies, I shall present a mobility model (Fig. 18-1) modified from the one presented in my book (1965). I will not be writing about the process of mobility itself, as much as of the changing and contrasting strategy sequence used to move from one local stratum to another. Hopefully, the diagram will help the reader to follow the scheme of generational mobility. I begin by considering a segment of a lower class kindred which has become localized. By "localized" I refer to a segment of a lower class kindred which has developed intra-community networks to exploit local economic resources, and which has sufficient exploitative ties to make spatial mobility difficult. In the course of localization, peasant concern with exploitation of surrounding natural resources transforms to a proletarian concern with the cash resources of a community. I refer to this situation as the first generation of vertical mobility, since localization is the first tactical move toward increased power over sociopolitical resources. This does not mean that upward mobility is the immediate design of those people who are characterized as "localized"—It does mean, however, that in a sequence of strategies, the basis of mobility is localization.

On the diagram the couple within the pyramid is, with the process of localization, becoming proletariat, while members of the dispersed personal kindred outside of the pyramid may be either proletariat or peasant, or both.

First Generation

In the first generation two complementary strategies are employed: (1) Settlers maintain open contracts within a circle of recognized kinsmen to provide social capital insurance. (2) They develop direct economic resources (shop, farm) at the local level to build tenuous economic autonomy within the community. Commercial activities keep the participants settled in one place, while serial dyadic contracts remain open with a dispersed personal kindred or overlapping personal kindreds. Although the successful, settled group makes more money than their relatives, the leveling effect of open symmetrical dyadic contracts with a number of kinsmen keeps the members of the first generation from advancing economically. Also, because their work (keeping a small shop, working a small farm, keeping on the good side of local politicians, and tax collectors) ties them to one place, their own spatial mobility is restricted, although they continue to contribute to the spatial mobility of others. The fluctuating money economy necessitates the combination of strategies, however, for even though economically leveled, the localized group is relatively secure. For example, during hard times I have seen an entire shop stocked with prestations (including bananas, pineapples, wooden bowls, canoe paddles, clay pipes, cigars, bark mats, rope, dynamite, dried fish, and fire fans) from hinterland relatives.

Second Generation

As children of the first generation reach adulthood, they may move to another town

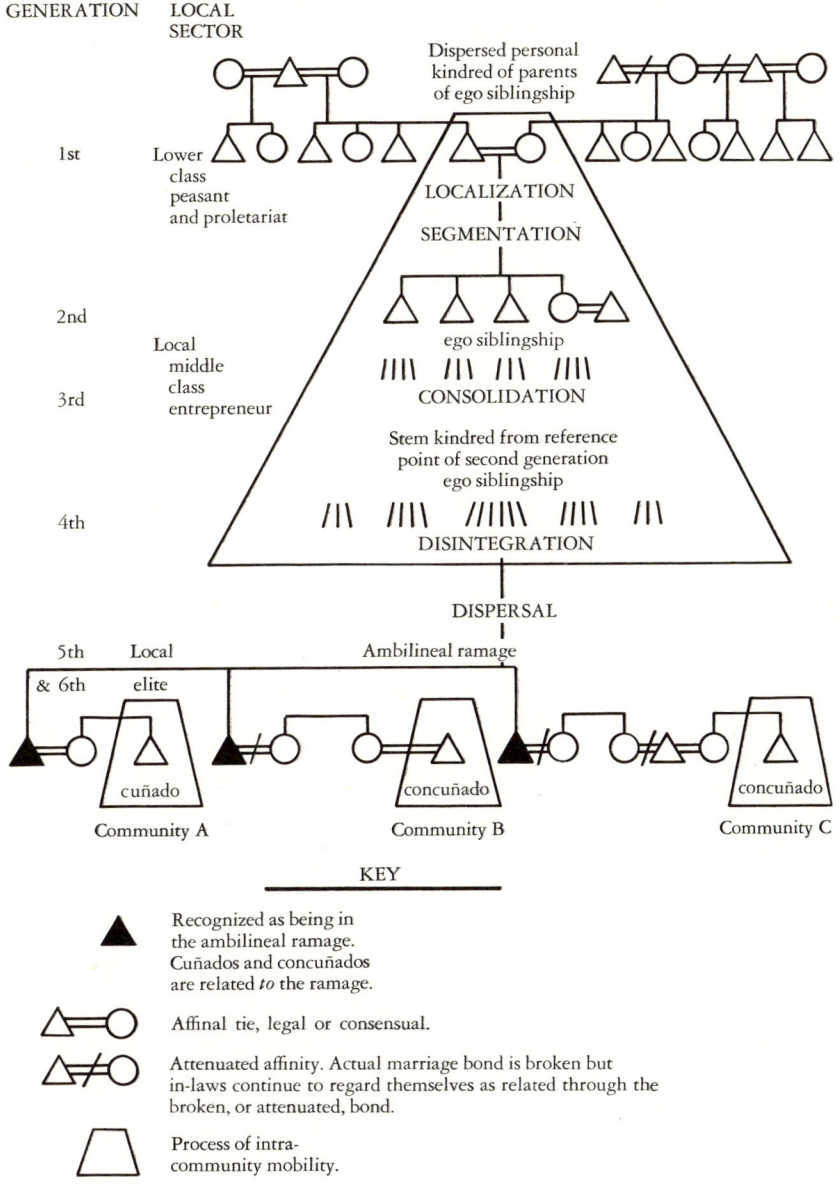

FIGURE 18-1. Kinship and Socio-economic Mobility: A Model

or settlement, or participate in the game of horizontal mobility. If they choose to stay, *and* if they seek economic advance, then a strategic rearrangement of capital resources *must* be made. The second generation success strategies may be stated in terms of liquidating dispersed social capital, thus providing for spatial mobility and developing localized sociopolitical capital to further upward socio-economic mobility. Political and social power within a community offer alternatives to the security of the dispersed network of kinsmen. Children of the settlers "cash in" their social capital with the dispersed kindred and invest time taken from direct economic pursuits to seek political influence. They incorporate non-kin into an economic unit through polygyny, thereby leaving themselves free for politics. While women tend the shop, buy or beg products to sell, work small farms, and engage in local gossip (sometimes leading to information about prospective new economic inputs from the externally generated cash economy), men loiter around the local officials' offices and homes, talk to the rural police, and perhaps give some information which may result in a bit of a "pay off" (*el mame* or *la ají*).

In time, party politics becomes increasingly important and men spend a good deal of their effort in learning about the networks of political influence with the inevitable economic parallels. Some capital is expended on the children's education and dress to enhance the social prestige of the rising groups. Finally, all able-bodied members of the *local* kindred, including affines, contribute to one another's economic advance. The contributing, reciprocating members define their own boundaries and let it be known throughout the community who is a member of the "family" and who is not. Ties are reckoned through the second generation siblingship, the family name of the male loci being used (the family name may be taken from the brother's father, or mother, or prestigious brother of one of their mothers).

Within a particular town the kindred is definitely established as upward-mobile, and members enter the local middle class as they continue shopkeeping and expand commercial interests. They are especially active in buying forest and sea products from lower class Negroes and Indians, people who would have dealt on a prestation basis with their parents, and marketing them later at a profit. Consensual polygyny, which reaches its height in this generation, makes possible considerable diversification of economic and political activities. Normally, only one wife will reflect the social prestige of her husband, while the others will further his economic well-being. The upward-mobile do not appear to be gaining in cash value, and claim never to have a *centavo* to loan or give, except within the kindred, and for political influence.

Third Generation

As the children of the second generation reach adulthood and begin to participate in the social, economic, and political life of the community, strategies again alter. By the third generation the kindred has achieved a prominence vis-à-vis other community members. As it takes on a corporate character, its perpetuation becomes dependent on consolidation of its socio-economic interests. The strategy adopted by the successful to allow consolidation without leveling side effects is to *be indirectly involved in everything*. The complementary tactics making up this strategy can be stated as follows: focus on genealogical ties within the "stem kindred" (Davenport 1959; Whitten 1965) (reckoning from the second generation siblingship); draw together in a section of town; compete for social honor within the community; break contracts with previous affines and their relatives except those very high in social honor and those with accessible economic capital; avoid direct political involvement and use symbols of social prestige together with money to influence political activities; and finally, make asymmetrical dyadic contracts upward with those people who control aspects of the economy, and with those competing with the controllers, and extend asymmetrical contracts downward to rising second generation kindreds and to lower class peasants and proletarians central to horizontal mobility. (These people are the loci for traditional labor organizations [see Whitten 1965:69–74].)

A sketchy example of such activities is drawn from San Lorenzo, Ecuador, during the time of the establishment of the coastal-highland link created by the Ibarra-San Lorenzo section of the Quito-San Lorenzo railroad. At this time newly arriving managerial and entrepreneurial highlanders badly needed wood for building. Young men, overtly "non-political," who were the children of the reference points of the then dominant middle class kindred (whom I shall call the Arisalas) offered to help the newcomers. By offering aid to the highlanders, these members achieved the favored bottom half of an asymmetrical contract. They then extended favors downward to lower class minga heads—they made loans, and opened a few political avenues of graft to the minga heads thereby increasing the rapidity of the latters' horizontal mobility.

At that time San Lorenzo had reached its period of most rapid growth and wood was at a premium. The *Junta Autónoma del Ferrocarril* (agency responsible for the development of the lands adjoining the railroad, as well as the railroad itself) had established a small sawmill in the center of town and needed timber. Also, the agency had to work on limited funds and could not afford to compete with the lumber speculators already at work in the area around San Lorenzo.

Newly arrived entrepreneurs from the Sierra charged with getting San Lorenzo moving soon found that the mention of the need for timber (or information) in one of the shops owned by the parents of the helpful young Arisala men often led to rapid delivery at a low cost. The highlanders did not know why or how the Arisala men did it, but they were happy with their timber and information about other commercial activities. In return for relatively effortless acquisition of timber and information, young men were given access to minor sources of graft (their parents refusing such direct access). The Arisalas became middlemen in Negro-mestizo social relations as well as economic middlemen.

Increased work opportunities produced an in-migration of young Costeño proletariat of the favored personal kindred of the minga heads: they became part of a labor force indirectly controlled by the middle class stem kindred through a series of dyadic contracts (see Whitten 1965:148–55). Eventually, some of these lower class Negroes severed their kinship ties and began to rise economically and socially.

In this case, the highland managers and entrepreneurs received timber, the lower class proletariat a guaranteed market for the fruits of their minga operation, and the Negro entrepreneurs (the local middle class) from the dominant stem kindred received favors that were necessary for continued mobility. All those involved benefited. This is only one abbreviated example of a standard way to accomplish something in the Pacific Littoral, although each organization, or adaptive sector, does not always receive such obvious benefits.

All the tactics described and briefly illustrated above insure the third generation stem kindred that most of the economic, social, and political advantages entering their residential community will flow through the group of kinsmen. Members of the stem kindred, in other words, strive to provide channels to economic, social, and political power. Affinity and consanguinity are manipulated symmetrically and asymmetrically to insure dominance for members of the stem kindred. Such manipulation seems terribly obscure and disorganized unless one knows what the economic advantages are at the community level; then the moves of people become quite understandable. Since I have described the process at length elsewhere (1965 : 148–67), I will not illustrate except to say that the easy flow of information on economics and politics through the stem kindred is contingent upon the obscurity of the activities, taken collectively, of members of the kindred. It is the responsibility of the members of the stem kindred to manipulate and remain obscure; their strategy is entrepreneurial in social and political capital, although they have merely become apparent *petit bourgeoisie* in economic affairs.

Fourth Generation

The system of mobility through a vertical sequence of strategies so far described, although adaptive to fluctuation in the money economy, is usually inadequate to sustain continuous rise to dominance beyond four generations by any family or kin unit. By the time they reach the fourth generation, it becomes increasingly clear that the sequence of strategies, adaptive to a marginal economic situation though it may be, does not usually provide a tactical basis for mobility into a sphere of economic security. (The adverb "usually" is used because of the unusual, but strategically important, exception suggested at the end of this paper.)

Members of the kindred, still reckoning from the second generation siblingship, remain in the local middle class and retain their respectability symbols and some upper class contacts, but their control of social and political affairs weakens to the point where they cease to be useful to the upper and lower classes. They still have social power, but their power in economic and political affairs is gone. Unlike the third generation, any tactic aimed at consolidation is disastrous. Because the kindred expands faster than the economy, even during periods of economic expansion, serial dyadic contracts within the stem kindred become impossible to fulfill. Smaller, rising, third-generation kindreds compete with them successfully. Factions develop that eventually create fission within the unit. The eventual dispersion of the kindred allows remaining members to hold on to whatever socio-economic position they still have for some time, but they are unable to perpetuate their middle class standing, as a unit, to the next generation.

Individually, members have a few alternatives: they can marry out into a rising kindred, or sometimes into the local upper class; they can become political figureheads, usually by being placed in office by the relatives of the girls they marry; or they can turn to radical politics, hoping to attract the attention of a powerful party. Usually, a person tries to accomplish *all three alternatives* with one move.

There is only one organizational strategy that can be effective (discussed below), and it is seldom recognized, or if it is, there are insufficient resources available to use it. People do not normally have access to the economic resources necessary to move from manipulation of social capital to direct economic competition. One cannot usually take the next step in which he would become a shipper, or a lumber dealer, or a large-scale cash farmer, or a large-scale commercial entrepreneur.

SUMMARY AND SUGGESTION OF A FURTHER ADAPTIVE STRATEGY

The vertical sequence of strategies of adaptive mobility discussed above can be summarized as passing through the following phases, proceeding through four generations:

1. Balance activities bringing direct economic gain at the local level with those maintaining social capital of a dispersed personal kindred (normal peasant strategy and first generation proletarian strategy).
2. Dispense with the dispersed social capital and invest in local social capital of close kinsmen and affines directly contributing to the acquisition of political and social power. This is normally done through polygyny, direct political activity and the accumulation of symbols of local social prestige (late first generation and early second generation proletarian strategy).
3. Consolidate economic, social, and political capital and serve as a necessary middle-range organization for economic, social, and political power. This is done by acquiring high prestige and using consanguinity, affinity, and money to manipulate local politics (late second generation, third generation, and early fourth generation entrepreneurial strategy).
4. Break all contracts within the kindred and marry out; cash in social prestige and economic and political power for their utility to a rising kindred, or to the local elite (fourth generation strategy of individual survival at acquired socio-economic level).

Within this developmental cycle of four major strategies, making up a vertical sequence, a variety of tactics may be used, depending upon local situations, personal skill, and available resources. The contrast in strategies through the four-fold sequence defines three distinct groupings, the local lower class peasant, local lower class proletariat, and local middle class entrepreneur. The four phases of the developmental sequence do not, however, coincide exactly with the three sectors, although the three sectors may be regarded, in developmental terms as making up three stages in a local socio-economic hierarchy.

Since *each of these strategies is contingent on successful competition during the previous generation*, the developmental cycle is not realized by every aspiring grouping of kinsmen. Looked at from within any community, however, I suggest that these strategies do describe the activities engaged in by persons in all walks of life (even the processes of spatial and horizontal mobility are partially contingent upon the activities of the upwardly mobile (see Whitten 1965), and that a concept of sequence of successful strategies helps an observer appreciate the organization within a regional section of the national lower class. Without such a model, an observer would likely speak of the lack of organization.

In this model of a developmental cycle of adaptive mobility strategies there remains an additional, rare phase, alluded to above, which is occasionally taken by some members of the fourth generation. It involves tactical, conscious, planned dispersal and investment in social capital of a dispersed ambilineal ramage, together with tactical, planned, deliberate obscurity in political affairs at the local level.

Some members of the disintegrating fourth generation local stem kindred find a means to direct economic involvement—they get enough money to become entrepreneurs in some business and quickly disperse, using the social power of their family name to gain access to important rising second and third generation stem kindreds in other communities, while setting up some business in the same or in a different community. Today, this seems to occur only in and around the large towns: Esmeraldas, Limones, Tumaco, Buenaventura, though some individuals are also found in smaller, but very old towns such as Barbacoas. They become local elite, ostensibly completely uninvolved in regional or community politics, known throughout a region for the respect accumulated through the four or more generations of successful mobility. Their *cuñados* and *concuñados*, that is (as Strickon [1962] reports for the *Criollo* or *Gaucho* in Argentina) their brothers-in-law, or the spouses of their in-laws or even the brothers-in-law of their brothers-in-law, are those men within the various communities who are either direct politicians, as members of the rising second generation kindreds, or behind the scenes manipulators of the third generation stem kindred, or both. The social prestige of having lateral ties to a socially and economically important "family name" insures a sufficient number of concuñados in every community for members of the ambilineal ramage; and since serial polygyny is the norm, the insurance is even more securely fashioned, because individuals continue profitable interaction with affinally related kinsmen, even after the formal affinal tie has been broken (for more data on "attenuated affinity" see Whitten 1967; this volume).

The local elite strategically manipulate local politics[6] to their own economic advantage without damaging their social position. They manipulate by using their economic and social power to influence politicians, who in turn are using political advantage to secure more economic gain and social prestige.

The local elite are freed from direct political involvement (they do not have to hold office, or lead a party, or lead a strike), and even indirect involvement in their residential communities (they leave the *immediate* behind the scenes politics to the local third generation rising strivers). Each member of the local elite is a member of the only dispersed ambilineal ramage within a broad region (such as the entire Province of Esmeraldas, Ecuador, or the southwest sector of Colombia, including both Nariño and Cauca). Collectively, the local elite improve their collective situation by making predictions of political behavior in the rain-forest coast to interested inlanders. For example, during a time of political unrest the local coastal elite might make a vague prediction that, given a movement to depose the President of the nation, the majority of Costeños, ordinarily not ostensibly interested in politics, would rally behind the local liberal leaders. Since the concuñado pattern normally includes politically liberal, radical, and conservative, predictions can, with proper manipulation, and a degree of deliberate uninvolvement, be self-fulfilling. Successful predictions of how the Negroes will behave gives a mystique to lowlands politics, and a certain inside "know-how" to the local elite. The prestige symbols of the local elite increase as some become poets, novelists, social commentators, artists, and collectors of archaeological artifacts. Their legal marriages are increasingly outward although their pattern of concubinage follows that of the coastal "serial polygyny," and their ethnic appearance becomes lighter. Each boom period advances the elite more as they take a direct part in the economic sphere of activity, while retaining their social and political capital to sustain them through times of relative depression. In other words, while any one or a few of the local elite may sustain heavy losses during a depression period, the ramage itself continues as a binder of elite Negroes and light Costeños.

CONCLUSION

In the Pacific Littoral, at least, the problem with a stratification model is that it differentiates local elite (as part of the national middle class) and lumps local entrepreneurial middle class, lower class peasant, and lower class proletariat (all as members of the national lower class). While such a model is accurate in predicting the control of large aggregates over their chances of competition in the economic sphere, it does not allow us to perceive the organization of activities within any community at a given moment.

I have suggested that a focus on the developmental sequence of successful strategies is more productive in understanding the dynamics of economics, social prestige, and politics at any given time within the Pacific Littoral of Colombia and Ecuador. In order to apply my model of successful strategies, however, it is necessary to know what the economic possibilities are, and also to discern the available social and political capital. One should know, to use a model of a developmental sequence of strategies, not only what people are doing and trying to do, but also what their *possibilities of success will be*. Methodologically, this involves, at some point, the development of a model which attempts to see daily activities as part of emergent organizations, and organizations as phases of a developmental cycle, the developmental cycle being a dynamic representation of a dominant aspect of social structure. The data for such a model are the qualitative data gained through genealogical method and the life history approach. No "new anthropology" is required, only a more creative, generalizing approach to data gained from proven methods.

The model presented in this paper is offered as predictive of the meanings and organizational functions of social activities of individuals in the Pacific Littoral of Colombia and Ecuador, provided that resources and context are known. If the method called for by the model does not satisfactorily produce the data necessary to predict under these circumstances, then further methodological refinements, and consequent modifications in the model, become necessary. The advantage of such a model is that it should direct us to data which can generate systematic modification. By so sharpening our sense of social reality a contribution to both theory and ethnography can be made.

NOTES

1. A preliminary version of this paper was prepared for the Central States Anthropological Society symposium, "Social Stratification in Latin America." Discussion, during and after the symposium, with Arnold Strickon, David Chapin, Joseph Whitecotten, John W. Bennett, and Iwao Ishino clarified many points. I wish to thank Dorothea Scott Whitten, Charles A. Valentine, and Alvin W. Wolfe for their comments on the revised manuscript. "Strategies of Adaptive Mobility" is reproduced by permission of the American Anthropological Association from the *American Anthropologist*, Vol. 71, No. 2.

2. I use this term in a way similar to that of Erasmus' (1961a) use of "culture capital." I do not use the approach of Meyer Fortes (1958) who refers to the total cultural heritage of a people as their "social capital." Social capital herein refers to the human resources upon which a person can depend, just as he may depend upon economic resources (i.e., money, goods).

3. For more information on the converging adaptation of Chocó and Cayapa Indian society, see Altschuler (1965 and 1967) and Faron (1961, 1962). In the case of the Cayapa, comparisons in support of my statement can be made with data from the early 1900's by referring to Barratt (1925).

4. Most of the generalizations presented in this paper are derived from the qualitative analysis of extensive genealogies and life-historical material. The method is essentially similar to that described by Leeds (1965). See the metholological discussion in the Introduction to Whitten (1965), and in Whitten (1969).

5. The remarkable structural similarity to the Japanese lumber *Nakama* work group (Bennett and Ishino 1963:176–200) should be noted, particularly since the Nakama group descends naturally from a paternalistic economy, while the *minga* organization functions to thwart the development of paternalism. Such remarkable convergence raises the question whether cultural traditions such as paternalism or its absence really function to structure work groups, or whether evolutionary adaptation to consistency in similar inputs of an externally generated cash economy may not be the critical molding devices.

6. In Buenaventura, Colombia, local politics seem to hinge on labor union organization, thereby introducing further complexity. To a lesser extent, this is also true of Tumaco and Esmeraldas.

Part three

"BLACK CULTURE" AND GHETTO ETHNOGRAPHY

Nineteen

BLACK CULTURE: MYTH OR REALITY?[1]

Robert Blauner

In their communities across the nation, Negro Americans are discussing "black culture." The mystique of "soul" is merely the most focused example of this trend in consciousness. What is and what should be the black man's attitude toward American society and American culture has become a divisive issue in the Negro protest movement (Berger 1967:54). The spokesmen for black power celebrate black culture and distinctiveness; the integrationists base their strategy and their appeal on the fundamental "American-ness" of the black man. There are nationalist leaders who see culture-building today as equal to or more important than political organization. From Harlem to Watts there has been a proliferation of black theater, art, and literary groups; the recent ghetto riots (or revolts as they are viewed from the nationalistic perspective) are the favorite material of these cultural endeavors. The spread of resistance to the draft and the Vietnam war seem to indicate an increasing tendency among blacks (as well as non-blacks) to reject certain basic values of American life. But as with so many of these apparent "tendencies," it is difficult to know whether this one portends an actual change in sentiment or instead reflects the new conditions that have lifted some of the past inhibitions against its expression.

The emergence of this cultural revitalization movement among American Negroes poses a number of dilemmas for the larger society. There are the problems of practice and policy for our educational, welfare, and political institutions and for their professional and administrative representatives. Also, an intellectual dilemma exists for the analysts of American society and its culture. The black culture movement flies in the face of certain basic assumptions upon which social scientists and liberal intellectuals have constructed the nation's official "enlightened" attitudes toward race relations and the Negro minority. Their primary tenet is that Negroes—unlike other minority groups—have no ethnic culture because the elimination of African ancestral heritages brought about total acculturation. Related to this is a second assumption that stresses poverty or *lower class* conditions as an explanation of whatever may be distinctive in the ghetto's subculture. The middle class character and mobility goals of most federal anti-poverty efforts follow from this tenet. Thus there is an apparent contradiction between what is happening in the black communities today and many social scientist's theoretical perspective on American Negro life. A re-examination of this standard sociological perspective on the ethnic character of Afro-Americans in the United States is needed, and will be undertaken in this essay.

The view that Negroes lack any characteristics of a distinctive nationality, that they are Americans and nothing else, has become almost a dogma of liberal social science. Gunnar Myrdal in his great study, *An American Dilemma* (1944), set the tone for the present outlook. In this influential and otherwise voluminous work there is no chapter on Negro cultural orientations and only the briefest treatment of the black community. Furthermore, Myrdal's statement that the Negro is "an exaggerated American" and that his values are "pathological" elaborations on general American values have been widely quoted for a generation (Myrdal 1944:927-30). In the Introduction to *The Peculiar Institution*, historian Kenneth Stampp (1956:vii) asserted that Negroes are "white men with black skins," even though his thorough scholarship raises troubling questions about this statement. And as recently as 1963, Glazer and Moynihan took "the Myrdal position" when they wrote "the Negro is only an American and nothing else. He has no values and culture to guard and protect"[2] (Glazer and Moynihan 1963:53).

It is misleading to give the impression that the standard position reflects only the vantage point of the white liberal sociologist. E. Franklin Frazier has been at least as influential as Myrdal in gaining acceptance for this outlook. Frazier entered the debate to counter the position of Melville Herskovits who, in his *Myth of the Negro Past*, imputes African origins to many, if not most, Negro American social and cultural patterns. Frazier's view was published as late as 1957 in the revised edition of his comprehensive work, *The Negro in the United States* (Frazier 1957a:680-81):

> As a racial or cultural minority the Negro occupies a unique position. He has been in the United States longer than any other racial or cultural minority with the exception, of course, of the American Indian. Although the Negro is distinguished from other minorities by his physical characteristics, unlike other racial or cultural minorities the Negro is not distinguished by culture from the dominant group. Having completely lost his ancestral culture, he speaks the same language, practices the same religion, and accepts the same values and political ideas as the dominant group. Consequently, when one speaks of Negro culture in the United States, one can only refer to the folk culture of the rural Southern Negro or the traditional forms of behavior and values which have grown out of the Negro's social and mental isolation. Moreover, many of the elements of Negro culture which have grown out of his peculiar experience in America, such as music, have become a part of the general American culture.
>
> Since the institutions, the social stratification, and the culture of the Negro minority are essentially the same as those of the larger community, it is not strange that the Negro

minority belongs among the assimilationist rather than the pluralist, secessionist or militant minorities. It is seldom that one finds Negroes who think of themselves as possessing a different culture from whites and that their peculiar culture should be preserved.

When Negro sociologists present community studies of southern towns and northern ghettos however, they describe distinctive institutions and unique ways of looking upon life and society that begin to read like the depiction of an ethnic culture.[3] Yet until recently, the positive assertion of Negro culture has been confined to nationalist and political circles: it has not been defended through analysis and evidence in the academic field. This is what makes *Urban Blues* by Charles Keil an important book. Keil, a white anthropologist, uses the blues singer and his audience as the raw materials to outline the distinctive traits and ethos of Negro-American culture. He finds the core of this culture in the "soul" ideology. Soul may be related to the more archetypal "wisdom-through-suffering" theme, but as Keil pieces it together, it suggests "that Negroes have a dearly bought experiential wisdom, a 'perspective by incongruity,'" that provides black Americans a unique outlook on life that cannot be shared by whites (Keil 1966: 170).

Keil's rich study, to which I shall return later, stimulated an incisive critical review by the sociologist Bennett Berger. In the context of general admiration for Keil's achievement, Berger attacks his major thesis at three pivotal points. First, he asserts that "soul" theorists like Keil, in romanticizing Negro life, miss the key fact that "black culture" is at bottom only an American Negro version of lower class culture. Second, analytical appreciation of this culture may be misplaced since it has no future. Lower class culture in America is no basis for the development of a national consciousness and ethnic solidarity. Since it will have no appeal to the socially mobile, it can only impede progress toward integration and equality. Third, this suggests for Berger that black cultural spokesmen are only confusing the intellectual atmosphere and obstructing Negro progress and racial harmony. As intellectuals and political men, they have the obligation to clearly specify what in Negro culture is to be affirmed, so that we all can see whether anything solid or meaningful is involved. But speaking so generally, if not demagogically, they fail to do so (Berger 1967:54-57).

The various positions discussed, from Myrdal to Frazier to Berger, share in common the idea that American Negroes have no ethnic culture. The first formulation asserts that Negro culture is American culture; the second and more recent positions argue that Negro orientations are southern regional or lower class. I suggest that this approach is based on a number of misconceptions about culture and ethnicity in modern American society. It reflects first a narrow usage of the sociologist's culture concept, but more importantly a mechanical application of the model of immigrant ethnic group assimilation to very different cultural experience. Second, it is a response to the complexity of Negro American life which is related to the many sources of black culture. It also reflects a denial of the prime role racism—and its residues, Negro political history—play in the process of cultural elaboration. Finally, it is based on a static, deterministic approach to cultural development, an approach which minimizes its open-ended quality and therefore underplays the role of consciousness and culture-building in affecting that development. Let us examine each of the issues in turn.

FIRST DIMENSION: THE UNIQUE CULTURAL PROCESS

There is a sociological plausibility to the argument that Negroes are only Americans with black skins. As Frazier stressed, the manner in which North American slavery developed—in contrast to Caribbean and South American slavery—eliminated the most central African traits, those elements of ethnicity which European and Asian immigrants brought to this country: language, dress, religions, and other traditional institutions, a conscious identification with an overseas homeland. Basic as is this critical difference, it misses the point in assuming that there is only one generic process—that model of European ethnic assimilation—through which nationality cultures and the dominant American ethos have interacted. What must be understood is the uniqueness of the Afro-American condition, an essential aspect of which has been a deviant cultural experience that to some degree is the reverse of those of the traditional ethnic minorities.

Howard Brotz has observed that the "no Negro culture" argument rests on the assumption that an ethnic group must possess three attributes: a distinctive language, a unique religion, and a national homeland (Brotz 1964:129–30). This position is also tied to what I regard as the classical concept of culture, a usage that is less and less applicable to the condition of any ethnic group in modernized mass society. This is the *holistic* view of culture, which points to the integrated way of life, that system of customs, institutions, beliefs, and values that fit together into some organic whole, perhaps dominated by a central ethos. This concept was of course developed from the study of primitive peoples. Yet it fairly well captures the unity of the social heritages that the various immigrant groups brought to America.[4] The parallel holistic cultures of the African peoples were destroyed in America because slaves from the diverse tribes, kingdoms, and linguistic groups were consciously separated so that language, religion, and national loyalties were attenuated (Frazier 1966:4–16). But ethnic cultures as organic, holistic ways of life did not last very long for the immigrant nationalities either. Today when we characterize Jews, Italians, or Greeks as ethnic groups, we are referring implicitly to a different notion of culture. This is the idea that the ethnic sub-cultures reside in a certain number of distinctive values, orientations to life and experiences and shared memories that co-exist within the framework of the general American life-style and allegiances. Most sociologists and laymen find little difficulty in calling American Jews an ethnic group despite the fact that in most of their institutional and cultural behavior Jews are nothing if not American middle class. But there are also distinctive cultural orientations, a peculiarly ethnic style in humor, for example, that came from a common historical and social experience.

Let us look more closely at the model of ethnic group assimilation that dominates sociological thinking about national cultures. The holistic way of life was introduced at the outset of the immigrant group's entry, or more accurately early in the peak periods of its immigration. It soon gave way to the demands of the American environment and the competition of the American ways of life. Typically after one generation an ethnic culture developed that combined old country and American ways, that was more fragmented and full of normative and value conflicts than the traditional culture, and yet still provided some round of life and center of community for the group. As time went on, the numbers of people in each group involved in the more traditional holistic culture declined, and the emerging ethnic–American culture tended to take on more and more characteristics of the larger society. Assimilation meant the modification or the giving up of certain ethnic institutions and culturally distinct values as the generations followed one another. Though life experience may have been incredibly subtle and complex, the sociological model that captures the immigrants' cultural experience is fairly simple. There are basically two variables, the traditional culture and the American values and conditions. The process tends to be a one-way, non-reversible one, from immigrant extra-national status to ethnic group assimilation, though Herberg and others have noted a tendency to reassert ethnic identity in the third generation. The means that move this process forward are occupational mobility and the ethnic's increasing contact with dominant institutions, especially education.

Very little of this fits the cultural experience of Afro-Americans. How a minority group enters the host society has fateful—if not permanent—consequences. The very manner in which Africans became Americans undermined traditional culture and social organization. The black man did not enter this country with a group identity as a Negro. This group category could only be formed by the slave-making operation which vitiated the meaning and relevance of the traditional, specific African identities.[5] Therefore, the cultural process could not be one of movement from ethnic group to assimilation, since Negroes were not an ethnic group. Instead, they were incorporated into a legal station that did not permit the group autonomy and the social and economic progress that accompanied assimilation of other minorities—a forced deculturation occurred, a spurious but not genuine acculturation. But at the same time, beginning with slavery, the group and culture-building process began among the black population, and the development of an ethnic group identity and distinctive culture has been going on ever since. But this cultural process is infinitely more complex than that of the immigrant ethnic groups. One reason is the general reversal in direction. But it is not a simple one-way process in the opposite direction, from "assimilation" to ethnic group. The black cultural experience more resembles an alternating current than it does a direct current. The movement toward ethnicity and distinctive consciousness has been paralleled by one inducing more "Americanization" in action and identity.[6] Sometimes these conflicting vectors characterize different time periods; sometimes they reflect different segments of the large and diversified black minority. But these contradictory cultural tendencies have occurred simultaneously and within the psyches and social orientations of the same individuals. Behind all this are many and various historical and social conditions that have produced Negro American culture. Black culture therefore cannot be understood in terms of the simplified two-variable model which is reasonably satisfactory for the ethnic groups.

SECOND DIMENSION: THE MANY SOURCES OF NEGRO AMERICAN CULTURE

The present essay will not attempt to characterize the contents of black culture. As I see it, this is a difficult if not impossible job for a white social scientist in today's

America. The job eventually will be done by the more appropriate workmen in this jurisdiction, the Negro intellectuals and scholars. Furthermore, it is my estimate that black culture is at present too much in flux for a systematic schematization to have much value. My task rather is to make some broad generalizations about the conditions in American life that have and are presently giving rise to distinctive Afro-American cultural orientations. Central to my argument against the conventional position is the thesis that the *ghetto sub-culture involves both lower class and ethnic characteristics*. Poverty is only one source of black culture, and as I shall attempt to prove, even the lower class traits and institutions in Negro life have been modified by strictly ethnic values. Among other sources of black culture are Africa, slavery, the South, Emancipation and northern migration, and above all, *racism*. That racist oppression provides the basis for a more elaborate and more ethnic cultural response than does class exploitation and lower class status is a central postulate of the present thesis.

Negro American culture is an ethnic as well as a class culture because the history of black people *in the United States* has produced a residue of shared collective memories and frames of reference. It is because black Americans have undergone unique experiences in America, experiences that no other national or racial minority or lower class group have shared, that a *distinctive* ethnic culture has evolved. Though this culture is overwhelmingly the product of American experience, the first contributing source is still African. Herskovits may have exaggerated the power of African continuities, but it seems plausible that some aesthetic and linguistic principles that underlie Negro-American music and dialect (as well as possibly some movement patterns and religious orientations) have their origins in those peoples, tribes, and kingdoms that supplied the slave trade. However, the importance of African patterns for American Negro ethnicity was greatly diminished by the fact that these orientations had to be transmitted largely on the subliminal level rather than through conscious awareness and identification. Recently, of course, with the emergence of independent African nations, a concern with this continent has become more prominent in the cultural symbolism of the black community and presumably also in the personal identities of many individual black men and women.[7]

The first great source of black culture in America is slavery. Here, under seriously restricting conditions, American Negroes began developing their own quasi-communities and their own codes of conduct (Stampp 1956). Here certain prevailing patterns such as ecstatic religion, mother-led families, anti-white attitudes, and the yearning for freedom and autonomy got their start. To slavery also the more negative adaptations and character-types—for example, the submission, timidity, fear, and manipulation embedded in the "Uncle Tom" orientation—owe their origins. It is these kinds of cultural adaptations that many nationalist leaders are trying to stamp out in their attacks on "the slave mentality."

Related to slavery as a second great source of Negro ethnicity is the sub-culture of the American South. Ralph Ellison (1965) and more recently Calvin Hernton (1966)[8] have pointed out how much of the black man's attitudes and cultural styles reflect the patterns of this region. Some aspects of Negro religion, "soul food," and linguistic styles are similar to poor white counterparts. But the black man also assimilated some of the values and the style of the southern ruling classes, though he was not always in a position to emulate them. Ellison has attributed the general aristocratic flavor of ghetto life-styles to this origin, as well as the American Negro's apparent lack of passion for business entrepreneurship. Still unexplored are the ways in which Afro-Americans themselves have shaped (rather than reflected) the sub-culture of the South; the black influence is probably more profound than generally recognized.

A further source was Emancipation: the promises, the betrayals, and the frustrations that followed upon release from servitude. There may be much in Afro-American patterns that still reflects a "freedman's culture"; I refer to the great mobility, the moving about and restlessness that characterizes the life patterns of an important minority (especially male) within this great minority group. This mobility, the promise of the North, the attractions of industry, and the push from a depleted southland, set the stage for ghetto life in the urban North. This is the source of black culture which is most clearly tied to poverty and lower class existence. And yet the Negro ghetto is different from the ethnic ghettos of the Irish, Jews, or Chinese because it comes out of a different history—from slavery, southern Jim Crowism, and a northern migration which only partly parallels the transoceanic search for a better life. *It is also different in its cultural impact because it exists in a racist society which strongly resists the assimilation of black Americans.* For this reason the Negro ghettos have served more as the setting for the flowering of a distinctive ethnicity, whereas the immigrant ghettos were actually way-stations in the process of acculturation and assimilation (Handlin 1951).

THE LOWER CLASS COMPONENT

The black ghettos are overwhelmingly made up of low-income people, and poverty is the first fact of life. This has naturally encouraged the view that the ghetto sub-culture is lower class culture, or the "culture of poverty," to use Oscar Lewis' now fashionable phrase. This interpretation is based on the liberal assumption that Negro Americans lack distinctive ethnic or national characteristics and on the social scientists' discovery that lower class groups in America share somewhat deviant orientations and ways of life that we call a sub-culture. Since black Americans are overwhelmingly in the low income population, whatever appears to be distinctive in the ghetto culture must be due to class status rather than ethnicity.[9]

In *Urban Blues*, the most exhaustive, serious treatment of Negro American culture up to now, Keil does not deal explicitly with the analytical problems of class and ethnic contributions. Working with the blues as his chief material, he identifies the ideology and behaviors associated with "soul" as the keystone of that culture. Bennett Berger, on the other hand, in his interesting review, bases his argument on the theory that ghetto culture is essentially lower class in character. I think Berger finds Keil's overplaced emphasis (from my viewpoint) on "soul" very convenient to his position, since this real and yet elusive cultural symbol of black America does contain many of the values, orientations, and virtues that have been historically attributed to the poor and downtrodden. As Berger (drawing from Keil) summarizes "soul," it has become the stereotype that flatters the oppressed Negro lower class and thus can serve as a compensation, an ideological palliative for its discontents (Berger 1967: 56):

> ... strong emotions and feelings, especially when shared with others; something pure, non-machined; staying power and wisdom through suffering; telling it like it is, being

what you are, and believing in what you do. The concept suggests further a tight intermingling of sex, love and reciprocal responsiveness which constitute the pattern of Negro Dionysianism, manifest in the swing of the blues-jazz-gospel musical milieu and in the brilliant, moving, linguistic innovations which spring from it. The pattern emphasizes the erotic, the frenetic, and the ecstatic—a pattern which when made ideological constitutes a claim to emotional depth and authenticity. . . .

As this capsule summary suggests, there are themes in ghetto life that can be identified in other lower class groups: for example, the Latin American poor described by Lewis or the immigrant ghettos of the Irish and the Poles. Some of these themes are a present-oriented and expressive style of life, characterized by minimal planning and organization. Religion is usually a more dominant value and release than politics; crime, hustling, rackets and other forms of "deviance" are commonplace. Economic pressures strain the family, and marginal employment tends to weaken the father's authority. Aggression and violence seem to be more frequent than in middle class neighborhoods. Expressive personal releases that some sociologists label "immediate rather than deferred gratifications"—sex, drinking, drugs, music—are emphasized in the lives of individuals. A sense of fatalism, even apathy or quasi-paranoid outlooks (the "world is against me") pervades the streets where the public life of the lower class sub-culture is set.[10]

That the black ghetto shares these traits with other lower class milieux and that these themes flow primarily from the condition of poverty I do not doubt. But that is not the whole story. Even the class characteristics gain an ethnic content and emphasis when people with unique problems live under similar conditions and associate primarily with one another for generations. The "expressiveness" of Negroes is more articulated and developed than the expressiveness of lower class Poles, for example. Not only music, but language, styles of dress, and movement also are more consciously cultivated. The religion of southern blacks has similar institutional origins to that of southern whites, but as Powdermaker observed in the 1930's, a Negro church service is totally different from a poor white one (Powdermaker 1939:259–60).

Berger correctly observes that lower class traits do not become institutionalized or legitimated.[11] But when class traits are modified and given ethnic content by a national group, they may become institutionalized—that is, conscious, expected, and infused with value (which can be positive or negative). Black Americans have long valued their folk music; today southern rural cuisine, modes of walking and talking, and even the alleged "supersexuality" of Afro-Americans are becoming symbols of group identity and cohesiveness. (The development of ethnic cultural values does not preclude, of course, ambivalence; the fact that many people may feel ambivalent toward these phenomena is no argument against their cultural reality. Just the contrary!) My argument can perhaps be best illustrated by the matriarchy controversy. Though some reactions to the "Moynihan report" may suggest otherwise, Negro people with whom I have discussed the matter are well aware that for centuries the mother has played a more dominent role in the black family and community than she does in the larger society. Unlike the situation with lower classes in which the matrifocal theme generally operates amid a value system that stresses patriarchy and therefore obscures the detection and confrontation of this trend, Afro-Americans *expect* to see women playing independent and powerful roles. Since the matriarchy is a conscious and expected reality, it is talked about, joked about, defended against, debated pro and con, and more and more actively acted upon, as, for example, in selecting the leadership of community anti-poverty boards and other political groups. It is becoming more and more infused with negative value. This type of cultural ferment in the black communities is not characteristic of lower classes—nor even of organized working classes in America—it indicates a dynamic of self-definition through which an ethnic group is shaping its character.

The class and the ethnic factors in Negro American culture are so intimately intermingled that they are very difficult to distinguish. The effort must be made, however, because the intellectual and social consequences of this apparently innocent distinction are considerable—as I shall suggest in my concluding section.

Racism

Perhaps the critical reader might agree that slavery, emancipation, and the southern heritage are a unique constellation that no other lower class minority group shared. Yet, these significant events are more than 100 years past, and the southern element weakens with migration and the modernization of the southern region. There is still much in the northern ghettos today that resembles the life conditions of the ethnic immigrants. All this is true and it might shatter my argument except for one fact. *A continuing racist theme, with powerful social structural consequences, has served to consolidate rather than to erase the distinctive experience of the past.* There is no other lower class group in America's pluralistic society that has met in the past or meets in the present the systematic barriers of categorical exclusion, blockage, and discrimination based on race and color. This has been such an omnipresent reality for Afro-Americans that just as the way in which black individuals have confronted the patterns of exclusion and denigration are central themes of their personal biographies, so the direct and indirect struggle against racism is the core of the history of the Negro group in this country. It is through this continuing struggle to surmount and change a racist social system—a struggle which began at least with emancipation, and has stepped up to new levels each generation after periods of decline up to the zenith of the present day—that black Americans have created a *political history*. This political history is the core of the emerging ethnic culture, and the clue to the contemporary revitalization movement which celebrates blackness.

Despite the cliches of the Kerner report, it is still difficult for most whites to accept the unpleasant fact that America remains a racist society. Such an awareness is also obscured by the fact that more sophisticated, subtle, and indirect forms, that might better be termed neo-racism, tend to replace the traditional, open forms that were most highly elaborated in the old South. By American racism, I refer to two key characteristics of our social structure. First, that the division based upon color is the single most important split within the society, the body politic, and the national psyche.[12] Second, that various processes and practices of exclusion, rejection, and subjection based on color are built into the major public institutions (labor market, education, politics, and law enforcement) with the effect of maintaining special privileges, power, and values for the benefit of the white majority.

Racism is not only a central though subterranean theme of American culture; its attitude toward black culture has had from the beginning a profound impact on the course of Negro ethnicity. Initially it alienated its slave population from African culture. A further manifestation of its destructive and exploitative character was the tendency to appropriate and use for profit the cultural creations of Negro Americans: jazz has been the classic example here, but the present day use of ghetto language is in the same vein.[13] And today the liberal ideologues deny the legitimacy, or even the existence, of those sub-cultural values that make up the black man's distinctive culture.

American racism has been the key reality that has encouraged the flowering of black culture. There are several related reasons for this. First, racism blocked the participation of Negroes in the dominant culture so that unfilled needs for symbols, meaning, and value had to be met elsewhere. Though for many years southern-oriented Negroes named their sons after George Washington and other presidents, the founding fathers have become negative symbols for a northern ghetto generation which is finding its cultural heroes elsewhere. Second, Negroes have perceived the fact (as Hernton [1966] has recently made explicit) that racism is no American aberration, but an institution built into the society and its cultural values. As possibilities for assimilation and acculturation opened up in certain areas, this created a difficult dilemma. How can one embrace a culture whose values and practices deny one's own humanity? Thus for the protection of self there was a need to maintain some distance from the dominant culture, if one were to avoid intense inner conflict. This structured conflict and ambivalence lies at the heart of much of the cultural products of American blacks—from anonymous blues to poetry and fiction. Thus the tensions of racism brought on a group experience that could be interpreted in creative terms. Finally, racism called forth social and political responses on a collective level aimed at transforming the American system in line with its equalitarian rhetoric. The legacy of this century-long battle against racism is the political history of Negroes in the United States. This shared political history is the solid core, the hard rock non-mystical aspect of Negro American culture.

A unique political history plays an essential role in the development and consolidation of ethnic groups, as well as nations.[14] For the Irish-American community in the late nineteenth and early twentieth centuries, Ireland's struggle against England and the heroes of this national movement were at the center of ethnic group values and concerns. As others have pointed out, the Jews may be the purest example of a group that has institutionalized its political history into cultural, ritual, and sacred values. The Old Testament depicts the political vicissitudes of the Jewish nation and the religious holidays memorialize this milennial struggle for liberation. Perhaps then the attempt of many black nationalist groups to memorialize the death of Malcolm X as an "official" holiday can be understood as a similar recognition of the relation between political history and national culture.

The content of Afro-American political history is beyond the scope of this essay. It is clear, however, that in the past decade there has been a significant change in the intensity and nature of this history—a change which lies behind the present-day ferment and renaissance of black culture. In the past, the Negro masses—like the lower orders of all colors and nations in most eras—were primarily passive politically, acted upon more than acting. After the 1954 Supreme Court decision (the last major turning point in American race relations that was initiated by an act of a "white" institution), blacks have become the primary active agents for change with respect to the nation's social structure. Since the mid-fifties Negroes have created the big news in domestic American history.[15]

But important as the decade is, it does not exhaust the contents of Negro political history that makes black culture a real sociological phenomenon rather than a group myth. Despite the fateful reciprocity of black and white in America (a theme that has been stressed in the essays of Baldwin [1955] and in the fiction of Faulkner and W. T. Kelley [1962]), Afro-Americans share a consciousness of a common past (and a concomitant national or ethnic identification) that white Americans simply are not privy to. How could whites perceive, react, and relate to slavery, emancipation, to the South and its history of Jim Crow and lynching, to early twentieth century race riots, and even to Montgomery and Watts in the same way as blacks? No matter how democratic our ideals and how sensitive our human capacities, we were *on the other side* sociologically and existentially.

The point I am laboring has been made most succinctly by a reflective blues singer, Al Hibbler. When Charles Keil (1966:152) asked him what it takes to make a soul singer, Hibbler listed three ingredients, "having been hurt by a woman," "being brought up in that old-time religion," and "knowing what that slavery shit is all about." In a nutshell, this is the essence of the Negro's distinctive political history that lies behind the autonomy of his ethnic culture—since no white American can really know "what that slavery shit is all about." Hibbler, of course, was not referring only to the past.

The black man's unique social-political experience also lies behind the other elements of Negro culture that have been recently stressed. The "soul" orientation can be discussed in its Dionysian aspects which emphasize its relation to poverty and lower class status. But it can also be looked at as a philosophy of life or world view that places tragedy, suffering, and forbearance in a more central position than does the dominant American ethos. The construction of an orientation toward inner experience that clashes with the more external instrumental orientation of our industrial culture reflects as much the racism that has excluded Negroes from American life as it does lower class status *per se*.

Another contribution of racism to Negro American culture is the prominence of *survival* as a focal concern in the black community. The preoccupation with survival is worth examining because of its remarkable salience and because it seems once again simply to reflect the conditions of poverty and lower class status. What do I mean by the "survival theme?" For one thing, it is very common for black people to express group pride by arguing that the white race would not have survived had we been subject to the past or present life conditions of American Negroes. This sense of tough resilience is one of the central themes in the blues and in the mystique of soul. In the ghetto there is consensus that the problem of every individual is "making it"; "How you makin' it, man?" is a common form of greeting. Interviews I have conducted in the black community suggest that "making it with dignity" is central to a leading concept of manhood. Finally, on the political level, black leaders are becoming concerned with the problem of group survival; a number of "Black Survival Conferences" have been convened on the West Coast.

Poverty and lower class existence *per se* also make survival an inevitable and insistent preoccupation. But the Afro-American's self-conscious concern with survival and "making it" only reflects in part subsistence needs. When black people talk about surviving, they are even more pointedly referring to the problem of maintaining life, dignity, and sanity in a racist society. The backdrop of the "making it" imagery is the presence of the Klan, lynch mobs, ghetto police, and the closed, restricted white power and economic structures. "Making it" appears to be a response to poverty and blocked economic opportunities, but "making it with dignity" is the response of a suppressed national group with their distinctive ethnic (read human) values to defend. Here I refer to the more subtle pressures of white institutions to make Negroes "tom," smile to fit conventional stereotypes, or more commonly today, to the pressures to change in middle class ways that acceptance and success seem to require. Right or wrong, these constraints are interpreted as forms of racism. The survival fears of the black politicos (which incidentally are commonly encountered among ordinary people in the ghettos today) are not directed at economic poverty. Right or wrong again, they sense that a racist plot to eliminate the black population is behind the birth control efforts aimed at Negro welfare clients, the Vietnam war and its draft policies, and even the alleged readying of concentration camps for ghetto rioters.

The gist of my argument in this section is that racist social relations have different cultural consequences from class relations, and therefore black culture cannot be forced into the Procrustean bed of lower class culture in the way that Marxists at one time and some liberal social scientists today want to reduce race relations to class relations. For several centuries in America, blacks have lived together in ways that are markedly different from the ways in which lower and working classes live together. This is largely because the manner in which Negroes have been compelled to relate to individual whites and to the larger society is so divergent from the typical relations of the lower classes to the middle classes or to that of the proletariat to a capitalist social order. Racism excludes a category of people from participation in society in a way different from class hegemony and exploitation. Racism insults, attempts to violate dignity and to degrade personalities in a much more pervasive and inclusive way than class exploitation—which in the U.S. at any rate has typically not been generalized beyond the "point of production." Racist oppression attacks men and manhood more directly and thoroughly than does class oppression. For these reasons racist and class oppression—while intimately related—still have diverse consequences for group formation, for the salience of identities based on these groups, and for individual and group modes of adaptation and resistance. Class exploitation does not *per se* stimulate ethnic and national cultures and liberation movements; colonialism and domestic racism do.

Oscar Lewis has recently pointed out that there is a complementary and conflicting relation between the culture of poverty and ethnic group cultures. The classical lower class "culture" characterized by apathy, social disorganization, aggression, sexuality, and other themes, lacks strong ethnic as well as organized political traditions. When an ethnic culture is viable or when political working class consciousness is cultivated (as Lewis believes has occurred among the Cuban poor), the culture of poverty with all its negative and problematic effects declines (Lewis 1966a:xlviii–xlvix). If Lewis is correct—and he makes sense to me—the black culture movement among American Negroes may represent the strengthening of ethnic consciousness, the ethnic cultural component, at the expense of lower class patterns. This strikes me as something that liberal social scientists and intellectuals would want to applaud and appreciate rather than meet with carping criticism.

THIRD DIMENSION: CULTURE-BUILDING AND ITS PRESENT-DAY ROLE

The fact that Negroes possess an ethnic culture does not make them less American, though it conditions their relation to American life in distinctive ways. There is no question but that the society's prevailing standards have been a major if not an overwhelming influence on ways of life in the black community. Precisely because black men were stripped of their traditional culture, language, and institutions, they were more vulnerable than other groups to American values. But since Negroes could never share fully and participate as equals in that way of life, they assimilated American values from a unique perspective, that of the outsider. As many Negro writers have pointed out, the majority of the black population never bought the big myths of America, no matter how much they desired their realization. Certainly Negro culture is American in that it accepts the desirability of money and the material accoutrements of affluence, probably even the suburban life-style. But there is a distinctive ethnic strain in the awareness of the social costs of these goods, in the sensitivity to the hypocrisy in American public and private life, to the gap between the ideal and reality. This long-term awareness appears to be changing into a more outspoken and outright rejection of American middle class values by at least a substantial (though unknown) number of young blacks today.

There is a remarkable paradox here in the phenomenon of Negro Americans more actively rejecting the society and its values at the very time when that social order has begun to open its doors to their participation. To some degree and in some cases this may be a "defense mechanism," a protection against the anxieties of openness, competition, and new possibilities. But from another point of view, the paradox is resolved if we understand the peculiarities of the Afro-American cultural experience set forth in the first section of this essay. In contrast with the situation of the immigrant ethnics, the period of integration and potential assimilation for Negroes is coinciding with the upsurge of the group's sense of peoplehood and with the institutionalization of its culture, rather than with the decline of these phenomena. The black man with mobility and integration chances is therefore torn in a deeper and more profound sense than was the "marginal man" second immigrant generation.

One reason why the existence of a Negro American *ethnic* (as opposed to the lower class ghetto) culture has been easily dismissed by social scientists and policy-makers may be a certain lack of focus and unity in Afro-American life-styles. These traditions, values, and patterns of social organization may not be as firm as were those of the immigrant nationality groups, though today black music, language, and cultural experience is more compelling in its power and influence than are the residual counterparts among the European ethnic groups. The black culture that has emerged has grown out of the soil of American life, and the time in which cultural evolution has been possible is relatively brief—perhaps a hundred years. In addition, our social structure does not easily provide the physical isolation and autonomy for groups to develop distinctive ways of life (only people like the Amish who have been able to isolate themselves in self-contained and economically sufficient rural pockets have shown quick results in ethnic development). On the one hand, America in its racist dimension excludes the black man and maintains the ghettoized communities that provide the groundwork for Negro ethnicity; with the other hand America in its inclusive, mass homogenizing dimension beckons black men and all others to identify with its material and ideal symbols and to participate in at least the middle levels of consumption and life-style.

This duality and the fact that Negro American culture has so many diverse sources contributes to the lack of clarity and unity. Compared once again to the immigrant groups upon which sociological models of ethnic group assimilation were built, the Negro minority is extremely large and highly differentiated. At the high points of immigrant ethnicity, most of these groups were small, their members concentrated in one or more cities and socially in the lower classes. During the period that black culture has been building up (including the present) the Afro-American minority continues to differentiate itself. The middle classes grow; new political and religious movements proliferate (e.g., the Muslims); the black population spreads out more evenly across the country—though predominantly now in the urban centers. The development of ethnic culture moves on at an uneven pace. New values and styles are born and institutionalized in the northern ghettos at the same time that southern-oriented values and styles lose their hold on many people. There is yet a final reason why Negro American culture has been relatively "invisible." Blacks have learned to respond to racist depreciation and opportunistic cultural appropriation by concealing many of their deeply held patterns from the white world. White America therefore has not been prepared to respond to any affirmation of black culture beyond the conventional and usually racist stereotypes. We are hearing so much about "soul" today because this old adaptation is dying as a new mood of pride motivates cultural spokesmen to celebrate rather than to deny black values.

To point out the ambiguities within Negro American culture is not to deny its existence. Nor are the black radicals necessarily misguided or visionary in their efforts to strengthen and consolidate it. For it is precisely this deviant, paradoxical character of black culture that makes it especially critical for the group formation and personal identity needs of its bearers. The immigrant ethnic groups had a clear-cut, holistic, traditional culture; this gave them an implicit strength and bargaining power in the game of assimilation and acculturation. They had something deep inside the group and individual to fall back upon in the event the American staircase became blocked or its climb too perilous. But the black man has faced the American colossus with an original culture that was shattered. And most important, racism is more profound in its destructive impact on personal identity than was the prejudice and discrimination leveled against the non-black outlanders.

Of course, the present cultural ferment in the Negro community is not a new thing. Well known is the Harlem renaissance of the 1920's, which saw the emergence of a group of self-conscious black intellectuals and artists, along with a somewhat parallel nationalist development in the political field—the Garvey movement. This earlier cultural renaissance came after the post-World War I setbacks to racial democratization, just as today's cultural movement gains its power from the limited successes and possibilities of the civil rights movement—specifically the failure of integration to become a social-economic reality. But if culture-building feeds on "back lash," this does not mean it is a temporary will-of-the-wisp that will die out when integration finally hits its stride. The very successes and social legitimation of the civil rights experience during the last ten years is beginning to teach some whites what most blacks have probably always known—that racism is not a dying phenomenon in American life, confined largely to decadent southern elites and their redneck allies. Unfortunately, it is only on the way out in these more blatant forms. In various and subtle ways, racism and neo-racism permeate the social institutions of society—North, South, West, and East. Thus the black culture movement is a reasonable response to the realities of a society and a people that—as they are at present organized in socio-economic and psychic structures—are not going to accept Afro-Americans without imposing ceilings on their possibilities to reach "the heights of a man." The stronger that Negro ethnic culture becomes, the greater the possibility for black people to utilize *both* group power and individual mobility to take what they can and give what will be accepted from this basically racist society—a process that in time will contribute to the transformation of this society and its racism. For in American life, ethnic culture is identity, and there is no individual or group progress without a clear sense of who one is, where one came from, and where one is going.[16]

The black consciousness and culture-building movements of today seem much more significant than the earlier Harlem development, though this for a non-historian can only be an impressionistic guess. Today's movement is more widespread; it is taking place in every major ghetto, not just New York. It encompasses large segments of the black bourgeoisie and working class masses, rather than primarily marginal people and intellectuals. The appeal of black culture seems *especially* strong today to the occupationally and socially mobile, a group which in the past tended to resist ethnic identification.

Mr. Berger, however, in the review referred to earlier, argues that the soul ideology cannot meet the needs of the upwardly mobile integrationists. It is, he asserts, a lower class mystique, and they are moving into the middle classes. I think that Professor Berger is dead wrong on this point. Even in America, people cannot live by bread (or television) alone. The mobile young blacks of today seem to be seizing upon the soul concept (and the related black power ideal) because they provide bulwarks of identity and identification in the face of the very anxieties of mobility and assimilation into the cultural vacuum of American life. My recent research and interviewing of community organizers and young college students from low-income ghetto origins suggests that this is so. Certainly, as Berger suggests, there may be new pressures to conform to militant postures and nationalist identifications in order to avoid charges of selling or copping out. But the external pressure point is over-emphasized when the need is so intrinsic. This may be why there is more active support for the black power radicals (as well as for Muslims) from the mobile Negroes, rather than from the "stable" lower classes in the ghetto. This again seems to reflect a change. It is said that a generation ago middle class Negroes rejected jazz, blues, gospel music, and all other signs of lower class and southern roots. Today I find middle class black youth keep their car radios tuned in to the soul music stations and switch them on automatically whether riding with whites or other Negroes.[17]

In the same review, Berger presents a criticism of the Negro cultural "radicals" that probably is representative of much white liberal and intellectual thinking on this matter. It is important to understand why he is presumptuous in his plaint that "once the radicals invoke the perspective and rhetoric of black culture, they place themselves under the intellectual obligation to concern themselves with clarifying precisely *what* patterns of Negro culture they are affirming, *what* sources of institutional support for these patterns they see in Negro social organization, and *how* these patterns may be expected to provide the bases of 'racial pride' and 'ethnic identity' sufficient to motivate the black masses to claim both their full rights as Americans *and* the nation's respect for their ethnicity" (Berger 1967:54). First he is asking the black intelligentsia to do for their sub-culture what American social scientists have not adequately accomplished for the society as a whole. The concept of culture—as well-taught undergraduates should know—is a very sticky and troubling concept. There is much scholarly controversy and uncertainty with regard to its essential features. American culture, furthermore, is a most vague and amorphous reality: it simply cannot be pinned down as neatly and conveyed to us as graphically as the ethnographer can describe the culture of a tribal people. This may be partly because we are all caught up in it; more probably it reflects the diversity, the contradictions, and even the weakness of meaning systems and central patterns in American life. Finally, as we have seen, Afro-American culture is an even more complex reality.

Berger has every right not to accept the key assumptions of the black power movement; we differ politically and I respect these differences. But he should at least be listening to what these men are saying, for one premise is most central to his pointed criticism of their "failings." As Carmichael reiterates and expresses personally in his dealings with the mass media, one of the essences of black power is self-definition. This means that Negroes select the time, place, and manner in which to reveal their plans and strategies outside their own group. Self-definition implies that whites no longer can demand that Negroes do this or that; they have an intellectual obligation to communicate with us only if they choose to become part of our general intellectual community, and for many, the present mood is to choose otherwise. But Berger misses the boat when he implies that black intellectuals are not striving for whatever clarity and specifity that is possible in the present situation. Ralph Ellison has long been calling for such an approach to the Negro cultural experience; conferences where such issues are hammered out have been taking place all over the country recently. But this has become an in-group matter; most of these meetings have been closed to white people. Berger is probably right that such discussions and clarification are essential for the cultural and political dynamics of the Negro movement today; I suspect many black leaders agree with him thus far. But we are not going to hear what is happening until they are good and ready. His demand (and there are many who would voice similar ideas) is out of order because our long used, behind the scenes *cartes blanches* have expired for sociological voyeurs like Berger and myself.

The demand that Negro spokesmen give us the low-down once and for all on black culture so that we can define our attitude toward it overlooks a reality that is more profound than the new nationalist definition on intergroup relations. It reflects a static approach to social and cultural reality. It assumes that Negro culture is *all there*, or all-determined, needing only to be fully detected so the chaff can be separated from the wheat. On the contrary, Negro culture—like all cultures but more so—is in *process*, it is a dynamic, open-ended phenomenon, and that is why it is becoming such a central concern of the protest movement. On the basis of the culture that has already been built up out of the American experience of the until recently relatively silent masses, a more self-conscious and explicit national culture is in the process of formation. This process involves the synthesis of the orientations of the ghetto masses with the articulations of the intellectual and political leaders. The middle classes and the marginal people are playing a crucial part as enunciators and systematizers of this culture. From this point of view, Berger and others cannot lightly dismiss the activities of such men as LeRoi Jones who affirm soul and other black mystiques. Whether or not their every statement is judicious and wise, these spokesmen have a historic hand at present in the development of black culture. They know "where it's at," and they are there where the action is, and they influence this cultural action process because Negro culture is not a finished, a determined, or a static thing.

The same is true for the notion of soul which Mr. Berger feels is becoming a stereotype. This does not tell us anything about its present or future significance. The cultural reality of an affirmed trait is not in its statistical or scientific reality but in what it does and accomplishes as a rallying point and symbol. As we have come to know unhappily in less ambiguous race relations situations, stereotypes have living effects whatever the scientist may do to deflate them. The fate, function, and thus reality of soul—like black power—remains to be revealed in the practical course of events. What soul is and becomes is therefore in part a product of the conscious decisions and political-educational activities of the cultural leadership of the Negro community and even more of the response of its less articulate masses. Its fate will not be determined by white social analysts.

Whites are no longer calling the shots on these matters that most deeply affect black Americans. This is the great and historic gain of a decade of Negro protest, culminating in the black power mood—which from this viewpoint is not as total a departure from the previous civil rights activity as most people assume. And this applies also to the intellectual and social science community's grappling with such issues as Negro culture. Yet even while our academic theorizing is no longer as central as it once may have been, the black political and cultural movement still operates within these American conditions that we affect. For this reason, white social scientists have a responsibility to probe deeply into the assumptions and consequences of our characterizations of race relations in this country. This I believe justifies the present essay.

Postscript on "Neo-racism"

The viewpoint that black culture is only a lower class life-style and Negro Americans have no ethnic traditions to value and defend falls within a liberal frame of reference that I call neo-racism—though its proponents abhor traditional racism. Superficially, this argument seems to say that blacks are as American as whites and therefore, their cultural orientations reflect their social class position. But as I have pointed out, this theory ignores the group-forming and culture-producing effects of racism and therefore, as an analytical position minimizes the reality of racial oppression. In addition, this position leads to an overconcern with the pathological features of the black community at the expense of its unique strengths and contributions, since the "culture of poverty" is generally (and correctly) seen in terms of the predominance of suffering and the destruction of choice and human possibility. If Negro culture is only lower class culture, then the common assumption that *all* black people want integration, mobility, and assimilation (middle class status) seems justifiable as a basis for institutional policy and it is not necessary to consult, to offer alternative choices or to respect individual diversity. Furthermore, this position is historically tied to past patterns of negating or appropriating the cultural possessions and productions of black people. The racist pattern was to destroy culture, to steal it for profit or to view it contemptuously or with amusement. The neo-racist equivalents today are to deny that any Negro culture exists or to envy and to desire those values which the black man creates and defends as his own. (Witness the pathetic need of many young and not-so-young liberal and radical "friends" of the Negro movement to feel that they, too, have "soul.") The denial of Afro-American ethnicity is the more serious form that white appropriation takes today. Through abstract and intellectual analysis, the social scientist attempts to undermine the claims of black Americans to a distinctive ethos and value system. The very existence of our possibility to so influence the cultural process among Negroes is based on the original alienation of the black man from his African traditions. Because colored Americans could only use the English language to carry on their business, their politics, and their intellectual life, their physical and moral communities became vulnerable to the penetration of white Americans in a way that other ethnic groups—insulated by exotic languages, religions, and other institutions—could escape. Thus, the original culture-stripping and the consequent appropriation of indigenous black culture laid open the Negro community to economic and political colonialism, to the contamination of group ideology by alien, pride-destroying perspectives, and to the participation of paternalistic whites in racial movements. It is time to permit the black community to define for itself its relationship to American culture and society.

NOTES

1. Space is not sufficient to mention everyone who made useful criticisms of an earlier draft. But most helpful were Lee Rainwater, Charles Keil, and Bennett Berger. Professor Berger's enthusiastic reaction to what was almost a polemical attack on his own position provided a welcome reminder that community of scholarship is not wholly a myth.

2. Glazer, it is true, views Negroes as an ethnic group rather than simply as a racial category. But for him the content of black ethnicity is only common interests and shared social problems. His account of Negro New York ignores the existence of a collective ethos, community social structure, and group institutions.

3. For example, Charles S. Johnson, *Shadow of the Plantation* (1934); St. Clair Drake and Horace Cayton, *Black Metropolis* (1945); and Hylan Lewis, *Blackways of Kent* (1955). The distinctive culture of Harlem also is emphasized in the writings of James Baldwin and Claude Brown, *Manchild in the Promised Land* (1965), though not in the scholarly study of Kenneth Clark, *Dark Ghetto* (1965).

4. One of the most comprehensive studies of the eastern European heritage of American Jews was written explicitly from the anthropologist's view of culture, Mark Zborowski and Elizabeth Herzog's *Life Is with People* (1952).

5. As Singer (1962) has pointed out, blacks at first were simply a social-legal category, rather than a group in sociological terms.

6. In his account of Harlem, Claude Brown emphasizes the cultural conflict between the traditional "down home" (southern) older generation and their more modern, urban-oriented offspring.

7. We can also assume that considerable ambivalence toward the African "homeland" remains. See Harold Isaacs, *The New World of Negro Americans* (1963), for an excellent treatment of attitudes toward Africa.

8. Hernton's stimulating collection of essays is surprisingly neglected; see *White Papers for White Americans* (1966).

9. For an excellent critique of attempts to characterize lower class culture, including the theory of Oscar Lewis, see Charles A. Valentine, *Culture and Poverty* (1968). Valentine systematically attacks the assumptions of the main students of lower class culture and shows how the pathological interpretation of lower class, including Negro, life-styles is based more on middle class preconceptions than on careful ethnography. Valentine helps clarify the concepts of culture and sub-culture, and contributes a devastating critique of Oscar Lewis' "culture of poverty" thesis.

10. Valentine makes the important point that students of lower class life have incorrectly characterized some of these traits that result from external conditions as elements of culture, when the idea of culture should be reserved for norms and values that the group sees as desirable. Thus, sporadic unemployment may be part of the life style of many in the lower class ghetto; it is not valued by the vast majority, however (Valentine 1968).

11. As many have pointed out, the organization of lower class people into Christian, Marxist, or trade union associations leads toward middle class socialization as much as the institutionalization of working class values.

12. If race is a more important division in present-day American society than that of class, this raises serious questions about the tendency to reduce Negro American culture to lower class culture.

13. For a thorough discussion of cultural exploitation see the original and perceptive analysis of Harold Cruse, *The Crisis of the Negro Intellectual* (1967).

14. Howard Brotz has pointed out that sects like the "Black Jews" and the "Black Muslims" attempt to latch themselves to a long and respectable political history as well as to unique religions because they understand how important for culture both these elements are. See his perceptive book, *The Black Jews of Harlem* (1964).

15. Berger notes that moderate civil rights groups like the NAACP do not accept the notion of a distinctive Negro culture. By restricting black culture to the "soul" complex and ignoring political history, he misses the point that they have willy-nilly played a part, and an important one, in developing this culture.

16. For the black man, this theme has been most fully elaborated in the philosophy of Elijah Muhammad and in the speeches of Malcolm X (see his *On Afro-American History*).

17. The young and the youthful are of course at the forefront of the black culture and black power movements. If Claude Brown is correct, E. Franklin Frazier may have had much to do with this generational change in the outlook of the "black bourgeoisie." Brown mentions that Frazier's lectures and his *Black Bourgeoisie* (1957b) had a great impact on his own thinking, and presumably that of other college students. Of course, there is a sense in which these mobile black youths did not have to be motivated to become different from their parents, since in America all young people are predisposed to reject their elders and break away from their life patterns. But in so clearly dissecting the group-denying and the self-negating hang-ups of their parents, Frazier also helped teach the young generation to identify with their own blackness and with the oppressed ghetto masses. Many of these middle class, college educated youth have taken on the task of attempting to organize politically, as well as to articulate self-consciously, the less conscious cultural values of the lower class black man.

Twenty

SOUL MUSIC AND BLUES: THEIR MEANING AND RELEVANCE IN NORTHERN UNITED STATES BLACK GHETTOS[1]

Michael Haralambos

The general aim of this paper is to assess the importance of music as a medium of communication in northern United States black ghettos. Major foci are the ascertaining of the range of meanings that may be associated with the music by the black listener, the various functions it may perform for the individual, and an examination of directions and changes in this music. Soul music, the most popular form of black music, will be examined, as will be blues, a more traditional form. It will be suggested that blues is not in accord with the contemporary mood of northern blacks, and that soul music has replaced it as their dominant form of musical expression.

Data were gathered over a two-and-a-half month period during the summer of 1968 in Chicago, Detroit, and New York. They come primarily from four sources: radio programs (the records played and the comments of the disc jockeys), the interviews with the disc jockeys, "live" music performances within the ghettos, and interviews with performers. These four sources will be used in part to cross check each other for reliability. Many of the data are illustrative and suggestive of the points made. However, they raise questions and provide directions for future research in an area where little research has been done, due in part to ignorance of its possible importance.

One radio station in each city was selected for study, WVON in Chicago, WCHB in Detroit, and WWRL in New York. The specifically stated purpose of all three stations is to reach a black audience. All claim to be the most popular station among blacks in their respective cities. Surveys conducted among the black radio audiences by an independent organization (The Pulse, Inc.) uphold these claims. The fullest figures available to the author are the "total radio audience estimates" for the black audience

TABLE 20-1

Number of Black Households in Detroit Reached in Average Quarter-hour Periods over a Five-day Week

Radio Station	6–10 A.M.	10–3 P.M.	3–7 P.M.	7 P.M.–12 MIDNIGHT
CKLW	2,400	2,560	2,880	960
WCHB	25,550	20,920	38,490	13,900
WCHD–FM	800	4,150	5,750	3,510
WGPR–FM	3,350	2,080	3,040	1,280
WJLB	11,180	9,740	11,340	3,350
WJR	2,400	1,440	2,400	800
Misc.	6,550	5,270	6,070	2,240
Total	52,230	46,160	69,970	26,040

Note: Adapted from The Pulse, Inc., Detroit City Michigan Negro Audience, February–March, 1968:6–7.

TABLE 20-2

Percentage Share of Each Radio Station of the Total Black Audience Reached at Least once a Week by Stations in Detroit and New York

DETROIT		NEW YORK	
Station	Percentage of Weekly Audience	Station	Percentage of Weekly Audience
CKLW	11.0	WABC	15.6
WCHB	65.4	WABC–FM	1.2
WCHD–FM	17.6	WCBS	9.9
WGPR–FM	9.8	WINS	24.6
WJLB	37.7	WLIB	18.5
WJR	5.0	WLIB–FM	7.0
All stations	100.0	WMCA	16.2
		WNBC	8.1
		WNEW	6.3
		WNEW–FM	1.9
		WNJR	8.4
		WOR	15.1
		WWRL	45.0
		All stations	100.0

Note: Adapted from The Pulse, Inc. Detroit Michigan Negro Audience, February–March, 1968:4.

Note: Adapted from *The Pulse, Inc.,* New York City Five County Survey Area, Negro Radio Audience, January–April 1968:5.

in Detroit. Table 20-1 gives estimates for the number of black households receiving broadcasts from particular radio stations from Monday to Friday during an average quarter of an hour for four time periods. The basis for naming particular radio stations in the survey is given as follows, "Stations achieving an average Monday–Friday quarter hour rating which is equivalent to a share of audience of 2.5% or greater are reported on the share page and in the ratings section.... All other stations are included in the miscellaneous category" (The Pulse, Inc., Detroit City Michigan Audience, February–March 1968:2). The survey was conducted from February 12 to March 19, 1968.

Directly comparable data to this for Chicago and New York were unobtainable. Some comparable data for Detroit and New York are available. Percentage shares of radio stations of the total black audience in respect to the number of different households reached in the course of a week is given in Table 20-2.

Surveys of black radio audiences in Chicago have not been taken by The Pulse, Inc. However, WVON in its advertising material makes certain claims with respect to the station's audience based on evidence from "A Survey of Brand Preferences among Chicago Negro Families," by J. S. Wright and C. M. Larson (University of Illinois, Chicago). The station asserts that "WVON named 'favorite station' by 64% of Chicago Negro households—more than double the percentage of the next four stations combined..." and "WVON reaches 90% of all Chicago Negro households every week..." (Ignore It and Lose 1968:7).

The available evidence clearly indicates that WVON (Chicago), WCHB (Detroit), and WWRL (New York) are the most popular radio stations among the black audience in their respective cities. These stations have certain factors in common that suggest the reasons for this popularity. Each station has six regularly featured disc jockeys; all are black. All stations broadcast twenty-four hours a day, seven days a week, and an average of 90% of their airtime is devoted to secular music. The vast majority of this music is vocal and almost all the singers are black. This is revealed by surveys of records played over three-week periods by these stations. From June 28 to July 18, 1968, disc jockeys at WVON selected the records they played from a possible 61, 56 of which are by black vocalists, 3 by black instrumentalists, and 2 by non-black vocalists. WCHB playlists from July 15 to August 4, 1968, show a total of 52 records, all by black vocalists (one was by Miriam Makeba, a black African). Records from WWRL playlists from August 8 to 28 total 73, of which 64 are by black vocalists (including one by Miriam Makeba), 4 by black instrumentalists, and 5 by non-blacks. Only one of these three stations (WVON) maintained detailed accounts of records broadcast over a lengthy period of time: evidence from this source is similar to that gained from the three-week surveys. During the year 1967 WVON played 774 vocal records, only 10 of which were by non-black artists.

The preference of black audiences for black music (hereafter referred to as "soul music," as it is called by the stations in this study) is emphasized by a brief look at the broadcasting format (Table 20-3) of other stations which figure in the New York and Detroit surveys. These stations were roughly classified in terms of their programs by members of the staff of WCHB (for Detroit) and WWRL (for New York).

Top 40 refers to the 40 best-selling

TABLE 20-3

Broadcasting Format of Radio Stations in Detroit and New York

DETROIT

Station	Style of Programs
CKLW	Top 40, with an emphasis on soul music
WCHD–FM	Jazz, mainly black instrumentalists
WGPR	Soul music, plus foreign language programs
WJLB	Soul music (WJLB's July 22, 1968 playlist contained 42 records, 39 by black vocalists, 2 by black instrumentalists, and 1 by a non-black vocalist) plus foreign language programs.

NEW YORK

Station	Style of Programs
WABC	Top 40
WABC–FM	"Middle of the road" music, instrumentals
WCBS	All news format
WINS	All news format
WLIB	Soul music
WLIB–FM	Jazz, mainly black instrumentalists
WMCA	Top 40
WNBC	"Middle of the road" music, talk/conversation
WNEW	"Middle of the road" music
WNEW–FM	Progressive jazz
WNJR (New Jersey)	Soul music
WOR	News, talk/conversation

records in the United States based on charts in *Billboard* and/or *Record World*, plus local surveys. Even on stations with a "Top 40" formats, however, there is a strong minority of soul music played. A three-week survey of the charts in *Record World* shows 15, 13, and 16 records, respectively, by black artists in the top 40 for the weeks beginning August 10, 17, and 24, 1968 (*Record World*, Vol. 23, No. 1105, 1968:30; No. 1106, 1968:95; No. 1107, 1968:25).

The rationale for using the radio station as a general gauge for the type of music that is popular with a black audience is that first, the gamut of present-day musical forms is available via this medium. Second, the physical ease of choice between these types of music is equalized on a radio. Third, in such a highly competitive industry, radio stations have to be highly sensitive to public tastes in order to stay in business. One factor that has not been taken into account is the number of AM-only radios in black households.

The music played on WVON, WCHB, and WWRL is termed "soul music," "blues" being an explicitly recognized sub-division. Only 5 out of the 61 records for the three-week survey period for WVON are blues (in the city, Chicago, which is considered the blues capital of the world). For WCHB (Detroit) the figures are 2 out of 52, for WWRL (New York) 5 out of 73. All informants agrees that blues is decreasing in popularity, at least in northern ghetto cities. Tentative answers to the reasons for the decrease are given by disc jockeys. The rationale for relying on their opinions is first, music is their business; second, many run dances, promote shows, work as disc jockeys in places of public entertainment (bars, etc.), and as M.C.'s introducing artists, and so are in constant touch with the musical tastes of the black public in their cities.

The major point made by the disc jockeys is that the blues as a musical form and the meanings associated with it, are no longer relevant to the general mood and conditions of blacks today. This is particularly true with respect to younger blacks. Ray Henderson of WCHB states:

> Music has changed. The younger set does not understand what the blues really mean. They're more concerned with doing the boo-ga-loo. You play a real blues tune and you'll find the youngsters with a frown, or some type of expression of displeasure.

Bill William (WCHB) refers to this association of the blues with the past, a past that to many appears undesirable to resurrect: "Most people who are rejecting the blues are definitely trying to throw away old clothes." Butterball, Jr. (WCHB) echoes this point and relates it to generally improved conditions.

> You try to push it out of your life.... In the old days they were really in a blues bag. The man was treatin' him so bad that he had to sing the blues, but it's not like that anymore so they don't have a leg to stand on.

Butterball (Bill Crane) of WVON refers to the sadness and misery associated with blues and the function of the latter as an emotional release for these feelings.

> Years ago people identified with all this sadness, all sadness.... Now people don't feel so oppressed or depressed. They know that there's people that are against them but they're no longer canned up or nailed down. Y'see now we can move freely even though sometimes we can't express ourselves freely.

Blues songs often relate the experiences of the singer without holding out any optimism for improvement of the individual or alleviation of conditions in the future. Hal Atkins (WWRL) makes this point.

> Blues generally relates an experience of something that has happened. Gospel tunes go a little beyond that ... to the thought that ... God gives us the hope and strength that a brighter day will come. But blues is just primarily an experience that maybe you or I had, and we're relating that particular experience with no particular outlook for anything in the future. We just become absorbed in a particular experience and buy into a sort of sadistic element.

Something of the reasoning and basis for the above comments may be clearly seen from the words of several blues songs recorded by the author at a blues concert (August 4 and 5, 1968) at the Regal Theater on Chicago's South Side. Albert King performed a song entitled "Born Under a Bad Sign." Excerpts follow:

> *Born under a bad sign,*
> *Been down since I began to crawl,*
> *If it wasn't for bad luck,*
> *You know I wouldn't have no luck at all.*
> *Hard luck and trouble,*
> *Been my only friend,*
> *I been on my own,*
> *Ever since I was ten.*
>
> . . .
>
> *I can't read,*
> *I didn't learn how to write,*
> *My whole life has been,*
> *One big fight.*

("Born Under a Bad Sign" by Booker T. Jones & William Bell. Copyright © 1967 by East/Memphis Music Corp.)

Another song by King, which drew a loud affirmative response from the audience, contained the lines,

*I've been down so long
That down don't bother me.*

("Down Don't Bother Me" by Albert King. Copyright © 1966 by East/Memphis Music Corp.)

Little Milton performed a song "Hard Luck Blues" in which he referred to his troubles and poverty, bemoaning the fact that his home was the highway, the ground his bed, and he had only the clothes on his back. His response to this hardship was to cry and conclude that he might as well be dead. In "Sweet Sixteen," Little Milton told a story of an unsuccessful love affair and the great trouble this had caused him. He reacted to his problems by admitting that he had no idea what was going to happen to him in the future. In "Feel So Bad," he again related a story of unsuccessful love. His response to the situation was to vacate the scene of his troubles—in other words, leave town. During "Blind Man," Little Milton shouted to the audience, "I want to tell you all I feel like the blind man."

A song by B. B. King entitled "Worry, Worry" contained the lines,

*Oh worry, worry, worry,
Worry's all I can do.*

("Worry, Worry" by B. B. King. Copyright by Modern Music Publishing Co., Inc.)

Fred Goree (WCHB) sums up the general feelings that the blues are somewhat of an anachronism in terms of today's times: "... today it's not the same kind of starvation and the real abject poverty that the old blues singers went through." Ray Henderson (WCHB) summarizes the attitude of particularly the younger blacks: "They say say hey! I'm not gonna be down, I'm gonna get up."

Thus, blacks see the blues as relating to a past era. Next, blues relates to a time of hardship and sadness which many don't particularly want to be reminded of. It is a musical form that starkly relates experiences and feelings without generally offering any hope of future improvement. As such, blues is a recognition and acceptance of the situation. The heritage of blues and its present-day expression is neither in tune with the material conditions of many in the northern ghettos, nor in harmony with their aspirations, expectations, and general mood.

Observations, particularly in Chicago, do suggest however, that there is still at least a strong black minority that supports blues. A blues concert in Chicago (August 4 and 5, 1968) promoted by E. Rodney Jones and Purvis Spann, disc jockeys at WVON, was well attended. The show featured Jr. Parker, Albert King, Little Milton, Bobby "Blue" Bland, and B. B. King, who were billed as the five greatest living blues singers, the latter being billed as "The King of the Blues." Five shows were given at the Regal Theater and they played to capacity (approximately 4,000) or near capacity audiences. About 80% of the audiences at two of the shows was estimated at over 30 years of age, about 50% over forty years. The audiences were fairly evenly divided in regard to the sexes. The advertised appearance (he was unable to perform) of Bobby "Blue" Bland at Prince Hall in the East Side ghetto of Detroit (July 21, 1968) drew a capacity crowd of about 1,500. (Again the breakdown of the audience with respect to age and sex was similar, though with a slightly higher proportion of people in their middle and late twenties. The audiences were made up entirely of blacks.)

However, judging from evidence from Detroit, this support for blues seems only to apply to the more famous singers. Little Sonny, generally accepted as the most popular locally based blues singer in Detroit and the only fully professional local blues singer, appears regularly at the Calumet Bar on 12th Street. Observations (July 18, 1968) showed, however, that only about 20% of his repertoire consists of blues. The main part of his act is devoted to soul music, and he features such songs as "Knock on Wood" (first recorded by Eddie Floyd) and "Chain of Fools" (first recorded by Aretha Franklin). Eddie Burns, another local Detroit blues singer, featured few blues in his act. He states that, "I don't play blues much now. Got to change with the times." He has a full-time day job. Other local blues singers such as Mr. Bo and Washboard Willie were not even performing during the author's three-and-a-half-week stay in Detroit. John Lee Hooker, a nationally known blues singer from Detroit, was in town during this period but did not appear before a black audience.

Chicago appears to be the major center for continuing support for blues in the North. One reason for their continuing popularity there is suggested by Enoch Gregory (WWRL).

> Chicago's a funny place. I lived there for a year and a half. . . . The blues in the later years have remained a musical entity more in the states of Mississippi, Alabama, and some parts of Louisiana and Arkansas, rather than in North Carolina, Virginia, South Carolina, Georgia, and Florida. The migration pattern has a great deal to do with it. The people in Mississippi and Alabama and those states go up to Chicago. The people in the coastal states come to Baltimore, Washington, D.C., and primarily New York. . . . So you find a deep appreciation for the blues in Chicago, and in spite of attempted revivals by program directors and show promoters here in New York, it does not exist in New York.

This is supported by evidence from Charles Keil's *Urban Blues*. At a blues concert on Chicago's West Side he interviewed a sample of the audience and found approximately one-third were from Mississippi, and "respondents from Mississippi, Arkansas, Tennessee and Alabama account for 75% of the sample (Keil 1966:155–56). The more famous living blues singers were born and raised in these states. B. B. King, Albert King, Little Milton, Muddy Waters, and Howling Wolf were born in Mississippi; Jr. Parker in Arkansas; and Bobby "Blue" Bland in Tennessee.

The evidence suggests that even today in the North the blues is somewhat removed in time and space from its origins and heyday, a point recognized by performers and audience. On August 3, 1968, Jr. Parker began a performance by shouting, "Everybody from Tennessee, Arkansas and Mississippi say yeah!" and was greeted by an affirmative roar from the audience. The following evening he shouted, "Everybody from Alabama and Mississippi say yeah!" which produced a similar response. Prefacing a blues entitled "Five Long Years," Jr. Parker said, "All right, we're gonna put you there, everybody got the blues tonight, we're gonna take you straight back to Jackson, Mississippi."

Little Milton introduced a blues with the words, "Time to go to school y'all, here we go," and when interviewed he said he meant, "This is the beginning, this is from way back." Jr. Parker stated that, "We always have to do the old standards like 'Five Long Years,' 'Driving Wheel,' 'That's Alright,' and 'Next Time You See Me.' They really go for these." Albert King went so far as to say that he now often prefers performing before a young white audience because he no longer enjoys "playin' this old time stuff."

What does the blues mean to those who still enjoy it today? Judging from the vocal responses of the audience at the Chicago concerts, both music and words have a deep emotional impact. Members of the audience constantly shouted words and phrases of affirmation, agreement, validation, encouragement, usually at the end of a line and during guitar and harmonica solos. After the first line of each song, a huge roar emitted from the audience indicating pleasure, recognition, and affirmation. The most common exclamation was "yeah!" A few of the other responses I recorded included, "sure 'nuff," "take your time son," "sing your song man," "sing it Bobby," "what you say," "say it again" (all during Bobby "Blue" Bland's performance). During B. B. King's performance responses included "play the blues man," "play it B.," "that's your song B. B., sing it," "take it down baby," "that's the truth," and "that's all right." Responses to the other artists were similar.

Disc jockeys maintain that a major feature of the blues is its graphic depicting of a stark reality. Ray Henderson (WCHB) states, "I don't feel badly about the blues. It's like Ray Charles' record of 'Tell the Truth,' and that's exactly what it is." Jay Butler (WCHB) says, "When B. B. King sings a blues song he tells it just like it is." This is echoed by Hal Atkins (WWRL) who states, "Sometimes I say on the radio, 'Blues ain't nothing but the truth,' and that's actually what it is. It's a true experience in life."

There is a belief that the blues singer is depicting situations he has actually experienced. Fred Goree (WCHB) summarizes the importance of this,

> Blues means like you have to have been through it, you have to have experienced it. ... If an artist can project the blues more than ninety percent of the time he's experienced everything he's singing about, and to really get the true picture and the true feeling an artist really has to have been through this kind of thing.

Blues singers themselves validate this point. Jr. Parker states, "Most of the things we sing about actually have happened to us, or to a neighbor, so this is what we go by." B. B. King states that his songs are based directly on his personal experiences and observations, "I've seen many people hurt, homes broken, people killed, people talked about, so today I sing about it." He more generally relates the blues to black experiences under the Jim Crow system in the South, "After you live under that system for so long, then it don't bother you openly, but way back in your mind it bugs you. . . . So you sing about it." Jr. Parker says about the former vital importance of the blues: "A lot of the time that was the only way we could express ourselves, through song, y'know."

The blues is important in crystallizing and synthesizing and expressing a mood or feeling. Lee Garrett (WGPR) recalled his earliest childhood memory: "The first thing I remember was waking up one morning about four o'clock and hearing my brother sing a blues, 'I feel so unnecessary.' It touched me and I wanted to imitate it, to learn it." During the Chicago concert Jr. Parker asked, "Do I have a witness out there?" and was answered by a chorus of assent. In his words, "You're asking if they really feel what you're doing."

The singers interviewed constantly referred to the importance of shared experiences, their recognition, and expression in a blues song and the implied understanding of their audience. Little Milton states,

> Some fans say that we were like spelling out a thing that they had wanted to say, but

then on the other hand it's kind've impossible to express it to the whole world what your situation really is, so I've tried my best to try... some people just don't have nobody and its a thing where you can feel you being represented and as the old folks used to tell me, you get it off your chest, you feel better.

B. B. King summarizes what many members of his audiences over the years have told him: "When I sing the blues the whole song may not be about the person, but there are certain things in it that they will recognize that have happened to them or some of their friends, and when this happen, then they feel it."

Despite the evident support for the blues, it seems reasonable to predict that it will die out as a black musical form at least in northern cities. Both audiences and singers average in age somewhere in their forties (B. B. King is forty-three). Either there must be a drastic change in the general mood and conditions of blacks in the North or else a specific change in their outlook toward blues. It is doubtful whether a change merely in the words of blues songs will bring them into line with present attitudes, because the associations are as much with the vehicle itself, the actual instrumental musical base, the melodies, and the style of singing, as with the words. Future acceptance of blues by a black majority in the North would entail a total restructuring and reconstituting of the meanings associated with the music.

From evidence based upon the music played on the radio stations, soul music is by far the most popular musical form with the black audience. The three-week surveys show that 91.8% of the music played on WVON is soul music, 96.2% for WCHB, and 93.2% for WWRL. These figures are based upon statements by radio station personnel of what they classify as soul music.

Explicit definition of what soul music actually is, as opposed to other forms of music, is difficult, because criteria used for classification by radio station personnel are largely subjective. Standard musical transcription fails to distinguish between soul music and other forms. Disc jockeys frequently made the point that most white artists recording or performing standard soul songs may achieve an accurate copy in terms of strict musical notation, but the final product does not have the overall sound, quality, and feeling of soul music. Particular songs in themselves cannot be irrevocably classified as soul music, or non-soul music. The Beatles' music, performed by themselves, is not classified as soul music. However, versions of their songs performed by particular singers—e.g., "Eleanor Rigby" by Ray Charles, "Ticket to Ride" by Willie Walker—are classified as soul music.

These points are made clearer by an examination of the criteria used in choosing the records for the above stations. Each station has a program director whose responsibility is to select records to be played over the air. All program directors are influenced in their choice of material by returns sent to the stations from record shops in black ghetto areas, listing best-selling records. Lucky Cordell, assistant manager of WVON, was program director of that station for a number of years. He states, "We play a sound rather than negroid music... our music is primarily by Negro artists. But this is because there are so few white artists that record our sound." Reggie Lavong, program director of WWRL, describes the principles upon which he bases his choice of records,

> It's difficult to put into words.... It's a thing that takes experience. It's a thing you've got to feel. It's not an exacting science, it's an esthetic thing. That's the final analysis, my

own ears and my own background and experience in the business.

Disc jockeys state that the only way to define soul music is by example, by an appreciation that comes from listening to the music and gaining an understanding and subjective feeling for the overall sound, so that one can point to a record and say "that is soul music," and one's classification will be in accord with that of others who have shared one's exposure to the music. This point is clearly brought out in a record by Marvin L. Sims entitled "Talkin' 'bout Soul," one of the records in the survey for WWRL. He defines soul music by example, mentioning the names of four of the most famous soul singers while the brass section and guitar play extracts from the arrangements of one of their most famous tunes.

Everybody talkin' 'bout soul,
How it make you feel now,
But I just wanna know baby,
Do they really know the deal now.
. . .
All you got to do is feel it,
I'm talkin' 'bout soul.
. . .
Now if you ask old James
He can tell you all about it.

(Brass riff and guitar phrase from "Papa's Got a Brand New Bag" by James Brown)
. . .
And Wilson Pickett say

(Brass introduction—with adapted harmony —from "In the Midnight Hour" by Wilson Pickett)
. . .
Memphis sound,
This is the best soul around,
And it kinda does somethin' to you,
When you hear Sam and Dave get down.

(Brass riff and guitar phrase from "Soul Man" by Sam and Dave)
. . .

Everybody remember the sound of the big O
The king of Memphis soul.

(Brass introduction from "Mr. Pitiful" by the late Otis Redding)

("Talkin' 'bout Soul" by Marvin L. Simms. Copyright © 1968 by Anthor Music Company.)

An explicit definition of soul music will not be given in this paper, and it is doubtful whether a satisfactory one will ever be produced. However, a number of the ingredients of soul music will be referred to, along with a fraction of the multiplicity of meanings and associations the music may have for the black listener.

In assessing the reasons for the popularity of soul music, the tradition of music as an expressive media for blacks is important. Something of the role of gospel music may be seen from E. Franklin Frazier's *The Negro Church in America*. He quotes one of the "famous" Ward Sisters on the subject of gospel music, ". . . it fills a vacuum in people's lives. For people who work hard and make little money it offers a promise that things will be better in the life to come" (Frazier 1966:74). Disc jockeys emphasized that aspects of gospel music and blues are present in the harmonies, rhythms, diction, and subject matter of present-day soul songs. They maintained that there is a basic continuity of "feeling" in all black American music, past and present. Ray Henderson (WCHB) alludes to the relationship between gospel and soul music: "They bring a similar response . . . both will bring on an emotional thing." Bill Williams (WCHB) states that soul music has "the same basic pattern" as blues and gospel and is ". . . definitely an outgrowth of these things. So when we hear a good gospel groove going in a record or some nice blues changes going . . . then this is soul music." There was general agreement that modern soul

TABLE 20-4
Summary of Statements Referring to the Music, Made by the Disc Jockeys During Sample One-hour Radio Broadcasts

STATION	DISC JOCKEY	A	B	C	D	E	F	G	H
WVON	Butterball	11	4	6	1	5	2	7	4
WVON	Joe Cobb	8	3	8	1	5	5	8	8
WVON	E. Rodney Jones	5	1	2		5	2	4	2
WVON	Ed Cook	6	2			9		2	4
WVON	Herb Kent	2				3			
WVON	Purvis Spann	8	1	3		3	3	3	1
WCHB	Ron White	3	1		1		2	4	2
WCHB	Jay Butler	5		2		1		2	1
WCHB	Ray Henderson	8	4	2		1	1	3	
WCHD	Bill Williams	3	1		1		2	4	2
WCHB	Fred Goree	7	3	7	4	4	2	5	2
WCHB	Butterball, Jr.	14	9	7	3	4	5	10	1
WWRL	Jerry B	6		2		1	2	5	4
WWRL	Hal Atkins	9	2	4	1	5	3	6	1
WWRL	Jeffrey Troy	6	1		2	1		5	4
WWRL	Frankie Crocker	7	1	2		1		6	4
WWRL	Al Gee	9	2	2	1	4	3	5	5
WWRL	Enoch Gregory	6		6	2	1	1	1	

music began about 1955 when Ray Charles made a secular song from the old gospel tune "This Little Light of Mine," which he rearranged and retitled "This Little Girl of Mine." A graphic illustration of the gospel tradition comes from a performance by Little Milton, one of the few blues singers who is equally at home singing soul music. During one song he shouted to the audience, "This is the time to get this church thing together. Clap your hands." The audience responded by clapping on the off beat (Chicago, August 3, 1968). This continuity of "feeling" may tend to explain why all ages are well represented in the black radio audiences. The estimated breakdown of the audience from 3 p.m. to 7 p.m. Monday to Friday, in terms of teen (12–17 years) men and women (18 and over) is for WCHB 26% teens, 36% men and 38% women (adapted from The Pulse, Inc., Detroit City Michigan Negro Audience, February–March 1968:3). For WWRL, 30% teens, 23% men and 47% women (adapted from The Pulse, Inc., New York City Five County Survey Area, Negro Radio Audience, January–April 1968:4).

Two major sources of data are used to ascertain something of the possible range of meanings and associations that soul music has for the black audience. First, there are the comments of the disc jockeys—one hour of each disc jockey's program was recorded and examined; second, disc jockeys were interviewed concerning soul music in general, and in particular about their explanations and interpretations of what they said over the air. Many of the disc jockeys' remarks during their programs refer directly or indirectly to the music. These are the "descriptions" of the music heard by the audience. The preceding chart (Table 20-4) is intended to summarize these data for one-hour time periods and to show that they are not isolated phenomena with respect to the particular disc jockey or with reference to the particular station. The categories or descriptive depositories were defined by the author, based upon the interpretations of the data given by the disc jockeys. Their criteria were used for assigning words, phrases, and longer passages to particular categories.

CATEGORY A

Category *A* is specific comment on particular lyrics of a song, usually the repetition of a phrase or the paraphrasing of a line in the song, generally in terms of agreement. This serves to emphasize and reinforce the message of the words; it complements and validates the message. For example, Ed Cook during a song by Charles Brown entitled "I'm Gonna Push On," comments as follows:

Yes, I'm gonna push on
A little longer

Yeah
You'd better believe it.

When interviewed Ed Cook stated:

> Well it's in reference to me and the people who listen to me... and what we're striving for, the civil rights fight in other words. I'm saying you'd better believe what he's saying, push on, don't give up to reach that goal, because if you give up you're lost, and it's something to verify what Charles Brown is trying to relate in that song.

CATEGORY B

Category *B* is general comment on the overall message of the lyrics of a song, usually a phrase of general agreement or support, such as "yes, yes, yes," "tell it like it is," "that's the truth." During a Clarence Carter record entitled "Slip Away" (the singer is asking a woman to slip away from her husband or boyfriend and join him for a short time), Joe Cobb said "That's all right, son." He states that he uses this phrase in regard to,

> ... a particular situation, something that would relate or touch an individual that's listening... we all like have had experience at this and if not we will. I'm saying that's all right, don't worry, in other words you aren't alone, there are millions of others, go ahead... which is like telling the audience too I feel the same way.

CATEGORY C

Category *C* is encouragement of the singer or instrumentalist, not directly related to the content of the words, but more to the mood of the piece—e.g., expressions such as "cook!" "burn!" "c'mon." Fred Goree exclaimed "cook!" during an instrumental entitled "The Mule" by the James Boys. He explains, "When I use the expression 'cook' it simply means work on it man, do it hard man, play your soul out... it's been around for a long time, it's like smokin', this cat is smokin'...."

Ray Henderson used the expression "c'mon" during "Woman Love" by Albert Washington. He states that it "comes from the church... the deacon say c'mon son if you're singing... or if you were testifying. It's more or less an encouraging thing.'

CATEGORY D

Category *D* is exhortation of the singer or instrumentalist to do something for the disc jockey or the audience; e.g., "Sock it to me," "give it to me." During Jimmy Ruffins "Don't Let Him Take Your Love from Me" Butterball Jr. shouted "Sock it to me," meaning "throw it all on me, let me have all of it...."

CATEGORY E

Category E is epithets of general approval of the singer and the song, phrases of general approbation—e.g., "WVON proudly presents the sound of soul, the soul of James Brown," After a Jimmy McCracklin song entitled "She's My Kinda Woman" Ed Cook said, "Well alright, there you heard my man Jimmy McCracklin." Ed Cook explains the connotations of the phrase "my man": "Like my brother, like my soul brother ... you might have an expression like my main man, well it means my brother whom I certainly can communicate with and sit down and have a drink with and have a ball."

CATEGORY F

Category F is comments which describe how the disc jockey feels in the context of the music, how the music is affecting him. During a record by the Esquires called "How Could It Be" Butterball Jr. exclaimed "Mercy!" He states that "it's a sound of relief, you really received all from a song that the person can put into it."

CATEGORY G

Category G is encouragement to the audience to participate in some way either in the mood of the song, or more specifically in terms of dancing (expressions such as "do it to it"), or asking the audience to relate the theme of the lyrics to their own experiences. Introducing Clarence Carter's "Slip Away" Joe Cobb said, "Let me see if I can put a strain on somebody's brain." He explains that "... someone out there might be listening and may be at this particular moment in a situation like this. And let me see if I can make someone think, in other words. Because I do believe this is a true story." During "Love Makes a Woman" by Barbara Acklin, Joe Cobb said "Do what you can do best this afternoon," meaning "I was speaking directly to the audience ... do any particular dance you can do best."

CATEGORY H

Category H is a residual category. General descriptions of the singer and song that do not fit neatly into the above categories; e.g., "Junior Wells explaining and entertaining."

The importance of the disc jockeys' comments over the air is that they are constantly explaining and emphasizing to the audience in the particular jargon of the disc jockey and in the dialect of the ghetto, the meanings and functions of the music. The fairly stereotyped and standardized words and phrases of the disc jockeys are frequently a short, hard version of the more explicit explanations of soul music they gave to the author.

The following statements taken from interviews are fairly representative of the opinions of all the disc jockeys. First, the lyrics of the songs, what is actually said, the content rather than the form. Jeffrey Troy states that "The songs definitely tell a story, something that people can relate to and identify with." Stories, in the words of Hal Atkins, that are "basically just what happens in life." Disc jockeys stress the association of the song with an individual's experiences, and the effect of this. Butterball states that "A person will say, well at least someone feels the way I feel at the present time, at least someone has been through what I've been through."

What is it about the lyrics that causes this? Ed Cook states "... the lyrics get to you in a realistic way and a simple way where everybody can understand what is being said." With respect to this idea of realistically reflecting a mood and describing a situation, Jerry B. says "Say like an illegitimate child, yes it's a natural thing, it's part of life, and James Brown or somebody like that wouldn't be afraid to say this to you in his music." Again, with reference to the form of the lyrics, the diction, phrasing, and choice of words is an important element of soul music. Fred Goree maintains,

> This is what it's all about too because it's like easy to relate.... And it's funny, even those artists who are well educated... purposefully revert back to the stereotype form and the bad pronunciation if I can call it that without sounding like I'm putting it down because I think this is where it's really at.

Bill Williams adds that "It's definitely a difference in communication, because there are certain ways that we say things to each other that we don't say when we're talking to a white person." In the words of a song of Little Richard entitled "I Got it" (1958), "It's not what you say, it's the way that you say it." Jerry B. discusses the importance of a phrase like "Uh, with your bad self" (the first line of "Say It Loud, I'm Black and I'm Proud" by James Brown),

> That's a catch thing with James Brown.... That's the type of statement that would make you feel proud. It's just about in all of James Brown's tunes... bad means the essence of good.... So when James Brown says "Uh, with your bad self," he acknowledges me, in other words he knows I'm trying to do something.

The next major point concerns the singer, and the belief that he has experienced what he is singing about, which adds impact to the message. Ed Cook states,

> The only way a singer can communicate with his audience is he will have had to live it or experience it. For example Ray Charles, he's experienced everything, he's blind, not only that he's Negro, he's been addicted to narcotics, he's lived it all.

The importance of this is stated by Hal Atkins.

> A man like James Brown, who has come from grief to glory, he has experienced just about everything that the poor man, the people in the ghetto areas are experiencing now, and he understands and knows how to reach them better than a Dr. Martin Luther King.

A further related point is the belief that soul singers are expressing their true feelings and emotions, and the accompanying spontaneity and immediacy of such a communication. In the words of Enoch Gregory:

> Soul singers get down to the profoundness of their inner self and bring this up into the tune. It's rare that you'll ever hear a live performance done twice the exact same way. This is because the human feeling, the current, immediate human feeling has so much to do with this thing called soul, and lines like James Brown saying "now get to that," it's the mood of the moment.

A basic prerequisite of the emotional impact of the words is the emotion conveyed by the singer's voice and the style of singing. In terms of a hierarchy this may be seen as the basic message. This point is made clear by Butterball.

> Soul music is music that expresses the feeling of the artist and you find a lot of groups that are singing, you can't even distinguish what they're saying, they're almost unintelligible, but the emotion, the feeling still gets across, *the message is across*.

In the same way instrumental soul music may have a similar impact. Again quoting Butterball, "It can be the music itself, the mood that the music is painting, and a guy say, ain't that the truth, that's what's happening baby." This point is developed by Fred Goree: "The guitar and the sax have a way of saying what you can't say orally. They can play it and you can feel it and you can say, yeah man, I know what you're talking about."

In summary, if we talk about the structure of soul music in a linear fashion, there are a series of prerequisites which must be met before the content of the lyrics is absorbed by the black listener. Although these elements are absorbed and appreciated as one, this being what the informants mean by the "overall sound" of soul music, various factors may be analytically separated and delineated in order of descending importance in the following manner: the instrumental musical base, the vocal style and emotional content of the voice, the pronunciation of the words, the choice of words, phrases and images, and finally what the words in and of themselves say. Via this vehicle the black audience is recognized and related to in its own terms, in its own "language," by a meaningful and emotion-laden medium.

One factor not yet discussed is the network of symbolism covered by the term "soul." A brief summary of definitions of and discussions about "soul" with informants will be given. Soul music, as its name implies, is said to have this quality of "soul." The most frequently stated connotations of the word are listed below. They generally relate to what has already been said about soul music.

1. "Soul" is communication and understanding. White singers played on black radio are often referred to as "blue-eyed soul brothers," meaning "you can communicate with him," "he feels the same way I feel."

2. "Soul" is an aspect of self, a possession. It is a quality one gains from experience, particularly the experience of being black, from "paying one's dues in life," from "coming up the hard way."

3. "Soul" is an expression of self, of "the whole self, the inner self." It is an expression of feeling, of emotion.

4. "Soul" is approbation. As an epithet it means good, pleasurable. It is a desirable quality for an individual to have.

5. "Soul" is a basic reality. It is "pure," "undiluted," "not watered down."

6. "Soul" is black. The word is often used as a synonym for black. Informants emphasized that the concept is rather fuzzy and its meaning derived from its use in the particular context rather than being gained from explicit definition.

Nineteen sixty-eight has seen an unprecedented innovation in the words of soul music. For the first time in the most popular form of black music, lyrics have explicitly and directly related to the civil rights issue. During 1968, records such as "We're a Winner" and "We're Rolling On" by the Impressions, "Free at Last" by James Barnes, "Together We Shall Overcome" by the Magictones and "Say it Loud, I'm Black and I'm Proud" by James Brown were released and played on black radio stations. "We're a Winner" contains the words:

We're a winner,
And never let anybody say,
Boy you can't make it

. . .

No more tears do we cry
And we have finally dried our eyes,
And we're moving on up

. . .

We're a winner
And everybody knows the truth,
We just keep on pushin'
Like your leaders tell you to.

("We're a Winner" by The Impressions. Copyright © 1968 by Curtom Record Company.)

James Brown's "Say it Loud" is replete with "catch" phrases.

Uh, with your bad self,
Say it loud, I'm black and I'm proud (× 2)
Some people say we got a lot of malice,
Some say it's a lot of nerve,
But I say we won't quit moving,
Until we get what we deserve,
We've been 'buked and we've been scorned,
We've been treated bad, as sure as you've been borned,
But just as it takes two eyes to make a pair,
We're not gonna quit until we get our share,
Say it loud, I'm black and I'm proud (× 2)
Whee it's hurting me, if it's alright, it's alright,
You're too tuff, you're tuff enough,
You're all right and you're out of sight,
Say it loud, I'm black and I'm proud (× 2)
I've worked on jobs with my feet and my hands,
But all that work I've done was for the other man,
Now we demand a change, we're tired of beating our
Heads up against the walls and working for someone else.
Say it loud, I'm black and I'm proud (× 2)
We're people and like the birds and the bees,
But we'd rather die on our feet, than keep living on our knees.
Say it loud, I'm black and I'm proud (× 2)

("Say It Loud, I'm Black and I'm Proud" by James Brown. Copyright 1968 by Dynatone Music. Used by permission of the publisher.)

The phrase "we'd rather die on our feet than keep living on our knees" is the complete antithesis of the lines from Albert King's blues, "I've been down so long, that down don't bother me." The important point is not the expression of these sentiments in and of themselves. Such sentiments have been expressed before 1968. The importance lies in the way they are expressed, by whom they're expressed (James Brown is referred to generally on black radio as "soul brother number one"), and the vehicle in which they are expressed. In view of the meanings associated with soul music and its widespread popularity and exposure, and its function as a medium of communication, these innovations in the lyrics are of great significance.

The material presented in this paper suggests that the area of black music, in particular soul music, is one which requires considerably more study. Publications to date are inadequate. Charles Keil's *Urban Blues* (1966) refers only to Chicago and contains little information about soul music. LeRoi Jones' *Blues People—the Negro Experience in White America and the Music that Developed from it* (1963) is a hopelessly unbalanced piece of work. Its two hundred and thirty-six pages contain not one mention of soul music, and scarcely a mention of modern blues. It is mainly concerned with jazz, Jones' forte. A glance at the tables at the beginning of this paper will reveal that jazz is of relatively minor importance. Jones somewhat remedies his omissions in his later work *Black Music* (1967). Although again the book is largely devoted to jazz, he does realize the importance of soul music. Jones writes (1967:186), "The world James Brown's images power is the lowest placement (the most alien) in the white American social order. Therefore, it is the blackest and potentially the strongest."

Finally, with respect to the broader issue of anthropological research and theory in the area of black America, two major points are suggested by data in this paper. First, what appears to be true for one area of communication may be true for others. This paper suggests that the meanings associated with black music by black Americans are distinct to that group. It suggests that far more sensitive research is needed into questions of the meanings black Americans associate with other forms, which may be outwardly similar to white American models. Second, it suggests that the question of whether or not there is a black

American culture, in relation to any other "culture," is an empirical question, and one that should be left open until further research can provide sufficient data to answer it.

NOTE

1. This research was financed by a grant from the Hill Family Foundation. It forms part of a larger project on movements of social transformation and revolutionary change under the direction of Professor Luther P. Gerlach.

Twenty-one

THE SOCIAL ORGANIZATION OF A MOVEMENT OF REVOLUTIONARY CHANGE: CASE STUDY, BLACK POWER

**Luther P. Gerlach
and
Virginia H. Hine**

This is a considerably modified version of a paper which will be published in a *Human Organization* special monograph edited by D. White and T. Weaver.

INTRODUCTION

The Black Power movement is a vastly significant social movement which is contributing to the transformation of the United States and its people, white as well as black. Certainly, it is important and exciting enough to be studied and discussed in and of itself, as so many observers as well as active members of the movement are doing.[1]

While we share in this specific interest in Black Power, we approach it as one of a class of events which we term "Movements of Protest, Revolutionary Change, and Personal Transformation," or, more simply, "Movements of Social Transformation" (M.O.S.T.).[2] We define such a movement as a group or collectivity of individuals who are *organized* and *ideologically* motivated for and *committed* to the purpose of implementing fundamental change and/or condemning present conditions, who are actively *recruiting* new participants, and whose influence is growing in real or perceived *opposition* to the established order within which it exists. We conceive of movements as functioning to challenge conventional wisdom and to muster and release energy which can be used to vitalize or to destroy people and institutions, depending upon the complex and dynamic interaction of a host of variables. The "established order" includes not only those who clearly profit from the maintenance of the status quo, but those who from apathy, caution, fear, dislike or other such motives are unwilling to be involved in movement activities although they might well profit from movement-generated change.

Analyses of social movements have characteristically explained them as consequences of certain social–environmental factors or preconditions of deprivation and disorganization in the established sociocultural system or in the personality of individuals. True believer Eric Hoffer (1951, 1963) is well known as an axe-grinding popularizer of such views. Linton (1943) and Wallace (1956) have contributed excellent anthropological classics of this type, while Lanternari (1963) follows a well-trodden path and shows how religious movements arise as a reaction to and compensation for oppression. Projects which seek to promote economic development and political reform to counter insurgent movements often are based upon stated or unstated assumptions that deprivation spawns insurgency, and insurgency is a malady to be eliminated through prophylaxis.

On the other hand, Brinton (1965) uses the historical record to show what also should be obvious from recent events in this country, namely, that revolutionary movements can flourish in an environment of moderate reform aimed at reducing deprivation. Disorganization and deprivation theory alone does not enable us to explain why the Black Power movement exploded in some cities which seemed most oriented to progress and reform in "race relations" [such as New Haven, discussed by Talbot (1968)], and not in other cities with apparently poorer records in this area. Similarly, it does not explain why the religious movement of Pentecostalism spreads in one Haitian village and not in a neighboring community equally poor and oppressed. Such theory also does not by itself explain why seemingly affluent and successful students are involved in radical protest across much of the United States. It is also not enough to follow Hoffer's lead (reported in the *Minneapolis Tribune*, Oct. 24, 1968) and simply write off the rebellion of the affluent as only a new form of fun and games for bored kids rather than a serious social movement.

If we are to build an adequate precondition model of movement origin and growth we should have to include the concept that deprivation is not merely economic and is "relative" to expectancy and perception, as do Aberle (1965) and Gurr (1967). Furthermore, we should need to consider the effect on movement development of establishment capabilities and limitations in social control and also recognize the role of "precipitating factors" (Eckstein 1964) acting as catalysts upon this critical mass of preconditions.

The development of an adequate model of the multivariant system which generates a movement is further complicated by the obvious fact that once a movement is under way it helps generate the very conditions which foster its continued growth. For example, a movement can produce an ideology which exacerbates perception of deprivation. It can increase social disorganization and grow in the ability to impose sanctions even as it reduces the control capability of the established order.

In time, perhaps someone will produce a definitive multivariant socio-environmental model of movement genesis and growth. Johnson (1966: 119–120) believes it to be impossible to construct a statistical measure which will predict the occurrence of a phenomenon as multiplex as a movement of revolutionary change. Instead, he aims to discover measures of the "disequilibrated social system," an approach which he feels provides "the potentially revolutionary situation."

Our own approach is to regard these socio-environmental conditions of deprivation, disorganization, disequilibration as at best movement-facilitating rather than sufficient or necessary. In our studies we have focused on the structure, function and process of the movement itself, rather than these facilitating conditions. We propose a movement model which includes a set of five key factors which are part of the movement rather than of its socio-environment. These factors are:

1. segmentary, decentralized and reticulate *organization*;
2. *recruitment* which exploits pre-existing social networks;
3. a commitment act and/or transforming experience;
4. a change-oriented and action-motivating *ideology* which transcends mere self-interest and offers (a) a vision of a better future, (b) heightened self-esteem, (c) a cognitive "filter" through which "objectively" negative feedback can be converted into positive reinforcement, proving that the movement is right;
5. the perception of real or imagined opposition against which the movement can unite and strive.

We might add that Friedrich (1969) proposes a model of "the causes of local agrarian revolt in Mexico" which combined some of what we term facilitating conditions with some (organization and ideology) of those we regard as internal movement factors. He also orders all of these in a causal sequence. We feel that such combination reduces analytical clarity.

Of course, it is only for purposes of analysis that we thus dissect a movement, divorce it from its matrix, and rather mechanically treat these five internal factors as separate entities. In the actual stream of movement events these factors interact dynamically, each both influencing and being influenced by each other in a complex developmental process of the type Maruyama (1965) describes as "deviation-amplifying mutual causal." Similarly and simultaneously, these factors interrelate dynamically with a range of external and facilitating conditions, including those mentioned above.

We have discussed this five factor movement model in other writings (Gerlach and Hine 1968a; 1969) and in a film, *People, Power, Change* (Gerlach 1968). In these publications we use data and ideas drawn chiefly from our 1965–1968 field research on the Pentecostal and Neo-Pentecostal religious movement in urban U.S.A., Colombia, Haiti, Jamaica and Mexico, and our 1967–1969 study of Black Power and quasi-movement collective response to Black Power in two North American cities. The model is proving eminently useful in our current study of middle class North Americans who are organizing at the grass roots to fight pollution and improve the quality of the environment. Various articles in the May 1969 *Minneapolis Tribune* refer to this activity as "the surging conservation movement" but we refer to it as "Participatory Ecology—a Movement in Embryo." In one of the two cities where we have studied it, we find that according to our model it displays movement-like characteristics in social organization, patterns of recruitment, and perception of opposition. It seems to be developing a motivating and transcending ideology (of ecology) but has yet to generate a commitment process. Applying our model, we have accurately predicted the rapid proliferation and segmentation of a variety of environmentally-oriented groups, and the interweaving of these groups to form a network of the type we describe below, for Black Power, and have previously described for Pentecostalism (Gerlach and Hine 1968a).

We have discussed movement organization and other aspects of our model in private conversation and public form with representative participants of the movements studied. Most have agreed that our model is useful, valid, and does not do injustice to the ways in which they and their brother participants interpret events. Following our explanation, most seem to appreciate that we are comparing generic form and process rather than specific substantive features of individual movements. Some, however, have objected to the type of movement we draw on for comparison. Pentecostals feel that their movement is "of the Lord" and some feel that as such it should not be compared with a movement "of man," like Black Power. Similarly, some participants in the Black Power movement argue that their sociopolitical movement should not be compared with Pentecostalism, which they often perceive as the very antithesis of a movement of change. In large part, this criticism reflects a lack of understanding of the variety of group types within the Pentecostal movement. It is as if someone evaluated Black Power simply on the basis of the activity of a branch of the NAACP or, at the other extreme, of a Black Panther group.

We should add here that Pentecostalism, as it has appeared in much of Black America, has indeed been an established religious system which has helped to conserve, justify and compensate for those traditions which have locked blacks into a position of subordination to white power. Similarly, some white Pentecostal churches, such as the Assemblies of God, are equally long-established and serve to help their members conform to main-line patterns. But our research clearly demonstrates that Pentecostalism is not limited to this conservative dimension. In the United States, the cutting edge of the Pentecostal movement, sometimes called Neo-Pentecostalism or the Charismatic Revival, consists of large numbers of independent, often "home-meeting" groups which recruit primarily from the white middle and upper-middle class. Many are newly formed groups and consist chiefly of new converts. This new Pentecostalism asks participants to change in ways which conflict with white middle class convention. It emphasizes deep personal involvement in religious practice, personal receipt of various supernatural gifts, including the gift of tongues, and personal behavioral transformation. As it grows both in the U.S.A. and the other areas where we have studied it, it characteristically threatens and draws opposition from established religious institutions: i.e., Voodoo in Haiti, mainline Protestant and Catholic denominations elsewhere. In some areas, this opposition extends to include political and economic sanction.

Similarly, the "conservation movement" as it has been known to many is not perceived as a movement of change but instead as a set of middle and upper class clubs which have their roots in the established order and which often "... prefer to treat developers and exploiters as basically good fellows deep down, whose consciences could be aroused (to conserve some of the environment) if only their feelings were not badly bruised" (Peterson 1969). These have thus supported rather than challenged conventional patterns of resource management. But our research suggests that in one area, at least, a more aggressive, often radical, set of "participatory ecology" groups are emerging to challenge conventional uses of the environment and to use unconventional and aggressive tactics to that end.

Thus, in Pentecostalism, Black Power, and potentially in "Participatory Ecology" we observe how groups which vary considerably in internal routinization, age, and tactics interweave to form a structure which we perceive as *segmentary, politically decentralized and reticulate*. We suggest that this may be the more basic structure of grass roots social movements, and that more centralized revolutionary movements, such as we find in Viet Nam, are special cases developed through modification of this general form.

In the balance of this paper we shall limit ourselves to a short analysis of this basic type of movement organization as we observed it in the Black Power movement. We shall describe this organization and point out its adaptive function in implementation of social change.[3] We shall not in this paper deal directly with the movement factors of recruitment, commitment, ideology or opposition, but refer the reader to our publications which do explicate these features.

PERSPECTIVE ON ORGANIZATION

Movement organization—that is, organization designed to implement personal and social change—parallels in many ways the well-known segmentary lineage systems found in many African, Middle-Eastern and Asian tribal societies. Each segment, or cell, in the body of the movement is an essentially independent entity, politically autonomous and economically self-supporting. Each displays a tendency to divide just as each is linked to other cells through various types of cross-cutting ties. Especially characteristic of movement organization are the counter-balancing processes of fission and fusion, of splitting in dispute or competition and relinking in alliance. These same processes and their adaptive utility have been well-described for a variety of African and Middle-Eastern societies by such scholars as L. Bohannan (1958), P. Bohannan (1954), Evans-Pritchard (1940), Eisenstadt (1959), Fortes (1963), Gluckman (1954), Middleton and Tait (1958), I. Lewis (1961), Kasdan and Murphy (1959), Sahlins (1961). To paraphrase Sahlins, these processes provide a mechanism for expansion into the domain over which others have established control. The segmentary system "divides" to push into the living space of its neighbors and then pulls together to apply concerted pressure and consolidate its gains.

Outsiders find it difficult to control such a system. British administrators in the earlier days of colonialism, attempting to come to terms with or dominate certain segmentary and acephalous or "headless" African tribes, probably felt as if they were reaching in to grasp the center of a bowl of jelly. These tribes did not have a single paramount leader and/or controlling bureaucratic administration through whom the British could operate. Chairmen of the Urban Coalitions of contemporary American cities, attempting to locate a "responsible" black leader who represents the Black Power movement, have many of the same feelings.

According to one popular view, the Black Power movement is wholly amorphous—a series of disconnected activities and spontaneous eruptions due to pent-up frustrations caused by prolonged deprivation. Other people assume some sort of central direction, pyramidal organization, and a defined chain of command—often imagined as leading through invisible channels to the Kremlin. Still others utilize an oversimplified version of the Weberian charismatic-leader–devoted-followers model. All of these popular views are inadequate.

DESCRIPTION OF VARIATION OF CELL TYPES

Observation of the movement in any single metropolitan area reveals a multitude of organizations of various sizes, of varying degrees of permanence, with different and often conflicting views of Black Power ideology, and utilizing very different means to achieve common goals. In one urban center we found such black initiated and black controlled organizations as:

— three community centers offering study and action programs for both youth and adults. They are moderate-to-militant in orientation. Two of them were inspired by, but are independent of, the first.
— a very conservative adult group organized in opposition to the militant effect of these community centers on their youth. This group competes with the community centers for direction of youth activities.
— a vocational and technical training center focused on solution of employment problems. Teachers represent the whole attitudinal continuum from militant separatists to conservative integrationists.
— three para-police patrol groups, two of which are equipped with squad cars, weapons, and other accoutrements of para-police activity. Two of these are all black, one is integrated. All compete for recognition as legitimate law-enforcement agencies.
— several Afro-American culture and history study groups.
— several so-called sensitivity-training groups which conduct seminars for bewildered whites —businessmen and community organization groups—who realize that they do not understand the problems or orientations of black Americans. Some of these groups have become prosperous businesses.
— a militant group dedicated to Frantz Fanon's concept of violence as a cleansing force. This group is arming itself and talking about techniques of urban guerilla warfare.
— a rumor control center which competes with the local Urban Coalition to be the clearing house for information about all pertinent activity in the area.
— several groups of university and high school students who meet regularly for discussion, are militant in orientation, and initiate confrontations by agitating for curriculum and administrative changes. These groups are capable of rapid organization for sizable demonstrations and sit-ins in response to any official act or policy decision that may have racial undertones.
— ad hoc groups, continually being formed in on-the-spot response to specific situations. Self-appointed leaders step forward to direct the demonstration and formulate demands. These groups often continue to meet after the initiating confrontation is resolved and become permanent study and action groups.

This is, of course, a very incomplete list, and is intended only to indicate the variety of local, autonomous groups which consider themselves part of the Black Power movement. There are also local chapters in many urban centers of nationally organized groups such as SCLC, SNCC, and CORE. Since Whitney Young's conversion to Black Power, reported in the August 9, 1968, issue of *Time*, local Urban Leagues may be considered Black Power groups representing the conservative end of the continuum. NAACP groups vary in the degree of militancy depending on the local personnel and on the strength of the affiliated youth groups. These organizations may be considered super-cells in the structure of the movement as a whole. Although local chapters of these organizations are directed to varying degrees by a central headquarters, their well-known leaders in no sense can be considered the leaders of the movement as a whole. There are too many local, independent groups who owe no allegiance to any body larger than themselves and who are often more significant in the effect of the Black Power movement at the local level than the more highly organized national groups.

Although all Black Power groups ascribe to a basic ideology of black pride, black unity, economic and political power for the black community, and self-determination, each group has its own ideological "bag," develops its peculiar style and stance and "does its own thing."

DECENTRALIZATION

Leadership in the Black Power movement in Weberian terms is charismatic rather than bureaucratic. As in acephalous tribal societies, power and authority tend to be disbuted among several of the most able and dedicated members of a group, of which one is recognized as *primus inter pares*, the "first among equals." A typical leader in this context achieves his status by building a personal following and displaying abilities and characteristics pertinent to situational needs and the expectations of his adherents and potential recruits. He must prove and continue to demonstrate his worth to maintain his status. One way to look at the segments which comprise the body of the movement might, indeed, be to consider them essentially the personal networks of leaders. Mayer's suggested approach to personal networks is useful in such analysis. However, it focuses on too limited a set of relationships and by itself would not show movement structure in adequate perspective. The reticulate structure of a movement is too broad in scope to be effectively analyzed as but the sum total of key individual networks. In any event, although leaders will fall, the movement will persist and most of the groups which they bossed will continue under new direction, often with little or no change in membership.

In his study of segmentary lineage systems, Sahlins (1961) points out that leadership in such systems is often situation specific and hence ephemeral. A man who proves himself as a war leader over a confederation of segments fighting a common foe is not necessarily able to work as a leader of this confederation or of its components in peace.

This situational aspect of leadership is characteristic of Black Power. Those qualities which enhance the leader's reputation in some types of militant and action oriented operations may not be pertinent to ensure maintenance of leadership under different conditions. A person may secure leadership over a group or collection of groups by his ability to "sock it to" "whitey," to mobilize and lead a short-run militant operation and obtain concessions from the establishment. But he may not have the ability to lead these groups in the more routine consolidation of gains, and hence might fade, at least for a time, into the background while persons with more pertinent organizational skills assume control—again temporarily.

Even where a person has both militant action-oriented and administrative-routinization skills, he may find it difficult to play both more or less simultaneously. Administering the ordinary activities of many of the Black Power groups often implies working to some degree with whites, taking their advice and funds (often with some strings attached or implied) and reducing overt manifestations of militancy. This leads other blacks to brand such leaders as Uncle Toms and accuse them of being co-opted by the system.

Occasionally, we find a leader who manages more or less simultaneously to play such administrative roles and more militant roles. We might note the example of one leader who has impressed us with his remarkable flexibility in this regard. He used his militant following to help him gain control of certain community development centers which are financed by the Federal Government. To maintain status as a militant and reward his loyal followers, he has had to behave in ways which conflicted with the expectations of the establishment and the bureaucratic and fiscal management requirements of his new office. To remain in office he has then had to convince government monitors that he is the man for the job, even when he has various charges pending against him for leading militant demonstrations. He has had to explain to them that if they replace him with a moderate black their development programs will not be able to "reach the militant youth." On the other hand, he has had to convince his militant followers that it is in their interests to support him so that he can control the centers. We are tempted to suggest that this movement environment selects leaders who can adapt to and manipulate such diverse pressures.

Although certain particularly charismatic and able leaders, like Stokely Carmichael, H. Rap Brown, Dick Gregory, Eldridge Cleaver, or the late Martin Luther King, are highly revered and widely influential at any one moment, the humblest new convert to the movement can perceive them as "soul brothers," not as "commanders of the faithful." Each has organizational power only over his own segment of the movement. To outsiders, such men often appear to be the key individuals without whom the movement would grind to a halt. But not one of them could be called the leader of the Black Power movement as a whole.

First, they quite clearly disagree upon such crucial matters as the goals of the movement and the means by which these goals should be achieved. Second, none of these leaders have a roster, or even know about, all of the groups who consider themselves to be participants in the Black Power movement.

Third, they can make no decisions which are binding upon all or even a majority of the participants in the movement.

Fourth, and this is most frustrating for representatives of the established order, *none of these leaders have regulatory powers over the movement*. City officials are often upset when well-known leaders whom they assume to have incited a riot, cannot control it, even when they are obviously working sleeplessly to do so. Officials then conclude either that the leader is not sincere in his efforts to stop the riot or that it got "out of hand" and beyond his original orders. In one recent riot, the governor of the state called in a well-known Black Power leader who had been speaking in the area to plead for an end to the violence. Local black leaders said afterwards that they felt this only made the situation worse. The assumption that local groups were under his control angered them.

A fifth manifestation of the acephalous nature of the movement is that there is no such thing as a card-carrying member of the movement, although some groups do have specific membership requirements. Participation in the movement is based on the experience of "having soul." There are no objective requirements for membership, and soul brothers recognize each other through a bond of subjectively perceived commitment. There is no leader, therefore, who can determine objectively who is or is not a member of the movement, let alone direct, regulate, or speak for the movement as a whole.

SEGMENTATION

Observation of the segmentary nature of movement organization suggests four basic ways in which cells split, merge, or proliferate.

First, movements characteristically include in the ideology a concept of personal power. In religious movements, this involves beliefs concerning the direct access to God from whom power is derived. In the Black Power movement, this concept is expressed in terms of "doing your own thing." Each individual, as well as each small group, is credited with and encouraged to manifest his own unique "bag" and to take initiative in acting to serve the cause of the revolution. This results in organizational splits over ideological or methodological approach and stimulates the gathering of new recruits to support each new venture.

Second, pre-existing socio-economic cleavages, factionalisms, and personal conflicts are carried over into the movement and increase the so-called "fissiparous" nature of the movement organization.

Third, movement members, especially those with leadership capabilities, compete for a broad range of economic, political, social and psychological rewards. Black Power leaders are continually vying with one another for funds elicited from the white community because of fear, guilt, or a genuine desire for social change. This personal competition results in continual splitting of cells, realignment of followers, and intensified recruitment of previously uninvolved blacks.

Fourth, segmentation of movement organization occurs over ideological differences which cannot be traced to previously existing socio-economic cleavages or personal conflicts. As we have pointed out in other papers, a truly committed movement participant experiences an intensity of involvement over ideological differences that the ordinary person does not feel unless his pocket book or his pride has been attacked. Ideological differences which are sufficient to produce organizational fission in the Black Power movement are such matters as: the concept of separatism versus the concept of integration, violence versus non-violence, the extent to which white supporters should be allowed to participate in black controlled groups, etc.

RETICULATION

The decentralized, segmentary, organizational structure of the Black Power movement owes its cohesion to linkages between the autonomous cells. Through these linkages the various cells intermesh to form a network which, following Mayer (1966), we regard as essentially "unbounded." That is, it ramifies extensively throughout Black American society and there are no well-defined limits to such extension. We identify five types of such linkage:

First, there are ties of kinship, friendship, and other forms of close association between individual members of different local Black Power groups. Often a single individual will be an active participant in more than one group as well. Even after an organizational split over some issue, previous ties of friendship tend to form loose linkages between the resulting splinter groups. Such ties form the basis for potential cooperative action in the face of large scale opposition at a future date.

Second, personal kinship or social ties between leaders of autonomous cells form networks that sometimes extend beyond the local community and tie independent groups in distant cities together.

Third, every movement has its travelling evangelists who criss-cross the country as living links in the reticulate network. Carmichael, Abernathy, McKissick, Cleaver, and others are only the better known of hundreds of spokesmen whose influence is spreading beyond their own local groups. When such an evangelist–organizer comes to town, members of many different local segments bury the hatchet temporarily to hear him speak and often act in concert under his ad hoc leadership in a specific activity such as a demonstration or march.

Closely related to the rally or the revival meeting of the traveling evangelist are the more permanent cross-cutting activities of the area-wide, regional or national "in-gathering." One example of the regional and national in-gathering is the Poor People's March. Another, somewhat earlier example, is the open housing demonstration of Father Groppi and the "Commandoes" in Milwaukee. An example of the area-wide gathering is what we shall call the "Freedom Week Coalition" which developed in the Winter and Spring of 1969 in one large metropolitan area which we studied. Freedom Week followed upon a black student, S.D.S.-supported, sit-in at a local university administration building, during which some property was damaged. The County Grand Jury indicted several black students as alleged leaders of the demonstration, charging them with "unlawful assembly, wilful destruction of property and inciting to riot." The manifest purpose of Freedom Week was to protest this Grand Jury action.

Participation in each of the above gatherings and activities cut across many divisions and drew support from various segments of the Black Power movement as well as from individuals and groups, black and white, not in the movement, but often linked to it through the "extra-movement linkages" which we discuss below.

If the local committees of such area, regional, and national associations continue, and become more permanent organizations, they will be roughly analogous to the age sets in acephalous African societies which cut across loyalties to the lineage segments (Eisenstadt 1959). In the sites of our research, Poor People's March Committees and Freedom Week Coalition Committees were composed of representatives of different local "lineages" in spite of serious differences in ideological and group practices.

While national Urban Leagues and NAACP chapters are better viewed as super cells, or maximal lineages within the segmentary structure, SNCC might be characterized as a cross-cutting structural mechanism. Individuals who are recruited for SNCC activities such as voter registration in Southern counties, come from and remain members of other local Black Power groups in their own cities.

A fifth and crucial cross-cutting linkage that provides movement unity are those basic beliefs which are shared by all segments of the movement, no matter how disparate their views on other matters. All movement ideologies are "split level" in the sense that there are a few basic themes and an infinite variety of interpretations and emphases. The variety of interpretation is the ideological basis for organizational fission. The few basic tenets are the ideological basis for fusion, enabling members of warring factions to conceptualize themselves as participants in a single movement or "revolution." These unifying tenets can be simply and forcefully condensed into a few credal statements, slogans, or battle cries such as: Black is beautiful, Black Power is Green Power, Racism is Whitey's hang-up, etc. Such statements express the core beliefs which make possible the system of inter-cell leadership exchange, temporary coalition on specific actions, a flow of financial and other material resources through non-bureaucratic channels, and an often surprising presentation of a united front in the face of external opposition. They are comparable to the common ancestor concept of the Arabs, Nuer, or Tiv, and

Somali peoples, who unified on this basis when necessary.

This, then, is the decentralized, segmentary, and reticulate social structure of the Black Power movement. It is a structure which "surprises" John Herbers, described by *Time Magazine* (June 6, 1969:53) as a "veteran civil rights reporter," because its various participants and "communities" display such "unity" of purpose "despite organizational fragmentation."

EXTRA-MOVEMENT LINKAGES

This structure is articulated to and gains in strength from various significant extra-movement linkages, in particular linkages to groups, organizations and persons in established white society. Here, again, these links ramify in an essentially unbounded, expanding web. Typically, participants in the Black Power movement will have various white or black friends, associates and other contacts who are not involved in the movement. These relationships may have been established through, or quite independently of, Black Power activities. A participant in any one movement cell may prevail upon his extra-movement friends and associates to aid him in ways which directly or indirectly help the movement locally or nationally. Through their relationships with any one participant, or cell, non-participants may be influenced to support the movement in word or deed. In turn, many such non-participants will use their own networks of friends, relatives, or associates either directly or indirectly to help them provide such support. As an example of these extra-movement linkages, we can note that personal associations of varying intensity among several dynamic black militant spokesmen and various white churchmen, community leaders, students, and university faculty in one urban center provided the primary and initial channels through which these black leaders were able to obtain financial and political support to establish a unique and controversial community center.

Concerned whites of varying background have also formed collectivities of varying composition and scale to generate changes in white society which they believe will be appropriate responses to legitimate black demands and complaints. In one city, the Urban Coalition and its various task forces provide an example of such "positive response groups."

Other response groups have been formed among church congregations, university faculty and students, suburban neighborhood populations and the like. Various black power cells are linked to these groups through a variety of interweaving relationships. Personal extra-movement association with members of such groups provides one important tie. Overlapping participation is another. For example, some blacks who are participants in one or more Black Power cells are also consultants to or participants in a number of these response groups. In one city studied, the integrated para-police patrol mentioned earlier provides an effective point of linkage between Black Power cells and white groups, since many patrol members also participate in a variety of other collectivities. Similarly, the Urban Coalition task forces provide a linkage juncture through which circles of involvement overlap and extend to new areas.

As is well known, Students for a Democratic Society (S.D.S.) often seek to join in common cause with militant Black Power groups. In part, they do this because Black Power activities so often zero in on the gap between the noble ideals expressed in the

American Dream and the harsher manifestations of real life in these United States. Thus, Black Power causes provide S.D.S. with ideological motive and justification for implementation of confrontation tactics. For example, as it has done in campuses across the country, S.D.S. was quick to join blacks in the University administration building takeover which gave rise to the events leading to Freedom Week, mentioned above. Furthermore, they were among the first of the many white groups to link with blacks to form the Freedom Week Coalition committees. In fact, they attempted to dominate this coalition and direct its activities to their ends. Black leaders had to remain alert and aggressive to retain control. More moderate whites, especially members of a university student association and various campus ministers and their student followers, helped block S.D.S. attempts at takeover.

In theory, at least, such extra-movement linkages and alliances can result in essentially balanced reciprocity in which movement and established order share about equally in accomplishment of objectives. Or, they can result in asymmetrical flows of energy, assistance, influence, authority, decision-making and control capability. We shall summarize this simply as "influence flow." We imply in the above discussion of extra-movement linkages that this influence flow is asymmetrical and presently favors Black Power. This has not always been the case. Many blacks perceive that whites controlled much of the Civil Rights struggle, just as they once dominated various key associations which were supposed to help Negroes make their way into the American mainstream. Blacks now strive to be masters of their own movement for their own ends. We have many examples in which whites voice and often accept the dictum that blacks must indeed achieve such self-determination and that whites must now be dutiful assistants and silent subordinates to black leaders. Hence, the preponderant direction of influence flow has been reversed, shifting from an earlier pattern in which the articulation of whites to Negro associations helped chiefly to perpetuate convention and white domination, to an opposite pattern in which blacks exploit such articulation primarily to gain white establishment support for Black Power goals. This shift is roughly coterminous with the shift from the Civil Rights phase to the Black Power movement.

Whether by design or accident, S.D.S. is attempting to generate another type of asymmetrical exchange with Black Power. S.D.S. claims to be working for the cause of "black liberation," yet it often seeks to use Black Power causes to further its own ends. These ends do not necessarily coincide with those of the Black Power movement, and they also conflict with convention and practice in the established order. Blacks appear to understand this situation well and to be able to employ the broad range of their extra-movement linkages more to the gain of their movement than to its cost.

In short, then, these extra-movement linkages and alliances help Black Power participants and groups to establish and maintain useful interrelationships with white society, to articulate to the community power structure or otherwise to muster enough support to negotiate advantageously with this structure.

EXAMPLES OF RETICULATION AND EXTRA-MOVEMENT LINKAGE

Freedom Week as mentioned above and the events which led up to it provide good examples of reticulation within the black movement and extra-movement extension. It developed as follows:

A black student group called Black Students Action Committee at the university took over part of the administration building to protest conditions and demand, among other things, the initiation of a Black Studies Program and special scholarship assistance for black students. Various other blacks on the campus, a few who are participants of other black student groups, joined in the action. Some members of the Black Students Action Committee had been "radicalized" and committed to Black Power through earlier involvement in two black community centers. A few were still participants in center activities. Through such links, other members of these centers came to the administration building, a few to criticize the takeover as "poorly planned and executed," but most to assist. Other blacks from the surrounding metropolitan area joined the action, some of whom are participants in one or more other Black Power groups. In time, yet other blacks appeared to act as mediators between these in the initial takeover and the university administration. Although the mediators did not agree with the tactic of takeover, they tended to share many Black Power goals and perspectives with the militants.

Various whites, especially S.D.S., then also appeared on the scene, ostensibly to help the black students. The issue was resolved through negotiation. But after some weeks, it exploded again when the county grand jury served alleged black "ringleaders" of the takeover with indictments charging them with unlawful assembly and wilful destruction of property, and inciting to riot. This was considered unjust interference by a broad segment of the black community in the city and by many whites. This grand jury action provided the "ideologically right" action against which a diverse array of black and white groups could form and unite in common cause. Individuals and groups combined in various demonstrations, culminating in a final and very large march (several thousands of marchers) from the university to the city center. Some of those on the march, including various church groups, were there both to protest the charges and to act as a counter balance to prevent extremist whites or blacks from precipitating a clash with the police or other violence.

ADAPTIVE FUNCTIONS

There is a popular bias, often shared by movement participants, against such a segmented structure as inherently weak. Factionalism and schism is viewed as a sign of weakness, ideological diversity is seen as divisive, and undirected proliferation of cells is deplored as duplication of effort. We have found, however, that *these characteristics are highly adaptive in situations of social change*. Bureaucratic centralization, while efficient, is not noted for producing rapid organizational growth, for inspiring depth of personal commitment, or for flexible adaptation to rapidly changing conditions. All of these are necessary to a successful movement aimed at implementing personal and social change. A decentralized, segmented, reticulate social structure is adaptive for five major reasons:

First, it prevents effective suppression by the opposition. Multiplicity of leadership and lack of centralized control ensures the survival of the movement even if leaders are jailed or otherwise removed. In fact, such action stimulates emergence of new leadership because of heightened commitment in the face of opposition. Autonomy and self-sufficiency of local cells make effective suppression of the movement extremely difficult. For every cell that is co-opted into the establishment, or eliminated, at least one more springs up. To the members of the establishment it can indeed appear like the *hydra* of mythology.

Second, factionalism and schism facilitates the penetration of the movement into a variety of sociological niches. Factionalism along lines of pre-existing socio-economic cleavages provides recruits from a wide range of socio-economic and educational backgrounds with a type of Black Power group they can identify with. The variety of ideological emphases and types of organizational structures produces an organizational smorgasbord which has something for everyone, no matter what his taste in goals or methods might be. A segmented social structure is designed for multi-penetration of all sociological levels and psychological types. As Marshall Sahlins (1961) noted of segmentary lineage systems, this type of social structure is well set up for predatory expansion.

The resultant multiplicity of cell types maximizes adaptive variation during a time of marked environmental change. As each cell does its "own thing" in its own way, each contributes to the success of the whole. As the black militant sociologist Nathan Hare (1968) explains, even Uncle Toms can be used by the movement to achieve movement purposes.

A third function of such a decentralized structure is what we have called the escalation of effort. This sometimes, but not always, involves personal competition between leaders. Often when a militant segment of the Black Power movement turns to violence, a host of moderate groups in the city benefit. On the grounds that they agree with the goals but not the means of the militants, representatives of the white power structure give recognition, money, jobs, and even some political power to some groups in the movement. Black pride, moderate or militant, is thus fostered. Furthermore, there is an increase in real power for the black community as a whole. This inspires a sort of escalating dynamism. Today's radical is tomorrow's Uncle Tom. As one segment of the Black Power Movement goes militant and attracts public attention, other segments are motivated to step out and upstage it. Thus demands which were once viewed as outrageous, soon appear to the so-called liberal whites as relatively moderate and reasonable. Gains for the whole movement are thus consolidated.

The most significant and undoubtedly the most adaptive function of segmentation and decentralized control is that it promotes innovation in the design and implementation of social, economic, and political change. The climate of such a social structure fosters entrepreneurial experimentation. Black Power sensitivity training groups are using innovative techniques in communicating the need for change across previously formidable barriers. As noted above, black action has stimulated the development of a multitude of white or interracial "positive response groups," which are experimenting with ways to make adaptive social change and facilitate face-to-face interracial communication. Some meet as housewives, some as church groups, some as joint action groups, Urban Coalition groups, university student and faculty groups, and the like. All of these efforts require social innovation, for existing institutions simply do not provide channels through which these people ordinarily meet on a face-to-face, talk-it-over basis.

The "buy black" concept which has sprung up in various cities across the nation has required innovation, as the white buyers usually live some distance from the black-owned stores they wish to support with their patronage. Black groups are experimenting with communal ownership of businesses, with tutorial programs in schools, and with the use of extra-party political organizations in certain localities. Para-police forces of black youth are springing up with varying degrees of success in many cities. The trial and error approach to social change facilitated by the segmented social structure of the Black Power Movement has inspired a similar type of social innovation among white positive response groups. All such innovators are finding that it must be a grass-roots attempt, using one-to-one communication and personal initiative. Normal bureaucratic channels appear to be useless for experimentation of this sort.

The fifth feature of such a social structure is closely related to the fourth. Innovation through trial and error results in a variety of adaptive and successful social "mutations." It also results in many failures. In fact, if social processes are at all analogous to natural processes, there are a good many more failures than successes. Under the pressure of selective adaptation, the maladaptive variant simply passes out of existence. This can only occur on the social level, however, within a decentralized, segmented social structure where the errors of one group have little if any effect on another. Members of a group that failed to find a viable answer to a problem can disband, reform under new leadership, or simply be absorbed into other groups. The movement goes on unabated. A social innovation that fails affects only those closely associated with it, and may indeed benefit others by showing them what will not work. Information about success and failure of such experiments flows rapidly through the reticulate network of the Black Power Movement and to and from white society and the established order across the extra-movement linkages.

SOME LIMITATIONS OF SEGMENTED STRUCTURES

Having stressed these adaptive characteristics, we should add that such a segmented structure does impose a psychic cost to leaders in the black community. The leaders of any movement component must be on their guard against those within or without their group who would displace them. Many leaders of militant groups must surely feel that in their respective followings they have the proverbial "tiger by the tail." Often they can lead only as long as they also follow. They must reflect and enunciate the ideas and demands of their groups. They can best introduce new ideas and actions if they make them appear logical projections of the group will. One important traveling Black Power spokesman indicated his keen understanding of these dynamics when he explained why he could not easily introduce to militant black groups ideas about the probable longer range disadvantages *to blacks* of separate, all black, Afro-American studies programs. He said that he would lose all power to influence and help his brothers if he appeared to block them—even though he was clearly motivated by a desire to help the black community. He pointed out that in speaking to them his ideas must "flow with theirs." If he deviates from this course, he will be cast aside in favor of other spokesmen. He did not disagree with our observation that black leaders are often under constraint to speak in a more militant fashion if in the presence of other blacks than if alone in conversation with a white man. They *must* keep up their image as aggressive militants.

It is likely that in some cities various black groups and black leaders will resort to violence or the threat of violence to force a centralization of local black power under one leader or one cell. We have some evidence of intimidation by militants of actual or presumed moderates or conservatives in order to accomplish this domination and unity. A real limitation in the "black capitalism" concept is that certain blacks will simply replace whites as economic masters in a black area and then become, with their followers, the objects of militant opposition.

It seems reasonable to hypothesize that some whites will see factionalism among black groups as a sign of weakness and seek to exacerbate such segmental conflict in order to limit Black Power. Such "divide and rule" actions will be perceived by blacks, increase the probability of conflict among black groups, and reduce the potential of segmentation to be adaptive to the total society.

SUMMARY

A movement like Black Power is neither an amorphous collectivity nor a centralized autocracy. Neither is it an imperfect bureaucracy that succeeds in spite of its lack of unity and duplication of effort. It is a different but adaptive form of social structure: decentralized, segmented and reticulate.

In any one area, a movement like Black Power is composed of groups which vary in size, scope, and duration of operations, militancy, routinization and autonomy.

Segmentation and proliferation of groups within a movement occurs because of a belief in personal access to power, because of pre-existing social cleavages, because of personal competition and because of ideological differences.

Leadership is ephemeral and weakly developed above a local group level just as organized activity above this level is ephemeral. As in acephalous, segmentary societies, leaders "build a name" and establish a following on the basis of personal qualities and skills and personally established social links and bonds. In spite of these centrifugal characteristics, these varying groups manifest sufficient cohesion and ideological unity to be perceived as a large scale movement. Such cohesion is obtained through a range of integrating, cross-cutting links, bonds, and operations, including ties between members and group leaders, by the activities of "traveling evangelists,' or spokesmen, large scale demonstrations and "in-gatherings," sharing of basic ideological themes and collective perception of, and action against, a common opposition.

Such an organization is adaptive in implementing social change because it makes the movement difficult to suppress, it affords maximum penetration of and recruitment from different socio-economic and sub-cultural groups, and it encourages social innovation and problem solving.

NOTES

1. See, for example, Bennet (1969), Barbour (1968), Carmichael and Hamilton (1966), Cleage (1969), Cleaver (1968a; 1968b), Dynes and Quarantelli (1968), Hare (1968), Hayden (1967), King (1967), and Murphy and Elison (1966), Talbot (1968), U.S. Riot Commission Report (1968), Wills (1968); to sample some representative approaches.

2. The research on which our study was based was financed by a large grant from the Hill Family Foundation, and smaller grants from Ferndale Foundation, McKnight Foundation and the U. of Minn. Graduate School.

3. In our study of movement structure we focus on groups as key components of a movement. For convenience' sake we have lumped diverse entities under the category "group." Following Chinoy (1961), a social group is identified by three attributes: patterned interaction, shared or similar beliefs, and values and consciousness of kind. We should, however, note the distinction that has been made between group and quasi- or incipient group by such scholars as Ginsberg (1934), Chinoy (1961), Mayer (1966). A quasi-group is defined by Ginsberg as a collectivity of individuals sharing mutual interests but lacking a "definite organization." It would be possible to take the entities which we lump together as groups and range them along a continuum of routinization from group at one end to quasi-group at the other. For the present we see no point in making such distinctions, however.

In addition to distinguishing between group and quasi-group, there are at least two major alternative approaches to movement structure which we might have taken.

a. Focusing on issues: We could have analyzed movement phenomena from the standpoint of key issues or events. For example, for Black Power we could focus on such issues as Afro-American studies or an open housing demonstration. In the case of participatory ecology, we could focus on such issues as protest over pollution of a river or the building of an airport near a wildlife area. In the case of Pentecostalism we could focus on specific revival missions. Then, in respect to any of these issues or events, we could examine the types of people or collectivities of individuals which come out for or against the issue.

b. Focusing on ego or leader-centered networks: Following Mayer (1966) or Barnes (1968) and others working in the area of network theory, we could focus on the ways in which specific individuals from any of the movements studied develop and use personal networks to accomplish a variety of personal and movement goals. Such study could trace ways in which these ego-centered networks intermesh through a wide variety of direct and indirect linkages. We note in this paper in the section on decentralized structure some limitations in leader-centered network theory.

A fully comprehensive study of movement organization might usefully include the above two foci as a complement to the focus on groups which we use in this paper. Certain directions for such analysis are described in the Introduction to this volume.

Twenty-two

MAKING THE SCENE, DIGGING THE ACTION, AND TELLING IT LIKE IT IS: ANTHROPOLOGISTS AT WORK IN A DARK GHETTO

Charles A. Valentine
and
Betty Lou Valentine

This is a modified version of a paper which will be published in a *Human Organization* special monograph edited by D. White and T. Weaver.

MAKING THE GHETTO SCENE IN 1968: WHY AND HOW?

Why Anthropology in the Ghetto?

This is an early report on the beginnings of a research project. We are a husband–wife team attempting to carry out a well-rounded urban ethnographic study. We have the indispensable aid of a contact man and initial rapport-builder, our 18-month-old son. As this is written (November, 1968), we have been in the field for four months. The area under study is an urban enclave which is notable for its poverty and its ethnically distinct populations. Its location is in a large metropolitan area in the northeastern United States. Its inhabitants belong mainly to non-white minorities.

We feel obligated by our relationship with the people under study not to identify the community further at the present time. For readers who may have been acquainted with plans and proposals that preceded this field work, we should add that the location of our research has shifted somewhat.

The work reported here rests on two main sets of basic assumptions. One is that solid and insightful knowledge of any human community is worth having. We believe this is true for humane as well as intellectual reasons. The second assumption is that such knowledge and understanding are particularly lacking for certain human categories in our society. Among these are our most disadvantaged groupings, preeminently black people of the poorer urban communities in the United States.

These deficiencies of knowledge are not a matter of quantity of information. There are vast bodies of recorded data on the least fortunate of our social groupings. The weaknesses of available knowledge have rather to do with frameworks of thought and outlook. Most of those who study and report on our darker ghettos do so from a thoroughly external viewpoint. This circumstance strongly influences the kinds of data gathered and the quality of understanding that emerges.

We have long felt that careful research by cultural anthropologists can provide a worthwhile start toward remedying these deficiencies. It has taken some time for this conviction to be translated into practical activity. We had to come to terms with considerable professional skepticism and negative advice about our plans. We also had to make the decision to go into the field without any normal research support.

These background factors make us feel that a preliminary field report is even more appropriate than might otherwise be the case. We want to let it be known that this kind of research is eminently possible. We also want to present our tentative but growing sense that this work is turning out to be very much worthwhile.

Our orientation can also be stated in slightly more formal terms of immediate objectives and long-range goals. One objective is to examine current ideas about culture patterns among low-income, urban, minority populations. A second aim is to investigate the nature of contemporary culture change among poor minority urbanites. Third, we hope to contribute to an understanding of the relationships between these populations and the wider society. While in the field a fourth aim has come to seem equally important: improving the quality of relevant public information for wide audiences.

One of our broader goals is to contribute to developing techniques and methods in urban anthropology. Second, we hope to play a part in advancing theory within the anthropology of complex societies. In both these connections we see much potential, but rather little achievement of insight thus far, from existing approaches and ideas. Finally, we are committed to an additional goal which stems directly from a value position. We believe that the fortunes and interests of the minority poor—indeed of the poor in general—should be rapidly and radically advanced. We therefore hope that whatever knowledge and understanding we may develop will contribute to present and future efforts by disadvantaged ethnic populations to promote their own advancement. We also hope that what we learn may help establish potential bases for more rational and humane public policies in our society as a whole.

Ways and Means of Making the Scene

The basis for all operations in this research is that we shall live for at least two years within the community and among the people under study. This kind of residential experience has, of course, long been a standard basis for anthropological work in small-scale societies. We believe that it is no less necessary in studying the urban sectors of a complex society. We find that a rounded perception of ongoing social life is largely impossible unless one is immersed in it day and night over a long period of time. Our first few months' experience has borne this out many times over.

We have so far found that participation in local life is the key technique for gathering data. Direct observation of behavior in its natural setting is the principal necessary supplement to participation. Indeed, these two approaches necessarily go hand in hand. No doubt interviewing and other forms of verbal elicitation will become more important as the work progresses. In the early months, when building initial rapport is vital, however, we have found that straightforward participation as neighbors and as interested citizens has been the most productive approach. We have always combined this with candid statements of our actual purpose for being in the community.

In a few months this orientation has produced rich records of immediate experience and observation. These materials are supplemented by much informant testimony in the form of largely unsolicited explanation and commentary. The topical areas of these data range from children's games, food customs, and adult entertainment patterns or associational networks, religious behavior, and infant care to non-legal traffics of various kinds and mass demonstrations under armed attack. On the other hand, we have yet to collect our first formal genealogy, record a single life history, or initiate an interaction which would be recognizable as a formal interview.

This approach has dangers as well as limitations. We have experienced many of these difficulties in a short period of time. There are first of all, the hazards of being treated as a member of the community by powerful outsiders. Significant outsiders range from bureaucrats to policemen, and so one must be prepared for problems extending from denial of normal social services to serious physical danger. Participation, more than other modes of study, involves the risk of cutting one's self off from one community faction by associating with another. Heavy reliance on participation increases the ever-present difficulty of keeping observer effects on the object of study to a minimum.

Living in a partisan community, rather than simply viewing it from a distance, adds other special qualities to normal research problems. It greatly sharpens the general problem of maintaining intellectual integrity in relation to controversial, value-laden materials. Participation leads to stronger emotional relationships—and perhaps more compelling ethical obligations—to the community than do more detached styles of research. Our experience leads us to reject the idea that involvement in community life necessarily makes one's work only advocacy. We do not feel that a participatory basis disqualifies the work as scholarship or science. The same experience, however, is teaching us to appreciate some of the pressures and strains of intensive participant observation. We are thus aware of factors that may lead others to see an opposition between participatory involvement and research which has integrity.

In spite of all this, however, choosing participation as the dominant research mode is the key to solving a most fundamental problem. We begin our research as outsiders in a community that has many reasons to be suspicious of outsiders. Yet in order to achieve our goals we must become, in effect, insiders. We have found that this requires being credible members of the community by actual performance. Suspicions that one is a detective or a spy are not affected by verbal assurances or protestations. On the other hand, these and similar fears of false pretense *do* yield to actual experience which shows that the researchers are credible neighbors and predictable community members.

We have found that initial anxieties as to our identities and motives have given way to a high degree of openness. A few early and mild expressions of direct hostility have been similarly resolved. Our approach has already passed several tests in the present research. One kind of expression is the spontaneous remark by a neighbor that she finds it hard to believe we have only been here a few months because she feels she has known us for a long time. Another indication is that quite a number of individuals who initially suspected us of being agents for dangerous external forces have now volunteered to describe those early perceptions. More significant, however, is the fact that we now receive considerable unsolicited information which would be quite dangerous to community members if it fell into the wrong hands. All in all, we now feel confident that substantially more behavioral and organizational settings are open to us than to the average member of the community.

DIGGING THE ACTION: EARLY IMPRESSIONS AND INTERPRETATIONS

Organization of the Local Community

We call the urban district whose people we are studying the community. In this we have adopted the usage followed by many local residents. Our area bears the same name it was given when it first became urban over a century ago. This name is in common usage today among both residents and outsiders. The territorial extent of the community is generally clear, though there is some local uncertainty about some of its boundaries. With one exception, on the other hand, the community is not recognized as an entity by any official agency outside the local area. The one exception is the complex of metropolitan establishments which administers public anti-poverty programs.

This community is inhabited by more than 100,000 people. Nearly three-quarters of this population are English-speaking Afro-Americans. The majority of these are North Americans, but West Indians are a significant minority. The largest remaining group are Spanish-speaking Latin Americans, chiefly from Puerto Rico. Much smaller local minorities—really little more than remnants—who have nevertheless long been established in the area include American Jews of Eastern European extraction, Yemeni Arabs, and a few Italians. Both in ethnic composition and in class structure our community appears to contrast quite sharply with adjacent predominantly Black and Latin districts. Here we have a very few resident Black professionals and no owners of large and comfortable homes, nor is there any numerically substantial white minority living within the community.

Available survey data indicate that the median family income of the community is well below official poverty lines. Except for a few recent public housing projects, virtually all housing was built well before World War II. Deterioration reaches literal ruin in many blocks. Community rates approach or exceed double the corresponding citywide indices for many factors associated with poverty. These include infant mortality, tuberculosis, venereal disease, aid to dependent children, and juvenile delinquency. Drug addiction and crimes against property are recognized throughout the community as major problems. Pupil achievement in every local school stands far below standard levels. While it might be difficult to demonstrate this with certainty, it is generally believed among local administrators and professionals that 80% of the community's residents are dependent on the welfare system.

There are major territorial divisions within this community which appear to be significant in the local social structure. We do not understand these divisions very well as yet. We are tentatively calling them sections, again in conformity with local usage. Section lines are probably conditioned by certain externally imposed spatial factors. These factors include variations in land use apparently dictated by outside economic forces. Also apparently involved are city policies with respect to residential locations for families supported by the welfare system.

On the other hand, sections certainly do not correspond to administrative areas established by extra-community bureaucracies. Indeed it is conspicuous that the territorial units set by supra-community agencies seldom bear any resemblance to entities of the local social structure. Most externally established boundary lines crosscut the community and chop up its sections in mutually inconsistent confusion. Among such lines are those of political and electoral districts, census tracts, police precincts, urban renewal areas, school districts, and the service areas of numerous other agencies.

The section in which we live and which we know best includes some 25 city blocks. The population here is probably somewhat less than 5,000. It displays an ethnic diversity similar to that of the community as a whole. The area is almost entirely residential or what might be better described as ex-residential: there are great stretches of abandoned tenements in advanced stages of decay or demolition. This is one of the poorest sections in the community. Public facilities are generally lacking or exist in varying states of dilapidation. Many public services are unpredictable or unobtainable.

Our own block is typical of this section, except that it has a relatively dense population. This is because comparatively few of its housing units are uninhabited. Over 600 people reside in this block. They include a somewhat higher proportion of black Americans than does the community as a whole. A large majority of our neighbors receive public assistance in various forms. Residents often refer to the block as their neighborhood. Many neighborly interactions and networks are confined—or at least focused upon—the personnel of the block. The block appears to be a more clearly established unit in the local social structure than the section.

Our investigation has proceeded at each of these three organizational levels: the block, the section, and the community. Many events occur and many organizations function in ways that anchor them clearly in one of these structural contexts. Other social entities are also emerging as promising units of study: households, kin groups, personal networks, age groupings, and numerous community institutions. At least preliminary contacts have been made and initial data have been gathered from sample units at all these levels. This whole social field also has many significant interconnections with extra-community groupings and forces. We are beginning to scrutinize these relationships as well.

The Community, Wider Scenes, and Familiar Images

At the present point in the field study, one general finding seems to be emerging. *It is proving difficult to find major community patterns that correspond to many of the sub-cultural traits often associated with poverty in learned writings about the poor.* Consider, for example, the lack of participation or disengagement from major institutions of the wider society commonly mentioned in this connection. In our community, on the contrary, there is continuous involvement with numerous public agencies and private establishments of the larger society. These include various levels of governmental institutions. They also include many types of commercial and financial enterprises. Only a few examples can be cited in this brief presentation.

Dealings with metropolitan welfare agencies are a major part of community life. Approaches to these agencies include patient acceptance of whatever is easily available, persistent group pressure for maximum benefits, and resourceful individual manipulation of the welfare system. Clinics and emergency wards of major hospitals available to the community are regularly crowded. This is true despite the fact that medical personnel feel the community people do not use medical facilities properly, while many local citizens feel the health institutions do not serve their needs either competently or equitably. Prominent among institutions of the wider society whose projections into the community receive widespread daily attention are the mass media, both printed and electronic. Community people participated heavily in the national and local elections of November, 1968. At the polling place in our section, this participation included considerable commentary, by electoral workers and voters alike. A frequent comment was that the whole exercise was undemocratic because few or none of the candidates were in any sense representative of the local community.

In spite of unemployment, under-employment, and low wages, other economic patterns do not appear as might be expected from familiar images. Few homes are bare of possessions, and most display at least minimal comforts and decorations. Durable goods such as household appliances are not rare. Some people with low incomes tell us that they own or share in ownership of land and other real property. Most of these holdings seem to be located in the southern United States or Puerto Rico. A minority of unknown proportions own the two-family city dwellings in which they presently live. Small bank accounts and other modest forms of savings are by no means unknown among our neighbors. This is especially true when such resources available through kin ties or other networks are taken into account.

Modest food reserves normally exist in most households. The predominant food-buying pattern involves a once-a-week shopping schedule. Constant indulgence in small purchases, which is often portrayed as part of a culture of poverty, is prominent here only among children and adolescents. Householders make considerable use of department stores as well as supermarkets, particularly those of the smaller type that exist in or near the community. These economic patterns are intertwined with extensive networks for obtaining and distributing resources which are quite unconventional or illicit in terms of overt middle-class values.

According to familiar models of subcultures among the poor, social organization beyond the household level is practically nonexistent. Within the community under study, however, there is a veritable plethora of organizations. These range from block associations to the area-wide community council. The council itself maintains both central agencies and neighborhood branches with social service functions. The council has more than 100 member organizations, though some of these exist largely on paper.

Churches and other religious institutions abound. Many of them are small and purely local, while others are large and affiliated with major national denominations. Among the more highly structured secular organizations are several varieties of youth groups, political clubs, ethnic cultural organizations, athletic associations, clubs for social entertainment, parent-teacher associations, lodges and other fraternal groups, and various categories of service organizations. Many either maintain or periodically initiate contacts outside the community.

We do not yet have sufficient information to make confident or extensive statements about many aspects of family life, cultural values, and kindred topics often dealt with in generalizations about the minority poor. Yet here too we have strong early impressions suggesting that many common expectations are not confirmed in this community. Many standards and orientations generally associated with the middle class are conspicuous among our neighbors. These cover such diverse areas as career aspirations, interpersonal etiquette, dress and grooming, expressed marital and domestic ideals, conceptions of kinship, life crisis rituals, and child-rearing patterns.

Change: Where It's At and Where It's Going

This is a heterogeneous and dynamic community. It bears little resemblance to the static uniformity often attributed to poverty ghettos. Along with the historically derived diversity of ethnic groupings, change is occuring at different rates in various segments of the populace. Many outward signs of cultural black nationalism—such as "natural" hair styles, "African" clothing, and associated speech styles—are common but by no means universal among Afro-Americans here. There is a less conspicuous, often more low-keyed cultural nationalism among some but not all Puerto Ricans. These trends appear to be much in flux and to touch many aspects of community life.

Materials for case studies in social change abound. An instance which we have followed closely emerged as developments outside the community closed down a public institution for child care located in our section. Scattered elements within a previously moribund citizens association coalesced in an effort to reopen the institution. This sectional group was aided a little by the community council and by minor connivance from a disaffected faction within an extra-community bureaucracy. However, it was mainly the local blacks and Latins who forced a physical opening of the establishment. Next they obtained the services of a skeleton staff of dissident and community-oriented professionals to re-establish the essential functions of the institution. Other necessary services, from janitorial to secretarial, were performed by a combination of citizen volunteers and personnel supplied by the community council. The citizens' group also publicized the reopening among residents of their section. Then the institution's clientele began returning and additional popular support for the whole effort developed.

All this was accomplished against active and powerful opposition from outside the community. In the process, the citizen group transformed itself, not only in personnel and leadership but also with respect to the group's goals and functions. It became a force for expression and implementation of local needs and demands in relation to public institutions heretofore entirely controlled from extra-community power centers. Central control was forcefully re-established within a few weeks, and many local activists were successfully co-opted with appointments to non-professional positions in the target institution. Nevertheless, the possibility exists that the institution itself may still undergo significant permanent changes in response to a resurgence of pressure along similar lines. In the meantime, some local people have learned from this attempt at creating change, and some have acquired new sources of income.

Many such local occurrences, in our area and elsewhere, are beginning to be viewed as a broad movement for social change. This is the movement for community control over the local operations of presently centralized public institutions. As the name indicates, the basic initiatives for change are quite local in their immediate scope. Yet there is also a growing consciousness of parallel interests and outlooks shared more widely. When the people in our section reopened a closed public institution and pressed for changes in its operation, they did not do this in the name of community control. Since that original initiative, however, some neighborhood people, encouraged by the community council, have begun to see their accomplishment in precisely those terms. This process has begun to create a sense of identification with a larger movement, as well as some organizational links with other groups in the community. This consciousness is expanding further as people learn that similar actions are occurring in many other communities.

The movement for community control has received notoriety in the news media with respect to recent disputes about public schools in New York City. In the area of our study, however, the institutional focus is much broader. While schools may have been a catalyst, there are beginnings of a parallel approach to health institutions, social service agencies, legal services, and police forces. Initiatives in these different sectors are at different stages of development. They are often pressed under different organizational sponsorships. Yet there is also much overlap and interconnection, developing in the direction of unified effort. The basic thrust of the movement as we have seen it is a demand that the local branches of major public institutions be made accountable to local groups which represent the publics that the institutions are supposed to serve.

This movement draws strength from long-standing dissatisfactions with the quality and relevance of local public institutions. Along with this goes a widespread conviction that the same types of institutions in affluent white communities are of a higher quality, more relevant to local needs, and more responsive to the popular will. Moreover, there are many memories of unavailing attempts by low-income minority groups to gain access to these putatively superior public facilities. These memories relate particularly to various schemes for integration.

Among the assumptions underlying all these perceptions and the resulting efforts for change are a number of value orientations common to dominant American culture. One such assumption is the belief that quality education is a principal key to achieving a comfortable and respected place in society. Another is the assumption that adequate health care is an essential to which every one is entitled. A third is that police agencies should serve and protect the community rather than prey on it. Such ideals persist in the face of long-standing conditions to the contrary. For example, it is well known throughout the community that the city police are deeply involved in payoffs and other forms of corruption that contribute directly to many forms of unlawful behavior and non-enforcement of criminal statutes. A very common reflection of local experience is that the same policemen who are so zealous in violently breaking up political demonstrations generally fail to protect householders, prevent muggings, or control the drug racket.

The movement for community control often combines a stress on ethnic identity with much emphasis on intergroup unity within the community. This is a combination which obviously involves the tension of potential contradiction. Moreover, opposition outside the community has had some success in cultivating pre-existing hostilities and suspicions between the community's ethnic segments.

A favorite tactic of this kind is for the external (generally white) opposition to suggest to Puerto Ricans the spectre of an oppressive Black Power under community control. Nevertheless, the movement as we have seen it does manage to unite individuals and groups representing a great range of ethnic, organizational, and ideological affiliations. Conservative clergymen and declared revolutionaries, black nationalists and Latin matrons, young militants and grandmotherly clubwomen do form working relationships in this effort. Perception of common interests and shared desire for change, together with mutual experience of coping with resistance, appear to bring people together.

The development of this movement is revealing with respect to relationships between the community and other sectors of society. Many institutional, bureaucratic, and political networks linking local districts to outside centers can be explored by observing the course of local initiatives for change. Forms of resistance mounted by political hierarchies, centralized bureaucracies, and professional associations are varied and instructive. The observer can learn much about the whole social field as local change advocates develop tactics to match central opposition measures ranging from administrative obfuscation to armed force.

Conceptions of the movement's goals differ among its diverse constituencies. Many neighborhood participants simply look forward to bringing particular institutions up to the standards of the wider society as these are understood locally. Some leaders envision a broadly revitalized community in which democratic processes will insure that all major institutions serve local interests. The desired long-range result is that today's slums and ghettos should become comfortable and dignified communities tomorrow. Other leaders project visions of more radical change. According to one such projection, local accountability of institutions is but a step on the way to total community self-determination. This in turn would lead to the establishment of a new non-white nation in North America. Such a program may sound utopian or disingenuous to outsiders. Yet it is by no means dismissed by everyone in the community under study or in similar areas elsewhere. We have been in local audiences numbering many hundreds and in citywide gatherings several thousand strong where lengthy disquisitions on the steps from community control to nationhood are set forth. These discussions are accorded rapt attention and enthusiastic applause.

Inside and Outside Views of the Changing Scene

Through the approaches outlined earlier, the structures and processes of our chosen community seem to be unfolding before us. We are of course not yet in a position to make fully defensible statements about the theoretical significance of our findings. Nevertheless, we do have a growing impression that prominent models of life among low-income minority Americans do not fit our data very well. Thus far, what we are living in the midst of just doesn't look or feel like what books and articles offer us as the "sub-culture of poverty," "lower-class structure," and kindred formulations.

These doubts are not confined to the specific inconsistencies between data and models cited earlier. There is also a strong feeling that some major qualities are ignored or denied by well known portrayals of life among the poor. There certainly are real contrasts between social patterns in our community and those of typical middle-class areas. Yet the essence of these contrasts does not seem to reside in the alleged subcultural differences so often suggested.

First, there are major areas of life in which local analogues of wider institutions are dilapidated or low-quality versions of standard culture elements common to the society as a whole. This type of difference is most conspicuous in those institutional areas where direct external control has long limited the quality and quantity of resources flowing into the community. Such seems to be the case with the local units of many centralized public institutions and facilities. Examples range from sanitation services which leave the community continuously heaped with refuse, to schools with substandard teaching staffs which fail to educate community children.

Further external determinants operate through other centralized institutions which devote disproportionately *large* measures of their resources to low-income districts. Most prominent here are the welfare establishment and the police. Like other wider institutional complexes already cited, these organizations tend to play a highly manipulative role with the general effect of preserving existing conditions within the community. To this inventory must be added the commercial and financial enterprises, equally controlled from outside the community in all major cases. Without any other stake in the local situation, they appear simply to profit from whatever money is available to local people and to demand heavy police protection for their property. It is difficult to avoid the conclusion that all these agencies and enterprises taken together establish and maintain the larger socio-economic environment to which the poor must adapt.

It is the quality of this adaptation by poor people that seems most distorted in many writings. Contrary to most descriptions of slums, life in the community where we are working is neither drab nor dull. We see much energetic activity, great aesthetic and organizational variety, quite a number of highly patterned and well displayed behavior styles. Apathetic resignation does exist, but it is by no means the dominant tone of the community. Social disorganization can be found, but it occurs only within a highly structured context. Individual pathology is certainly present, but adaptive coping with adversity is more common. Positive strengths (often ignored in the literature) include the ability to deal with misfortune through humor, the capacity to respond to defeat with renewed effort, recourse to widely varied sacred and secular ideologies for psychological strength, and resourceful devices to manipulate existing structures for maximum individual or group benefit. Perhaps least expectable from popular models is the capacity to mobilize initiatives for large-scale change, like the movement for local control.

Both ethnic contrasts and social stratification are certainly among the most arresting dimensions of human variation continually demanding our attention. Yet the shape and dynamism of human affairs in this community seem to correspond only here and there with major delineations of these dimensions in anthropological publications. Our experience strengthens our conviction that class structures, part-societies, subcultures, and revitalization movements are conceptions of great importance for understanding our complex society. Yet we are developing an equally impelling sense that these conceptions may serve as hardly more than labels for unsolved theoretical problems.

This inadequacy of expert and specialist formulations is matched by the failure of another professional field. This is the incapacity of lay and popular media to record or communicate either the texture or the flux of life in our community. Recently there has been unprecedented attention by the mass media and other public information sources to minority communities and poverty areas. Nevertheless, the phenomena reported in this paper have generally either received no attention from the media or have been projected in a form that is difficult to recognize from within the community. Because so many community members follow the news media closely, these projections cause confusion and anger.

Leaders and followers alike increasingly believe that media policies thrust newsmen and information organs into active alliance with the resistance to community-oriented change. This experience has gradually led to exclusion of reporters from some otherwise public events. It has also produced forceful insistence that certain types of events which have been systematically ignored should be covered by the news people. The press and electronic media are thus now being added to the list of centralized institutions over whose local operations community forces demand a measure of control. The negative or exclusionist aspect of this initiative has so far been more effective than the positive demands for expanded coverage or more accurate coverage. As might be expected, it is far easier to bar journalists from a gathering than to influence the policies of their editors and publishers.

This situation has stimulated us to make a running study comparing observed events with projections from the metropolitan information media. Our preliminary conclusion is that citizens dependent on the media cannot obtain a remotely accurate perception of what is going on in this community. In this metropolitan area—like most in the United States—the general public is increasingly called upon to make political judgments with respect to minority peoples and poverty districts. Thus far our experience indicates that these public judgments must be made almost entirely without benefit of valid empirical information.

Neither the failure of the news media nor the inadequacies of the specialized published material can be ascribed to lack of interest or effort. Both seem to have in common a lack of appropriate conceptual frameworks. We suspect, however, that the common difficulty has another origin which is at once simpler and more profound. This is a problem of incomplete perception which is in turn part of a limitation on total experience. How many American newsmen, and how many social scientists, have recently lived a significant segment of their own lives as part of a low-income minority community? The numbers must be both absolutely and proportionally insignificant.

The question thus arises as to what kind of qualifications by experience are relevant to the task of portraying and interpreting the communities at issue here. How well are most writers and others who describe, analyze, and generalize about the life of the minority poor in the United States actually qualified in terms of experience? This problem takes on special significance for anthropologists. We may apply traditional ethnographic criteria to the question of qualifications for producing valid presentations of sociocultural realities. One need not necessarily challenge the legitimacy of all other perspectives. One need only ask whether the absence of an anthropological perspective may help explain the sense of unreality that arises when available portrayals are compared with direct experience in ghetto slums.

The overlapping publics who read books and articles on social science and follow the popular media are in serious need of valid information. They need the opportunity to form realistic conceptions about what is going on in disadvantaged minority communities in the United States. The need for these phenomena to be accurately perceived and meaningfully interpreted by the public at large is equally serious from the viewpoints of non-white poverty areas. White America and the darker ghettos are already engaged in a struggle which may easily have wholly destructive results if some degree of realistic knowledge and humane understanding is not established for the national public as a whole. Anthropology has risen to similar challenges in past times and different contexts. It may soon be too late for a comparable response to the present national crisis.

Who Gets the Information—and for What?

In closing we wish to raise one further issue which is also directly related to our present research experience. This is an issue which has been dealt with in recent discussions and resolutions by the anthropological association. We believe anthropologists must take care not to confuse or contaminate the provision of socially useful information with an intelligence function serving the existing concentrations of power and privilege in our society. Researchers may certainly proceed from, or be influenced by, quite a variety of ideological viewpoints. This need not cast any doubt either on the intellectual worthiness of their work or on its utility and relevance to human welfare. There is, however, one value position which *cannot* be reconciled by any humane judgment with direct experience of ghetto existence: support—active, passive, or "neutral" —for the socio-economic and political status quo as it exists in the communities of the minority poor.

We would venture to say that every adult in the community we are studying knows or feels this in one way or another— allowing for a wide range of individual and group variations on the theme. More concretely, we have never met a ghetto inhabitant who positively accepts all aspects of the ghetto as it exists. Consequently, it seems to us that nothing could be more contrary to the underlying ethical values of anthropology than to provide information of certain kinds to certain agencies. We must refuse to supply data or make reports to increase the resources of any agency that functions, for whatever reason, to prolong the existing sociopolitical position of the minority poor. Among institutions which have been shown in the past to have such functions are some which are common sources of research funds, including certain governmental agencies and a number of private foundations.

We are convinced that any anthropologist in a situation like ours must uncompromisingly refuse to contribute to the political operations of such agencies. It seems to us that any other position on this particular point would be a betrayal of the fundamental contract—explicit or implicit—between the anthropologist and the people he studies. This position may, of course, conflict with the obvious fact that public information can be used by anyone. Then the individual scholar must exercise his judgment and take full responsibility for weighing the probable effects of publication, or particular forms of publication, on community welfare. The specifics of this concluding argument are clearly open to much discussion. With this in mind we invite comment.

TELLING IT LIKE IT IS: POSTSCRIPT, 1969

Making It: *Performance and Proving Oneself*

Comments by others and reflections of our own, since this paper was first composed, lead us to offer a few further thoughts. Some of these expand upon matters already dealt with briefly. Others broach new problems.

Before we undertook this fieldwork we were repeatedly told, either directly or by implication, that what we hoped to do would be extremely risky and probably impossible. The burden of this prediction seemed to be a notion that the angry ghetto would make it quite unfeasible to achieve the necessary rapport and at the same time subject us to serious personal danger. No doubt those who felt this way took into account the fact that one of us is black, and the other is not. Indeed we have been given strong reason to believe that sources of financial support avoided funding our work at least partly because of doubts along these lines. We went into the field with one half academic salary, but without any supporting grant; funding began to materialize only when we had demonstrated that our field situation was viable.

There are probably many reasons why such fears about this kind of fieldwork are so wide of the mark. We expect to write about this at length later. Here it is only possible to touch on one important aspect of a complex situation. We are convinced that one factor above all others has enabled us to succeed in the early months of our work. That is, our empathy with the community under study is real, strong, and active. This means, first of all, that in our own block we are neighbors in the full sense that we actively share the discomforts and misfortunes as well as the adaptations and pleasures of living here. So for example, when large amounts of looted foodstuffs flowed into the neighborhood toward the end of a particularly lean month, the people knew that we were just as glad as they to be included in the distributional networks of the block. As our son learns to talk, people use him to predict the number for the day, and if this little ritual should ever pay off it is quite predictable that we will be asked to share in the proceeds.

One early event went far toward establishing our rapport with the neighborhood. Our tenement apartment was broken into and the few possessions that combined some value with ready salability (including all our field equipment) were stolen. Every local household is fully familiar with this kind of event, and sharing this experience immediately established the beginnings of important bonds. In this context it may be mentioned that our 1967 model car, always parked in our block, is never locked and all the neighbors know this. (This block is one among very many in which stolen autos are stripped and left as empty but expressive hulks.) The neighbors also know that our vehicle is frequently available for errands ranging from shopping trips and outings for children to transportation to public demonstrations.

This quality of involvement has additional implications in relation to public events beyond the confines of the block-neighborhood. When local community people resort to activist behavior in service of their movements for social change, we have to be there too. We insist that our role as anthropologists makes it impossible for us to become leaders or initiators in these situations. Yet we feel just as strongly that the same role requires us to be genuine and trustworthy followers of community initiatives. So we have spent a good deal of time as observers in the middle of mass street demonstrations, sometimes under heavy constabulary aggression. And when community people have physically captured local institutions from centralized bureaucratic control, we have again been with the people. Though still eschewing leadership functions, we have worked long and hard with others to restore the operation of such captured establishments—e.g., repairing plumbing and wiring sabotaged by the external opposition or doing office work.

No one reading this should underestimate the risks entailed by these courses of behavior. Notice, however, that the principal threats we worry about do not come from the angry ghetto. They come rather from external agencies such as police forces. Most important, this is understood by the people we work with every day. Mutual respect and trust are thus based on shared experience. The legitimacy of our role as as participant observers is not established by any ascribed status or external authentication. On the contrary, it develops from achieving, in the local setting, an observably consistent pattern of actual behavior. As a result of these approaches, we are not only living *in* the community but becoming a functioning part *of* it. We believe that this enables us to explore a living social entity as no other technique could.

The barriers to be overcome are not confined to generalized suspicion toward outsiders. They also include local forms of ethnic self-assertion, black nationalism and separatism, complex and powerful anti-white feelings, and hostilities specifically directed at academic researchers as such. Most of these orientations are not universal in our chosen community, but they are all present in quite significant forms. The important point here is that the approach we have described has succeeded well in spite of these barriers. This remains true even though one of us is white and we have never disguised our identity as social scientists. We do not wish to exaggerate our success in this regard. There are important local organizations to which we have only very limited access because of highly developed hostilities toward one or another of the wider social categories to which we belong. Whether these barriers will dissolve in time remains to be seen; because of our experience thus far we are confident that at least some of them will. Six months of this experience has given us a strong feeling that the impenetrability of the angry ghetto is currently being greatly exaggerated by outsiders.

Yet like any community with boundary-maintaining mechanisms, this one too sets requirements for any would-be member who seeks full and free access. Much of the quality of these requirements can be communicated through an experience that is vividly remembered by the lighter member of our team. In a ticklish situation early in our field work, a black man who knew us only slightly could have been helpful; instead he said, "Any white man gotta *prove* himself to me." (Knowledge of both the man and the situation convinces us that he might just as well have said, "Any broad with some higher degree gotta prove herself to me—I don't care if she *is* black.") Today, however, this man is one of our many friends in the community. There have been a number of important subsequent occasions when he has vouched for us to others who did not know us as well as he came to.

Somehow we have "proved" ourselves to this man and to a great many like him—

though as already noted, not to everyone. And we have done this without compromising our commitments as anthropologists, at least as we see these commitments. Perhaps the essential point is that, ultimately, the community test is one of performance, not of ascription whether by racial category, class status, or what-have-you. Possibly, it is this more than anything else which middle class and white Americans misunderstand when they overestimate the impenetrability of the darker ghettos today. At the same time, it is certainly a strong tentative conclusion of our brief experience that any serious attempt to enter into today's aroused black communities would be futile or worse for an outsider who does not take the test of performance seriously and empathetically.

Running It Down, or Writing It Up

Closely connected with all this is a phenomenon of field work which we did not anticipate. We feel that this may well be increasingly important for anthropologists working in circumstances like ours. Not long ago anthropologists became concerned about the consequences and implications of emerging literacy among their once nonliterate subjects, including the possibility that the objects of study might begin to read some of the reports written about them. Our situation has taken us well beyond that stage, as indeed must by now be the case for many urban anthropologists.

Writing is the principal output of our special role in the community of which local people are aware. There is much interest in this at several different levels. A not infrequent formulation, usually delivered with a beguiling smile, is, "Hey man, how's the book coming, and is my name in it?" (Among other things, this provides many opportunities to repeat that we would not dream of writing a book about this community until we had lived here for a good two years.) We have also begun to receive direct requests to record individual first-person life stories for possible publication.

Another level of response is illustrated by the behavior of a local man who happened to be present when the version of this paper delivered at a scholarly meeting was being prepared. He showed great interest in hearing what was going to be said to the professional audience. So we did a practice delivery for him, and his reactions were instructive. The less complimentary references to the community at first angered him, he said, but he felt that everything in the paper was true, and taking it altogether he was glad we were "telling it like it is."

The most complex and demanding outgrowth of our function as writers, however, has emerged in relation to public events connected with one of the community movements for change. Musing angrily or despondently on the distortions and misrepresentations of the news media, local people began to suggest that we help set the record straight. They wanted us to do this by publishing accounts of recent developments from a community viewpoint. This suggestion made us recognize that we were uniquely qualified by circumstances to do what was asked.

So we produced several published descriptions and analyses, drawing on the systematic comparison of news reports and direct observation of events mentioned earlier. These publications are anonymous and will not be cited here, for reasons which we hope are obvious. They are known in the community, however, and local reactions to them are quite significant for our work. Community leaders and others have said spontaneously that our accounts are accurate and valuable. In one or two cases it has been specifically mentioned that we report community faults and weaknesses as well as virtues or strengths, and this is again presented as "telling it like it is."

It is perhaps unnecessary to point out that this makes us privy to a great deal that is hidden from outsiders. The principal point we wish to make is that we have found it necessary to extend the commitments of participant involvement to the work of writing as well as other aspects of our research. This is not to be taken lightly, for it is undoubtedly a delicate and difficult task. It does produce great rewards in terms of the primary object of the research, to obtain a full and deep picture of all possible aspects of community life. Yet it confronts us, as perhaps nothing else could, most sharply and directly with several interrelated issues: of scientific objectivity, scholarly integrity, and the influence of values upon research. This experience tears away from our minds' eyes any vestiges there may have been of the veil of "value-free social science." It brings home most forcefully and concretely the need for effectively combining empirical accuracy of a high order with a genuine commitment to humane valuation of community interests and welfare. Any lingering, naïve hopes of detachment have to be abandoned, while safeguards against factual inaccuracy or distortion must be redoubled.

The local response to knowledge of us as persons and to published results of our work has led to a group action which illustrates these problems. This is a formal action approving extension of our research to an area of the movement for community control which had a long-standing ban on all research. Naturally this gives us a warm sense of both personal and professional success. Yet it also makes us more aware of the dangers of becoming mouthpieces for a segment of the community, however sympathetic we may feel toward that segment. In this respect we count heavily on our already established reputation for reporting phenomena as we see them, even if in some respects they may not reflect credit on local groups or institutions. We also muster all ability to listen to and respect other points of view on these issues. Special recognition and requests of this kind tempt us to neglect many other aspects of our holistic study where comparable rewards may not be immediately forthcoming. In this connection we point out our own research needs, commitments, and values. Moreover, we attempt to remind community people of the accurate images we have projected because as anthropologists we are concerned with the *entire* community.

REFERENCES CITED

ABERLE, DAVID
- 1965 A note on relative deprivation theory as applied to millenarian and other cult movements. *In* Reader on comparative religion, W. A. Lessa and E. Z. Vogt, eds. New York: Harper & Row.

ABRAHAMS, ROGER D.
- 1962a The changing concept of the Negro hero. The Golden Log, Austin: Publications of the Texas Folklore Society.
- 1962b Playing the dozens. Journal of American Folklore 75: 209–20.
- 1964 Deep down in the jungle... Negro narrative folklore from the streets of Philadelphia. Hatboro, Pa.: Folklore Associates.
- 1967 The shaping of folklore traditions in the British West Indies. Journal of Inter-American Studies 9: 456–80.
- 1968a Speech mas' on Tobago. *In* Tire Shrinker to Dragster. Austin: Publications of the Texas Folklore Society No. 34.
- 1968b "Pull out your purse and pay:" St. George mumming from the British West Indies. Folklore 7: 172–201.

ADAMS, RICHARD N.
- 1959 On the relation between plantation and "creole cultures." *In* Plantation systems of the New World. Washington, D.C.: Pan American Union.
- 1964 Rural labor. *In* Continuity and change in Latin America, J. J. Johnson, ed. Stanford: Stanford University Press.
- 1965 Introduction (to the section on social organization). *In* Contemporary cultures and societies of Latin America, Dwight B. Heath and Richard N. Adams, eds. New York: Random House.
- 1967 The second sowing: power and secondary development in Latin America. San Francisco: Chandler.

AGUIRRE BELTRÁN, GONZALO
- 1946 La población negra de México (1519–1810). Mexico City: Ediciones Fuente Cultural.

1958 Cuijla, esbozo etnográfico de un pueblo negro. Mexico, D.F.: Fundo de cultura Económica.

ALBERT, ETHEL
1964 "Rhetoric," "logic" and "poetics", in Burundi: cultural patterning of speech behavior. American Anthropologist 66: No. 6, pt. 2: 35–54.

ALLAND, ALEXANDER, JR.
1967 Evolution and human behavior. New York: Natural History Press.

ALLEN, W. F., C. P. WARE, AND L. M. GARRISON
1867 Slave songs of the United States. New York: A. Simpson and Co.

ALLEYNE, MERVYN
1967 *Review of* Beryl Loftman Bailey, Jamaican Creole syntax: a transformational approach. Caribbean Studies 6: 92–94.
1968 The cultural matrix of Caribbean dialects. Paper presented at the conference on creolization and pidginization of language. Mona, Jamaica, April 9–12, 1968.

ALTSCHULER, MILTON
1965 Notes on Cayapa kinship. Ethnology 4: 440–47.
1967 The sacred and profane realms of Cayapa law. International Journal of Comparative Sociology 8: 44–54.

ANDERSON, ROBERT T., AND BARBARA GALLATIN
1965 Bus stop for Paris. New York: Doubleday.

ANGELLI, JOHN D.
1962 The rimland–mainland concept of culture areas in Middle America. Annals of the Association of American Geographers 52: 119–29.

ANTONOVSKY, A.
1956 Toward refinement of the marginal man concept. Social Forces 35: 57–62.

APTHEKER, HERBERT
1943 American Negro slave revolts. New York: Columbia University Press (copyright 1952 by International Publishers).

ATWOOD, E. BAGBY
1953 A survey of the verb forms of the Southeastern United States. Ann Arbor: University of Michigan Press.

AZEVEDO, THALES DE
1956 Classes sociais e grupos de prestígio na Bahia. Arquivos da Universidade de Bahia, Faculdade de Filosofia No. 5.

BACHOFEN, J. J.
1861 Das Mutterrecht. Basel: Benno Schwabe.

BAILEY, BERYL LOFTMAN
1965 Toward a new perspective in Negro English dialectology. American Speech 40: 171–77.
1966 Jamaican Creole syntax: a transformational approach. Cambridge: Cambridge University Press.

BALDWIN, JAMES
1955 Notes of a native son. Boston: Beacon Press.

BALLANTA-TAYLOR, N. G. J.
1925 St. Helena island spirituals. New York: G. Schirmer.

BANTON, MICHAEL G.
1957 West African city: a study of tribal life in Freetown. Oxford: Oxford University Press.
1966 The social anthropology of complex societies, ed. New York: Praeger.
1967 Race relations. New York: Basic Books.

BARATZ, JOAN
n.d. Language in the economically disadvantaged child: a perspective. Ms.

BARBOUR, FLOYD B.
1968 The black power revolt. Boston: Porter-Sargent Publications.

BARNES, J. A.
1954 Class and committees in a Norwegian island parish. Human Relations 7: 39–58.
1968 Networks and political process. *In* Local-level politics, M. J. Swartz, ed. Chicago: Aldine.

BARRETT, SAMUEL A.
1925 The Cayapa Indians of Ecuador, 2 vols. New York: Heye Foundation.

REFERENCES CITED

BASCOM, WILLIAM R.
  1941 Acculturation among the Gullah Negroes. American Anthropologist 43: 43–50.
  1944 The sociological role of the Yoruba cult group. Memoir 63, American Anthropological Association.
  1951 The Yoruba in Cuba. Nigeria 37: 14–20.
  1952 The focus of Cuban Santería. Southwestern Journal of Anthropology 6: 64–68.
  1955 Urbanization among the Yoruba. American Journal of Sociology 60: 446–54.
  1964 Melville Jean Herskovits (1895–1963). American Sociological Review 29: 278–79.

BASTIDE, ROGER
  1958 Le condomblé de Bahia (rite Nagô). Paris, The Hague: Mouton.
  1959 Sociologia do Folclore Brasileiro. São Paulo: Editora Anhambi.
  1961a Dusky Venus, Black Apollo. Race 3: 10–18.
  1961b Les Religions Africaines au Brésil. Paris: Presses Universitaires de France.
  1965 Le syncrétisme en Amérique latine, Bulletin St. Jean-Baptiste 5: 166–71.
  1967 Les Amériques noires, les civilisations africaines dans le nouveau monde. Paris: Payot.

BASTIEN, RÉMY
  1951a La familia rural Haitiana. Mexico, D.F.: Libra.
  1951b Haití: ayer y hoy. Cuadernos Americanos 10: 153–63.
  1964 Procesos de aculturación en las Antillas. La Revista de Indias 95–96: 177–96.

BECKWITH, MARTHA
  1923 Some religious cults in Jamaica. American Journal of Psychology 34: 32–45.
  1929 Black roadways: a study of Jamaican folklife. Chapel Hill: University of North Carolina Press.

BELSHAW, CYRIL S.
  1957 The great village: the economic and social welfare of Hanuabada, an urban community in Papua. London: Routledge & Kegan Paul.

BENDER, D. R.
  1967 A refinement of the concept of household: families, co-residence, and domestic functions. American Anthropologist 69: 493–504.

BENDIX, REINHARD, AND SEYMOUR M. LIPSET
  1966 Class, status, and power: social stratification in comparative perspective. 2nd ed. New York: The Free Press.

BENNETT, JOHN W., AND IWAO ISHINO
  1963 Paternalism in the Japanese economy. Minneapolis: University of Minnesota Press.

BENNETT, LERONE, JR.
  1964 The Negro mood. New York: Ballantine Books.
  1969 Confrontation on the campus. Ebony 23 (7): 27 ff.

BENZ, ERNST
  1968 Ergriffenheit und Bessessenheit als Grundformen religiöser Erfahrung. Paper presented to Symposium, Bad Homburg, May 2–5.

BERDIE, RALPH F.
  1947 Playing the dozens. Journal of Abnormal and Social Psychology 42: 120–21.

BERGER, BENNETT M.
  1967 Soul searching: *review of* Urban blues, by Charles Keil. Trans-action 4: No. 7, 54–57.

BERGER, PETER L., AND THOMAS LUCKMANN
  1966 The social construction of reality. Garden City, N.Y.: Doubleday.

BERNARD, JESSIE
  1966 Marriage and family among Negroes. Englewood Cliffs, N.J.: Prentice-Hall.

BERNARD, L. L., AND J. S. BERNARD
  1928 The Negro in relation to other races in Latin America. Annals of the American Academy of Political and Social Sciences 140: 306–18.

BIESANZ, JOHN AND MAVIS
   1950 Race relations in the Canal Zone. Phylon 11: 23–30.
   1951 Race relations in Panama and the Canal Zone: a comparative analysis. American Journal of Sociology 57: 7–14.
   1953 Schools in the Panama Canal Zone. Michigan Education Journal 33: 432–34.
   1955 The people of Panama. New York: Columbia University Press.

BILLINGSLEY, ANDREW
   1968 Black families in white America. Englewood Cliffs, N.J.: Prentice-Hall.

BIRDWHISTELL, RAY
   1952 Introduction to kinetics. Washington, D.C.: Department of State, Foreign Service Institute.
   1966 The American family: some perspectives. Psychiatry 29: 203–12.
   1968a Body behavior and communication. In International Encyclopedia of the Social Sciences. New York: Macmillan and Free Press.
   1968b Communication as a multi-channel system. In International Encyclopedia of the Social Sciences. New York: Macmillan and Free Press.

BLACKING, JOHN
   1961 The social value of Venda riddling. African Studies 20: 1–32.

BLAKE, JUDITH
   1961 Family structure in Jamaica: the social context of reproduction. New York: The Free Press.

BLAU, PETER M.
   1964 Exchange and power in social life. New York: Wiley.

BLOOMFIELD, LEONARD
   1933 Language. New York: Holt.

BOAS, FRANZ
   1911 The mind of primitive man. New York: Macmillan.
   1916 Tsimshian mythology. Washington, D.C.: 31st Annual Report, Bureau of American Ethnology, 1909–1910.
   1935 Foreword. In Mules and men, by Zora Neale Hurston. Philadelphia: Lippincott.
   1940 Race, language and culture. New York: Macmillan.

BOHANNAN, LAURA
   1958 Political aspects of Tiv social organization. In Tribes without rulers, John Middleton and David Tait, eds. London: Routledge & Kegan Paul.

BOHANNAN, PAUL
   1954 The migration and expansion of the Tiv. Africa 24 (1): 2–16.

BONTEMPS, ARNA
   1944 Rock, church, rock. In Anthology of American Negro literature, Sylvester C. Watkins, ed. New York: Random House.

BOTKIN, B. A., ED.
   1945 Lay my burden down: a folk history of slavery. Chicago: University of Chicago Press.

BOTT, ELIZABETH
   1957 Family and social network. London: Tavistock.

BOURGUIGNON, ERIKA
   1959 The persistence of folk belief: some notes on cannibalism and zombis in Haiti. Journal of American Folklore 72: 36–46.
   1964 More on the equine subconscious: comment on Utley's comment on Gladwin. American Anthropologist 66: 1391.
   1965 The self, the behavioral environment and the theory of spirit possession. In Context and meaning in cultural anthropology: in honor of A. Irving Hallowell, Melford E. Spiro, ed. New York: The Free Press.
   1967 Religious syncretism among New World Negroes. Paper presented at annual meeting of the American Anthropological Association, Washington, D.C.
   1968a World distribution and patterns of possession states. In Trance and possession states, Raymond Prince, ed. Proceedings, Second Annual Con-

ference, R. M. Bucke Memorial Society, Montreal.
1968b Final report, a cross-cultural study of dissociational states, Project MH 07463, submitted to the National Institute of Mental Health, The Ohio State University Research Foundation, Columbus, Ohio.
1968c Trance dance. Dance Perspectives 35: 1–61.
1969 Maladie et possession: éléments pour une étude comparative. Colloque international sur les cultes de possession. Paris.

BOURGUIGNON, ERIKA, AND LOUANNA PETTAY
1964 Spirit possession, trance and cross-cultural research. *In* Proceedings of the annual meeting of the American Ethnological Society, June Helm, ed. Seattle: University of Washington Press.

BOWEN, ELENORE SMITH (pseud. LAURA BOHANNAN)
1954 Return to laughter. New York: Harper.

BOYER, RUTH
1964 The matrifocal family among the Mescalero: additional data. American Anthropologist 66: 593–602.

BRAITHWAITE, LLOYD
1953 Social stratification in Trinidad. Social and Economic Studies 2: 5–175.
1960 Social stratification and cultural pluralism. *In* Social and cultural pluralism in the Caribbean, Vera Rubin, ed. Annals of the New York Academy of Sciences 83: 816–31.

BRINTON, CRANE
1965 Anatomy of a revolution. Englewood Cliffs, N.J.: Prentice-Hall.

BROOKS, CLEANTH
1935 The relation of the Alabama-Georgia dialect to the provincial dialects of Great Britain. Baton Rouge: Louisiana State University Studies, No. 20.

BROTZ, HOWARD
1964 The Black Jews of Harlem. New York: The Free Press.

BROWN, CLAUDE
1965 Manchild in the promised land. New York: Macmillan.

BRYCE-LAPORTE, R. S.
1962 Social relations and cultural persistence (or change) among Jamaicans in a rural area of Costa Rica. M.A. thesis, University of Puerto Rico.
1967 *Review of* M. G. Smith's version of pluralism—the questions it raises. Comparative Studies in Society and History 10: 114–20.
1968 The conceptualization of the American slave plantation as a total institution. Ph.D. dissertation, University of California, Los Angeles.

BURTON, ROGER V., AND JOHN W. M. WHITING
1961 The absent father and cross-sex identity. Merrill-Palmer Quarterly 7: 85–95.

CAINES, CLEMENT
1804 The history of the General Council and General Assembly of the Leeward Islands which were convened for the purpose of investigating and ameliorating the condition of the slaves throughout those settlements and effecting a gradual abolition of the slave trade, vol. 1. St. Christopher: Basseterre.

CALLEY, MALCOLM
1956 The economic life of mixed-blood communities in northern New South Wales. Oceania 26: 200–13.

CAMARGO, CANDIDO PROCOPIO FERREIRA DE
1961 Kardecismo e Umbanda. São Paulo: Livraria Pioneira Editôra.

CARIBBEAN QUARTERLY
1956 Trinidad carnival issue. Caribbean Quarterly 4: Nos. 3–4.

CARMICHAEL, STOKELY, AND CHARLES HAMILTON
1966 Black power. New York: Vintage.

CARR, ANDREW
1953 A Rada community in Trinidad. Caribbean Quarterly 3 (1): 36–54.

CARVALHO-NETO, PAULO DE
1962 Antología del Negro Paraguayo. Anales de la Universidad Central 41,

346: 37–66. Quito: Editorial Universitaria.

1965 El Negro Uruguayo (hasta la abolición). Quito: Editorial Universitaria.

CHAMBERS, E. K.
1933 The English folk-play. Oxford: Oxford University Press.

CHARTERS, SAMUEL
1965 The poetry of the blues. New York: Oak Publications.

CHAYANOV, A. V.
1966 The theory of peasant economy. Homewood, Ill.: Dorsey.

CHINOY, ELY
1961 Society. New York: Random House.

CHOMSKY, NOAM
1965 Aspects of the theory of syntax. Cambridge, Mass.: M.I.T. Press.
1966 Cartesian linguistics. New York: Harper & Row.

CLARK, KENNETH
1965 Dark ghetto. New York: Harper & Row.

CLARKE, EDITH
1957 My mother who fathered me. London: Allen and Unwin. (Re-issued in 1966 with a new Foreword by M. G. Smith.)

CLEAGE, ALBERT
1969 The black messiah. New York: Sheed and Ward.

CLEAVER, ELDRIDGE
1968a Soul on ice. New York: Ramparts and McGraw-Hill.
1968b Playboy interview. Playboy 15 (12): 89 ff.

COHEN, YEHUDI
1968 Man in adaptation: the cultural present. Chicago: Aldine.

COLBY, B. N.
1966 Ethnographic semantics: a preliminary survey. Current Anthropology 7: 3–32.

COLEMAN, JAMES S., AND GABRIEL A. ALMOND, EDS.
1960 The politics of developing areas. Princeton: Princeton University Press.

CONKLIN, HAROLD C.
1955 Hanunóo color categories. Southwestern Journal of Anthropology 11: 339–44.

CONOT, ROBERT
1967 Rivers of blood, years of darkness. New York: Bantam.

COULTHARD, G. R.
1968 Parallelisms and divergencies between "Négritude" and "Indigenismo." Caribbean Studies 8: 31–55.

COURLANDER, HAROLD
1960 The drum and the hoe: the life and lore of the Haitian people. Berkeley and Los Angeles: University of California Press.
1963 Negro folk music U.S.A. New York: Columbia University Press.

COURLANDER, HAROLD, AND RÉMY BASTIEN
1966 Religion and politics in Haiti. Washington, D.C.: Institute for Cross-Cultural Research.

CROWLEY, DANIEL J.
1956a Tradition and individual creativity in Bahamian folktales. Ph.D. dissertation, Northwestern University.
1956b The traditional masques of carnival *and* The midnight robbers. Caribbean Quarterly 4: 194–223, 263–74.
1958–59 L'héritage Africaine dans les Bahamas. Presence Africaine: 41–58.
1959 Toward a definition of calypso. Ethnomusicology 3: 55–66, 117–24.
1960 Cultural assimilation in multiracial society. *In* Social and cultural pluralism in the Caribbean, Vera Rubin ed. Annals of the New York Academy of Sciences 83: 850–54.
1962 Negro folklore. An Africanist's view. Texas Quarterly 5: 65–71.
1966 I could talk old story good: creativity in Bahamian folklore. Berkeley and Los Angeles: University of California Press.
1967 The view from Tobago: national character in folklore. *In* Folklore international, D. K. Wilgus, ed. Hatboro, Pa.: Folklore Associates.

CRUSE, HAROLD
    1967 The crisis of the Negro intellectual. New York: William Morrow.

CURME, GEORGE
    1935 Parts of speech and accidence. Boston: Heath.

DA COSTA EDUARDO, OCTAVIO
    1948 The Negro in northern Brazil. A study in acculturation. Seattle: University of Washington Press.

DALLAS, ROBERT CHARLES
    1803 The history of the Maroons from their origins to the establishment of their chief tribe at Sierra Leone, 2 vols. London: Straham.

DARK, PHILIP J. C.
    1954 Bush Negro art: an African art in the Americas. London: Alec Tiranti.

DAUER, ALFONS M.
    1958 Der Jazz, seine Ursprunge und seine Entwicklung. Kassel: Erich Roth Verlag.

DAVENPORT, WILLIAM
    1959 Nonunilinear descent and descent groups. American Anthropologist 61: 557–72.
    1960 Jamaican fishing: a game theory analysis. New Haven: Yale University Publications in Anthropology No. 59.

DAVIS, HASSOLDT
    1952 The jungle and the damned. New York: Duell, Sloan & Pearce.

DECAMP, DAVID
    1967 Mock-bidding in Jamaica. *In* Tire Shrinker to Dragster. Austin: Publications of the Texas Folklore Society.
    1968 Paper presented at the conference on creolization and pidginization of language. Mona, Jamaica, April 9–12, 1968.

DERBYSHIRE, ROBERT L., EUGENE B. BRODY, AND CARL SCHLEIFER
    1963 Family structure of young adult Negro male patients: preliminary observations from urban Baltimore. Journal of Nervous and Mental Disease 136: 245–51.

DESPRES, LEO A.
    1964 The implications of nationalist politics in British Guiana for the development of cultural theory. American Anthropologist 66: 1051–77.
    1967 Cultural pluralism and nationalist politics in British Guiana. Chicago: Rand McNally.

DICKIE-CLARK, H. F.
    1966 The marginal situation. London: Routledge & Kegan Paul.

DILLARD, J. L.
    1962 Some variants in concluding tags in Antillean folktales. Caribbean Studies 2: 16–25.
    1963 Beginning formulas for Antillean folktales. Caribbean Studies 3: 51–55.
    1964 The writings of Herskovits and the study of the language of the Negro in the New World. Caribbean Studies 4: 35–41.

DOLLARD, JOHN
    1939 The dozens: dialect of insult. American Imago 1: 3–25.

DORSAINVIL, J. C.
    1931 Vodou et névrose. Port-au-Prince: Impr. "La Presse."

DORSON, RICHARD
    1956 Negro folktales in Michigan. Cambridge, Mass.: Harvard University Press.
    1958 Negro tales from Pine Bluff, Arkansas, and Calvin, Michigan. Bloomington: Indiana University Press.
    1959 American folklore. Chicago: The University of Chicago Press.

DOUGLASS, FREDERICK
    1968 Narrative of the life of an American slave. New York: New American Library.

DRAKE, ST. CLAIR
    1966 The racial and economic status of the Negro in the United States. *In* The Negro American, Talcott Parsons and Kenneth B. Clark, eds. Boston: Beacon Press.

DRAKE, ST. CLAIR, AND HORACE R. CAYTON
    1945 Black metropolis, a study of Negro

life in a northern city. New York: Harcourt, Brace.

DUBOIS, W. E. B.
1908 The Negro family. Atlanta: Atlanta University Press.

DYNES, RUSSELL, AND E. L. QUARANTELLI
1968 What looting in civil disturbances really means. Trans-action 5 (6): 9–14.

ECKSTEIN, HARRY, ED.
1964 Internal war: problems and approaches. New York: The Free Press.

EDDY, ELIZABETH M., ED.
1969 Urban anthropology: research perspectives and strategies. Athens: University of Georgia Press.

EDMONSON, MUNRO, et al.
1960 Nativism and syncretism. New Orleans: Middle American Research Institute, Publication No. 19.

EDWARDS, CHARLES L.
1895 Bahama songs and stories. Memoirs of the American Folklore Society No. 3.

EISENSTADT, S. N.
1959 Primitive political systems: a preliminary analysis. American Anthropologist 61: 200–220.

ELDER, JACOB
1966a Kalinda—song of the battling troubadours of Trinidad. Journal of the Folklore Institute 3: 192–203.
1966b Evolution of the traditional calypso of Trinidad and Tobago: a sociohistoric analysis of song change. Ph.D. dissertation, University of Pennsylvania.

ELKINS, STANLEY
1959 Slavery: a problem in American institutional and intellectual life. Chicago: University of Chicago Press.

ELLISON, RALPH
1965 Interview. In Who speaks for the Negro, by Robert Penn Warren. New York: Random House.

EMBREE, EDWIN R.
1945 Brown Americans: the story of a tenth of a nation. New York: Viking.

EPISCOPAL CHURCH
1963 Diocese of California, Division of Pastoral Services, Study Commission on Glossolalia, Preliminary Report.

EPSTEIN, A. L.
1961 The network and urban social organization. Human Problems in British Central Africa 29: 29–62.

ERASMUS, CHARLES J.
1950 Patolli, parchisi and the limitation of possibilities. Southwestern Journal of Anthropology 6: 369–87.
1956 Culture structure and process: the occurrence and disappearance of reciprocal farm labor. Southwestern Journal of Anthropology 12: 444–69.
1961a Man takes control. Minneapolis: University of Minnesota Press.
1961b *Review of* Andrew H. Whiteford, Two cities of Latin America: a comparative description of social classes. American Anthropologist 63: 843–45.
1967 Upper limits of peasantry and agrarian reform: Bolivia, Venezuela and Mexico compared. Ethnology 4: 349–80.

ESCALANTE, AQUILES
1964 El Negro en Colombia. Bogotá: Universidad Nacional de Colombia, Monografías Sociológicas No. 18.

ETZIONI, AMITAÏ
1961 A comparative analysis of complex organizations. New York: The Free Press.

EVANS-PRITCHARD, E. E.
1940 The Nuer. Oxford: Clarendon Press.

FALLERS, LLOYD A.
1965 Bantu bureaucracy: a century of political evolution among the Basoga of Uganda. Chicago: University of Chicago Press.

FARON, LOUIS C.
1961 A reinterpretation of Chocó society.

Southwestern Journal of Anthropology 17: 94–102.
1962 Marriage, residence and domestic group among the Panamanian Chocó. Ethnology 1: 13–37.

FEATHER, LEONARD
1964 A talk with Mahalia Jackson. *In* American Folk Music Occasional Publications No. 1, Chris Strachwitz, ed. Berkeley.

FERGUSON, CHARLES A.
1959 Diglossia. Word 15: 325–40.

FERGUSSON, C. B.
1948 A documentary study of the establishment of the Negroes in Nova Scotia between the War of 1812 and the winning of responsible government. Halifax: Public Archives.

FERNANDES, FLORESTAN
1964 A integracão do negro a sociedade de classes. Faculdade de Filosofia, Ciencias e Letras da Universidade de São Paulo.

FINNEGAN, RUTH
1967 Limba stories and story-telling. Oxford: Oxford University Press.

FIRTH, RAYMOND
1951 Elements of social organization. Boston: Beacon Press. (Paperback edition cited, 1963.)
1956 Two studies of kinship in London. London: Athlone Press.

FISHER, MILES MARK
1953 Negro slave songs in the United States. New York: Citadel Press.

FORTES, MEYER
1949 Time and social structure: an Ashanti case study. *In* Social structure: studies presented to A. R. Radcliffe-Brown, Meyer Fortes, ed. London: Oxford University Press. (Reprinted 1963, New York: Russell and Russell.)
1953 The structure of unilineal descent groups. American Anthropologist 55: 17–41.
1958 Introduction. *In* The developmental cycle in domestic groups, Jack Goody, ed. Cambridge Papers in Social Anthropology No. 1, Cambridge University Press.
1963 The political system of the Tallensi of the northern territories of the Gold Coast. *In* African political systems, M. Fortes and E. E. Evans-Pritchard, eds. London: Oxford University Press. (First ed., 1940.)

FORTIER, ALCÉE
1895 Louisiana folk-tales. Memoirs of the American Folklore Society 2.

FOSTER, GEORGE
1961 The dyadic contract: a model for the social structure of a Mexican peasant village. American Anthropologist 63: 1173–92.
1963 The dyadic contract in Tzintzuntzan II: patron–client relationships. American Anthropologist 65: 1280–94.

FRAKE, CHARLES
1961 The diagnosis of disease among the Subanun of Mindanao. American Anthropologist 63: 113–32.
1962 Cultural ecology and ethnography. American Anthropologist 64: 53–59.
1964 Notes on queries in ethnography. American Anthropologist 66: No. 6, pt. 2, 132–45.

FRANCISCO, SLINGER (THE MIGHTY SPARROW)
n.d. Dan is the man in the band *In* The Sparrow, King of Calypso, MGM E-4259.

FRANCO, JOSÉ L.
1961 Afroamérica. Havana: Junta Nacional de Arqueología y Etnología.

FRANKENBURG, RONALD
1966 British communities. Harmondsworth: Penguin Books.

FRAZIER, E. FRANKLIN
1932 The Negro family in Chicago. Chicago: University of Chicago Press.
1934 Traditions and patterns in Negro family life in the United States. *In* Race and culture contacts, E. B. Reuter, ed. New York: McGraw-Hill.
1939 The Negro family in the United States. Chicago: University of Chi-

cago Press. Revised and abridged edition 1948. New York: Dryden. Paperback edition of 1948 edition 1966, Chicago: University of Chicago Press.
1942 The Negro family in Bahia, Brazil. American Sociological Review 7: 465–78.
1949 The Negro in the United States. New York: Macmillan. Second edition published 1957.
1957a The Negro in the United States, rev. ed. New York: Macmillan.
1957b Black bourgeoisie. Glencoe, Ill.: The Free Press.
1957c Introduction. In Caribbean studies: a symposium, Vera Rubin, ed. Seattle: University of Washington Press.
1963 The Negro church in America. New York: Schocken Books.
1966 The Negro family in the United States, revised and abridged edition. Chicago: University of Chicago Press.

FREILICH, MORRIS
1961 Serial polygyny, Negro peasants and model analysis. American Anthropologist 63: 955–75.
1969 Marginal natives: anthropologists in cross cultural research. New York: Harper & Row.

FREYRE, GILBERTO
1964 The masters and the slaves: a study in the development of Brazilian civilization. New York: Knopf. (Originally published as Casa grande e senzala, 1946. This edition is an abridgment of the 1956 translation.)

FRIEDLAND, W. H., AND DOROTHY NELKIN
1967 Migrant labor as a form of intermittent social organization and as a channel of geographical mobility. Report to the U.S. Department of Labor, Washington, D.C.: mimeo.

FRIEDRICH, PAUL
1969 Causes of local agrarian revolt in Mexico. Paper presented at the University of Minnesota, Department of Anthropology. May 29, 1969.

FROBENIUS, LEO
1913 The voice of Africa, 2 vols. London: Hutchinson.

FRUCHT, RICHARD
1967 A Caribbean social type: neither "peasant" nor "proletarian." Social and Economic Studies 16: 295–300.

FURNIVALL, J. S.
1948 Colonial policy and practice. London: Cambridge University Press.

GANS, HERBERT J.
1967 The Negro family: reflections on the Moynihan report. In The Moynihan report and the politics of controversy, Lee Rainwater and William L. Yancey, eds. Cambridge, Mass.: M.I.T. Press.

GEERTZ, CLIFFORD, ED.
1963 Old societies and new states. New York: The Free Press.

GEERTZ, HILDRED
1959 The vocabulary of emotion. Journal for the Study of Interpersonal Processes 22: 225.
1961 The Javanese family: a study of kinship and socialization. New York: The Free Press.

GERLACH, LUTHER P., PRODUCER
1968 Film: People, power and change: a study of movements of revolutionary change. 16 mm., sound/color, 29 minutes. Minneapolis: University of Minnesota Audio-Visual Education Service.

GERLACH, LUTHER P., AND VIRGINIA HINE
1968a Five factors crucial to the growth and spread of a modern religious movement. Journal for the Scientific Study of Religion 7: 23–40.
1968b The mobilization of human resources to save natural resources: movement dynamics in action. Prepared for presentation at a conference of the Minnesota Association for Conservation Education, Minneapolis, November 20, 1968. Working paper.

REFERENCES CITED

1969 Prometheus unbound: a study of movements of revolutionary change. Indianapolis: Bobbs-Merrill.

GIGLIONI, G.
n.d. The population and housing problem on the sugar estates of British Guiana. Georgetown, B.G.: The Argosy Company.

GINSBERG, MORRIS
1934 Sociology. London: Butterworth.

GLAZER, NATHAN, AND DANIEL PATRICK MOYNIHAN
1963 Beyond the melting pot. Cambridge, Mass.: M.I.T. Press.

GLUCKMAN, MAX
1954 Political institutions. *In* The institutions of primitive society, E. E. Evans-Pritchard, ed. Glencoe, Ill.: The Free Press of Glencoe.
1965 Politics, law, and ritual in tribal society. Chicago: Aldine.

GOFFMAN, ERVING
1959 The presentation of self in everyday life. Garden City, N.Y.: Doubleday.
1961a Asylums. Garden City, N.Y.: Doubleday.
1961b Encounters. Indianapolis: Bobbs-Merrill.
1963 Behavior in public places: notes on the social organization of gatherings. New York: The Free Press.

GOLDBERG, MILTON
1941 A qualification of the marginal man theory. American Sociological Review 6: 52–58.

GOLDKIND, VICTOR
1961 Sociocultural contrasts in rural and urban settlement types in Costa Rica. Rural Sociology 26: 365–80.

GOLDSCHMIDT, WALTER, ED.
1959 The anthropology of Franz Boas: essays on the centennial of his birth. American Anthropological Association Memoir #89, 61: No. 5, pt. 2. San Francisco: Chandler.

GONZÁLEZ, A. E.
1922 The black border: Gullah stories of the Carolina coast. Columbia, S.C.: The State Company (Reprinted 1964).
1924 The captain: stories of the black border. Columbia, S.C.: The State Company.

GONZÁLEZ, NANCIE L.
1965 The consanguineal household and matrifocality. American Anthropologist 67: 1541–49.
1969 Migration and modernization: adaptive reorganization in the Black Carib household. Seattle: University of Washington Press.

GOODENOUGH, WARD H.
1962 Kindred and hamlet in Lakalai. Ethnology 1: 5–12.
1965a Yankee kinship terminology: a problem in componential analysis American Anthropologist 67: No. 6, pt. 2, 259–87.
1965b Rethinking "status" and "role:" toward a general model of cultural organization of social relationships. *In* The relevance of models for social anthropology, Michael Banton, ed. New York: Praeger.

GOODY, JACK, ED.
1958 The developmental cycle in domestic groups. Cambridge Papers in Social Anthropology No. 1. London: Cambridge University Press.

GOUGH, KATHLEEN
1952 A comparison of incest prohibitions and rules of exogamy in three matrilineal groups of the Malabar coast. International Archives of Ethnography 46: 81–105.
1959 The Nayars and the definition of marriage. Journal of the Royal Anthropological Institute of Great Britain and Ireland 89: 23–34.

GOVEIA, E. V.
1965 Slave society in the British Leeward Islands at the end of the eighteenth century. Caribbean Series No. 8. New Haven and London: Yale University Press.

GRAUER, VICTOR
1965 Some song style clusters: a prelimin-

ary study. Ethnomusicology 10: 265–71.

GREAVES, I.
1959 The plantation in world economy. In Plantation systems in the New World. Washington, D.C.: Pan American Union.

GREEN, A. W.
1947 A reexamination of the marginal man concept. Social Forces 26: 167–71.

GREEN, PAUL
1928 Wide fields [stories, sketches and plays]. New York.

GREENFIELD, SIDNEY
1966 English rustics in black skin: a study of modern family forms in pre-industrialized society. New Haven: College and University Press.

GULICK, JOHN
1967 Tripoli: a modern Arab city. Cambridge, Mass.: Harvard University Press.

GUMPERZ, JOHN J.
1967 On the linguistic markers of bilingual communication. Journal of Social Issues 23: 48–57.

GUMPERZ, JOHN J., AND DELL HYMES, EDS.
1964 The ethnography of communication. American Anthropologist 66: No. 6, pt. 2.

GURR, TED
1967 The conditions of civil violence. Princeton, N.J.: Center of International Studies.

HALL, EDWARD T.
1963 A system for the notation of proxemic behavior. American Anthropologist 65: 1003–26.
1966 The hidden dimension. New York: Doubleday.

HALL, GWENDOLYN MIDLO
1969 Africans in the Americas. Negro Digest 18: No. 4, 35–44.

HALL, ROBERT A., JR.
1950 African substratum in Negro English. American Speech 25: 51–54.
1966 Pidgin and creole languages. Ithaca, N.Y.: Cornell University Press.

HAMMEL, EUGENE A.
1964 Some characteristics of rural village and urban slum populations on the coast of Peru. Southwestern Journal of Anthropology 20: 346.
1965 A transformational analysis of Comanche kinship terminology. American Anthropologist 67: No. 6, pt. 2, 65–105.

HANDLIN, OSCAR
1951 The uprooted. New York: Little, Brown. (Paperback edition 1957.)

HANNERZ, ULF
1969 Soulside: inquiries into ghetto culture and community. New York: Columbia University Press.

HARE, NATHAN
1968 New role for Uncle Toms. Negro Digest 17: 14–19.

HARRIS, JOEL CHANDLER
1881 Uncle Remus: his songs and his sayings. New York: D. Appleton.

HARRIS, MARVIN
1956 Town and country in Brazil. New York: Columbia University Press.
1960 Adaptation in biological and cultural sciences. Transactions of the New York Academy of Sciences, Series II, 23: 59–65.
1964a Racial identity in Brazil. Luso Brazilian Review 1: 21–28.
1964b Patterns of race in the Americas. New York: Walker.
1968 The rise of anthropological theory: a history of theories of culture. New York: Crowell.

HARRIS, MARVIN, AND CONRAD KOTTAK
1963 The structural significance of Brazilian racial categories. Sociologia 25: 203–09.

HASTINGS, JAMES
1963 Dictionary of the Bible. Rev. ed. by Frederick C. Grant and H. H. Rowley. New York: Scribner.

HAYDEN, TOM
1967 Rebellion in Newark. New York: Vintage.

HAYNES, J. A.
1954 The economic importance of the

sugar industry to British Guiana. *In* Booker's sugar, report of the Booker Brothers. McConnell and Company.

HEARN, LAFCADIO
1885 Gombo zhébes: a little dictionary of creole proverbs, selected from six creole districts. New York: Coleman.
1890 Two years in the French West Indies. New York: Harper.

HEATH, DWIGHT B., AND RICHARD N. ADAMS, EDS.
1965 Contemporary cultures and societies of Latin America. New York: Random House.

HELM, JUNE
1962 The ecological approach in anthropology. American Journal of Sociology 68: 630–39.

HENNEY, J. H.
1967 Trance behavior among the Shakers of St. Vincent. Working paper No. 8, cross-cultural study of dissociational states. Columbus: Department of Anthropology, The Ohio State University.
1968a "Mourning," a religious ritual among the Spiritual Baptists of St. Vincent: an experience in sensory deprivation. Working paper No. 21, cross-cultural study of dissociational states. Columbus: Department of Anthropology, The Ohio State University.
1968b Spirit possession belief and trance behavior in a religious group in St. Vincent, British West Indies. Ph.D. dissertation, The Ohio State University.

HENRIQUES, F. M.
1953 Family and colour in Jamaica. London: Eyre & Spottiswoode.

HENRY, JULES
1965 White people's time, colored people's time. Trans-action 2 (3): 31–34.

HERNÁNDEZ DE ALBA, GREGORIO
1946 The highland tribes of southern Colombia. *In* Handbook of South American Indians, Julian H. Steward, ed. Bureau of American Ethnology Bulletin 143, Washington, D.C.: Smithsonian Institution.

HERNTON, CALVIN
1966 White papers for white Americans. New York: Doubleday.

HERSKOVITS, MELVILLE J.
1924a What is race? The American Mercury 2 (6): 207–10.
1924b The racial hysteria. Opportunity II (18): 166–68.
1925a The color line. The American Mercury 6 (22): 204–08.
1925b The Negro's Americanism. *In* The new Negro, Alain Locke, ed. New York: Charles and Albert Boni.
1926 On the relation between Negro–White mixture and standing in intelligence tests. Pedagogical Seminary and Journal of Genetic Psychology 33: 30–42.
1927 The Negro and the intelligence tests. Hanover, N.H.: Sociological Press.
1929 Race relations in the United States, 1928. American Journal of Sociology 34: 1129–39.
1930a The culture areas of Africa. Africa 3: 59–77.
1930b The Negro in the New World: the statement of a problem. American Anthropologist 32: 145–55. Reprinted in The New World Negro, 1966, Melville J. Herskovits.
1930c The anthropometry of the American Negro. Columbia University Contributions to Anthropology 11. New York: Columbia University Press.
1932 Race relations. American Journal of Sociology 36: 976–82.
1933 Race relations. American Journal of Sociology 38: 913–21.
1935a Social history of the Negro (illustrated). *In* Handbook of social psychology, Carl Murchison, ed. Worcester, Mass.: Clark University Press.
1935b What has Africa given America? New Republic No. 1083: 92–94. Reprinted in The New World Negro, 1966, Melville J. Herskovits.

1937a African gods and Catholic saints in New World Negro belief. American Anthropologist 39: 635–43.

1937b Life in a Haitian valley. New York: Knopf.

1938 Dahomey, an ancient West African kingdom. New York: J. J. Augustin.

1938–39 The ancestry of the American Negro. American Scholar 8: 84–94.

1940 *Review of* The Negro family in the United States by E. Franklin Frazier. The Nation 150: No. 4, 104–05.

1941 The myth of the Negro past. New York: Harper. Paperback edition 1958, Boston: Beacon Press.

1943a Some next steps in the study of Negro folklore. Journal of American Folklore 56: 1–7. Reprinted in The New World Negro, 1966, Melville J. Herskovits.

1943b The Negro in Bahia, Brazil: a problem in method. American Sociological Review 8: 394–402.

1943c The southernmost outposts of New World Africanisms. American Anthropologist 45: 495–510.

1945a Trinidad proverbs. Journal of American Folklore 58: 195–207.

1945b Problem, method and theory in Afro-American studies. Afroamerica 1: 5–24. Reprinted, Phylon 7: 337–54, 1945. Also reprinted in The New World Negro, 1966, Melville J. Herskovits.

1946 Drums and drummers in Afro-Brazilian cult life. The Musical Quarterly 30: No. 4, 477–92. Reprinted in The New World Negro, 1966, Melville J. Herskovits.

1948a The contribution of Afroamerican studies to Africanist research. American Anthropologist 50: 1–10.

1948b Man and his works. New York: Knopf.

1960 The ahistorical approach to Afroamerican studies. American Anthropologist 62: 559–68. Reprinted in The New World Negro, 1966, Melville J. Herskovits.

1964 The American Negro: a study in racial crossing. Midland paperback, Bloomington: Indiana University Press. First published in 1928, Knopf.

1966 The New World Negro, F. S. Herskovits, ed. Bloomington: Indiana University Press.

HERSKOVITS, MELVILLE J. AND FRANCES S.

1934 Rebel destiny: among the Bush Negroes of Dutch Guiana. New York: McGraw-Hill.

1936 Suriname Folk-lore (with transcriptions of Suriname songs and musicological analysis by Dr. M. Kolinski). Columbia University Contributions to Anthropology 27. New York: Columbia University Press.

1943 The Negroes of Brazil. Yale Review 32: 263–79.

1947a Trinidad village. New York: Knopf.

1947b Afro-Bahian religious songs; folk-music of Brazil. Pamphlet accompanying Album XIII, Library of Congress, Recording Laboratory, Music Division, Washington, D.C.

HERZOG, ELIZABETH

1967 Is there a "breakdown" of the Negro family? *In* The Moynihan report and the politics of controversy, Lee Rainwater and William L. Yancey, eds. Cambridge, Mass.: M.I.T. Press.

HERZOG, GEORGE, AND C. G. BLOOAH

1936 Jabo proverbs from Liberia. London: International Institute of African Languages and Cultures.

HILLERY, GEORGE, JR.

1963 Villages, cities and total institutions. American Sociological Review 28: 779–90.

HOETINK, H.

1967 The two variants in Caribbean race relations: a contribution to the sociology of segmented societies. London: Oxford University Press. (Translated by Eva M. Hooykaas from De

Gespleten Samenleving in het Caribisch Gebied [1962], Assen, Netherlands.

HOFFER, ERIC
1951 The true believer. New York: Harper & Row.
1963 The ordeal of change. New York: Harper & Row.

HOGG, DONALD
1960 The convince cult in Jamaica. *In* Papers in Caribbean anthropology, Sidney Mintz, ed. Yale University Publications in Anthropology, No. 58. New Haven: Yale University Press.
1964 Jamaican religions: a study in variation. Ph.D. dissertation, Yale University.

HOMANS, GEORGE C.
1950 The human group. New York: Harcourt, Brace.
1961 Social behavior, New York: Harcourt, Brace.

HOROWITZ, MICHAEL
1967 Morne-Paysan: peasant village in Martinique. New York: Holt, Rinehart and Winston.

HORTON, JOHN
1967 Time and cool people. Trans-action 4: 5–12.

HUDSON, RANDALL O.
1964 The status of the Negro in northern South America, 1820–1860. Journal of Negro History 49: 225–39.

HUNT, ROBERT C.
1965 The developmental cycle of the family business in rural Mexico. Proceedings of the American Ethnological Society. Seattle: University of Washington Press.

HUNTER, GUY, ED.
1965 Industrialization and race relations: a symposium. London: Oxford University Press.

HURAULT, JEAN
1961 Les Noirs réfugiés Boni de la Guyane française, Mémoire 63, Institut français d'Afrique Noire, Dakar.
1965 La vie matérielle de noirs réfugiés Boni et des Indiens Wayana de Haut-Maroni (Guyane Française). Paris: ORSTOM (Office de la Recherche Scientifique et Technique Outre-Mer.)

HURSTON, ZORA NEALE
1934 Jonah's gourd vine. Philadelphia: Lippincott.
1935 Mules and men. Philadelphia: Lippincott.
1938 Tell my horse. Philadelphia: Lippincott.
1942 Dust tracks on a road: an autobiography. Philadelphia: Lippincott.

HUTCHINSON, HARRY W.
1957 Village and plantation life in northeastern Brazil. Seattle: University of Washington Press.

HYMES, DELL
1967 Models of interaction of language and social setting. Journal of Social Issues 23: 8–28.

ICEBERG SLIM
1967 Pimp: the story of my life. Los Angeles: Holloway House.

ISAACS, HAROLD
1963 The new world of Negro Americans. New York: Day.

JACKSON, BRUCE, ED.
1967 The Negro and his folklore in 19th century periodicals. Austin: University of Texas Press.

JACKSON, GEORGE P.
1943 White and Negro spirituals, their life span and kinship. New York: J. J. Augustin.

JAHN, JANHEINZ
1961 Muntu: the new African culture. New York: Grove Press.

JAYAWARDENA, CHANDRA
1967 Conflict and solidarity in a Guianese plantation. London: Athlone Press.

JEKYLL, WALTER
1907 Jamaican song and story. London: David Nutt.

JENSEN, ADOLF ELLEGARD
1963 Myth and cult among primitive

peoples. Translated by Marianna Tax Choldin and Wolfgang Weissleder. Chicago: University of Chicago Press.

JOHNSON, CHALMERS
1966 Revolutionary change. Boston: Little, Brown.

JOHNSON, CHARLES S.
1934 Shadow of the plantation. Chicago: University of Chicago Press.

JOHNSON, GUY B.
1930 Folk culture on St. Helena island, South Carolina. Chapel Hill: University of North Carolina Press. Reprinted 1968, Hatboro, Pa.: Folklore Associates.
1940 Preface to Drums and shadows: survival studies among the Georgia coastal Negroes. Athens: University of Georgia Press.
1968 Folk culture on St. Helena island, South Carolina. Hatboro, Pa.: Folklore Associates. (With new preface.)

JOHNSON, JAMES WELDON
1925 The book of American Negro spirituals. New York: Viking.
1926 The second book of Negro spirituals. New York: Viking.
1968 Black Manhattan. New York: Atheneum. (First published in 1930.)

JOHNSTON, SIR HARRY
1910 The Negro in the New World. London: Methuen.

JONES, LEROI
1963 Blues people. New York: Morrow.
1967 Black music. New York: Morrow.

JOY, LEONARD
1967 One economist's view of the relationship between economics and anthropology. In Themes in economic anthropology, Raymond Firth, ed. A.S.A. Monograph No. 6. New York: Praeger.

KAHL, JOSEPH B.
1957 The American class structure. New York: Rinehart.
1965 Social stratification and values in metropoli and provinces: Brazil and Mexico. América Latina 1: 23–35.

KAHN, MORTON C.
1931 Djuka: the Bush Negroes of Dutch Guiana. New York: Viking.

KARPE, KENNETH LEE
n.d. Album notes to Ray Charles at Newport. Atlantic Record 1289.

KASDAN, L., AND R. F. MURPHY
1959 The structure of parallel cousin marriage. American Anthropologist 61: 17–29.

KATZIN, MARGARET
1959 The Jamaican country higgler. Social and Economic Studies 8: 421–40.
1960 The business of higglering in Jamaica. Social and Economic Studies 9: 297–331.

KAY, P.
1963 Aspects of social structure in a Tahitian urban neighborhood. Journal of the Polynesian Society 72: 325.

KEIL, CHARLES
1966 Urban blues. Chicago: University of Chicago Press.

KELLEY, WILLIAM T.
1962 A different drummer. Garden City, N.Y.: Doubleday.

KING, CHARLES E.
1945 The Negro maternal family: a product of an economic and a cultural system. Social Forces 24: 100–04.

KING, JAMES F.
1945 Negro slavery in New Granada. In Greater America: essays in honor of Herbert Eugene Bolton. Berkeley: University of California Press.

KING, MARTIN LUTHER, JR.
1967 Where do we go from here? Boston: Beacon Press.

KING, WOODIE, JR.
1965 The game. Liberator 5: 20–25.

KLASS, MORTON
1961 East Indians in Trinidad. New York: Columbia University Press.

KLATZKO, BERNARD
n.d. Album notes to In the Spirit, Nos. 1 and 2. Origin Jazz Library Records, OLJ 12, OLJ 13.

REFERENCES CITED

KOTTAK, CONRAD
    1963 Race relations in Arembepe. Columbia-Cornell-Harvard-Illinois Summer Field Studies Program, mimeo.
    1966 The structure of equality in a Brazilian fishing community. Ph.D. dissertation, Columbia University.

KRAPP, GEORGE PHILLIP
    1924 The English of the Negro American, Mercury 2: 190–95.
    1928 The English language in America. New York: The Century Co.

KREHBIEL, H. E.
    1914 Afro-American folksongs. New York: G. Schirmer.

KUNSTADTER, PETER
    1963 A survey of the consanguine or matrifocal family. American Anthropologist 65: 56–66.

KUPER, HILDA, ED.
    1965 Urbanization and migration in West Africa. Berkeley: University of California Press.

KURATH, HANS
    1928 The origin of dialectal differences in spoken American English. Modern Philology 25: 385–95.

L AND P BROADCASTING CORPORATION
    1968 Ignore it and lose. Chicago: L & P Broadcasting Corporation.

LABAT, PÈRE
    1724 Nouveau voyage aux Isles de l'Amérique, 2 volumes. The Hague: P. Husson.

LABOV, WILLIAM, PAUL COHEN, AND CLARENCE ROBINS
    1965 A preliminary study of the structure of English used by Negro and Puerto Rican speakers in New York City. Cooperative Research Project No. 3091, Washington, D.C.: Office of Education.

LAMMING, GEORGE
    1960 The pleasures of exile. London: Michael Joseph.

LANIGAN, MRS.
    1944 Antigua and the Antiguans, 2 volumes. London.

LANTERNARI, VITTORIO
    1963 The religions of the oppressed. Translated by Lisa Sergio. New York: Knopf.

LEACH, EDMUND
    1954 Political systems of highland Burma. London: Bell.

LEACOCK, SETH
    1964a Ceremonial drinking in an Afro-Brazilian cult. American Anthropologist 66: 344–53.
    1964b Fun-loving deities in an Afro-Brazilian cult. Anthropological Quarterly 37: No. 3, 94–109.

LEEDS, ANTHONY
    1965 Brazilian careers and social structure: a case history and model. *In* Contemporary societies and cultures of Latin America, Dwight B. Heath and Richard N. Adams, eds. New York: Random House.

LEIGHTON, ALEXANDER
    1959 My name is legion. New York: Basic Books.
    1965 Poverty and social change. Scientific American 212: No. 5, 21–27.

LEIRIS, MICHEL
    1955 Contacts des civilisations en Martinique et en Guadeloupe. Paris: UNESCO.
    1958 La possession et ses aspects théâtraux chez les Ethiopiens de Gondar. L'Homme, 1. Paris: Plon.

LENSKI, GERHARD
    1966 Power and privilege: a theory of social stratification. New York: McGraw-Hill.

LEVY, M. J., JR., AND LLOYD A. FALLERS
    1959 The family: some comparative considerations. American Anthropologist 61: 647–51.

LEWIS, HYLAN
    1955 Blackways of Kent. Chapel Hill: University of North Carolina Press.
    1967 The family—resources for change. *In* The Moynihan report and the politics of controversy, Lee Rainwater

LEWIS, I. M.
and William L. Yancey, eds. Cambridge, Mass.: M.I.T. Press.

LEWIS, I. M.
1961 A pastoral democracy: a study of pastoralism and politics among the Northern Somali of the Horn of Africa. London: Oxford University Press.
1966 Spirit possession and deprivation cults. Man 1: 307–29.

LEWIS, OSCAR
1959 Five families: Mexican case studies in the culture of poverty. New York: Basic Books.
1961 The children of Sánchez. New York: Random House.
1966a La vida: a Puerto Rican family in the culture of poverty, San Juan and New York. New York: Random House.
1966b The culture of poverty. Scientific American 215: No. 4, 19–25.

LEYBURN, J. G.
1941 The Haitian people. New Haven: Yale University Press.

LHERMITTE, JEAN
1946–7 Essai sur les phenomènes de possession démoniaque. Encephale 36: 261–81.
1963 True and false possession. Trans. P. J. Hepburne-Scott. New York: Hawthorn (orig. 1956).

LIEBOW, ELLIOT
1967 Tally's corner: a study of Negro streetcorner men. Boston: Little, Brown.

LINTON, RALPH
1937 One hundred percent American. The American Mercury 40: 427–29.
1943 Nativistic movements. American Anthropologist 45: 230–40.

LISCANO, JUAN
1950 Folklore y cultura. Caracas: Avila Gráfica.

LITTLE, KENNETH
1966 West African urbanization: a study of voluntary associations in cultural change. Cambridge: Cambridge University Press.

LOCKE, ALAIN
1925 The new Negro, paperback edition 1968. New York: Atheneum.

LOFLIN, MARVIN D.
1967 On the structure of the verb in a dialect of American Negro English, University of Missouri Center for Research in Behavior, Technical Report No. 26.

LOMAX, ALAN
1959 The rainbow sign. New York: Duell, Sloan, and Pearce.
1960 The folk songs of North America in the English language. New York: Doubleday.
1962 Song structure and social structure. Ethnology 1: 425–51.
1967a Special features of the sung communication. In Essays on the verbal and visual arts, June Helm, ed. Seattle: University of Washington Press.
1967b The good and the beautiful in folksong. Journal of American Folklore 80: 213–35.

LOMAX, ALAN et al.
1968 Folksong style and culture. Washington, D.C.: American Association for the Advancement of Science.

LOMAX, JOHN, AND ALAN LOMAX
1960 Folk song, U.S.A. New York: New American Library.

LOPREATO, J.
1965 How would you like to be a peasant? Human Organization 24: 298.

LOUNSBURY, FLOYD
1965 Another view of the Trobriand kinship categories. American Anthropologist 67: No. 6, 142–85.

LOWENTHAL, DAVID
1967 Race and color in the West Indies. Daedalus, 96 (2): 580–626.

LOWIE, ROBERT H.
1912 The principle of convergence in ethnology. American Anthropologist No. 14.

REFERENCES CITED

1947 Primitive society. New York: Boni and Liveright.

LUDWIG, ARNOLD
1968 Altered states of consciousness. *In* Trance and possession states, Raymond Prince, ed. Proceedings of the second annual conference of the R. M. Bucke Memorial Society, Montreal.

LYLE, W. H., AND ARNOLD LUDWIG
1964 Tension induction and hyper-alert trance. Journal of Abnormal and Social Psychology 69: 70–76.

MCBRIDE, GEORGE
1937 Plantation. *In* Encyclopaedia of the Social Sciences, Vol. IX. New York: Macmillan.

MCCORMICK, MACK
1960 The dirty dozens. The unexpurgated folksongs of men. Arhoolie record album.

MCDAVID, RAVEN I., JR.
1955 The position of the Charleston dialect. Publications of the American Dialect Society 23: 35–49.
1967 Historical, regional and social variation. Journal of English Linguistics 1: 35–43.

MCDAVID, RAVEN I., JR., AND VIRGINIA MCDAVID
1951 The relationship of the speech of American Negroes to the speech of American whites. American Speech 26: 2–17.

MCGALE, EDWARD
1957 Report to the government of British Guiana on employment, unemployment and underemployment in the colony in 1956. Geneva: International Labour Office.

MCGREGOR, PEDRO
1967 Jesus of the spirits. New York: Stein and Day.

MAILER, NORMAN
1969 Looking for the meat and potatoes— thoughts on Black Power. Look, January 7: 57–60.
n.d. The white Negro. San Francisco: City Light Books.

MALCOLM X
1965 The autobiography of Malcolm X. New York: Grove Press.
1967 On Afro-American history. New York: Merit Publishers.

MALLOL DE RECASSENS, JOSÉ, AND MARIA ROSA Y RECASSENS
1963 Estudios comparativos de vivienda en Bueraventura y Puerto Colombia. Revista Colombiana de Antropología 12: 295–328.

MANGIN, WILLIAM
1967a Las comunidades alteñas en la América Latina. Instituto Indigenista Interamericano, Serie Antropología Social No. 5, Mexico.
1967b Squatter settlements. Scientific American 217: No. 4, 21–29.

MANN, J. W.
1957 The problem of the marginal personality. Thesis, University of Natal.

MARRIS, PETER
1961 Family and social change in an African city: a study of rehousing in Lagos. London: Routledge & Kegan Paul.

MARSHALL, A. H.
1955 Report on local government in British Guiana. Georgetown, B.C.: The Argosy Company.

MARS, LOUIS
1946 La crise de possession dans le vaudou: essai de psychiatrie comparée. Port-au-Prince: Bibliothèque de l'Institut d'Ethnologie.

MARUYAMA, MAGOROB
1965 The second cybernetics: deviation amplifying mutual causal processes. American Scientist 51 (2): 164–179.

MARWICK, M. G.
1965 Sorcery in its social setting: a study of Northern Rhodesian Ceŵa. Manchester: Manchester University Press.

MASON, JULIAN
1960 The etymology of buckaroo. American Speech 35: 51–55.

MAYER, ADRIAN C.
1966 The significance of quasi-groups in

MAYR, ERNST
    1963 Animal species and evolution. Cambridge, Mass.: Harvard University Press.

MAYS, BENJAMIN E.
    1968 The Negro's God. New York: Atheneum. (First published by Chapman & Grinnell, 1938.)

MEILLASSOUX, CLAUDE
    1968 Urbanization of an African community: voluntary associations in Bamako. Seattle: University of Washington Press.

MELNICK, MIMI CLAR
    1967 "I can peep through muddy water and spy dry land": boasts in the blues. *In* Folklore international, D. K. Wilgus, ed. Hatboro, Pa.: Folklore Associates.

MENCHER, JOAN P.
    1962 Changing familial roles among South Malabar Nayars. Southwestern Journal of Anthropology 18: 230-45.

MENNESSON-RIGAUD, ODETTE
    1946 The feasting of the gods in Haitian vodû. Primitive Man 19: 1-58.
    1953 Voudou haitien. Quelques notes sur les réminiscences Africaines. *In* Les Afro-Américains, Pierre Verger, ed. Mémoire 27, Institut français d'Afrique Noire, Dakar.

MERCIER, P.
    1954 The Fon of Dahomey. *In* African worlds: studies in the cosmological ideas and social values of African peoples, Daryll Forde, ed. London: Oxford University Press.

MERIZALDE DEL CARMEN, B.
    1921 Estudio de la costa Colombiana del Pacífico. Bogotá: Imp. del Estado Mayor General.

MERRIAM, ALAN P.
    1951 Songs of the Afro-Bahian cults, a musicological analysis. Unpublished Ph.D. dissertation, Northwestern University.
    1959 African music. *In* Continuity and change in African cultures, W. R. Bascom and Melville J. Herskovits, eds. Chicago: University of Chicago Press.
    1963 Obituary: Melville J. Herskovits, 1895-1963. Ethnomusicology 7: 79-82.
    1964a Obituary: Melville Jean Herskovits. American Anthropologist 66: 83-91.
    1964b The anthropology of music. Evanston, Ill.: Northwestern University Press.

MERRILL, GORDON C.
    1958 The historical geography of St. Kitts and Nevis. Mexico, D.F.

MERTON, ROBERT K.
    1957 Social theory and social structure (revised and enlarged). Glencoe, Ill.: The Free Press.

MESSENGER, JOHN
    1959 The role of proverbs in a Nigerian judicial system. Southwestern Journal of Anthropology 15: 64-73.

MÉTRAUX, ALFRED
    1959 Voodoo in Haiti. Trans. Hugo Charteris. New York: Oxford University Press.

METZGER, DUANE, AND GERALD WILLIAMS
    1966 Some procedures and results in the study of native categories: Tzeltal firewood. American Anthropologist 68: 389-407.

MIDDLETON, JOHN, AND E. H. HENKER, EDS.
    1963 Witchcraft and sorcery in East Africa. London: Routledge & Kegan Paul.

MIDDLETON, JOHN, AND DAVID TAIT, EDS.
    1958 Introduction. *In* Tribes without rulers. London: Routledge & Kegan Paul.

MILLER, ELIZABETH W.
    1966 The Negro in America: a bibliography. Cambridge, Mass.: Harvard University Press.

the study of complex societies. *In* The social anthropology of complex societies, Michael Banton, ed. New York: Praeger.

MILLER, WALTER B.
  1958 Lower class culture as a generating milieu of gang delinquency. Journal of Social Issues 14: 5–19.
MINTZ, SIDNEY W.
  1956 Cañamelar: the subculture of a rural sugar plantation proletariat. *In* The people of Puerto Rico, Julian H. Steward, ed. Urbana: University of Illinois Press.
  1959a Internal market systems as mechanisms of social articulation. Proceeding of the Annual Spring Meeting of the American Ethnological Society 20–30. Seattle: University of Washington Press.
  1959b The plantation as a sociocultural type. *In* Plantation systems of the New World. Washington, D.C.: Pan American Union.
  1961 Pratik: Haitian personal economic relationships. Proceedings of the Annual Spring Meeting of the American Ethnological Society 54–63. Seattle: University of Washington Press.
  1964 Melville J. Herskovits and Caribbean studies: a retrospective tribute. Caribbean Studies 4: 42–51.
  1966 The Caribbean as a socio-cultural area. Cahiers d'Histoire Mondiale 9: 912–37.
MINTZ, SIDNEY W., AND WILLIAM DAVENPORT, EDS.
  1961 Caribbean social organization. Social and Economic Studies 10: No. 4, special number.
MISCHEL, F. O.
  1958 A Shango religious group and the problems of prestige in Trinidad Society. Unpublished Ph.D. dissertation, The Ohio State University.
MISCHEL, WALTER, AND FRANCES MISCHEL
  1958 Psychological aspects of spirit possession. American Anthropologist 60: 249–60.
MITCHELL, J. CLYDE
  1966 Theoretical orientations in African urban studies. *In* The Social anthropology of complex societies, Michael Banton, ed. New York: Praeger.
MONEYPENNY, ANNE, AND BARRIE THORNE
  1964 Bibliography of Melville J. Herskovits. Appended to Alan P. Merriam, Melville Jean Herskovits: 1895–1963. American Anthropologist 66: 91–109.
MOORE, J. C.
  1965 Religious syncretism in Jamaica. Practical Anthropology 12: 63–70.
MOREAU DE SAINT MÉRY, LOUIS ÉLIE
  1797 Description topographique, physique, civile, politique et historique de la partie Française de l'île Saint-Domingue, 2 vols. Philadelphia.
MÖRNER, MAGNUS
  1966 The history of race relations in Latin America: some comments on the state of research. Latin American Research Review 1: No. 3, 17–44.
  1967 Race mixture in the history of Latin America. New York: Little, Brown.
MORSE, R. M.
  1962 Some characteristics of Latin American urban history. American Historical Review 57: 317.
MOYNIHAN, DANIEL PATRICK
  1965 The Negro family: the case for national action. Washington, D.C.: Government Printing Office. Prepared for the Office of Policy Planning and Research of the Department of Labor.
  1968 Letter to the Editor. Trans-action 6: 63.
MUHAMMAD SPEAKS
  1967 Published by Muhammad's Mosque No. 2, 436 E. 79th St., Chicago, Ill., Dec. 15.
MURDOCK, GEORGE PETER
  1949 Social structure. New York: Macmillan.
  1959 Africa, its people and their culture history. New York: McGraw-Hill.
  1967 Ethnographic atlas: a summary. Ethnology 6, 2.

MURPHY, JEANETTE ROBINSON
  1899 The survival of African music in America. Popular Science Monthly 55: 660–72.
MURPHY, RAYMOND J., AND HOWARD ELISON, EDS.
  1966 Problems and prospects of the Negro movement. Belmont, Calif.: Wadsworth.
MURPHY, ROBERT F., AND JULIAN H. STEWARD
  1956 Tappers and trappers: parallel processes in acculturation. Economic Development and Cultural Change 4: 335–55.
MYRDAL, GUNNAR
  1944 An American dilemma. New York: Harper. Republished 1964, New York: McGraw-Hill, 2 vols.
NASH, MANNING
  1963 Burmese Buddhism in everyday life. American Anthropologist 65: 285–95.
NATH, DWARKA
  1950 A history of Indians in British Guiana. London: Thomas Nelson and Sons.
NETTL, BRUNO
  1965 Folk and traditional music of the western continents. Englewood Cliffs, N.J.: Prentice-Hall.
NEUMANN, PETER
  1961 Eine verzierte Kalebassenschüssel aus Suriname. Veröffentlichungen des Museums für Völkerkunde zu Leipzig, Heft 11: 481–98.
  1965a Zur Funktion des Bassia in der gesellschaftlichen Organisation der Buschneger Surinames. Abhandlungen und Berichte des Staatlichen Museums für Völkerkunde Dresden, Bd. 24: 61–72.
  1965b Bemerkungen zu einigen Rechtsauffassungen der Buschneger Surinames. Abhandlungen und Berichte des Staatlichen Museums für Völkerkunde Dresden, Bd. 25: 1–15.
  1967 Wirtschaft und materielle kultur der Buschneger Surinames: Ein Beitrag zur Erforschung afroamerikanischer Probleme. Abhandlungen und Berichte des Staatlichen Museums für Völkerkunde Dresden, Bd. 26.
NEWMAN, STANLEY
  n.d. The gouster: a functional analysis of a ghetto role. Ms.
NORTON, ARTHUR A.
  1921 Linguistic persistence. American Speech 6: 149.
OBERG, KALERVO
  1955 Types of social structure among the lowland tribes of South and Central America. American Anthropologist 57: 472–87.
ODUM, HOWARD W., AND GUY B. JOHNSON
  1925 The Negro and his songs: a study of typical Negro songs in the South. Chapel Hill: University of North Carolina Press.
  1926 Negro workaday songs. Chapel Hill: University of North Carolina Press.
OESTERREICH, T. G.
  1922 Die Bessessenheit, Halle: Wendt and Klauwell. (Possession, demonical and other.) Trans. D. Ibberson, reprint edition 1966. New York: Universe Books.
OLIVER, PAUL
  1965 Conversation with the blues. New York: Horizon.
ORTIZ, FERNANDO
  1912 Les chansons et la musique de la Guyane néerlandaise. Journal de la Société des Americanistes de Paris (N.S.) 9: 27–39.
  1916 Hampa Afro-cubana: Los Negros esclavos, estudio sociológico y de derecho público. Havana: Revista Bimestre Cubana.
  1917 Hampa Afro-Cubana: los Negros brujos. Madrid: Editorial América.
  1924 Hampa Afro-cubana: Glosario de Afronegrismos. Havana: Imprenta "El Siglo xx."
  1940 Contrapunteo Cubano del tabaco y del azúcar. Habana: Jesus Montero.
  1947 Cuban counterpoint: tobacco and sugar. New York: Knopf.
  1950 La Africanía de la música folklórica

REFERENCES CITED

de Cuba. Habana: Ministério de Educación, Dirección de Cultura.
1952–55 Los instrumentos de la música Afrocubana, 5 vols. Habana.

ORTIZ, SUTTI
1967 Colombian rural market organization: an exploratory model. Man 2: 393–414.

OSSOWSKI, STANISLAW
1963 Different conceptions of social class. *In* Class, status, and power, Reinhard Bendix and Seymour M. Lipset, eds. New York: The Free Press.

OTTENHEIMER, HARRIET J.
1965 Blues: pattern and variation. Paper presented to the Society for Ethnomusicology, Albuquerque, New Mexico.

OTTERBEIN, KEITH F.
1965 Caribbean family organization: a comparative analysis. American Anthropologist 67: 66–79.
1966 The Andros islanders. Lawrence: University of Kansas Press.

PAN AMERICAN UNION
1959 Plantation systems of the New World. Social Science Monographs, No. 7, Washington, D.C.

PAREDES BORJA, VIRGILIO
1963 Suma de la historia de los conocimientos médicos en el Ecuador: I (?–1914). Medicina y Ciencias Biológicas Quito 1: 43–51.

PARES, RICHARD
1950 A West India fortune. London: Longmans, Green. Reprinted 1968, Hamden, Conn.: Archon.

PARO, PAULINE
1957 Survey of family expenditures, 1956. Geneva: International Labour Office.

PARRINDER, GEOFFREY
1952 Religion in an African city. London: Oxford University Press.

PARRISH, LYDIA
1942 Slave songs of the Georgia Sea Islands. New York: Farrar, Straus. Reprinted 1965, Hatboro, Pa.: Folklore Associates.

PARSONS, ELSIE CLEWS
1918 Folk-tales of Andros Island, Bahamas. Memoirs of the American Folklore Society No. 13.
1923a Folk-lore from the Cape Verde Islands. Memoirs of the American Folklore Society No. 15.
1923b Folk-tales of the Sea Islands, South Carolina. Memoirs of the American Folklore Society No. 16.
1933–35, Folklore of the Antilles, French
1943 and English. Memoirs of the American Folklore Society 26, vols. I, II, III.

PARSONS, TALCOTT, AND KENNETH CLARK, EDS.
1965 The Negro American. Boston: Beacon Press.

PAVY, DAVID
1967 The provenience of Colombian Negroes. Journal of Negro History 47: 36–58.

PEARSE, ANDREW
1955 Aspects of change in Caribbean folk music. UNESCO International Folk Music Journal 7: 29–36.
1956 Mitto Sampson on calypso legends of the nineteenth century. Caribbean Quarterly 4: 250–62.

PEDERSON, LEE A.
1968 Middleclass Negro speech in Minneapolis. Orbis 17: 347–53.

PENARD, F. P., AND A. P. PENARD
1912 Surinaamsch bijgeloof. Iets over winti en andere natuurbegrippen. Bijdragen tot de taal-, land-, en volkenkunde van Nederlansch-Indie 67: 157–83.

PERANIO, ROGER
1961 Descent, descent line, and descent group in cognatic social systems. Proceedings of the American Ethnological Society 1961: 93–114.

PETERSON, HAROLD
1969 Brower power awaits the verdict. Sports Illustrated April 14: 36 ff.

PETTIGREW, THOMAS F.
1964 A profile of the Negro American. Princeton: Van Nostrand.

PFEIFFER, W. M.
 1968 Personal communication.
 n.d. Andere rituelle Versenkungs-und Ausnahmezustände. Ms.
PICKFORD, GLENNA RUTH
 1956 American linguistic geography: a sociological appraisal. Word 12: 211–33.
PIERSON, DONALD
 1942 Negroes in Brazil. Chicago: University of Chicago Press.
 1955 Race relations in Portuguese America. *In* Race relations in world perspective, Andrew W. Lind, ed. Honolulu: University of Hawaii Press.
PITT-RIVERS, JULIAN
 1967 Race, color, and class in Central America and the Andes. Daedalus 96 (2): 542–59.
PLOTNICOV, LEONARD
 1967 Strangers to the city: urban man in Jos, Nigeria. Pittsburgh: University of Pittsburgh Press.
POLGAR, STEVEN
 1960 Biculturation of Mesaquakie boys. American Anthropologist 62: 232–33.
POLLAK-ELTZ, ANGELINA
 1966 Afrikanische Relikte in der Volkskultur Venezuelas. Freiburg im Breisgau.
 1967 Notizen über den Batuquekult der Neger in Porto Alegre. Mitteilungen der Anthropologischen Gesellschaft in Wien 96/97: 138–46.
 1968 The devil dances in Venezuela. Caribbean Studies 8: 65–73.
POUSSAINT, ALVIN F.
 1967 A Negro psychiatrist explains the Negro psyche. The New York Times, Aug. 20, Section 6: 52 ff.
POWDERMAKER, HORTENSE
 1939 After freedom. New York: Viking.
PRESSEL, ESTHER
 1968a Structure, belief, and ritual behavior in Umbanda (a preliminary report of field research in São Paulo, Brazil). Cross-cultural studies of dissociational states, working paper No. 19. Department of Anthropology, The Ohio State University.
 1968b Dissociational states in Umbanda: a function of cognitive dissonance. Cross-Cultural Studies of Dissociational States, Working Paper No. 23, Department of Anthropology, The Ohio State University.
PRICE, RICHARD
 1964 Magie et pêche à la Martinique. L'Homme 4: 84–113.
PRICE, THOMAS J., JR.
 1954 Aspectos de estabilidad y desorganización cultural de una comunidad isleña del Caribe Colombiano. Revista Colombiana de Antropología No. 2.
 1955a Estado y necesidades de las investigaciones Afro-Colombianas. Revista Colombiana de Antropología 3: 11–36.
 1955b Saints and spirits: a study of differential acculturation in Colombian Negro communities. Ann Arbor: University Microfilms.
 1966 *Review of* Norman E. Whitten, Jr., Class, kinship, and power in an Ecuadorian town: the Negroes of San Lorenzo. American Anthropologist 68: 1548.
PRICE-MARS, J.
 1928 Ainsi parla l'oncle. Paris: Impr. de Compiègne.
PUCKETT, NEWBELL NILES
 1926 Folk beliefs of the southern Negro. Chapel Hill: University of North Carolina Press.
THE PULSE, INC.
 1968a Detroit City, Michigan, Negro audience, February–March.
 1968b New York City five county survey area, Negro radio audience, January–April.
RAINWATER, LEE
 1966a Crucible of identity: the Negro lower-class family. Daedalus 95 (2): 172–216.

REFERENCES CITED

1966b Work and identity in the lower class. *In* Planning for a nation of cities, Sam Bass Warner, Jr., ed. Cambridge, Mass.: M.I.T. Press.

RAINWATER, LEE, AND WILLIAM L. YANCEY, EDS.
1967 The Moynihan report and the politics of controversy. Cambridge, Mass.: M.I.T. Press.

RAMOS, ARTHUR
1935 O folk-lore Negro do Brasil. Rio de Janeiro.
1937 As culturas Negros nova mundo. Rio de Janeiro: Companhia editoria nacional.
1939 The Negro in Brazil. Washington, D.C.: Associated Publishers, Inc.

RAPER, ARTHUR F.
1968 Preface to peasantry. New York: Atheneum. (First published 1936, University of North Carolina Press.)

RECORD WORLD
1968 Vol. 23, No. 1105, 1106, 1107. New York: Intro Publishing Co.

REISMAN, KARL
1967 Linguistic values and cultural values in a West Indian village. Paper presented at 66th annual meeting, American Anthropological Association, Washington, D.C.

REISS, I. L.
1965 The universality of the family: a conceptual analysis. Journal of Marriage and the Family 27: 443–53.

ROACH, JACK L., AND ORVILLE R. GURSSLIN
1967 An evaluation of the concept "culture of poverty." Social Forces 45: 383–92.

ROBERTS, JOHN
1964 The self-management of cultures. *In* Explorations in cultural anthropology, Ward H. Goodenough, ed. New York: McGraw-Hill.

RODMAN, HYMAN
1963 The lower-class value stretch. Social Forces 42: 205–15.

RODRIGUES, NINA
1900 L'animisme fétichiste des Nègres de Bahia. Bahia: Reis Brazil.

ROGLER, L. H., AND A. B. HOLLINGSHEAD
1961 The Puerto Rican spiritualist as a psychiatrist. American Journal of Sociology 67: 17–21.
1965 Trapped: families and schizophrenia. New York: Wiley.

ROHRER, JOHN H., AND MUNRO S. EDMONSON
1960 The eighth generation grows up. New York: Harper & Row.

ROMNEY, A. KIMBALL, AND ROY D'ANDRADE
1964 Cognitive aspects of English kin terms. American Anthropologist 66: 146–70.

ROSE, ARNOLD
1944 The Negro in America. New York: Harper. (Beacon paperback published in 1956.)

ROWLEY, C. D.
1966 The New Guinea villager. New York: Praeger.

RUBEL, A. J.
1964 The epidemiology of folk illness: *susto* in Hispanic America. Ethnology 3: 268–83.

RUBIN, VERA
1959 Introduction. *In* Plantation systems of the New World. Washington, D.C.: Pan American Union.

RUBIN, VERA, ED.
1957 Caribbean studies: a symposium. Seattle: University of Washington Press.
1960 Social and cultural pluralism in the Caribbean. Annals of the New York Academy of Sciences 83: 791–916.

RUBIO, ANGEL
1957 Las plantaciones en Panamá. Paper presented at a seminar on plantation systems in the New World. Washington, D.C.: Pan American Union (mimeographed).

SAHLINS, MARSHALL D.
1961 The segmentary lineage: an organization of predatory expansion. American Anthropologist 63 (2): 322–45.
1964 Culture and environment. *In* Horizons of anthropology, Sol Tax, ed. Chicago: Aldine.

1965a On the sociology of primitive exchange. *In* The relevance of models for social anthropology, Michael Banton, ed. New York: Praeger.

1965b On the ideology and composition of descent groups. Man 65: 104–06.

SARGANT, WILLIAM

1959 Battle for the mind (rev. ed.). London: Pan Books.

SAVANNAH UNIT, GEORGIA WRITER'S PROJECT (WPA)

1940 Drums and shadows: survival studies among the Georgia coastal Negroes. Athens: University of Georgia Press.

SAXON, LYLE, EDWARD DREYER, AND ROBERT TALLANT

1945 Gumbo ya-ya: a collection of Louisiana folk tales. Boston: Houghton Mifflin.

SCARBOROUGH, DOROTHY

1925 On the trail of Negro folksongs. Cambridge, Mass.: Harvard University Press. Reprinted 1963, Hatboro, Pa.: Folklore Associates.

SCHNEIDER, DAVID M., AND E. K. GOUGH, EDS.

1961 Matrilineal kinship. Berkeley: University of California Press.

SESSIONAL PAPER NO. 5

1959 Paper of the Second Legislative Council on British Guiana's 1960–64 Development Programme. Georgetown, B.C.: The B.G. Lithographic Co.

SHIBUTANI, TAMOTSU, AND KIAN W. KWAN

1965 Ethnic stratification: a comparative approach. New York: Macmillan.

SHORRIS, EARL

1966 Ofay. New York: Dell.

SHUY, ROGER W.

1968 Detroit speech: careless, awkward, and inconsistent, or systematic, graceful, and regular? Elementary English 45: 565–69.

SIMPSON, GEORGE E.

1945 The belief system of Haitian vodun. American Anthropologist 47: 35–59.

1955a Political cultism in West Kingston, Jamaica. Social and Economic Studies 4: 133–49.

1955b The Ras Tafari movement in Jamaica: a study of race and class conflict. Social Forces 34: 167–70.

1956 Jamaican revivalist cults. Social and Economic Studies 5: i–ix, 321–42.

1962a Folk medicine in Trinidad. Journal of American Folklore 75: 326–40.

1962b The Shango cult in Nigeria and Trinidad. American Anthropologist 54: 1204–29.

1965 The Shango cult in Trinidad. San Juan: Institute of Caribbean Studies. Caribbean Monograph Series, No. 2.

1966 Baptismal, "mourning," and "building" ceremonies of the Shouters of Trinidad. Journal of American Folklore 79: 537–50.

SINGER, L.

1962 Ethnogenesis and Negro Americans today. Social Research 29: 419–32.

SKINNER, ELLIOT P.

1955 Ethnic interaction in a British Guiana rural community: a study in secondary acculturation and group dynamics. Ph.D. dissertation, Columbia University.

SMITH, M. G.

1953 Some aspects of social structure in the British Caribbean about 1820. Social and Economic Studies 1 (4): 57–79.

1955 A framework for Caribbean studies. Caribbean Affairs Series. Jamaica: University College of the West Indies.

1957a Dark puritan: the life and work of Norman Paul (in two parts). Caribbean Quarterly 5: Nos. 1 and 2.

1957b Introduction. *In* My mother who fathered me, Edith Clarke. London: George Allen and Unwin.

1957c The African heritage in the Caribbean. *In* Caribbean studies: a symposium, Vera Rubin, ed. Seattle: University of Washington Press.

1960 Social and cultural pluralism. *In* Social and cultural pluralism in the

REFERENCES CITED

    Caribbean, Vera Rubin, ed. Annals of the New York Academy of Sciences No. 83.

1962a Kinship and community in Carriacou. New Haven: Yale University Press.

1962b West Indian family structure. Seattle: University of Washington Press.

1963 Dark puritan. Kingston: Department of Extra-mural Studies, University of the West Indies.

1965 The plural society in the British West Indies. Berkeley and Los Angeles: University of California Press.

SMITH, RAYMOND T.

1956 The Negro family in British Guiana. London: Routledge & Kegan Paul.

1963 Culture and social structure in the Caribbean: some recent work on family and kinship studies. Comparative Studies in Society and History 6: 24–46.

1967 Social stratification, cultural pluralism and interaction in the West Indies. *In* Special issue of Caribbean Studies on Caribbean integration, Thomas G. Mathews and Sybil Lewis, eds. Rio Piedras, P.R.: Institute of Caribbean Studies, University of Puerto Rico.

SMITH, RAYMOND T., AND C. JAYAWARDENA

1958 Hindu marriage customs in British Guiana. Social and Economic Studies 7:178–94.

1959 Marriage and family amongst East Indians in British Guiana. Social and Economic Studies 8:321–76.

SMITH, T. WATSON

1899 The slave in Canada. Nova Scotia Historical Society Collection, Vol. 10 Halifax, N.S.

SOLIEN, NANCIE L.

1958 The consanguineal household among the Black Carib of Central America. Ann Arbor: University Microfilms.

SOLIEN DE GONZÁLEZ, NANCIE L.

1961 Family organization in five types of migratory wage labor. American Anthropologist 63:1264–80.

SOUTHALL, AIDAN

1961 Social change in modern Africa. London: Oxford University Press.

SOUTHEY, ROBERT

1925 The life of Wesley and the rise and progress of Methodism, 2 vols. London: Oxford University Press (originally published 1825).

SPIRO, MELFORD E.

1954 Is the family universal? American Anthropologist 56:839–46.

STAMPP, KENNETH

1956 The peculiar institution. New York: Random House.

STEWARD, JULIAN H.

1938 Basin-plateau aboriginal sociopolitical groups. Bureau of American Ethnology Bulletin No. 120.

STEWARD, JULIAN H., ROBERT A. MANNERS, ERIC R. WOLFE, E. PADILLA SEDA, SIDNEY W. MINTZ, AND R. L. SCHEELE

1956 People of Puerto Rico. Urbana: University of Illinois Press.

STEWART, WILLIAM A.

1962 Creole languages in the Caribbean. *In* Study of the role of second languages in Asia, Africa and Latin America, Frank A. Rice, ed. Washington, D.C.: Center for Applied Linguistics.

1965 Urban Negro speech: sociolinguistic factors affecting English teaching. *In* Social dialects and language learning, Roger W. Shuy, ed. Champaign, Ill.: National Council of Teachers of English.

1966 Observations on the problems of defining Negro dialect. *In* Conference on the language component in the training of teachers of English and reading: views and problems. Washington, D.C.: Center for Applied Linguistics and the National Council of Teachers of English.

1967 Sociolinguistic factors in the history

of American Negro dialects. The Florida FL Reporter 5: No. 2.
1968 Continuity and change in American Negro dialects. Reprinted *in* Readings in American dialectology, Harold B. Allen and Gary N. Underwoods, eds.

STOCKING, GEORGE W., JR.
1968 Race, culture, and evolution. New York: The Free Press.

STONEQUIST, EVERETT
1937 The marginal man. New York: Scribners.

STRACHWITZ, CHRIS
1964 An interview with the Staples family. American Folk Music Occasional Paper No. 1, Chris Strachwitz, ed. Berkeley.

STRICKON, ARNOLD
1962 Class and kinship in Argentina. Ethnology 1: 500–15.

STURTEVANT, WILLIAM
1964 Studies in ethnoscience. American Anthropologist 66: No. 6, pt. 2, 99–131.

SZWED, JOHN F.
1966 Musical style and racial conflict. Phylon 27: 358–66.
1968 Negro music: urban renewal. *In* Our living traditions: an introduction to American folklore, Tristram P. Coffin, ed. New York: Basic Books.

TALBOT, ALLEN
1968 The lessons of New Haven, the erstwhile model city. Psychology Today 2 (3): 22–27.

TALLANT, ROBERT
1946 Voodoo in New Orleans. New York: Macmillan. (Collier paperback published 1962.)

TAX, SOL, ED.
1952 Acculturation in the Americas. Chicago: University of Chicago Press.
1964 Horizons of Anthropology. Chicago: Aldine.

TAYLOR, DOUGLAS MACRAE
1951 The Black Caribs of British Honduras. New York: Viking Fund Publications in Anthropology, No. 17.
1957 Review, Élodie Jourdain, Du Français aux parlers Créoles et le vocabulaire du parler Créole de la Martinique. Word 13: 357–68.
1959 On function vs. form in "non-traditional" languages. Word 15: 485–88.
1960 Language shift or changing relationships? International Journal of American Linguistics 26: 155–61.
1963 The origin of West Indian creole languages: evidence from grammatical categories. American Anthropologist 65: 800–14.
1964 Review, Antoon Donicie and Jan Voorhoeve, Sarama Kaanse Woordenschat. International Journal of American Linguistics 30: 434–39.

TERAN, FRANCISCO
1966 Geografía del Ecuador. Quito: Editorial Colón.

THIBAULT, JOHN W., AND HAROLD H. KELLEY
1959 The social psychology of groups. New York: Wiley.

THOMAS, PIRI
1967 Down these mean streets. New York: Knopf.

THOMPSON, EDGAR T.
1959 The plantation as a social system. *In* Plantation systems of the New World. Washington, D.C.: Pan American Union.

TIME MAGAZINE
1969 Los Angeles: bitter victory. June 6, 1969. 93 (23): 29 ff.
1969 Reporters: ghetto news. June 6, 1969. 93 (23): 53.

TURNER, LORENZO D.
1949 Africanisms in the Gullah dialect. Chicago: University of Chicago Press.

UNITED NATIONS
1956 Demographic yearbook special topic: ethnic and economic characteristics. Statistical Office of the United Nations, Department of Economic and

Social Affairs. New York: United Nations.
1963 Demographic yearbook special topic: population census statistics II. Statistical Office of the United Nations, Department of Economic and Social Affairs. New York: United Nations.

U.S. RIOT COMMISSION REPORT
1968 New York: Bantam.

VALENTINE, CHARLES A.
1968 Culture and poverty. Chicago: University of Chicago Press.

VAN DEN BERGHE, PIERRE L.
1967 Race and racism: a comparative perspective. New York: Wiley.

VAYDA, ANDREW P., AND ROY A. RAPPAPORT
1968 Ecology, cultural and noncultural. *In* Introduction to cultural anthropology, James A. Clifton, ed. New York: Houghton Mifflin.

VERGER, PIERRE
1957 Notes sur le culte des orisa et vodun à Bahia, la Baie de tous les Saints au Brésil et à l'ancienne Côte d'Esclaves en Afrique. Mémoire 51, Institut français d'Afrique noire, Dakar.

WAGLEY, CHARLES
1957 Plantation America: a culture sphere. *In* Caribbean studies: a symposium, Vera Rubin, ed. Seattle: University of Washington Press.
1965 On the concept of social race in the Americas. *In* Contemporary cultures and societies of Latin America, Dwight B. Heath and Richard N. Adams, eds. New York: Random House.

WAGLEY, CHARLES, ED.
1952 Race and class in rural Brazil. Paris: UNESCO.

WAGLEY, CHARLES, AND MARVIN HARRIS
1958 Minorities in the New World. Six case studies. New York: Columbia University Press.

WALLACE, ANTHONY F. C.
1956 Revitalization movements. American Anthropologist 58: 264-81.
1966 Religion: an anthropological view. New York: Random House.

WALLACE, ANTHONY F. C., AND JOHN ATKINS
1960 The meaning of kinship terms. American Anthropologist 62: 58-80.

WATERMAN, RICHARD A.
1943 African patterns in Trinidad Negro music. Ph.D. dissertation, Northwestern University.
1952 African influence on the music of the Americas. *In* Acculturation in the Americas, Sol Tax, ed. Chicago: University of Chicago Press.

WATERMAN, RICHARD A., AND WILLIAM R. BASCOM
1949 African and New World Negro folklore. *In* Dictionary of folklore, mythology and legend, Maria Leach, ed. New York: Funk & Wagnalls.

WATSON, JEANNE
1958 A formal analysis of sociable interaction. Sociometry 21: 269-81.

WEBER, MAX
1958 From Max Weber: essays in sociology. Trans. and edited by H. H. Gerth and C. Wright Mills. New York: Oxford University Press.

WEINSTEIN, EUGENE A., AND PAUL DEUTSCHBERGER
1963 Some dimensions of altercasting. Sociometry 26: 454-66.

WELDING, PETE
1967 Tapescripts: interview with Rev. Robert Wilkins, T7-155. John Edwards Memorial Foundation Newsletter 2: 54-60.

WELSCH, ERWIN K.
1965 The Negro in the United States: a research guide. Bloomington: Indiana University Press.

WENTWORTH, HAROLD, AND STUART BERG FLEXNER
1960 Dictionary of American slang. New York: Crowell.

WEST, ROBERT C.
1952 Colonial placer mining in Colombia.

Baton Rouge: Louisiana State University Press.

1957 The Pacific lowlands of Colombia: a Negroid area of the American tropics. Baton Rouge: Louisiana State University Press.

WESTERMAN, GEORGE

1948 A study of the socioeconomic conflicts in the Canal Zone. Panama City, R.P.: National Civic League.

1954 School segregation on the Panama Canal Zone. Phylon 15: 276–88.

WHITE, LESLIE

1966 The social organization of ethnological theory. Rice University Studies, Monograph in Cultural Anthropology 52, No. 4. Houston: Rice University Press.

WHITE, NEWMAN I.

1928 American Negro folk-songs. Cambridge, Mass.: Harvard University Press. Reprinted 1964, Hatboro, Pa.: Folklore Associates.

WHITEFORD, ANDREW

1960 Two cities in Latin America: a description of social classes. Beloit, Wis.: Logan Museum Publications in Anthropology No. 9.

WHITING, JOHN W., AND IRVING L. CHILD

1953 Child training and personality. New Haven: Yale University Press.

WHITTEN, NORMAN E., JR.

1962 Contemporary patterns of malign occultism among Negroes in North Carolina. Journal of American Folklore 75 (298): 311–25.

1965 Class, kinship, and power in an Ecuadorian town: the Negroes of San Lorenzo. Stanford: Stanford University Press.

1967a Música y relaciones sociales en las tierras bajas colombianas y ecuatorianas del Pacífico: estudio sobre micro-evolución sociocultural. América Indígena 27: 635–65.

1967b Afro-Hispanic music from western Colombia and Ecuador. Ethnic Folkways Library FE 4376.

1968 Personal networks and musical contexts in the Pacific lowlands of Colombia and Ecuador. Man 3: 50–63.

1969 Network analysis and processes of adaptation among Ecuadorian and Nova Scotian Negroes. In Marginal Natives: Anthropologists at Work, Morris Freilich, ed. New York: Harper & Row.

WHITTEN, NORMAN E., JR., AND AURELIO FUENTES C.

1966 ¡Baile marimba! Negro folk music in northwest Ecuador. Journal of the Folklore Institute 3: 168–91.

WHYTE, WILLIAM F.

1943 Street corner society. Chicago: University of Chicago Press.

WILGUS, D. K.

1959 Anglo-American folksong scholarship since 1898. New Brunswick: Rutgers University Press.

WILLS, GARRY

1968 The second Civil War. New York: New American Library.

WILSON, CHARLES

1947 Empire in green and gold. New York: Holt.

WILSON, PETER J.

n.d. Caribbean crews. Ms.

1969 Reputation and respectability: a suggestion for Caribbean ethnology. Man 4: 70–84.

WOLF, ERIC R.

1955 Types of Latin American peasantry. American Anthropologist 57: 452–71.

1957 Closed corporate peasant communities in Mexico and central Java. Southwestern Journal of Anthropology 13: 1–8.

1966 Peasants. Englewood Cliffs: Prentice-Hall.

WOLPOFF, M. H.

1968 Telanthropus and the single species hypothesis. American Anthropologist 70: 477–93.

WOOFTER, T. F., JR.

1930 Black yeomanry: life on St. Helena Island. New York: Holt.

REFERENCES CITED

YINGER, J. MILTON
    1960 Contraculture and subculture. American Sociological Review 25: 625–35.

YOUNG, A.
    1958 The approaches to local self-government in British Guiana. London: Longmans, Green.

YOUNG, MICHAEL, AND PETER WILLMOTT
    1957 Family and kinship in East London. Glencoe, Ill.: The Free Press.

YOUNG, FRANK W., AND RUTH CY YOUNG
    n.d. The differentiation of family structure in rural Mexico. Ms.

ZBOROWSKI, MARK, AND ELIZABETH HERZOG
    1952 Life is with people. New York: International Universities Press.

ZELINSKY, WILBUR
    1949 The historical geography of the Negro population of Latin America. Journal of Negro History 34. (2): 153–221.

ZEMPLÉNI, A.
    1966 La dimension thérapeutique de culte des rab. Ndöp. Tuuru et Samp, rites de possession chez les Lébou et les Wolof. Psychopathologie Africaine 2: 295–439.

PICTURE CREDITS FOR PICTORIAL ESSAY

PAGE 1 — Paul Conklin

PAGE 2
- *Top* Ruth & Hassouldt Davis—Rapho Guillumette Pictures
- *Bottom Left* Muriel & Malcomb Bell
- *Bottom Right* Muriel & Malcomb Bell

PAGE 3
- *Top* Richard Price
- *Bottom Left* William LaVarre — Black Star
- *Bottom Right* Ruth & Hassouldt Davis—Rapho Guillumette Pictures

PAGE 4
- *Top* Ruth & Hassouldt Davis—Rapho Guillumette Pictures
- *Bottom Left* Ruth & Hassouldt Davis—Rapho Guillumette Pictures
- *Bottom Right* Richard Price

PAGE 5
- *Top* Thomas Price
- *Bottom* Ingeborg de Beausacq — Pix

PAGE 6
- *Top* Michael Semak—Pix
- *Bottom* Marvin Harris

PAGE 7
- *Top* Caio Garrubba — Rapho Guillumette Pictures
- *Bottom* Marvin Harris

PAGE 8
- *Top* Christa Armstrong — Rapho Guillumette Pictures
- *Bottom Left* Carl Purcell
- *Bottom Right* Pix

PAGE 9
- *Top Left* Norman E. Whitten, Jr.
- *Top Right* Paul-Henri Bourguignon
- *Bottom* Charles M. Rafshoon—Pix

PICTURE CREDITS

PAGE 10
- *Top* Michael Semak—Pix
- *Bottom* Stern—Black Star

PAGE 11
- *Top* Calogero Cascio — Rapho Guillumette Pictures
- *Bottom Left* Norman E. Whitten, Jr.
- *Bottom Right* Paul Conklin

PAGE 12
- *Top Left* Norman E. Whitten, Jr.
- *Top Right* Norman E. Whitten, Jr.
- *Bottom Left* Carl Purcell
- *Bottom Right* Nancie González

PAGE 13
- *Top* James Newberry
- *Bottom* Norman E. Whitten, Jr.

PAGE 14 Richard Bellak

PAGE 15 Richard Bellak

PAGE 16
- *Top Left* Richard Bellak
- *Top Right* Camera Press—Pix
- *Bottom Left* Burk Uzzle — Magnum Photos
- *Bottom Right* Burk Uzzle — Magnum Photos

PAGE 17
- *Top* Burk Uzzle — Magnum Photos
- *Bottom* George W. Gardner

PAGE 18 Richard Bellak

PAGE 19
- *Top Two Rows* Richard Bellak
- *Next to Bottom of Page* Wolf von dem Bussche
- *Bottom* Peter S. Dole

PAGE 20
- *Top Left* Camera Press—Pix
- *Top Right* James Newberry
- *Bottom* Norman E. Whitten, Jr.

PAGE 21
- *Top Left* Charles Gatewood
- *Top Right* Paul-Henri Bourguignon
- *Bottom* Dr. Georg Gerster—Rapho Guillumette Pictures

PAGE 22
- *Top Left* Anne Bolt—Black Star
- *Middle Right* Norman E. Whitten, Jr.
- *Bottom* Richard Bellak

PAGE 23
- *Top* Norman E. Whitten, Jr.
- *Middle* Norman E. Whitten, Jr.
- *Bottom* Lac Bouchage — Rapho Guillumette Pictures

PAGE 24
- *All* James Newberry

PAGE 25
- *All* James Newberry

PAGE 26
- *Top* Roger Abrahams
- *Bottom* John Messina

PAGE 27
- *Top* Paul-Henri Bourguignon
- *Bottom* Lilo Raymond

PAGE 28
- *Top* Bill Wingell
- *Bottom Row* Don Charles Blom

PAGE 29
- *Top* Charles Gatewood
- *Middle* Laurence Kirkland
- *Bottom Row* Don Charles Blom

PAGE 30
- *Top* Calogero Cascio — Rapho Guillumette Pictures
- *Bottom* S. Harrison—Camera Press—Pix

PAGE 31
- *Top* Luther Gerlach
- *Middle* Wolf von dem Bussche
- *Bottom* Charles Gatewood

PAGE 32 Ruth-Marion Baruch

INDEX

Aberle, David, 386
Abernathy, Ralph, 393
Abrahams, Roger D., vii, 21, 39, 156, 158, 159, 161, 163-179, 221, 303, 318, 320
Acklin, Barbara, 379
Adams, Richard N., 44, 45, 329, 331
Adaptation, concepts of, 24, 38, 41-49, 51-52, 264-265
Adaptive strategies, 24, 40, 52; *see also* Ecuador, Guyana
Africa, 25, 26
African culture: *see* Culture
African food, 3, 7
African gardeners, 192
African Hunters, 182, 183, 185-186, 189, 191-192, 196, 197
African music, 9, 181-201, 213, 216
Africanisms, 3-5, 11, 25-30, 34, 36, 40, 63, 119, 264; *see also* Herskovits, Melville J.
Africans in the New World, distribution of, 7, 17
Afro-American, definition of, 3-5, 18-19
Agrarian Reform Law (Ecuador), 248
Aguardiente: *see* Rum
Alabado, 67, 208-211, 214
Alagoas, Brazil, 76
Alland, Alexander, 48, 264
Allen, W. F., 31
Allusion, 139-140
Altered states of consciousness, 88
Aluku, the, 63, 64-66
Aluku tongo, 65
Aluminium Ltd., 267
Alvo, 77, 78, 82, 83, 85
Ambato, Ecuador, 247
Ambulantes, 252
American Anthropological Association Symposium (1967), 34-40, 58
American Dilemma, An (Myrdal), 23, 54, 348
American Folklore Society, 31, 32
American Indians, 13, 36, 40, 50, 52, 64, 68, 87, 235, 245-246, 248, 256-259, 265
Anamat, Trinidad, 315
Andros Islands, Bahamas, 315, 321
Angelli, John D., 105

Anglicanism, 87, 94, 111, 112
Animism, 93
Anthropomorphic spirits, 89
Antigua, 40, 129-144, 171
Antonovski, A., 289
Anxiety, 115
Aptheker, Herbert, 34
Arabs, the, 191, 197, 406
Arensberg, Conrad, 194
Arrollo de Piedra, Colombia, 67
Arrullos, 206-208, 211
Articles of Capitulation, Guyana, 270
Asson, ritual of taking the (becoming a priest), 95
Atkins, Hal, 371, 374, 379, 380
Atkins, John, 85
Atwood, E. Bagby, 122, 125
Aucaners, the, 64
Avocados, marketing of, 247, 248-251, 252-254, 255-256
Azevedo, Thales de, 75

Baby Drill (dance), 175
Bachofen, J. J., 304
Bahamas: *see* Andros Islands
Bahia, Brazil, 76, 95
Bahima kingdom, 188
Baile de respeto (dance), 205
Bailey, Beryl Loftman, 121, 137
Bakkanenge, 64
Bakra (Bakka), 64, 70, 122
Baldwin, James, 357
Ballanta-Taylor, N. G. J., 32
Bananas, 192
Banton, Michael G., 46
Bantu, the, 182, 186, 188, 189, 193, 197
Baptists, 37, 88, 91, 95, 98, 99
Baratz, Joan, 122
Barbados, 171
Bargaining, 250-256, 257-259
    three stages in, 253
Barnes, James, 316, 381
Barranquilla, Colombia, 69
Bascom, William R., 91, 95
Bastide, Roger, 28, 37, 45, 49, 96
Bastien, Rémy, 37
Bauxite, 267

Beatles, the, 375
Beckwith, Martha W., 33-34, 112
Bedouins, the, 196
Bedwardite sect, 112
Bell, William, 371
Bende, 70
Bender, D. R., 304
Benedict, Ruth, 33
Benjinite Church, 104, 111-113, 114
Bennett, John W., 21
Bennett, Lerone, Jr., 227
Benz, Ernst, 92
Berbice River, 265, 270
Berdie, Ralph F., 320
Berger, Bennett, 347, 349, 353-354, 361-363
Bernard, Jessie, 41
Bible, the, 37, 92-93, 113, 356
Bilingualism, 129
Billboard, 370
Billingsley, Andrew, 41
Birdwhistell, Ray, 319
Birth control, 358
Black, definition of, 19
Black capitalism, 399-400
Black Carib, 44, 236-239
Black culture, 11, 19, 347-366
Black ghetto, 52-53, 313-327, 403-418
Black Music (Jones), 382
Black Muslims: *see* Muslims
Black Panthers, 388
Black power, 85, 242, 362, 385-401
    adaptive functions, 397-399
    decentralization, 391-392
    extra-movement linkages, 395-397
    organization of, 389-391
    reticulation, 393-395, 396-397
    segmentation, 392-393, 399-400
Black Roadways: A Study of Jamaican Folklife (Beckwith), 33
Black Students Action Committee, 397
Black Survival Conferences, 358
Blake, Judith, 41, 331
Bland, Bobby "Blue," blues singer, 372, 373, 374
Blauner, Robert, vii, 52, 347-366
Blooah, C. G., 141
"Blood" (Slim), 147

INDEX

Bloomfield, Leonard, 121, 122
Bluefields, Nicaragua, 69
Blues, 165, 220-226, 357, 367-384
Blues People—The Negro Experience in White America and the Music That Developed from It (Jones), 382
Bo, Mr., blues singer, 373
Boas, Franz, 13, 24, 31, 32, 33, 55
Bogotá, Colombia, 69
Bohannan, Laura (Elenore Bowen), 141, 389
Bohannan, Paul, 389
Bolivian Yungas, 18
Bongo celebration, 170, 171
Boni, the, 63, 64-66
    language, 65
    prevarication, 65
    religious ceremonies, 66
    wakes, 66
Bontemps, Arna, 225
Booker Brothers, 267
"Born Under a Bad Sign" (Jones and Bell), 371
Botkin, B. A., 34
Bott, Elizabeth, 316
Bourguignon, Erika, vii, 20, 21, 35-38, 51, 87-101
Bowen, Elenore: *see* Bohannan, Laura
Boyer, Ruth, 235
Brain-washing, 94
Branco, 77, 78, 79, 80, 81, 82, 85
Branco africano, 77
Branco amarelo, 77
Branco indio, 77
Branco mestiço, 77
Branco nagó, 77
Branco sarará, 77
Brasilia, Brazil, 76
Brazil, 35, 36, 37, 38, 42, 43, 46, 75-86, 87, 89, 96
Brinton, Crane, 386
Brooks, Cleanth, 40, 121
Brotz, Howard, 350
Brown, Charles, 378
Brown, Claude, 154-155
Brown, H. Rap, 392
Brown, James, 376, 379, 380, 381, 382
Brown, Roy, 372

Bryce-Laporte, Roy Simon, vii, 38, 51, 103-118
Buddhism, 87
Buenaventura, 214
Bukra: *see* Bakra
Bureau of American Ethnology, 13
Burns, Eddie, 373
Burton, Roger V., 318
Bushinenge, 64
Bushinenge tongo, 65
Bushman culture, 188, 189-191
"Butches," in Panama, 108, 113-114
Butler, Jay, 374
Butterball (Bill Crane), 371
Butterball, Jr., 371, 379

Cabo, 83
Cabo verdes, 77, 78, 85
Caboclo preto, 77
Caines, Clement, 94
Caiso Mas, 167, 170
Cali, Colombia, 332
Calley, Malcolm, 235
Calypso, 165, 226
Camargo, Candido Procopio Ferreira de, 37
Cameroun, Africa, 122
Canada, 42, 43, 46, 173
Cantadoras (singers), 207, 208, 209
Cantometrics, 39, 181-201
    three basic models, 188
Caribbean: *see* West Indies; *see also* Bahamas, Carriacou, Cuba, Haiti, Jamaica, Martinique, Nevis, Puerto Rico, Tobago, Trinidad
Carmichael, Stokely, 51, 225, 362, 392, 393
Carnegie Project, 23, 54
Carr, Andrew, 36-37
Carriacou, 41, 58, 59
Cartagena, 69
Carter, Clarence, 378, 379
Cataleptic trance, 96
Categorical social relationships, 11-12, 24, 46-47, 68, 204
Catholicism, 27, 37, 70, 87, 88, 89, 94-95, 97, 98, 110, 112, 113, 207, 211, 388
Cauca, Colombia, 203
Cayenne, French Guiana, 50, 64

INDEX

Cayton, Horace R., 303
Ceará, Brazil, 76
"Chain of Fools," 373
Chambers, E. K., 173
Charismatic Revival, 388
Charles, Ray, soul singer, 374, 375, 377
Charleston, 125
Charters, Samuel, 220
Chicago, 146-162, 367, 369, 370, 371, 372, 373, 374, 375, 377, 379
Chigualo, 206-208, 214
Chinese, 36, 87, 269, 279, 353
Chinese Pidgin English, 126
Chocó, Colombia, 66, 203, 331
Chomsky, Noam, 85, 142
Chota River Basin, Ecuador, 247
Chota Valley Negroes, 245-261
Christmas, 173, 176, 177
Chromolithographs, 95
Civil rights, 55-56, 242
Clark, Kenneth, 52
Clarke, Edith, 28, 241, 315
Claro, 77, 82, 85
Claro branco, 77
Cleaver, Eldridge, 392, 393
Cobb, Joe, 378, 379
Coconuts, 273
Colby, B. N., 85
Coleman, James S., 263
Colombia, 18, 41, 42, 43, 47, 48, 51, 52, 203-217, 226, 246-247, 387
    adaptive mobility in, 329-344
    economy, 203
Colombian coastal villages, 63, 66-68
Columbia University, 13
Common law marriage, 297
Communal villages, 279-281
Community studies, 54, 55, 56-57, 349
Compadrazgo (ritual co-parenthood), 249, 250, 251, 255
Compulsory Education Ordinance (Guyana), 279, 283
Confu (Obeah cult), 94
Congress of Racial Equality (CORE), 390
Conklin, Harold C., 85
Conot, Robert, 146, 150, 154

Consanguineal household, 232, 236-237; see also Matrifocality
Conversion, 94
Convince cult, 112
Cook, Ed, 378, 379, 380
Cooke, Sam, 225
Copping a plea, 155-156, 162
Cordell, Lucky, 375
Corn Islands, Nicaragua, 69
Costeños (from Ecuador and Colombia), 332-343
Coulthard, G. R., 50
Courantyne River, Guyana, 265
Courlander, Harold, 37, 89
"Cowboys and the Indians" plays, 174
Crane, Bill: see Butterball
Credit, 251-252, 335, 338
Creole, 40, 51, 65
    definition of, 38
    meaning of, 136-140
    status of, 136-140
    as symbol, 140-141
Creole languages, 120, 121, 122, 123, 125, 126, 129, 132, 136-140
Creolization, 121, 139
Crise de loa, 88
Crise de possession, 88
Crowley, Daniel J., 20, 35, 38, 39, 170, 226
Cuba, 88
Cultural focus, 28, 39, 56, 214-215
Cultural materialist strategy, 42-43
Cultural spheres, 57
Culture, 11, 14, 48, 347
    African and Afro-American, 3, 7-8, 14, 18, 28, 35, 44, 51, 57, 129, 155, 181-201
    and physique, 4, 7, 12
    and poverty: see Poverty, culture of
    and society, 9-10, 29
Curme, George, 122
Currulao (dance and music), 204-206, 214, 226
Cushite, 191, 196
Cushitic pastoralism, 196
Cushitic song style, 196

INDEX

Daelman, Jan, 133
Dahomey, Africa, 89, 95, 196
Dallas, Robert Charles, 43
Dance hall music, 211-213, 214
D'Andrade, Roy, 85
Dark Puritan (Smith), 37
Davenport, William, 41, 48, 207, 209, 337
DeCamp, David, 129, 175
De-creolization, 121
Demerara River, Guyana, 265, 270
Demoniac possession, 91, 98, 99
Department of Córdoba, Colombia, 66
Derbyshire, Robert L., 317
Despres, Leo A., viii, 48, 49, 50, 51, 52, 263-286
Dessunin (ritual), 91
Detroit, 367-369, 370, 371, 372-373, 374, 375, 376, 377
Deutschberger, Paul, 318
Developmental cycle, 330-331
Dialect Atlas approach, 121
Dictionary of the Bible (Hastings), 92-93
Dillard, J. L., viii, 39, 40, 51, 119-127
Dinka, 196
Dipi, 65
Dipitaki, 65, 70
Dissociation, 87-101
Djuka, the, 64
Dollard, John, 320
Domestic domain: *see* Household composition
Dominican Republic, 173
Dorsainvil, J. C., 26
Dorson, Richard, 34
Douglass, Frederick, 152
"Down Don't Bother Me" (King), 371-372
Down These Mean Streets (Thomas), 155
Drake, St. Clair, 41, 303
Drinking behavior, 295, 297, 324, 354
Drugs, 354, 406
DuBois, W. E. B., 305
Duppies (spirits), 113
Dyadic contracts, 211-213, 333

East Indians, 36, 87, 268, 274, 276-279, 281-286

East London, 235
East Sudanic song style, 196
Eckstein, Harry, 386
Ecology, 52, 246, 265-286
    participatory, 387
Ecuador, 18, 39, 41, 42, 43, 47, 48, 50, 51, 52, 203-217, 226
    adaptive mobility in, 329-344
    black traders of north highland, 245-261
        cooperation, 254-256
        ecological context of marketing, 246-248
        ethnic identity, 256-259
        process of trading, 248-252
        social relations within market place, 252-254
        sources of conflict, 254-256
    economy, 203
Edmonson, Munro, 30, 317
Education, 68, 70, 275, 406, 410
Edwards, Charles L., 31
Egypt, 189
Eisenstadt, S. N., 389, 394
El Rabo, Panama, 107-109
Elder, Jacob, 170
"Eleanor Rigby" (Beatles), 375
Elkins, Stanley, 34
Ellipsis, 137
Ellison, Ralph, 8-9, 10, 352, 353, 362
Emancipation, 353-355
English language, 136-140
Episcopalians, 104, 110-111, 113, 116
Epstein, A. L., 316
Erasmus, Charles J., 44, 58, 294, 329, 335
Escurinho, 77
Escuro, 77
Esmeraldas, Ecuador, 203, 214
Esmeraldas River, 331
Esquires (singing group), 379
Essequibo River, Guyana, 270
Ethiopia, 91, 182, 188, 193, 196
Ethnographic Atlas (Murdock), 181, 194
Ethnography of Communications, The (Gumperz and Hymes), 145-146
Ethnohistory, self-image and, 63-73
Evans-Pritchard, E. E., 331, 389

Evolution, 43-49, 263, 264, 265
Exorcism, 91, 99

Faaka tiki, 66, 72
Faith healing, 97
Fallers, Lloyd A., 303, 335
Family, 41, 49, 205-206, 210, 214, 231-244, 303-311, 313-314; *see also* Household composition
Fancy Costume Mas', 170
Farvar, Mary 21
Faulkner, William, 135, 357
Federal Writer's Project, 34
Fergusson, Charles A., 43
Fernandes, Florestan, 85
Fertility, 193
Fischer, Ann, 14
Fisher, Miles Mark, 34
Fisherman's Fete, 171
Flexner, Stuart Berg, 155
Folk Beliefs of the Southern Negro (Puckett), 25
Folk illness, 99
Folklore, 30-35, 39, 58, 67-68, 113-114, 164
Fon, the, 89, 91, 95, 96, 99
Ford, Henry, 2
Fortes, Meyer, 30, 57, 233, 330, 389
Fortier, Alcée, 31
Foster, George, 212, 213, 333, 335
Foxx, Redd, 160
Frake, Charles, 85
Franklin, Aretha, 225, 373
Franklin, Benjamin, 119
Frazier, E. Franklin, 28, 51, 56, 225, 241, 303, 305, 313-314, 324, 348-349, 350, 376
Freedom Week Coalition, 394, 396-397
Freilich, Morris, 206, 239, 315
French and American Canals (in Panama), 115
Friedland, W. H., 291
Friedrich, Paul, 387
Frobenius, Leo, 91, 92
Frucht, Richard, 44
Fuentes C., Aurelio, 204, 205

Gambling, 295

Gans, Herbert J., 314
Garrett, Lee, 374
Garrison, Lucy McKim, 31
Gause's exclusion principle, 287
Geertz, Hildred, 235, 241, 263
Georgetown, Guyana, 270, 273, 283-285
Gerlach, Luther, viii, 49, 52, 385-401
Gestures, 132-133, 135
"Giant Despair and Christian" play, 174
Giglioli, G., 268
Gillette, Cynthia, 22
Glazer, Nathan, 348
Glosador (singer), 205
Glossolalia, 92, 93, 97, 112
Gluckman, Max, 330-331, 389
Goffman, Erving, 257, 295
Goldkind, Victor, 241
González, A., 32
González, Nancie L., viii, 28, 41, 44, 52, 231-244, 304, 305
Goodenough, Ward H., 85, 209, 330
Good-talkers, 166
Goody, Jack, 304, 330
Goree, Fred, 372, 374, 378, 380, 381
Gospel music, 220-226
Gossip, 204, 213, 252
Gough, Kathleen, 236, 303
Goveia, E. V., 94
Granman, 65, 66
Grauer, Victor, 181
Great Britain, 171, 172, 173, 269, 270-271
Greaves, I., 105
Greeks, 350
Green, Paul, 124
Greenfield, Sidney, 30
Gregory, Dick, 160, 392
Gregory, Enoch, 373, 380
Gripping, 155-156
Groppi, Father, 394
Guayaquil, Ecuador, 50, 332
Guayllabamba River, 247
Guianas, 87, 88
Guinea Coast, 182, 197, 201
Gullah, 67, 122, 125-126
  dialect, 119, 120
  recordings by Reeves, 125
Gumperz, John J., 129, 145-146

INDEX

Gurr, Ted, 386
Gursslin, Orville R., 324-325
Guyana, 36, 48, 52, 63, 64-66
   differential adaptations, 263-286
   environmental zones, 265-267
   micro-cultural evolution, 263-286
   plantation environments, 267-269, 276-279
      adaptive strategies, 276-279
      capital, 268
      markets, 269
      technology, 268-269
   plural society of, 285-286
   urban environments, 273-276, 282-285
      adaptive strategies, 282-285
      capital formation, 275-276
      education, 275
      employment, 274-275
      population, 274
      power structure, 276
   villages as environments, 269-273, 279-282
      adaptive strategies, 279-282
      capital, 272-273
      labor, 271-272
      land, 271, 272
      markets, 273
      population, 272
      technology, 273

Hacienda, 248
Haiti, 26-27, 33, 36, 40, 51, 88, 89-100, 182, 197, 200-201, 254, 264, 386, 387, 388
Haitian Creole language, 122, 123
Hall, Robert A., Jr., 120, 121
Hallucinations, 95
Hammel, Eugene A., 85, 235
Hannerz, Ulf, viii, 49, 52, 124, 313-327, 353
Haplology, 137
Haralambos, Michael, viii, 39, 50, 52, 367-384
"Hard Luck Blues" (Brown), 372
Hare, Nathan, 398
Harris, Ann, 21
Harris, Joel Chandler, 31, 32-33
Harris, Marvin, viii, 28, 36, 42, 45, 46, 49, 51, 75-86
Hastings, James, 92-93
Hausa, the, 191

Hawaiian Creole language, 122
Haynes, J. A., 267
Head-washing ritual (Haiti), 91, 95
Hearn, Lafcadio, 9, 31
Helm, June, 264
Henderson, Ray, 371, 372, 374, 376, 378
Henker, E. H., 100
Henney, J. H., 37, 95
Henriques, F. M., 30, 241
Henry, Jules, 37, 331
Herbers, John, 395
Hernton, Calvin, 352, 356
Herskovits, Frances S., 24-25, 26, 37, 91, 95, 98, 264; see also Herskovits, Melville J.
Herskovits, Melville J., 4, 13, 20, 23-30, 33, 34, 35, 36, 37, 38, 39, 40, 41, 42, 44, 54, 55, 56, 57, 58, 87, 89, 91, 95, 98, 116, 120, 121, 130, 131, 133, 135, 163, 197, 219, 264, 313, 348, 352
   critical review of his works, 25-30, 54
Herzog, George, 141, 314
Hibbler, Al, 357
Hinduism, 87
Hine, Virginia H., 49, 52, 385-401
Hoetink, H., 45
Hoffer, Eric, 386
Hogg, Donald, 112
Holiday, Billie, 134
Hollingshead, A. B., 87
Holy Ghost, 93
Homans, George C., 115
Honduras, 51, 132
Hooker, John Lee, 373
Horton, John, 155, 161-162
Household composition, 40-41, 57, 59, 214-215, 232-233, 303-311; see also Family
   distinction between family and household, 233-234
Howling Wolf, 373
Hausipungueros, 248
Humor, 299-300
Hunt, Robert C., 330
Hurault, Jean, 66
Hurston, Zora Neale, 33, 220, 221
Hutchinson, Harry W., 28
Hymes, Dell, 129, 141, 145-146

Hypodescent, 75, 86
Hypoglaecemia, 95

Ibarra, Ecuador, 249
Ibo, the, 89
Iceberg Slim, 146, 147, 148, 151, 153, 154, 155
Imbabura, Ecuador, 246
Impressions, The, singing group, 381
"In the Midnight Hour" (Pickett), 376
India, 188, 196, 197, 268
Indian Pidgin English, 126
Indians: *see* American Indians; East Indians
Indigenismo, 50
Indio moreno, 77
Indio preto, 77
Indirection, 141
Indonesians, 87
Ingi, the, 64
Interlacustrine kingdoms of Africa, 188
Intonation, 137
Irish, 353, 354, 356
Italians, 350, 406

Jackson, Bruce, 31
Jackson, George Pullen, 34, 197
Jackson, L'il Son, 223-224
Jackson, Mahalia, 223
Jamaica, 33, 36, 88, 95, 112, 137, 331, 387
Jamaican revivalists, 94
James Boys, 378
Japan, 188
Japanese Fan Drill, 175
Jaquith, James R., 21
Jaquith, Rose Marie, 22
Java, 235
Jayawardena, Chandra, 278, 298
Jazz, 8, 382
Jekyll, Walter, 31
Jensen, Adolf Ellegard, 92
Jews, 52, 350, 353, 356, 406
Jiving, 149, 151, 152, 153-154, 162
"Johnny's So Long at the Fair," 172
Johnson, Chalmers, 386
Johnson, Guy B., 21, 32, 34
Johnson, James Weldon, 32
Johnson, Robert, 221
Johnston, Sir Harry H., 23-24

Jokes, 299-300
Jones, Booker T., 371
Jones, E. Rodney, 372
Jones, LeRoi, 363, 382
Jourdain, Elodie, 123
Journal of American Folklore, 31
Jukes, 291-292, 295
Jump-up Church, 104, 110, 111-112
Junta Autónoma del Ferrocarril, 339

Kahl, Joseph B., 329
Kahn, Morton, 26
Kalinda, 170
Kanuku Mountains, Guyana, 265
Kanzo ritual, Haiti, 95
Kardec, Alan, 37
Kasdan, L., 389
Katzin, Margaret, 250
Kay, Paul, 235
Keil, Charles, 28, 39, 221-222, 224, 316, 317, 318, 325, 349, 353, 357, 373, 382
Kelley, W. M., 357
Kembé (spirit possession), 91
Kerner Report, 355
King, Albert, 371-372, 373, 382
King, B. B., 372, 373, 374, 375
King, Charles E., 304, 305
King, Martin Luther, Jr., 225, 392
King, Woodie, 154
Kinship, 44-45, 206-211, 234, 303-304, 311, 336-341
Klass, Morton, 87
Klatzko, Bernard, 221
Klumpp, Kathleen M., viii, 50, 52, 245-251
Kochman, Thomas, viii-ix, 40, 48, 49, 51, 145-162, 320
Kottak, Conrad, 75
Krapp, George Phillip, 40, 119, 120, 121
Krehbiel, H. E., 32
Kumina cult, 112
Kunstadter, Peter, 236
Kurath, Hans, 119-120
Kwakwani, Guyana, 265

Lamming, George, 141
Landman, Bette E., 20

INDEX

Language
    ambiguity in West Indies, 129-144
    the Boni, 65
    Colombian coastal villages, 67
    English, 136-140
    ethnography of black American speech behavior, 145-162
    Haitian Creole, 122, 123
    Hawaiian Creole, 122
    Indian Pidgin English, 126
    Melanesian Pidgin, 122
    Non-Standard Negro dialects, 119-127
    Panama Canal Zone, 104
    Portuguese Trade Pidgin, 122
    Pidgin English, 120, 121, 125, 126
    Quechua, 2
    San Andrés, 68, 69, 70-71
    Saramaccan, 131-132
    Spanish, 67
Lanternari, Vittorio, 386
Larson, C. M., 369
Latacunga, Ecuador, 247
Lavé tête: see Head-washing ritual
Lavong, Reggie, 375-376
Lay My Burden Down (Botkin), 34
Leach, Edmund, 331
Leacock, Seth, 35
Leeward Islands, 94, 171
Leiris, Michel, 36, 91
Lenski, Gerhard, 329, 331
Levy, M. J., Jr., 303
Lewis, Cudjo, 33
Lewis, Hylan, 314
Lewis, I. M., 91, 389
Lewis, Oscar, 235, 241, 353, 354, 358-359
Lhermitte, Jean, 91
Liebow, Elliot, 49, 161, 316, 317
Life in a Haitian Valley (Herskovits), 26
Limones, Ecuador, 214
Lindley, A. B., 125
Linguistic Atlas tradition, 121-122
Linguistic continua, 129
Linguistic maps, 124-125
Linton, Ralph, 386
Little Milton, 372, 373, 374-375, 377
Little Richard, 380
Little Sonny, 373

Locke, Alain, 25
Loflin, Marvin D., 123
Lomax, Alan, ix, 21, 39, 51, 181-201, 204, 220, 221, 223, 224
Lopreato, J., 235
Lounsbury, Floyd, 85
Love and Friendship (Lindley), 125
Lowenthal, David, 45
Lowie, Robert H., 305
Ludwig, Arnold, 88, 96
Lyle, W. H., 96

McBride, George, 105
McConnel and Company, 267
McCormick, Mack, 158, 161
McCracklin, Jimmy, 379
McDavid, Ravin I., Jr., 120, 123, 124, 126
McGale, Edward, 274
McGregor, Pedro, 37
Mackenzie, Guyana, 265
Macking, 147
McKissick, Floyd, 393
Madagascar, 182, 188, 196
Madeira, 268
Magictones, 381
Mailer, Norman, 40, 314
Makeba, Miriam, 369
Malaysia, 192, 197
Malcolm X, 4, 146, 152, 153, 154, 356
Malinowski—Radcliffe-Brown controversy, 115
Mallol de Recassens, José, 331
Mangin, William, 59, 242
Marginality, 17, 41, 43, 44, 48, 49, 289-301
Marimba dance, 204-206, 226
Markets: see Guyana, Ecuador
Mars, Louis, 88
Marshall, A. H., 272
Martinique, 36
Maruyama, Magorob, 387
Marwick, M. G., 100
Masculinity, 314-324
Masking, 129, 131
Mason, Julian, 120
Matawey, the, 64
Mather, Cotton, 119
Matrifocality, 41, 44, 231-244, 280, 304-305, 314-316, 318, 326-327

Mauritania, 188
Mayer, Adrian C., 45, 204, 316, 391, 393
Mayr, Ernst, 264, 286
Melanesian Pidgin English, 122
Melnick, Mimi Clar, 224
Mencher, Joan P., 238
Mennesson-Rigaud, Odette, 89
Men-of-words, 163-166
Mercier, P., 91
Merriam, Alan P., 204, 213
Merrill, Gordon C., 171
Merton, Robert K., 104
Mescalero Apache, 231, 235
Mesmer, Franz, 93
Mestizos, 245-246, 248, 251, 252, 256-259, 332
Methodism, 92, 93-94, 98
Métraux, Alfred, 36, 89, 131
Metzger, Duane, 85
Mexico, 329, 387
Middleton, John, 100, 389
Migrant farm workers, 289-301
   conflicting tendencies, 297-300
   leveling tendency in camps, 294-297
   marginality of, 292-294
   migrant labor system, 290-292
Migration, 59, 234, 289-301
Miller, Walter B., 317
Minga, 335
Minimax, 48
Minneapolis Tribune, 386, 387
Mintz, Sidney W., ix, 1-16, 26-27, 41, 87, 235, 245, 246, 254, 267
Mischel, Frances, 37, 38
Mischel, Walter, 37, 38
Missionaries, 69, 70, 93-94
Mississippi Freedom Democratic Party, 139
"Mr. Pitiful" (Redding), 376
Mitchell, J. Clyde, 45, 47-48, 204, 316
Mitchell, Joseph, 15
Moore, J. C., 94
More, Hannah, 174
Moreau de St. Méry, Louis Elie, 36
Moreno, 43, 77, 84, 85
Moreno cabo verde, 77
Moreno caboclo, 77
Moreno claro, 77, 85
Moreno escuro, 85
Moreno escuro claro, 77
Moreno mestiço, 77
Moreno preto, 77
Moreno sarará, 77
Mörner, Magnus, 45
Morse, R. M., 7, 241
Moslem Sudan, 182, 188
Moslems: *see* Muslims
Mounting by spirits, 89, 97
Mourning ritual, 95, 96
Movements of Social Transformation (M.O.S.T.), 385
Moynihan, Daniel Patrick, 41, 303, 348
Moynihan report, 50, 60, 314, 354
Mozambique, 51
Muddy Waters, blues singer, 373
Mulato, 77, 84, 85
Mulato branco, 77
Mulato caboclo, 77
Mulato indio, 77
Mulato mestiço, 77
Mulato sarará, 77
Mules and Men (Hurston), 33
"Mummies" play, 173-174
Murdock, George Peter, 181, 192, 194, 196, 209
Murphy, Robert F., 47-48, 389
Music, 9, 67, 181-201, 203-217
   adaptation, 219-227
   sketch map of style areas, 195
   social relationships and, 204-213
   song style areas, 196
Muslims, 51, 87, 97, 360, 362
Myalism, 112
Myrdal, Gunnar, 23, 54, 348
Myth of the Negro Past, The (Herskovits), 13, 20, 23-24, 27, 28, 29, 63, 197, 348

Nago, the, 89
Nariño, Colombia, 203
Nasalization, 137, 138
Nath, Dwarka, 269, 271, 272, 281
National Association for the Advancement of Colored People (NAACP), 388, 390, 394

INDEX

Nayar, 236, 237, 238
Ndoep cult, 91
Negro branco, 77
Negro Church in America, The (Frazier), 376
Negro Family in British Guiana, The (R. T. Smith), 314
Negro mulato escuro, 77
Negro preto, 77
Negro in the United States, The (Frazier), 348-349
Negro-Pygmy song style, 193
Negro's Americanism, The (Herskovits), 25
Nelkin, Dorothy, ix, 48, 49, 52, 289-301
Neo-Pentecostalism, 387, 388
Neo-racism, 364
Neoteric societies, 44, 242
Netherlands, 270
Nettl, Bruno, 216, 219
Networks, 43-48, 59, 204, 215, 227, 232, 316-317, 325, 401
Nevis, 51, 171-176
   intersexual involvements, 172
   plays, 173-175, 177
   sugar fortunes, 171-172
New Amsterdam, Guyana, 270, 273, 283-285
New Guinea, 232
New York, 367, 368, 369, 370, 371, 373, 374, 375, 377, 410
Newfoundland, Canada, 132
Nicaragua, 69
Nigeria, 122
Nigerian Plateau, 182
Nilotic song style, 196
North African musical style, 196
North Carolina, 21, 124-125
Norton, Arthur A., 40
Nova Scotia, Canada, 41, 47, 58
Novenario ritual, 208-211
Nubians, the, 188, 189, 196
Nuer, the, 196

Obeah, 70, 104, 110, 113, 114, 131
Oberg, Kalervo, 43, 58
Oceania, 192, 197
Odum, Howard W., 32
Oesterreich, T. G., 91
Oliver, Paul, 221, 223-224

Optional assimilations (in Creole languages), 137
Orinoco Delta, Venezuela, 265
Ortiz, Fernando, 31, 246
Ossowski, Stanislaw, 329
Ottenheimer, Harriet J., 221
Otterbein, Keith F., 41, 239, 315, 321
Overacceptance (process in acculturation), 136

Pacific Littoral (Ecuador and Colombia), 43, 47, 329-344
   dyadic contracts, 333
   economic structure, 331-332
Pan American Highway, 246, 247
Panama, Republic of, 104, 105, 106
Panama Canal Zone, 38, 69, 103-118
   El Rabo, 107-109
   judicial-police system, 106
   language, 104
   plural arrangements, 104-107
   power structure, 104-107
   prestige and popularity, 108-109, 111, 114
   race relations, 104-107
   stratification, 104-107
   U.S. control, 104-105
Panama Railroad, 115
"Papa's Got a Brand New Bag" (Brown), 376
Paramaka, the, 64
Paramaribo, Surinam, 50, 64, 65
Pares, Richard, 171
Pari, 196
Parker, Jr., 372, 373, 374
Paro, Pauline, 276
Parrinder, Geoffrey, 91
Parrish, Lydia, 221
Parsons, Elsie Clews, 32, 33
Pastoralism, 196
Patois, 70
Patrilocal residence, 278
Pearse, Andrew, 39
Peculiar Institution, The (Stampp), 348
Pederson, Lee A., 126
Pelto, Pertti, 21
Penard, A. P., 31
Penard, F. P., 31
Pentecostalism, 37, 97, 98, 386-388
People, Power, Change (film, Gerlach), 387

Peranio, Roger, 203
Performance patterns, 164-166
Pernambuco, Brazil, 76
Peterson, Harold, 388
Pettay, Louanna, 88
Pettigrew, Thomas F., 317
Pfeiffer, W. M., 88, 92
Philadelphia, 164, 165
Pickett, Wilson, soul singer, 376
Pickford, Glenna Ruth, 121
Pidgin English, 120, 121, 125, 126
Pierson, Donald, 7, 46, 75
Pina (punishment), 64
Pitt-Rivers, Julian, 45
Plantation environments, 267-269, 276-279
    adaptive strategies, 276-279
    capital, 268
    markets, 269
    technology, 268-269
Plantations, 6, 17, 57
Playing the dozens, 165
Plural societies, 50, 51, 57, 86, 105-107, 109, 118, 263, 285-286; *see* M. G. Smith
Plymouth, Tobago, 168-171
Pocomania cult, 112
Polgar, Steven, 116
Polhemus, Ted, 21
Polish ghetto, 354
Polygyny, 205-206, 239, 342
Polynesia, 188
Poor People's March, 394
Popayán, Colombia, 329
Portuguese Trade Pidgin, 122
Possession trance, 88-100
    demonic, 91, 98, 99
    essential aspect of, 93
Poussaint, Alvin F., 149-150, 153
Poverty, culture of, 11, 50, 58-59, 358-359, 365
Powdermaker, Hortense, 30, 354
Predestination, 134
Pressel, Esther, 37
Preta, 78, 80
Preto, 19, 77, 78, 79, 82, 85
Preto amarelo, 77
Preto claro, 77
Preto louro, 77

Preto mestiço, 77
Preto moreno, 77
Preto negro, 77
Preto sarará, 77
Prevarication, 65
Price, Richard, 36
Price, Thomas J., ix, 20, 51, 63-73, 133-135, 331
Price controls, 252
Price-Mars, J., 26, 31
Proprietary villages, 279-281
Protestantism, 37, 87, 88, 91-95, 97, 98, 99, 100, 116, 386-388
Providencia, San Andrés (Colombia), 68
Puckett, Newbell Niles, 25, 32
Puerto Ricans, 87, 264, 293, 406, 408, 409, 411
Pulse, The, Inc., 367-369, 377
Pygmies, African, 188, 189-191, 193

Querétaro, Mexico, 329
Quito, Ecuador, 246, 247, 249, 250, 252-254

Race: *see* Categorical social relationships
Race, Culture, and Evolution (Stocking), 24
Race relations: *see* Categorical social relationships
Race Relations (Banton), 46
Racial identity, calculus of, 75
Racism, 352, 355-359, 364, 394
Rada, 89
Radio, 65, 367-383
Rainwater, Lee, 41, 303, 314
Ramzy, Nadia, 21
Rapping, 146-149, 161, 162
Rappaport, Roy A., 264
Record World, 370
Redding, Otis, 225, 376
Reeves, Dick, 125
Reichard, Gladys, 33
Reinterpretation, 27, 28, 129-130
Reisman, Karl, ix, 21, 39, 40, 51, 63, 129-144
Reiss, I. L., 303
Relexification, 122, 123, 125
Religion, Caribbean variants, 87-100, 103-118

INDEX

Religious music, 220-226
Remodeling, 130, 131-132, 133, 135
Repetitive trances, 94
Resignation, 134, 135
Respondedoras: *see* Cantadoras
Retention, 27
Retreat, 95-96
Return to Laughter (Elenore Bowen), 141
Reynolds Metals Corporation, 267
Rhyming, 165
Rice, 272, 273, 281, 282, 285
Riobamba, Ecuador, 247
Ritual dissociation, 87-101
Roach, Jack, 324-325
Rodman, Hyman, 324
Rogler, L. H., 87
Rohrer, John H., 30, 317
Romney, A. Kimball, 85
Rowley, C. D., 232
Rubel, Arthur J., 99
Rubio, Angel, 105
Ruffins, Jimmy, 379
Rum, 207, 208, 213
Running it down, 148, 154-155, 161, 162
Rupununi Savannahs, Guyana, 265

Sahara, 182, 184-186, 193
Sahlins, Marshall D., 44-45, 48, 237, 250, 389, 391, 398
"St. George and the Turk" play, 173
St. John the Baptist play, 98
St. Kitts, 171
St. Peter's Day, 171
St. Vincent Island, 37, 88-99
Saints, 68, 94-95, 210-211
Saloon music and dance, 211-213, 214, 226-227
San Andrés, Colombia, 63, 68-71
San Gabriel, Ecuador, 247
San Juan River, Colombia, 331
San Lorenzo, Ecuador, 214, 339
San Roque market place, Ecuador, 252-254
São Paulo, Brazil, 76
Saramaca, the, 64, 133
Saramaccan language, 131-132
Sarará, 77, 78, 83, 85
Sargant, William, 94

"Say It Loud, I'm Black and I'm Proud" (Brown), 382
Scarborough, Dorothy, 32, 221
Schneider, David M., 304, 305
SCLC (Southern Christian Leadership Conference), 390
Scotland, 235
SDS (Students for a Democratic Society), 395-396, 397
Sea Islands (Georgia and South Carolina), 119, 120, 125, 126
Seizure, 92
Self-image, ethnohistory and, 63-73
Senegal, Africa, 91
Service, Elman R., 2
Seventh Day Adventists, 37, 70
Shaker ritual, 89-97
Shakers, 37, 88, 91-95, 98, 99
Shango, 37, 91, 97, 98
Shibutani, Tamotsu, 116
Shilluk, 196
Shluh, 188, 189
Shorris, Earl, 161
Shouterism, 37, 91
Shucking, 149-154, 162
Shuy, Roger W., 125
Signifying, 156-157, 162
Simpson, George E., 37, 89, 91, 94, 95, 97, 98, 112
Sims, Marvin L., 376
Slave Songs of the United States (Garrison), 31
Slavery, 3, 5-7, 8, 17, 36, 43, 63, 64, 68, 235, 265, 271, 313, 314
  gesture and, 133
  patterns of kinship under, 280
  as a source of black culture, 350-352, 355
Slim, Iceberg: *see* Iceberg Slim
Smith, M. G., 27, 28, 29-30, 35, 37, 39, 41, 42, 50, 63, 91, 116, 133, 239, 264, 304, 305
Smith, Raymond T., 28, 29, 44, 133, 134, 235, 241, 278, 280, 314, 330
Smith, T. Watson, 43
SNCC (Student Nonviolent Coordinating Committee), 390, 394
Social security, 294

Solien, Nancie L., 28, 235, 236; *see also* González, Nancie L.
Solien de González, Nancie L., 239; *see also* González, Nancie L.
Sorcery, 97, 98, 99
Soul (the term), 124, 347, 349, 357, 364
Soul food, 352
"Soul Man" (Sam and Dave), 376
Soul music, 367-384
Sounding, 157-159, 160, 165
South African musical style, 196
South Italian peasants, 235
Southern Christian Leadership Conference (SCLC), 390
Southey, Robert, 93, 94
Spain, 67-68
Spann, Purvis, 372
Speaking in tongues: *see* Glossolalia
Speech Band, 167, 170, 174
Speech behavior: *see* Language
Speech Mas', Tobago, 167-168, 177
Spirits, 88, 89, 99-100
   anthropomorphic, 89
   categories of, 99
   mounting by, 89, 97
   possession trance, 88-100
      demonic, 91, 98, 99
      essential aspect of, 93
Spiritual death, 95
Spiritualism, 87, 88
Spirituals, 8; *see also* Arrullos
Spiro, Melford E., 303
Sranan Tongo, 122
Stack, Carol B., ix, 47, 49, 52, 241, 303-311
Stampp, Kenneth, 348, 352
Steward, Julian H., 48, 264
Stewart, William A., 21, 39, 120, 121, 122, 124, 125, 126
Stick-fight dance, 170
Stocking, George W., Jr., 24
Stonequist, Everett, 289
Stovall, Babe, 221
Strachwitz, Chris, 221
Streams of Power, 97-98
Street and Gangland Rhythms, 155, 156
Strickon, Arnold, 342

Student Nonviolent Coordinating Committee (SNCC), 390, 394
Students for a Democratic Society (SDS), 395-396, 397
Sturtevant, William, 85
Sudan, Africa, 182
Sugar, 6, 171-172, 247, 248, 267-269, 271-272, 277, 279
Surinam, 51, 63-66, 121, 122, 131-132, 264
"Survey of Brand Preferences among Chicago Negro Families" (Wright and Larson), 369
Survival, 40, 357-358
Syncretism, 28, 35-38, 131
   definition of, 27
Szwed, John F., ix, 17-60, 219-227
Szwed, Sue, 21-22

Tait, David, 389
Takitaki, 65, 67
Talbot, Allen, 386
Talbot, George, ix-x, 21
"Talkin' 'bout Soul" (Simms), 376
Talley's Corner (Liebow), 316
Tapanahoni, 64
Target workers, 296
Tax, Sol, 28
Taxes, 252, 280-281
Taylor, Douglas Macrae, 122, 123, 131-132
Tea Meetings, Nevis, 173, 175-177
Television, 297, 322
Tell My Horse (Hurston), 33
Teran, Francisco, 247
Third Locks Project, Panama, 115
"This Little Girl of Mine," 337
Thomas, Piri, 155
"Ticket to Ride" (Beatles), 375
Time Magazine, 390, 395
Tobago, 166-171
Torbellino (song and dance), 205
Townsend, Henry, 223
Trance, 88
   cataleptic, 96
   possession, 88-100
      demonic, 91, 98, 99
      essential aspect of, 93

INDEX

repetitive, 94
visionary, 98
Transformational-Generative syntacticians, 123
Transvaluation, 131
Trinidad, 27, 36, 37, 39, 51, 87-89, 91, 95, 97, 98, 166-168, 170, 226, 264
    beach life, 168-169
    economy, 168
Trinidad Village (Herskovits), 27, 29
Troy, Jeffrey, 379
Trumping, 94
Tuareg, 189, 191
Tulcán, Ecuador, 247
Tumaco, Colombia, 214
Tumba, La: *see* Alabado
Turner, Lorenzo D., 40, 120, 121

Último alabado, 208-211
Umbanda, 37-38
Uncle Remus: His Songs and His Sayings (Harris), 31
United Fruit Company, 115
United States of America, 42, 75, 85, 87, 163-166, 173, 241
    black culture, 347-366
    black ghetto, 403-418
        males of, 313-327
    Black Power, 385-401
        adaptive functions, 397-399
        decentralization, 391-392
        extra-movement linkages, 395-397
        organization of, 389-391
        reticulation, 393-395, 396-397
        segmentation, 329-393, 399-400
    blues, 165, 220-226, 357, 367-384
    control of the Panama Canal Zone, 104-105
    ethnography of speech behavior, 145-162
    migrant farm workers, 289-301
        conflicting tendencies, 297-300
        leveling tendency in camps, 294-297
        marginality of, 292-294
        migrant labor system, 290-292
    Non-Standard Negro dialects, 119-127
    soul music, 367-384
    urban residence and family organization, 303-311

Urban anthropology, 59-60
Urban Blues (Keil), 221, 316, 349, 353, 373, 382
Urban League, 390, 394

Valentine, Betty Lou, x, 52-53, 403-418
Valentine, Charles A., x, 11, 21, 41, 49, 51, 52-53, 324, 403-418
Valle, Colombia, 203
Vayda, Andrew P., 264
Velorio, 211; *see also* Arrullo
Verde, 83
Verger, Pierre, 91, 95
Vietnam War, 347, 358
Village environments, 269-273, 279-282
    adaptive strategies, 279-282
    capital, 272-273
    labor, 271-272
    land, 271, 272
    markets, 273
    population, 272
    technology, 273
Violence, 298
Virgin Islands, 88, 173
Visionary trances, 98
Vodû, 36-38, 89-99, 388
    innovation in, 90
Vodû necklace, 95
Voodoo: *see Vodû*

Wagley, Charles, 28, 36, 45, 46, 57, 75, 105, 246
Wakes, 66, 67, 166, 206-211
Wales, 94
Walker, Willie, 375
Wallace, Anthony F. C., 37, 85, 223, 386
Ward Sisters, 376
Ware, Charles P., 31
Wari, the, 130
Washboard Willie, blues singer, 373
Washington, Albert, 378
Waterman, Richard A., 204
Watson, Jeanne, 320
Watusi (Watutsi), 188, 191
WCHB (Detroit), 367, 369, 370, 371, 372, 374, 375, 376, 377

Weber, Max, 331
Weinstein, Eugene A., 318
Welding, Pete, 221
Wentworth, Harold, 155
"We're a Winner" (The Impressions), 381
Weskos, the, 122
Wesley, Charles, 93
Wesley, John, 93-94
West, Robert C., 43
West Indians, 103-118, 406
West Indies, 40, 88, 98, 108, 111, 121, 226, 233, 235, 268
   Carnival, 166-168, 170
   character qualities, 130
   cultural ambiguity in, 129-144
   gestures in, 132-133
   linguistic ambiguity in, 129-144
   patterns of performance in, 163-179
      men-of-words, 163-166
      Nevis, 51, 171-176
      social uses of, 176-178
      Tobago, 166-171
   symbolic expression, 131
West Sudan, 196
White, Douglas, 78
White, Newman I., 32
White Negro, The (Mailer), 314
Whites, 64, 65, 67, 69, 70
   standards of beauty, 68
Whiteford, Andrew, 329
Whiting, John W., 318
Whitten, Norman E., Jr., x, 17-60, 203-217, 220, 226, 239, 329-344
Whitten, Sibby, 21-22

"Whupping the game," 147-149, 151, 152
Wide fields (Green), 124
Wilgus, D. K., 32
Wilkins, Robert, 221
Williams, Bill, 371, 376, 380
Williams, Dr. Eric, 165, 169
Williams, Gerald, 85
Willmott, Peter, 235, 308
Wilson, Charles, 105
Wilson, Peter, 133
Wolf, Eric R., 9, 261
Wolfe, Alvin W., 21, 34
"Worry, Worry" (King), 372
Wright, J. S., 369
WVON (Chicago), 367, 369, 370, 371, 372, 375, 377, 379
WWRL (New York), 367, 369, 370, 371, 373, 374, 375, 377

Xhosa, 191

Yams, 192
Yoruba, the, 89, 91, 95, 96, 98, 99, 130, 135
Young, A., 270, 271, 272, 277, 279
Young, Frank W., 329
Young, Michael, 235, 308
Young, Ruth Cy, 329
Young, Whitney, 390

Zar cult, 91
Zelinsky, W., 7
Zempleni, A., 91
Zombi, 99
Zulu, the, 191